Frommer's®

Ecuador & the Galápagos Islands

3rd Edition

by Eliot Greenspan

WILEY

Wiley Publishing, Inc.

ABOUT THE AUTHOR

Eliot Greenspan is a poet, journalist, musician, and travel writer who took his backpack and typewriter the length of Mesoamerica before settling in Costa Rica in 1992. Since then, he has worked steadily as a travel writer, freelance journalist, and translator, and has continued his travels in the region. He is the author of *Frommer's Belize, Frommer's Costa Rica, Costa Rica For Dummies, Frommer's Costa Rica Day By Day,* and *Frommer's Guatemala,* as well as the chapter on Venezuela in *Frommer's South America.*

Published by:

WILEY PUBLISHING, INC.

111 River St.
Hoboken, NJ 07030-5774

ISBN 978-0-470-94951-1 (paper); ISBN 978-1-118-10030-1 (ebk); ISBN 978-1-118-10031-8 (ebk); ISBN 978-1-118-10032-5 (ebk)

Editor: Myka Carroll with Ian Skinnari
Production Editor: Jonathan Scott
Cartographer: Nick Trotter
Photo Editors: Cherie Cincilla, Richard Fox, Alden Gewirtz
Production by Wiley Indianapolis Composition Services
Front Cover Photo: Galapagos Island Iguana, Galapagos Islands ©Frans Lanting Studio/Alamy Images
Back Cover Photo: Cotopaxi Volcano, Quito, Ecuador ©Robert Frerck/Odyssey/Robert Harding World Imagery

For information on our other products and services or to obtain technical support, please contact our Customer Care Department within the U.S. at 877/762-2974, outside the U.S. at 317/572-3993 or fax 317/572-4002.

Wiley also publishes its books in a variety of electronic formats. Some content that appears in print may not be available in electronic formats.

Manufactured in the United States of America

5 4 3 2 1

CONTENTS

15 ECUADOREAN WILDLIFE 382

LIST OF MAPS

ACKNOWLEDGMENTS

I got some very valuable support and input on this book from friends and experts in Ecuador and abroad. For the third edition running, Danielle Leyla Walters made many valuable contributions and corrections. I would also like to thank Patricio Tamariz and Paola Tama of the Ecuadorian Ministry of Tourism. Dominic Hamilton of the Metropolitan Touring was once again a huge help, while Alfonso Tandanzo of Surtrek also shone. Finally, *muchas gracias* are due to Myka Carroll, my editor, for her patience, understanding, and deft editorial touch.

—Eliot Greenspan

HOW TO CONTACT US

In researching this book, we discovered many wonderful places—hotels, restaurants, shops, and more. We're sure you'll find others. Please tell us about them, so we can share the information with your fellow travelers in upcoming editions. If you were disappointed with a recommendation, we'd love to know that, too. Please write to:

Frommer's Ecuador & the Galápagos Islands, 3rd Edition
Wiley Publishing, Inc. • 111 River St. • Hoboken, NJ 07030-5774
frommersfeedback@wiley.com

ADVISORY & DISCLAIMER

Travel information can change quickly and unexpectedly, and we strongly advise you to confirm important details locally before traveling, including information on visas, health and safety, traffic and transport, accommodation, shopping and eating out. We also encourage you to stay alert while traveling and to remain aware of your surroundings. Avoid civil disturbances, and keep a close eye on cameras, purses, wallets and other valuables.

While we have endeavored to ensure that the information contained within this guide is accurate and up-to-date at the time of publication, we make no representations or warranties with respect to the accuracy or completeness of the contents of this work and specifically disclaim all warranties, including without limitation warranties of fitness for a particular purpose. We accept no responsibility or liability for any inaccuracy or errors or omissions, or for any inconvenience, loss, damage, costs or expenses of any nature whatsoever incurred or suffered by anyone as a result of any advice or information contained in this guide.

The inclusion of a company, organization or Website in this guide as a service provider and/or potential source of further information does not mean that we endorse them or the information they provide. Be aware that information provided through some Websites may be unreliable and can change without notice. Neither the publisher or author shall be liable for any damages arising herefrom.

FROMMER'S STAR RATINGS, ICONS & ABBREVIATIONS

Every hotel, restaurant, and attraction listing in this guide has been ranked for quality, value, service, amenities, and special features using a **star-rating system.** In country, state, and regional guides, we also rate towns and regions to help you narrow down your choices and budget your time accordingly. Hotels and restaurants are rated on a scale of zero (recommended) to three stars (exceptional). Attractions, shopping, nightlife, towns, and regions are rated according to the following scale: zero stars (recommended), one star (highly recommended), two stars (very highly recommended), and three stars (must-see).

In addition to the star-rating system, we also use **seven feature icons** that point you to the great deals, in-the-know advice, and unique experiences that separate travelers from tourists. Throughout the book, look for:

special finds—those places only insiders know about

fun facts—details that make travelers more informed and their trips more fun

kids—best bets for kids and advice for the whole family

special moments—those experiences that memories are made of

overrated—places or experiences not worth your time or money

insider tips—great ways to save time and money

great values—where to get the best deals

The following **abbreviations** are used for credit cards:

AE	American Express	**DISC**	Discover	**V**	Visa
DC	Diners Club	**MC**	MasterCard		

TRAVEL RESOURCES AT FROMMERS.COM

Frommer's travel resources don't end with this guide. Frommer's website, **www.frommers. com**, has travel information on more than 4,000 destinations. We update features regularly, giving you access to the most current trip-planning information and the best airfare, lodging, and car-rental bargains. You can also listen to podcasts, connect with other Frommers. com members through our active-reader forums, share your travel photos, read blogs from guidebook editors and fellow travelers, and much more.

THE BEST OF ECUADOR

Ecuadoreans like to boast that their country is really four distinct destinations: the Galápagos Islands, the Amazon basin, the high Andean sierra, and the Pacific coast. In fact, it's much more. With so much physical and cultural variety, there are plenty of excellent experiences and adventures for any type of traveler.

Quito offers up both colonial gems and modern pleasures in a compact urban environment. Cuenca is another colonial treasure, with the Inca ruins of Ingapirca nearby. You can visit not only the rainforests of the Amazon basin, but also the cloud forests of Mindo, Tandayapa, San Isidro, and Bellavista; the dry forests of the southern Pacific lowlands; and the high-altitude paramo of the Central highlands. Those Central highlands are home to numerous colonial-era haciendas that have been converted into lovely and cozy hotels and inns. Active travelers can ride horses on the Andean plains or mountain-bike down the slopes of active volcanoes. Bird-watchers can add to their list from the more than 1,600 species found here.

Below is a selective list of some of the best that Ecuador has to offer.

THE best PURELY ECUADOREAN TRAVEL EXPERIENCES

o **Stepping Back in Time in Colonial Quito:** Founded in 1534, Quito was the first city to be declared a World Heritage Site by UNESCO. Its Old Town seems in many ways to have changed little over the centuries. Walk the rough cobblestone streets and visit the numerous beautifully restored colonial-era churches, monasteries, convents, private mansions, and public plazas. You'll feel as if you've traveled back in time. See chapter 5.

o **Straddling the Equator:** The country isn't called Ecuador for nothing—the Equator passes right through it. Don't miss the chance to have your photo taken with one foot in either hemisphere. There are several popular tourist attractions and marked spots where you can do this. My favorite is **Quitsato Mitad del Mundo Monument** (© 09/9701-133; www.quitsato.org), located just off the highway from Quito to Otavalo. See p. 130.

The Best of Ecuador

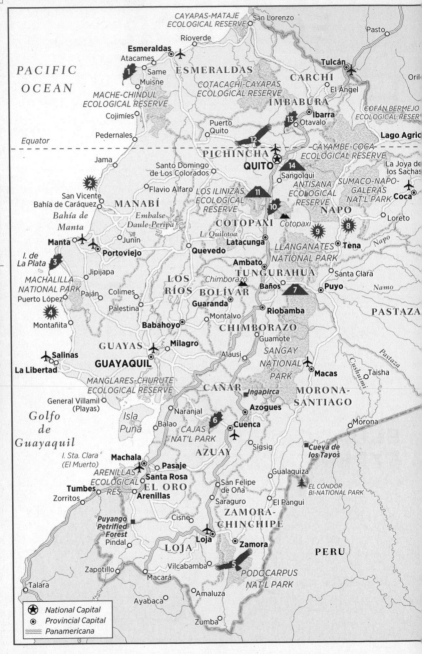

THE BEST OF NATURAL ECUADOR

THE BEST OUTDOOR ADVENTURES

THE BEST BIRD-WATCHING

THE BEST FAMILY DESTINATIONS

o **Eating Cuy:** You'll see them roasting on spits at little stands along the highways, or on sidewalks in cities and towns. You'll also find them on the menus of some of Ecuador's fanciest restaurants. It's guinea pig to you and me. The skin is served crisp and crackling, and you'll have to work to get much meat from *cuy*. But when it's good, it's moist and flavorful. See restaurant reviews throughout the book.

o **Searching for the Fountain of Youth in Vilcabamba:** The small and isolated village of Vilcabamba is said to have a disproportionately high number of centenarians. Most folks credit the clean water, air, and living. While it may not actually add years to your life, this is a great place to come for a quiet getaway with superb scenery. And whether or not there's any science behind it, a spa treatment or two at **Hostería Izhcayluma** (© 07/3025-162; www.izhcayluma.com) will definitely cure whatever's ailing you at the moment. See chapter 8.

o **Starting Off Your Day with a Glass of Tree-Tomato Juice:** Don't be put off by the name or think that it tastes anything like a traditional tomato. A tree tomato (*tomate de árbol* or *tamarillo*) is a unique fruit served just about every which way in Ecuador. My favorite is the juice, although you'll also find tree tomatoes in salads; cooked into jam; or boiled, peeled, sweetened, and served as dessert.

o **Riding a Train Past the Devil's Nose:** Earthquakes, landslides, and volcanic eruptions have wiped out most of the rail line that used to connect Quito to Guayaquil. One remaining operational section is also one of the most spectacular, a white-knuckle ride of sharp switchbacks and hairpin turns down the side of a steep rock mountain affectionately known as the Devil's Nose. See p. 191.

o **Buying a Panama Hat:** You shouldn't leave the country without buying one of these stylish straw wonders, which are made in Ecuador, not Panama (for an explanation, see p. 205). Cuenca is currently the primary center for production of Panama hats; **Homero Ortega P. & Hijos** (© 07/2809-000; www.homeroortega.com) is that city's top manufacturer. True aficionados might even head to the small towns of Montecristi (p. 268) or Jipijapa to find their special *superfino* headpiece. See chapter 8.

o **Drinking Chicha:** Homebrewed liquor made from fermenting corn, potatoes, *yuca,* and just about anything else on hand, *chicha* is consumed by indigenous peoples throughout the Andean highlands as well as in the lowland forests of El Oriente. Most *chicha* is relatively mild, but if you drink enough of it, you'll definitely feel its effects—especially at high altitudes. See chapter 7.

o **Visiting the Amazon Basin:** While officially just tributaries of the great river, the lowland rainforest rivers of eastern Ecuador form an important part of the Amazon basin. This area is loaded with impressive wildlife, and it's home to traditional indigenous tribes. You'll get to interact with both on any trip here. See chapter 11.

THE best OF NATURAL ECUADOR

o **Cuicocha Lake:** Formed thousands of years ago in the extinct crater of a massive volcano, this beautiful, clear blue lake is a popular destination. You can choose between hiking around the rim of the crater or scrambling down for a boat ride on the waters of the lake. The lake is named after the popular dish *cuy* (guinea pig), because locals thought the islands in its center resembled guinea pigs. See p.134.

o **Cotopaxi National Park:** With 33,393 hectares (82,481 acres) surrounding the park's namesake and emblematic volcano, this is Ecuador's most popular national park, after the Galápagos. At 5,897m (19,342 ft.), the snow-covered Cotopaxi is the country's second-highest peak and one of the highest active volcanoes in the world. Tour options here range from leisure hikes at lower elevations to full-on summit climbs, with other options including mountain biking, horseback riding, and camping. The best general tour operators running trips to Cotopaxi are **Metropolitan Touring** (© 02/2988-200; www.metropolitan-touring.com) and **Surtrek** (© 866/978-7398 in the U.S. and Canada, or 02/2500-530 in Ecuador; www.surtrek.com). For hard-core climbing and adventures, try **Safari Ecuador** (© 02/2552-505; www.safari.com.ec). See chapters 4 and 7.

o **Cajas National Park:** Located just outside Cuenca, this beautiful national park is famous for its 232 high montane lakes and misty cloud forests. It is also an excellent place for hiking and bird-watching. Easily accessible, it's a great change of pace from the cobblestone streets, colonial-era churches, and Panama hat shops of Cuenca. See p. 213.

o **Isla de la Plata:** The crowning jewel of **Machalilla National Park** is Isla de la Plata, an offshore island often touted as "the poor man's Galápagos." Whether or not that's an appropriate or even worthy moniker, Isla de la Plata offers excellent bird-watching and wildlife viewing and snorkeling. What's more, from late June to early October, you have a good chance of seeing humpback whales on the boat ride out to the island. On land, Machalilla has some fabulous trails and beaches. See chapter 9.

o **The Beaches West of Atacames:** In general, Ecuador is not a great beach destination. It certainly can't hold a candle to beaches found in the Caribbean, South Pacific, or even Mexico or Costa Rica. However, the relatively short section of Pacific coast west of Atacames has several small and beautiful beaches. Sua and Same are my favorites, and Tonsupa, Tonchigue, and Galera are also pretty. For someplace really unique and isolated, you can head to the small island of Muisne. See chapter 10.

o **The Rainforests of Ecuador's El Oriente:** When Amazon rainforests are mentioned, most people think of Brazil. But Ecuador's El Oriente is a vast area of lowland tropical rainforest that is part of the Amazon basin. In fact, Francisco Orellana, who first named and navigated the Amazon River, began his long journey here in Ecuador. Over 500 species of birds and some 15,000 species of flora can be found here, as well as freshwater dolphins, 11 different species of monkeys, anacondas, caimans, and jaguars. See chapter 11.

o **The Galápagos Islands:** Ecuador's prime attraction is a naturalist's paradise. In fact, if we were talking religion, this would be Holy Ground. It was here that Charles Darwin developed many of his ideas that would later emerge as the theory of natural selection and the theory of evolution. Not only are the Galápagos famous for their wildlife—on land, in the sea, and in the air—but this unique and isolated volcanic archipelago is also a living geology laboratory. See chapter 12.

THE best HISTORICAL SITES & MUSEUMS

o **Iglesia de San Francisco (Old Town; Quito):** Quito's first church, San Francisco remains one of its most impressive, especially when you factor in the attached monastery, museum, massive altar, and wide stairway ascending from the plaza.

The church and its ornate interior are in the midst of a major restoration, which should only make this classic, colonial-era church that much more impressive. See p. 107.

o **La Compañía de Jesús (Old Town; Quito):** There's so much gold and gold leaf adorning this unbelievably ornate 17th-century baroque church that I often feel the need for sunglasses. In fact, the Jesuits who built this church incorporated several sun symbols, which some say was a nod to the Incas who preceded them on this spot. The level of detail and artistry on display here is unparalleled. See p. 109.

o **Museo Nacional del Banco Central del Ecuador (New Town; Quito):** Ecuador's largest museum is also arguably its best. The anthropological and historical displays of the pre-Columbian inhabitants are extensive, interesting, and beautifully displayed. There are also very good collections of colonial-era and religious art, as well as a fine representation of Ecuador's best modern art and artists. See p.111.

o **Fundación Guayasamín (Bellavista, Quito):** Oswaldo Guayasamín was Ecuador's greatest and most famous modern artist. His striking large paintings, murals, and sculptures had an impact on artists across Latin America and around the world. This extensive museum displays both his own work and pieces from his private collection. Combined with the neighboring **Capilla del Hombre,** this is a must-see for any art lover or Latin American history buff. See p. 112.

o **Museo del Convento de la Concepción (Riobamba):** Housed in the rambling rooms of a colonial-era convent, this museum has an impressive collection of 18th-century religious art and artifacts. Rooms formerly occupied by prospective nuns are now filled with beautiful paintings, sculptures, ceremonial clothing, and jewels. See p. 189.

o **Catedral Nueva (Cuenca):** This massive cathedral took over 80 years to complete. Its two towering blue domes dominate the skyline of Cuenca, especially when viewed from one of the hillside lookouts outside town. Don't miss a chance to tour its beautiful inside, which has white marble floors, stained-glass windows, and a Renaissance-style main altar. See p. 201.

o **Museo del Banco Central (Cuenca):** This modern museum features an excellent collection of archaeological finds and relics, ethnographic displays, and colonial-era figurative·and religious art; it's also built right on top of a major Inca ceremonial site that has been semiexcavated. As if that weren't enough, there are extensive botanical gardens here, a small aviary, and llamas roaming the grounds. See p. 202.

o **Ingapirca (outside Cuenca):** Ingapirca is the greatest surviving Inca ruin in Ecuador. A visit here will allow you to appreciate the famous Inca masonry, with its seemingly impossibly tight joints. Even before the Incas arrived, this spot was inhabited by the Cañari, and some of their original constructions are also on display. The site is believed to have been sacred to both the Cañari and Incas. See p. 214.

o **La Tolita (North Pacific coast):** This unique archaeological site is found on a small island outside San Lorenzo. It is believed that it was inhabited by one of the oldest pre-Columbian cultures, a people skilled at working with gold, silver, and even platinum. One whole beach here contains millions of shards of ancient pottery. See p. 286.

o **Museo Antropológico y de Arte Contemporáneo (Guayaquil):** Large, modern, and well laid out, this is Guayaquil's best museum. There are extensive archaeological collections here from all over Ecuador, as well as a wonderful wing dedicated to contemporary Ecuadorean art. One of the best features of this museum is its prized location at the northern end of Guayaquil's Malecón, allowing easy access to both the popular riverside boardwalk and neighboring Cerro Santa Ana. See p. 236.

THE best OUTDOOR ADVENTURES

o **Climbing Volcán Cotopaxi:** Although it's actually only the second-highest peak in the country, Cotopaxi is Ecuador's most coveted summit. At 5,897m (19,342 ft.), this is no leisurely climb, yet most people in reasonably good condition, with the proper guides and acclimation, can reach the top. The views on the way up, at the summit, and coming back down are spectacular. **Adventure Planet Ecuador** (© 02/2863-086; www.adventureplanet.ec) and **Safari Ecuador** (© 02/2552-505; www.safari.com.ec) are two excellent local operators who can get you to the snowcapped summit. See chapters 4 and 7.

o **Playing Cowboy or Cowgirl on the High Mountain Paramo:** In Ecuador, cowboys are called *chagras*, and the *chagra* tradition is alive and well. Whether you sign on for a short ride or actually get to join in a roundup of wild bulls or horses, you'll feel like a *chagra* as you ride your steed over the rugged scrub of the high Andean paramo. **Hacienda La Alegría** (© 02/2462-319; www.haciendalaalegria.com) offers multiday rides. See chapters 4 and 7.

o **Watching Whales Breach & Breed off the Pacific Coast:** From late June to early October, humpback whales congregate in large numbers off Ecuador's Pacific coast. They come to the warmer waters from Antarctica to mate, give birth, feed, and nurse their young. The whales here are very social, and they often give spectacular displays of breaching. Whale-watching tours are offered up and down this coastline, but **Salinas** and **Puerto López** are your best bases for setting out on a whale-watching excursion. See chapter 9.

o **Surfing Lonely Waves Along Ecuador's Pacific Coast:** Surfers love isolated or undiscovered breaks, and Ecuador is loaded with them. In fact, even the most crowded breaks here could be considered deserted by California standards. Beach and point breaks can be found up and down the Pacific coast. Montañita and Canoa are the country's top surfing destinations and good bases to use for your search for the perfect wave. See chapters 4, 9, and 10.

o **White-Water Rafting & Kayaking:** With high Andean peaks plunging down to coastal lowlands in two directions, Ecuador is blessed with a host of white-water rivers perfect for rafting and kayaking. The small town of Tena, in El Oriente, is the country's hot spot for these sports, with easy access to everything from Class III to Class V rapids. The most popular rivers are the Upper Napo, or Río Jatunyacu, and the Río Misahuallí. There are also opportunities accessible from Quito and other cities around the country. **Ríos Ecuador** (© 06/2886-727 in Tena, or 02/2904-054 in Quito; www.riosecuador.com) is an excellent operator with offices in both Tena and Quito. See chapters 4 and 11.

o **Scuba Diving in the Galápagos Islands:** While most visitors spend their time marveling at the turtles, iguanas, boobies, and finches, diving the Galápagos may just provide the archipelago's most rewarding wildlife-viewing opportunities. The rich and protected waters here are home to large quantities of sea life, from schools of hammerhead sharks, to manta rays, to large masses of jacks, barracuda, and other schooling fish. Lucky divers enjoy playful encounters with sea lions and penguins. Your best bet for enjoying the diving is to sign up for a cruise on a dedicated dive boat. You can also book dive trips out of Puerto Ayora or Puerto Baquerizo Moreno. See chapters 4 and 12.

THE best BIRD-WATCHING

o **Enjoying the Mists and Multitude of Species Found in the Cloud Forests of Mindo, Tandayapa & Bellavista:** Cloud forests are unique ecosystems, renowned for their biological abundance. Located less than 2 hours north of Quito, the cloud forests of Mindo and Bellavista are rich and rewarding stops for birders and nature lovers of all stripes. Over 400 species of birds have been recorded here, and experts believe the actual count is much higher. **Satchitamia Lodge** (© 02/3900-907 or 02/2555-144; www.sachatamia.com) and **San Jorge de Tandayapa Lodge** (© 877/565-2596 toll-free in the U.S. and Canada, or 02/3390-403 in Ecuador; www.eco-lodgesanjorge.com) are two excellent lodges from which to base your bird-watching expeditions of this area. See p. 125, as well as chapter 4.

o **Spotting Some of the More Than 600 Species in Podocarpus National Park:** This remote national park runs from a high of 3,700m (12,136 ft.) down to some 1,000m (3,280 ft.) above sea level, and contains ecosystems that range from high paramo to cloud forest and rainforest. The most common jumping-off points for visiting here are Loja and Vilcabamba. If you're looking for an excellent personal guide, contact Jorge Luis Mendieta, at **Caminatas Andes Sureños** (© 07/2673-147; www.vilcabamba.org/caminatasandessurenos.html). See p. 221.

o **Catching Sight of Hundreds of Species in El Oriente:** The midelevation and lowland rainforests of Ecuador's El Oriente are prime bird-watching areas. Many lodges in this region have on-site bird species lists that number 400 or more. Several species of macaws frolic overhead, while the prehistoric hoatzin inhabits the low branches of riverside trees. Just about any of the lodges in El Oriente can be considered top bird-watching destinations, but I recommend the **Napo Wildlife Center** (www.napowildlifecenter.com), which has a couple of parrot licks right on their grounds, where as many as several thousand mixed-flock parrots may gather on any day to extract minerals and nutrients from an exposed clay riverbank. See chapter 11.

o **Seeing Endemic Species on the Galápagos Islands:** What can you say? From the 13 species of Darwin's finches, to the only subtropical penguin, to the unique flightless cormorant, the Galápagos provide the greatest one-stop spot to check off a whole host of once-in-a-lifetime birds from your life's list. In fact, around half of all the bird fauna on the Galápagos is endemic, meaning you can see them only here. See chapter 12.

THE best DESTINATIONS FOR FAMILIES

o **El Teleférico & Vulqano Park** (Quito; © 02/3250-076): If you spend any time in Quito, and if you have kids in tow, this is a must-stop. The fast and thrilling ride up the mountain in this cable-car gondola is usually enough to put a smile on most kids' faces, and there's also an amusement park (Vulqano Park) at the base of the cable car. See p. 106.

- **Hacienda La Alegría** (Aloag; ☎ **02/2462-319;** www.haciendalaalegria.com): This beautiful old hacienda is also a working farm. Kids can watch and even lend a hand when the cows are milked. Horseback riding is the specialty, and they have particularly good horses, trails, and trainers for introducing young riders to the sport. Their safety concern and record are exemplary. See p. 162.
- **Baños de Agua Santa:** While best known as a backpacker and adventure-travel hot spot, Baños is also great for kids. Vacationing Ecuadorean families come here, and many of the hotels and resorts cater to families. **Sangay Spa-Hotel** (☎ **03/2740-490;** www.sangayspahotel.com) has a ton of excellent facilities and activities geared toward all ages. See chapter 7.
- **Hostería Alándaluz** (south of Puerto López; ☎ **04/2780-690;** www.alandaluz hosteria.com): An environmentally conscious and eclectic collection of rooms and bungalows on a beautiful spot along the Pacific coast, this place is very popular with Ecuadorean families. In addition to the beach and pools, there's plenty to keep kids and parents alike entertained. See p. 192.
- **The Galápagos Islands:** Many of the Galápagos cruise ships and tour companies offer specific family-oriented tours. There is a ton to see and do, and plenty of science, nature, and adventure to keep the whole family interested and entertained. **Tauk** (☎ **800/788-7885** in the U.S. and Canada; www.tauck.com) is an excellent soft-adventure company with distinctive family package tours to the Galápagos. See chapter 12.

THE best LUXURY HOTELS

- **JW Marriott Hotel** (Quito; ☎ **888/236-2427** in the U.S. and Canada, or 02/2972-000 in Ecuador; www.marriotthotels.com): With an imposing glass-atrium-covered lobby, gorgeous rooms, attentive service, and good restaurants, this is one of the top business-class hotels in Ecuador. The pool, spa, and recreational facilities are excellent, as are the business services. See p. 90.
- **nü house** (Quito; ☎ **02/2557-845;** www.nuhousehotels.com): Hip and contemporary, this hotel sits right on the popular Plaza Foch, at the center of all the action in New Town. A host of great shops, restaurants, bars, and clubs is just outside its doors. See p. 92.
- **Hotel Patio Andaluz** (Quito; ☎ **02/2280-830;** www.hotelpatioandaluz.com): This place just oozes colonial-era charm. The spacious restored old mansion features two large interior courtyards. Accommodations are supercomfortable, and the service is excellent. Plus, it's located in the heart of Old Town, right off Plaza de la Independencia (Plaza Grande). See p. 95.
- **Sheraton Quito** (Quito; ☎ **800/325-3535** in the U.S. and Canada, or 02/2970-002 in Ecuador; www.sheraton.com): Large and plush rooms, a great spa, meticulous attention to detail, and fabulous service have made the Sheraton one of my favorite hotels in Quito. The facilities are all top-notch, and the location makes it one of the closest hotel options to the airport. See p. 98.
- **La Mirage Garden Hotel & Spa** (Cotacachi; ☎ **800/327-3573** in the U.S. and Canada, or 06/2915-237 in Ecuador; www.mirage.com.ec): Arguably the most exclusive and opulent boutique hotel in the country, La Mirage offers refined accommodations, fine dining, and a spectacular spa. If that's not enough, a range of excellent hikes and adventure activities is available, and Otavalo is just a few minutes away. See p. 140.

o **Samari Spa Resort** (outside Baños de Agua Santa; ☏ **03/2741-855;** www. samarispa.com): This plush and luxurious hotel and spa sits at the base of Volcán Tungurahua, on the outskirts of Baños. Rooms have all the modern conveniences (a rarity in this area), and there are beautiful design touches throughout. The spa is large and expansive. See p. 183.

o **Hotel Oro Verde Guayaquil** (Guayaquil; ☏ **04/2327-999;** www.oroverdehotels. com): Located in the center of the city, close to all the parks, museums, and scenic riverside walkways, this is the top hotel in Guayaquil. Rooms have all been beautifully remodeled, and the service is refined and attentive. See p. 207.

o **Palmazul** (San Clemente, Manabi; ☏ **05/2615-018;** www.manabihotel.com): My favorite beach hotel on the mainland, this place has large, light, and airy rooms; a fabulous restaurant; friendly service; and a fantastic location on a quiet stretch of sand. See p. 272.

o **Finch Bay Hotel** (Santa Cruz Island, Galápagos; ☏ **877/534-8584** in the U.S. and Canada, or 02/2988-200 reservations office in Quito; www.finchbayhotel. com): The only beachfront hotel on Santa Cruz is also the best. You'll be pampered and well looked after at this posh and secluded resort hotel. You'll also feel apart from the hustle and bustle that often characterizes tourism in the Galápagos. See p. 342.

o **Iguana Crossing** (Isabela Island, Galápagos; ☏ **800/217-9414** in the U.S. and Canada, or 02/6046-800 in Ecuador; www.opuntiagalapagoshotels.com): Set on the remote and lesser-visited Isabela Island, this boutique hotel has beautiful rooms, a host of modern amenities, and a great in-house restaurant. See p. 355.

THE best MODERATELY PRICED & BUDGET HOTELS

o **Hotel Vieja Cuba** (Quito; ☏ **02/2906-729;** www.hotelviejacuba.com): Beautifully restored and wonderfully located, this Mariscal-district hotel provides great value. Hardwood floors, mosaic-tile bathrooms, a central courtyard fountain, and an excellent restaurant are just some of the perks. See p. 94.

o **Hotel San Francisco de Quito** (Quito; ☏ **02/2287-758;** www.sanfranciscode quito.com.ec): Offering tidy and comfortable rooms in a wonderfully preserved 17th-century converted home, this is my favorite budget option in Quito. This hotel is situated in the heart of Old Town. You get colonial charm and a great deal all in one. See p. 96.

o **La Posada del Quinde** (Otavalo; ☏ **06/2920-750;** www.posadaquinde.com): This laid-back hotel is my favorite haunt in Otavalo. Just a few blocks away from Plaza de los Ponchos, it's a calm oasis in a bustling little town. See p. 138.

o **Hacienda Guachala** (Cangahua, Cayambe; ☏ **02/2363-042;** www.guachala. com): Dating back to 1580, this rustic old hacienda provides all the colonial-era vibe and experience offered up by its fancier brethren, at very reasonable prices. The rooms are quite rustic, but you'll have the undeniable feeling of staying at what was once a thriving colonial-era hacienda. A host of tours and activities is available, including a number of horseback-riding adventures. See p. 142.

o **Hostal La Posada del Arte** (Baños de Agua Santa; ☏ **03/2740-083;** www.posada delarte.com): Artistic touches abound in this cozy and friendly *hostal*. The best rooms here have waterfall views from private balconies, although all guests get to enjoy the view from the shared rooftop patio. See p. 184.

- **Hacienda El Porvenir** (Cotopaxi; © 02/2041-520; www.tierradelvolcan.com): Wonderfully located on the flat paramo just below Volcán Cotopaxi, this humble hostel and working ranch offers comfortable and inviting rooms from which to explore the surrounding area. See p. 163.

- **Posada del Angel** (Cuenca; © 07/2840-695; www.hostalposadadelangel.com): It's hard to believe you can find such a charming room in such a charming converted old colonial home for such a bargain. The building is over 120 years old, yet the place is lively and cheery. There are a couple of classic interior courtyards and second-floor lounge areas. If you want more privacy and a bit of a view, ask for a room on the third or fourth floor. See p. 209.

- **Manso Boutique Hostal** (Guayaquil; © 04/2526-644; www.manso.com.ec): Located right on Guayaquil's riverfront Malecón Simón Bolívar, this boutique hotel offers up well-designed and -equipped rooms in a remodeled old downtown building. The restaurant here is also excellent. See p. 240.

- **Farallón Dillon** (Ballenita; © 04/2953-611; www.farallondillon.com): Set on a steep hillside above a beautiful stretch of beach, this eclectic and rambling hotel is one of the most unique along the Ecuadorean coast. Antiques and nautical memorabilia abound, the views are fabulous, and the restaurant is excellent. See p. 248.

- **Hotel Casablanca** (Puerto Barquerizo Moreno, Isla San Cristóbal; ©/fax 05/2520-392; jacquibaz@yahoo.com): When you can score a bayfront room with a balcony on the Galápagos Islands for under $100, you know you've found a good deal. Accommodations here have loads of unique artistic touches. See p. 352.

THE best ECOLODGES & HACIENDAS

Two distinct yet, in some ways, similar lodging options in Ecuador are small, converted old haciendas and isolated ecolodges. While the haciendas tend to be located on the high Andean plains, the ecolodges are mostly found in the Oriente or the Amazon basin. Both tend to be small and isolated, and nature-viewing and active adventure activities are the order of the day.

- **Hacienda Cusín** (San Pablo del Lago, Otavalo; © 06/2918-013; www.hacienda cusin.com): This 17th-century hacienda was sold originally at auction in Spain by King Phillip II. It's located just outside Otavalo, beside the pretty San Pablo Lake. Accommodations, food, and service are all top-draw, and the surrounding gardens and volcano views are delightful. See p. 141.

- **Hacienda Zuleta** (Angochahua, Imbabura; © 06/2662-182; www.hacienda zuleta.com): With sprawling grounds; a working cheese, cattle, and horse farm; and the largest original entrance plaza of any hacienda in Ecuador, this place exudes authenticity. Once the home of President Galo Plaza, and still in his family, the hacienda offers wonderful and comfortable rooms, tasty family-style meals, and a host of tour options. Horseback riding is excellent here. They also have a condor rescue project on their grounds. See p. 144.

- **Black Sheep Inn** (Chugchilán, Cotopaxi; © 03/2708-077; www.blacksheepinn. com): This isolated high-altitude ecolodge is built on a hillside overlooking a beautiful river canyon. Situated about midway along the famed Quilotoa Loop, this is hands-down the best place to stay while taking part in the hiking, biking, trekking, and other adventures available in this pretty and pristine area. See p. 169.

- **Hacienda Leito** (outside Patate, Baños; ✆ 03/2859-329; www.haciendaleito. com): This isolated hacienda provides a fabulous mix of old and new. The original ranch building, with its original cobblestone driveway, central fountain, and antique artworks and furnishings, is a classic example of a colonial-Spanish hacienda. But the extensive spa, up-to-date rooms, and free Wi-Fi let you know you're in the 21st century. See p. 175.

- **Hacienda San Augustín de Callo** (Lasso, Cotopaxi; ✆/fax 02/2906-157; www. incahacienda.com): My pick for the most unique hacienda in Ecuador, this place is built upon the ruins of both an Inca palace and a colonial-era monastery. Some of the rooms here have walls laid by Inca masons, with their distinctive stone work. All are stunning and unique, with artistic touches that range from hand-painted murals to working stone fireplaces. See p. 161.

- **Albergue Abraspungo** (Km 3.5, Vía Guano, Riobamba; ✆ 03/2364-031; www. abraspungo.com.ec): Located on the outskirts of Riobamba, in the shadow of Chimborazo peak, this place oozes country charm. The restaurant and service here are excellent, and a number of activities are available. See p. 191.

- **Kashama** (outside Santo Domingo de los Colorados; ✆ 02/2773-193; www. kashama.com): This is a beautiful and relaxing jungle lodge and spa set on the shores of the Río Blanco. Creative design elements and arty touches abound. The inviting pool features a tall, sculpted waterfall, and the excellent spa here offers a wide range of treatments and cures. All sorts of tours and adventures are also offered. See p. 294.

- **Napo Wildlife Center** (lower Río Napo; ✆ 866/750-0830 in the U.S., or 02/6005-893 reservation office in Quito; www.napowildlifecenter.com): Run as a joint venture with the local Añangu Quichua community, this is one of the top ecolodges in the Amazon basin. The 12 lakefront bungalows are rustically luxurious, and the guides, food, and service are superb. Tours and adventures are offered, including visits to local indigenous communities and tours of the rivers, lagoons, and creeks of this lowland rainforest region. See p. 308.

- **Kapawi Ecolodge & Reserve** (on the Río Pastaza; ✆ 02/6009-333; www.kapawi. com): This pioneering ecolodge is located deep in the Amazon rainforest among the villages of the Achuar tribe. You can reach Kapawi only on a private charter flight, and the isolation is part of the charm. Beautiful cabins (built on stilts over a black-water lagoon), great food, and fantastic guides don't hurt, either. This place provides a top-notch Amazon rainforest experience. See p. 320.

THE best BED-AND-BREAKFASTS & SMALL INNS

- **Hotel Café Cultura** (Quito; ✆/fax 02/2224-271; www.cafecultura.com): Hip and European in feel, this cozy Mariscal hotel features unique artistically designed and decorated rooms, an excellent restaurant, and super service. Hand-painted murals abound, and many of the bathrooms are works of art themselves. See p. 90.

- **Mansión del Angel** (Quito; ✆ 800/327-3573 in the U.S., or 02/2557-721 in Ecuador; www.mansiondelangel.com.ec): With crystal chandeliers, Oriental rugs, and four-poster beds, this refined boutique hotel offers all the elegance and style of a bygone era. Located on a side street about halfway between the Mariscal district and Old Town, this place is a quiet and calm oasis in a busy city. See p. 97.

○ **Villa Colonna** (Quito; © 02/2955-805; www.villacolonna.ec): This six-room converted mansion oozes style and class. Rooms are plush, with a sense of Colonial-era splendor, and the hotel's rooftop terrace is a beautiful spot to take in some sweeping views of the Old Town's impressive architecture. See p. 96.

○ **Mansión Santa Isabella** (Riobamba; © 03/2962-947; www.mansionsanta isabella.com): This new boutique hotel offers warm and inviting rooms right in the heart of Riobamba, just blocks away from the city's famous train station. The central interior courtyard is a quiet oasis, and the hotel's wine cellar and bar is arguably Riobamba's best nighttime haunt. See p. 192.

○ **Mansión Alcázar** (Cuenca; © 800/327-3573 in the U.S. and Canada, or 07/2823-918 in Ecuador; www.mansionalcazar.com): Like the Santa Lucía (below), this charming little hotel is housed in a remarkably well-restored old colonial mansion. The Alcázar has a gorgeous garden with several sumptuous sitting areas and lounges, and one of the best restaurants in Cuenca. See p. 206.

○ **Hotel Santa Lucía** (Cuenca; © 07/2828-000; www.santaluciahotel.com): Set right in the heart of colonial Cuenca, in a house that dates to 1859, this is one of the best boutique hotels in Ecuador. The colonial vibe is maintained throughout, but the rooms also feature plasma-screen televisions and free Wi-Fi. The central courtyard here is home to a towering magnolia tree, as well as an excellent restaurant. See p. 207.

○ **Mansión del Río** (Guayaquil; © 04/2565-827; www.mansiondelrio-ec.com): This new boutique hotel has an enviable location fronting the river in the heart of Guayaquil's trendy and artistic Las Peñas neighborhood. The rooms and common areas are plush and overflowing with colonial-era charm and sophistication. See p. 239.

○ **Vistalmar** (Manta; © 05/2621-671; www.hosteriavistaalmar.com): From the two large jade horses near the entrance to the large Buddha sculpture in the main lounge area, you'll be struck at every turn by the art, sculpture, and decor here. When that stops piquing your interest, you can marvel at the ocean views from the hillside perch. See p. 270.

○ **El Faro Escandinavo** (San Lorenzo, south of Manta; © 09/1122-336; www.elfaro escandinavo.com): Set on a lovely stretch of nearly deserted beach, the eight individual bungalows here are inviting yet understated. The service and attention are very personalized. See p. 271.

○ **Hamadryade Lodge** (south of Tena; © 800/327-3573 in the U.S. and Canada, or 08/5909-992 in Ecuador; www.hamadryade-lodge.com): With just four individual cabins, this new boutique lodge adds a touch of class and style to the generally more rustic offerings found in the Ecuadorean Amazon basin. See p. 314.

○ **Red Mangrove Adventura Lodge** (Puerto Ayora, Isla Santa Cruz, Galápagos; © 888/254-3190 in the U.S. and Canada, or 05/2526-564 in Ecuador; www. redmangrove.com): Located right on the bay, this hip hotel offers up the best rooms right in Puerto Ayora. A rambling structure filled with nooks and crannies, the hotel boasts tasteful and comfortable rooms and the best restaurant on the island. These folks also run hotels on Isla Floreana and Isla Isabela. See p. 343.

THE best RESTAURANTS

o **Azuca Latin Bistro** (Quito; ℭ 02/2907-164): Loud and lively most of the time, this spot serves up excellent *nuevo latino* fare. Mojitos are the specialty drink, and there's quite a variety of them on the menu here. See p. 99.

o **Theatrum** (Quito; ℭ 02/2571-011; www.theatrum.com.ec): With elegant ambience, an inventive menu, and a wonderful setting overlooking Plaza Sucre, this is one of my favorite restaurants in Quito. If you're lucky, you can combine a meal here with a show or concert at Teatro Sucre. See p. 101.

o **Zazu** (Quito; ℭ 02/2543-559; www.zazuquito.com): Brash and bold, Quito's hippest restaurant is also one of its most satisfying. The Peruvian-born chef uses his native sensibility, fresh local ingredients, and ample imagination to create a consistently successful string of new and exciting dishes. Just about everything on the menu shines, but my favorite way to dine here is to trust the chef and sign on for his nightly tasting menu. See p. 103.

o **Hacienda Rumiloma** (Quito; ℭ 02/2548-206): It's definitely worth the short taxi ride to this elegant and eclectic restaurant on the slopes of Volcán Pichincha. The menu is broad, inventive, and wonderfully executed. And the cozy dining room features an excellent view of the city below. See p. 103.

o **Café Pachamama** (Otavalo; ℭ 06/2920-750): Housed inside a popular hotel, this is my favorite restaurant in Otavalo. The healthy and creative international cuisine is served in a cozy and inviting ambience. Locally grown organic produce is used wherever possible. This is a welcome treat for breakfast, lunch, or dinner. See p. 143.

o **Café Mariane** (Baños de Agua Santa; ℭ 03/2740-936): I know Baños is a backpacker and budget-hound hangout, but even if that description fits you, be sure to treat yourself to an elegant French-Mediterranean meal at the best little restaurant in town. See p. 185.

o **Casa Alonso** (Cuenca; ℭ 07/2823-918): A young, creative chef has turned the hotel restaurant inside the elegant Mansión Alcázar into one of the best fine-dining experiences to be found in Ecuador. Using local ingredients and tweaking traditional recipes, the menu here is adventurous and extremely pleasing. See p. 210.

o **Tiestos** (Cuenca; ℭ 07/2835-310): Most of the dishes here are cooked in clay pots, or *tiestos*, which are taken from the small open kitchen right to the table in this festive and almost always packed restaurant. The food itself is rich and rewarding. See p. 211.

o **Lo Nuestro** (Guayaquil; ℭ 04/2386-398): Elegant and relaxed, this is the best place in Guayaquil to enjoy classic Ecuadorean cooking in a refined setting. The restaurant is located a little outside downtown, but it's definitely worth the ride. See p. 242.

o **Asia de Cuba** (Guayaquil; ℭ 04/2838-068): Guayaquil is experiencing a major boom in high-end dining, and this Latin-Asian fusion spot is a highlight. The decor is chic and contemporary, the bar is well stocked and beautiful, and the food hits all the right marks. See p. 242.

o **Martinica** (Manta; ℭ 05/2613-735): Creative and hip, this homey restaurant stands head and shoulders above the rest in Manta. The eclectic fusion menu is bolstered by a wide-ranging wine list. See p. 271.

o **Sea Flower Restaurant** (Same; ℭ 06/2733-369): It's almost worth a trip to Ecuador's Pacific coast just to dine at this delightful spot. Presentations are eye-catching, and the food lives up to the fanfare. Be sure to have a reservation—this place fills up fast. See p. 190.

o **The Marquis Restaurant** (Tena; ✆ 05/06/2886-513): Aside from a few fancy lodges with an imported chef, dining in the Ecuadorean Amazon region is pretty dire. This downtown Tena restaurant is a striking exception to the rule, with homemade pastas, excellent steaks, and a good wine list, to boot. See p. 313.

o **Angermeyer Point Restaurant** (Puerto Ayora; ✆ 05/2527-007): With a wraparound wooden deck fronting the water on Puerto Ayora's Academy Bay, this restaurant has a spectacular setting. With a wide-ranging menu, the dining here is pretty good, too. See p. 345.

THE best SHOPPING & MARKETS

o **Olga Fisch Folklore** (Quito; ✆ 02/2541-315; www.olgafisch.com): Olga Fisch was a pioneer in recognizing and promoting the artistry of Ecuador's artisans and craftspeople. She helped them refine and improve some of their designs. Today her shop/gallery remains the top place to go for the best selection of high-end products. You'll find everything here, from clothing to ceramics, to paintings. You can get chess sets with pieces carved from *tagua* nuts, or fine original silver and gemstone jewelry. See p. 115.

o **Tianguez** (Quito; ✆ 02/2570-240; www.sinchisacha.org): Housed in a mazelike series of rooms that feel like catacombs under the San Francisco church, this is my favorite place to shop for handicrafts. Just about every corner and region of the country is represented here, with pieces from the various Amazon basin indigenous tribes, as well as primitive paintings from artisans of the central Sierra. You can buy trinkets for next to nothing, or fine works that will make a dent in your wallet. See p. 115.

o **Otavalo Market** (Otavalo): This is the most famous market in Ecuador, and perhaps in all of South America. Indeed, it's the place to come for all sorts of locally made crafts, including alpaca sweaters, rugs, and wall hangings, as well as a wide range of wood work, primitive paintings, and jewelry. Musicians can pick up some pan pipes or a *charango*. See p. 133.

o **San Antonio de Ibarra:** It seems as if everyone in this little town in Imbabura province is a woodcarver. Many of the works produced here are religious in theme, and often of monumental proportion. Still, you can get plenty of decorative and functional pieces, and some that are easy enough to carry home with you (the others can be shipped). See p. 147.

o **Cuenca:** From Panama hats to locally produced handicrafts, fine art works to unique jewelry pieces, Cuenca holds its own against Quito and Otavalo as one of the top shopping cities in the country. Of particular interest are visits to the actual Panama hat factories and the studio of renowned ceramic artist Eduardo Vega. See chapter 8.

o **Galería Aymara** (Puerto Ayora; ✆ 05/2526-835; www.galeria-aymara.com): This place has an amazing collection of decorative and functional pieces culled from artists and craftspeople from the Galápagos, mainland Ecuador, and other South American countries. See p. 342.

THE best AFTER-DARK FUN

- **Mariscal District** (Quito): The 4- to 5-square-block area known as Mariscal, in the heart of Quito's New Town, is chock-full of bars, clubs, discos, and restaurants. It's busy here every night of the week, but especially Thursday through Saturday. Consider starting off on Plaza Foch with a pub crawl, but be careful and use common sense, because crime against tourists is not unheard of here. See p. 119.

- **Café Arte** (Ibarra; ✆ 06/2950-806): The otherwise sleepy and mostly forgotten city of Ibarra is home to one of the country's best boho bars and coffeehouses. This place has excellent and widely varied entertainment most weekend nights. See p. 150.

- **Baños de Agua Santa:** As befits a bustling backpacker and adventure-tourist town, Baños has a rocking nightlife. If the rumblings of Volcán Tungurahua keep you up at night here, stroll down Calle Eloy Alfaro, where you'll find a string of bars, clubs, discos, and *peñas*. See p. 185.

- **Café Eucalyptus** (Cuenca; ✆ 07/2849-157): Great tapas, an excellent wine list, locally produced tap beer, and top-notch call liquors combine with a warm and welcoming ambience to make this hands down the top after-dark gathering spot in Cuenca. I like the couch seating near the fireplace, but the bar is also a good place to settle in. Or, if you're looking for a little more privacy, head to the second floor. See p. 213.

- **Montañita** (South Pacific coast): In addition to their prowess on the sea, surfers are legendary for their après-surf sessions. Montañita is the top surfer town in Ecuador, and its raucous nightlife is fed by the flood of local and international surfers. Lately, they've been pulling out all the stops on the weekend closest to a full moon. See p. 252.

- **Night Tours** (El Oriente): Most neotropical forest dwellers are nocturnal. Animal and insect calls fill the air, and the rustling on the ground all around takes on new meaning. Night tours are offered at most, if not all, of the rainforest nature lodges in the Ecuadorean Amazon basin. Many use high-powered flashlights to catch glimpses of various animals. See chapter 11.

- **Puerto Ayora** (Galápagos Islands): Puerto Ayora has a surprisingly lively, albeit limited, nightlife and bar scene. **Bongo Bar** (✆ 05/2526-264) is the most happening place in town at night. It's located on a rooftop and opens at 4pm but usually doesn't get busy until after 8pm. See p. 346.

THE best WEBSITES ABOUT ECUADOR

- **Latin America Network Information Center** (http://lanic.utexas.edu/la/ecuador): This site contains a collection of diverse information about Ecuador. Hands down, it's the best place for Web browsing, with helpful links to a wide range of tourism and general information sites.

- **Pure Ecuador** (www.ecuador.travel): This is the official website of the Ecuadorean Ministry of Tourism. There's a lot of information here, although much of it is quite basic, and the format can be hard to navigate at times.

- **Hip Ecuador** (www.hipecuador.com): This is a large and comprehensive tourism site in English, with loads of useful information, recommendations, and links.

- **Quito** (www.quito.com.ec): Quito's official tourism bureau maintains an excellent bilingual site, loaded with useful and current information.
- **U.S. Embassy in Quito** (http://ecuador.usembassy.gov): This is the official website of the United States Embassy in Quito. This site has plenty of good information, even for non-U.S. citizens, including regular news updates and travel advisories.

ECUADOR IN DEPTH

2

Ecuador is a nation of extremes, a nexus of the Northern and Southern hemispheres, a link between the Old and New worlds. Centuries of Inca, Andean, and Amazonian indigenous civilization yielded to Spanish colonial rule, which was followed by independence, modernization, and, most recently, decades of tumultuous government. All of this has given Ecuador's economy, politics, crafts, architecture, languages, and religious customs one primary trait: profound variety. Ecuador is one of the smallest countries in South America, but with nearly 15 million residents, it's home to an ethnically and culturally diverse population.

For travelers, all this variety translates into myriad opportunities to explore and enjoy this multifaceted country. During a visit here, you'll have ample and easy access to hefty doses of awe and adventure, whether floating down the Amazon in a dugout canoe; touring through colonial churches or plazas; hiking along snowcapped volcanic peaks or in dense jungles; dodging piranhas or anacondas; searching for howler monkeys in the rainforest or for giant condors soaring above the Andes; learning Quichua in a Quiteño language school (or listening to it spoken in a mountainous village near Riobamba); or viewing the woodcarvings, paintings, Panama hats, woven tapestries, and clothing of contemporary indigenous craftspeople or the stone temples, carvings, and fortresses of ancient Inca empires.

And of course, there are the Galápagos Islands. Some 1,000km (621 miles) off the country's Pacific coast, the islands are still home to the emblematic and endemic giant Galápagos tortoises that were around when Charles Darwin arrived here in 1831. Among other species that call the Galápagos home are marine and land iguanas, sea lions, albatrosses, and the famous blue-footed boobies. It's not surprising that this magical archipelago inspired a scientific theory that would change how human beings understand the natural world.

ECUADOR TODAY

The government of President Rafael Correa represents a radical change from the decades of oligarchic, military, and post-military rule. With the dissolution of the nation's congress and the drafting of a new constitution in 2008, Correa set the country on a new road forward. But that road, like so many in the country, is bumpy, winding, and steep—and not yet entirely paved. Chaos and turmoil have come to define Ecuadorean politics, and an October 2010 police uprising did nothing to dispel that perception.

People

Long-lasting Inca and Spanish empires, followed by centuries of unstable national governments, have produced an ethnically, linguistically, and economically divided Ecuador. Around 65% of the country's almost 15 million people are *mestizo*—of mixed Spanish-Amerindian heritage. Amerindians make up a full 25% of the population, with blacks accounting for 3%, and 7% falling into the "Caucasian/other" category.

There are 11 indigenous groups, each with its own language and customs. The largest is the Andean Quichua, over two million strong. They are joined in the equatorial Andes by the Otavaleños, Salasaca, and Saraguros. The shaman traditions of the Incas are carried on in the rainforest by the Huaorani, Zaparo, Cofán, lowland Quichua, Siona, Secoya, Shuar, and Achuar peoples. The nation's black population traces its ancestry to slaves who were brought to work on coastal sugar plantations in the 1500s. The Afro-Ecuadorean community is famous for its marimba music and lively dance festivals.

The population is about equally divided between the central highlands and the low-lying coastal region. Over the last few decades, there has been a steady migration toward the cities, and today 60% of Ecuadoreans reside in urban areas. Hundreds of thousands of people emigrated from Ecuador following the financial crisis at the beginning of the millennium; the U.S. State Department estimates that more than two million Ecuadoreans currently reside in the United States, and large populations of Ecuadorean immigrants can be found across Europe, particularly in Spain.

Economy

The Ecuadorean economy depends heavily on the export of petroleum, which represents around 50% of the country's export earnings and almost a third of the government's revenues. Agriculture is strong as well. Ecuador is the world's largest banana exporter, accounting for more than 30% of the world's banana supply and shipping out roughly 260 million cases of the fruit in 2010. Other crops include cocoa, coffee, cut flowers, rice, and sugar cane. Tourism and manufacturing are also important.

Per-capita income in Ecuador is around $4,000 per year. The gap between rich and poor is wide. Estimates vary as to what percentage of the population lives below the poverty line, but most agree the rate is at least 35% and perhaps as high as 60%. Though social turmoil has been somewhat muted, considering how vast the economic inequality is, economic weakness is not without its obvious social costs. The poverty rate helps explain, for instance, the number of young Ecuadoreans in gangs: over 65,000, by some estimates.

The nation's dependence on petroleum production has been a boon, but it leaves the country vulnerable to the frequent swings in global prices. Ecuador suffered a massive economic crisis in 1999, with its GDP contracting by more than 6%. The adoption of the dollar as the national currency in 2000, replacing the rapidly devaluating sucre, was highly controversial, and though it led to the end of hyperinflation, it also resulted in a perceived loss of national sovereignty. After robust economic growth in 2007 and 2008, it was estimated that the GDP contracted in 2009, and it was projected to be sluggish in 2010. Moreover, economic policies under the Correa government, including the unilateral termination of more than a dozen bilateral investment treaties, has put a huge damper on both domestic and foreign investment in the country.

Politics

Social and economic divisions have significantly affected Ecuador's political landscape. National politics are fractured along geographic, ethnic, and ideological lines. The country has more than two dozen official political parties.

In recent decades, the instability of Ecuador's executive branch has drawn international attention. Between 1996 and 2006, seven presidents attempted to govern the nation. They all failed to ameliorate the political volatility, because of either a hostile Congress, a military coup d'état, or what many Ecuadoreans considered the president's sheer mental incompetence.

After a decade that saw power most often change hands through military intervention or presidential resignation, free and popular elections were held in autumn 2006, with 13 candidates vying for office. Because no candidate obtained a high enough percentage of the vote to win in the first round, a runoff election took place in November 2006. It pitted banana tycoon Alvaro Noboa, who had campaigned unsuccessfully in 1998 and 2002, against former finance minister Rafael Correa, a left-leaning populist. Correa defeated Noboa and announced plans to hold a referendum that would lead to the drafting of a new constitution. In a national referendum held in September 2008, Ecuadoreans voted by a large margin to ratify the new constitution. (In Latin America, political movements routinely write new constitutions when they come to power.)

President Rafael Correa's PAIS Alliance (Alianza PAIS) party controls a majority of the seats in the Constituent Assembly (national congress), giving it broad powers to enact legislation. Other parties represented include the Ecuadorean Roldosist Party (Partido Roldosista Ecuatoriano), the Institutional Renewal Party of National Action (Partido Renovador Institucional de Acción Nacional), the January 21 Patriotic Society (Partido Sociedad Patriótica 21 de Enero), and the Social Christian Party (Partido Social Cristiano).

LOOKING BACK: ECUADOR HISTORY

Early History

Human presence in the Andes region dates perhaps as far back as 20,000 B.C.—making South America the last continent on Earth, with the exception of Antarctica, to be inhabited. Evidence of the first hunter-gatherer societies in Ecuador dates back to 10,000 B.C., and methods of crop cultivation began to develop around 3600 B.C.

Though its partial influence began to spread from what is now Peru around A.D. 1200, the Inca empire held uncontested dominion over the Andes region only from 1438 to 1533. In Quichua, it was known as *Tawantin Suyu,* or "Land of the Four Regions." At its height, it encompassed an estimated 15 million people belonging to roughly 100 ethnic or linguistic communities; it covered an area of over 6,000 sq. km (2,317 sq. miles), within which were more than 25,000km (15,500 miles) of roads.

Inca warrior Pachacuti and his son Topa Yupanqui, descendants of the first Sapa Inca, Manco Capac, began to extend the empire into what is now Ecuador in 1463. The 11th Sapa Inca, Huayna Capac, completed the conquest of Ecuador, extended the empire into present-day Chile and Argentina, and took a special interest in the city of Quito, which his father, Tupac Yupanqui, rebuilt. When Huayna Capac died

More Like Dogs Than Like Gods

Conventional wisdom holds that the Incas believed the Spaniards were gods and capitulated to the invaders out of holy fear. This may have been true in some cases. Not so for Atahualpa. The Sapa Inca had heard of these strange visitors who had wool on their faces, like an alpaca or a sheep, and considered them subhuman, akin to animals.

They must have been fairly stupid, thought Atahualpa, if they walked around wearing metal pots on their heads—and they never even used the pots for cooking. It was the Inca's lack of fear, rather than his excess of it, that clouded his judgment, initially leading him to greet the Spaniards with dancers rather than with soldiers.

of either smallpox or malaria during a military campaign in 1527, a war of succession began between his sons, Huáscar and Atahualpa.

Shortly after his father's death, Huáscar seized control of Cusco and captured Atahualpa. Legend has it that the crafty Atahualpa escaped with the help of a little girl, returned to Quito, and began recruiting his father's best generals to serve alongside him. Atahualpa's forces were eventually victorious, but the triumph was short-lived: While he was resting in hot springs near Cajamarca, a former swineherd from western Spain named Francisco Pizarro stopped by for a visit.

Spanish Conquest

At the end of 1531, Francisco Pizarro set out from Panama with fewer than 200 men and arrived on the coast of Ecuador. He spent some months gathering precious stones and gold in order to finance reinforcements, and then he led his expedition inland.

On November 16, 1532, 168 Spaniards led by Pizarro attacked the imperial army of the Incas at Cajamarca, almost 80,000 soldiers strong. Despite reports of having felt quite scared the night before, the Spaniards slaughtered over 7,000 Incas and captured the emperor, Atahualpa. The supposed justification for the attack was Atahualpa's rejection of Christianity (a Spanish friar had presented him with a Bible, but the emperor said he could not hear what the book said and tossed it to the floor).

The Spaniards considered Atahualpa useful for subduing the rest of the population and kept him alive, though imprisoned. While under their watch, he learned to speak some Spanish and play chess. But after receiving over 20 tons of gold and silver, Atahualpa's captors garroted him.

Quito fell to the Spanish in mid-1534, effectively ending resistance from the Inca armies. The conquistadors continued to loot, pillage, kill, and torture the indigenous population as they swept across the continent, though they were not able to implement a unified system of colonial rule until more than 20 years after capturing Atahualpa. Once established, Spanish dominion was largely peaceful, though in no way just.

Colonial Rule

When Spanish colonial rule began in 1544, Ecuador was part of the Viceroyalty of Peru. It joined the new Viceroyalty of Nueva Granada in 1720. Quito became an *audiencia real* in 1563, allowing for direct relations with the Spanish crown and circumventing the regional government in Lima. ("Quito" referred not just to the city, but encompassed all of present-day Ecuador, reaching into northern Peru and southern Colombia.)

In Spanish colonial society, racial divisions were enshrined in law. *Peninsulares* (Spaniards living in the New World who were born in Spain) occupied the top of the economic and political pyramid, followed by *criollos* (descendants of Spaniards born in the New World), *mestizos* (those of mixed Spanish and Amerindian ancestry), *mulatos* (those of mixed Spanish and African ancestry), Amerindians, *zambos* (those of mixed Amerindian and African ancestry), and finally blacks. Individuals from the latter three groups were often enslaved outright. In Ecuador, the population soon became heavily *mestizo*, with less indigenous predominance than in Peru or Bolivia, but significantly more than in Argentina or Chile.

These racial divisions formed the basis for the economic system, the *encomienda*. In exchange for defending the territory, Spanish settlers were granted ownership not only of the land, but also of the people living on it. The indigenous population, therefore, was forced into slavery on plantations. In 1542, Spanish friar Bartolomé de las Casas convinced the Spanish crown to institute the New Laws, granting some protection to indigenous peoples. But despite these protections, forced labor largely continued.

And no law could protect against the most pernicious Spanish import: disease. The diseases the Europeans brought devastated the Incas and all other indigenous societies in the Western Hemisphere. Some scholars estimate that there were 20 million Native Americans in the New World prior to the arrival of the Spanish. Nearly 95% of them were wiped out after the conquistadors arrived, falling to diseases such as plague, typhoid, and smallpox, to which they had no natural resistance. The Western Hemisphere was essentially emptied of its native population. While the Incas were vanquished militarily, after the imposition of colonial rule, the effect of European diseases was severe and far-reaching.

Independence

Criollo discontent with the exclusive rule of *peninsulares* reached a boiling point in the early 19th century, and a mood of reform swept across New Spain. A sharp economic downturn contributed to that mood.

In October 1820, a *criollo* junta led by José Joaquín Olmedo declared Quito independent from Spain and appealed to the independence movements in Venezuela and Argentina for support.

At the time, rebellion was sweeping the Western Hemisphere. Simón Bolívar, El Libertador, defeated a Spanish army at Carabobo in Venezuela on June 24, 1821, clearing the way for the independence of modern-day Venezuela, Colombia, Panama, and Bolivia. On September 15, 1821, Gabino Gaínza, the Spanish captain general of Central America and a rebel sympathizer, signed the Act of Independence, which broke Mexico's and Central America's ties with Spain.

Bolívar sent troops and skilled officers to Olmedo, and an Ecuadorean army led by José de Sucre Alcalá won a decisive victory against the Spanish at Pichincha on May 24, 1822. Hours later, the Quito Audiencia formally surrendered to Sucre.

Ecuador immediately joined the Republic of Greater Colombia, led by Bolívar, but separated from that federation in 1830 following Bolívar's resignation as president. The Republic of Ecuador was born.

The Early Republic

In 1832, Ecuador annexed an archipelago about 970km (599 miles) off its coast—the Galápagos. Originally used as a prison colony, the islands soon became populated by a group of farmers and artists. In 1835, the British survey ship HMS *Beagle* sailed by, carrying a young naturalist named Charles Darwin. He published *On the Origin of Species,* a landmark in human thought, in 1859.

Following independence, Ecuador's political landscape was rocky. It quickly came to be dominated by two parties, the Liberals and the Conservatives. Apart from the geographic differences between the two (the Liberals drew their strength from coastal populations, while the Conservatives represented the country's heartland and highlands), one issue defined their rivalry and Ecuadorean politics for more than a century after the creation of the republic: the role of the Roman Catholic Church in society.

With backing from the Church, Conservative politician Gabriel García Moreno rose to power in the 1860s. García Moreno strove to achieve universal literacy among the citizenry and forged a close relationship with the clergy, granting asylum to exiled Jesuit priests.

Before being assassinated with a machete by a Colombian immigrant, García Moreno inspired deep resentment among the Liberals, who favored secular government, closer ties with the United States, and freer markets.

The political conflict soon became a military one: In 1895, Ecuador erupted in civil war between the Liberals and Conservatives. The Catholic Church urged its loyal members to take up arms against the Liberals but later declared neutrality in the conflict. By the end of the year, the Liberals were victorious and formed a government under President Eloy Alfaro.

Intermittently serving until his assassination in 1911, Alfaro was best known for instituting a firm separation of church and state. Whereas religious paintings had adorned the walls of public buildings during García Moreno's term, Alfaro replaced them with secular art. The president's other reforms included the establishment of civil rights such as freedom of speech, the legalization of civil marriage and divorce, the building of the first railroad from Guayaquil to Quito, and the construction of many public schools. Today he is remembered as a national hero.

A Rocky Century

All the while, Ecuador's economy was changing. By the early 20th century, cocoa had taken over as the dominant crop, responding to a worldwide boom in demand. But over-reliance on the crop led to trouble. In 1925, the cocoa market plummeted and a bloodless political coup removed the Liberals from power. Contemporary observers might think today's political climate in Ecuador is volatile, but the 1930s were much worse: 14 chief executives served during the depressed decade.

The end of World War II and a global banana boom heralded a brighter future for Ecuador. Between 1948 and 1952, exports of the golden fruit grew from $2 million to $20 million. The political climate was relatively mild in the years following the war's end, with three freely elected presidents completing their terms between 1948 and 1960.

These stable conditions did not last, though. The banana boom ended in 1959, bringing a severe economic downturn in its wake. In 1963, a military junta deposed the sitting president, Carlos Julio Arosemena, who himself had pressured sitting president José María Velasco into resigning 2 years earlier. Velasco soon returned to the presidency, assuming dictatorial powers in 1970, only to be overthrown by another military junta in 1972.

Using revenues from Ecuador's newly successful oil export industry, the junta invested in land reform and industrialization. But in the midst of the global oil crisis of 1979, a successor junta allowed for a democratic transition to power. A charismatic young politician from Guayaquil named Jaime Roldós Aguilera won the presidency by a landslide, but his reform efforts were curtailed 2 years later when his plane crashed.

An economic and humanitarian crisis struck the country in 1987 in the form of a devastating earthquake in northeast Ecuador. The disaster interrupted oil exports, crippling the economy.

Though Ecuador's economy intermittently grew and contracted during the 20th century, the country itself followed a single trend: It shrank. Starting in 1904, Ecuador began to lose a substantial amount of its territory in small-scale conflicts with its neighbors. The most serious was the 1941 war with Peru, which resulted in Peru's temporarily occupying two-thirds of Ecuador. Though Peru eventually withdrew after the signing of the Río de Janeiro Protocol in 1942, the ambiguous border between the two nations remained a point of contention. In 1995, the two countries began the so-called "Cenepa War," prompting shock and outrage from the international community. A ceasefire was quickly established, but a final treaty would not be signed for several more years.

A Revolving Door at the Presidential Palace

Change seems to be a consistent factor in Ecuadorean politics—since the return to democracy in 1979, no party has captured the presidency through an election more than once—but the period between 1997 and 2006 was as tumultuous as any during the last century. Seven presidents took office during that 10-year period, intermittently swept in and out of power by the ballot of the people, the vote of the National Congress, or the barrel of a gun.

In 1996, Ecuadoreans elected Abdalá Bucaram, from the Guayaquil-based center-right Ecuadorean Roldosista Party (PRE), to what was supposed to be a 4-year term. He campaigned on promises to institute populist economic policies and check the influence of the nation's oligarchy, but once in office, his administration was widely criticized for corruption. Less than a year into his term, Bucaram was impeached by the National Congress on the grounds that he was mentally incompetent to serve. Fabián Alarcón, at the time the leader of the Congress, was named interim president, which was reinforced by the electorate in a May 1997 referendum.

A year later, the nation went to the polls once more to choose a replacement president to serve a full 4-year term. Quito Mayor Jamil Mahuad, of the Popular Democracy Party, narrowly defeated banana magnate Alvaro Noboa in a runoff election, taking office on August 10, 1998, the same day that a new constitution went into effect. Mahuad was lauded for negotiating a peace treaty with Peru to end the half-century-old border conflict, but his successes ended there. A sharp decline in the price of oil sent Ecuador's economy into a tailspin in 1999, leading Mahuad to propose adopting the U.S. dollar as the country's official currency in order to curtail inflation. Huge demonstrations swept Quito, and on January 21, 2000, protestors stormed the National Congress building, proclaiming a three-person junta to be Ecuador's new ruling body.

Military commanders intervened and negotiated a deal whereby Mahuad would step down to make way for his vice president, Gustavo Noboa, to take office. Mahuad announced his resignation and endorsed his successor in a televised address, and Congress ratified the succession.

Noboa brought little in the way of policy change from his predecessor. He followed through on Mahuad's plan to dollarize the economy and negotiated a deal for the construction of the country's second major oil pipeline using private financing.

Lucio Gutiérrez, formerly an army colonel and member of the ruling junta of January 21, won the presidential election of 2002 and took office in January of the following year. The conservative fiscal policies he implemented stood in stark contrast to his populist campaign promises, and when demonstrations began to shake the capital, Gutiérrez declared a state of emergency and replaced the Supreme Court. On April 20, 2005, Congress declared that he had "abandoned his post," and stripped him of it. Gutiérrez went into exile, leaving Vice President Alfredo Palacio to take over. He carried out no major reforms during his term.

In 2006, Ecuador went to the polls once more, and elected Rafael Correa, a center-left economist. Despite major changes, including hotly contested national referendums to approve the drafting and subsequent ratification of a new constitution, the first couple of years of the Correa administration were relatively calm. However, that changed dramatically in an October 2010 national strike and alleged coup attempt, from which Correa was rescued safe and sound. In the wake of these events, Correa's public approval rating shot up to 75%, and he was granted the perfect pretext to solidify his agenda and clean house, which he is maximizing to the fullest.

In April 2011, a diplomatic spat between the United States and Ecuador resulted in each country expelling the other's ambassador. The dispute erupted when a confidential cable released by WikiLeaks quoted U.S. ambassador Heather Hodges claiming that a former police chief was well known to be deeply corrupt, and that it was likely that President Correa was aware of this. Correa declared Hodges a persona non grata and withdrew her credentials. The United States responded in kind by expelling Ecuadorean ambassador Luis Gallegos.

ART & ARCHITECTURE

Ecuador's culture is arguably as varied as its population and politics. Mainstream culture is a mix of Amerindian, Spanish, African, North American, and other Latin American influences. Its mixed heritage has ensured the existence of a wide array of arts and crafts, literature, architectural styles, and musical rhythms.

Art

Ecuadorean artists range from folk artisans working in a variety of forms, materials, and traditions to modern painters, sculptors, and ceramicists producing beautiful representational and abstract works.

  The Work of God or the Devil?

As legend has it, a stonemason named Cantuña enlisted the Devil's help in constructing a chapel near Iglesia de San Francisco in Quito in the late 18th century. When the Devil came to collect Cantuña's soul as payment for the work, thinking the project had been completed, the mason showed him that the church was, in fact, missing a single stone. The Devil returned to Hell angry and empty-handed.

Pre-Columbian artisans produced a wide range of pottery, paintings, sculpture, and gold and silver work. Intact pottery figurines dating from 3000 B.C. were discovered in the coastal village of Valdivia and are still on display in several museums. After the arrival of the Spanish, art became increasingly influenced by Christianity. Paintings from colonial times can still be seen in many churches and museums. During the 17th and 18th centuries, painters of the **Quito School** began to combine Spanish and indigenous influences, but this movement fell out of favor following independence, when the focus shifted to formalist depictions of the great heroes of the revolution and the social elite.

Ecuador's most prominent modern artist is **Oswaldo Guayasamín** (1919–99), whose powerful paintings—often of just faces and hands—evoke the lives, struggles, and suffering of the country's indigenous population.

Indigenous woven tapestries and clothing are still available for sale throughout the country, as are fine basketwork, leatherwork, woodcarving, ceramics, and jewelry. The most famous indigenous craft is the **Panama hat,** as much a must-buy in Ecuador as cigars are in Cuba.

Galleries, shops, and markets in Quito, Otavalo, Ibarra, Cuenca, and Guayaquil carry a wide range of locally produced art and crafts; see chapters 5, 8, and 9 for more information.

Architecture

Ecuador's buildings offer a charming mix of old and new. Quito is perhaps the South American colonial capital that has changed the least since Spanish rule. The city's very impressive colonial churches were built in the baroque style, including **La Compañía de Jesús, Iglesia de Santo Domingo,** and **Iglesia de San Francisco.** Several neoclassical and Beaux Arts buildings also survive from the beginnings of the republic.

Some of the most beautiful buildings in Ecuador are also found in Cuenca. **La Inmaculada,** the city's main cathedral, was completed in 1885 and houses a famous painting of the Virgin Mary, along with modern stained glass. The city's other cathedral, **El Sagrario,** was completed in 1557 and built over Inca ruins, some of which are still visible. Several other colonial and colonial-esque buildings dot the historic city, including the district **Supreme Court.**

In Guayaquil, Ecuador's largest city, fire wiped out most of the old colonial buildings, and today modern high-rises coexist with tin-roof slums, though poverty is not laid as bare as in other urban areas of Latin America.

 A Man, a Plan, a Misnomer: The Panama Hat

Don't let the name fool you: Panama hats are made in Ecuador. The tradition of millinery in Ecuador is long and proud. By the 16th century, the Incas had used the *Carludovica palmata* plant to create headwear, and the hats continued to have a place in Ecuador's culture after the Spanish conquest. In a famous painting of St. James the Great from the 17th century, made by an anonymous artist of the Cusco School, the mighty apostle is portrayed wearing a typical Ecuadorean hat while bounding on his horse, slaying Moors. For more about these unique items, see p. 205.

Though not as elaborate as the structures in Peru, some Inca ruins are still visible today in Ecuador. The principal Inca site here is **Ingapirca,** near Cuenca. The stone structure is small but well preserved. Other sites include **Rumicucho,** near Quito; **La Tolita,** near Esmeraldas; and **Tomebamba,** in Cuenca.

ECUADOR IN POPULAR CULTURE: BOOKS, MUSIC & FILMS

Literature

Though Ecuador's literary tradition is not world famous, neither is it barren. Ecuador has produced some excellent literary talents. Unfortunately, Ecuadorean authors are not widely read outside the country, at least not in comparison with writers from other parts of Latin America. Many Ecuadorean works aren't translated, and those that are can be difficult to come by.

Quito is also saturated with a different kind of literature: graffiti. As a local saying goes, *No hay muros blancos*—there are no blank walls in Quito. Graffiti writing is taken far more seriously here than elsewhere in the world, with politicians, writers, and journalists frequently quoting the social, political, and poetic sentiments expressed on the walls. An oft-quoted graffiti expression is *"Es más fácil describir lo que no es amor"* ("It's easier to describe what isn't love"). Think about that for a while.

RECOMMENDED BOOKS

The Ecuador Reader, edited by Carlos de la Torre and Steve Striffler ★★, is an excellent and broad introduction to the history, culture, and politics of Ecuador. If you want to break things down into periods, start with the award-winning *The Conquest of the Incas,* by John Hemming ★, which deals with Ecuador and Peru's Inca history; or the newer *The Last Days of the Incas,* by Kim MacQuarrie. These books are well complemented by *Indians, Oil and Politics: A Recent History of Ecuador,* by Allen Gerlach ★, a brilliantly descriptive account of the country's more contemporary history, political conditions, and rise of its indigenous movements. While not confined to Ecuador, I think every traveler to Latin America should read Eduardo Galeano's *Memory of Fire* ★★★ (W.W. Norton & Co., 1998). This astonishing achievement tells the history of the Americas in a poetic prose and unique style that redefines the form, function, and potential of nonfiction history.

Ecuador's Jorge Icaza (1906–79) was one of the 20th century's most notable authors. His seminal work, *Huasipungo* (1934), tells of the exploitation suffered by the local indigenous peoples at the hands of their colonizers; it's an excellently written, extremely insightful critique on Ecuadorean society. Its English translation is titled *The Villagers* ★. Demetrio Aguilera Malta is another distinguished author whose first and most successful work of magical realism, *Don Goyo,* has been compared to Gabriel García Márquez's *One Hundred Years of Solitude.* Following this success, Aguilera Malta's *Babelandia* somewhat satirically yet comically tells of the kidnapping of a corrupt general in a Latin American dictatorship by a group of guerillas. Enrique Gil Gilbert's *Our Daily Bread* is another novel that received international critical acclaim in the mid–20th century. *Juyungo,* penned by the late Adalberto Ortiz (1914–2003), incorporates elements of Afro-American culture and identity, as well as telling of the exploitation and discrimination faced by Afro-Americans within a Latin American society.

Another notable work of Ecuadorean fiction is Jorge Enrique Adoum's **Entre Marx y una Mujer Desnuda** (*Between Marx and a Naked Woman*), a clever novel about novels and about Ecuadorean society as a whole. Although not yet translated, it was made into a 1995 film by Camilo Luzuriaga, and you can sometimes find a subtitled copy of the film at better video stores (see below).

Regarding contemporary literature, Abdón Ubidia's celebrated novel **Wolves' Dreams** emerged in the 1980s as a superb insight into Ecuador's political and economic realities in the context of an attempted bank robbery. Eliécer Cárdenas's novels signify a break with tradition on the country's literary scene in an attempt to dig up an Ecuador buried and forgotten; his most celebrated, critically acclaimed realist work is **Polvo y Ceniza** (*Dust and Ashes*), which has been translated into a number of languages.

For an outsider's perspective, you might pick up **The Ecuador Effect**, by David E. Stuart, a fictionalized account of the author's anthropological and human rights work in the country during the 1970s.

For natural history and wildlife buffs, my all-time favorite book is **Tropical Nature**, by Adrian Forsyth and Ken Miyata ★★★. This is a lively collection of tales and adventures by two neotropical biologists; a lot of their research was carried out in Ecuador. The best all-purpose field guide for those visiting the country is David L. Pearson and Les Beletsky's **Traveller's Wildlife Guide: Ecuador and the Galápagos Islands** ★★. *Amazon Wildlife*, by Hans Ulrich Bernard, is a visual, detailed guide on jungle life. For bird lovers, **Common Birds of Amazonian Ecuador**, by Chris Canday and Lou Jost, provides a good overview; for more detailed descriptions and a comprehensive listing of species for the whole country, grab Robert Ridgely and others' **The Birds of Ecuador. Birds, Mammals and Reptiles of the Galápagos Islands**, by Andy Swash and Rob Still, is a fully illustrated, colorful, descriptive, yet user-friendly guide to Galápagos fauna and birdlife.

Perhaps the most common book ordered by those heading to the Galápagos Islands is a reprint of Charles Darwin's **The Voyage of the Beagle.** Running a close second is Darwin's **On the Origin of Species by Means of Natural Selection.** I also recommend David Quammen's **The Song of the Dodo** ★★, which is admittedly tangential to Ecuador and the Galápagos, but really gives you a good sense of the foundation of the theory of evolution, as well as its impact, implications, and current development.

Music

A variety of musical traditions come together in Ecuador. In Afro-Ecuadorean folk culture, the marimba is king. The traditional music of the Andes features a variety of wind instruments—such as the guaramo horn, the pifano and pinkullo flutes, and panpipes (*rondador*)—supported by guitar, charango, and percussion. Its distinctive pentatonic scales give it a very haunting feel. And the song "El Condor Pasa" ("The Condor Flies By") is recognizable to many visitors, having been made a minor hit by Simon & Garfunkel, with the familiar lyric starting off, "I'd rather be a hammer than a nail."

Songs in mainstream contemporary folk music fall into one of three forms. The first is *pasillo*, a slow variant on the waltz played with guitar and rondin flute. The second is *pasacalle,* a dance rhythm, and the third is *yarabi,* a sentimental style that has retained its popularity for generations.

Urban *discotecas* spin salsa and merengue, though a newer style called *reggaetón* is starting to dominate. *Reggaetón* is a combination of hip-hop and Jamaican dancehall reggae whose firmest roots are in Panama, though the music was popularized in Puerto Rico. In recent years, it has skyrocketed in popularity in Puerto Rico, the Dominican Republic, and most Central and South American nations, as well as among Latinos in the United States. City bars feature those rhythms as well as pop and *rock en español.*

Film

Ecuador doesn't have a major film industry, but it does produce a small number of independent local films each year. Some of these can be found online or at better-stocked video stores. Sebastian Cordero is the country's most prominent director, with **Crónicas** (*Chronicles,* 2004)—starring John Leguizamo—and **Ratas, Ratones, Rateros** (*Rats, Big Rats, and Rat Catchers,* 1999) ★ to his credit. **Qué Tan Lejos** (*How Far Away,* 2006) ★★, by Tania Hermida, was met with critical acclaim; it tells the story of two young women forced to hitchhike to Cuenca when a worker's strike stops bus traffic. Another film sometimes available is **Entre Marx y una Mujer Desnuda** (*Between Marx and a Naked Woman,* 1995) ★★, directed by Camilo Luzuriaga and based on a novel by Jorge Enrique Adoum.

Perhaps the most relevant film for English-speaking visitors is the 2005 docudrama **End of the Spear** ★, directed by Jim Hanon. Although filmed mostly in Panama, this movie tells the tale of the 1956 Waoroni killing of five missionaries in Ecuador's Amazon basin. The movie even includes cameos by several of the surviving members of the missionary families and members of the Waoroni tribe involved in the events.

Several major releases were either entirely or partially filmed in Ecuador. These include the Academy Award–nominated **Maria Full of Grace** (2004) ★★★, John Malkovich's **The Dancer Upstairs** (2003) ★, and **Proof of Life** (2000), starring Russell Crowe and Meg Ryan.

LLAPINGACHOS, CUY & PILSENER: ECUADOREAN FOOD & DRINK

Given the variety that defines Ecuadorean culture, art, geography, and politics, it would be logical to assume the country also offered a fair amount of culinary variety; however, the typical cuisine nationwide relies heavily on potatoes, rice, and beans. Coastal cuisine differs most from that of the mountainous regions, with an emphasis on seafood, spices, and coconut milk. The major cities of Quito, Guayaquil, and Cuenca all have sophisticated dining scenes, with a range of restaurants serving contemporary takes on Ecuadorean classics and a host of international cuisines.

Meals & Dining Customs

Ecuadoreans tend to eat three meals a day, in similar fashion and hours to North Americans. Breakfasts tend to be served between 6:30 and 9am, lunch between noon and 2pm, and dinner between 6 and 10pm. Most meals and dining experiences are quite informal. In fact, there are only a few restaurants in the entire country that could be considered semiformal, and practically none require a jacket or tie, although you could certainly wear them in Quito's or Guayaquil's finer establishments.

FOOD

BREAKFAST The typical breakfast in Ecuador is quite simple, usually anchored by scrambled eggs and potatoes or rice. Pancakes are often an option, though they might be oilier and crispier than the pancakes you're used to. Breakfast is often served with fruit, toast, corn tortillas, and coffee.

SANDWICHES & SNACKS Empanadas—small deep-fried pastries stuffed with meat or potatoes—are ubiquitous. Tamales, a mixture of cornmeal, meat, and spices wrapped in banana leaves, are widely available, as are *humitas,* a similar preparation that's steamed in a corn husk. The filling for *humitas* also tends to be simpler, usually consisting of just the mashed corn, cheese, and perhaps some egg. *Llapingachos* are popular potato-cheese patties found all across the country. You can also get traditional sandwiches, often served on sliced white bread, as well as American-style burgers.

SOUPS Ecuador takes its soup seriously. Soup is served with almost every lunch and dinner, both at restaurants and in private homes. During Lent, Ecuadoreans make *fanesca,* a milky broth served with fish, green beans, lima beans, and a bean called *chocho.* On the coast, you'll find *caldo,* a general term for soup, which can be either *aguado* (water based, thin, and usually containing meat) or *caldo de leche* (cream soup, usually with vegetables). *Menestra* is a thicker lentil stew often served with both vegetables and either meat or fish. *Locro* is a potato-cheese soup, and *sopa de tomates con plátanos,* tomato soup with plantains, is quite popular.

MEAT & POULTRY Ecuadoreans eat a fair amount of meat and poultry. Chicken and pork are the most popular, though you might encounter other meats you have not tried before. For instance, a common Ecuadorean delicacy is *cuy,* or roast guinea pig. You might even get to pick the pig you'll be eating. *Cuy* with potatoes is a common street food in the sierra region. Travelers should not order wild game unless they are certain it is farmed rather than hunted.

SEAFOOD Seafood is often available inland, though it is most plentiful and best on the coast, where shrimp, lobster, and a variety of fish are always on the menu. The coastal region is famous for its *ceviche,* a cold concoction of fish, conch, and/or shrimp marinated in lime juice and seasonings. The marinade is said to "cook" the fish or seafood. *Ceviche* is a great treat for lunch or as an appetizer. Also be sure to try *bollos de pescado,* fish and peanuts wrapped in banana leaves.

VEGETABLES The potato is the king of Ecuadorean cuisine. It is eaten at almost every meal and as snacks. But these aren't your basic Idaho Russets; you'll find over 200 varieties of potatoes in the Andean region, from tiny spuds no bigger than a peanut to larger varieties as big as a large orange, with colors ranging from yellow to brown to purple to blue. Chile peppers are used heavily, especially chopped and mixed with onion and salt to form *salsa de ají,* which is offered alongside most meals. Along with broccoli, palm hearts, cassava, and asparagus, you might come across *malanga* (also known as *yautía*), a starchy yam native to the tropics. *Patacones,* or fried plantains, are frequently served as side dishes on the coast.

FRUITS Ecuador has a wealth of delicious tropical fruits. The most common are bananas, mangoes, papayas, and pineapples. Other fruits you might find include *maracuyá* (passion fruit), *naranjilla* (a cross btw. an orange and a tomato), and *guanábana* (soursop—a misleading name), a sweet white fruit whose pulp makes for fabulous fruit shakes.

DESSERTS   Ecuador doesn't have a very extravagant dessert culture. *Bien me sabe* is a coconut dessert native to the country. Flan, a custard, comes in coconut and caramel flavors, and *tres leches* is a very sweet, runny cake that almost falls into the custard category. All types of sweets and candies are available.

DRINK

BEVERAGES   Most major brands of soft drinks are available, as are fresh juices (*jugos*) made with papaya, pineapple, mango, *maracuyá* (passion fruit), *naranjilla* (a cross btw. an orange and a tomato), or my personal favorite, *tomate de árbol* (tree tomato, a ubiquitous sweet-and-sour local fruit said to be good for the heart and for reducing cholesterol). Ask for them in milk (*en leche*) or water (*en agua pura*), and *sin hielo* (without ice) if you want to be extra sure you're not drinking tap water.

Unfortunately, it can be hard to find very good coffee in Ecuador, even though the country grows the crop natively, as most of the best beans are shipped abroad.

WATER   Do not drink the tap water in Ecuador, even in the cities, as disease-causing organisms are endemic. Ask for bottled drinking water (*agua pura* or *agua purificada*) at your hotel, and whenever you can, pick up a bottle of spring or purified water (available in most markets) to have handy. You also would do well to brush your teeth with purified water or, just for the fun of it, with beer.

BEER, WINE & LIQUOR   Ecuador's brewing industry is dominated by two companies. The first, known as Cervecería Nacional on the coast and Cervecería Andina in the highlands, makes the country's most popular beer, a pale lager called **Pilsener.** **Clausen** is similar, with higher alcohol content, and **Club** is a lighter, blonde pilsner. The competing company is Cervecería Suramérica, based in Guayaquil. Their big brew is **Biela,** a pale lager, which some prefer to Pilsener. As far as I'm concerned, no one is ever going to pin a medal on these beers, but after a long day of hiking through the hot jungle or sierra, any one of them will hit the spot.

No good wine is made in Ecuador, though quality bottles imported from Argentina, Chile, Italy, and France are available. Decent rum can be found at moderate prices; try **Ron Castillo** or **Ron San Miguel** (5 or 7 years).

If you want to expose your throat to something a little more painful, have a shot of *aguardiente*—Spanish for "fire water"—a strong spirit (60–100 proof, or more if it's homemade) made from fermented sugarcane and all but officially considered the national liquor of Ecuador. It's widely popular throughout the rest of South America as well.

In the course of your travels, you may have the chance to sample several traditional alcoholic concoctions. If you come upon Ecuadoreans in full fiesta, they may be drinking *canelazo,* a mixture of boiled water, sugarcane alcohol, lemon, sugar, and cinnamon typical of the Andean region. In some communities the traditional beverage *chicha,* made from fermented maize or cassava, is not complete until the person who is preparing it has chewed the ingredients and spit them back out. Make sure you find your *chicha* from a nonchewing source.

Other alcoholic beverages available in Ecuador include *guarapo,* also made from cane; *anisados,* liquor flavored with anis; *secos,* cheap and flavorless alcohol good for mixing; **Espíritu del Ecuador,** a fruity, golden liquor; and *rompope,* a Latin American version of eggnog, often bought prespiked with rum.

WHEN TO GO

Peak Season

The peak seasons for travelers to Ecuador last from mid-June to early September and from late December to early January, because most American and European visitors have vacation time during these months. Cruises in the Galápagos are booked solid during these times of year. But since Ecuador is hardly Disney World, you'll always be able to find a room (or a berth on a ship), and the country never feels overcrowded. Ecuador is great throughout the year, so whenever you visit, you won't be disappointed.

Climate

There are four distinct geographical zones in Ecuador, all subject to their own weather patterns.

In the **Galápagos,** from June to September, the air and water are chilly and the winds can be a bit rough. October through May, the air and water temperatures are warmer, but you can expect periodic light rain almost daily.

On the **coast,** the rainy season lasts from December to May; this season is marked by hot weather and high humidity. The cooler air temperature from June to September attracts whales and dolphins to the waters off the coast. In an odd anomaly, it's actually much sunnier during the rainy season, with a pattern of sunny mornings and early afternoons, followed by distinct and heavy showers or storms in the late afternoons. The dry season is often characterized by dense and heavy overcast skies that feel as if they want to let loose but never do.

In **Quito and the highlands,** the weather is coolest June through September (the dry season), but it's only a few degrees colder than during the rest of the year. Keep in mind that although Quito is practically on the Equator, the temperature can get quite cool because it's at such a high altitude. The city has an average high of 19°C (66°F) and an average low of 10°C (50°F). Throughout the rest of the highlands, the temperature is similarly consistent, with average highs and lows mostly determined by the altitude.

In the rainforests and lowlands of **El Oriente,** it rains year-round, but the rain is especially hard from late December to April. The driest period is October through December. The temperature in the jungle can reach 27° to 32°C (81°–90°F) during the day; it's a bit cooler at night.

Holidays

Official holidays in Ecuador include New Year's Day (Jan 1), Easter, Labor Day (May 1), Simón Bolívar Day (July 24), National Independence Day (Aug 10), Guayaquil Independence Day (Oct 9), All Souls' Day (Nov 2), Cuenca Independence Day (Nov 3), and Christmas Day (Dec 25). The country also closes down on some unofficial holidays, including Carnaval (Mon and Tues prior to Ash Wednesday), Battle of Pichincha (May 24), Christmas Eve (Dec 24), and New Year's Eve (Dec 31). The founding of Quito (Dec 6) is observed as a holiday only in Quito.

Ecuador Calendar of Events

Most of the events listed below are more traditions than organized events—there's not, for instance, a Día de los Muertos PR Committee that readily dispenses information. In many cases, I give a more detailed description of the events listed below in the appropriate destination chapters throughout the book. Beyond that, you can contact the **Ecuadorean Tourism Ministry** (© **02/2507-559;** www.vivecuador.com). Your best bet is probably to contact hotels or tour agencies in the destination where the event or festivities take place.

For an exhaustive list of events beyond those listed here, check http://events.frommers.com, where you'll find a searchable, up-to-the-minute roster of what's happening in cities all over the world.

FEBRUARY

Carnaval (Carnival), nationwide. Public concerts, parades, city fairs, and heavy drinking are all part of the festivities. In many cities, water, egg, and/or flour fights are part of the tradition. The city of Guaranda (p. 194) is particularly famous for its Carnaval celebrations, as are Esmeraldas (p. 282) and Ambato (p. 170). During the week or so just before the start of Lent.

APRIL

Holy Week, nationwide. Religious processions are held in cities and towns throughout the country. Quito's Good Friday procession through Old Town is especially large and ornate, with large floats, thick clouds of incense, and numerous devotees, some of whom quite vigorously flagellate themselves. Week before Easter.

JUNE

Inti Raymi, countrywide. The indigenous peoples of South America have always revered the sun. The Inca have left intact their celebration of the summer solstice, or Inti Raymi. It is celebrated nationwide, but especially throughout the northern Sierra, with Otavalo having the most famous celebrations. In Otavalo, Inti Raymi festivities blend into and overlap with the Catholic celebration of San Juan de Batista (St. John the Baptist) on June 24.

JULY

Fiestas de Guayaquil, Guayaquil. The country's largest city throws a large party for itself each July. Wild street parties, concerts, fireworks, and overall festivities last for at least a week on and around the official holiday, although in many ways, this party is merely a prelude to the October celebrations of the city's Independence Day. July 26.

SEPTEMBER

Fiestas de Mama Negra, Latacunga. This generally sleepy central Sierra city comes alive with a vengeance during its celebrations of the Virgen de la Merced (Virgin of Mercy), better known locally as Mama Negra (Black Mama). Each year, Ecuadoreans flock to Latacunga and fill its streets with dancing and parades, fireworks, and carnival rides. The festivities are unique in their mixing of indigenous, Spanish, and even African influences. September 23 and 24.

OCTOBER

Independencia de Guayaquil (Guayaquil Independence Day), Guayaquil. Some say these are the largest civic parties in the country. Quiteños would probably disagree, but suffice it to say that Ecuador's largest city throws an appropriately large party to celebrate its independence day. Festivities include parades, rodeos, fireworks, and street parties, for several days on either side of the actual date of October 9.

NOVEMBER

Día de los Muertos (Day of the Dead), countrywide. Ecuadoreans honor their dead with flowers and joyful remembrances. Many head to cemeteries, but the vibe is far from somber. November 2.

DECEMBER

Fiestas de Quito, Quito. The capital city pulls out all the stops in early December to commemorate the city's founding. Celebrations last through the first and most of the second week of December. Concerts and street fairs can be found all over the city. Bullfights are held in Plaza de Toros, with famous bullfighters coming from Spain and Mexico. A general air of celebration pervades the entire city. December 6 is the official date.

Christmas Eve, Cuenca. Obviously, the entire country celebrates Christmas, but the colonial city of Cuenca is famous for its Christmas Eve tradition of holding elaborate parades, with nativity scenes and other religious iconography on massive floats. December 24.

Años Viejos (Old Years), countrywide. In addition to the general debauchery and celebration, New Year's Eve is marked by an interesting tradition throughout Ecuador: Puppets and effigies symbolizing all that is bad or negative from the previous year are constructed, using old rags, sawdust, gunpowder, and fireworks as stuffing. Throughout the night, they sit on doorways and sidewalks. They are set on fire at the stroke of midnight, as part of the celebrations. December 31.

THE LAY OF THE LAND

Ecuador sits near the top of the South American continent, straddling the Equator. It covers an area of just under 256,000 sq. km (98,842 sq. miles), about the size of the state of Colorado. It is bordered on the north and east by Colombia, on the south and east by Peru, and on the west by the Pacific Ocean. The country includes the Galápagos Islands, 970km (601 miles) due west from the mainland coast.

There are three primary geographic regions in Ecuador, plus the Galápagos. The first is La Costa (The Coast), the low-lying area that runs the length of the Pacific coastline. Fertile plains and rolling rivers lead into pleasant Pacific beaches.

The rugged center of the country is called La Sierra (The Mountains), with the **Andes** running all the way from north to south. The Andes, the longest mountain chain in the world, appeared around 5 million years ago. A German naturalist named Alexander von Humboldt visited Ecuador in the early 19th century and named this central region "Avenue of the Volcanoes." At an elevation of 5,897m (19,342 ft.), **Volcán Cotopaxi,** with its almost perfectly symmetrical cone—a beautiful one, at that—is the world's fourth-highest active volcano. **Volcán Sangay** and **Volcán Guagua Pichincha** are numbers 9 and 10 in the world, respectively. (No. 1 is Ojos de Salado, on the border btw. Argentina and Chile.)

Finally, El Oriente (The East) runs from the edge of the Andes to the borders with Colombia and Peru and contains a chunk of the **Amazon rainforest.** This area covers over 25% of the country's landmass but is home to less than 5% of its human population.

The Galápagos archipelago consists of 13 large islands, 17 islets, and several dozen ancient rock formations scattered over 7,500 sq. km (2,896 sq. miles) of ocean. Though famous for its beaches, active volcanoes also rise from several of the islands, reaching altitudes of up to 1,600m (5,248 ft.).

Flora & Fauna

The biodiversity within Ecuador's borders is stunning. While it makes up only .02% of the world's landmass, it contains an amazing 10% of the world's plant species.

GENERAL resources FOR RESPONSIBLE TRAVEL

In addition to the resources for Ecuador listed above, the following websites provide valuable wide-ranging information on sustainable travel.

○ **Responsible Travel** (www. responsibletravel.com) is a great source of sustainable travel ideas; the site is run by a spokesperson for ethical tourism in the travel industry. **Sustainable Travel International** (www. sustainabletravelinternational.org) promotes ethical tourism practices and manages an extensive directory of sustainable properties and tour operators around the world.

○ **Carbonfund** (www.carbonfund. org), **TerraPass** (www.terrapass. org), and **Cool Climate** (http:// coolclimate.berkeley.edu) provide info on carbon offsetting, or offsetting the greenhouse gas emitted during flights.

○ **Greenhotels** (www.greenhotels. com) recommends green-rated member hotels around the world that fulfill the company's stringent environmental requirements. **Environmentally Friendly Hotels** (www.environmentallyfriendly hotels.com) offers more green accommodations ratings.

○ **Volunteer International** (www. volunteerinternational.org) has a list of questions to help you determine the intentions and nature of a volunteer program. For general info on volunteer travel, visit **www.volunteerabroad. org** and **www.idealist.org**.

Conservation International has listed Ecuador as one of just 17 "megadiverse" countries on the planet. Cataloging of the nation's biological treasures is far from complete, and already scientists have counted 3,800 species of vertebrates, 1,550 species of birds, 320 species of mammals, 350 species of reptiles, 375 species of amphibians, 800 species of freshwater fish, and 450 species of marine fish. Ecuador is a birdwatcher's paradise. A full 18% of the world's bird species can be found in Ecuador, more per square meter than in any other Latin American country. In fact, although Brazil is 30 times Ecuador's size, Ecuador has just as many species of birds. And last but not least, there are over a million species of insects in Ecuador (they're not all ugly—6,000 species are butterflies).

See "Tips on Health, Safety & Etiquette in the Wilderness," in chapter 4, for information on enjoying Ecuador's natural wonders. In chapter 15, you'll find an illustrated wildlife guide.

SUSTAINABLE TOURISM

Ecuador is a pioneering and still-evolving sustainable tourism destination. With large indigenous populations and a wide range of fragile ecosystems, including both the Galápagos Islands and Amazon basin, it's both natural and necessary that Ecuador develop the means to implement and promote sustainable and ethical practices. Some of the small hotels, isolated nature lodges, and tour operators around the

sustainable PROPERTIES IN ECUADOR

Following is a selection of hotels, boats, and tour operators either certified by the Smart Voyager program or that I feel are making real efforts to implement sustainable practices. Throughout the book, I try to highlight hotels, as well as restaurants and other attractions, that pay more than mere lip service to sustainability.

Quito & Side Trips:
Hotel Patio Andaluz (p. 95)
Hotel Real Audiencia (p. 96)
San Jorge Eco-Lodge and Biological Reserve (p. 124)
Satchitamia Lodge (p. 125)
Septimo Paraíso (p. 125)
Bellavista Cloud Forest Reserve (p. 125)
Termas de Papallacta (p. 126)
Metropolitan Touring (p. 121)
Surtrek (p. 121)

The Northern Sierra:
Runa Tupari Native Travel (p. 132)
La Posada del Quinde (p. 138)
Las Palmeras Inn (p. 139)
Hacienda Cusín (p. 141)
Ali Shungu Mountain Lodge (p. 140)
Casa Mojanda (p. 141)
Hacienda Zuleta (p. 144)

The Central Sierra:
Hacienda Hato Verde (p. 161)
Hacienda El Porvenir (p. 163)
Hostería Tambopaxi (p. 163)
Black Sheep Inn (p. 169)
Hacienda Manteles (p. 176)
Luna Runtun Adventure Spa (p. 183)

Cuenca & The Southern Sierra:
Hostería Izhcayluma (p. 225)
Madre Tierra (p. 225)

Guayaquil & The Southern Coast:
Hamaca Tours & Expeditions (p. 237)
Hotel Oro Verde Guayaquil (p. 238)
Manso Boutique Hostal (p. 240)
Hostería Alándaluz (p. 253)
Mantaraya Lodge (p. 256)
Hostería Mandála (p. 258)

Northern Pacific Coast & Lowlands:
Chirije (p. 277)
Kashama (p. 294)
Tinalandia (p. 294)

El Oriente:
Cofán Nation (p. 300)
Napo Wildlife Center (p. 308)
Sani Lodge (p. 308)
Manatee Amazon Explorer (p. 309)
Yachana Lodge (p. 314)
Cotococha Amazon Lodge (p. 315)
Las Cascadas (p. 319)
Kapawi Ecolodge & Reserve (p. 320)

The Galápagos Islands:
Ecoventura (p. 330)
Metropolitan Touring (p. 331)
M/V Celebrity Xpediton (p. 331)
S/S Mary Anne (p. 332)
Finch Bay Eco Hotel (p. 342)
Red Mangrove Adventura Lodge (p. 343)
Royal Palm Hotel (p. 343)

country are pioneers and dedicated professionals in the sustainable tourism field. Other hotels, lodges, and tour operators are honestly and earnestly jumping on the bandwagon and improving their practices. Still others are simply "green-washing," using the terms *eco, green,* and *sustainable* in their promo materials, but doing little real good in their daily operations.

In 2010, Ecuador was ranked near the top for countries in the Americas in the Environmental Performance Index (EPI; http://epi.yale.edu). Despite this, the substantial amounts of good work being done, and ongoing advances being made in the field, Ecuador faces severe environmental threats. One of the greatest threats is contamination and long-lasting pollution from oil exploration and extraction.

Smart Voyager (www.smartvoyager.org) is the principal international certification program, working on comprehensive evaluations of hotels and tourism operators in Ecuador. The **Rainforest Alliance's Sustainable Trip** (www.sustainabletrip.org) site is another good place to go to research Ecuadorean operators and properties. This site mostly duplicates the Smart Voyager recommendations, but I find the format and search capabilities far more user-friendly.

Recycling is just beginning to gather momentum in Ecuador. You can now occasionally find separate bins for plastics, glass, and paper on town and city streets, at national parks, and at the country's more sustainable hotels and restaurants. This is a nascent phenomenon, but I expect it to continue to grow and spread. Your hotel will be your best bet for finding a place to deposit recyclable waste, especially if you choose a hotel that has instituted sustainable practices.

While sustainable tourism options are expanding in Ecuador, organic and sustainably grown fruits and vegetables (as well as coffee) are just beginning to become available. Very few restaurants feature organic produce, although hopefully that will change in the near future.

Several of the tour operators listed in the "Organized Adventure Trips" section in chapter 4 (p. 55) have trips specifically geared toward ecotourists. You might also focus on specific hotels and lodges that have an ecotourism bent or have implemented sustainable practices, such as those I recommend in the box below.

Finally, another great way to make your tourism experience more sustainable is to volunteer. For specific information on volunteer options in Ecuador, see "Volunteer & Study Programs," in chapter 4.

See "The Lay of the Land," earlier in this chapter, for additional information on the various ecosystems and geographical highlights you'll find around the country. For information on Ecuador's national parks, turn to chapter 4.

SPANISH-LANGUAGE PROGRAMS

Ecuador is one of the most popular places to study Spanish in South America. It is also one of the least expensive. A vast majority of the schools are found in Quito, although many have sister institutions in other cities and tourist towns around the country, such as Baños, Manta, Cuenca, and Otavalo.

If you are just looking to brush up on your existing knowledge of the language or to learn the basics to get by during your stay, most schools are happy to tailor their programs according to your requirements, offering courses ranging in length from 1 week to a year, from 2 to 8 hours a day. The majority of Spanish institutes also offer programs combining home-stays with local Ecuadorean families, as well as volunteer placements, workplace internships, cultural activities, and/or excursions to Ecuador's coastal, Amazon, and Andean regions included with the language tuition. The home-stays include a private room and either two or three meals daily taken with the family. One-on-one tuition or group classes, always with native speakers, cost approximately $6 to $12 an hour, depending on the institution and the specific program.

Qualifications obtained upon completion of courses range from diplomas accredited by the Ecuadorean Ministry of Education and Culture to those recognized on an international level and accredited by Spain's Instituto Cervantes. Some of the schools have reciprocal relationships with U.S. and European universities, so you can even arrange for college credit.

Listed below are some of the better-established Spanish-language institutes in Quito, many of which have sister schools in other popular tourist destinations. Study programs in such destinations are usually organized through their Quito offices. Guayaquil has very few Spanish institutes, primarily because most tourists head for Quito, and the *castellano* spoken in Guayaquil is generally more difficult to understand, particularly for the beginner.

The popular **Amazonas Spanish School** ★★, Jorge Washington 718 and Avenida Amazonas, Edificio Rocaforte, Quito (© 02/2504-654; www.eduamazonas.com), was established in 1989. This academy boasts that all of its teachers have a minimum of 6 to 7 years of teaching experience. They emphasize language study combined with travel, offering homestays, tours, and volunteer programs. They also offer Spanish classes in various popular destinations, including Quito, the Galápagos, and El Oriente, and on the coast.

Beraca Spanish School, Av. Amazonas 11–14 and Pinto, 2nd Floor; in Quito's New Town; and García Moreno 858, No. 3, between Sucre and Espejo, in Quito's Old Town (© 02/2906-642; www.beraca.net), has been operating since 1993. They provide the option of studying at either of their well-located campuses. Home-stays with Ecuadorean families or in private apartments can also be arranged.

Bipo & Toni's ★★, Carrión E8–183 and Leonidas Plaza, Quito (© 02/2556-614 or 02/2500-732; www.bipo.net), is a Spanish academy with small-group and private classes. They also offer organized excursions, Latin dance classes, volunteer work opportunities, and home-stays. The institute has a good library, a garden with barbecue, and its own restaurant-bar, providing a friendly and interactive environment for its students.

Cristóbal Colón Spanish School, Colón Oe-2-56 and Versalles, Quito (© 02/2506-508; www.colonspanishschool.com), is one of Quito's most popular modern Spanish schools. They offer primarily one-to-one classes, but they also have organized excursions, volunteer work opportunities, and the option of studying in several sister schools located around the country. Classes usually last 4 hours, but more flexible schedules can be arranged.

Galápagos Spanish School, Av. Amazonas 884 and Wilson, Quito (© 02/2565-213; www.galapagos.edu.ec), offers one-on-one instruction through 10 levels or personalized courses, with the option of completing the Ministry's diploma. Private classes, local home-stays, and a variety of optional tours and activities are available.

Instituto Superior de Español ★★, Darquea Terán 1650 and Avenida 10 de Agosto, Quito (© 02/2223-242; www.instituto-superior.net), has been in business since 1988 and offers flexible Spanish courses in six locations around the country, including Quito, Otavalo, El Oriente, and the Galápagos. They emphasize extracurricular activities through an extensive program of excursions and events. Specialized courses in business Spanish and Latin American literature and history are also on the agenda.

Simón Bolívar ★, Mariscal Foch E9–920 and Avenida 6 de Diciembre, Quito (© 02/2234-708; www.simon-bolivar.com), is rated as "one of Ecuador's top schools" by members of the reputable South American Explorers Club. They offer home-stays and volunteer placements, a "Discover Ecuador" program, and various excursions. The institute also has schools in Cuenca, in El Oriente, and along the Pacific coast.

SUGGESTED ECUADOR ITINERARIES

Ecuador has numerous natural attractions and a broad mix of stunning historical sights and exhilarating adventure activities to keep you busy. On a trip to Ecuador, you can visit rainforests, cloud forests, lowland mangrove forests, snowcapped peaks, high Andean paramo, active volcanoes, perfectly preserved colonial-era churches, and Inca and Cañari ruins. You can go horseback riding, mountain biking, trekking, surfing, and white-water rafting. The bird-watching is world class. And, of course, there are the Galápagos Islands. Ecuador is also a relatively compact country, which makes visiting several destinations during a single vacation both easy and enjoyable.

By far the fastest and easiest way to get around the country is by small commuter aircraft. Most major tourist destinations in Ecuador either are serviced by reasonably priced domestic airlines or are commonly reached on a package tour that includes charter air transportation.

Driving is another option, though one that demands serious consideration. Most major destinations are at least 3 to 5 hours from Quito by car, and some are even farther. Moreover, the roads here are often in terrible shape and unmarked (as are many intersections), and Ecuadorean drivers can be reckless and rude. One interesting option is **Rent 4WD.com ★** (© **02/2544-719;** www.rent-4wd.com), where $198 per day gets you a large, modern 4WD vehicle; unlimited gas and mileage; and an English-speaking driver. See p. 359 for more information on driving around Ecuador.

The following itineraries are blueprints for fabulous vacations. You can follow them to the letter, or you might decide to use one or more of them as outlines and fill in the blanks with other destinations, activities, and attractions that suit you.

THE REGIONS IN BRIEF

The Republic of Ecuador sits near the northwestern corner of South America. It's bordered by Colombia to the north, Peru to the south and east, and the Pacific Ocean to the west. The Galápagos Islands, which straddle the Equator, are located about 966km (599 miles) to the west, in

The Regions in Brief

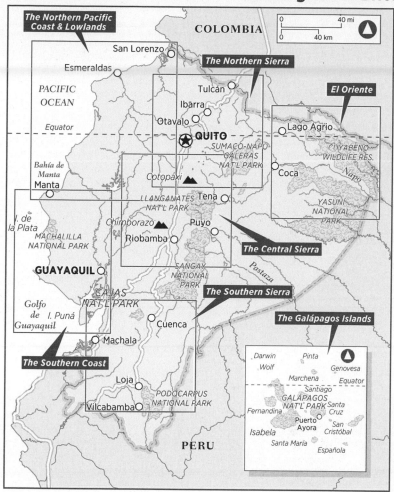

The Northern Pacific Coast & Lowlands
COLOMBIA
San Lorenzo
Esmeraldas
The Northern Sierra
PACIFIC OCEAN
Tulcán
Ibarra
El Oriente
Otavalo
QUITO
Lago Agrio
Equator
SUMACO-NAPO-GALERAS NAT'L PARK
CUYABENO WILDLIFE RES.
Napo
Bahía de Manta
Cotopaxi
Coca
Manta
LLANGANATES NAT'L PARK
Tena
YASUNÍ NATIONAL PARK
I. de la Plata
Chimborazo
Puyo
MACHALILLA NATIONAL PARK
Riobamba
The Central Sierra
GUAYAQUIL
SANGAY NATIONAL PARK
Pastaza
CAJAS NAT'L PARK
The Southern Sierra
Golfo de Guayaquil
I. Puná
Cuenca
The Galápagos Islands
Machala
Darwin Pinta
Wolf Genovesa
Marchena Equator
The Southern Coast
Santiago
GALÁPAGOS NAT'L PARK Santa Cruz
Loja
Fernandina
PODOCARPUS NATIONAL PARK
Puerto Ayora San Cristóbal
Vilcabamba
Isabela
Santa María
Española
PERU
0 40 mi
0 40 km

the Pacific Ocean. The country covers an area of 272,046 sq. km (105,038 sq. miles), making it roughly the same size as Colorado.

QUITO Situated at some 2,850m (9,348 ft.), Quito is the second-highest capital city in the world (after La Paz, Bolivia). It may be the capital of Ecuador, but it's actually the second-most-populous city in the country (after Guayaquil). Still, it's a major transportation hub, so most visitors begin and end their trips to Ecuador here. Quito is one of the more charming cities in South America, and there's plenty to see and do. **Old Town,** with its wonderfully preserved colonial-style buildings, was declared a World Heritage Site by UNESCO in 1978—the first city to earn the designation. **New Town** is a lively cosmopolitan area, with all the modern amenities you would expect to find in a world-class destination.

3

SUGGESTED ECUADOR ITINERARIES

The Regions in Brief

THE NORTHERN SIERRA   Just north of Quito, the Equator cuts across Ecuador and forms the border that roughly defines the country's northern Sierra, or highlands. **Imbabura** is the first province you hit, and one of the country's prime tourism destinations. In Imbabura, you can explore the colorful artisans market of **Otavalo,** as well as nearby towns, where you'll find the workshops and homes of many of the artisans who supply this fabulous market. In addition, this region is one of high volcanic mountains and crater lakes. There are great hiking opportunities, especially at such beautiful spots as **Cuicocha Lake** and **Mojanda Lakes.** Farther north lie the province of Carchi and the small border town of **Tulcán,** a gateway (albeit a rather dangerous one) to Colombia.

THE CENTRAL SIERRA   The central Sierra covers the area south of Quito. **Cotopaxi National Park** is a little more than an hour south of Quito, and it's one of the most popular attractions on mainland Ecuador. Active travelers can climb to the summit of the highest active volcano in Ecuador (and one of the highest in the world), while anybody can marvel at its imposing beauty from the high-altitude paramo all around the park. The central Sierra contains many isolated, colonial-era haciendas that have been converted into fabulous hotels and lodges. Most offer a variety of active tour options, with horseback riding often being the mainstay. **Baños** and **Riobamba** are the primary tourist towns of the central Sierra. Travelers head to Baños mainly for both relaxation and active adventures. The city, which is nestled at the bottom of active Volcán Tungurahua, offers great hiking and biking opportunities, as well as easy access to great white-water rafting. You can also take a soothing soak in one of the hot springs, or pamper yourself with spa treatments. Riobamba is much less visited, and there's not much to do here besides catch the popular **Nariz del Diablo (Devil's Nose)** tourist train, which takes you on a spectacular journey along the winding switchbacks of a steep rock face, or set out to summit **Chimborazo,** the country's highest peak, at 6,310m (20,697 ft.).

CUENCA & THE SOUTHERN SIERRA   **Cuenca** is the largest and most interesting city in the southern highlands. Like Quito, it is filled with colonial-era homes and churches, and was declared a World Heritage Site by UNESCO. Cuenca was also the second-most-important city in the Inca empire (after Cusco). Nearby, you can explore **Ingapirca,** an archaeological site with both Inca and pre-Inca ruins. Cajas National Park is located only an hour outside Cuenca, and farther south lies the small city of **Loja,** one of the oldest cities in Ecuador. South of Loja is the even more remote village of **Vilcabamba,** famed for the health and longevity of its residents. Many come here seeking to sip from the town's fountain of youth; others use it as a jumping-off point to visit the wild **Podocarpus National Park.**

GUAYAQUIL & THE SOUTHERN COAST   **Guayaquil** is Ecuador's largest city. Chiefly a port and industrial city, Guayaquil is reinventing itself at a dizzying pace. The city's attractive riverside walk, **Malecón Simón Bolívar,** has served as the anchor for a minirenaissance. Guayaquil boasts several excellent museums, as well as top-notch hotels, restaurants, and bars. To the west of Guayaquil lies the **Ruta del Sol** (Route of the Sun), a string of beach resorts, small fishing villages, and isolated stretches of sand. Surfers come here to find that endless wave, and sun worshippers can get the perfect tan. At the north end of the Ruta del Sol is **Machalilla National Park.** The sleepy town of **Puerto López,** just outside the park, is a gateway to the park's mainland sections, as well as to **Isla de la Plata,** which is home to a rich variety of wildlife and which is often called the "Poor Person's Galápagos."

NORTHERN PACIFIC COAST & LOWLANDS Ecuador's northern coast and its surrounding lowlands are often neglected or avoided by most tourists, although Ecuadoreans are well aware of this area's charms. The beaches around **Esmeraldas** and **Atacames** are by far the prettiest in the country. The seaside city of **Bahía de Caráquez** is a picturesque and peaceful place with a safe and scenic bayside Malecón. At the southern end of this section of coast is **Manta,** the country's second-largest port and former home to a controversial U.S. airbase. **Santo Domingo de los Colorados,** a bit inland, serves as a major crossroads and little-known gateway to a couple of beautiful and isolated nature lodges.

EL ORIENTE The eastern region of Ecuador, known as El Oriente, is a vast area of lowland tropical rainforests and jungle rivers. It's considered part of the Amazon basin because the rivers here all feed and form the great Amazon River just a little farther downstream. The wildlife and bird-watching here are phenomenal; visitors have a chance to see hundreds of bird species and over a dozen monkey species, as well as anaconda, caiman, and freshwater dolphins. For the most part, the indigenous people in this region escaped domination by both the Incas and the Spanish, so they have been able to maintain their ancient rituals and traditions. Most visitors explore this area by staying at one of many remote jungle lodges, some of which are surprisingly comfortable. English-speaking guides will take you to local villages, as well as show you the incredible diversity of wildlife here.

THE GALÁPAGOS ISLANDS The Galápagos Islands, located about 970km (599 miles) off the coast of Ecuador, are one of nature's most unique outdoor laboratories. The unusual wildlife here helped Charles Darwin formulate his theory of natural selection. Fortunately for modern-day visitors, not much has changed since Darwin's time, and the islands still offer visitors the chance to get up close and personal with a wide variety of unique and endemic species, including giant tortoises, marine iguanas, penguins, sea lions, albatrosses, boobies, and flightless cormorants. The best way to explore the area is on a cruise ship or yacht. Note, however, that this isn't your typical cruise destination. Trips involve packed days of tours and activities, some of them strenuous. A more relaxing option would be to base yourself at a resort in Santa Cruz (the most populated island in the Galápagos) and take select day trips to the islands of your choice.

ECUADOR IN 1 WEEK

Let me level with you: Unless you are coming here only to visit the Galápagos, a week is just not enough time to see all of what Ecuador has to offer. If you are coming just to visit the Galápagos, however, 1 week is perfect—and you might even get to squeeze in a day or so in Quito and/or Guayaquil.

Having said this, I'm not including the Galápagos in the following itinerary. Instead, it takes you to several of Ecuador's top destinations and attractions, with everything from high-altitude hiking in the paramo to a rainforest extravaganza in the Amazon basin.

Note: The following 1-week itinerary includes 8 days, the first of which is considered a "travel day," when you'll likely arrive in Quito in the evening.

Days 1 & 2: Quito ★★

Many international flights arrive in Quito in the late afternoon or early evening, so you'll need to book yourself into a hotel for 2 nights to enjoy 1 full day of sightseeing in the capital. Get to bed as early as possible so you can be rested and out the door early on Day 2. After breakfast at your hotel, spend the morning touring **Old Town.** Visit the magnificent **Iglesia de San Francisco ★★** (p. 107), which dates back to 1535, and allow yourself a good 45 minutes to get a feel for the city's oldest church and its attached museum.

A few minutes' walk away, **La Compañía de Jesús ★★★** (p. 109) Jesuit church features an incredibly ornate interior that shows baroque and Moorish influences. Nearby, **Casa del Alabado ★★** (p. 104) is a wonderful new museum with a fantastic collection of pre-Columbian artifacts. Housed in a restored colonial-era mansion, this museum takes about 40 minutes to visit. **Casa Museo María Augusta Urrutia ★** (p. 105) is another perfectly preserved 19th-century mansion worthy of at least a 45-minute visit. As the sun warms the cool morning air, take some time to stroll around Old Town and end up at **La Plaza de la Independencia** (p. 109), which was the city's main square in the 16th century. Break for a cup of coffee at one of the many sunny cafes on or around the plaza.

Next, grab a taxi and head to **El Panecillo,** where you'll see the Virgin of Quito (p. 107). It's a 10-minute ride up a steep hill. From here, standing below the immense winged Virgin, you have a sweeping view of Old Town and the rest of the city. Right next to the monument is **PIM's Panecillo** (p. 101), a great place to enjoy local cuisine for lunch while you continue to enjoy the view. Remember to drink lots of bottled water, especially in the early afternoon, when the sun is at its highest and the atmosphere its driest.

After lunch, take a taxi to **Fundación Guayasamín ★★★** (p. 112), named after the country's most famous and influential artist, Oswaldo Guayasamín. Expect to spend at least 1½ hours here and at the nearby **Capilla del Hombre ★**. At both, you'll find original works by Guayasamín, as well as pieces from his personal collection.

You should be pretty beat by now, so head to **Plaza Foch** (p. 119) in the **Mariscal district** of **New Town** for a late-afternoon or early evening cup of coffee or a cocktail. If the weather is good, grab an outdoor table on the plaza at **Coffee Tree** (p. 119), or at **Azuca Latin Bistro ★** (p. 99) if you're feeling more like a mojito. If you're lucky, a jazz band will be playing on the plaza right in front of you.

For dinner, be sure to have reservations at **Zazu ★★★** (p. 103), the best and hippest spot in Quito. You can end the meal with dessert or a drink at their popular little laid-back bar. If you have the energy, pull out all the stops and head back to the Mariscal district's many bars and clubs to see where the night and your whims lead you.

Days 3 & 4: Otavalo ★★ & Imbabura Province

After your grueling sightseeing day in Quito, it's time to leave the city behind and unwind in the highlands of the northern Sierra for a couple of days. The roughly 2-hour drive is leisurely and scenic, and should include a stop at **Quitsato Mitad del Mundo** (p. 122), where you can have your photo taken with one foot in each of Earth's hemispheres.

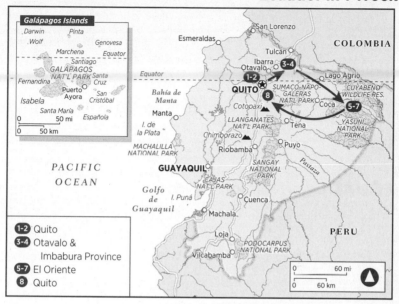

Galápagos Islands

Darwin · Pinta
Wolf · Genovesa
Marchena · Equator
Santiago
GALÁPAGOS
NAT'L PARK · Santa
Fernandina · Cruz
Puerto · San
Ayora · Cristóbal
Isabela
Santa María · Española

0 — 50 mi
0 — 50 km

San Lorenzo
Esmeraldas
Tulcán
Ibarra
Otavalo **3-4**
1-2
QUITO ✪
Equator
Bahía de
Manta
Cotopaxi ▲ **8**
Manta
LLANGANATES
NAT'L PARK
I. de
la Plata
Chimborazo ▲
MACHALILLA
NATIONAL PARK
Riobamba

PACIFIC
OCEAN

GUAYAQUIL
Golfo
de
Guayaquil
I. Puná
Machala

CAJAS
NAT'L PARK

SANGAY
NATIONAL
PARK

COLOMBIA

Lago Agrio
SUMACO-NAPO-
GALERAS
NAT'L PARK · Coca **5-7**
CUYABENO
WILDLIFE RES.
Tena
Puyo
YASUNÍ
NATIONAL
PARK

Cuenca

PERU
PODOCARPUS
NATIONAL PARK
Vilcabamba
Loja

0 — 60 mi
0 — 60 km

1-2 Quito
3-4 Otavalo &
Imbabura Province
5-7 El Oriente
8 Quito

I recommend **Hacienda Cusín** ★★ (p. 141), a rambling, serene inn set amid 4 hectares (10 acres) of lush gardens, on the outskirts of **Otavalo** ★★. In the distance, Volcán Imbabura makes for a breathtaking backdrop. Have lunch on the sun-splashed terrace and perhaps take a siesta afterward. In the afternoon, choose from a variety of activities, including horseback riding in the nearby hills, taking a Spanish lesson, or meandering in the lovely gardens. A candle-lit dinner is served in the cozy dining room, which makes for a perfect ending to a relaxing day. If you feel like going out for a gourmet dinner, make reservations at and take a taxi to **La Mirage Garden Hotel** ★★★ (p. 140), one of the finer restaurants in Ecuador. The drive takes about 20 minutes.

On Day 4, spend your morning perusing the artisans market at **Otavalo** ★★★ (p. 133), a 15-minute taxi ride away, and shop to your heart's content. Then stop by **Peguche** (p. 137) to visit some of the best weavers in Ecuador, before heading up to **Hacienda Pinsaquí** ★ (p. 141) for lunch at one of the region's most picturesque and historic haciendas. If you have the energy after lunch, take a taxi up to **Lago Cuicocha** ★★ (p. 134) and hike around the rim of this beautiful volcanic crater lake, or take a more relaxing boat ride on its waters.

In the evening, you can either spend a quiet night at Hacienda Cusín or head back into Otavalo for dinner at **La Posada del Quinde** ★★ (p. 138) and maybe catch some live music at **Peña la Jampa** ★ (p. 144). Whatever you choose, be sure to get a good night's rest, because you'll have to wake early in order to drive back to the Quito airport for your flight to the Amazon.

Days 5–7: Head for the Amazon Basin ★★

Just about all the rainforest lodges in Ecuador's El Oriente offer 4-day, 3-night package excursions, perfect for giving you a good sense of the culture, environment, and wildlife of this amazing region. I recommend either **Kapawi Ecolodge & Reserve** ★★★ (p. 320) or **Napo Wildlife Center** ★★ (p. 308). Both have excellent facilities, guides, and tour options.

Day 8: Saying *Adios*

Your flight back to Quito from the Amazon won't get in until around midday, which is probably too late for your connecting flight back home. If you have extra time, head to **Mercado Artesanal La Mariscal** (p. 114) to buy some last-minute souvenirs and gifts, or squeeze in a visit to **Museo Nacional del Banco Central del Ecuador** ★★ (p. 111).

ECUADOR IN 2 WEEKS

While it may seem like a lot of time, you'll still just be scratching the surface if you spend 2 weeks in Ecuador. You'll visit Quito and the Sierra, the lovely colonial city of Cuenca, and then, after spending a week in the enchanting Galápagos Islands, you'll have just enough time for an overnight in Guayaquil, one of South America's most up-and-coming cities. If you can tack on a few more days, or opt for just a 3-day cruise of the Galápagos, then you'll have enough time to take a 4-day, 3-night tour to El Oriente, Ecuador's lush Amazon region (chapter 11), spend some time at one of the beautiful old haciendas found throughout the central Sierra (chapters 6 and 7), or head out to the Pacific coast from Guayaquil (chapter 9).

Days 1–4: Quito ★★, Otavalo ★★ & Imbabura Province

This itinerary starts off exactly as "Ecuador in 1 Week" does. Follow the first 4 days of that itinerary, as described above.

But on Day 5, instead of leaving early from Hacienda Cusín for a flight to the Amazon, you'll leave early for a flight to Cuenca.

Day 5: Cuenca ★★★

Your 1-hour flight will bring you to Cuenca, one of Ecuador's most charming colonial cities. If you're seated on the left side of the plane, and if there's a break in the clouds, you'll probably get a great view of Volcán Cotopaxi on the way.

By the time you arrive and settle into your hotel, you should be ready for lunch. I recommend that you head to **Villa Rosa** ★★ (p. 210), a beautiful and elegant restaurant serving creative takes on classic Ecuadorean dishes. After lunch, visit **Museo del Banco Central** ★★ (p. 202). The museum contains an extensive art and archaeology collection and is located on the site of a major Cañari and Inca ceremonial center. After touring the museum, be sure to walk around the ruins and their botanical gardens.

From the museum, take a taxi to **Mirador de Turi,** a strategic lookout with a beautiful view of Cuenca and its broad valley. Be sure to combine a visit here with a stop at **Taller E. Vega** ★★ (p. 204), the gallery and workshop of one of the country's most prominent ceramic artists.

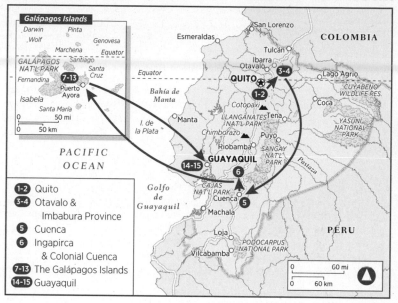

Galápagos Islands

Darwin · Pinta
·Wolf · Genovesa
Marchena · Equator
GALÁPAGOS · Santiago
NAT'L PARK · Santa
Fernandina · **7-13** · Cruz
Isabela · Puerto
Ayora
Santa María

0 ___ 50 mi
0 ___ 50 km

PACIFIC
OCEAN

Esmeraldas · San Lorenzo · COLOMBIA
Tulcán · Ibarra
Otavalo · **3-4** · Lago Agrio
Equator · **QUITO** · CUYABENO
WILDLIFE RES.
Bahía de · **1-2** · Coca
Manta · Cotopaxi
Manta · LLANGANATES Tena · YASUNÍ
I. de · NAT'L PARK · NATIONAL
la Plata · Chimborazo · Puyo · PARK
Riobamba · SANGAY
GUAYAQUIL · NAT'L
14-15 · **6** · PARK · Pastaza
Golfo · CAJAS
de · NAT'L PARK · **5**
Guayaquil · Cuenca
Machala
Loja · PERÚ
PODOCARPUS
Vilcabamba · NATIONAL PARK

0 ___ 60 mi
0 ___ 60 km

1-2 Quito
3-4 Otavalo &
Imbabura Province
5 Cuenca
6 Ingapirca
& Colonial Cuenca
7-13 The Galápagos Islands
14-15 Guayaquil

At some point during the day, be sure to sign up for a half-day tour to Ingapirca for the following day. Your hotel desk is probably your best bet. Otherwise, contact **Hualambari Tours** ★ (p. 200) or **TerraDiversa** ★ (p. 20).

For dinner, head for the trendiest and best restaurant in town, **Tiestos** ★★★ (p. 211), which serves rich and rewarding dishes served in the same ceramic vessels (*tiestos*) that they are cooked in. If you have any energy left, head for a nightcap at the **Wunderbar Café** ★ (p. 213), located just off Calle Larga midway down a flight of steep stairs to the Río Tomebamba.

Day 6: Ingapirca ★ & Colonial Cuenca ★★★

You'll probably leave just after breakfast for your trip to Ingapirca (p. 214), the Machu Picchu of Ecuador. Located about a 2-hour drive north of Cuenca, Ingapirca is the largest and most significant archaeological site left by the Incas in Ecuador. It was built on the ruins of a Cañari settlement, and you will see evidence of their culture and architecture here as well. Your tour will likely include lunch, but you should be back in Cuenca with plenty of time to further explore its colonial core.

Start at the colorful **Flower Market** (p. 201) and continue from there to the main square, **Parque Calderón** (the heart of Cuenca). Be sure to visit the Gothic-Romanesque **Catedral Nueva** ★★ (p. 201), with its exquisite white marble floors. Then catch a taxi from the square to the most interesting and best-known factory in the country, **Homero Ortega P. & Hijos** ★★★ (p. 205), which makes some of the highest-quality Panama hats in the world. You'll get to see how they do it, as well as shop at slightly discounted prices in their showroom store.

For your last night, I recommend combining dinner and nightlife by heading to **Café Eucalyptus** ★★ (p. 211), where you can dine on a range of exotic tapas while mingling with the crème de la crème of Cuenca.

Days 7–13: The Galápagos Islands ★★★

Getting to the Galápagos from Cuenca will require an early morning departure with a change of planes in Guayaquil. The flight to Guayaquil is only 30 minutes, and from there to the Galápagos, it's exactly 1½ hours. A 7-day cruise on one of the 100 vessels plying the waters of these magical islands is the best way to visit the Galápagos; the typical itinerary includes a visit to two islands a day—one in the morning and one in the afternoon. See chapter 12.

Day 14: Guayaquil ★

Because all flights from the Galápagos first land in Guayaquil, spend your last night in Ecuador in this economically vibrant and up-and-coming city, the country's largest. Flights from the Galápagos arrive in the early afternoon, leaving you enough time to check into your hotel and stroll over to **Malecón Simón Bolívar** ★★ (p. 234). You may want to visit the **Museum of Anthropology and Contemporary Art** ★★ (p. 236), or take a long walk in the interesting neighborhood of **Cerro Santa Ana** ★★★ (p. 235). Climb to the top for a sweeping view of the city. For your last evening in Ecuador, head over to **Lo Nuestro** ★★ (p. 242), the city's best restaurant focusing on traditional cuisine.

Day 15: Fly Home

It's unlikely you'll have much time during your last morning in Guayaquil, but if you do, head to **Parque Histórico Guayaquil** ★ (p. 237), a small theme park with a re-creation of colonial-era homes and haciendas, as well as lovely gardens.

ECUADOR FOR FAMILIES

Ecuador is not a particularly kid-friendly destination. There are few attractions and activities that appeal to youngsters, and very few hotels here have well-developed kids' programs. But youngsters and teens, especially the adventurous and inquisitive, will do great in Ecuador. The biggest challenge to families traveling with children is travel distances, as well as the logistical difficulties of moving around within the country, which is why I recommend going with two organized tour options, combined with a stay at a hacienda near Quito.

Day 1: Arrive & Head for Happiness

Alegría means "happiness" in Spanish, and I'd make my family's first stop **Hacienda La Alegría** ★ (p. 162). This colonial-era hacienda, still a working farm, specializes in horseback-riding tours, including a comprehensive and conscientious program for teaching beginners and young riders. The hacienda is only an hour or so from Quito's airport, making it possible to come here from all but the latest-arriving flights.

Days 2 & 3: Saddle Up, Partners

Depending on the skills, experience, and abilities of your family, a wide range of **horseback rides** can be arranged. Beginners will probably stay pretty close to

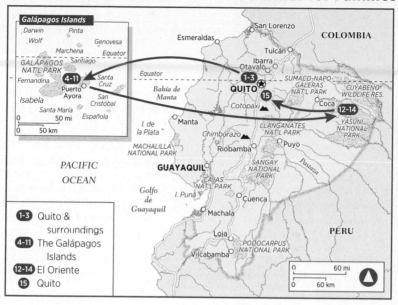

the hacienda, at least on the first day or so. More experienced riders can venture farther afield, through neighboring towns, villages, and countryside, and even up into the high Andean paramo. In addition to riding, kids can take part in various farm chores, including milking cows.

You'll probably want to spend your third night in Quito, because early the following morning you'll be catching a flight to the Galápagos.

Days 4–11: Cruise the Galápagos Islands ★★★

The Galápagos Islands are an excellent destination for families. Kids of all ages—as well as adults—can't help being awed by the close and constant contact with wildlife. Several cruise operators specialize in family packages to the Galápagos; this is a good way to give your kids some extracurricular class time in the natural sciences. They'll have so much fun, they won't realize how much they're learning. **Tauck** ★★ (p. 331) is a first-rate tour company with several family-oriented itineraries to the Galápagos.

Days 12–14: The Amazon Basin ★★

You can continue your clandestine classes in the natural sciences by following the Galápagos with a 3-day tour to one of the isolated nature lodges in Ecuador's Amazon basin. (To get here, you'll have to fly back to Quito first.) I recommend **Kapawi Ecolodge & Reserve** ★★★ (p. 320), which has excellent guides, comfortable accommodations, and a wide range of tour and activity options. In addition to the chance to see wild caiman, anacondas, bats, and an amazing abundance of bird and insect life, you can take night hikes and try your hand at fishing for piranhas.

Day 15: Quito ★★

Your return flight to Quito from the Amazon won't get you in until around mid-day, which is probably too late for your connecting flight back home. If you have time, take everyone to **El Telefériqo,** a high-speed cable car that will whisk you to the top of Volcán Pichincha. At the base of the cable car is **Vulqano Park,** where your family can enjoy amusement park rides and mingle with Quiteño families (p. 106).

ECUADOR FOR ADVENTURE TRAVELERS

Ecuador is an underexploited adventure tourism destination, with much to offer. The following itinerary packs a lot of adventure punch into a single week. This is a basic outline; if you want to do more high-altitude climbing, trekking, mountain biking, horseback riding, or kayaking, schedule that in place of one of the activities that doesn't get your adrenaline pumping.

Day 1: Arrive & Settle into Quito

If your flight gets in early enough and you have time, head to Old Town and visit some of the colonial-era treasures this UNESCO World Heritage Site has to offer. See the suggested itinerary "Quito in 3 Days," below, for sights to see and restaurant recommendations.

Days 2–4: Head for the Hills

Parque Nacional Cotopaxi is Ecuador's premier high-mountain park and home to the country's second-highest peak. The rustic yet very comfy **Hacienda El Porvenir ★** (p. 163), right at the northern entrance to the national park, makes an excellent base for exploring this area. You'll need at least a day or two to acclimate if you plan on climbing Cotopaxi. The hacienda can arrange a number of adventures, including high-altitude trekking and camping, mountain biking, horseback riding, and, of course, summit climbs of Cotopaxi and several other nearby peaks. They also have a zip-line canopy tour at one of their sister lodges.

You'll want to head back to Quito for your final night of this leg, because you'll be getting up early to head to the Galápagos.

Days 5–7: Dive with Hammerhead Sharks

Sure, the wildlife viewing and natural history are fabulous draws and reason enough to visit the Galápagos Islands, but scuba divers know that this is one of the prime diving destinations on the planet. The isolated location, fishing regulations, and ocean currents have blessed this archipelago with abundant sea life. Large schools of all sorts of fish are the mainstay, and it's common to encounter hammerhead sharks—I've seen them on every one of my dives here. If you're lucky, you might also bump into a manta ray, whale shark, sea turtle, or dolphin. You'll almost certainly have a sea lion swim right up to your face. If you're going specifically to dive, I recommend staying in Puerto Ayora and doing daily dives with one of the local operators, such as **Sub-Aqua ★** (p. 341). Because you're not supposed to fly soon after diving, talk with your dive master, and if necessary,

Ecuador for Adventure Travelers

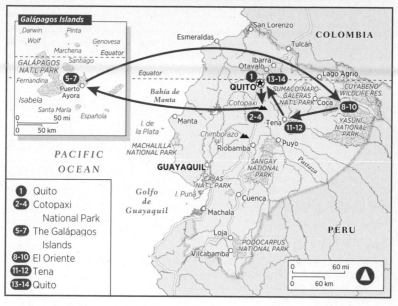

spend your final day **surfing** Ola Escondida (Hidden Wave) and Punta Barba Negra (Black Beard Point). See p. 342.

Days 8-10: Go Native in the Amazon Basin with the Cofán Nation

No adventure tour to Ecuador would be complete without a visit to the lowland rainforests of El Oriente. There are plenty of ways to visit Ecuador's Amazon basin, but those with a real sense of adventure will do so by booking directly with the **Cofán Nation ★★** (p. 300), one of the local tribes. Cofán guides lead multiday tours through the area around **Cuyabeno Wildlife Reserve ★★**, emphasizing hands-on experiences that get you into the lifestyle, tradition, and culture of the Cofán people.

Days 11 & 12: Get Wet & Wild

From the northern part of El Oriente, head south to Tena and spend some time on the rivers. Tena is Ecuador's capital for **white-water rafting** and **kayaking.** There are a number of local operators in town; **Ríos Ecuador ★★** (p. 312) is one of the most reputable, with options ranging from relatively gentle Class III floats to kayak outings on raging Class IV and Class V sections.

Day 13: Return to Quito & Prepare to Say Goodbye

If you're traveling by land, make a stop at Papallacta on your way back to Quito. After all your adventure travel, you'll appreciate—and perhaps desperately need—a few hours soaking in the hot springs at **Termas de Papallacta** ★★★ (p. 126). Papallacta is just off the road, along the main route between Tena and Quito.

Day 14: Fly Home

Your flight will probably leave early in the morning, but if you have time, head to **Mercado Artesanal La Mariscal (Mariscal Artisans Market)** to buy last-minute souvenirs and gifts.

QUITO IN 3 DAYS

Surrounded by towering Andean peaks and volcanoes, Quito is a compact and accessible city with a host of interesting sights, as well as great dining and shopping opportunities. Three days is a perfect amount of time to visit many of the capital's best museums and attractions, while sampling some of the city's many great restaurants. You even have time to visit the artisans market in nearby Otavalo and to have your picture taken straddling the Equator.

Day 1: Taking in Old Town

Many international flights arrive in Quito in the late afternoon or early evening, so this actually begins the day after your arrival. Following breakfast at your hotel, spend the morning touring Old Town. Visit the magnificent **Iglesia de San Francisco** ★★ (p. 107), which dates back to 1535, allowing a good 45 minutes to get a feel for the city's oldest church and its attached museum.

A few minutes' walk from here is **La Compañía de Jesús** ★★★ (p. 109) Jesuit church, which features an incredibly ornate interior mixing baroque and Moorish influences. Nearby, **Casa Museo María Augusta Urrutia** ★ (p. 105) is a perfectly preserved 19th-century mansion worthy of at least a 45-minute visit. Pope John Paul II visited here, so you shouldn't miss it. **Casa del Alabado** ★★ (p. 104) is a wonderful new museum with a fantastic collection of pre-Columbian artifacts. Housed in a restored colonial-era mansion, this museum takes about 40 minutes to visit. After all those museums and churches, and as the day begins to warm up, head to **La Plaza de la Independencia** (p. 109), the city's main square in the 16th century. (Old Town is safe to get lost in during the day, but at night I don't advise venturing far from Plaza de la Independencia on foot.) Break for a cup of coffee at a sunny cafe on or around the plaza—there are plenty of spots to choose from.

While walking around Plaza de la Independencia, see if there's a show on that night at **Teatro Nacional Sucre;** if there is, buy a ticket and make a pre-show dinner reservation at **Theatrum** ★★★ (p. 101).

El Panecillo (p. 107) is where you'll want to head next; it's a 10-minute ride up a steep hill. From here, standing below the immense winged virgin, you have a sweeping view of Old Town and the rest of Quito. Right next to the monument is **PIM's Panecillo** (p. 101), a great place to enjoy local cuisine and the view. I suggest returning to your hotel for a rest, because your body is probably not acclimated to the altitude and you may get tired easily. Remember to drink lots of bottled water, too, especially in the early afternoon, when the sun is at its highest and the atmosphere at its driest.

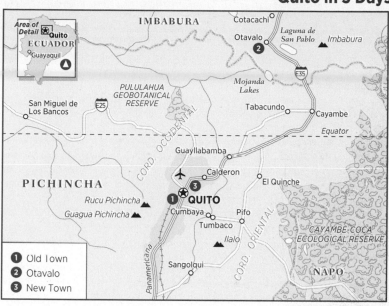

After your dinner (and hopefully a show), sit at the bar in stylish **Plaza Grande** ★★ for a nightcap.

Day 2: A Side Trip & Some Shopping

For your second day, sign up for a day trip to **Otavalo,** home to Ecuador's most famous **artisan market** ★★★ (p. 133). The market is most extensive and active on Saturday, but it's pretty impressive any day of the week.

Your tour should include lunch at one of the area's historic haciendas, as well as stops at any number of nearby attractions, such as Lago Cuicocha, Cascada Peguche, Lagunas de Mojanda, and Parque Condor. Be sure your tour includes a stop at **Quitsato Mitad del Mundo Monument** (p. 130).

For dinner, head to **Zazu** ★★★ (p. 103), arguably the best restaurant in Quito, for a taste of cutting-edge fusion cuisine.

Day 3: Time for New Town

After breakfast, head for **Parque El Ejido** (p. 113) and work off a few calories walking around this pretty city park. If it's a weekend, you'll have a chance to shop for Ecuadorean crafts and clothing at the outdoor market here. Otherwise, you can head to the nearby **Mariscal Artisans Market** or to **Olga Fisch Folklore** ★★ (p. 115), a high-end shop nearby. This is a good chance to pick up any last-minute gifts.

Next, head to **Museo Nacional del Banco Central del Ecuador** ★★ (p. 111), the country's biggest and most extensive museum. If you have the time, stop in at **Museo Mindalae** ★★ (p. 111).

For lunch, head to Plaza Foch and have lunch at one of the restaurants ringing this open-air plaza in the heart of the Mariscal district. I recommend the *nuevo latino* cuisine at **Azuca Latin Bistro** ★★ (p. 119).

After you eat, take a taxi to **Fundación Guayasamín** ★★ (p. 112), named after the country's most famous and influential artist. Expect to spend at least 1½ hours here, which may include a brief stop at the charming museum-cafe for a coffee and a sweet empanada.

For dinner, head up the flanks of Volcán Pichincha to the stunning and romantic restaurant at **Hacienda Rumiloma** ★★ (p. 103), which serves up excellent food in a cozy and stylish room with a stunning view of the city below. If you've got the energy, pull out all the stops and do a bar-and-club crawl in the Mariscal district of New Town. Begin at **Plaza Foch** (p. 119), and see where the night takes you.

THE ACTIVE VACATION PLANNER

E cuador's varied landscapes, culture, and natural beauty combine to make it a world-class destination for everything from bird-watching to sport fishing, from scuba diving to white-water rafting. Outdoor outfitters take full advantage of the country's diversity. For example, horseback-riding tours include stays in colonial haciendas, mountain-biking excursions stop at indigenous markets, and a golf course doubles as a bird-watching garden.

The fact that Ecuador's ocean, islands, mountains, forests, rivers, lakes, and beaches are packed into a relatively small territory allows travelers to sample an array of outdoor activities on a single trip. This chapter lays out the options, lists the best tour operators for each activity, and provides an overview of the country's national parks and protected areas. I also list some volunteer programs and other options for those who want to contribute to the preservation of the country's natural treasures.

ORGANIZED ADVENTURE TRIPS

Organized ecotourism or adventure-travel packages, arranged by operators in either the United States or Ecuador, are a popular way of combining varied activities. Bird-watching, horseback riding, biking, and hiking can be done in conjunction with visits to national parks or indigenous communities.

Traveling with a group has several advantages over traveling independently: Your accommodations and transportation are arranged, and most (if not all) of your meals are included in the cost of a package. If your tour operator has a reasonable amount of experience and a decent track record, you should proceed to each of your destinations quickly, without the snags and long delays that those traveling on their own can occasionally face. You'll also have the opportunity to meet like-minded souls who are interested in nature and active sports. Of course, you'll pay more for the convenience of having all your arrangements handled in advance.

In the best cases, groups are small (8–15 people) and tours are escorted by knowledgeable, bilingual guides. Be sure to ask about difficulty levels when you're choosing a tour. Although most companies offer "soft adventure" packages for those in moderately good but not phenomenal shape, others focus on more hard-core activities geared toward seasoned athletes or adventure travelers.

U.S.-Based Adventure-Tour Operators

These agencies and operators specialize in well-organized and coordinated tours that cover your entire stay. Many travelers prefer to have everything arranged and confirmed before arriving in Ecuador, and this is a good idea for first-timers and during the high season.

Abercrombie & Kent ★★ (✆ **800/554-7016** in the U.S. and Canada; www. abercrombiekent.com) is a luxury-tour company that offers upscale trips around the globe, and it has several Ecuador tours on its menu. It offers a selection of Galápagos cruises in combination with attractions on the Ecuadorean mainland or in Peru, as well as family-oriented tours perfect for those traveling with children. Service is personalized and the guides are top-notch.

Aventouras ★ (✆ **800/930-2846** in the U.S. and Canada; www.aventouras. com) is a small-scale adventure-tour operator that specializes in off-the-beaten track destinations, using local guides and staying in small environmentally conscious and sustainable hotels and lodges.

Backroads (✆ **800/462-2848** in the U.S. and Canada; www.backroads.com) is a U.S.-based adventure-tour operator specializing in hiking and biking tours that combine active endeavors with varied cultural pursuits and stays at plush inns and bed-and-breakfasts. Their Ecuador multisport outing includes biking, hiking, and kayaking in the central and northern Sierra, as well as in the Galápagos Islands.

Bike Hike Adventures (✆ **888/805-0061** in the U.S. and Canada, or 604/731-2442; www.bikehike.com) is a Canada-based company specializing in multiday, multi-adventure tours for small groups. They have several different offerings in Ecuador; most include a mix of activities, including hiking, mountain biking, river rafting, and wildlife viewing. Many tours also include some volunteer work.

Butterfield & Robinson ★★ ☺ (✆ **866/551-9090** in the U.S. and Canada; www.butterfield.com) is another company specializing in the very high-end market. One of its most interesting options is a Galápagos cruise designed for families with children over 8 years old. The trip provides a wealth of activities and adventures for parents and children to enjoy both together and apart.

Nature Expeditions International ★ (✆ **800/869-0639** in the U.S. and Canada; www.naturexp.com) specializes in educational and "low-intensity adventure" trips tailored to independent travelers and small groups. These folks have a steady stream of programmed departures, or they can customize a trip to your needs.

Overseas Adventure Travel ★★ (✆ **800/493-6824** in the U.S. and Canada; www.oattravel.com) has good-value natural history and "soft adventure" itineraries with small groups and naturalist guides. They offer a 15-day package that combines the Amazon with the Galápagos Islands, as well as optional extensions to the Central highlands.

In addition to these companies, many environmental organizations, including the **Sierra Club** (✆ **415/977-5522** in the U.S. and Canada; www.sierraclub.org) and **Smithsonian Institute** (✆ **877/338-8687** in the U.S. and Canada; www.smithsonian journeys.org), periodically offer organized trips to Ecuador.

Ecuador's National Parks & Protected Areas

U.K.-Based Tour Operators

Imaginative Traveller (© **44/1473-667-337** in the U.K.; www.imaginative-traveller.com) is a good-value operator specializing in budget student, group, and family travel. Their offerings in Ecuador focus on both wildlife and cultural themes. Several trips combine visits to Ecuador with stops in other South American countries. These trips range in duration from 9 to 31 days.

Journey Latin America ★ (© **020/8747-8315** in the U.K.; www.journeylatin america.co.uk) is a large British operator specializing in Latin American travel. They offer a range of escorted tours around Latin America, including quite a few that touch down in Ecuador. They also design custom itineraries and often have excellent deals on airfare.

Ecuadorean Tour Operators

Because most foreign-based operators subcontract their tours to established Ecuadorean companies, travelers can sometimes save money by booking directly with those outfitters in Ecuador. Packages may be 20% to 30% less expensive this way, but they're still not cheap—you still pay for the convenience of having all your arrangements handled for you.

Scores of agencies in Quito offer a selection of adventure options, ranging from white-water rafting to mountain climbing, to bird-watching at a nature lodge in the Amazon basin. Although it's generally quite easy to arrange a day trip at the last minute, longer tours often leave on set dates or when there are enough interested people. So it pays to check websites or call companies before you leave home.

Latin Trails ★ (✆ 800/747-0567 in the U.S. and Canada; www.latintrails.com), an American-Ecuadorean company, specializes in adventure and off-the-beaten-path tourism of Ecuador and other Andean nations. They offer a selection of Galápagos cruises, as well as overland adventures and Amazon expeditions, at competitive prices. They have permanent offices and staff in Ecuador.

Metropolitan Touring ★★ (✆ 02/2988-200; www.metropolitan-touring.com) is the country's largest tour operator. Many foreign tour operators subcontract most or all of their programs to Metropolitan, which maintains a full and very varied offering of fixed-departure and custom-designed tours.

Safari Ecuador ★ (✆ 02/2552-505; www.safari.com.ec) offers various Galápagos cruises, an array of Amazon adventures, Andean camping safaris, and mountain climbing.

Surtrek ★★ (✆ 866/978-7398 in the U.S. and Canada, or 02/2500-530 in Ecuador; www.surtrek.com), one of the country's best tour operators/wholesalers, offers everything from mountain-bike tours to white-water rafting and can customize combination tours.

ACTIVITIES A TO Z

This section describes the best places to participate in a given sport or activity and lists tour operators and outfitters. If you want to focus on only one active sport during your stay in Ecuador, these companies are your best bets for quality equipment and knowledgeable service.

Adventure activities and ecotourism inherently carry risks and dangers, which vary according to the sport. Over the years, there have been deaths and dozens of minor injuries from white-water rafting and mountain climbing, which is why I include only the most reputable companies here. If you have any doubt about the safety of the guide, equipment, or activity, opt out. Moreover, know your limits and abilities, and don't exceed them.

Biking

Ecuador offers varied biking options. Rentals in Baños and certain beach towns provide the option of heading off on your own. The highlands have a better climate for biking and are traversed by countless dirt tracks, with seemingly unlimited options for mountain biking, but there is a real potential for getting lost, which makes guided tours a good option. Some travelers fly their bike down and explore on their own, avoiding the country's main roads. Various tour companies—most of them based in Quito—provide the highway transport, bilingual guides, and logistical support.

TOUR OPERATORS & OUTFITTERS

Aries Bike Company ★★ (© 02/2380-802; www.ariesbikecompany.com) has an array of guided tours that last anywhere from 1 day to 2 weeks. Those itineraries range from challenging rides over the rugged countryside surrounding Ecuador's highest peaks, or around the crater lake of Quilotoa, to more leisurely downhill routes.

Safari Ecuador ★ (© 02/2552-505; www.safari.com.ec) offers mountain-bike safaris around Volcán Cotopaxi and to indigenous villages, including a back-road trip from Quito to the market town of Otavalo.

Surtrek ★★ (© 866/978-7398 in the U.S. and Canada, or 02/2500-530 in Ecuador; www.surtrek.com), one of the country's biggest tour operators/wholesalers, has mountain-bike tours ranging from 1 day to 2 weeks.

Bird-Watching

Ecuador is one of the best places in the world for bird-watching. With approximately 1,659 species, counting resident species and migrants, the country has a greater diversity of birds than China or India and nearly twice as many bird species as the United States. Though the neighboring nations of Colombia and Peru may boast more species, no nation in the world has as great a diversity of birdlife in as small an area as Ecuador. The country holds approximately one-sixth of the world's bird species in an area about the size of Colorado and gives birders the possibility of spotting more different species in a week or two than they would have just about anywhere else.

Ecuador's varied feathered creatures are scattered across its main geographical regions: the Sierra, Oriente, Pacific coast and lowlands, and Galápagos Islands. For birding purposes, the Andes could be further broken down into the highlands, Pacific cloud forest, and Amazon cloud forest. The Andean condor may be the **Sierra**'s avian king, but the highlands' smaller species are also quite impressive and much easier to see, especially the varied tanagers and hummingbirds. Birdlife in the Andes varies depending on the altitude, with some species found only around the peaks and high-altitude paramo, and others found only in the Sierra's valleys. There is also a good bit of difference between the birdlife of the northern highlands and that of the country's southern mountains.

The **cloud forests** of Ecuador's Andes are considered one of the planet's biodiversity "hot spots," with a greater diversity of birds than just about anywhere else in the world.

The **Oriente,** or Amazon basin, is home to some amazing birds, including colorful toucans, macaws, and jacamars, as well as the unusual hoatzin. Whereas the Oriente is relatively homogenous, the country's **Pacific lowlands** have a greater variety of habitats, which translates into more bird species, with the Chocó rainforest to the north giving way to tropical dry forest in the southwest, which is home to such species as the Pacific parrolet and the Ecuadorean trogon. The **Galápagos Islands** are often a birder's top spot in Ecuador, with a mix of endemic species, such as Darwin's famous finches, and common species such as the blue-footed booby and the red-billed tropicbird.

If you're serious about birding, you'll definitely want pick up a copy of the *Birds of Ecuador Field Guide,* by Robert Ridgely, Paul Greenfield, and Frank Gill, as well as a pair of gas-sealed binoculars. While the field guide is helpful, you'll get much more out of your time in the woods if you are accompanied by a naturalist guide; fortunately, Ecuador's best tour operators and nature lodges have some very experienced, dedicated birding guides. The following specialty tour operators tend to use designated lodges, several of which organize their own tours.

U.S.-BASED TOUR OPERATORS

Exotic Birding (𝓒 877/247-3371 in the U.S. and Canada; www.exoticbirding.com) specializes in bird-watching tours with very small groups (usually six people) to several Latin American countries. The company offers occasional 2-week tours in Ecuador that combine the highlands, cloud forest, and Amazon basin.

Field Guides ★ (𝓒 800/728-4953 in the U.S. and Canada, or 512/263-7295; www.fieldguides.com), a specialty bird-watching travel operator, offers long tours of Ecuador and stays at nature lodges for small groups accompanied by expert guides. The company's 18-day "Jewels of Ecuador" tour travels across the highlands and Pacific. They also offer a 2-week "Rainforest & Andes" trip, as well as tours that concentrate on the highlands, Galápagos, and southwest Ecuador.

Victor Emanuel Nature Tours ★ (𝓒 800/328-8368 in the U.S. and Canada, or 512/328-5221; www.ventbird.com), a well-respected, small-group operator specializing in bird-watching, runs several Ecuador trips. These folks offer a variety of tours, generally focusing on one or two bioregions.

Wings (𝓒 888/293-6443 in the U.S. and Canada, or 520/320-9868; www.wingsbirds.com) is a specialty bird-watching travel operator with more than 35 years of experience in the field. It offers various 1- and 2-week packages with small groups at nature lodges in the cloud forest and Amazon basin.

ECUADOREAN TOUR OPERATORS & LODGES

Andean Birding (𝓒 401/369-8623 in the U.S., or 09/418-4592 in Ecuador; www.andeanbirding.com) was founded by an American and a Swede who have dedicated most of their lives to studying birds. They invest 10% of their profits in conservation and research. They offer a wide range of small-group tours to a wide range of habitats and ecosystems throughout the country.

Bird Ecuador (𝓒 02/2906-769; www.birdecuador.com) is a small tour company owned by the same people who run Cabañas San Isidro, one of Ecuador's better birding spots. They offer various tours that combine stays at San Isidro, which is in the cloud forests of eastern Andes, with time at lodges in other parts of the country, including their sister Guango Lodge, near Papallacta.

San Jorge Eco-Lodge & Biological Reserve ★★ (𝓒 877/565-2596 toll-free in the U.S. and Canada, or 02/3390-403 in Ecuador; www.eco-lodgesanjorge.com) is a lodge near Quito that offers a "magic bird circuit" tour to its private forest reserves that protect various forest types. See p. 124.

Mindo Bird Tours ★ (𝓒 866/787-9901 in the U.S. and Canada, or 09/7351-297; www.mindobirds.com.ec) is an Ecuadorean tour operator founded by a British biologist; Mindo uses tourism profits to finance research and conservation. They have a good selection of tours to different regions of Ecuador for groups of no more than 10 people for competitive prices. Custom tours are also available.

Tinalandia (𝓒 02/2449-028; www.tinalandia.com) is a pretty lodge set in private cloud-forest reserve in northwest Ecuador; bird-watching is the specialty here. More than 350 bird species have been spotted on that hotel's grounds, among them an array of hummingbirds, tanagers, manikins, cotingas, parrots, and other colorful creatures. They also offer day trips to other birding spots in the area.

Tropical Birding ★★ (𝓒 800/348-5941 in the U.S. and Canada, or 09/9231-314 in Ecuador; www.tropicalbirding.com) is a leading operator specializing in birding

HUMMINGBIRD heaven

The first winged creatures to capture a traveler's imagination may be the legendary condor or the multicolored macaws, but Ecuador's varied and abundant hummingbirds could well be its most impressive avian attraction. With more than 130 different species of hummingbirds, the country vies with Colombia for the distinction of having the most hummingbird species in the world. And because that diversity is spread from one end of the nation to the other, you are likely to encounter hummingbirds wherever you travel—from the rugged mountain slopes, to the lush jungles, to the patio of your Quito hotel.

The world's 330 hummingbird species are all found only in the Americas, and they can be spotted anywhere from Alaska to Tierra del Fuego, but Ecuador lies at the center of the region. With more than a third of the planet's hummers packed into a tiny fraction of its landmass, Ecuador is nothing less than hummingbird heaven.

It is feasible for a birder to spot more than a dozen different kinds of hummingbirds in one morning. The best places to observe them are gardens, plenty of which can be found on the grounds of the country's best hotels. Ecuador's hummingbird rainbow includes the green-crowned wood nymph, the sparkling violet-ear, the amethyst-throated sun angel, the purple-crowned fairy, and the violet-tailed sylph, which has long blue-green tail feathers that trail behind it when it flies.

The country is home to the Andean swordbill, which has the proportionally longest beak of any bird in the world—a 10-centimeter (4-in.) bill on a 13-centimeter (5-in.) body—which allows it to suck nectar from the long tubular flowers that it pollinates. Ecuador also has several species with inordinately long tails, such as the black-tailed trainbearer and the booted racket-tail, which has two bare-shafted tail feathers tipped with green discs. The country is also home to the largest species in the hummer family, called the giant hummingbird, though with a length of 20 centimeters (8 in.) and a weight of ⅔ ounce, the name does seem an exaggeration.

It may be hard to focus your binoculars on them before they zip away, but when you get a good look at one of the country's hummingbirds in direct sunlight, its colors are simply amazing. As they hum about from blossom to blossom and chase each other around, these high-powered, iridescent beauties are bound to impress you, and if you find a spot where several species congregate to feed, you are set for an entertaining morning.

tours around the world. They happen to be based in Ecuador, giving them particular expertise in the bird-watching here. These folks specialize in small group tours, with highly skilled guides.

Camping

During the dry months, the Andes and Pacific coast provide excellent camping conditions. Camping is allowed in many of the country's protected areas, but infrastructure is largely lacking and access is often difficult. Outdoor outfitters offer tours that include overnights in tents, usually at the end of a day of hiking, biking, horseback riding, or white-water rafting.

Safari Ecuador ★ (℡ 02/2552-505; www.safari.com.ec) runs a series of African-style safaris in the Andean paramo using 4WD vehicles. In addition to high-altitude camping, activities include day hikes and horseback riding easy enough to be appropriate for families. Expeditions last anywhere from 2 days to 2 weeks.

Surtrek ★★ (℡ 866/978-7398 in the U.S. and Canada, or 02/2500-530 in Ecuador; www.surtrek.com), one of the country's biggest adventure and ecotour companies, offers various Andes and Amazon hiking tours that include the option of camping.

Canopy Tours

The canopy tour—an activity that involves gliding along steel cables between platforms perched high in trees—was invented in Costa Rica but has spread to other countries, Ecuador among them. It is estimated that some two-thirds of the tropical rainforest's species live in the canopy (the uppermost, branching layer of the forest), and biologists who pioneered study of that biodiversity developed some of the techniques now used in canopy tours. Nevertheless, the tours are more about adrenaline rushes than about observing or learning about wildlife.

Mindo Canopy Adventure (℡ 08/5428-758; www.mindocanopy.com) is one of the best zip-line operations in the country, with 13 different cables strung through the beautiful forests around Mindo.

Mindo Ropes & Canopy (℡ 09/1725-874; www.mindoropescanopy.com) features a total of 12 zip-line cables traveling a total of 2,650m (8,692 ft.) through the cloud forests just outside of Mindo.

El Cañón del Salto Canopy Tour (℡ 02/2041-520; www.tierradelvolcan.com) is run by the folks at Hacienda El Porvenir (p. 163) and features seven different cable runs, with the longest being some 420m (1,378 ft.) long.

Cruising

Most of Ecuador's cruising options are centered in the Galápagos (see chapter 12), where dozens of yachts and catamarans offer 1- to 2-week tours to the archipelago's attractions. These cruises are focused on the fascinating fauna, and most offer the option of snorkeling or scuba diving, whereas some boats cater exclusively to scuba divers (see "Diving & Snorkeling," below).

Celebrity Cruises ★★★ (℡ 800/647-2251 toll-free in the U.S. and Canada, or 316/554-5961; www.celebritycruises.com) keeps their posh 296-foot Celebrity Xpedition in the Galápagos Islands year-round. Their 10-day packages include 3 nights at the JW Marriott in Quito, two pre-cruise and one post-cruise.

Ecoventura ★ (℡ 800/633-7972 in the U.S. and Canada, or 04/2839-390 in Ecuador; www.ecoventura.com) is a good choice for an economical trip to the Galápagos, with four first-class ships and excellent local guides.

Galacruises Expeditions (℡ 02/250-9007; www.galacruises.com) has five boats in the Galápagos, ranging from older, less-expensive yachts to luxury catamarans. They can also book Galápagos cruises on various other vessels.

KLEIN Tours ★ (℡ 888/810-6909 in the U.S., or 02/2430-345 in Ecuador; www.kleintours.com) is one of the original cruise operators in the Galápagos, currently offering up three first-class ships.

Linblad Expeditions ★★ (℡ 800/397-3348 in the U.S. and Canada; www.expeditions.com), a luxury-oriented agency committed to environmental protection, offers first-class Galápagos cruises with highly trained naturalist guides on the

National Geographic Explorer, the *National Geographic Islander,* and the *National Geographic Polaris.*

Metropolitan Touring ★★★ (© 888/572-0166 in the U.S. and Canada, or 02/2988-200 in Ecuador; www.metropolitan-touring.com) offers Galápagos cruises on three privately owned luxury ships. They also offer the option of pairing a cruise with time at their Finch Bay Hotel, on Santa Cruz Island, or with an array of packages on the mainland.

The rustic **Manatee Amazon Explorer** ★ (© 02/3360-887; www.manatee amazonexplorer.com) runs 3-, 4-, and 7-night ecocruises on the **Napo River,** the Amazon tributary where Francisco de Orellana began his journey that led to the big river's discovery. Accommodations are snug, but the guides and itinerary are first class. The cruise includes daily boat trips up smaller rivers and hikes into the rainforest, where you are likely to see everything from wooly monkeys to blue and gold macaws. See p. 309.

Tauck ★★ (© 800/788-7885 in the U.S. and Canada; www.tauck.com) is a soft-adventure company catering to higher-end travelers. They offer various Galápagos cruises, including a family package, and an add-on to package to Peru.

Diving & Snorkeling

In addition to being a phenomenal place to spot fauna on hikes and boat rides, the **Galápagos Islands** are a world-class scuba-diving destination. Unlike popular areas such as the South Pacific and Caribbean, the Galápagos don't have coral reefs, because the water is too cold. They do have a lot of marine life, including manta rays, sea lions, penguins, sea turtles, iguanas, at least five species of sharks, and hundreds of other fish species, many of them endemic to the archipelago. Galápagos cruises generally offer snorkeling or scuba diving; keep in mind that the water is chilly and most people need a wet suit. A handful of boats catering to experienced divers offer cruises that include any of 30 dive sites over the course of 1 to 2 weeks. Two to four daily dives are complemented with island excursions. All divers must pay the one-time $100 national park admission fee and port fees.

The best months for diving are November through April, when seas are calmer and the water is less cold: 18° to 23°C (64°–73° F). However, even then, many dive sites experience strong currents, surges of cold water that can get as low as 10°C (50°F), and visibility that can get as low as 3m (9¾ ft.), though it averages 6 to 24m (20–79 ft.). Many of the dives are relatively deep. Night dives are prohibited in the Galápagos. Divers need to prove that they are experienced and have been diving recently in order to join trips. They will also need to use a full wet suit, often with hood. Because of the nature of the diving here, I recommend taking a dive boat with Nitrox facilities. If you aren't already Nitrox certified, you can take the course onboard and dive with Nitrox tanks during the trip. Nitrox will allow you increased time below the surface, an important consideration with these predominantly deep dives.

Various ships offer dive cruises to the northern islands that include comfortable accommodations, good food, and creature comforts. The best and most challenging dive spots are located around the archipelago's northern islands, especially **Wolf Island** and **Darwin Island,** but because the main attractions are on the southern islands, excursions that combine divers with nondivers tend to stay in the south.

A less expensive option is to stay on Santa Cruz or on San Cristóbal and take day trips with a local dive operator. Though the best dive spots are too far north to reach on anything other than a live-aboard ship, there are dozens of excellent dive spots within a 20- to 90-minute boat trip from **Santa Cruz,** including Gordon's Rocks, where schools of hammerhead sharks sometimes congregate. The conditions in the south are also less demanding, and local dive schools offer basic certification and resort dives for novices. See chapter 12 for more about diving in the Galápagos.

Though the Galápagos has Ecuador's best diving, the **Pacific coast** also has its share of dive spots, the best of which is around **Isla de la Plata,** an offshore island about 2 hours by boat from Puerto López. Dubbed the "poor man's Galápagos," Isla de la Plata has many of the same fish, including white-tipped sharks and manta rays, as well as plentiful birdlife. From June to October, dive trips to the island can be complemented with whale-watching. See chapter 9.

DIVING BOATS & OPERATORS

Aggressor **Fleet Limited ★★** (© **800/348-2628** in the U.S. and Canada, or 04/2681-950; www.aggressor.com) runs 1-week cruises for 14 divers to the islands' best spots on its two identical 30m (98-ft.) boats: the *Galápagos Aggressor I* and *II.* Boats include Nitrox facilities, film developing, and underwater-camera rental.

Exploramar Diving ★★ (© **02/2564-342** or 05/2300-123; www.exploradiving. com), an Ecuadorean company with dive centers on Santa Cruz Island and in Puerto López, Manabí, offers a selection of diving packages for the Galápagos and Isla de la Plata, as well as PADI certification courses.

Galápagos Sub-Aqua ★ (© **05/2526-633;** www.galapagos-sub-aqua.com), an Ecuadorean company in Puerto Ayora, is the archipelago's oldest dive center. They offer PADI certification courses, land-based packages, and cruises custom-designed to divers' experience levels.

Machalilla Tours ★ (© **05/2300-234** or 09/4925-960; www.machalillatours. org) is an excellent local operator based out of Puerto López. They offer diving trips to sites around Isla de la Plata, as well as off the coast of Manabí.

M/S *Galapagos Sky* ★ (© **800/633-7972** in the U.S. and Canada, or 04/2839-390 in Ecuador; www.ecoventura.com) is a dedicated dive boat carrying a maximum of 16 divers. Top-notch dive masters, food, and Nitrox facilities make this the second-best diving option in the Galápagos, after the *Aggressor* boats (see above).

Scuba Iguana (© **05/2526-497;** www.scubaiguana.com) is an excellent operator, offering an array of day trips out of Puerto Ayora, as well as diving certification courses.

Fishing

Ecuador is one of the world's great overlooked deep-sea-fishing destinations. The ocean is remarkably rich in marine life, thanks to the Humboldt Current, which pulls nutrients off the ocean bottom through a process called upwelling, keeping the water full of plankton. A vibrant food chain ends in massive marlins, sailfish, sharks, and whales. The country has few sport-fishing operators, but their catch logs are as impressive as those of charter boats in the Caribbean, Mexico, or Costa Rica. The Galápagos archipelago and Pacific coastal waters hold abundant Pacific sailfish, tuna, wahoo, mahimahi, and blue, black, and striped marlin.

The calmest conditions are from December to May, but the fishing stays good from June to November, when it can be chilly in the Galápagos. Temperatures are more consistently tropical along the coast, where marlin and sailfish abound, especially around Isla de la Plata.

SPORT-FISHING CHARTERS

Galápagos Sport Fishing ★ (www.galapagosfishing.com) will help you put together fishing trips to the Galápagos. Fishing is done with local, licensed fishermen. Rates run around $1,500 per day for a full day of fishing, on a boat that can hold up to four anglers, and include all gear, tackle, breakfast, lunch, drinks, and snacks. Hotel stays, transfers, and other incidentals are extra, but everything can be arranged and facilitated by these folks.

Machalilla Tours ★ (© 05/2300-234 or 09/4925-960; www.machalillatours. org) operates sport fishing out of Puerto López and along the Manabí coast.

Pesca Tours ★ (© 04/2772-391; www.pescatours.com.ec) offers sport-fishing charters out of the beach town of Salinas.

Hang Gliding & Paragliding

Hang gliding and paragliding are popular from the mountains above Quito—namely, Pichincha—and the cliffs above Canoa and the tiny town of Crucita, both on the Manabí coast. While experienced pilots should be happy with the conditions, novices can also try the paragliding on a tandem flight, which can provide an unforgettable, bird's-eye view of the coast or highlands.

The Belgian-owned operator **Terranova Trek** (© 02/2253-327; www.terranova trek.com) offers tandem flights in the Quito area, advice, transportation, and support for pilots with their own gear, various paragliding courses, and a package tour for experienced pilots that includes flights in both the mountains and on the coast, as well as visits to national parks and other attractions. Tandem flights cost just $60, whereas the 16-day tour costs $1,650. These folks also offer lessons and certification courses.

Parapente Crucita (© 05/2340-334; www.parapentecrucita.com), in the paragliding mecca of Crucita, has a hostel and flight school, rents equipment, provides transportation to the bluffs, and offers 10-minute tandem flights for $35. A 5-day paragliding course costs $350.

Hiking

From its jungle trails to its highland tracks, Ecuador's hiking options are virtually limitless. In many places, the terrain is challenging, the altitude a serious consideration, or the forest thick, which is why organized hikes are quite popular. Stays at the nature lodges of the Oriente and the cruise down the Napo River include guided hikes through the rainforest, while options in the Andes range from short hikes through the countryside around mountain lodges to acclimation and summit hikes on the slopes and peaks of snowcapped volcanoes, and full-on trekking safaris to some of the country's most remote protected areas.

Popular trips include walks on the well-marked trails of the Pasochoa Reserve, near Quito; treks up the slopes of Cotopaxi or Chimborazo; or hikes around the crater lake of Cuicocha or down a section of the old Inca trail to the ruins of Ingapirca. Hikers who want to do it on their own should pick up the book *Trekking in Ecuador,* by Robert and Daisy Kunstaetter. When planning a hiking expedition, it is good to pay attention to the country's regional rainy seasons. Though the Sierra is largely sunny from June to September and partially sunny in December and January, the eastern peaks and valleys are influenced by the inclement climate of the Oriente, where the wettest months are June, July, and August. The wettest months on the country's Pacific side are February through May.

HIKING OUTFITTERS

The Black Sheep Inn ★★ (© 03/2708-077 or 09/9635-405; www.blacksheep inn.com), beautifully located in Chugchilán, Cotopaxi, offers guests guided day hikes around Quilotoa Lake and through the surrounding countryside. See p. 169.

Safari Ecuador ★ (© 02/2552-505; www.safari.com.ec) runs multiday hiking trips for serious hikers to the remote indigenous village of Tigua, around Cotopaxi and Antisana national parks, and up several of the country's secondary peaks that can serve as acclimatization hikes for further mountaineering expeditions.

Surtrek ★★ (© 866/978-7398 in the U.S. and Canada, or 02/2500-530 in Ecuador; www.surtrek.com) offers a dozen 3- to 6-day treks through some of the country's most spectacular regions, complete with pack horses and a cook. Among the tours are a 5-day trek around Volcán Cotopaxi and the Ilinizas peaks, a trek on the Inca Trail, and 4 days in Podocarpus National Park.

Horseback Riding

Ecuador's horseback-riding tradition stretches back to 1534, when Spanish conquistadors rode the first horses into the country. During the colonial era, a thriving ranching culture developed in the Sierra, where cattle and horses took over pastureland that once supported herds of llamas and alpacas. That heritage is still visible at the country's traditional haciendas, where *chagras,* or Ecuadorean cowboys, round up cattle in traditional garb.

For visitors, horseback-riding opportunities range from an array of day trips to equestrian packages that let you ride from hacienda to hacienda, or participate in a roundup. Trail rides can take you past amazing scenery, including the highland paramo, snowcapped volcanoes, Andean dwarf forest, or lush cloud forest. Horseback-riding enthusiasts have the option of staying at one of the country's traditional cattle ranches, such as Hacienda La Alegría or Hacienda Zuleta, or joining one of various horseback tours that visit two or more haciendas.

HORSEBACK-RIDING OUTFITTERS

Equitours (© 800/545-0019 in the U.S. and Canada; www.ridingtours.com), of Wyoming, sells a 9-day horseback tour of Ecuador, which includes 7 days of riding and overnights at various historic haciendas.

Hidden Trails (© 888/987-2457 in the U.S. and Canada; www.hiddentrails. com), a U.S. tour agency that specializes in equestrian vacations, offers various riding packages in Ecuador that combine nights in traditional haciendas with camping or overnights in rustic farmhouses. Their tours include rides through cloud forest and highland paramo, trips around Volcán Cotopaxi, overnights at various historic haciendas, and participation in traditional horse or cattle roundups.

Ilalo Expeditions ★ (© 09/7778-399 or 02/2484-219; www.ilaloexpeditions. com), an Ecuadorean outfitter, offers 1-day rides near Volcán Cotopaxi or to the summit of extinct Volcán Ilalo, and an 8-day ride along the Avenue of the Volcanoes, with overnights in historic haciendas and country inns. They also have a 2-week "Inca Imperial" tour that combines horseback riding in Ecuador and Peru with trips to the Galápagos and Machu Picchu.

HACIENDAS

There are scores of haciendas around Ecuador, but the following specialize in horseback riding.

Hacienda El Porvenir ★★ (© **02/2041-520** or 09/4980-121; www.tierradel volcan.com) is a working ranch set on the outskirts of Cotopaxi National Park, with great horses and almost endless high Andean terrain just outside its gates. See p. 163.

Hacienda Hato Verde ★ (©/fax **03/2719-348** or 09/5978-016; www.hacienda hatoverde.com) is a cozy and artfully done little inn housed in a converted old hacienda near the base of Volcán Cotopaxi. The owners here take their horseback riding seriously. See p. 161.

Hacienda La Alegría ★★ (© **02/2462-319** or 09/9802-526; www.hacienda laalegria.com), a 20th-century horse ranch south of Quito, offers guests various horseback-riding tours through the surrounding countryside, as well as other outdoor activities. See p. 162.

Hacienda Pinsaquí (© **06/2946-116;** www.haciendapinsaqui.com), near the market town of Otavalo, is a historic hacienda founded in 1790 that specializes in horseback riding, with trips to nearby indigenous communities or to the summit of Volcán Imbabura. See p. 141.

Hacienda Zuleta ★★★ (© **06/2662-182;** www.zuleta.com), a colonial 1,780-hectare (4,398-acre) hacienda about 2½ hours north of Quito, has more than 90 horses. Their horses are a unique mixture of Andalusian, thoroughbred, and quarter horses, and offer a remarkably smooth ride. Guests can choose from an ample selection of guided trail rides through pasture, cloud forest, and paramo. See p. 144.

San Jorge Eco-Lodge & Biological Reserve (© **877/565-2596** toll-free in the U.S. and Canada, or 02/3390-403 in Ecuador; www.eco-lodgesanjorge.com), in the mountains near Quito, has more than 20 horses and various trail rides from which guests can choose. See p. 124.

Mountain Climbing

Ecuador may not have the world's highest mountains, but thanks to the accessibility of the country's big peaks and its supply of experienced, bilingual climbing guides, it is one of the great mountaineering destinations. The country's popularity among climbers has grown steadily since the British mountaineer Edward Whymper—the first to ascend many of Ecuador's mountains—chronicled his experiences in an 1892 book called *Travels Amongst the Great Andes of the Equator.* But you don't need to read Whymper to be inspired enough to want to climb one of Ecuador's massive snow-capped volcanoes, which dominate the landscape in much of the northern Sierra.

The country's highest peaks are divided between eastern and western cordilleras that flank a fertile central valley, known as the "Avenue of the Volcanoes." The view from the summit of one of those mountains on a clear morning is truly breathtaking—if you've got any breath left to take after making the climb. But even a hike to the edge of one of their glaciers, or an ascent that fails to reach the summit, can provide an unforgettable experience.

Ecuador has peaks that are technically difficult enough to challenge experienced climbers, but it is also an excellent place for an introduction to the sport, thanks to the existence of various mountaineering schools. Because the country's second-highest peak, Cotopaxi, is a relatively young, conical volcano, it presents a technically simple climb that is accessible to climbers with various levels of experience. If you're in good shape and acclimate quickly, it is feasible for you to take an introductory course and end up climbing Cotopaxi within a week's time.

Whether you are an experienced climber or a mountaineering novice, safety is always the priority, which means climbing only with trained, experienced guides. The

THE big PEAKS

Climbers have dozens of mountains to choose from in Ecuador, but most head up the same peaks, especially the two highest—Chimborazo and Cotopaxi—which may be ascended by several groups at once during the driest months. Here are the biggest and most popular peaks:

Chimborazo (6,310m/20,697 ft.) This massive, glacier-encrusted peak 150km (93 miles) south of Quito has five summits, the highest of which is named for Whymper, who believed it was the tallest mountain in the world when he ascended it in 1880. It has claimed the lives of many climbers and requires experience and acclimation. Best weather: June to January.

Cotopaxi (5,897m/19,342 ft.) A perfectly conical, snowcapped volcano less than an hour south of Quito, Ecuador's second-highest mountain is also its most popular climb. Though technically straightforward, the ascent demands good physical conditioning, ice axes, crampons, and ropes. It can be climbed year-round, but the best weather is in December, January, and July to September.

Cayambe (5,790m/18,991 ft.) Ecuador's third-highest peak, this extinct volcano north of Quito is climbed less frequently than Cotopaxi because it has crevasses and suffers from more inclement weather and avalanches. Nevertheless, qualified mountain guides regularly lead successful ascents there. Best weather: July and August.

Antisana (5,704m/18,709 ft.) Ecuador's fourth-highest peak, Antisana towers over the eastern edge of the Andes, which means it is more influenced by Amazon-basin weather. The surrounding scenery of lakes and forest and the abundance of Andean condors make this a good area for hikers—but the frequent clouds and crevasses near the summit make it a difficult peak to climb. Best weather: December and January.

El Altar (5,319m/17,446 ft.) This massive, extinct volcano with nine summits is a challenging technical climb complicated by frequent inclement weather, but even if you don't make the summit, you'll enjoy the impressive scenery on the lower slopes. Best weather: December to May.

Tungurahua (5,023m/16,475 ft.) Located within Sangay National Park, remote Tungurahua is an active volcano that was part of the climbing circuit for years when it was dormant, but massive eruptions in 2006 knocked it off the circuit, at least for the time being.

popularity of the sport has resulted in an overabundance of companies offering climbing tours, many of which are of dubious quality. The minimum training your guide should have is that required for membership in ASEGUIM, the Ecuadorean Mountain Guides Association; it's preferable, though, that a guide has had some training abroad as well. That said, there is no substitute for experience, so if you are going to attempt an ascent of a big peak, make sure your guide has climbed it at least a dozen times.

The most popular peaks have large refuges at their bases with kitchen facilities and rooms full of bunks, where climbers hit the sack early in order to start their ascent around midnight. Climbing outfitters reserve bunks, provide transportation, and take care of dinner. Serious climbers will want to pick up a copy of the book *Climbing and Hiking in Ecuador*, by Rob Rachowiecki, Mark Thurber, and Betsy Wagenhouser.

MOUNTAINEERING OUTFITTERS

Adventure Planet Ecuador (© 02/2863-086; www.adventureplanet-ecuador. com) offers guided ascents of the country's highest peaks and mountaineering tours that range from to a 6-day "soft climbing" package to a 3-week tour that combines ascents of five volcanoes with a rainforest trip.

Compañía de Guías de Montaña ★★ (© 02/2901-551; www.companiade guias.com.ec), started by a group of Ecuadorean climbing guides 17 years ago, offers guided ascents of most of the country's big mountains and 9- to 15-day packages that combine acclimation and ascents of several summits with general sightseeing.

Ecuadorian Alpine Institute (© 02/2565-465; www.volcanoclimbing.com), a local climbing and trekking outfitter, organizes ascents for experienced climbers and offers mountaineering training for beginners and intermediate climbers.

Safari Ecuador ★ (© 02/2222-505; www.safari.com.ec) organizes ascents of the country's main climbing peaks and runs Andes Climbing School, which offers an introduction to the sport and acclimatization programs.

Spas

Ecuador has a limited spa selection, but those that are listed here feature such unusual extras as hummingbird gardens, lush cloud forests, or the opportunity to complement massages and other treatments with outdoor activities.

Arasha Resort ★ (© 02/2449-881; www.arasharesort.com) is sequestered in the cloud forest near Mindo, about 2 hours from Quito. It offers an array of stress-relieving therapies, as well as a lot of exposure to soothing Mother Nature.

Hotel Termas de Papallacta ★★★ (© 02/6005-586 at the hot springs, or 02/2568-989 for reservations in Quito; www.termaspapallacta.com), on the eastern slope of the Andes, is an hour from Quito. This hotel and hot springs offers a rich yet affordable spa experience in an attractive valley known for its bird-watching. See p. 126.

La Mirage Garden Hotel & Spa ★★★ (© 800/327-3573 in the U.S. and Canada, or 06/2915-237 in Ecuador; www.mirage.com.ec), on the outskirts of the tranquil colonial town of Cotacachi, is a luxury hotel and spa where the massages and aromatherapy can be complemented by contemplating the hummingbirds that abound in the hotel's extensive gardens. See p. 140.

Luna Runtun Adventure Spa ★★ (© 03/2740-655; www.lunaruntun.com), an attractive hotel and spa in the mountains above Baños, offers a range of massages, skin care, and hair care, as well as a selection of outdoor activities that include hiking, horseback riding, and mountain biking. See p. 183.

Piedra de Agua ★★★ (© 07/2892-496; www.piedradeagua.com.ec) is a gorgeous new spa located on the outskirts of Cuenca. Literally carved into a field of red volcanic rock in places, this place has hot and cool mineral pools, steam baths, and volcanic mud treatments. See p. 203.

Samari Spa Resort ★★★ (© 03/2741-855; www.samarispa.com) is a beautiful resort hotel on the outskirts of Baños, with a delightful and luxurious spa offering up a range of treatment options. See p. 183.

Surfing

Ecuador is one of the world's best-kept surfing secrets. Between the Galápagos Islands and the Pacific coast, the country has at least 50 surf spots where the waves consistently break overhead. The coastal water is warm, especially from December to

June, but the Galápagos are wet suit territory pretty much year-round. The best surfing months are December through June, when the ocean is often glassy in the morning and the sky is usually clear. From June to November, the water gets choppier and cold, especially in the Galápagos, and onshore winds can further complicate conditions, though the mainland experiences days with good conditions year-round.

Galápagos surfing is considerably more expensive, due to logistics and lodging costs, but the islands have few surfers and the waves are consistently overhead and uncrowded. San Cristóbal Island has about five breaks, most of which are over volcanic-rock platforms; though pleasant from January to May, the water gets cold here during the June-to-December rainy season. The U.S. company **Wave Hunters Surf Travel** ★★ (✆ 760/494-7392 in the U.S.; www.wavehunters.com) offers 1-week surfing packages that include the flight from Guayaquil, lodging at the Canoa Surf Resort, and transportation to surf breaks and cost $1,800 to $2,550.

Pacific coast surfing is considerably less expensive and offers more options. The coast has about 50 breaks, most of which lie between Manta and Salinas and along the coast south of Salinas. **Montañita,** a tubular right point break, is one of the best. **Casa del Sol Surf Camp** (✆ 09/2488-581; www.casadelsolmontanita.com; p. 252), in Montañita, offers accommodations, surf tours of coastal breaks, and instruction for novice surfers. **Río Chico,** north of Montañita, has an excellent left break when there is a southwest swell. Las Tunas, near Ayampé, is a fun beach break that can easily be surfed from **Finca Punta Ayampé** ★ (✆ 09/1890-982; www.fincapuntaayampe.com), an ecolodge that offers surf tours, whale-watching, and other activities. **Salinas** has several breaks nearby, the best of which is a reef break, in front of a military base, that is accessible only by boat. **San Mateo,** near Manta, is a long, consistent left that can get very big. **Canoa,** on the northern coast, has a good beach break that can be fun for beginners and experienced surfers alike. **Mompiche,** south of Esmeraldas, is an intense left that breaks over lava rock—for experienced surfers only.

Waterways Travel ★ (✆ 888/669-7873 in the U.S. and Canada; www.waterwaystravel.com) sells packages ranging from a week at Casa del Sol—either surfing Montañita or touring nearby breaks—to more deluxe packages that combine a tour of various coastal breaks with a week in the Galápagos or exclusive surf stays in the Galápagos.

Whale-Watching

From late June to early October, the ocean off Ecuador's Pacific coast is the breeding area for hundreds of humpback whales, which migrate there from the icy waters around Antarctica. Boat tours out of Salinas, Puerto López, and other ports offer an opportunity to observe those amazing creatures, the largest of which are 15m (49 ft.) long and can weigh as much as 50 tons. Whale-watching tours may include a stop at Isla de la Plata, an offshore island where thousands of seabirds nest.

WHALE-WATCHING OUTFITTERS
Exploramar Diving (✆ 02/2564-342 or 05/2300-123; www.exploradiving.com), in Puerto López, offers whale-watching tours on its dive boats during the whale-watching season.

Guacamayo Tours (✆ 05/2691-107; www.guacamayotours.com) runs inexpensive whale-watching tours out of Bahía de Caráquez.

Machalilla Tours ★ (✆ 05/2300-234 or 09/4925-960; www.machalillatours.org) is my favorite operator in Puerto López; they offer whale-watching excursions throughout the whale-watching season.

Pesca Tours ★ (② 04/2402-504; www.pescatours.com.ec) is the best operator to contact if you are staying in Salinas and want to head out to spot a whale.

White-Water Rafting & Kayaking

As might be expected from a country with massive mountains and copious rainfall, Ecuador has world-class conditions for white-water rafting and kayaking. What makes those sports even more exciting in Ecuador is the fact that its rivers flow though tropical forests that are home to hundreds of bird species and other animals. And some river trips can be combined with visits to traditional indigenous communities.

Thanks to almost year-round rainfall, the eastern slope of the Andes boasts one of the highest concentrations of rivers in the world. Those boulder-strewn waterways flow from the cloud forest down to the rainforest, winding through lush valleys and gorges, past waterfalls, massive trees, and an array of flora and fauna. The western slope of the Andes also has some popular rivers that are more accessible, but their water levels are high enough for rafting only from January to May.

Río Toachi, in the western Andes, is conveniently close to Quito and easy enough for beginners, which makes it the country's most rafted river. A strong Class III/IV river, it can be run from January to May but flows through inhabited areas and farmland, which means its waters suffer from some pollution. **Río Mulaute,** a Class III river to the north of the Toachi, can be run as a 1- or 2-day trip. The upper **Río Blanco,** another Class III river farther north of the Toachi, flows through a less developed, forested valley, making it a more pleasant trip. A good trip for beginners and experienced rafters alike, it is far enough from Quito to be a 2-day trip but is navigable only from January to May. The lower Río Blanco, after its confluence with the Toachi River, can be run year-round but is not as pristine as the Upper Blanco.

On the eastern slope of the Andes is the upper **Río Napo,** a Class III Amazon tributary that flows past amazing tropical forest. Its 25km (16-mile) white-water route is an exhilarating day trip that can be done year-round from Tena. **Río Misahuallí,** another eastern Andes river, is a gorgeous Class IV route that offers the country's most impressive and challenging white-water experience. Some rafting experience is required for this river, which can be navigated only at low water from October to March and which includes a portage around Casanova Falls. **Río Upano,** another Amazon tributary that flows through dense rainforest and spectacular Namangosa Gorge, then past indigenous villages, is a multiday trip, with rapids ranging from Class II to Class IV. **Río Jatunyacu** is a long and lively Class III white-water route perfect for beginners and nature enthusiasts. **Río Anzu** has an easier Class II/III white-water route that is perfect for families or beginners. **Río Quijos,** a difficult Class IV river east of Quito, is a popular route for experienced rafters and kayakers; it was the site of the 2005 World Rafting Championship.

RAFTING OUTFITTERS
Agencia Limoncocha ★ (② 06/2887-583; http://limoncocha.tripod.com) is an all-purpose Tena-based tour operator that runs river trips on most of the local white-water routes.

Ríos Ecuador ★★ (② 06/2886-727 in Tena, or 02/2904-054 in Quito; www. riosecuador.com) runs rafting trips on the Upper Napo and Misahuallí rivers, and an easy trip down the Class-II-to-III Río Anzu that is perfect for nature lovers and families. They also teach kayaking.

River People Rafting ★ (© 06/2887-887; www.riverpeoplerafting.com), a small outfitter based in Tena, runs rafting and kayaking trips on the Napo and Misahuallí rivers and on the Class IV Río Intag, east of Otavalo. They also have a kayaking school.

Small World Adventures ★★ (© 800/585-2925 in the U.S. and Canada; www.smallworldadventures.com), a Colorado company with a river lodge near Tena, runs multiday advanced rafting and kayaking trips on the Quijos, Misahualli, and Jatunyacu rivers. Small World is an especially good company for kayakers.

Yacu Amu Rafting (© 02/2904-054; www.raftingecuador.com), a well-established Quito-based rafting and kayaking outfitter, offers rafting trips on the most popular rivers, as well as a 2-day trip on the challenging Quijos and a 4-day trip down the wild Upano. They also offer kayaking tours and instruction.

ECUADOR'S TOP NATIONAL PARKS & BIORESERVES

Ecuador has nearly 30 national parks and preserves that together protect all of its varied ecosystems and approximately 17% of the national territory. Those protected areas cover everything from the country's highest mountains to the blue depths of the Galápagos archipelago, and include vast expanses of Amazon rainforest, misty cloud forest, and paramo, as well as the mangroves and threatened tropical dry forest of the Pacific lowlands. Several of the largest protected areas stretch from the Sierra down to the Pacific lowlands or Amazon basin, in which case they protect a series of different but interconnected life zones—important for the many animals that migrate seasonally between the mountains and lowlands.

Most of the country's protected areas are remote, undeveloped tropical forests, with few services or facilities available for visitors. Others, however, offer easier access to the country's varied natural wonders. Because most parks have limited or no infrastructure, and access can be difficult, it's usually best—and, in some cases, obligatory—to visit them on an organized tour. Many parks have farms or villages within them, most of which existed before those protected areas were created. And as is all too common in developing countries, hunting, illegal logging, mining, and even oil exploration take place in some of Ecuador's parks and reserves.

Most of the national parks charge $10 to $20 for admission, but it costs a hefty $100 to enter Galápagos National Park. At parks where camping is allowed, there is usually an additional charge of around $5 per person per day. The following section is not a complete listing of all of Ecuador's national parks and protected areas, but rather a selective list of those parks that are of greatest interest and accessibility. Those protected areas are grouped according to the regions they lie in: the Sierra, Oriente, Pacific lowlands, and Galápagos. You'll find detailed information about food and lodging options near some of the individual parks in the regional chapters.

The Sierra

Cajas National Park ★★   Located in the western Andes near the city of Cuenca, Cajas National Park comprises a vast expanse of paramo—a high-altitude ecosystem dominated by grasses and bushes—dotted with 232 lakes, rocky peaks, and patches of cloud forest. The area is generally cool and misty, but when the sun burns through, it can be quite warm, and the rugged landscape is impressive. It is home to several duck species, the gray-breasted toucan, and the Andean condor, as well as wild llamas. The park also holds the ruins of pre-Columbian buildings and the remains of the Inca Trail. Guided tours to Cajas are recommended, since an expert's knowledge can help you spot and identify wildlife, and there is a real risk of getting lost there when it's foggy. Admission costs $10, and camping is permitted for an extra fee of $4 per night.

Location: 32km (20 miles) west of Cuenca. See chapter 8.

Cayambe-Coca Ecological Reserve

This important protected area stretches from the icy heights of Volcán Cayambe, the country's third-highest peak, down to the rainforest of the Amazon basin. It covers almost 403,103 hectares (995,664 acres) and protects an array of ecosystems that, when combined, are home to a wealth of wildlife. More than 900 bird species have been identified in the park, ranging from the Andean condor to the cock of the rock. The park's western sector is centered on Cayambe, a glacier-topped giant that is one of the country's more difficult climbing peaks. Volcán Reventador, farther to the east, is a 2-day hike but lies in a lush area rich in wildlife. The park's upper sector holds several popular lakes, such as Laguna de San Marcos and Laguna Puruhanta. Access to the park's lower forest is available near Papallacta and at Cascada San Rafael, a spectacular waterfall above Coca.

Location: 75km (47 miles) northeast of Quito.

Cotacachi-Cayapas Ecological Reserve

One of the country's biggest protected areas, covering more than 204,420 hectares (504,917 acres), the Cotacachi-Cayapas Reserve is also one of its most important, owing to the diversity of wildlife zones that it protects. The reserve stretches down from the paramo west of Ibarra to the lowland rainforest of the Chocó region, comprising a series of ecosystems that are home to such rare species as the spectacled bear and ocelot, and more than 500 bird species, including the Chocó toucan, great green macaw, and Andean condor. But most of the reserve's natural wonders are inaccessible to all but the most dedicated hikers. Other areas, however, are very accessible, such as **Laguna Cuicocha ★★**, a beautiful crater lake that can be reached by a paved road, a short trip from Otavalo or Cotacachi. The lagoon has two islands that can be visited on a boat ride, and a trail that skirts the crater's edge provides impressive vistas. Admission costs $5. Nearby Volcán Cotacachi can be reached via a 4WD track that leaves the main road near the lake. The Lagunas de Pinan, another of the park's Sierra attractions, are surrounded by relatively well-preserved paramo.

Location: 18km (11 miles) west of Cotacachi. See chapter 6.

Cotopaxi National Park ★★★

This is one of Ecuador's most popular parks, thanks to its proximity to Quito and the majesty of its volcano. The park is dominated by awe-inspiring Volcán Cotopaxi, a 5,897m (19,342-ft.) snow-draped cone that is Ecuador's second-highest peak and its most popular mountaineering spot. The park's 33,393 hectares (82,481 acres) are traversed by a series of dirt tracks that provide the opportunity for hiking, mountain-biking, or horseback-riding trips, but most people visit spots close to the park's small museum and main ranger headquarters. Other destinations inside the park include the Laguna de Limpiopungo, where you might see Andean gulls, American coots, Andean lapwings, paramo rabbits, or perhaps a herd of wild llamas or horses grazing in the nearby plains. El Salitre, a pre-Inca site near the northern entrance, has an excellent volcano view. A trail near the lake leads to the smaller Volcán Rumiñahui, a 2-hour hike away, which is sometimes visited by Andean condors. The pine forest near the park entrance is the product of a reforestation project, but hikers or riders who make it to the volcano's eastern slope can explore native cloud and Andean dwarf forests that hold an array of birdlife and other animals.

The park admission costs $10 and camping costs $2, but be forewarned: It can get very cold at night. The climbers' refuge at the volcano's base is accessible by 4WD vehicle, plus a short hike; a bunk there costs $10. But few guests actually sleep here, as most summit attempts begin around 11pm to midnight; you hike through the night to reach the peak in the early morning light and to descend before bad weather moves in.

Location: 60km (37 miles) south of Quito. See chapter 7.

Ilinizas National Park   Spread over 149,000 hectares (368,030 acres) in the country's northwest Sierra, the bulk of Ilinizas is remote, unexplored wilderness. Two of its sites, however, receive a fair amount of visitors: the crater lake Quilotoa and the twin Ilinizas peaks. The bright blue Laguna Quilotoa lies in a deep crater, a hiking trail around the edge of which makes for an excellent day hike—a popular tour offered by nearby lodges and outfitters. The ascent of the Ilinizas peaks, the highest of which stands at 5,263m (17,263 ft.), is popular with mountaineers. The smaller Iliniza Norte is a relatively easy climb good for acclimatization before attempting the country's highest peaks, but Iliniza Sur is an experts-only technical climb. A refuge at their base has two dozen bunk beds and a basic kitchen.

Location: Quilotoa is 15 minutes from the town of Zumbagua. See chapter 7.

Podocarpus National Park ★★   Off the beaten path, Podocarpus covers a vast swath of the southern Sierra stretching from the paramo down to the rainforest. Its 146,280 hectares (361,312 acres) consequently contain an array of life zones, giving the park some of the greatest biodiversity of any of the country's protected areas. It is named for the endemic coniferous podocarpus trees that abound in its Andean forests, known locally as *romerillo*. But those conifer forests are just one of an array of ecosystems protected within the park, which include highland lakes, paramo, cloud forest, and rainforest. Its resident flora and fauna include the rare mountain tapir, a tiny deer called the *pudú*, and more than 600 species of birds, including such threatened species as the umbrella bird, bearded guan, and coppery-chested jacamar. The park also protects a large petrified forest in Puyango, more than 100 Andean lakes, and the headwaters of southern Ecuador's principal rivers.

Podocarpus is best visited from Loja, which lies close to its upper sector, or Zamora, which is closer to its cloud forests. The park's Cajanuma Administrative Center is 14km (8¾ miles) south of Loja. A refuge 8km (5 miles) uphill from there has about 10 bunk beds, whereas the Lagunas del Compadre, a dozen lakes with a camping area, is about a 2-day hike in. Access to the park's lower sector is available via the Bombuscara ranger station near Zamora; the sector also has a shelter with dorm accommodations. The loop trail, called Sendero Higuerones, is an excellent bird-watching route. The admission fee is $10 per person per day, camping costs an additional $3 per person in a tent, and a bunk at one of the shelters costs $5 per person per night.

Location: 14km (8¾ miles) south of Loja and 6km (3¾ miles) south of Zamora. See chapter 8.

Sangay National Park ★★   Sangay is one of the country's two parks to be declared a UNESCO World Heritage Site, along with the Galápagos. The park, which spreads out over almost 518,000 hectares (about 1.3 million acres) to the southeast of Baños, is a hiker's paradise, but is also accessible on horseback or mountain bike.

Its natural attractions include 324 lakes; the volcanoes of Altar, Sangay, and Tungu-rahua; and a wealth of rare flora and fauna. Sangay and Tungurahua volcanoes are both sporadically active, and thus too dangerous to climb, though Tungurahua's occasional incendiary performances can by enjoyed from miles away. Altar, an extinct volcano that is Ecuador's fifth-highest peak, is a popular climbing and trekking destination where there are lush forests, waterfalls, and a crater lake. Together with adjacent Llanganates National Park, Sangay National Park protects an array of ecosystems ranging from Andean paramo to lush rainforest; these areas are home for hundreds of bird species and such rare and endangered fauna as the spectacled bear, mountain tapir, and condor. Sangay National Park can be accessed from Baños, Riobamba, Puyo, and other towns of the central and southern highlands. Admission is $10. All of the hotels and tour agencies in the region offer trips and tours here.

Location: Sangay National Park is a broad swath of high sierra stretching south and east from Baños and Riobamba. This massive park can be entered from various points, but the most popular entrance is the northern entrance, located about 70km (43 miles) of Baños. See chapter 7.

El Oriente

Cuyabeno Wildlife Reserve ★★ This wildlife reserve is one of the largest and richest in Ecuador, with over 655,781 hectares (1.6 million acres) of lowland rainforest in the northeast corner of the country. It is very wet, with numerous oxbow lagoons, streams, and rivers, the largest of which is Río Aguarico. Access to the park is by boat, and as you explore its smaller waterways, you may see gray river dolphins, caimans, monkeys, marmosets, macaws, toucans, or hoatzins, an unusual bird found only in the Amazon basin.

This area also is home to the Siona, Cofán, and Quichua indigenous communities, several of which are accustomed to receiving visitors. The best way to visit the reserve is on day trips from one of the lodges along the Aguarico River, which are several hours by bus and boat to the east of Lago Agrio, an oil town that's a 30-minute flight from Quito. Tour and lodging prices usually include the reserve's $20 admission fee.

Location: 30km (19 miles) east of Lago Agrio. See chapter 11.

Yasuni National Park ★★ Ecuador's biggest national park, Yasuni covers almost 962,000 hectares (2.4 million acres) of lowland rainforest to the south of Río Napo, in the country's eastern extreme. Its jungle is drained by hundreds of lakes, streams, and rivers, such as the Yasuni, Tiputini, and Shiripuno, all of which flow into Río Napo. Those smaller waterways offer the best access to Yasuni, and exploration of them offers opportunities to spot some of area's rare wildlife, which includes pink river dolphins, tapirs, capybaras, giant river otters, anacondas, harpy eagles, various types of macaws, and approximately 500 other bird species.

Yasuni is also home to the Huaorani, an indigenous group that has had contact with Western civilization only since the mid–20th century. The only way to visit the park is from one of the nearby nature lodges or on the *Manatee Amazon Explorer* (p. 309). Those companies will arrange payment of the $25 park entrance fee and provide naturalist guides who help spot wildlife and explain the local ecology. Unfortunately, Yasuni wilderness and its Huaorani inhabitants are threatened by oil companies, loggers, and poor farmers, all of which are slowly looting the park of its natural treasures.

Location: 250km (155 miles) east of Quito. See chapter 11.

SEARCHING FOR wildlife

Animals in the forests and paramos are predominantly nocturnal. When they are active in the daytime, they are usually elusive and on the watch for predators. Birds are easier to spot in clearings or secondary forests than they are in primary forests. Unless you have lots of experience in the tropics, your best chance of an enjoyable walk through the forest is with a trained and knowledgeable guide.

Here are a few helpful hints:

o **Listen.** Pay attention to rustling in the leaves; whether it's monkeys or birds up above or coatis on the ground, you're most likely to hear an animal before you see one.

o **Keep quiet.** Noise will scare off animals and prevent you from hearing their movements and calls.

o **Don't try too hard.** Soften your focus and allow your peripheral vision to take over. This way you can catch glimpses of motion and then focus in.

o **Bring your own binoculars.** It's a good idea to practice a little first, to get the hang of them. It would be a shame to be fiddling around and staring into space while everyone else in your group *oohs* and *aahs* over a trogon or honeycreeper.

o **Dress appropriately.** You'll have a hard time focusing your binoculars if you're busy swatting mosquitoes. Light, long pants and long-sleeved shirts are often your best bet. Comfortable hiking boots are a real asset, except where heavy rubber boots are necessary. Avoid loud colors; the better you blend in with your surroundings, the better your chances of spotting wildlife.

o **Be patient.** The jungle isn't on a schedule, though your best shot at seeing forest fauna is in the very early morning and late afternoon.

o **Read up.** Familiarize yourself with what you're most likely to see. Most nature lodges and ecotourism-based hotels have wildlife field guides and bird books, although if you're serious about this, it's always a good idea to have your own copy. The best of the bunch for most would be David Pearson and Les Beletsky's *Ecuador and the Galápagos Islands: Traveler's Wildlife Guide.* Also, bird-watchers will want to purchase a copy of *Birds of Ecuador Field Guide,* by Robert Ridgely, Paul Greenfield, and Frank Gill. Be forewarned, though, that the latter book is extremely hefty.

The Pacific

Galápagos National Park ★★★ The crown jewel of Ecuador's national parks system, Galápagos is not just the country's most visited park—it is the reason most people travel to Ecuador. This 14-million-hectare (35-million-acre) marine park was the country's first protected area and remains its most important. Its endemic birds, giant tortoises, and marine iguanas are biological icons, and their archipelago is of such global importance that UNESCO designated it a World Heritage Site. The ability to follow in Darwin's footsteps and marvel at such biological oddities as swimming iguanas, flightless cormorants, and finches that drink blood is a dream come true for many nature lovers. A week spent exploring this park, whether on a cruise or from one of the hotels, is one of the world's great outdoor experiences. Park admission costs $100. .

Location: 970km (599 miles) west of continental Ecuador. See chapter 12.

Machalilla National Park ★★ The only major protected area in Ecuador's Pacific lowlands, Machalilla encompasses some of the last surviving expanses of tropical dry forest in the country. The park's approximately 55,000 hectares (135,850 acres) of dry forest include a mix of endemic plants, such as the ivory palm, as well as more common cactuses and kapok trees. During the dry season, many of the park's trees and bushes drop their foliage, which gives the area a desertlike appearance but makes it easier to spot wildlife. The park is home to animals such as the black howler monkey, the collared peccary, and the endangered brocket deer, as well as some 270 bird species that include such rarities as the gray-cheeked parakeet and the Esmeraldas wood star. The park also contains various archaeological sites of the pre-Columbian Valdivia culture.

In addition to the dry forest, Machalilla protects a stretch of coastline that contains sea-turtle nesting beaches and the offshore islands of Isla Santiago and Isla de la Plata, which are important seabird nesting sites. The park's more than 128,000 hectares (316,160 acres) of protected ocean are rich in marine life, offering the country's best scuba diving outside the Galápagos Islands, and are a feeding and breeding area for humpback whales from June to October. Tour companies in Puerto López and Salinas offer boat trips to Isla de Plata for whale-watching, snorkeling, or scuba diving. The park's forests, beaches, and archaeological sites can be easily visited on day trips from Puerto López, where the park administration is based. You can pay the $15 admission there.

Location: 224km (139 miles) northwest of Guayaquil. See chapter 9.

TIPS ON HEALTH, SAFETY & ETIQUETTE IN THE WILDERNESS

Much of what is discussed below is common sense. For more detailed information, see "Health," in chapter 13.

Although most tours and activities are safe, there are risks involved in any adventure activity. Know and respect your physical limits before undertaking any strenuous activity. Be prepared for extremes in temperature and rainfall and for wide fluctuations in weather. A sunny morning hike can quickly become a cold and wet ordeal, so it's usually a good idea to carry along some form of rain gear when hiking in the rainforest or high paramo, and to have a dry change of clothing waiting at the end of the trail.

Avoid sunburn and sunstroke—be sure to bring along plenty of sunscreen and a hat when you're not going to be covered by the forest canopy. And don't be fooled by an overcast sky; I've been burned to a crisp on what seemed to be extremely cloudy days in Ecuador.

Altitude sickness is perhaps the biggest concern for visitors to Ecuador, especially those taking part in active adventures in the highlands and paramos. Altitude sickness is caused by reduced concentrations of oxygen in the air at higher altitudes. Symptoms include headache, fatigue, stomach upsets, dizziness, and sleep disturbance. Shortness of breath, quickened pulse, and general malaise can also occur. Exertion and alcohol consumption can worsen the symptoms. Altitude sickness affects everyone differently. Some will feel its effects in Quito at 2,850m (9,348 ft.) above sea level, while others will find no noticeable effects in the capital. Almost everyone will feel some effects over 4,000m (13,120 ft.). It is essential to stay fully hydrated, and with time, often a day or two, most people will acclimate to all but the most extreme altitudes. In serious cases, you should try to head to a lower altitude as soon as possible.

If you visit any of the country's rainforests or cloud forests, particularly in the lowlands, remember that it really *is* a jungle out there. Don't go poking under rocks or fallen branches. Snakebites are very rare, but don't do anything to increase the odds. If you do encounter a snake, stay calm, don't make any sudden movements, and *do not* try to handle it. Also avoid swimming in major rivers or lagoons unless a guide or local operator can vouch for their safety. Those in El Oriente may have caimans, electric eels, or piranhas.

Bugs and bug bites will probably be your greatest health concern in the Ecuadorean lowlands and beaches, and even they aren't as much of a problem as you might expect. Bugs are primarily an inconvenience, although mosquitoes can carry malaria or dengue. Strong repellent and proper clothing will minimize both the danger and the inconvenience; you might also want to bring along some cortisone or Benadryl cream to soothe itching. At the beaches, you may be bitten by *pirujas* (sand fleas); these nearly invisible insects leave an irritating welt. Try not to scratch, because this can lead to open sores and infections. *Pirujas* are most active at sunrise and sunset, so you might want to cover up or avoid the beaches at these times.

And remember: Whenever you enter and enjoy nature, you should tread lightly and try not to disturb the natural environment. There's a popular slogan well known to most campers that certainly applies here: "Leave nothing but footprints; take nothing but memories." If you must take home a souvenir, take photos. Do not cut or uproot plants or flowers. Pack out everything you pack in, and *please* do not litter.

ECOLOGICALLY ORIENTED VOLUNTEER & STUDY PROGRAMS

Below are some institutions and organizations working on ecology and sustainable development projects.

Earthwatch Institute (✆ 800/776-0188; www.earthwatch.org) organizes volunteers to go on research trips to help scientists collect data and conduct field experiments in a number of scientific fields. Expeditions to Ecuador range from studies of cloud-forest birds to efforts to eliminate the exotic species that threaten the ecological equilibrium of the Galápagos Islands. Fees for food and lodging average around $2,450 to $3,000 for an 11-day to 2-week expedition, excluding airfare.

Ecuador Volunteer (✆ 02/2557-749; www.ecuadorvolunteer.org), a Quito-based organization that connects volunteers with nonprofit organizations, usually has a long list of positions available, ranging from teaching in small communities, to building low-income housing, to aiding in the protection of wildlife in national parks and reserves around the country, including the Galápagos Islands.

Global Volunteers (© 800/487-1074 in the U.S.; www.globalvolunteers.org) is a U.S.-based organization that offers a unique opportunity to travelers who've always wanted a Peace Corps–like experience but can't make a 2-year commitment. For 2 to 3 weeks, you can join one of its working vacations in Ecuador. A certain set of skills, such as engineering or agricultural knowledge, is helpful but by no means necessary. Each trip is undertaken at a particular community's request, to complete a specific project. However, be warned: These "volunteer" experiences do not come cheap. You must pay for your transportation, as well as a hefty program fee, around $2,495 for a 2-week program.

Habitat for Humanity International (© 800/422-4828 in the U.S. and Canada; www.habitat.org) is a nonprofit, nondenominational Christian volunteer organization specializing in building individual housing for needy folks around the world. Habitat sometimes runs organized Global Village programs here. It usually costs between $1,400 and $1,800 per person for a 2-week program, including room, board, and in-country transportation (but not airfare to Ecuador).

Idealist ★ (© 646/786-6886 in the U.S.; www.idealist.org), a Web portal of volunteer and employment opportunities with nonprofit organizations around the world, often lists more than a dozen environmental volunteer positions in Ecuador.

Jatun Sacha (© 02/2432-240; www.jatunsacha.org) is an Ecuadorean environmental foundation that manages private biological reserves in various parts of the country and works with local communities to involve them in conservation. They accept a steady flow of volunteers who help with field research, teach English, and perform other tasks for fees that are a fraction of what big U.S. volunteer programs charge.

Maquipucuna (© 706/542-2923 in the U.S., or 02/2507-200; www.maqui.org) is a private biological reserve and ecotourism lodge in the northern Pacific lowlands that is administered by the University of Georgia. They accept volunteers to help with conservation and research projects; volunteers pay $450 per month for food and lodging. The reserve protects an important expanse of the endangered Chocó rainforest.

QUITO

Ecuador's capital, Quito, sits on a long, level plateau in a valley between towering Andean peaks. It is a city of striking beauty and stark contrasts. Sebastián de Benalcázar founded Quito in 1534. If he were to walk the streets of Old Town today, he might still feel right at home—notwithstanding the gridlock traffic. Many of the original colonial structures here have been magnificently preserved and restored. Quito was—and still is—a city of grand churches with detailed, hand-carved facades and altars. It is a place where 500-year-old buildings, which have survived earthquakes and volcanic eruptions, open onto medieval-style courtyards, complete with columned archways and stone fountains. In 1978, Quito was declared a UNESCO World Heritage Site, the first city to earn that designation.

5

But that's only one side of Quito. If Benalcázar were to venture a few kilometers north, the glass skyscrapers, electric trolleys, and early-20th-century mansions would make his head spin. Quito is a city of wonderful juxtapositions and stark contrasts. It's a place where you can travel to the past but still enjoy modern-day comforts. The living museum that is Old Town nicely complements New Town's modern-art and archaeology museums. Spend a few leisurely days here, and you can enjoy the best of both worlds. You can also travel to colorful indigenous markets, a unique cloud forest, or one of the world's highest active volcanoes—all within 2 hours of the city.

Although Quito is Ecuador's capital, it is only the second most populous city in the country, with under two million residents; Guayaquil has more people and is more important to the country's economy. In fact, there's a fierce and ongoing rivalry between the two cities (p. 228). Still, Quito is far more charming and cosmopolitan, and it has more museums, sights, restaurants, and clubs. The city gets its name from the pre-Inca Quitu tribe that inhabited this valley. Before Benalcázar arrived, the Incas had converted Quito into a major city. Instead of allowing the buildings and treasures to fall into Spanish hands, though, Inca warrior Rumiñahui ordered the city razed and burned in 1526.

Remember that, at 2,850m (9,348 ft.) above sea level, Quito is one of the highest capital cities in the world, and the air is much thinner here. Many visitors quickly feel the effects of the high altitude. Drink plenty of water and do not overdo it as your body acclimates.

ORIENTATION
Arriving

BY PLANE   All flights into Quito land at **Aeropuerto Internacional Mariscal Sucre** (© 02/2944-900; www.quiport.com; airport code: UIO). The airport is about 8km (5 miles) from the heart of New Town. Right before you exit the international terminal, you'll find several information desks. I recommend ordering and paying for your taxi here, then taking your receipt to one of the many taxis waiting outside the terminal. Taxis shouldn't cost more than $10. In fact, most rides to downtown hotels are around $5 to $8. You will find yellow taxis waiting as you exit anywhere in the airport.

For more information on arriving in Quito, see "Getting There" in chapter 13. Note that the new international airport, being built on the outskirts of downtown, is slated to open in mid-2011.

BY BUS   Quito has two major bus terminals. **Terminal Terrestre Quitumbe** (© 02/3988-200) is located on the southern outskirts of the city and handles bus traffic to all southern destinations, including the central and southern highlands, the Pacific coast, and El Oriente. **Terminal Terrestre Carcelén** (© 02/3961-600) is located on the northern outskirts of the city and services all northern destinations, including all of the northern highlands. Taxis are almost always available at both terminals. If you don't have much luggage, you can get into downtown via the city's mass transit trolley and bus system, although you'll need to be careful of pickpockets and thieves. Quitumbe is the final stop on the city's Trolebus line, while Carcelén has regular bus connections to the city's Ecovia line.

Visitor Information

Corporación Metropolitana de Turismo (**Metropolitan Tourism Corporation;** www.quito.com.ec) runs a few helpful information desks at strategic spots around Quito. You'll find one of their desks at **Mariscal Sucre Airport** (© 02/3300-163), after you clear immigration and just before you exit Customs. This is a good place to pick up an excellent free map of Quito, as well as a host of promotional materials. Their **main office** (© 02/2572-445) is in Old Town, at the corner of García Moreno and Mejía (in the Palacio Municipal). These folks also have desks at Museo Nacional del Banco Central (p. 111) and at Parque Gabriela Mistral in the Mariscal district.

The nonprofit **South American Explorers** ★★ (© 02/2225-228; www.saexplorers.org/clubhouses/quito), Jorge Washington 311, at the corner of Leonidas Plaza, is perhaps the best source for visitor information and a great place to meet fellow travelers. The offices are staffed by native English-speakers who seem to know everything about Ecuador. Membership costs $60 a year per person ($90 per couple). Members have access to trip reports (reviews of hotels, restaurants, and outfitters throughout Ecuador written by fellow travelers) and a trip counselor, as well as a host of discount offers. If you aren't a member, the staff can give you basic information that will get you on your way.

Local travel agencies are excellent sources of information. **Metropolitan Touring** ★★ (© 02/2988-200; www.metropolitan-touring.com), **Safari Ecuador** ★

(☏ 02/2552-505; www.safari.com.ec), and **Surtrek** ★★ (☏ 866/978-7398 in the U.S. and Canada, or 02/2500-530 in Ecuador; www.surtrek.com) are some of the best and most helpful.

City Layout

Quito is a long and thin city set in a long and thin valley. It runs 35km (22 miles) from north to south and just 5km (3 miles) from east to west. Most of the city's attractions are located in two areas: **Old Town** and **New Town.** Old Town, at the southern end of the city, is where you'll find most of the historic churches, museums, and colonial architecture. New Town, which is sort of the center of the city, has the greatest concentration of restaurants, bars, shops, and hotels.

Warning: All parts of Quito can be dangerous at night. Avoid dark and deserted areas, and take taxis, even when traveling relatively short distances.

The Neighborhoods in Brief

Most visitors will not venture far from Old Town and New Town, except to head out of the city, or to and from the airport, which lies in the heart of northern Quito.

OLD TOWN

Close to the southern extreme of downtown Quito lies Old Town. Also called **El Centro Histórico (Historic Center),** this is the colonial-era core of Quito. Much of it has survived over the centuries, almost unchanged. Here you will find Quito's classic old churches, theaters, monasteries, and convents. Popular public plazas include **Plaza de la Independencia, Plaza de San Francisco, Plaza de Santo Domingo,** and **Plaza del Teatro.** Although Old Town is hilly in places, it's easy to walk around this compact area and visit its major attractions on foot.

On the southern extreme of Old Town is **Terminal Terrestre de Cumandá,** Quito's main bus terminal. And just to the southwest of Old Town is **El Panecillo,** a high hill crowned with a large sculpture of a winged Virgin.

NEW TOWN

New Town is located south of Parque La Carolina and north of Parque El Ejido. As the name suggests, this is a modern and mostly upscale section of Quito, with many of the city's better hotels. New Town's main commercial street is **Avenida Amazonas,** where a host of banks and travel agencies are located.

La Mariscal, a subsection of New Town, is where you will find a dense concentration of clubs, bars, restaurants, Internet cafes, and backpacker hotels—the area is informally referred to as Gringolandia because of its popularity with tourists. **Plaza Foch** (also called Plaza del Quinde) is ground zero for La Mariscal district. La Mariscal is bounded by Avenida Amazonas, Calle Luis Cordero, Avenida 6 de Diciembre, and Calle Ventimilla.

La Floresta lies just to the east of La Mariscal, across Avenida 12 de Octubre and up a small rise. It's an upscale section of downtown with a mix of high-rise apartments and condos, neo-colonial-style mansions, hotels, restaurants, and shops. This area has recently seen a rapid rise in the number of high-end restaurants and is one of the city's better destinations for dining. The area gets its name from the former Urrutia family's Hacienda La Floresta that once occupied this area. **La Universidad Católica (Catholic University)** is located toward the southern end of La Floresta, while **Swissôtel Quito** is at its northern edge.

NORTH OF NEW TOWN

While both Old Town and New Town lie toward the southern end of Quito's long, narrow valley, many of the city's two million inhabitants live north of New Town. This is also the area where much of the city's

BREAKING THE code

Feeling a little bewildered by Quito's street address system? Well, you should be. While it's actually pretty logical, there are plenty of anomalies and certain addresses that correspond to a previous system. To add to the confusion, Ecuadoreans only occasionally use the *calle* (street) and *avenida* (avenue) designation. More often than not, addresses are given with the street or avenue's name, but no indication of whether it's a street or avenue. Introduced in 1998, the capital's newer street-numbering system is prefixed by one of the following letters: **N,** indicating that the street is situated north *(norte)* of Calle Rocafuerte in Old Town; **S,** meaning south *(sur)* of Old Town; or **E,** indicating east *(este),* or **OE,** meaning west *(oeste),* depending on which side of 10 de Agosto the street is located. A hyphenated number follows, and then the name of the nearest cross-street or avenue. The first of these

hyphenated numbers is actually the building number, while the second number indicates the number of meters the house or building is from the cross-street. For example, consider González Suárez N27–142 and 12 de Octubre. The building is found on González Suárez street, north of Calle Rocafuerte. The building number is 27, and it is roughly 142m (466 ft.) from Avenida 12 de Octubre. This new street-numbering system has principally been adopted in the north of the city and has proven difficult to implement in the south, owing to the nonperpendicular streets. Addresses in Old Town may have neither a letter indicator nor a hyphenated number, although the nearest cross-street will always be given. Both address systems are currently in use. Luckily, just about every taxi driver in Quito can find any address using either the new or old system.

industry is located. The neighborhoods here are often crowded, poor, and working class, and of little interest (and considerable danger) to most tourists. Exceptions include the trendy neighborhoods of **Guapulo** and **Bellavista.** The latter is where you find **Fundación Guayasamín** and **Capilla del Hombre.**

The **Mariscal Sucre International Airport** is located north of New Town. But

because the hotels of New Town are really just minutes away, there has been no real tourism or hotel development right near the airport. In fact, the area around the airport is mostly industrial and run-down.

The other main attraction and the geographic heart and civic soul of the area north of New Town is **Parque La Carolina,** a large, well-kept city park, with a host of facilities for sports and recreation.

GETTING AROUND
By Taxi

The streets of Quito swarm with taxis—my preferred means of transport here. Taxis are cheap, costing only $2 to $3 for a ride within Old or New Town and $4 to $7 for longer distances. Drivers are required by law to use a meter, but it's obviously not a strict law because few taxis use them. If the taxi has a meter *(taxímetro),* insist that the driver use it. Alternatively, ask your hotel desk or a trusty local what your ride should cost and negotiate an appropriate price beforehand. Quito can be dangerous

Quito

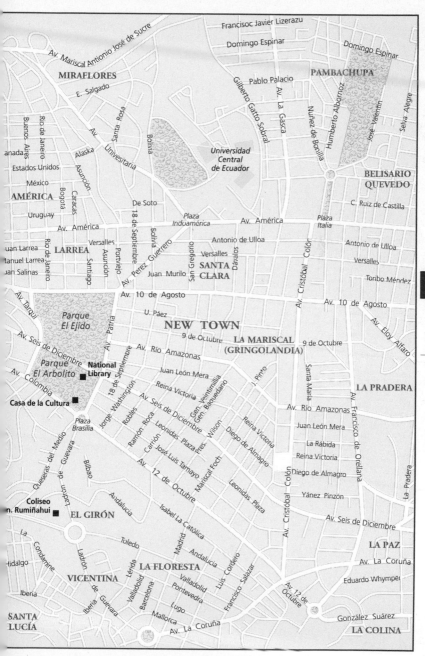

at night, so it's best to take a taxi wherever you go, no matter how short the distance. The staff at most restaurants, hotels, and bars will be happy to call a cab for you. In case you need to call one yourself, try **City Taxi** (© **02/2633-333**), **Taxi Amigo** (© **02/2222-222**), or **Taxi Express** (© **02/2500-600**).

By Trolley

Three electric trolley lines run north-south through Quito, connecting Old Town with New Town. In New Town, the **Trole** runs along Avenida 10 de Agosto, which is a few blocks west of Avenida Amazonas. When it reaches Old Town, it travels along Avenida Guayaquil. To reach Plaza de la Independencia, be sure to get off at the Plaza Grande stop. The **Ecovía** is much more convenient if you want to start your journey in New Town; it runs along Avenida 6 de Diciembre, one of the major streets. Unfortunately, when it reaches Old Town, it stops several blocks east of the colonial core, and it's a bit of an uphill hike to the heart of the action. If you want to avoid this hike, transfer to the Trole at the Simón Bolívar stop. **Metrobus** is the third line, and it runs along the western edge of town, along Avenida América. All three of these trolley lines cost 25¢ for a one-way trip. The turnstiles accept only exact change, but fortunately, all stations have change machines. Trolleys run from around 5am until midnight. *Warning:* Pickpockets frequently operate on crowded trolleys and buses, so be careful.

By Bus

Quito has an extensive and very complicated system of city buses. In New Town, buses run along Avenida Amazonas and Avenida 12 de Octubre. If you're going only a short distance along these streets, it's easy to hop on a bus (just flag it down). But beware: Once you pass Avenida Colón, the buses go off in many convoluted directions. Short rides cost 25¢. Overall, it's much easier to travel through Quito by taxi, which is inexpensive and safe, and will take you exactly where you need to go. Depending upon where you are in the city, a taxi ride to or from either one of the main bus terminals should run you between $5 and $10.

On Foot

Besides walking around specific and compact neighborhoods or circuits, such as Old Town or the Mariscal section of New Town, Quito is not a friendly city for walkers. Most of the streets are in a state of near-constant gridlock, sidewalks are narrow and irregular, and car and bus fumes, along with street crime, are real problems. Luckily, taxis are plentiful and very inexpensive (see "By Taxi," above).

By Car

I highly discourage you from renting a car to get around Quito. Navigating a strange city is difficult enough, and many of Quito's streets are narrow and in a nearly constant state of gridlock. Moreover, taxis (see "By Taxi," above) are plentiful and inexpensive.

If you're set on renting a car in Quito, **Budget** (© **02/3300-979;** www.budget-ec. com) and **Hertz** (© **02/2254-257;** www.hertz.com) have offices downtown and at the airport; cars can also be delivered to most hotels in Quito. Car rentals will run you $45 to $150 per day, depending on the type of vehicle. For more information about renting a car in Ecuador, see p. 86.

[FastFACTS] QUITO

Airport See "Arriving," above.

American Express In Ecuador, American Express travel service is represented by **Global Tours** (☎ 02/2265-222; www.globaltour.com.ec), located on Av. República El Salvador 309 and Calle Suiza.

Babysitters Your hotel front desk is your best bet for finding a babysitter.

Banks You'll have no trouble finding a bank in Quito. Branches are common all over the city, especially in the more affluent and touristy areas. Numerous bank branches and ATMs can be found in the popular Mariscal and Old Town areas.

Bookstores **Café Libro** (☎ 02/2503-214; www.cafelibro.com), Leonidas Plaza N23–56, between Wilson and Veintimilla; and **Libri Mundi** (☎ 02/2521-606; www.librimundi.com), Juan León Mera N23–83 and Wilson, are the two best bookstores in Quito. Both have excellent selections of tropical biology, bird, and flora books, as well as books on Ecuadorean history and culture, in both English and Spanish. Libri Mundi actually has a half-dozen or more storefronts around Quito. For a wide selection of new and used books in English, **Confederate Books** (☎ 02/2527-890), Calama 410 and Juan León Mera, is your best bet.

Car Rentals See "Getting Around," above.

Cellphones There are several competing cellphone companies in Ecuador. All have numerous outlets and dealers across the city, including at the airport, and all these outlets and dealers sell prepaid GSM chips that can be used in any unlocked triband GSM cellphone, as well as new phones with or without calling plans. An activated chip, with a dollar or two of calling time, runs just $7 to $9. If you're not carrying your own GSM phone, you are probably best off just buying one. Scores of storefronts around town, including those at the airport, sell already activated phones, with a few dollars of calling time loaded onto the chip. After that, you simply buy prepaid minutes at any cellphone or pharmacy store around the country. The cheapest of these phones costs around $30, activated and ready to go, with a few bucks' worth of calling time included.

The main cellphone companies in Ecuador are **Porta, Movistar,** and **Alegro.** Porta and Movistar have the best coverage.

Currency Exchange The U.S. dollar is the official currency of Ecuador. If you have euros, pounds, Canadian dollars, or any other currency, your best bet is to exchange them for dollars prior to leaving for Ecuador. However, all the major banks in Ecuador will exchange the major currencies for dollars, for a small service fee. And most ATMs in Ecuador will give you dollars at the official exchange rate, even if your home account is in another currency. See "Money & Costs," in chapter 13, for more information.

Dentists Call your embassy for a list of recommended dentists, or check out the Consular Section of the website of the U.S. Embassy in Quito (http://ecuador.usembassy.gov), which recommends local dentists as well.

Doctors Contact your embassy for information on doctors in Quito, or check out the Consular Section of the website of the U.S. Embassy in Quito (http://ecuador.usembassy.gov), which has a list of recommended doctors and specialists. You can also head to one of the major hospitals in town. See "Hospitals," below.

Drugstores A drugstore or pharmacy is called a *farmacia* in Spanish. **Fybeca** is the largest chain of pharmacies in Ecuador. You can call Fybeca's toll-free line (☎ 1800/2392-322; www.fybeca.com) 24 hours a day for home delivery.

Embassies & Consulates See "Fast Facts: Ecuador," p. 363.

Emergencies In case of an **emergency**, call ☎ **911**

or 101. You can reach an **ambulance** at ☎ **09/2739-801** or 02/2442-974. For the **tourist police,** call ☎ **02/2543-983;** the headquarters are located at Roca and Reina Victoria. You can reach the **Cruz Roja (Red Cross)** by dialing ☎ **131.**

Express Mail Services

Most hotels can arrange for express mail pickup. Alternatively, you can contact **DHL** (☎ **02/3975-000;** www.dhl.com), **FedEx** (☎ **02/6017-818;** www.fedex.com), **EMS** (☎ **1700/267-736;** www.correosdelecuador.com.ec), or **UPS** (☎ **02/3960-000;** www.ups.com).

Eyeglasses

Look for the word *óptica.* There are *ópticas* all over Quito. Your best bet is to ask your hotel concierge or manager. **Optica Los Andes** (☎ **1800/678-422;** www.opticalosandes.com.ec) is the largest chain, with storefronts across the city.

Hospitals

Hospital Vozandes (☎ **02/2262-142;** www.hospitalvozandes.org; Villalengua 267 and 10 de Agosto) and **Hospital Metropolitano** (☎ **02/3998-000;** www.hospitalmetropolitano.org; Mariana de Jesús and Occidental) are the two most modern and best-equipped hospitals in Quito. Both have 24-hour emergency service and English-speaking doctors.

Internet Access

Internet cafes can be found all over Quito, particularly in the Mariscal and Old Town neighborhoods. Rates run 50¢ to $1 per hour. Many hotels either have their own Internet cafe or allow guests to send and receive e-mail. A few are starting to add wireless access, either for free or for a small charge.

Laundry & Dry Cleaning

Most folks rely on their hotel's laundry and dry-cleaning services, although these can be expensive. Alternatively, head to the Mariscal district, where there are several self-serve and full-service laundromats. Try **Rainbow Laundry** (☎ **02/2237-128**), on Espejo 761 between Flores and Montufar, or **Super Lavado** (☎ **02/2502-987**), on Pinto E6–24 and Reina Victoria.

Maps

Corporación Metropolitana de Turismo (Metropolitan Tourism Corporation; ☎ **02/2572-445;** www.quito.com.ec) hands out excellent city maps of Quito at all of its desks, including one at **Mariscal Sucre Airport** (☎ **02/3300-163**), located just before you leave the immigration and Customs area. Other map sources in Quito include hotel gift shops and bookstores.

Photographic Needs

Film is generally more expensive in Ecuador, so bring as much as you will need from home. I also recommend that you wait to have your film processed at home, but if you must develop your prints here, or if you need to pick up film, batteries, or storage cards, try **Ecuacolor** (☎ **02/2460-731;** www.ecuacolor.com) or **Fujifilm** (☎ **02/2241-069;** www.fujifilm.com.ec), both of which have numerous outlets around town.

Police

Throughout Ecuador, you can reach the police by dialing ☎ **101** in an emergency. The tourist police (☎ **02/2543-983** in Quito) can also help sort out your problems.

Post Office

The **main post office** (☎ **02/2561-240;** www.correosdelecuador.com.ec) is located in New Town at Av. Eloy Alfaro 354 and 9 de Octubre. There's also a convenient post office in Old Town (☎ **02/2959-875**) on Calle Espejo 935, between Guayaquil 935 and Espejo. Perhaps the most conveniently located post office is on the ground floor of the Torres de Almagro Building, on the corner of Avenida Cristóbal Colón and Reina Victoria (☎ **02/2508-980**). Most post offices in Ecuador are open Monday through Friday from 8am to 12:30pm and 2:30 to 6pm, and Saturday from 8am to 2pm. It costs around $1 to mail a letter to the United States or Canada, and $1.40 to Australia and Europe. From time to time, you can buy stamps at kiosks and newsstands. But your best bet is to see if your hotel will provide stamps and post your mail, or do it yourself at the post office, especially because there are no public mailboxes.

Restrooms These are known as *sanitarios* or *servicios sanitarios* or *servicios higiénicos*. The latter usage is often abbreviated as "S.S.H.H." You might also hear them called *baños*. They are marked *damas* (women) and *hombres* or *caballeros* (men). Public restrooms are rare to non-existent, but most big hotels and public restaurants will let you use their restrooms.

Safety Pickpocketing and petty crime are problems in Quito. But if you keep an eye on your belongings and exercise caution, you should be fine. Never put anything valuable in your backpack. Also be careful on all public buses and trolleys. At night, Quito can be dangerous, especially in the touristy areas—take a taxi, even if you're going only a short distance. Because the streets in Quito are often deserted at night, I recommend walking in the middle of them to prevent someone from jumping at you from a hidden doorway. Report all problems to the **tourist police** office, on Roca and Reina Victoria (② **02/2543-983**). Also see "Police," under "Fast Facts: Ecuador," on p. 363.

Taxes All goods and services are charged a 12% value-added tax. Hotels and restaurants also add on a 10% service charge, for a total of 22% more on your bill. There is an airport departure tax of $41.80.

Taxis See "Getting Around," above.

Time Zone Quito is on Eastern Standard Time, 5 hours behind Greenwich Mean Time (GMT). Daylight saving time is not observed.

Useful Telephone Numbers For directory assistance, call ② **104;** for a local operator, dial ② **105;** and for an international operator, call ② **116,**

Water Always drink bottled water in Ecuador. Most hotels provide bottled water. The better restaurants use ice made from boiled water, but always ask, to be on the safe side.

Weather At 2,850m (9,350 ft.), Quito enjoys consistently mild to cool temperatures year-round. Daytime high temperatures average 18° to 21°C (64°–70°F), while evening lows average 7° to 13°C (45°–55°F). As with much of the rest of the Andean highlands, Quito experiences two distinct seasons: dry (June–Sept) and wet (Oct–May). The dry season is called summer *(verano),* the wet season winter *(invierno).* There's also a so-called "little summer" throughout much of December and early January. April is the rainiest month.

WHERE TO STAY

Because the Mariscal Sucre Airport is located in downtown Quito—and there are really no good options right at the airport—I don't include a section on accommodations near the airport. The hotels in New Town and La Floresta are approximately 10 to 15 minutes from the airport, depending on traffic, while those in Old Town are some 20 to 25 minutes away.

In New Town
EXPENSIVE

In addition to the places listed below, **Holiday Inn Express** (② **02/2997-300;** www.hiexpress.com) is a sharp business-class hotel, well located on Avenida Orellana, that is contemporary and well equipped.

Finally, the folks at **Café Cultura** (see below) are in the midst of remodeling a historic mansion in the Mariscal district that should be a fabulous luxury boutique option open to the public sometime in mid-2011.

Anahi Boutique Hotel ★ 🏨 Every room in this hotel is unique, and many have been designed or decorated by a prominent contemporary Ecuadorean artist. Some are real gems, while others—like the Pop suite—may a bit too bold or quirky for some tastes, so be sure to check out photos of your room before booking. My favorites include the Inca room, which comes with a large private balcony, and the Vidrio suite, which features beautiful glass works and decorations. One of the best features here is the glassed-in fourth-story rooftop terrace, with wonderful views of the city all around.

Tamayo 687 y Wilson, Quito. www.anahihotelquito.com. © **02/2501-421.** 15 units. $110–$150 double. AE, DC, MC, V. Free parking. **Amenities:** Restaurant; lounge; Jacuzzi; room service; sauna; all rooms smoke-free; free Wi-Fi. *In room:* A/C, TV, hair dryer, minibar, free Wi-Fi.

Hilton Colón Quito ★

When the Hilton Colón opened, in 1967, it was the only high-end hotel in town. It quickly became a major cultural and business meeting spot for locals and visitors alike. Today it faces stiff competition from both large chains and small boutique hotels. Still, the Hilton is a good and well-located choice—it's right near Parque El Ejido, Casa de la Cultura, and the business center of the city. It is particularly popular as a quick overnight base for folks heading to or from the Galápagos or other far-flung destinations in the country. The rooms and suites here are quite spacious, and all have been steadily remodeled and updated. Those on the lower floors, however, are susceptible to street noise. This hotel is always a beehive of activity, yet the service is superb.

Amazonas N1814 y Patria, Quito. www.hilton.com. © **800/445-8667** in the U.S. and Canada, or 02/2560-666 in Ecuador. Fax 02/2563-903. 300 units. $139–$189 double; $229–$319 suite. AE, DC, MC, V. Free parking. **Amenities:** 4 restaurants; bar; lounge; casino; free airport shuttle; babysitting; concierge; executive/club floor; small health club; Jacuzzi; midsize outdoor pool; room service; sauna; smoke-free floors. *In room:* A/C, TV, hair dryer, minibar, MP3 docking station, free Wi-Fi.

Hotel Café Cultura ★ 📷

In the heart of New Town, the Café Cultura is definitely one of the most unique and interesting hotels in Quito. This old, beautifully renovated house is one of the hippest hotels in the city. All the rooms have hand-painted designs on the walls and their own personal touches. No. 25 has a tree growing through it; no. 1 has a fireplace, French doors, painted furniture, and a claw-foot tub. My favorite room is no. 2, which has a beautiful sitting nook, with wraparound floor-to-ceiling windows. In general, the bathrooms are also excellent and eclectic, although some are a bit small. There's a lovely restaurant adjacent to the lobby, complete with hardwood floors, flickering candles, and a roaring fireplace.

Robles 513 y Reina Victoria, Quito. www.cafecultura.com. ©/fax **02/2224-271** or 02/2558-889. 26 units. $109 double; $149 suite. AE, DC, MC, V. Free parking. **Amenities:** Restaurant; lounge; room service; all rooms smoke-free; free Wi-Fi.

JW Marriott Hotel ★★

The JW Marriott features some of the best rooms and facilities in town. Service is top-notch, the restaurants are excellent, and the large pool—with a Jacuzzi island and waterfalls—makes you feel as if you're at a tropical resort. You enter each room through a carved wooden door that looks as though it should open onto an old Quito courtyard. Most rooms offer views of either the city or the volcanoes. (If you can, opt for the volcano view; avoid rooms with views of the glass-enclosed lobby.) **La Hacienda restaurant** offers delicious local specialties in an elegant setting, while **Don Porfirio** serves up excellent Mexican cuisine. The lobby features a sushi bar to round out the culinary offerings. The gym here is large and well equipped with a regular slate of classes and activities.

Av. Orellana 1172 y Av. Amazonas, Quito. www.marriotthotels.com. © **888/236-2427** in the U.S. and Canada, or 02/2972-000 in Quito. Fax 02/2972-050. 257 units. $139–$259 double; $289 junior suite.

Old Town

ACCOMMODATIONS ■
El Relicario del Carmen **19**
Hotel Catedral Internacional **22**
Hotel Real Audiencia **11**
Hotel San Francisco de Quito **12**
La Casona de San Miguel **4**
La Posada Colonial **17**
Mansión del Angel **29**
Patio Andaluz **18**
Plaza Grande **25**
Villa Colonna **24**

DINING ◆
Café Mosaico **28**
El Rincón de Cantuña **18**
El Tianguez **6**
La Casa de los Geráneos **3**
Mea Culpa **17**
Octava de Corpus **27**
PIM's Panecillo **1**
Theatrum **13**

ATTRACTIONS ●
Casa del Alabado **5**
Casa Museo María Augusta Urrutia **9**
El Centro Cultural Metropolitano **7**
El Panecillo **1**
El Sagrario **14**
Iglesia de la Merced **21**
Iglesia de San Francisco **6**
La Basílica del Voto Nacional **26**
La Compañía de Jesús **8**
La Plaza de la Independencia **15**
Museo Camilo Egas **25**
Museo de la Ciudad **2**
Museo Fray Pedro Gocial **6**
Museo Histórico Militar "Casa de Sucre" **10**
Teatro Bolívar **23**
Teatro Nacional Sucre **13**

5 QUITO Where to Stay

91

AE, DC, MC, V. Valet parking $2 daily. **Amenities:** 5 restaurants; bar; babysitting; concierge; executive/club floors; health club; Jacuzzi; large pool; room service; sauna; smoke-free floors; free Wi-Fi. *In room:* A/C, TV, hair dryer, Internet for a fee, minibar.

nü house ★★　This boutique hotel is stylish and chic. And it's hard to beat the location. The striking exterior, with horizontal wood slats, has a commanding perch above the heart and soul of the Mariscal district, right on Plaza Foch. Rooms are decidedly contemporary, with wood floors, stone bathrooms, flatscreen televisions, and artsy fixtures and furnishings—although the eclectic and minimalist design paradigm here might throw in a Victorian-style love seat where you least expect it. Suites all feature two small balconies, one overlooking Plaza Foch and another off the master bedroom, as well as a deep two-person tub and separate shower. In addition to the hip **Q restaurant** attached to the hotel, the owners here run several other excellent restaurants on Plaza Foch and around the Mariscal district.

Foch E6-12 y Reina Victoria, Quito. www.nuhousehotels.com. ✆ **02/2557-845.** 57 units. $129 double; $189 suite. Rates include breakfast. AE, DC, MC, V. Free parking. **Amenities:** Restaurant; bar; concierge; room service; smoke-free rooms; free Wi-Fi. *In room:* A/C, TV, hair dryer, free high-speed Internet, minibar.

MODERATE

Hostal Fuente de Piedra I　Not to be confused with the somewhat less charming Hostal Fuente de Piedra II, this is a good little hotel located on a quiet street close to everything. A serene courtyard with a trickling fountain leads to small, simply furnished rooms with exposed stone in some and large picture windows in others. The bathrooms are clean and good-size, though none have tubs. There's a small balcony with reading chairs for guests on the second floor and a very cozy restaurant with fireplace on the ground floor.

Wilson 211 y Tamayo, Quito. www.ecuahotel.com. ✆/fax **02/2900-323** or ✆ 02/2559-775. 19 units. $64 double. Rates include full breakfast. AE, MC, V. **Amenities:** Restaurant; bar; lounge; free Wi-Fi. *In room:* TV.

Hostal La Rábida　Hostal La Rábida is in an old home on a quiet street, away from the bustle, yet still close to the Mariscal action. The rooms are lovely, if a bit small, with brass or iron beds (one even has a canopy) and luxurious white down comforters. The spacious bathrooms come complete with old-fashioned wood sinks and antique fixtures. Room no. 11 has a patio and beautiful blue-and-white wallpaper, while room no. 2—my favorite—has a large second-floor terrace. The beautiful breakfast room/restaurant opens onto a small garden. Overall, the hotel has a refined British feel—the walls are covered with botanical prints and old maps, Oriental carpets complement the hardwood floors, and every evening a fire burns in the very cozy living room.

La Rábida 227 y Santa María, Quito. www.hostalrabida.com. ✆ **02/2222-169.** Fax 02/2222-720. 11 units. $68–$75 double. AE, DC, MC, V. Free parking. **Amenities:** Restaurant; bar; room service. *In room:* TV, free Wi-Fi.

Hotel Río Amazonas　At 10 stories, this modern business hotel towers over the Mariscal district. As you walk through the glass doors, marble floors and a broad marble reception desk greet you. Rooms are tidy, and most are spacious and modern. Try for a room on a higher floor, to take advantage of the views and get away from the street noise. This hotel does a brisk business with tour and events groups, and is often quite busy.

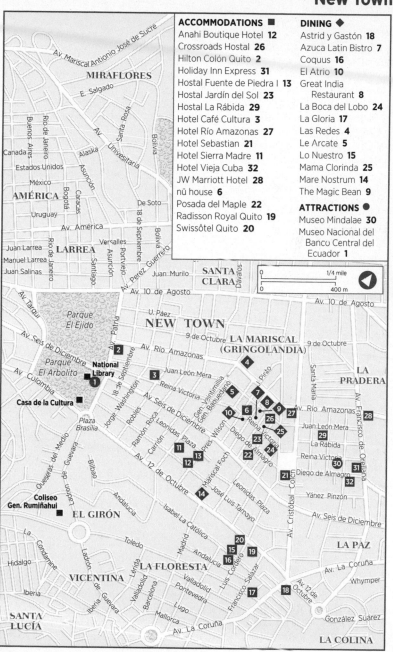

ACCOMMODATIONS ■
- Anahi Boutique Hotel **12**
- Crossroads Hostal **26**
- Hilton Colón Quito **2**
- Holiday Inn Express **31**
- Hostal Fuente de Piedra I **13**
- Hostal Jardín del Sol **23**
- Hostal La Rábida **29**
- Hotel Café Cultura **3**
- Hotel Río Amazonas **27**
- Hotel Sebastian **21**
- Hotel Sierra Madre **11**
- Hotel Vieja Cuba **32**
- JW Marriott Hotel **28**
- nü house **6**
- Posada del Maple **22**
- Radisson Royal Quito **19**
- Swissôtel Quito **20**

DINING ◆
- Astrid y Gastón **18**
- Azuca Latin Bistro **7**
- Coquus **16**
- El Atrio **10**
- Great India Restaurant **8**
- La Boca del Lobo **24**
- La Gloria **17**
- Las Redes **4**
- Le Arcate **5**
- Lo Nuestro **15**
- Mama Clorinda **25**
- Mare Nostrum **14**
- The Magic Bean **9**

ATTRACTIONS ●
- Museo Mindalae **30**
- Museo Nacional del Banco Central del Ecuador **1**

0 — 1/4 mile
0 — 400 m

5

QUITO | Where to Stay

Cordero 1342, on the corner of Av. Amazonas, Quito. www.hotelrioamazonas.com. ℓ **888/790-5264** in the U.S. and Canada, or 02/2556-666 in Ecuador. Fax 02/2556-670. 74 units. $89 double; $120 suite. AE, DC, MC, V. Free parking. **Amenities:** Restaurant; bar; room service; free Wi-Fi. *In room:* TV, hair dryer, minibar.

Hotel Sebastián ★   This well-located business-class hotel offers tidy, well-maintained rooms, excellent service, and good value. The decor is almost stately, although slightly dated, with gold bedspreads and subdued colors on the walls. Free Wi-Fi reaches every nook and cranny in the hotel. Rooms on the higher floors have great views, especially those on the south side, from which you can see Volcán Cotopaxi on a clear day. With its own filtering system, this is one of the few hotels in Quito—or in the country, for that matter—to offer safe drinking water straight from the tap. The small gym here is surprisingly well equipped.

Diego de Almagro 822 y Cordero, Quito. www.hotelsebastian.com. ℓ/fax **02/2222-300** or 02/2222-400. Fax 02/2222-500. 55 units. $75 double; $95 junior suite. AE, DC, MC, V. Free parking. **Amenities:** Restaurant; bar; small gym; room service. *In room:* TV, hair dryer, free Wi-Fi.

Hotel Sierra Madre ★ ✈   Located just outside the central bustle of the Mariscal district, this hotel offers clean and cozy rooms in two separate three-story "towers" of an old restored building. Most of the rooms feature wood floors, colonial-style furnishings, and original artworks. The best rooms in the house, nos. 11 and 12, are top-floor affairs with high ceilings and large private corner terraces with great views. If you don't land one of these, you can still enjoy the hotel's common terrace areas. The staff and tour desk here are very helpful and friendly.

Veintimilla 464 y Luis Tamayo, Quito. www.hotelsierramadre.com. ℓ **02/2505-687.** Fax 02/2505-715. 21 units. $55–$63 double. AE, DC, MC, V. Free parking. **Amenities:** Restaurant; bar; free airport transfers; room service; all rooms smoke-free. *In room:* TV, hair dryer, free Wi-Fi.

Hotel Vieja Cuba ★   This lovely old colonial house has been renovated with style and flair. A soothing fountain in the courtyard and gleaming hardwood floors lead to cozy rooms with exposed brick and modern wood beds. The rooms are simple but rustic and comfortable, although not for those who favor a soft bed. Bathrooms have nice mosaic tiles and showers with great pressure. Everything is very clean and kept in tip-top shape. The larger doubles come with either a sitting area or a fireplace; suite no. 11 has a nice sitting area downstairs and a loft bedroom upstairs with a small balcony. The Orisha restaurant downstairs offers homemade Cuban dishes and great mojitos, and the owners also run a couple of other Cuban-themed bars and restaurants in the neighborhood, including La Bodeguita de Cuba (p. 118).

Diego de Almagro 1212 y La Niña, Quito. www.hotelviejacuba.com. ℓ **02/2906-729.** Fax 02/2520-738. 26 units. $78 double; $112 suite. Rates include breakfast. MC, V. **Amenities:** Restaurant; bar; room service. *In room:* TV, hair dryer, free Internet.

INEXPENSIVE

In addition to the place listed below, **Posada del Maple,** at Juan Rodríguez E8–49 and 6 de Diciembre (ℓ **02/2544-507;** www.posadadelmaple.com), is another top choice for backpackers.

Hostal Jardín del Sol ✈   The "Garden of the Sun" hotel offers inexpensive and basic accommodations and is conveniently located close to many of New Town's bars and restaurants. The friendly, welcoming staff seems to genuinely care about making your stay as pleasant as possible. Units are small but clean and simply furnished, with wood beds and tiny bathrooms with tiled floors. Some rooms have balconies with limited views of Quito; a few have yellow walls as bright as the sunshine (thus the hotel's name).

Jose Calama 166 y Diego de Almagro, Quito. www.hostaljardindelsol.com. © **02/2230-941.** Fax 02/2230-950. 23 units. $45 double. Rates include full breakfast and taxes. AE, DC, MC, V. Free parking. **Amenities:** Restaurant; bar; room service; free Internet. *In room:* TV, free Wi-Fi.

In Old Town

Quito's Old Town is in the midst of a major renaissance. Whereas several years ago, I cautioned visitors against staying in this area, today you will find excellent hotel options in various price ranges and a vastly improved security situation. That said, taxis definitely should be used after nightfall.

VERY EXPENSIVE

In addition to the places listed below, the folks at Metropolitan Touring are planning to open a beautiful boutique hotel right on Plaza San Francisco in mid-2011. **La Casona de San Miguel** (© **02/2988-200;** www.casonasanmiguel.com) will have 31 rooms in a colonial-era mansion that at one time served as the residence for several presidents.

Hotel Patio Andaluz ★★★   This stately hotel is a fabulous option in the center of Quito's colonial core. Rooms are spread around the perimeters of two large central courtyard areas. The rooms are all large and elegant, with wood floors, Persian rugs, antique-style furniture and beds, large desks, and 37-inch flatscreen televisions. Most units have windows opening onto one of the two central courtyards (a few face the street). The suites are all two levels, with a bedroom on one level and a comfortable sitting room on the other. But suites have only one bathroom, and sometimes it's located on the level with the sitting room, so if you like your bathroom just steps away from your bedroom, be sure to request that arrangement. My favorite room here is no. 401, a fourth-floor room with incredible panoramic views of the Basilica and Ichimbia hill.

Av. García Moreno N6-52, btw. Olmedo and Mejía, Quito. www.hotelpatioandaluz.com. © **02/2280-830.** Fax 02/2288-690. 31 units. $200 double; $250 suite. Rates include breakfast buffet. AE, DC, MC, V. **Amenities:** Restaurant; bar; lounge; smoke-free rooms; free Wi-Fi. *In room:* A/C (in some), TV.

Plaza Grande ★★   Housed in the meticulously restored former home of one of Quito's founding fathers, this stylish hotel is opulent and grand. The all-suite hotel fronts Plaza de la Independencia (Plaza Grande), and the best rooms have large windows and French doors overlooking the plaza. All rooms feature soundproofed windows and doors, 42-inch flatscreen televisions, Jacuzzi tubs in large bathrooms with heated floors, and fine cotton linens and down comforters. The decor is refined, with heavy drapes, plush furnishings, fine fabrics, and tasteful art and tapestries on the walls. The hotel's restaurants and wine cellar match the high standards set by the rooms, and the spa is small but delightful. Prices here are well above those at most other high-end hotels in Quito—in most cases, more than two to three times as high as other upscale options. But no other Quito hotel can match Plaza Grande's intimacy, history, location, and luxury.

On Plaza de la Independencia, Av. García Moreno N5-16 y Chile, Quito. www.plazagrandequito.com. © **888/790-5264** in the U.S. and Canada, or 02/2510-777 in Ecuador. Fax 02/2510-800. 15 units. $550–$675 suite; $2,200 presidential suite. AE, DC, MC, V. Free valet parking. **Amenities:** 3 restaurants; cafe; bar; lounge; concierge; room service; sauna; small, well-equipped spa *In room:* A/C, TV, hair dryer, minibar, free Wi-Fi.

Villa Colonna ★★★ 🎁 This intimate and luxurious option offers up personalized attention, plush rooms, and a prime location in the heart of Old Town. Rooms are spread around a classic old converted home, with an atrium roof over a tranquil central courtyard. Floors are brilliantly varnished wood, covered at most turns by ornate Oriental rugs. Antiques and tasteful artworks abound. Breakfasts are memorable, but the best feature here is the rooftop terrace, with a wonderful view both day and night of the red tile roofs and church towers of colonial Quito.

Benalcázar 1128, btw. Oriente and Esmeraldas, Quito. www.villacolonna.ec. ☎ 02/2955-805. 6 units. $300 double. Rates include full breakfast. MC, V. Parking nearby. **Amenities:** Lounge; concierge; smoke-free rooms. *In room:* TV, hair dryer, free Wi-Fi.

MODERATE

Another good option in this category is **El Relicario del Carmen** (Venezuela 1041 and Olmedo; ☎ 02/2289-120; www.hotelrelicariodelcarmen.com), a midsize hotel housed in a colonial home that dates to 1705.

Hotel Real Audiencia ★ This Old Town classic offers clean, comfortable rooms at good prices. The best rooms are spacious and come with views. No. 2A is a corner suite with a fabulous view of Santo Domingo Plaza, while no. 301 is a floor higher up, with more panoramic views. One of the best features of this hotel is its top-floor restaurant with wraparound picture windows and a view of Santo Domingo Plaza and El Panecillo, although the view outshines the food. The owners aim to be socially and culturally conscious, with solar panels to heat their water, solid-waste recycling, and educational programs for local youths. You'll get a slight discount and free airport transfers if you book directly online with them.

Bolívar Oe-318 at the corner of Guayaquil, Quito. www.realaudiencia.com. ☎ 02/2952-711. Fax 02/2580-213. 32 units. $55 double; $66 junior suite; $90 Manuela Sáenz Suite. Rates include full breakfast and taxes. AE, DC, MC, V. **Amenities:** Restaurant; bar. *In room:* TV; free Wi-Fi.

INEXPENSIVE

In addition to the places listed below, **La Posada Colonial** (☎ 02/2280-282; www.posadacolonial.com.ec) is a good option in this price range, just steps away from the Compañía de Jesús and Plaza de la Independencia.

Hotel Catedral Internacional Once a rock-bottom backpacker joint, this centrally located budget hotel has been spruced up quite a bit. Rooms are all compact and carpeted, with wood furnishings, faux-stucco walls, and 24-inch LCD televisions. Nos. 1 through 4 front the street and are some of the few options with exterior windows. While this brightens things up and adds a bit of charm, it also makes these rooms noisier. There's also an atrium-covered central courtyard area with a simple restaurant, and the service here is friendly and attentive.

Mejía 638, btw. Cuenca and Benalcázar, Quito. www.hotelcatedral.ec. ☎ 02/2955-438. Fax 02/2557-890. 15 units. $49 double. Rate includes full breakfast. AE, MC, V. **Amenities:** Restaurant. *In room:* TV, free Wi-Fi.

Hotel San Francisco de Quito 🎐 This is my favorite budget option in Old Town. Housed in a 17th-century converted residence, the hotel has rooms on the second, third, and fourth floors that rise above a classic central stone courtyard with stone fountain. Rooms vary considerably in size, so try to see a few first. Most have varnished wood floors, although a few are carpeted. No. 32 is the best room in the house. A large suite with fireplace and kitchenette, it's located on the fourth floor and has excellent views in several directions.

Sucre Oe3-17, at the corner of Guayaquil, Quito. www.sanfranciscodequito.com.ec. © **02/2287-758** or 02/2951-241. 32 units. $42 double; $48 suite. Rates include breakfast. MC, V. **Amenities:** Restaurant; Jacuzzi; sauna; steam room. *In room:* TV, free Wi-Fi.

Between Old and New Towns

Mansión del Angel ★★★ 🎁 This is the most elegant and refined boutique hotel in Quito. The lobby, rooms, and common areas are full of gorgeous antiques, handmade wood furniture, art, crystal chandeliers, and gilded mirrors. All the rooms have canopy beds, hand-carved moldings, Oriental carpets, and plush bedspreads. The best rooms have a separate sitting area and private balcony letting out onto the hotel's lush gardens. A formal English tea is served every afternoon, which is a good way to meet other guests, and a hot water bottle is placed at the foot of your bed each night, which is a good way to ward off the Quito cold. There are plans to build a full-service spa here during 2011. *Note:* This is a new location for a longstanding hotel.

Calle Los Ríos N13-134 y Pasaje Ascencio Gándara, Quito. www.mansiondelangel.com.ec. © **800/327-3573** in the U.S., or 02/2557-721. Fax 02/2237-819. 15 units. $150–$300 double. Rates include full breakfast, afternoon tea, and taxes. MC, V. Parking nearby. **Amenities:** Restaurant; concierge; room service; all rooms smoke-free. *In room:* TV, hair dryer, free Wi-Fi.

In La Floresta

EXPENSIVE

In addition to the hotel listed below, the **Radisson Royal Quito** (© **800/967-9033** in the U.S. and Canada, or 02/2233-333; www.radisson.com), at Cordero 444 and 12 de Octubre, is another dependable high-end choice in La Floresta.

Swissôtel Quito ★★ This is yet another excellent large business-class hotel. The rooms are very modern, with a touch of classic Danish design: sleek blond-wood paneling; cream-colored striated wallpaper; and stylish wood desks, dressers, and closets. The bathrooms are very spacious and have double sinks and contemporary fixtures. The pool area is attractive but pretty small. You'll get all the typical services and amenities of a high-end business hotel. The Swissôtel doesn't feel as new or hip as the Marriott or Sheraton, but it does have a good location, excellent service, and one of the best hotel health clubs in Quito.

Av. 12 de Octubre 1820 y Luis Cordero, Quito. www.swissotel.com. © **02/2567-600.** Fax 02/2568-080. 275 units. $180–$220 standard; $220–$290 deluxe; $350–$500 suite. Free valet parking. AE, DC, MC, V. **Amenities:** 4 restaurants; 2 bars; babysitting; concierge; executive/club floors; state-of-the-art health club; Jacuzzi; small indoor-outdoor pool; racquetball and squash courts; room service; sauna; spa; outdoor tennis court; smoke-free floors. *In room:* A/C, TV, hair dryer, free Internet, minibar.

North of New Town

EXPENSIVE

Hotel Dann Carlton ★★ 🎁 The Dann Carlton is understated and elegant, and bills itself as a boutique hotel because it offers all the charm and personal service that you'd find at a small hotel. The accommodations are spacious and come with dark-wood furnishings, built-in closets, and subtle green, earthy tones. The marble bathrooms are sparkling. Rooms at the back of the hotel, especially those on the higher floors, have sumptuous views of the city, El Panecillo, Parque La Carolina, and the volcanoes. The location is a tiny bit out of the way, but the neighborhood is quiet and safe, and the huge Parque La Carolina is just outside the door. These folks offer free airport pickup and drop-off, too.

Av. República de El Salvador N34–377 y Irlanda, Quito. www.danncarltonquito.com. ℭ **02/2249-008.** Fax 02/2448-807. 212 units. $135–$150 double; $170–$200 suite. AE, DC, MC, V. Free valet parking. **Amenities:** Restaurant; bar; casino; concierge; executive/club floors; well-equipped gym; Jacuzzi; room service; sauna; smoke-free floors. *In room:* TV, CD player, hair dryer, minibar, free Wi-Fi.

Sheraton Quito ★★★ The Sheraton gets my nod for best high-end business-class hotel in the city. The facilities are top-notch and service is impeccable. Rooms are ample and equipped with all the modern conveniences, including 32-inch flatscreen televisions and MP3 docking stations. The "club-level" rooms come with a host of perks and complimentary services, and they are worth the splurge. The "extended stay" suites here come with a washer-dryer combo—good for families with young kids. The well-equipped gym, located on the top floor of one of the towers, allows you to take in the wonderful views as you try to burn some calories. This is one of the closest downtown hotels to the airport, and despite being geared to business travelers, it's perfectly suited for casual travelers and tourists as well.

Av. República de El Salvador N36–212 y Naciones Unidas, Quito. www.sheraton.com. ℭ **800/325-3535** in the U.S. and Canada, or 02/2970-002 in Ecuador. Fax 02/2433-906. 170 units. $210 double; $250 junior suite; $250–$320 extended-stay suite. AE, DC, MC, V. Free valet parking. **Amenities:** 2 restaurants; bar; lounge; concierge; executive/club floors; well-equipped gym; Jacuzzi; room service; sauna; smoke-free floors. *In room:* A/C, TV, hair dryer, minibar, MP3 docking station, Wi-Fi for a fee.

In the Foothills Overlooking Quito

VERY EXPENSIVE

Hacienda Rumiloma ★★ 🎒 The views and accommodations at this rustically luxurious lodge—housed on the grounds of a colonial-era hacienda—are spectacular. Although it's just 10 minutes or less from downtown, this volcano-side hotel feels worlds away. All the rooms are large and unique, with extravagant and ornate decor. Adobe walls, red-tile floors, brass sinks, and exposed beam-and-brick ceilings are combined with an abundance of antiques, artwork, and eccentric design touches, including hand-painted ceramic toilets. The common areas are equally ornate and artistic, and the hacienda has almost 40 hectares (99 acres) of land, including both primary and secondary forest. The **restaurant** here (see below) is also excellent.

Obispo de la Madrid, Quito. www.haciendarumiloma.com. ℭ **02/2548-206** or 09/9703-130. 8 units. $305 double; $345 family suite. Rates include breakfast. AE, DC, MC, V. Free parking. **Amenities:** Restaurant; bar; free airport transfers; concierge; room service; smoke-free rooms. *In room:* No phone.

WHERE TO DINE

In New Town

MODERATE

El Atrio ★★ FUSION Located on the second floor of a building overlooking Plaza Foch, this understated and elegant little restaurant is a bit of a hidden gem. The menu features a long list of creative dishes. Most of the dishes are named after a Catholic saint. The sea bass Santa María is prepared in a ginger and coconut sauce, and served over quinoa. For lighter fare, there are sandwiches and pastas. When the weather accommodates, I suggest grabbing one of the outdoor tables on the balcony overlooking the plaza, although you won't go wrong inside, which has seating on a couple of levels, with soft lighting, plush furnishings and decor, and windows all around.

Reina Victoria N24–67 y Foch, on Plaza Foch. ℭ **02/2520-581.** Reservations recommended. Main courses $7–$16. AE, DC, MC, V. Daily 11am–midnight.

La Boca del Lobo ★ 🛍 INTERNATIONAL/FUSION   As much a bar and lounge as a restaurant, this is one of the most unique spots in Quito. Several dining rooms are spread over several levels here. All are bright, upbeat, and artsy. A tree grows through one room, just off a sunken dining area whose edges are lined with pillow-covered benches. At 55 pages, the menu ranges far and wide, with everything from duck nachos to chicken curry, beef stroganoff, and moussaka. It's almost as eclectic as the decor. The food is pretty good and portions are large, although, in general, as far as the cuisine goes, their ambition exceeds their execution. Still, you'd be hard pressed to find a more charismatic joint for a few drinks and something to eat.

Calama 284 y Reina Victoria. ℂ **02/2234-083.** www.labocadellobo.com.ec. Reservations recommended. Main courses $7.30–$19. AE, DC, MC, V. Daily 5–11pm.

Mare Nostrum ★★ SEAFOOD   Dimly lit with a distinctly medieval feel, this is one of Quito's top seafood restaurants, and it has been for decades. Specialties include bouillabaisse, paella, and other seafood stews. The *arroz del capitán* features rice, prawns, mussels, clams, squid, octopus, and any other fresh seafood available that day, and is mixed with coriander, soy sauce, and onions; the coconut shellfish is prepared with local tropical flavors. Also available are Chilean mussels, lobster, and calamari. The sea bass in a butter-and-garlic sauce is succulent. Whatever you order, you probably won't be disappointed—the chef has a knack for throwing together different flavors from the sea. And you certainly won't leave hungry, as portions are substantial. There are three separate dining rooms; I always try to get a seat within view of but not too close to the fireplace in the principal dining room.

Mariscal Foch E10-5 y Tamayo. ℂ **02/2528-686.** www.marenostrumquito.com. Reservations recommended. Main courses $6–$22. AE, DC, MC, V. Daily noon–4pm and 7–10:30pm.

INEXPENSIVE

In addition to the places listed below, a host of simple restaurants are geared toward the backpacker crowd. For tasty Indian food, try **Great India Restaurant** (ℂ **02/2238-269**), on José Calama E4–54, between Juan León Mera and Avenida Amazonas. For pastas and pizzas, head to **Le Arcate** (ℂ **02/2237-659**; www.le arcate.com), on Baquedano 358 and Juan León Mera.

Azuca Latin Bistro ★★ NUEVO LATINO   Set right on Plaza Foch, this new joint is upbeat and chic. It's a great spot for everything from drinks and appetizers to more filling fare—and it's open 24 hours daily. You'll find indoor seating, as well as a host of tables under shade umbrellas right on the plaza. Don't miss the appetizer of barbeque ribs in a tamarind and guava glaze. As a main dish, the traditional Cuban *ropa vieja,* a plate of seasoned shredded beef, is a standout. There's a long list of cocktails, with a variety of specialty mojitos offered. I recommend the *mojito apasionado,* which has passion-fruit juice added. This place features live music or DJs Thursday through Saturday.

Plaza Foch. ℂ **02/2907-164.** Main courses $8–$11. AE, DC, MC, V. Daily 24 hr.

Las Redes ★ SEAFOOD   This is a good alternative to the more formal, and more pricey, Mare Nostrum (see above). Plus, this place serves the best *ceviche* in Quito. You can order any type of *ceviche,* from clams to octopus, fish, or shrimp. The chefs here also do an excellent job with all sorts of seafood. One of the specialties is the *gran mariscada,* an enormous, beautiful platter of assorted sizzling seafood. The *arroz con mariscos* (yellow rice with peppers, onions, mussels, clams, shrimp, calamari, octopus, and crayfish) is also delicious. Even though Las Redes is on one of the busiest streets of Quito, the simple wood tables and fishnets hanging from the ceilings make you feel as though you are at a local seafood joint on the coast.

Av. Amazonas 845 y Veintimilla. ℂ 02/2525-691. Reservations recommended. Main courses $5–$12. AE, DC, MC, V. Mon–Sat 11am–11pm.

The Magic Bean ★ ☺ BREAKFAST/INTERNATIONAL   The Magic Bean is a cozy cafe that would be at home in any college town in the United States, say, in Santa Cruz, California, or Boulder, Colorado. It's not fancy, but it has a pleasant setting with a couple of small dining rooms and covered outdoor tables. The fare is typical cozy cafe food—pancakes, French toast, sandwiches, bagels, omelets, fresh fruit drinks, salads made with organic lettuce, and freshly brewed coffee. Overall, the food is quite good. Just beware: The pancakes are enormous! More hearty options range from grilled local trout to filet mignon. They do a lot of kabobs here, with everything from steak, chicken, and pork, to mahimahi and shrimp grilled on a spear. They even have a children's menu and free Wi-Fi. Though it's more popular as a restaurant, the Magic Bean also functions as a hostel.

Mariscal Foch 681 y Juan León Mera. ℂ 02/2566-181. www.magicbeanquito.com. Sandwiches $4–$7; main courses $4.75–$12. AE, DC, MC, V. Daily 7am–11pm.

Mama Clorinda ECUADOREAN   This enormously popular restaurant opened in 2004 and immediately garnered a loyal following. Simplicity is the theme here; the food, not the atmosphere, is the attraction. The focus is on hearty and traditional recipes from the highlands, including *seco de chivo* (goat stew), *llapingachos* (potato-cheese patties), and *guatita* (beef, potato, and peanut stew). All varieties of grilled pork are also available, as well as roasted chicken served with *elote* (corn on the cob) and mashed potatoes. This is not a good place for a vegetarian because even the mashed potatoes are cooked with pork fat (which is the traditional Ecuadorean way to cook them). Finish off your meal with a silky coconut flan or a fresh-fruit salad.

Reina Victoria 1144 y Calama. ℂ 02/2544-362. www.mamaclorinda.com. Main courses $4–$9. MC, V. Daily noon–9pm.

In Old Town

In addition to the places listed below, you'll do well at the elegant courtyard restaurant **El Rincón de Cantuña** (ℂ 02/2280-830) inside the hotel Patio Andaluz (see "Where to Stay," earlier in this chapter). You might also try **Octava de Corpus** ★★ (ℂ 02/2952-989; www.octavadecorpus.com), Calle Junín E2–167, which is spread over several rooms in an old colonial home, with antiques and artwork everywhere and a fabulous wine cellar. Consider also **La Casa de los Geráneos** (ℂ 02/2283-889), Calle La Ronda OE 1–134, which has a lovely courtyard and indoor seating in an ancient home of the historic Calle La Ronda.

Two of the restaurants listed below, Café Mosaico and PIM's Panecillo, are actually located a little bit outside and above the center of Old Town, but for practical purposes—and for the views they provide of Old Town—they are included here. A taxi to either of these restaurants from Old Town should not cost more than $3 or $4.

EXPENSIVE

Mea Culpa ★ INTERNATIONAL   This restaurant commands one of the most beautiful settings in Old Town. On the second floor of a building that overlooks Plaza Grande, Mea Culpa is one of Quito's grandest restaurants—so grand, in fact, that they require "business casual" attire (although exceptions are sometimes made at lunch), and it's best to dress up if you come here. You'll definitely want to be in the front room, with large windows overlooking the plaza (try to reserve a window table). Main courses include everything from simple pastas and steaks, to pork tenderloin in a raspberry sauce, to an ostrich filet flambéed in brandy and served with a maple-soy-apple reduction. The modest wine list leans heavily on Chilean and Argentine vineyards, but with some interesting and less common selections.

2nd floor of the Palacio Arzobispal, on Plaza de la Independencia, García Moreno y Chile. ℭ **02/2951-190.** www.meaculpa.com.ec. Reservations recommended. Main courses $12–$26. AE, DC, MC, V. Mon–Fri 12:30–3:30pm and 7–11pm; Sat 7–11pm.

Theatrum ★★★ INTERNATIONAL Housed on the second floor of the Teatro Sucre, this elegant restaurant is formal and stylish. The dining room is long and narrow and has high ceilings and minimal decor, with bold black chairs, white-clothed tables, and heavy red drapes. The grilled tuna is a good bet, as is the rack of imported New Zealand lamb chops. Two separate five-course tasting menus are available for $39. Presentations are artsy, without being overdone. Another option is to head to their wine bar, where you can sample from their extremely extensive wine list and order a range of tapas, or appetizers. If you reserve in advance, be sure to ask about their offer of free transportation.

Teatro Nacional Sucre, Calle Manabí, btw. Guayaquil and Flores. ℭ **02/2571-011.** www.theatrum.com.ec. Reservations recommended. Main courses $11–$28. AE, DC, MC, V. Sun–Fri 12:30–4pm and 7–11:30pm; Sat 7–11:30pm.

MODERATE
PIM's Panecillo 📷 ECUADOREAN/INTERNATIONAL You might recognize this spot from a segment of *The Amazing Race: All-Stars.* The food here is relatively pedestrian, but you're most likely coming here for the view. Located just off the *Virgen de Quito* monument, atop the Panecillo hill, it has plenty of seating with a view, both in the multileveled main dining room and in the heated outdoor areas. The menu is massive and ranges from hamburgers and sandwiches to a wide selection of meat, poultry, and seafood options. You can get a pepper steak or trout in almond sauce. There's a good children's menu, which includes chicken nuggets and mini-hamburgers. These folks have another branch, with an equally stunning view, in the Centro Cultural Itchimbía (ℭ **02/3228-410**), on the top of the Itchimbía hill, and another at Isabel Catolica 915 (ℭ **02/2221-875**), in La Floresta.

Calle Melchor Aymerich, on top of Panecillo hill. ℭ**02/3170-878.** www.grupopims.com. Reservations recommended. Main courses $9–$20. AE, DC, MC, V. Mon–Sat noon–midnight; Sun noon–6pm.

INEXPENSIVE
Café Mosaico ★ 📷 INTERNATIONAL Set high on a hill overlooking Quito, Mosaico is run by an Ecuadorean-Greek-American family. Settle at a table inlaid with hand-painted mosaic tiles and take in the spectacular view. Greek dishes like moussaka and souvlaki are delicious. The vegetarian lasagna is excellent, and there's a good selection of delicious sandwiches, including a turkey club. Reservations are not accepted, and this place fills up fast; be prepared to wait for a table. The best time to come here is late afternoon during the week, before the after-work crowd arrives. That way, you'll score a table fast, get to see the place during the day, and also take in the incredible view as the city lights up after dark. The restaurant has a large telescope for stargazing at night and downtown spying during the day. A taxi here should cost under $5.

Manuel Samaniego N8–95 y Antepara, Itchimbía. ℭ **02/2542-871.** www.cafemosaico.com.ec. Reservations not accepted. Main courses $4.50–$14. MC, V. Tues 1–11pm; Wed–Mon 11am–11pm.

El Tianguez ★ 🍴 ECUADOREAN   This is the perfect place in which to have a quick meal when you're spending the day in Old Town visiting the sights. Just below Iglesia de San Francisco, the large outdoor cobblestone patio has a sweeping view of Plaza de San Francisco. The indoor dining room is very small, and it can get a bit cramped when it's full, but the atmosphere is friendly and convivial and the staff works hard to keep everybody happy. The food here is simple and delicious. Order a *plato típico,* and you'll get a sampling of local specialties: empanadas, *humitas,* fried *yuca,* and fried pork. For something lighter, there's a good selection of large salads and sandwiches and fresh-squeezed fruit juices. Live Andean music is here Wednesday through Saturday, beginning at 9pm.

Below Iglesia San Francisco, Plaza de San Francisco. ✆ **02/2954-326.** Reservations not accepted. Main courses $4–$8. AE, DC, MC, V. Mon–Tues 9:30am–6:30pm; Wed–Sat 9:30am–midnight; Sun 9:30am–10pm.

La Floresta & North of New Town

You'll find a wide range of good, and mostly high-end, restaurants clustered in La Floresta and spread throughout the northern sections of the city. **Chez Jerome** ★★ (✆ **02/2904-391;** www.chezjeromerestaurante.com), Whymper N30–96 and Coruña, is a standout spot for classic French cuisine. **Lo Nuestro** ★ (✆ **02/2563-438;** www.lonuestro.com.ec), Isabel la Católica N24–535 and Luis Cordero, is the Quito branch of a longstanding Guayaquil favorite (p. 242), serving up traditional Ecuadorian fare. The new **Coquus** ★★ (✆ **02/2902-446**), Pasaje Moeller E12–25 and Isabel la Católica, is getting raves for its unique version of New Ecuadorian cooking.

Astrid y Gastón ★★ (✆ **02/2506-621;** www.astridygaston.com), Av. Coruña N32–302 and González Suárez, is the Quito branch of groundbreaking Peruvian fusion stars Astrid and Gastón. For Italian fare, I recommend **Carmine** ★ (✆ **02/3332-829;** www.carmineristorante.com), Catalina Aldaz N34–208 and Portugal, while **La Gloria** ★★ (✆ **02/6006-841;** www.lagloria.com.ec), Valladolid N24–519 and Francisco Salazar, serves up a creative, contemporary take on Mediterranean cuisine. Finally, in the Bellavista neighborhood, **Alma** ★★ (✆ **02/2252-248;** www.alma.com.ec), Calle Monitor 188 and Quiteño Libre, is a classy spot in a converted home that caters to discerning diners, with Italian-inspired fusion cuisine.

EXPENSIVE

Il Risotto ★ ITALIAN   Semiformal and almost always packed, this longstanding option is one of the top Italian restaurants in town. The menu is dauntingly long and covers cuisines from all regions of Italy—I like coming with a group so I can taste a wide range of the choices. The heart and soul of the menu is a range of pastas and risi. Everything is very well done. I like the *risotto salmone e rucola* (salmon and arugula) and the house penne, which comes in a thick tomato sauce with eggplant, capers, anchovies, and both green and black olives. For something more exotic, try a risotto with frogs' legs. More substantial entrees include *capretto alla messinese,* a goat dish cooked with tomatoes, rosemary, and potatoes, as well as veal Bolognese. There's an inviting antipasti buffet and a less outstanding dessert buffet. The wine list is long but much heavier on Chilean and Argentine offerings than on those from Italy. Try to grab a window table in the main dining room, which features wood floors and a few Tiffany-style lamps. There's a cozy but viewless dining room below the main room that is used for overflow.

Eloy Alfaro N34-447 y Portugal. ✆ **02/2246-850.** Reservations recommended. Main courses $10–$30. AE, DC, MC, V. Mon–Fri noon–3pm and 6:30–11:30pm; Sun noon–3:30pm and 6:30–10:30pm.

Los Troncos Steak House ARGENTINE STEAKHOUSE   Fronting Parque La Carolina, this is where Ecuadorean businesspeople meet for power lunches and where families come to sample some of the best grilled meat in town. When you walk into the restaurant, you'll pass the huge grilling area, where juicy steaks, pork loin, chicken breasts, sausages, and other savory meat specialties roast over hot coals. I recommend the *parrillada* (grilled) special so that you can sample everything on the menu, including the above-mentioned meats, plus *riñón* (kidney) and *morcilla* (blood pudding). You can also order everything individually. The charcoal fire gives all the meat a delicious flavor. Vegetarians can eat here, too; there's a large selection of pastas, soups, and salads, including an impressive salad bar.

Av. de los Shyris 1280, btw. Suecia and Portugal. © **02/2437-377.** Reservations recommended. Main courses $8-$30. AE, DC, MC, V. Mon-Sat noon-11pm; Sun noon-4pm.

Zazu ★★★ FUSION   Hip and eclectic, this restaurant gets just about everything right. Chef Rafael Peréz uses fresh, local ingredients whenever possible, and flavor always takes precedence over presentation—although presentations are always creative and often unexpected. Start things off with the rose petal salad, with organic rose petals, mixed greens, and a lychee vinaigrette. For a main dish, I recommend *langostinos Zazu,* which are cooked tempura style and then served with a sauce made with six types of chilies and a green-mango side salad. Perhaps the best way to dine here is to go with the chef's nightly tasting menu ($35–$40). Quito's hippest crowd gathers at the bar here, which serves up a wide range of martinis and mixed drinks, including a couple of very tasty original concoctions.

Mariano Aguilera 331 y La Pradera. © **02/2543-559.** www.zazuquito.com. Reservations recommended. Main courses $10-$28. AE, DC, MC, V. Mon-Fri 12:30-11:30pm; Sat 7-11:30pm.

MODERATE

Zao ★★ 🍽 PAN-ASIAN   This new restaurant is owned and run by the folks behind Zazu (see above). The menu runs the gamut of Asian cooking cultures, with everything from Vietnamese summer rolls to pad thai, and from kung pao chicken to samosas and sushi. Everything is excellently and authentically done, with slightly ornate presentations. Still, the portions are hearty and the prices are excellent. I recommend starting things off with the Chinese hamburgers, three ground-pork sliders served with an Asian-spiced aioli. The large, stylish dining room features white walls and wood floors, and is divided into three sections by intricately carved wood screens. One section is a popular bar, which gets rocking on weekends, with live DJs and late-night revelry.

Eloy Alfaro N10-16 y San Salvador. © **02/2523-496.** www.zaoquito.com. Reservations recommended. Main courses $7-$12, including tax and service. AE, DC, MC, V. Mon-Sat 12:30pm-midnight; Sun 12:30-3pm.

In the Foothills Overlooking Quito

Hacienda Rumiloma ★★ 🏨 FUSION   If you're not staying at this lovely mountain retreat (p. 98), I highly recommend coming up for dinner. The large dining room features heavy wood and stone-top tables, exposed wood beams, and a host of artwork and antiques. They have one of the original 18th-century wooden sculptures by Bernardo de Legarda, used as a model for the El Panecillo monument. The menu features a broad mix of creative contemporary concoctions. And it's hard to go wrong with any of them. You can start off with a tuna carpaccio or some Ecuadorean stone crabs. For a main course, I recommend the lamb "La Cantera," which is marinated for 3 days and then slow-roasted. After dinner, savor a brandy while taking in the view, or head downstairs to the hotel's Irish-style pub for some aged single malt.

Obispo de la Madrid. *©* **02/2548-206.** Reservations recommended. Main courses $12–$25. AE, DC, MC, V. Mon–Sat 11am–11pm; Sun 10am–9pm.

WHAT TO SEE & DO

It's hard to hit all of Quito's major attractions in 1 day, although if you are really pressed for time, you can pack in a lot of them, especially if you focus first on Old Town. I recommend getting an early start and visiting the Old Town highlights of Iglesia de San Francisco, La Compañía de Jesús, and Casa Museo María Augusta Urrutia. During the midday break, when many attractions close for lunch and siesta, you could head up to El Panecillo for panoramic views of the city and lunch at PIM's (p. 101). In the afternoon, head over to Fundación Guayasamín and the Capilla del Hombre. End your day with a sunset ride on El Teleférico, with its sweeping view of the city. This is a pretty good and packed 1-day tour, although it leaves out Museo Nacional del Banco Central, which takes several hours to tour properly.

In Old Town

In addition to the places listed below, it's worth taking a walk along the recently restored **Calle La Ronda ★★**. Once the city's "red light" district and home to its poets, painters, and troubadours, it now has a series of art galleries and functioning workshops. Stop in and see how the traditional ornate devotional candles are made. Calle La Ronda is located at the southern end of Old Town, running parallel and beside Avenida Morales, bounded by Avenida Maldonado to the east and García Moreno to the west. A good way to visit Calle La Ronda is to begin at **Museo de la Ciudad ★** (*©* **02/2283-879;** www.museociudadquito.gov.ec), on García Moreno E1–47 at the western end of the street. The museum is housed in a meticulously restored old building, with several permanent historical exhibits, as well as a beautiful chapel, excavated catacombs, and regularly changing traveling or temporary shows and exhibits. Admission is $3.

Tip: One of the best ways to tour Old Town is on a guided excursion led by a bilingual member of the **Metropolitan Police Force** (*©* **02/2570-786;** Palacio Municipal, on Venezuela at the corner of Espejo). Tours leave daily from Plaza Grande at 10am and 2pm, and cost $15 for adults, $7.50 for children and seniors, including attraction entrance fees. Tours last for 2½ hours and take in many of the major sights, although a couple of different itineraries are offered, so check with them in advance. These folks also offer a night tour at 7pm, which costs $8.

Casa del Alabado ★★ 🎁 This new museum houses a fantastic collection of pre-Columbian artifacts. The restored mansion that houses this museum dates to 1671, although pieces on display go back as far as 4000 B.C. At any one point, some 500 pieces—drawn from a private collection 10 times that size—are on display, while rotating temporary exhibits are also often part of the offering. Exhibition rooms are spread around two floors of this old home, with a wonderful stone-tiled central court-yard where you can have a light bite or cup of coffee, and a second interior garden courtyard. Most of the works are ceramic, with everything from functional pieces to ornate religious figures, to purely artistic endeavors.

Note: Guided tours are available in English at $5 for two people, and an additional $1 per person for every other person in your group. A self-guided book is available for

THE QUITO school OF ART

The mid-16th-century Council of Trent mandate was clear: Art was to be used to convey Catholic doctrine and Christian themes to an illiterate, pagan populace. Early religious art that appeared throughout the Spanish colonies in South America carefully reflected traditional European themes and styles, as taught by Franciscan and Dominican monks to indigenous or mestizo artists.

After a century of standard, if uninspiring, copies of Christ on the cross and somber Virgins, a creative transition took place that the early Catholic fathers never envisioned. As the indigenous artists gained confidence and Catholicism became firmly rooted in the New World, religious paintings and sculptures became increasingly detailed and dramatic. In Quito, artists began incorporating more passionate elements into their works. Vivid crucifixes revealed Christ in excruciating detail—flayed, bones exposed, with a face distorted in agony. It was an almost rebellious reflection of the suffering of a conquered people.

The Quito School of art matured into a distinctive original style known for its exquisite detail of expression—statues had glass eyes, real hair, and rich fabrics overlaid with layers of gold leaf, for example.

By the time the colonial stranglehold weakened over an increasingly free-thinking Latin America, this graphic suffering and drama had given way to more native influences; Christ became swarthier, and llamas, cuyes (guinea pigs), parrots, and condors began to populate the landscapes in Catholic art.

Many of Quito's churches and museums display, or are examples themselves of, this idiosyncratic school: Visit the stunning, gold-draped Iglesia de la Compañía de Jesús, Iglesia de San Francisco, and Museo de Arte Colonial to see surviving examples. You might also want to visit Escuela Taller (✆ 02/**2373-890**), Montufar 352 and Pereira, which is housed in an old maternity hospital in heart of colonial Old Town; it functions as a training center for young artists working in traditional arts of wood carving, painting, metal works, and intricate inlays.

$2. Most of the written display information is in both Spanish and English. Allow about 40 minutes to visit the museum.

Calle Cuenca 335 y Bolívar. ✆ 02/**2280-940.** www.precolombino.com. Admission $4. Tues–Sat 9:30am–5:30pm; Sun and holidays 10am–4pm.

Casa Museo María Augusta Urrutia ★   This delightful museum allows visitors to envision what it must have been like to live in a 19th-century Spanish-style mansion in Old Town. When you enter the house, you immediately find yourself in a gorgeous courtyard. Not much has been changed since Doña María Augusta Urrutia lived here, so the dramatic entry that you see is probably what the Pope and many other world leaders also experienced when visiting this home. (Doña María devoted much of her life to philanthropy with a Catholic bent.) The house is surprisingly modern, with a full bathroom and modern kitchen appliances, but there are also a cold storage room, a wood-burning stove, and the oldest grain masher in Ecuador. The interior is gorgeous, featuring antique European furniture, a bed that belonged to General Sucre, hand-painted wallpaper, stained-glass windows, handcrafted moldings, murals on the walls, and Belgian tiles. There is also an incredible collection of Ecuadorean art, much of it by painter Victor Mideros.

GETTING high IN QUITO

One of the city's most popular attractions is **El Teleférigo** ★, with six-person cable cars that transport you up the side of Volcán Pichincha to 4,050m (13,284 ft.). The quick climb over 1,000m (3,280 ft.) takes all of 8 minutes. At the top, you have a magnificent view of the city and surrounding snow-covered peaks. Most folks recommend coming early, as that's when you'll have the best shot at a clear view. The air is thin up here, but don't worry: The ambitious and very modern complex includes an oxygen bar to replenish the weary traveler, along with several viewing platforms. You'll also find souvenir stands and shops, and a couple of restaurants and fast-food outlets.

If crowds bother you, avoid visiting here on the weekends (and public holidays), when it's packed to the gills. That said, this attraction is enormously popular with Ecuadorean families, and it's a wonderful cultural experience just to be out among the locals. People wait patiently in line just to get a glimpse of their city from an elevated perspective. You can escape the crowds by taking one of the marked paths on a stroll through the shrubby highlands. If you have kids in tow, you might want to return to the base of the mountain, where you'll find an amusement park, **Vulqano Park,** complete with roller coasters, all kinds of rides, arcades, and video games. However, this park is a bit run-down and forlorn for an amusement park.

The cable car operates Monday to Thursday from 10am to 8pm and Friday through Sunday from 9am to 11pm. Foreign visitors pay $8.50 for adults and $6.50 for children, but this is equivalent to the local rate for a "fast pass," which jumps you to the front of the line. Admission to Vulqano Park is free, and prices for the rides average around 75¢ to $1.50.

To get here, take a 15-minute taxi ride from the center of Quito. Tell the driver to take you to El Teleférigo at Vulqano Park. The taxi ride should cost $5 to $8. For more information, call ✆ **02/2222-997.**

Note: Guided tours are available in English. Just ask for a guide when you enter. Most of the written display information is in both Spanish and English. Allow about 40 minutes to visit the whole house.

García Moreno N2-60, btw. Sucre and Bolívar. ✆ **02/2580-103.** Admission $2 adults, $1 students and seniors, 50¢ children 11 and under. Tues–Sat 10am–6pm; Sun 9:30am–5:30pm.

El Centro Cultural Metropolitano This bustling public center is housed in a 400-year-old complex that contains several extensive public libraries, a museum, and performance spaces. The galleries on the main floor are used for temporary exhibitions and are free to the public. One of my favorite gallery spaces is the large open courtyard, covered with a high glass ceiling. Upstairs you'll find **Museo Alberto Mena Caamaño.** Few museums in the world can boast that they were both a prison and a university—this museum is one of them. Instead of prisoners or students, however, this space now houses a modest collection of colonial art. Your entrance fee gets you a bilingual guided tour; the guide will also take you to the old Jesuit residences and the basement area that used to house the prisoners. There's a simple cafeteria on the ground floor that makes a good coffee-break spot. Allow about a half-hour here.

Corner of Espejo y García Moreno. ✆ **02/2584-362.** www.centrocultural-quito.com. Free admission to the center; museum $1.50 adults, 75¢ students, 50¢ children and seniors. Tues–Sun 9am–4:30pm.

El Panecillo (Virgin Monument) 📷 From a distance, the hill that hosts a huge statue of the winged virgin does indeed look like a *panecillo* (small bread roll). Because it's directly south of the city, this hill was an ideal spot to construct the 45m-high (148-ft.) *Virgen de Quito,* an enlarged copy of Bernardo de Lagarda's *La Virgen de Quito* sculpture that is on display on the main altar in the San Francisco church. The Panecillo stands at about 3,000m (9,840 ft.), so you can also see the sculpture from the center of Quito.

The significance of the Panecillo hill dates back to Inca times, when it was known as Shungoloma (Hill of the Heart). Before the Spanish arrived, the Incas used this hill as a place to worship the sun. Later, from 1812 to 1815, the Spanish constructed a fortress here to control what was going on down below. These days, most people come up here for the 360-degree views of Quito. *Tip:* For the best vistas, try to get here early in the morning (around 10am), before the clouds settle in around the nearby mountains. On a clear day, you can see Cotopaxi in the distance. This is a relatively quick ride from Old Town, and a taxi should cost only about $3 each way. A half-hour is all you'll need to take in the sights.

El Panecillo, south of Old Town. Admission to enter the grounds $1; admission to climb to the top of the monument $1. Mon–Fri 9am–6pm; Sat–Sun 9am–5pm.

El Sagrario ★ This 17th-century church was once part of the nearby cathedral. It's a mishmash of different architectural styles, from baroque to neoclassical. The Solomonic columns on the outside are both Ionic and Gothic. Inside you can see the Moorish influence in the painted domes, with their striking frescos. As you enter El Sagrario, look down—you will see crypts. (Those with crossbones mean that the body buried there died of smallpox.) The second door is regarded as a colonial-era masterpiece; it was painted with liquid gold leaf and designed with vegetables and fruits, including pineapples, which are considered an indigenous welcome symbol. The lovely and intricate rococo altarpiece is also impressive—it took 12 years to build. Give yourself 15 minutes here (a half-hour, if you want to linger).

Around the corner from the cathedral on García Moreno 881, near Espejo. ☏ **02/2284-398.** Free admission. Mon–Sat 7:30am–5:30pm; Sun 7:30am–1pm and 5–6pm.

Iglesia de la Merced It's believed that after the expulsion of the Moors from Spain, in 1492, many Moorish artists sought refuge in South America. The current Iglesia de la Merced, a delightful example of Moorish design, dates from only 1737, but it was originally built in 1538. The resplendent gold-leaf altar, designed by the great Bernardo de Legarda, is pure baroque, while the ornate stucco work is mainly Moorish. Many of the oil paintings are by Víctor Mideros, one of the greatest Ecuadorean artists of the 20th century. If you have time (and it's still early in the morning), you can head around the corner to the convent, which dates back to the early 16th century and still houses the church's priests. Some of the highlights include the Neptune sculpture in the stone fountain and the 17th-century sun clock above the dome. The convent is open Monday through Saturday from 8 to 10:30am; the entrance is on Mejía near the corner of Cuenca. You'll need only 5 to 10 minutes here.

Chile, near the corner of Cuenca. ☏ **02/2280-743.** Free admission. Mon–Fri 7:30am–noon and 2–6pm; Sat 6:30am–noon.

Iglesia de San Francisco ★★ San Francisco was the first church built in Quito. Construction began in 1535, just 1 month after the Spanish arrived. (It took more than 100 years to finish.) You'll notice that Plaza San Francisco is distinctly sloped;

Touring Iglesia de San Francisco

Iglesia de San Francisco closes at noon, earlier than most of the other churches in Old Town, and it doesn't open again until 3pm. So if you're trying to see everything in Old Town in one morning, be sure to visit San Francisco first. If you can't make it before 11:30am, you can visit Museo Fray Pedro Gocial, the museum connected to the church (p. 110).

for several hundred years, it was assumed that it followed the shape of the earth. However, a group of archaeologists have discovered that San Francisco was built over an Inca temple, which is the reason the actual church is much higher than other structures in Quito. As you walk up the stairs from the plaza to the church, you can't help but notice how wide the stairs are. Supposedly the architects designed the stairs this way so that as you approach the church, you have to keep your eyes on your feet to watch where you're going—in other words, you are forced to bow your head in respect.

Like La Compañía (see below), San Francisco is an important baroque church, but the latter is much larger and, for some reason, feels much more somber. The ceilings have a beautiful Moorish design. In the entryway, as in La Compañía, you will notice images of the sun, which were used to lure indigenous people to the Christian religion. Throughout the church are combinations of indigenous and Catholic symbols. For example, the interior is decorated with angels in the shape of the sun—and the faces of these angels have distinct Indian characteristics.

The baroque altar in the front of the church has three important sculptures: The top is *El Bautismo de Jesús* (*The Baptism of Jesus*); the bottom is a representation of *Jesús de Gran Poder* (*Almighty Jesus*); and the middle is probably one of the most important sculptures in Ecuador, the original *La Virgen de Quito* (*The Virgin of Quito*), designed by Bernardo de Legarda. (*La Virgen de Quito* was the model for the huge winged angel on the Panecillo; p. 107.) Plan to spend between 30 minutes and an hour here.

Plaza San Francisco. © **02/2281-124.** Free admission. Mon–Sat 7am–noon and 3–5:30pm; Sun 7am–noon.

La Basílica del Voto Nacional   Work on the basilica began in 1883 and is still unfinished. Visitors are permitted inside this concrete marvel, which is modeled on Paris's Notre-Dame. The large central nave feels cold, with so much unfinished concrete, but if you look up, you'll see fabulous stained-glass works all around. Be sure to stop into the small side chapel, La Capilla de Sacramento, which features a mosaic tile floor, painted walls, columns, and a beautiful high altar of Mary. Most people, however, come here for the spectacular aerial views of the Old City and to see *La Virgen de Quito* in the distance. For the best views, you have to pay to take the elevator or climb the 90m (295 ft.) to the top of the towers. **Note:** The elevators don't always work, and the final "ladders" to the top are very narrow and quite steep. As you cross the bridge to enter the towers, look for the carved condors—the stonework is impressive and the condors appear ready to fly away. The basilica is also famous for its mystical gargoyles in the form of local Ecuadorean icons, such as pumas, monkeys, penguins, tortoises, and condors that guard the outsides of the church. There is a cafe on the third floor—a good place to catch your breath after taking in the breathtaking views. Plan to spend 30 to 40 minutes here.

Carchi 122, at the corner of Calle Venezuela. © **02/2289-428.** Admission $2 to visit the top of the towers. Daily 9am–5pm.

La Compañía de Jesús ★★★   This Jesuit church is one of the great baroque masterpieces in South America. All the work took 160 years to complete (1605–1765). The facade won't fail to impress you—the carvings are unbelievably detailed. Notice the Solomonic columns, symbolic of the Catholic doctrine that life's journey starts at the bottom (on Earth), but by following the holy path, it ends at heaven.

Almost every inch of the interior has intricate decorations. When you enter La Compañía, look for the symbols of the sun in both the main door to the church and the ceiling. The sun was a very important Inca symbol, and the Spanish thought that if they decorated the entryway with indigenous symbols, it might encourage local people to join the church. The walls and ceilings of La Compañía are typical of Moorish design—you will see only geometric shapes, no human forms. The building has been under renovation for the past several years, and some of the gold leaf on the ceiling and walls has been restored to its original luster. Natural sunlight and candlelight really bring out an angelic brilliance.

Concerts are sometimes held inside this church, and the acoustics and setting are haunting. If you happen to be in Quito on November 1 (Day of the Dead), you can also visit the catacombs here. Plan to spend between 30 minutes and an hour.

On García Moreno, near Sucre. © **02/2584-175.** www.ficj.org.ec. Admission $2. Mon–Fri 9:30am–5:30pm; Sat 9:30am–4pm; Sun 1:30–4:30pm.

La Plaza de la Independencia ★   Also called **La Plaza Grande,** this became the main square of Quito in the 16th century. Afraid the Incas might poison their water supply, the Spanish set up their own protected well here, and this plaza subsequently became the social center of town. It also served as a central market and bullfighting area. Today Old Town's main square is bordered by the Government Palace to the west, City Hall to the east, the Archbishop's Palace to the north, and the cathedral to the south.

The **Government Palace ★** is the most interesting building on the plaza. Don't be intimidated by the chain-link fence in front of the palace; everyone is welcome to walk inside the main area—just tell the guard that you're a curious tourist. Once you walk into the main entry area, you get a sense of the Spanish/Moorish architecture. Look straight ahead, and you'll see the impressive 1966 mural by Guayasamín, of Orellana discovering the Amazon.

City Hall is probably the least impressive structure on the plaza. It was built in 1952, in the Bauhaus style. The **Archbishop's Palace** was built in 1852; it was formerly the mayor's house. You can now walk inside and see the Andalusian- and Moorish-inspired courtyard; note that the floor of the courtyard is made from the spines of pigs. This area is now an informal crafts market. The **cathedral** dates from the 16th century. Inside is a good collection of art from the Quito School, including works by Caspicara and Manuel Samaniego. You can visit the cathedral Monday through Saturday from 6 to 10am. The square is most beautiful at night, when all the buildings are lighted up.

Plaza de la Independencia is bordered by Calle Venezuela to the east, García Moreno to the west, Chile to the north, and Espejo to the south. To get to the plaza from the Trole, get off at the Plaza Grande stop and walk 1 block on either Calle Espejo or Chile.

Colorful Quito

When a smallpox epidemic hit Quito in 1756, the government ordered all buildings be painted with white limestone, which was then believed to be a disinfectant. From that time until the late 1980s, all buildings in Quito were white. Everything changed when the mayor of Quito discovered that most Quiteños felt that Old Town was *too* white. Out came the art historians, who did extensive research, uncovering the true colors of all the colonial structures in the city. Now most of the buildings have been restored to their pre-1756 luster.

Museo Camilo Egas ★ Famed Ecuadorean *indigenista* (indigenist) painter Camilo Egas is featured in this small but striking museum. Housed in a colonial-era home with massive adobe walls and a beautiful central courtyard, the collection features a broad selection of Egas's work. Part of the international vanguard of painters of the early 20th century, Egas spent time in New York, Rome, Madrid, and Paris, where his works were influenced by contemporary trends and styles—expressionism, surrealism, cubism, and abstract expressionism. He knew and hung out with Picasso, Braque, Matisse, and de Chirico. Through it all, his primary subject matter was the Andean indigenous peoples of Ecuador and neighboring countries. Give yourself 45 minutes at this museum.

Venezuela 1302, at the corner of Esmeraldas. ℂ **02/2572-012.** Admission $1. Tues–Fri 9am–5pm; Sat–Sun and holidays 10am–4pm.

Museo Fray Pedro Gocial (San Francisco Museum and Convent) This museum, attached to the San Francisco church (p. 107), allows visitors to see the convent as well as the church's choir. Tour guides also will show you some of the pieces of the church's fantastic colonial art collection. I highly recommend a visit to the choir. Here you can see the church's original wood ceiling, as well as a beautiful wood-inlaid "lyric box" that was used to hold up the music for the singers in the choir. You will also experience Manuel Chile Caspicara's famous crucifix, which dates back to 1650–70. It is said that Caspicara tied a model to a cross to learn how to realistically represent Christ's facial and body expressions; the glass eyes are piercing. Plan to spend 45 minutes here.

Plaza San Francisco, Cuenca 477 y Sucre. ℂ **02/2281-124.** Admission $2. Mon–Fri 9am–1pm and 2–6pm; Sat 9am–6pm; Sun 9am–1pm. Visits only by guided tour, which leave on an as-needed basis. English-language tours are available.

Museo Histórico Militar/"Casa de Sucre" This museum will appeal to both history and military buffs. The house dates from the 17th century, but the house's namesake, the Independence hero Mariscal Antonio José de Sucre, lived here from 1828 until his death in 1830. On the ground floor, in the Sala de Armas, you can see swords, pistols, and bayonets that all belonged to him. There is also a stable with old-fashioned saddles on display. On the second floor, you can visit the original brick kitchen with two cold storage rooms. The *archivo* is where Sucre received visitors; the desk is original. Sucre's bedroom doesn't contain his original bed, but look at the walls—you'll notice that they have slats, which allowed Sucre to move the walls of his room closer together in order to preserve heat. Most of the tours are in Spanish, but even if you can't understand your guide, you can get a good picture of what it must have been like to live in Old Town in the 19th century. Plan on spending about 45 minutes here.

Venezuela 573, at the corner of Sucre. © **02/2952-860.** Admission $1. Tues-Fri 8am-4pm; Sat 9am-1pm.

In New Town

Museo Mindalae ★★ This excellent museum features five floors of displays dedicated to the traditional arts and crafts of Ecuador. Baskets, weavings, musical instruments, tools, weapons, pottery, clothing, and more are shown within their historical, geographic, and cultural contexts. There's a heavy emphasis on works from the Amazon basin tribes, although Andean and coastal communities are also represented. A central column of sunlight passes through the center of all five floors, through heavy, clear Plexiglas inlays in the floor. On the top floor, you'll find a representation of a shamanic ceremonial space. Most display explanations are in English, French, and Spanish. And the informative videos shown are available in English (but you may have to ask for them to switch languages). This museum has an excellent gift shop, where you can buy contemporary examples of many of the artifacts on display. Plan to spend between 45 minutes and an hour here.

Reina Victoria N26-166 y La Niña. © **02/2230-609.** www.sinchisacha.org. Admission $3 adults; $1.50 children. Mon-Sat 9:30am-5:30pm; Sun 10:30am-4:30pm.

Museo Nacional del Banco Central del Ecuador ★★ ☺ This huge and enormously rich museum offers visitors an opportunity to learn about the evolution of Ecuador—its human and natural history, as well as its art. When you see all the artifacts, archaeological finds, and works of art displayed chronologically, you get a profound sense of the country not commonly found in museums that focus on one era or type of exhibit. *Tip:* To see everything in this massive museum, you really need at least 4 hours; I recommend taking a guided tour.

If you visit the museum from beginning to end, you will start at the **Archaeological Gallery.** On display are artifacts dating from 11,000 B.C., as well as dioramas, which explain the beliefs and lifestyle of a wide range of pre-Columbian and pre-Inca peoples. One of the most striking exhibits here is a Cañari mummy, though the **Golden Court** ★★ is my favorite exhibit. Because many indigenous groups worshipped the sun, they used gold to create masks, chest decorations, and figurines to represent the sun. The fine details are really amazing—many of the pieces in this gallery are a sight to behold.

You can see the influence of the sun and the veneration of women in the work displayed in the **Colonial Art Gallery,** which contains pieces from 1534 to 1820. Much of the colonial art here combines the rich ornamentation popular in pre-Columbian art with the severe polychrome style of European art. You'll probably also notice that a lot of pieces in this gallery are quite bloody and gory—an attempt to scare the indigenous people into believing in the Christian God. I find the colonial-era art is displayed better here—with better lighting and explanations—than at Museo Fray Pedro Gocial (see above).

After independence from Spain, Ecuadorean artists began to eschew religious symbolism. In the **Republican Art Gallery,** you can see this transition. Instead of gory religious art and paintings of the Virgin, for example, you'll find lifelike portraits of Ecuador's independence heroes. One of my favorites is *Retrato de Simón Bolívar (Portrait of Simón Bolívar).*

On a whole different plane is the **Contemporary Art Gallery,** where you'll find everything from peaceful landscapes from the early 20th century to Oswaldo Guayasamín's tortured and angry portraits, as well as a wide range of modernist works by prominent Ecuadorean artists such as Pilar Bustos, Camilo Egas, Theo Constante, and Enrique Tabara. In addition to the above galleries, the museum hosts temporary art exhibits. And in the same building, there is a **Museum of Musical Instruments,** which is a lot of fun if you're traveling with kids.

Av. Patria, btw. 6 de Diciembre and 12 de Octubre. © **02/2223-258.** Admission $2 adults, $1 students and children. Mon–Fri 9am–5pm; Sat–Sun and holidays 10am–4pm. Free multilingual guided tours are available throughout the day, and most of the displays are in both Spanish and English.

North of New Town

The following two nearby attractions are expected to one day be joined in a relatively massive museum, workshop, and cultural center.

Capilla del Hombre (Chapel of Mankind) ★   A few blocks from the Fundación Guayasamín (see below), this impressive structure is in many ways the culmination of the work and dreams of Ecuador's great modern artist, Oswaldo Guayasamín. Guayasamín, who died in 1999 at the age of 90, had wanted to open the museum on the first day of the new century, but financial problems and construction delays postponed its opening until November 2002. Dedicated to "man's progress through art," the architecturally intriguing, nonsectarian chapel houses many of the artist's paintings, murals, and sculptures, as well parts of his personal collection of colonial art, archaeological finds, and contemporary art. Inca and indigenous mythological beliefs are incorporated into the design of the building, which is three levels tall and uses the number 3 for various motifs and architectural elements. The eternal flame in the chapel's altar is dedicated to those who died defending human rights (or the rights of man, which explains the name of the museum). Guayasamín himself is buried here, beneath a tree he planted, which has been renamed El Arbol de la Vida (The Tree of Life). Allot yourself about an hour to view the museum.

Corner of Mariano Calvache and Lorenzo Chávez, Bellavista. © **02/2448-492.** www.guayasamin.org. Admission $3, or $5 combined with the Fundación Guayasamín. Tues–Sun 10am–5:30pm.

Fundación Guayasamín ★★★   This powerful museum displays the works and art collections of Oswaldo Guayasamín, one of Ecuador's most famous artists. The museum has three sections. **El Museo Arqueológico (Archaeology Museum)** houses Guayasamín's collection of pre-Columbian art. The artist once said, "I paint from 3,000 or 5,000 years ago." It's interesting to see both his collection and his inspiration. Keep an eye out for the sitting shamans and tribal chiefs, and the jugs with the intricately carved faces.

Across the courtyard is **Museo de Arte Moderno (Museum of Modern Art)** ★, which displays Guayasamín's own work. Most impressive is his art from 1964–84 entitled *La Edad de la Ira (The Age of Anger)*, which represents his dismay over violence in the world, and in South America, in particular. One of the most dramatic pieces is the three-paneled *Homenaje a Víctor Jara (Homage to Víctor Jara)*. Jara was a Chilean guitarist and Communist Party supporter who was tortured and killed by General Pinochet's army during the 1973 military junta. Military officers cut off his hands to try to stop his protest songs, but it took a machine gun to silence him. The images of a skeleton playing a guitar have a tremendous impact.

In **Museo de Arte Colonial,** you can view Guayasamín's incredible collection of colonial art. The majority of the pieces are from the Quito School; they give viewers a good idea of the art created by the first inhabitants of Quito. The collection contains more than 80 crucifixes.

There is also a nice patio (with a great view) and a cafe on the premises. It doesn't take more than an hour to explore the whole museum. Take a taxi here (about $3–$4) from the heart of New Town).

Calle José Bosmediano 543, Bellavista (Batán). ℂ **02/2465-265.** www.guayasamin.org. Admission $3, or $5 combined with the Capilla del Hombre. Mon–Fri 10am–5pm.

OUTDOOR ACTIVITIES & SPECTATOR SPORTS

Quito is a big, sprawling city, so it's hard to do anything truly outdoorsy within the city limits. The large, central Parque La Carolina is the best spot for outdoor sports and activities. Your best bet, though, is to travel an hour or two outside the city, where you can hike, climb, trek, white-water raft, and mountain bike. Also see "Side Trips from Quito" (p. 121) and chapter 4.

BICYCLING ★★   Quito is not particularly amenable to bicycles. However, all this changes on Sundays, when over 10km (6¼ miles) of main arteries are closed off to vehicular traffic and converted into a Ciclovia. Starting around the southern bus station Terminal Terrestre Quitumbe, the traffic-free path runs all the way north beyond the airport, utilizing major avenues such as avenidas Venezuela and Guayaquil (through Old Town), Amazonas (through New Town), and even parts of the Pan-American highway (near the airport). For more information, and even to rent a bicycle, check in with the folks at **Ciclopolis** (ℂ 02/2901-920; www.ciclopolis.ec) or one of the mountain-biking tour operators listed in the Active Vacation Planner.

BULLFIGHTING   The once-popular and -proud tradition of bullfighting is now very rarely performed publicly in Quito, except during the Fiestas de Quito, the first week of December. Bullfights are held at **Plaza de Toros** (ℂ 02/3161-660; www.plazabelmonte.com), north of the intersection of Avenida Amazonas and 10 de Agosto. Although it gets little use, the bullring is rather spectacular. Built in 1960, it can hold 15,000 (and it's usually full for a bullfight). Tickets can be picked up at the bullring and run $2 to $15.

JOGGING   The downtown Parque La Carolina is your best bet for jogging. This large, central city park has several jogging paths, and you'll usually find plenty of fellow joggers around. The much smaller Parque El Ejido is another option.

SOCCER   Soccer, or *fútbol*, is the principal spectator sport in Ecuador. Soccer season in Quito lasts March through December. Most important games take place at **Estadio Olímpico Atahualpa** (ℂ 02/2224-410), on 6 de Diciembre and Avenida Naciones Unidas. Game day is usually Saturday or Sunday. General admission seats cost $2; the good seats go for $10 to $15. You can buy tickets at the stadium on the day of the game. To get there, take the Ecovía trolley line to the Estadio stop.

TENNIS   If you're not staying at a hotel with its own courts, Parque La Carolina open-air public courts are your best bet. They are free of charge and awarded on a first-come, first-served basis. They fill up very fast on weekends and tend to be busy on weekdays as well.

SHOPPING

While the majority of Ecuador's most famous and sought-after shopping occurs outside Quito—in Otavalo and Cuenca, and at small Andean markets—you can still find ample opportunities for successful and rewarding shopping in the capital.

THE SHOPPING SCENE As in the rest of the country, the shopping scene in Quito mainly consists of local handicrafts (alpaca sweaters, tapestries, figurines, pottery, hats, and jewelry) made by indigenous Ecuadorean artists. Some of the stuff you'll find is mass-produced or of poor quality. But if you know where to go (see below), there are some great shops that support local indigenous groups. You'll also find more high-end shops here than in other parts of the country.

MARKETS While nothing compares to the various weekly local markets held in towns and cities across the Andes, or to the world-famous market in Otavalo (p. 122), a couple of longstanding markets are worth hitting in Quito, especially if you can't visit any of the others.

In New Town, **Mercado Artesanal La Mariscal (Mariscal Artisans Market)** is a tight warren of permanent booths selling all sorts of arts, crafts, and clothing. You should definitely be picky here—there are a lot of mass-produced and mediocre wares for sale. But if you shop carefully, you can find plenty of high-quality goods. You can bargain a little, but not too much. Located on Jorge Washington, between Reina Victoria and Juan León Mera, it's open daily from around 10am until 7pm. A similar option is available on weekends all along the north end of **Parque El Ejido.**

MODERN MALLS Much of the local shopping scene has shifted to large megamalls. Modern multilevel affairs with cineplexes, food courts, and international brand-name stores are becoming ubiquitous. The biggest and most modern of these, called *centros comerciales* in Spanish, include **Centro Comercial El Jardín** (℃ 02/2262-350), at Avenida Amazonas and Avenida de la República; **Centro Comercial Iñaquito** (℃ 02/2252-510; www.cci.com.ec), at Avenida Amazonas and Naciones Unidas; and **Centro Comercial Quicentro** (℃ 02/2464-526; www.quicentro.com), at Avenida 6 de Diciembre and Avenida Naciones Unidas. Although they lack the charm of small shops and galleries found around Quito, they are a reasonable option for one-stop shopping; most contain at least one or two art galleries and crafts shops, along with a large supermarket, which is always the best place to stock up on coffee, local liquors, and other nonperishable foodstuffs.

Shopping A to Z
ART GALLERIES
Centro Cultural Artes This small, stylish gallery has rotating exhibits of modern Ecuadorean and other Latin American artists. They often host workshops and classes. Veintimilla 560 y 6 de Diciembre. ℃ **02/2548-494.**

Marsu Arte This high-end gallery carries an extensive collection of Ecuadorian and Latin American artists. The main gallery is listed here, but they also have storefront galleries in the JW Marriott and Swissôtel Quito hotels. Av. 6 de Diciembre 4475 y Portugal. ℃ **02/2458-616.** www.marsuarte.com.

BOOKS
Café Libro ★★ This is my favorite bookstore in Ecuador. They have an extensive collection of books in Spanish and English, with loads of books on natural history and tropical biology, as well as a fabulous collection of Ecuadorean and Latin American

literature. Poetry readings, lectures, and concerts are often held here. Leonidas Plaza N23—56, btw. Wilson and Veintimilla. ℰ **02/2503-214.** www.cafelibro.com.

Confederate Books Specializing in English-language books, this place buys and sells just about anything you may want in English. It offers the largest selection of English-language reading, especially novels and easy-reading books for travelers. Calama 410 y Juan León Mera. ℰ **02/2527-890.**

Libri Mundi Similar to Café Libro for quality, quantity, and selection, this is another excellent bookstore in the Mariscal district. Housed in a rambling old home, it stays open through siesta. Juan León Mera N23—83 y Wilson. ℰ **02/2521-606.** www.librimundi.com.

HANDICRAFTS

Andinarte This is one of the better souvenir stores in colonial Old Town. Located in the busy Pasaje Arzobispal shopping center, just off Plaza Grande, you'll find everything from T-shirts and alpaca weavings to wood and *tagua* carvings. Pasaje Arzobispal Shopping Center, Venezuela N5—41 y Mejía. ℰ **02/2512-513.**

Galería Latina Like Olga Fisch (see below), Galería Latina specializes in high-quality handicrafts. You'll find great pottery and a nice selection of alpaca sweaters, in addition to silver and gold jewelry, textiles, and even some antiques. Also open Sunday. Juan León Mera N23-69 (833) y Veintemilla. ℰ **02/2540-380.** www.galerialatina-quito.com.

Olga Fisch Folklore ★★ As an artist, Olga Fisch had a very keen eye, and she worked with a variety of Ecuadorean indigenous groups to produce carpets, figurines, jewelry, and decorative arts that were grounded in tradition yet also contemporary. This store carries high-end art, crafts, and clothing, and the prices reflect the difference in quality that you'll find between the offerings here and those at the street markets. A nonprofit museum here supports the development of these arts in indigenous communities. I suggest that you visit the museum first to get an idea of the local artisan traditions—it will help you understand what you are looking at in the showroom. In addition to the main shop, Olga Fisch has several other storefronts around Quito, including inside the Quicentro mall, as well as at Hotel Patio Andaluz (p. 95), in Puerto Ayora, Galapagos, and inside both the Guayaquil and Quito airports. It's open during siesta. Av. Colón E10-53 y Caamaño. ℰ **02/2541-315.** www.olgafisch.com.

Tianguez ★★ Tianguez showcases products similar to those you'll find at Olga Fisch and Galería Latina, including masks, ceramics, and pieces inspired by pre-Columbian artisan traditions. *Tianguez* means "market" in Quichua, and it's an especially appropriate name because the store is housed in a sprawling, mazelike old market in Old Town under Iglesia de San Francisco. It feels like the catacombs in Rome. A not-for-profit organization, Sinchi Sacha, runs Tianguez and Museo Mindalac (p. 111) and supports indigenous and *mestizo* artisan groups. Plaza San Francisco. ℰ **02/2570-240.** www.sinchisacha.org.

JEWELRY

In addition to the places listed below, you'll find excellent arty jewelry for sale at Fundación Guayasamín (see above).

Ag Joyería Featuring a broad selection of silver and stone jewelry from across Ecuador and other Latin American countries, this place also features antiques and other craft items. Juan León Mera 614 y Reina Victoria. ℰ **02/2550-276.**

Ari Gallery ★★ This place carries a collection of handmade original pieces in both silver and gold, some based on traditional indigenous motifs, and others

completely modern. Bolívar Oe6–23 y Benalcázar, Plaza San Francisco. ✆ **02/2284-157.** www.
ushinajewellery.com.

LEATHER GOODS

Aramis   A small local chain, these folks carry a range of high-quality locally produced leather works and leather wear. In addition to the main shop listed here, there
are outlets in the Centro Comercial Espiral, on Avenida Amazonas and Jorge Washington. Av. Amazonas N24–142 y Mariscal Foch. ✆ **02/2542-559.**

MUSIC

You'll see CDs of Ecuadorean pop and traditional Andean folk music for sale at many
gift shops around Quito. You'll also see hawkers selling CDs on the streets around the
city, though most of them are poor-quality bootlegs. For the best selection, head to
the local outlet of **Tower Records** (✆ **02/2920-415**), in the Centro Comercial
Quicentro.

PANAMA HATS

Ortega P. & Hijos ★   This is the local outlet for renowned Cuenca hat manufacturer Ortega and Sons. If you aren't able to get to Cuenca or to the other traditional
Panama hat–making cities of Montecristi and Jipijapa, this is where you should pick
up your *superfino*. If you really wait until the last minute, you can visit their outlet at
the airport, but the selection there is reduced, and the prices inflated. Isabel la Católica
N24–100 y Madrid. ✆ **02/2526-715.** www.homeroortega.com.

TEXTILES

Magic Hand Crafts ★   With an excellent selection of alpaca sweaters, this is the
place to come if you're looking for something better than street-market quality. These
folks work directly with weavers and producers, and have some unique designs you
won't find elsewhere. Juan León Mera N24–237 y Cordero. ✆ **02/2542-345.**

QUITO AFTER DARK

From elegant opera performances to dirt-cheap all-you-can-drink bars, Quito offers a
range of nocturnal activities for visitors and locals alike. The Mariscal sector, the hub
for partying and dining out, has restaurants and "here today, gone tomorrow" pubs and
clubs pumping out popular salsa and infectious reggaetón beats until daybreak. To
find out what's going on while you're in town, pick up a copy of *Quito Cultura,* a
monthly Spanish-language events guide that includes theater listings, concerts, and
general cultural events. You can often find this small magazine in hotel lobbies or at
the nearest tourist information office. For English listings, visit **www.quito.com.ec**.

   In 2001, the city government issued a law stating that all bars and clubs must close
at midnight on weekdays and 2am on weekends. But this is only sporadically
enforced, and many clubs have found ways around it, including declaring themselves
private parties.

   Warning: Remember that, at night, Quito can be quite dangerous, especially near
the bars and clubs. Take a cab, even if it's only for a few blocks—and be sure it's a
registered, official taxi.

The Performing Arts

Quito has a relatively important performing-arts scene, and the majority of theaters
are located in Old Town. Performances include traditional theater pieces, political
satire, ballets, dance shows, classic opera, and comedies.

The **National Symphonic Orchestra** (✆ 02/2502-814; www.sinfonicanacional. gov.ec) performs weekly in different venues around town, including some colonial churches. Every Wednesday at 7:30pm, **Ballet Andino Humanizarte** (✆ 02/2226-116) performs traditional Andean dances at the Fundación Cultural Humanizarte, on Leonidas Plaza N24–226 between Lizardo García and Baquerizo Moreno. **Ballet Folclórico Nacional Jacchigua** ★ (✆ 02/2952-025; www.jacchiguaesecuador. com) performs traditional dances and songs on Wednesday and Friday nights at 7:30pm at the Teatro Demetrio Aguilera Malta in Casa de la Cultura Ecuatoriana. Tickets cost $30 per person and can be purchased directly on their website, via **Metropolitan Touring** (✆ 02/2988-200; www.metropolitan-touring.com) or through your hotel tour desk or concierge.

The restored **Teatro Nacional Sucre** ★★ (✆ 02/2951-661; www.teatrosucre. com), in Old Town's Plaza del Teatro Manabí N8–131, between Guayaquil and Flores, first opened its doors in 1867; it's Quito's most popular theater and offers a varied and exciting events program including contemporary theater, ballet, electronic-music performances, and opera. Free concerts and street shows put on by the theater frequently take place just outside, on Plaza del Teatro. Despite being almost completely destroyed by a fire in 1999, the restored neoclassic **Teatro Bolívar** (✆ 02/2583-788; www.teatrobolivar.org), on Pasaje Espejo 847 and Guayaquil in the Old Town, continues to host and produce a range of cultural events, including theater, dance, music, and Latin American cinema.

Another important outlet for the performing arts is **Casa de la Cultura Ecuatoriana** (✆ 02/2902-272; www.cce.org.ec), on 6 de Diciembre N16–224 and Patria. Founded in the 1940s by writer, politician, and diplomat Benjamin Carrión ("If we can't be a military or economic power, we can, instead, be a cultural power fed by our rich traditions"), the Casa offers an extensive repertoire of events, including rock concerts, art exhibitions, and performances by the National Symphonic Orchestra. It also houses one of the city's most important museums, **Museo Nacional del Banco Central del Ecuador** (p. 111), which contains important archaeological artifacts, as well as an extensive collection of Ecuadorean traditional and contemporary artwork.

The **Teatro del CCI,** at CCI Iñaquito, Avenida Amazonas on 6 de Diciembre N16–224 and Patria, is a fine example of a modern theater with the latest technology in sound and lighting; it offers up a mix of contemporary dance, theater, and music.

Quito is a popular destination among international artists. Recent concerts have featured Colombian star Shakira and pop group the Jonas Brothers. The majority of large blockbuster concerts are held at **Coliseo Rumiñahui** (Ladrón de Guevara and Toledo), **Casa de la Cultura Ecuatoriana** (see above), **Plaza de Toros** (see "Bull-fighting," above), or the much larger **Estadio Olímpico Atahualpa** (see "Soccer," above). Check local papers or www.tuboleta.com.ec for listings and ticket outlets.

For a more mellow vibe, check out **Casa de la Música** (✆ 02/2261-965; www. casadelamusica.ec), at Valderrama and Avenida Mariana de Jesús. It hosts traditional, folkloric, classical, and jazz concerts and recitals, including performances by visiting international artists and orchestras.

Quito's cultural panorama changes quite dramatically during the first week of December, when **Fiestas de Quito,** celebrating the founding of the capital, transforms the city into one huge party. Festivities include profoundly Spanish traditions such as bullfighting in Plaza de Toros and flamenco dancing. Copious amounts of alcohol consumption accompany live music in *chivas* (open-air trucks with traditional bands carrying beer-swigging partygoers through the city streets); and the city comes to a standstill with never-ending street parades.

For the duration of August, Quito is also host to a popular arts festival offering a substantial list of art exhibitions, theater, and dance in cultural institutions all over the capital. Almost all performing arts events are done in Spanish. For 3 days in late September, there's **Quitofest** (www.quitofest.com), a free festival of rock, pop, reggae, ska, and alternative music, featuring large outdoor concerts at Parque Itchimbía, overlooking the city.

LIVE MUSIC

Quito has an active and vibrant live music scene. A number of bars and clubs regularly have bands and musicians performing. The city's scene, popular with local musicians trying to gain a larger following, is varied and includes jazz, salsa, pop, rock, metal, and alternative, among other musical styles.

A good place to look for live music ranging from jazz to rock is the restaurant and bar **El Pobre Diablo ★** (② 02/2235-194; www.elpobrediablo.com), in La Floresta on the corner of Isabel La Católica N24–274 and Galavis. Some of Ecuador's most influential bands and musicians include Muscaria, Convicto, Descomunal, Fausto Mino, Sudakaya, Geraldo Moran, Sal y Mileto, Luis Rueda, Juan Fernando Velasco, and Hector "El Napo" Napolitano.

The Club, Music & Dance Scene

There is certainly no shortage of places to let loose on the dance floor in Quito. Most popular among Quiteños are salsa, electronic, and reggaetón rhythms. You'll be harder pressed to find a decent selection of rock, alternative, or jazz clubs.

Quiteños and visitors alike mainly flock to the Mariscal sector to check out the capital's nightlife. With a range of restaurants, bars, and clubs, Mariscal is certainly Quito's hottest party spot. The majority of clubs are located around the streets Calama, Mariscal Foch, and Reina Victoria, or a few blocks north around Pinta and Santa María. In addition to the places listed below, another favorite among partygoers is **Cats** (② 02/2566-461), Lizardo García E7–56 and Diego de Almagro, a happening spot pumping out international dance and techno with a small cover charge. Thursday night there's live Cuban music and dancing at **La Bodeguita de Cuba ★** (② 02/2542-476), Reina Victoria 1721 and La Pinta.

Acid Lounge ★   Local DJs spin electronic, chillout, house, and drum and bass tunes here most nights. Guest DJs play on Fridays with a $5 cover charge, and Saturdays feature a live band playing acid jazz, followed by an open jam session, $2 cuba libres, and no cover charge. Av. Orellana E9–26 y Pinzón. ② 09/5834-262.

Blues ★   One of Quito's most popular venues, this is a relatively large retro-style club playing classic rock and contemporary dance tracks. Weekends are mainly dedicated to live DJs spinning electronic dance tunes. Depending on the night, cover charges range from $10 to $15. República 476 y Pradera. ② 02/2223-206. www.bluesestodo.com.

Flashback ★★   This is Quito's classiest and most popular retro joint, with '80s and '90s tunes dominating the playlists. The crowd here is a mix of young students and slightly older professionals, the dress code is on the smarter-casual side, and the locals absolutely rave about this place. Cover can cost up to $30 including an open bar. Av. Gonzalez Suarez N27–185 y Muros. ② 02/3226-922. www.flashback.com.ec.

La Bunga   This is a hip party spot with a medium-size dance floor and a varied music selection, including anything from Latino rhythms to rock, ska, hip-hop and cumbia. Guys are always charged the $5 admission fee, while women get in free before 11pm. Francisco de Orellana 899 y Yánez Pinzón. ② 02/2904-196.

PLAZA FOCH: GROUND zero IN MARISCAL

The heart and soul of Quito's nightlife, the Mariscal district has been dubbed "Gringolandia" by those who flock to the area to drink and dance the night away with the city's tourists and resident foreigners. Plaza Foch (also known as Plaza Quinde)—which has been transformed from a seedy, run-down intersection to a pristine plaza—is the area's star attraction. Its excellent selection of bars and international restaurants targets visitors in search of more upscale nightspots. In addition to hitting the bars, clubs, and restaurants right on the plaza, you can use the plaza as a great starting place for a bar or club crawl through the rest of the Mariscal district. Plaza Foch frequently hosts free, open-air live shows, including performances by rock bands, dance groups, and percussion and jazz ensembles. With alfresco dining at several different spots, under tall heater lamps to keep the Quito nighttime chill at bay, the funky European-style Plaza Foch is especially packed on weekends, so arrive early to get a good outdoor seat. The following are a couple of my favorite spots on the plaza.

Oceana Club Lounge ★   A contemporary lounge, Oceana is all the rage with Quito's young, restless, and chic. Cover charge is $5 on weekdays and $10 on weekends; free entry for women before 11:30pm. Corner of Reina Victoria and Joaquin Pinto. ℭ 02/2906-594. www.oceanaecuador.com.

Seseribó ★   This is *the* club for salsa lovers. Probably the best and most popular *salsateca* in Quito, Seseribó pumps out infectious Latino beats in a packed party atmosphere. A cover charge of $6 to $10 is common. Veintimilla 352 y 12 de Octubre, basement of Edificio Girón. ℭ 02/2563-598.

Azuca Latin Bistro ★★   In addition to being a top-notch Nuevo Latino restaurant on the plaza, this place has one of Quito's best bar and club scenes. A variety of mojitos and contemporary cocktails are on offer, and there's usually a live band or DJ. Just next door, and up a flight of stairs, you'll find their very popular sister bar, Azuca Beach, which oozes Caribbean-style vibes and even features a sand-covered floor where you can kick off your shoes. Plaza Foch and Reina Victoria. Azuca Bistro: ℭ 02/2907-164. www.azucabistro.com. **Azuca Beach:** ℭ 02/2550-825. www.azucabeach.com.

Coffee Tree ★   With front-row seats of the plaza's frequently staged live performances, and a big screen showing all the important *fútbol* games, this cafe/bar is extremely popular among locals and tourists alike. Two-for-one offers change every day, the drinks list is extensive, and the menu is pretty good for bar food. Try their ice-cold Pilsener on tap. They are open 24 hours on weekends. Plaza Foch and Reina Victoria. ℭ 02/2565-521. www.quitocoffeecompany.com.

The Bar Scene

Catering to all tastes, Quito's bar scene is extensive, offering options ranging from British-style beer pubs to sophisticated wine bars, and just about everything in between. The majority of places are situated in the Mariscal district. The renovated Plaza Foch is generally targeted toward those in search of classier venues (see "Plaza Foch: Ground Zero in Mariscal," above), while the majority of other bars, from funky cafes to laid-back bars, are located in and around the streets Calama, Reina Victoria, and Juan León Mera. With such a variety of options in one area, the Mariscal is perfect for a pub crawl, although it can sometimes get a little dodgy after dark, so it's advisable not to go alone. Bars usually charge a cover only if there is live music or another type of special event. The line between a bar and a club in Quito is sometimes a little blurry. Many bars pump up the volume as the night goes on and become happening party spots.

Bungalow 6 The best thing about this bar-cum-club is that it frequently hosts live music, featuring some of Quito's best reggae artists such as Alma Rasta. Apart from that, this is a colorful party spot playing a selection of contemporary and classic tunes with a small dance floor, busy bar, and vibrant atmosphere. Corner of Calama and Diego de Almagro. ✆ **08/5194-530.** www.bungalow6ecuador.com.

Finn McCool's One of Quito's more popular Irish pubs, this traditional joint is frequented by locals, expats, and passing travelers alike. To spice things up, they hold regular quiz nights, show sports on a large screen, and serve up hearty grub, including stews, bangers and mash, and fish and chips. Diego de Almagro N26–64 y Joaquin Pinto. ✆ **02/2564-953.** www.irishpubquito.com.

Ghoz A cozy bar playing rock from the '60s, '70s, and '80s, Ghoz offers nine pool tables, three foosball tables, and checkers, chess, backgammon, Jenga, and board games. La Niña 425 y Reina Victoria. ✆ **02/2556-255.** www.ghoz.com.

Naranjilla Mecánica ★★ The name of this club translates as "Clockwork Orange." Lavishly decorated and housing permanent art exhibitions, this is a great place for indulging in delicious cocktails while lounging on the comfy sofas and beanbag chairs. They play ambient grooves. Tamayo N22–43 y Veintimilla. ✆ **02/2526-468.** http://lanaranjillamecanica.blogspot.com.

Red Hot Chili Peppers ★ Although this is principally a Mexican restaurant renowned for its massive and mouthwatering fajitas, by night it is also a small and relatively laid-back bar serving the best frozen margaritas in the city. Foch 713 y Juan León Mera. ✆ **02/2557-575.**

Reina Victoria Pub ★★ As Quito's most authentic British-style pub, with a fireplace, pool table, and dartboard, Reina Victoria serves good old traditional pub grub and beer on tap in a genuinely comfy atmosphere. Check out their British-style pub quiz held every Wednesday. Reina Victoria 530 y Roca. ✆ **02/2226-369.**

Turtle's Head ★ Boasting the best beer in town, with various options on tap, this British-American–style pub has its own on-site brewery, pool table, darts, and table soccer, as well as tasty pub food—ideal for homesick British or American visitors. La Niña 626 y Juan León Mera. ✆ **02/2565-544.**

The Gay & Lesbian Scene

Although homosexuals are guaranteed protections and rights under the Ecuadorean constitution, attitudes toward the gay and lesbian community here still lag behind those of North America and Europe, principally owing to Ecuador's being a staunchly Catholic country. As a result, gay and lesbian nightlife is not particularly well publicized, although it's by no means nonexistent. Quito has a few homosexual hot spots, including those listed below. For a detailed lowdown and the latest happenings on Quito's gay and lesbian scene, check out **www.quitogay.net** or **http://quito.queercity.info**.

Matrioshka ★★ As one of Quito's best-established openly gay clubs, Matrioshka has a great party vibe and is one of Quito's better discos. This is a popular party spot for gays and lesbians, as well as for straight revelers. Cover charge is around $5, with a drink included. Pinto 376 y Juan León Mera. ℭ **08/4898-695.**

Tercer Milenio ★ Popular among the younger gay crowd, and reputedly a good pick-up joint, Tercer Milenio (formerly known as Bohemio, and often called El Hueco by locals) is Quito's longest-standing gay club. It pumps out popular dance tunes with a good party atmosphere. Baquedano 188 y 6 de Diciembre. No phone.

Cinemas

Quito has its fill of mainstream cinemas, as well as one or two alternative picture houses. Hollywood blockbusters, usually in their original English with Spanish subtitles, are most popular among moviegoers, as is Latin American cinema mainly consisting of Argentinean, Chilean, and Mexican productions. Two multiplexes, **Multicines,** Avenida Amazonas and Naciones Unidas, inside the CCI shopping mall (ℭ **02/3802-195;** www.multicines.com.ec), and **Cinemark,** Avenida de la República and América (ℭ **02/2260-301;** www.cinemark.com.ec), are your best bets for new releases. If alternative cinema is more your cup of tea, check out the excellent **Ocho y Medio,** Valladolid N24–353 and Vizcaya, near La Floresta (ℭ **02/2904-720;** www.ochoymedio.net), Quito's only independent picture house showing *cine arte,* classics, Latin American cinema, foreign films, and musical and dance productions. It also hosts the Eurocine film festival every May. Ocho y Medio also publishes the country's most extensive self-titled cinema guide, free of charge every month.

Casinos

Gambling is legal in Ecuador, but only in hotels, and the majority of casinos operate a free-entrance, free-drink policy. The city's most popular casinos are **Hotel Casino Plaza Caicedo,** Av. Shyris 1757 and Naciones Unidas (ℭ **02/2445-305;** www. hotelcasinoplaza.com), with 176 slots and 25 table games; **Hotel Casino Hilton Colón Quito,** Avenida Patria and Amazonas (ℭ **02/2501-919**), with 91 slots and 12 table games; and **Casino Montecarlo,** on Roca E4–122 and Amazonas (ℭ **02/2994-000;** www.casinomontecarlo.ec), which is located inside Hotel Mercure and is open 24 hours Thursday through Saturday.

SIDE TRIPS FROM QUITO

The legion of Quito-based tour agencies and just about every hotel desk can arrange any number of tour options, such as trips to Cotopaxi National Park. The most popular day trips out of Quito are probably to **La Mitad del Mundo** (see below and chapter 6), **Cotopaxi National Park** (see below and chapter 7), and the **market in Otavalo** (see below and chapter 6).

If you don't go with your hotel's tour desk or in-house agency, I recommend **Metropolitan Touring** ★★ (ℭ **02/2988-200;** www.metropolitan-touring.com), **Safari Ecuador** ★ (ℭ **02/2552-505;** www.safari.com.ec), and **Surtrek** ★★ (ℭ **866/978-7398** in the U.S. and Canada, or 02/2500-530 in Ecuador; www. surtrek.com).

Guided Tours & Adventures

In addition to the tours and adventures listed below, see chapter 4 for detailed information on **mountain biking, bird-watching, white-water rafting, climbing and**

trekking, and **horseback riding.** In each section, you will find recommended operators. In just about every case, you will find a Quito-based tour operator with day trips you can participate in for all of these different adventure sports and activities.

COTOPAXI NATIONAL PARK Almost every travel agency in Quito offers some sort of day trip to Cotopaxi National Park. Most are only moderately strenuous and feature a hike from the parking lot to the *refugio*. You definitely will *not* have time to hike up to the summit. If you want to hike, horseback ride, or mountain-bike around Cotopaxi National Park, be sure to ask your organizer what exactly the tour includes. A whole host of options are available. Most tours include lunch at a typical hacienda or inside the park at Tambopaxi. ***Note:*** On almost all tours, you will have to pay an additional $10 national park fee. Guided tours to Cotopaxi run $40 to $90 per person, depending on group size, length of tour, and other factors.

Alternatively, you can organize a day trip to Cotopaxi on your own. You can hire a taxi in Quito for $60 to $90 round-trip. Once you reach the parking lot (1½ hr. from Quito), you can then hike up to the *refugio* or glacier at your own pace while the taxi waits for you. This is my preferred way of visiting Cotopaxi. For more information, see chapter 7.

OTAVALO MARKET Though Saturday is the main market day, most Quito-based operators offer daily excursions to nearby Otavalo, and there's plenty of good shopping in here any day of the week. There's also a lot to see and do around the town. Most tours last all day, with a stop at the artisans market, as well as visits to any number of nearby attractions, including Cuicocha Lake, Peguche Waterfall, Mojanda Lakes, and Condor Park. Most tours include lunch at one of the area's historic haciendas.

Guided tours to Otavalo run $25 to $75 per person. The price varies depending on group size, what's included, where you have lunch, length of tour, and other factors. For more information, see chapter 6.

Destinations & Attractions Close to Quito
LA MITAD DEL MUNDO (THE MIDDLE OF THE WORLD)

It's one of the most common souvenir photos taken in Ecuador: A visitor with one foot in either hemisphere, straddling the Equator. **Ciudad La Mitad del Mundo ★** (© **02/2396-871;** www.mitaddelmundo.com) is a tourist complex set up on the site where, in 1736, French explorer and scientist Charles-Marie de la Condamine made his final calculations to determine the precise equatorial line. With modern GPS technology, we now know that de la Condamine erred by some 180m (600 ft.).

The centerpiece of the Ciudad La Mitad del Mundo is a large, trapezoidal monument topped with a large globe. At the top of the monument is a viewing area, reached by an elevator, with great views of the surrounding mountains and countryside. My favorite attraction here is the large scale model of colonial-era Quito, called **Museo del Quito en Miniatura (Quito in Miniature).** This is a great way to get your bearings before touring around the colonial core. On the site, you'll also find a **Museo de Etnografía (Ethnography Museum),** with displays about Ecuador's various indigenous tribes and peoples, as well as a small **Planetarium.** All around are tourist shops and souvenir stands, snack bars, and restaurants. The whole place was built with a mock-colonial styling, sort of a miniature Epcot version of colonial Quito. Frequent shows of folkloric music and dance are performed. Quiteños flock here on Sundays.

Ciudad La Mitad del Mundo is open Monday through Thursday from 9am to 6pm, and from Friday through Sunday from 9am to 7pm. Admission is $2. Admission to

Area of Detail — Quito
ECUADOR
Guayaquil

IMBABURA

Cotacachi
Otavalo
Laguna de San Pablo
Imbabura
E35

San Miguel de Los Bancos
PULULAHUA GEOBOTANICAL RESERVE
Mojanda Lakes
Tabacundo
Cayambe
E25
2
3
4
Equator
1 Mindo
Guayllabamba

PICHINCHA
Rucu Pichincha
Guagua Pichincha
5 ★ QUITO
Calderon
El Quinche
Cumbaya
Pifo
Tumbaco
Ilalo
CAYAMBE-COCA ECOLOGICAL RESERVE
NAPO
Toachi
Sangolqui
Cord. Oriental
6
Pasochoa
Aloag
E20
Machachi
Sincholagua
PASOCHOA WILDLIFE REFUGE
Aloasi
Rumiñahui
COTOPAXI
Iliniza Norte
Iliniza Sur
E35
COTOPAXI NATIONAL PARK
Cord. Occidental
Panamericana

Bellavista Cloud Forest Reserve **2**
La Mitad del Mundo **4**
Mindo-Nambillo Protected Forest **1**
San Jorge Eco-Lodge and Biological Reserve **5**
Tandayapa **3**
Termas de Papallacta **6**

5

QUITO | Side Trips from Quito

the Ethnographic Museum is an additional $3, while a visit to the Planetarium is $1.50.

Separate from the main Mitad del Mundo attraction, but just a few hundred yards away, is **Museo Solar Intiñan ★★ (Intiñan Solar Museum; ✆ 02/2395-122;** www.museointinan.com.ec). This interesting spot has a series of exhibits and ongoing experiments relating to the geography, astrology, and natural sciences of the region. Try your hand at balancing an egg on its end, and watch how water flows down a drain on either side of the Equator. You can also test your accuracy with a blow gun. The museum is open daily from 9:30am to 5pm. Admission is $3.

For a unique hotel experience, you can stay in the basic yet comfortable **Pululahua Hostal (✆ 09/9466-636;** www.pululahuahostal.com), which is built inside the circular crater of the extinct Volcán Pululahua, just a few kilometers beyond the Midad del Mundo monument. A similar, somewhat more upscale choice is **Crater Hotel ★ (✆ 02/2439-254;** www.elcrater.com), which is wonderfully situated along the rim of the volcano's crater.

For an alternative—and very precise—visit to the equatorial line, visit **Quitsato Mitad del Mundo Monument ★ (✆ 09/9701-133;** www.quitsato.org; p. 130), which is on the road to Otavalo.

GETTING THERE Located some 23km (14 miles) north of Quito, near San Antonio de Pichincha, Ciudad La Mitad del Mundo is connected to Quito by a well-paved road. Just about every tour agency and hotel desk in Quito offers a half-day tour here. Prices range from $10 to $30, depending on how exclusive the tour is, how many attractions it takes in, and whether lunch or admission fees are included in the price.

A taxi ride here from Quito should run about $10 to $15 each way. Regular buses, marked MITAD DEL MUNDO, leave from the Cotocallao stop of the Metrobus trolley line. The trolley costs 25¢, and the bus costs an extra 50¢. Be sure to stay on the bus until you reach the actual monument, its final stop.

SAN JORGE ECO-LODGE & BIOLOGICAL RESERVE ★

This mountain lodge just outside Quito gives you the best of several worlds. The original building here is an old hacienda once owned by former President Eloy Alfaro. The **San Jorge Eco-Lodge and Biological Reserve ★** (© 877/565-2596 toll-free in the U.S. and Canada, or 02/3390-403 in Ecuador; www.eco-lodgesanjorge. com) offers a wide array of tours and activities. Bird-watching, hiking, and horseback riding are the main draws, and all are excellent. These folks own four private nature reserves, which cover a number of distinct ecosystems, including high barren plains, high-altitude rainforest, montane cloud forest, and subtropical midelevation rainfor-est. More than 1,000 bird species have been recorded throughout the reserves.

Doubles at the lodge cost $77 to $150. The owners also have separate nature lodges in the cloud forests outside of Mindo (see below), in the transition forest of Tandayapa (see below), in the rainforests of Milpe, and in the high-elevation cloud forests of the Cosanga-Yanayaca Wildlife Reserve. My favorite lodge of theirs is **San Jorege de Milpe ★★**, which offers simple rooms in a dense forest overlooking a thickly forested ravine. If you venture to hike into the ravine, you'll be able to visit two spectacular jungle waterfalls and swim in their cool pools. These folks offer a range of bird-watching and hiking tours that visit various combinations of their lodges, ranging in time from 1 to 15 days.

GETTING THERE The ecolodge is only around 20 minutes from Quito's Mariscal Sucre International Airport, making it a reasonable alternative to city hotels, espe-cially for nature enthusiasts. The hotel offers transportation to the lodge for $18 per person each way.

CLOUD FORESTS: MINDO, TANDAYAPA & BELLAVISTA ★★

Hiking through a cloud forest is one of the most exciting and rewarding side trips you can take from Quito. Within 2 hours, you can escape the city and find yourself in a magical ecosystem where near-constant mist, as opposed to heavy rains, nourishes a dense mix of trees, lichen, and epiphytes. Cloud forests are some of the most biologi-cally diverse places on Earth. Over 400 bird species have been recorded in the area, including the golden-headed quetzal, tanager finch, and, my favorite, Chocó toucan. In addition, you will have the opportunity to hike to remote waterfalls, ride inner tubes on pristine rivers, take a zip-line canopy tour, and marvel at the rich array of orchids, butterflies, bromeliads, and flowers.

While the easy access makes this a potential (and popular) day-tour destination, I recommend spending at least a night or two. There are several lovely lodges in this region, with excellent naturalist guides and a host of tour and activity options. In addition to bird- and wildlife-viewing, tour options include horseback riding, moun-tain biking, and visits to local butterfly farms.

The most popular cloud forest destination is the tiny town of Mindo. Much of the cloud forest around Mindo is protected in **Bosque Protector Mindo-Nambillo (Mindo-Nambillo Protected Forest),** administered by **Amigos de la Naturaleza** (© 08/5638-011; www.amigosdemindo.blogspot.com). While most of the reserve is closed to the public, there are ample private reserves and publicly accessible trails through Mindo's cloud forests. The Mindo-Nambillo reserve was the source of controversy a few years ago, when the government ran an oil pipeline right through it, despite the objections of tourism and environmental groups. Today the forest is recuperating and covering up much of the damage caused by the pipeline.

Aside from hiking the misty cloud forests and looking for birds and other wildlife, there's plenty to do in this area. Mindo is home to two thrill-packed zip-line canopy tours, **Mindo Canopy Adventure** (© 08/5428-758; www.mindocanopy.com) and **Mindo Ropes & Canopy** (© 09/1725-874; www.mindoropescanopy.com). Both offer an adrenaline-packed ride on a dozen or so zip-line cables strung between large rainforest trees in the forests here; both charge $15 per person.

Another popular adventure activity in the area is **riding inner tubes** on any number of rivers that run through the area. All of the hotel tour desks and local tour operators can help you arrange for a tubing outing, for between $6 and $15 per person. And for a mellower time, be sure to check out the butterfly spectacle at **Mariposas de Mindo** (© 09/7511-988; www.mariposasdemindo.com), a small hotel, restaurant, and butterfly garden on the outskirts of town. A tour of their butterfly exhibit costs just $3.

The best hotel here is the gorgeous **Satchitamia Lodge ★★** (© 02/3900-907 or 02/2555-144; www.sachatamia.com), which is set on a high spot just off the main highway, at Km 77 via Quito-La Independencia right near the turnoff for the town of Mindo. Plush rooms, an indoor pool, and over 100 hectares (247 acres) of protected forest laced with trails make this my top choice in the region. Rates here run between $70 and $86 double, including a full breakfast.

Another excellent option is the lovely **Septimo Paraíso** (© 09/3684-420, or 02/2893-160; www.septimoparaiso.com), which is set amid lush forest along the entrance road, on the outskirts of Mindo.

Finally, if you want to stay in the small town itself, your best option by far is **Casskaffesu** (© 02/2170-100; www.caskaffesu.com), a delightful and well-run hostel and cafe in the heart of Mindo.

You also have several options in the Bellavista and Tandayapa area. One of the better options here is the **Tandayapa Bird Lodge ★** (© 02/2447-520; www.tandayapa.com), which was built by and for bird-watchers and is run by the folks behind **Tropical Birding** (www.tropicalbirding.com). A similar option is the **San Jorge de Tandayapa Lodge ★** (© 877/565-2596 toll-free in the U.S. and Canada, or 02/3390-403 in Ecuador; www.eco-lodgesanjorge.com), which is run by the folks from the **San Jorge Eco-Lodge and Biological Reserve** (see above). This new lodge features cozy, large rooms with large floor-to-ceiling windows.

The 720-hectare (1,778-acre) **Bellavista Cloud Forest Reserve** (© 02/2116-232 or 09/9490-891; www.bellavistacloudforest.com) is privately owned and has a variety of accommodations options, from private cabins to dorm rooms in the top of a large geodesic dome. It's not fancy, but the views over the forest canopy are dramatic, the food is excellent, and the nature guides will open up your eyes to a whole different world. Rates run $50 to $80 per person, including three meals, but a whole host of package options are available, including meals, tours, and transportation.

GETTING THERE You can usually arrange transportation with your hotel or lodge. Alternatively, a taxi from Quito should run around $50 to $70. Mindo is serviced by a couple of daily buses from Quito. **Cooperativa Flor de Valle** (© 02/2527-435) has buses leaving Quito's northern bus terminal, Terminal de Norte La Ofelia, at 8:20am and 4pm, and returning at 6:30am and 2pm. On weekends and holidays, there are additional buses and a slightly varied schedule. The ride takes around 2½ hours, and the fare is $3.50.

It's a little more complicated to travel to Bellavista on your own: You have to take the bus from Quito to the small town of Nanegalito, where you can arrange for a truck-taxi to Bellavista. From Nanegalito, it's about a 45-minute ride to Bellavista. The ride should cost about $15 for the whole vehicle, which can hold up to six passengers. Any bus from Quito to Mindo, Puerto Quito, or San Miguel de los Bancos can drop you off in Nanegalito.

PAPALLACTA ★★★

Situated at an altitude of 3,300m (10,824 ft.), and containing some wonderful lush green scenery, the small village of Papallacta boasts the country's most plush and picturesque **hot springs**—a must while in Ecuador, especially if you've been doing any strenuous hiking or bumpy horseback riding. Papallacta is less than 2 hours from Quito by car or bus, but far from the capital's hustle and bustle; it's along the road to Lago Agrio and is an excellent, relaxing day trip from the city, or the perfect stop-off spot to or from El Oriente.

The mineral-rich baths are believed to possess healing powers; locals swear by them, claiming that they alleviate a number of medical conditions, ranging from kidney ailments to arthritis. While there are a couple of inexpensive and basic hot springs options in and around the village, I highly recommend the considerably larger and far better maintained **Termas de Papallacta ★★★** (© 02/6005-586 at the hot springs, or 02/2568-989 for reservations in Quito; www.termaspapallacta.com), a couple of kilometers outside the center. They have exceptional pool and spa facilities, a hotel, and a restaurant. Take in the breathtaking views of the hilly landscape and, on a cloudless day, the majestic snowcapped Volcán Antisana (5,753m/18,870 ft.).

This complex houses various thermal pools ranging from frost-bitingly freezing to utterly scorching, all well maintained and with water changed on a daily basis. You can opt to enter either the *balneario* (daily 6am–11pm; admission $7; lockers 50¢) or the **spa area** (daily 9am–6pm; admission $18), which is generally less crowded and also has a sauna, a steam room, and hydromassage pools. In addition, the spa area offers a range of treatments, including massages, facials, clay body wraps, and aromatherapy at an extra charge. *Tip:* If at all possible, visit midweek, because this place fills up most weekends.

Termas de Papallacta is also an excellent lodging option. The rustically plush rooms and cabins are spacious and comfy, with minimalist mountain decor. A double, including entrance to the *balneario,* costs $130 to $150 per night. But the real advantage of spending the night here is that rooms are surrounded by scores of hot pools for the exclusive, around-the-clock use of hotel guests.

If you're looking for something less pricey, check out **Hostería La Pampa de Papallacta** (© 06/2320-624; www.hosteltrail.com/pampallacta), which has clean and stylish rooms with private bathrooms featuring spring-fed Jacuzzi tubs, at $60 to $75 for a double, including breakfast.

Papallacta's surrounding areas are great for horseback riding, hikes, and nature walks. Inquire at your hotel's reception desk or at the Termas de Papallacta's own Exploratorio research center, located next to the hot springs; they provide information on local flora and fauna, maps, and naturalist guides, and even organize excursions to the Cayambé-Coca Reserve or rafting tours on Río Quijos.

At an altitude of over 3,000m (9,840 ft.), Papallacta can get pretty cold after dusk; be sure to pack warm clothing if you're staying overnight.

Your best bet for food is the excellent **restaurant** at **Termas de Papallacta,** whose specialty is local, freshly caught trout. A snack bar sells sandwiches and light bites right at the hot springs. Outside the complex, you can head down the dirt track to any of the relatively inexpensive *almuerzo* eateries, all of which offer typical Ecuadorean fare, including fish; trout is on the menu everywhere. The **restaurant** at **Hostería La Pampa de Papallacta** serves rather tasty dishes.

GETTING THERE   The easiest ways to get here are to join an organized tour or to arrange transportation and an overnight stay with the Termas de Papallacta itself. Alternatively, any bus heading to Baeza, Tena, or Lago Agrio (via Baeza) will drop you off in the village of Papallacta (or, better yet, at the entrance road to the hot springs, a little before the village). From the well-marked turnoff here, it's a little over 1.5km (1 mile) to the hot springs. If you're coming by bus, you'll probably have to walk this last bit, unless you're lucky enough to flag down a ride. Buses leave from Quito's southbound Terminal Terrestre Quitumbe (© 02/3988-200) for Lago Agrio roughly every hour from 6am to 10:30pm. Two main bus lines, **Transportes Baños** (© 02/3824-843) and **Putumayo** (© 02/3824-807), make the run, and both will drop you off near the entrance to Termas de Papallacta. The ride takes around 2 hours, and the fare is $2.50. From the drop-off point, you'll need to take a local taxi to the actual hot springs, about a mile uphill.

If you're driving, take the highway (E20) east out of Quito toward Baeza. To get to E20 from downtown Quito, head north on Avenida Eloy Alfaro to Avenida de los Granados, and then turn right. This road becomes Hwy. E20. Follow any signs to Papallacta, Tumbaco Baeza, or El Oriente. Papallacta is about 65km (40 miles) southeast of Quito. The ride takes about 1½ hours.

THE NORTHERN SIERRA

The Equator cuts across Ecuador not far north of Quito. Besides delineating the planet's hemispheres—and determining which way water circles before heading down a drain—this line forms the rough boundary for Ecuador's northern Sierra.

The crown jewel and most popular destination of these northern highlands is the small, busy city of **Otavalo,** which has a world-famous artisans market. Besides doing some shopping, be sure to visit a few of these artisans' workshops and studios, which are spread around various neighboring towns and villages.

Several of the country's better haciendas and boutique resort hotels are here, too, and the area is great for hiking, mountain biking, and horseback riding. In particular, **Cuicocha Lake** and the **Mojanda Lakes** are fabulous spots for hikers of any ability, while the **Intag Cloud Forest Reserve** is a must-see destination for serious bird-watchers.

North of Otavalo lies the busy little city of **Ibarra** and its satellite suburb of **San Antonio de Ibarra,** where you'll find some of the best woodcarving craftsmen in all of Ecuador. From Ibarra, the Pan-American Highway continues north to **Tulcán** and the Colombian border.

OTAVALO ★★

95km (59 miles) N of Quito; 515km (319 miles) NE of Guayaquil; 537km (333 miles) N of Cuenca

Otavalo is one of Ecuador's most popular destinations. The locals, known as Otavaleños, have been famous for their masterful craftsmanship for centuries, and the artisans market here is world-renowned, and for good reason. Otavaleños still wear traditional clothing and cling to their heritage. Men wear their long, straight, black hair in distinctive ponytails, while married women wear multistrand gold-bead necklaces. Saturday is the main market day, when the impressive market spills out over much of this small city. But luckily for travelers with tight schedules, the market has become so popular that it now takes place on the other 6 days of the week, too, albeit on a smaller scale. In addition to shopping at Otavalo's market, you can explore the back roads of the province and visit local studios. Some of the smaller towns specialize in specific crafts: **Cotacachi,** for example, is known for leather work, **Peguche** for its weaving, and **San Antonio de Ibarra** for its age-old woodcarving techniques.

Even nonshoppers will love Otavalo and its surroundings. The town has an almost perfect setting. It's nestled in the Sunrise Valley in the shadow of two protective volcanoes, **Cotacachi** and **Imbabura.** According to local legend, Cotacachi is the area's symbolic mother, and Imbabura is the father standing watch. To feel the inspirational powers of Mother Nature, I recommend spending a few days exploring the area, breathing in the fresh air, gazing at the dark-blue waters of the local crater lakes, and standing in awe of the snow-covered volcanoes. Plus, after you find the perfect alpaca sweater, you can wear it as you stroll around **Cuicocha Lake** or hike in the mountains.

Essentials
GETTING THERE
BY PLANE The closest airport with regular traffic is Quito's **Aeropuerto Internacional Mariscal Sucre** (② 02/2944-900; www.quiport.com; airport code: UIO). From the airport, you can take a taxi or minivan shuttle to Otavalo (see below).

BY BUS Buses leave Quito's northern bus terminal, **Terminal Terrestre Carcelén** (② 02/3961-600), roughly every 10 minutes between 5am and 8pm, with

The Pan-American Highway north of Quito passes right through the Equator close to Km 55. On your left, as you drive toward Otavalo, you'll see a cluster of souvenir stands and a small concrete globe allegedly sitting right on the equatorial line. Avoid the temptation to pull over here, and head a few hundred feet farther to **Quitsato Mitad del Mundo Monument** (℃ 09/9701-133; www.quitsato.org), which is on the right side of the road, at latitude 0° 0' 0".

Opened in 2006, this attraction was built and is run by the folks at Hacienda Guachala (p. 142). The centerpiece is a tall spire that works as one of the world's most accurate sundials. Stone inlays mark the cardinal directions, as well as the solstice limits and the exact equatorial line. As far as I know, this is the most precise of the Mitad del Mundo (Middle of the World) attractions in Ecuador, and if you have a GPS, bring it to check. At noon, the spire casts absolutely no shadow in any direction, and on the equinoxes, the shadow falls precisely on the equatorial line. The monument's Solar Culture Museum houses an audiovisual exhibition on the history, geography, and astronomy of the Middle of the World. The monument is open daily from 8:30am to 5:30pm. Admission is $1 for adults, 50¢ for children 13 to 18, and 25¢ for students, seniors and children 12 and under.

less frequent departures during off hours. Two former rivals, **Cooperativa Los Lagos** and **Transportes Otavalo** (℃ 02/2479-124), have joined forces and now have a virtual monopoly on this route—although buses may be labeled with either name. The ride takes 2 to 2½ hours, and the fare is $2. Buses to Ibarra and Tulcán drop off folks along the highway just outside of town and do not enter the main bus terminal of Otavalo.

Otavalo's main bus terminal, Terminal Terrestre, is located on Quito and Atahualpa, about 8 blocks (a 15-min. walk) from Plaza de los Ponchos. Taxis are always available at the bus terminal.

BY SHUTTLE   Every hotel desk and tour agency in Quito sells day tours to Otavalo and shuttle tickets aboard minivans and buses. The rate runs around $7 to $15 per person each way for just transportation, and around $30 to $60 for a day tour, including lunch. These shuttles and tours will pick you up at most hotels in Quito.

If your hotel desk can't set one up for you, **Metropolitan Touring ★★** (℃ 02/2988-200; www.metropolitan-touring.com) has a variety of day tour options to Otavalo costing $90 to $115 per person, including lunch. For private tours, the cost is $354 for one person or $410 for two. Another good option for tours to Otavalo is **Grayline Ecuador** (℃ 800/490-0593 in the U.S. and Canada, or 02/2907-577 in Ecuador; www.graylineecuador.com), which offers day trips to Otavalo beginning at around $50.

BY TAXI   A taxi holding up to four passengers should cost $50 to $60 from Quito to Otavalo.

BY CAR   To reach Otavalo by car, take the Pan-American Highway (E35) north out of Quito. It's a fairly straight shot, and Otavalo is located just off the highway. You will pass first through the towns of Calderón and Cayambe. There are two $1 tolls between Quito and Otavalo. The ride takes around 1½ hours.

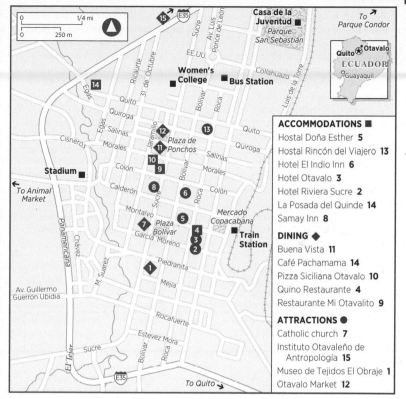

GETTING AROUND

It's easy to get around Otavalo and the surrounding area by taxi and local bus. Taxis are plentiful. A ride anywhere in the city of Otavalo itself should cost only $1.

If you're traveling farther afield and looking to explore Imbabura province, taxis can be hired for $6 to $10 per hour. A one-way taxi fare to Cotacachi or San Antonio de Ibarra should cost $6 to $8.

If you need a taxi, call **Taxis El Jordán** (© **06/2920-298**), **Taxi Express** (© **06/2927-777**), or **Taxi Yamor** (© **06/2921-475**).

Most of the surrounding communities, towns, and cities are connected to Otavalo by **local bus service.** Buses leave Otavalo every 5 minutes or so for Ibarra. Other buses head to Intag, Cayambe, El Quinche, Peguche, and Cotacachi. Your best source of information is to simply head to the bus station on Atahualpa and Ordoñez. Bus rides to nearby towns or villages run 15¢ to 50¢.

ORIENTATION

Otavalo is a compact city. Streets here are set on a grid running at an approximately 45-degree angle to true north. The main arteries through town are the parallel streets of Sucre and Bolívar, which run from southwest to northeast. There are two main

Sunny Otavalo

Otavalo is practically on the Equator. It's also located at about 2,700m (8,856 ft.) above sea level. The sun here is extremely powerful. To top it all off, in the main market, there is not a trace of shade. Be sure to bring plenty of **sunscreen** and a **brimmed hat,** and carry water with you at all times. It gets very hot, so dress appropriately—light pants and a short-sleeved shirt will be fine. If you plan on heading out to Cuicocha Lake, you'll also need a sweatshirt (it gets cold up there).

plazas of note. **Parque Bolívar** is located on the southwestern end of the city and is Otavalo's civic center, with the main Catholic church on its northwest side and the municipal hall on its southwest side. The streets that border Parque Bolívar are Sucre and Bolívar, on two opposite sides, and Juan Montalvo and García Moreno. Toward the northeastern edge of the city lies **Plaza de los Ponchos,** which is ground zero for the weekly market, and which has become a de facto artisans market every day of the week. The Pan-American Highway skirts the city to the north.

VISITOR INFORMATION

The **Otavalo Chamber of Tourism** (**Cámara de Turismo de Otavalo;** ✆ 06/2921-994) runs a helpful information office from the third floor of a building on Calle Sucre, between Quiroga and Quito. You'll find another, similar and more conveniently located **iTur** office run by the **Municipal Tourism Office** (**Oficina Municipal de Turismo;** ✆ 06/2927-230; www.visitotavalo.com) on the corner of Quiroga and Modesto Jaramillo. Your best bet, though, is your hotel tour desk or a local tour agency.

My favorite local agency is **Runa Tupari Travel** ★★, located right on Plaza de los Ponchos, between Sucre and Quiroga (✆ 06/2925-985; www.runatupari.com), which offers tours to indigenous communities and the surrounding lakes, as well as cycling, horseback riding, and volcano-trekking tours. A not-for-profit organization, Runa Tupari supports rural indigenous communities.

FAST FACTS   If you need to contact the **police,** dial ✆ 101 or 06/2920-101. The main hospital in Otavalo, **Hospital San Luis** (✆ 06/2920-444 or 06/2920-600), is located on Sucre and Estados Unidos. The **post office** (✆ 06/2920-642 or 06/2923-520) is adjacent to Plaza de los Ponchos, on the corner of Sucre and Salinas; it's on the second floor. (Yes, it looks as though the building has been condemned, but it hasn't, so head up the stairway and walk past the miniconstruction site to the post office.)

Banks are abundant in Otavalo. There's a **Banco Pichincha** (✆ 06/2920-214), Bolívar 614, near García Moreno; and a **Banco del Pacífico** (✆ 06/2923-301), Bolívar 4–86, at the corner of García Moreno. You'll find another branch of Banco Pichincha, Sucre 413, just north of Plaza de los Ponchos between Quiroga and Quito.

There are plenty of pharmacies around downtown Otavalo. **Farmacia Otavalo** (✆ 06/2920-716), Colón 510, between Sucre and Juan Jaramillo, is very helpful, as is **Sana Sana** (✆ 06/2924-944), on Sucre and Pedraita. Pharmacies work on a *turno* system, which means that each pharmacy periodically takes responsibility for being open 24 hours.

It's easy to find an Internet cafe in Otavalo; there are over a half-dozen within 2 blocks of Plaza de los Ponchos.

What to See & Do in & Around Otavalo

Aside from wandering around and shopping the outdoor markets (see below), there are few noteworthy tourist attractions in Otavalo, although the surrounding towns, villages, and countryside are ripe with opportunities for sightseeing, shopping, and adventure activities.

IN TOWN

If you tire of the hustle, bustle, and commerce of the artisans market on Plaza de los Ponchos, head for the more peaceful Parque Bolívar. You can grab a bench in the gardens here or venture into the city's main **Catholic church.** Although very plain from the outside, the church features a small but ornate gold-leaf and gold-painted altar, as well as a pretty tiled ceiling.

To learn about the process of weaving used by the artisans in and around Otavalo, head to **Museo de Tejidos El Obraje** (© 06/2920-261), which was set up by Don Luis Maldonado and his wife. It has exhibits about the local weaving tools and techniques, as well as displays on the daily lives of the Otavaleños. This little museum is located on Calle Sucre 6–08, just across from the Sana Sana pharmacy. It is open Monday through Saturday from 8am to noon and from 3 to 5pm. Admission is $2. They also offer classes on weaving.

On the campus of the University of Otavalo, just north of town across the Pan-American Highway, is **Instituto Otavaleño de Antropología** (**Otavalo Institute of Anthropology;** © 06/2920-461), which has a modest collection of archaeological relics and finds, as well as a library and bookshop. But I recommend that you spend your precious time enjoying the other sites and activities around town, and get your archaeological fix at Museo Nacional del Banco Central in Quito (p. 111). The institute is open Tuesday through Friday from 9am to noon and 2:30 to 6pm, and on Saturday from 9am to noon. Admission is free.

OTAVALO MARKET ★★★ Because there are often several simultaneous markets taking place, it's probably most accurate to talk about Otavalo's "markets." The artisans market presents some of the best bargains in Ecuador and, just as important, some of the best people-watching. On Saturday, almost the entire city becomes one big shopping area, and itinerant vendors set up stalls on every available speck of sidewalk and alleyway. It's not just for tourists, either; Ecuadoreans come here from miles away to sell and buy high-quality, handmade goods. The Otavaleños are extremely friendly and helpful, and they wear beautiful traditional clothing. Overall, this is one of the most colorful markets in Ecuador, and the handicrafts are of excellent quality.

Some of the most interesting buys available here include handmade alpaca sweaters, soft alpaca scarves, wool fedoras, colorful straw bags, hand-embroidered blouses, ceramics, tapestries, fresh pineapple, and llamas. Yes, llamas. Early in the morning on Saturday, there is an animal market, where you can exchange your cow for a llama or simply buy a dozen chickadees. To get to the animal market from the main plaza, walk down Sucre or Bolívar to Morales. Take a right on Morales and walk straight for about 5 blocks and cross the bridge. Turn right after the bridge and then take a left at the next main street. The animal market is about a half-block up. Get here early (around 7 or 8am) because the market closes down at 10am. There is also an excellent fresh-produce market on Plaza 24 de Mayo.

Though Saturday is market day, there is a relatively complete market every day on Plaza de los Ponchos. Whenever you visit, you'll find the same great crafts on sale here and the same beautiful people selling them. *Tip:* I find that the Saturday market is a bit overwhelming; in fact, I prefer coming on a Wednesday or Sunday, when the market still has great variety but when I don't have to visit innumerable stands to be sure that I have found the perfect bag or hat. You might also be able to bargain better on an off day, as fewer tourists mean less demand and sellers are often a bit more flexible if they really want to make a sale.

Shoppers should expect to do some bargaining; don't be shy, it's part of the culture. The Otavaleños are wily and determined negotiators, and since asking prices are usually quite low, most visitors don't have the stomach for hard bargaining. Still, I've found that prices will usually drop between 20% and 40% without too much haggling.

EXPLORING THE AREA

Many of the textiles and crafts sold in Otavalo's markets are produced in the towns and villages nearby. Outside Otavalo, you can visit weavers' studios in Peguche, leather shops in Cotacachi, and woodcarving workshops in San Antonio de Ibarra.

Nature lovers should also take note: With snow-covered Volcán Cayambe overhead and green mountains in the distance, Imbabura province is a place of stunning beauty. There are several excellent hiking possibilities in the area, including one from Otavalo to the Peguche waterfall, and a 4-hour hike around Cuicocha, a picturesque crater lake. All the travel agencies and tour desks in Otavalo can arrange hiking, trekking, and horseback-riding excursions to a range of beautiful and off-the-beaten-path spots in the area, as well as guided tours to the towns and artisans workshops all around outlying towns and villages.

Runa Tupari Native Travel ★★, located right on Plaza de los Ponchos between Sucre and Quiroga (© **06/2925-985;** www.runatupari.com), and **Dicency Viajes,** on the corner of Sucre and Colón (© **06/2921-217**), are the two best agencies in town. Both offer a wide range of tours, hikes, and adventure activities around the area, including guided tours to all the sites and destinations listed below, as well as organized climbs of Mount Cotacachi (4,939m/16,199 ft.).

CUICOCHA LAKE ★★   Cuicocha is a sparkling blue crater lake formed about 3,000 years ago when the crater of the lake's namesake volcano collapsed during an eruption. The crater was covered with snow, which eventually melted and formed the lake. When the Incas came here, they thought that one of the islands in the middle looked like a *cuy* (guinea pig), hence the name Cuicocha (Guinea Pig Lake). You can take a motorized boat ride out and around the two islands in the middle of the lake, although you can't get off and hike on them. From the boat, along the shores and in the shallows, you will see *totora,* the reed used in this area for making baskets and floor coverings. A 20- to 40-minute boat ride should cost no more than $3 or $4 per person. Be sure to bring a warm sweater—the wind here can be vicious.

I prefer hiking here to riding around on a boat (although you can certainly do both). An 8km (5-mile) trail loops around the rim of the crater, which takes about 4 hours to circle. But even if you walk along it for only 5 or 10 minutes, you'll be able to see Otavalo, Cotacachi, Cayambe, and all the volcanoes of Imbabura province. The setting and views are consistently striking. There's a small visitor center near the end of the road leading from Quiroga to Cuicocha that has some basic exhibits on the geography, geology, and local history of the lake and serves as the administration center for this entrance into the Cotacachi-Cayapas Ecological Reserve, of which Cuicocha is a part. Admission is $1 to visit the lake, $5 to visit other areas of the reserve. For more information on the Cotacachi-Cayapas Reserve, see chapter 4.

ACCOMMODATIONS
& DINING ■
Ali Shungu Mountain
  Lodge **6**
Casa Mojanda **8**
Hacienda Cusín **10**
Hacienda Guachala **12**
Hacienda Pinsaquí **3**
Hacienda Zuleta **11**
La Mirage Garden
  Hotel & Spa **2**
Las Palmeras Inn **7**

ATTRACTIONS ●
Cuicocha Lake **1**
Mojanda Lakes **9**
Parque Condor **5**
Peguche Waterfall **4**

Cuicocha Lake is located about 16km (10 miles) west of the town of Cotacachi. Although a paved road leads almost to the crater's edge, no public transportation is available from Otavalo directly to Cuicocha.

Tip: I recommend taking a guided tour here, as robberies of unaccompanied tourists have been reported. If you're doing it on your own, it's best to hire a taxi in Otavalo for the full trip, or to take a bus from Otavalo to Cotacachi or Quiroga and then hire a cab. If you hire a cab, be sure to either pay for the wait time or designate a time for your return ride.

COTACACHI ★★   Known as the Ciudad de Paz (City of Peace), Cotacachi is a sleepy little pueblo on the outskirts of Otavalo with incredible vistas. From here, you can see snow-covered Volcán Cayambe and the lush green mountains in the distance. But most folks don't come here for the views, because Cuicocha, about 10 minutes up the road, offers much better views. People do, however, come here to shop. Cotacachi is famous for the **leather stores** that line **Avenida 10 de Agosto ★★**. Offerings range from wallets and purses to shoes and clothing. Equestrian enthusiasts can shop for handmade saddles. The quality varies widely, but if you search hard enough, you are bound to find some excellent work and great bargains. There is also

OTAVALO globalized

There's a fair chance you'll have seen them on the streets or public plazas of cities around the world: a group of Otavaleños performing traditional Andean music and selling woven textile goods and other handicrafts. Known by both the Incas and Spanish conquistadors as talented weavers, Otavaleños are an indigenous group who live throughout much of Imbabura province but who are named after the town with the world-famous Saturday textile market. They have woven their way into the history books, and their enduring culture stands out as a unique success story in a time of globalization and diminishing ethnic identity.

With an official government seal of approval, Otavaleños and their craftsmanship were promoted—beginning in the 1950s—as part of a nascent tourism drive. Dutch artist Jan Schreuder, an Ecuadorean resident at the time, searched out pre-Columbian designs to incorporate into rugs, wall hangings, and ponchos; bizarrely, he is also responsible for the Escher knock-offs and more modern motifs that are still seen today.

Things took off in the 1970s with increased international tourism. Peace Corps assistance helped hone styles and colors to suit "foreign" tastes, and the Otavalo market became a must-do for everyone visiting Ecuador. With typical enterprise, Otavaleño weavers have embraced market trends and set forth: to Colombia, the United States, Europe, and as far away as Asia and Australia. With a strong independent streak and plenty of business acumen, they use no middlemen. The traditionally dressed Otavaleños sitting on an international flight to Amsterdam will have financed their flights, woven and bartered for their merchandise, and will keep all the profits from sales.

Otavaleños proudly display their culture; in fact, this is part of their successful "brand image." Quichua is their first language, although most also speak Spanish and many master other tongues as well. The men's long, braided hair is such a strong cultural symbol that Otavaleño men are not required to cut it off when they enter the Ecuadorean armed forces. Women wear embroidered white blouses, wool skirts, and many necklaces made of gold or red beads; the size, color, and quantity of the beads all carry cultural significance.

Many Otavaleño youngsters travel abroad—a rite of passage into the globalized world. The majority return home and add their experience and earnings to one of the world's most prominent indigenous groups.

---

a small museum here, **Museo de las Culturas** (© 06/2951-945), García Moreno 13–41, in the center of Cotacachi, which exhibits ethnographical, historical, archaeological, and musical pieces from the region. It's open Tuesday through Friday 9am to noon and 2 to 5pm, and Saturday 2 to 5pm. Admission is $1. Cotacachi is about 15km (9¼ miles), or 15 minutes, from Otavalo. You can easily take a public bus from the station in Otavalo, or hire a taxi for about $5 to $7 each way.

A robust building boom has hit Cotocachi in recent years, as expatriates and retirees from North America flock to this quaint and tranquil town. If you're looking to stay in Cotocachi, check out the delightful **Casa Luna** (© 06/2914-000; www.casaluna-cotacachi.com) or **Yellow Guest House** (©/fax 02/3440-327 or © 09/7591-395; reservas@yellowguesthouse.com), a cheery and well-run option in an old wooden home painted a bright, upbeat yellow.

PEGUCHE   Peguche is home to some of the best weavers in Ecuador. If you stop in the main square, you can start off by visiting the gallery and workshop of José Cotacachi, a master weaver. Peguche is also famous for its musical instruments. You'll find various shops that specialize in making single-reed flutes and *rondadores* (pan-pipes), as well as guitars and *charangos* (a mandolin-like instrument with five pairs of strings). Traditionally, the back of a *charango* is made from an armadillo shell. If you visit the town on a guided tour (which I highly recommend), you will explore the back streets of Peguche and visit the homes of some of the town's best weavers, while also learning about the old-fashioned process of spinning wool.

Just outside the town is **Peguche Waterfall** ★, a popular spot for tourists and locals alike. Peguche Waterfall is a tall and powerful torrent of water with lush vegetation on either side. Near the foot of the falls, you'll find broad, grassy areas with picnic tables and bench seating. Paths take you around the area, including one that goes to the top of the falls, with a sturdy wooden bridge taking you directly over the rushing water. The Peguche Waterfall plays an important role each year in the concurrent festivals of Inti Raymi and San Juan de Batista, which coincide with the summer solstice. Locals of both indigenous and Catholic faiths come to the falls for ritual baths at this time of year. If you fancy staying overnight or simply stopping for a bite to eat right in Peguche, check out **Hostal Aya Huma** (© **06/2690-333;** www.ayahuma.com), which has rustic rooms, serves up traditional and international cuisine, and holds spiritual cleansing workshops.

This tiny town is located about 10 minutes by car from Otavalo. A taxi should cost $5 each way, and you can also walk to the falls from town in about 45 minutes. The route is well worn and popular; just ask one of the locals to point you in the right direction.

MOJANDA LAKES ★   After Cuicocha Lake, the Mojanda Lakes offer some of the best and most scenic hiking around Otavalo. The extinct Volcán Fuya Fuya stands majestically above the three high mountain lakes, creating a beautiful setting. This is a great spot for bird-watching: More than 100 species of birds are found here, including the giant hummingbird and the endangered Andean condor. Mojanda Lakes are located about 30 minutes south of Otavalo. A taxi here costs about $12 each way.

PARQUE CONDOR ★ ☺   Although you'll find Andean condors on display here, you'll find a whole host of other bird species as well. The emphasis is on raptors, with a variety of local raptor species represented, including various different owls. Several large birds are brought out by trainers and allowed to fly each day at 11:30am and 4:30pm. The park is set on a high hillside with a lovely view over Laguna San Pablo, the Otavalo Valley, and Volcán Imbabura. There's a small restaurant with great views, as well as a children's playground.

Parque Condor (© **06/2924-429;** www.parquecondor.org) is located outside Otavalo near El Lechero and Peguche. It is open Tuesday through Sunday from 9:30am to 5pm. Admission is $2. A taxi ride here from Otavalo should cost no more than $5 each way.

INTAG ★   This is a region of beauty and conflict. The hills, mountains, valleys, and ravines here are covered in rich cloud forests, and they're home to a wide array of wildlife and hundreds of bird species. Small communities get by on subsistence farming and coffee production. But large mining interests, led by Ascendant Copper, have their eyes and heavy machinery aimed at the mineral wealth that lies beneath the ground, and the Intag region has been ground zero for a tense and sometimes violent clash between local activists, environmental organizations, and Ascendant Copper. The **Intag Cloud Forest Reserve** (© 06/2648-509; www.intagcloudforest.com) is owned and run by Carlos Zorrilla, who has been a leader in trying to preserve the environment and ecosystems here. The bird-watching is phenomenal, and Carlos and his crew are great guides. Accommodations are available in rustic rooms inside the reserve. Water is heated by passive solar energy, and all meals are vegetarian. Depending on the size of your group, rates run around $44 per person per day, including three meals and a guided hike daily.

The Intag Cloud Forest Reserve is located several hours, over rough dirt roads, from Otavalo. You absolutely need a prior reservation to stay here, and they aim for a minimum of eight people in a group. When making your reservation, Carlos and company will arrange transportation or give you detailed information on how to arrive in your own vehicle or via public transportation.

Those looking to volunteer or help out with the conservation efforts should contact **DECOIN** (www.decoin.org), an organization that works closely with indigenous communities in the region on a range of environmental and social issues, including mining and sustainable tourism.

OUTDOOR ACTIVITIES

Hiking trails abound here. One of my favorite hikes is the 4-hour trek around Cuicocha Lake. Keep in mind, however, that robberies have been reported in the area, so it's best to do the trail with a guide. You can also hike from Cuicocha to the Mojanda Lakes, up Volcán Cotacachi, or around the Mojanda Lakes and up Volcán Fuya Fuya. Both **Dicency Viajes** (© 06/2921-217) and **Runa Tupari Native Travel** ★★ (© 06/2925-985; www.runatupari.com) can provide experienced guides and help organize your hiking excursions. These tour agencies also offer **horseback-riding trips.** One of the most popular is the trail around Cuicocha Lake. A half-day trip costs $40 to $75 per person.

LEARN THE LANGUAGE

If you want to learn some Spanish, check in with the **Otavalo Spanish Institute**, Av. 31 de Octubre 476 and Juan de Salinas, 3rd Floor, which offers a variety of intensive plans with one-on-one instruction, a homestay with a local family and three meals daily, and various extracurricular activities (© 02/2921-404; www.otavalo spanish.com). They even offer classes in Kichwa. Rates run $180 to $275 per week, depending upon the number of hours of study per day.

PAMPER YOURSELF

If you're looking for some pampering or want to shake off the stress of traveling, head to the spa at **La Mirage Garden Hotel & Spa** ★★★ (see below). The spa facilities and treatments here are fabulous, and the prices are pretty reasonable. After your treatment, you can spend as much time as you like in their lovely atrium covered pool and Jacuzzi.

Where to Stay in Otavalo

MODERATE

La Posada del Quinde ★★ Recently renamed and under new management, this ever-popular hotel is a definite step up from most of the downtown options. Formerly Hotel Ali Shungu, the large two-story building is built in a broad horseshoe around a large garden that attracts hummingbirds and other bird species. The rooms are simple but comfortable, with firm beds, electric heaters, and colorful art and handicrafts hanging from the walls. The two family suites are big, with two bedrooms and spacious living areas; they are located on the second floor and have large, inviting balconies. In addition to the rooms, all public indoor areas here are smoke-free. The **Café Pachamama** restaurant here (see "Where to Dine in and Around Otavalo," later in this chapter) is one of the best in town.

Calle Quito y Calle Migue Egas, Otavalo. www.posadaquinde.com. ✆ **06/2920-750.** 20 units. $60 double; $125–$200 apt. Rates include full breakfast. DC, MC, V. Parking nearby. **Amenities:** Restaurant; bar; all rooms smoke-free; free Wi-Fi. *In room:* No phone.

Las Palmeras Inn ★★ ☺ This charming inn is a sister operation to the plush Hacienda Cusín (see below). Just a 20-minute walk from the main downtown hustle and bustle, the hotel is housed in a 150-year-old colonial hacienda in the green mountain foothills above Otavalo. Rooms are decorated with Andean crafts, and most feature working fireplaces stoked with roaring eucalyptus logs each night. The hotel offers outdoor dining on its pretty veranda. There are great views from around the grounds, which boast lush perennial gardens growing a host of tropical fruits, and a sprinkling of hammocks strung up and inviting you to take a midday siesta. The grounds are extensive here and feature a volleyball court and soccer field. Services for guests include Hawaiian massages, Spanish classes, and horseback riding.

Las Palmeras de Quichinche, 2km (1¼ miles) from Otavalo town, sector Quichinche. www.laspalmeras inn.com. ✆/fax **06/2922-607.** 15 units. $60–$120 double. Rates include full breakfast. DC, MC, V. Free parking. **Amenities:** Restaurant; lounge; room service; free Wi-Fi. *In room:* No phone.

INEXPENSIVE

In addition to the places listed below, **Hotel Riviera Sucre** (✆ **06/2920-241;** www.rivierasucre.com) is an excellent option in this price range, at $32 for a double, including breakfast. This hotel is located in a lovely old building on García Moreno 380, on the corner of Roca. Alternatively, check out the colonial-style **Hostal Doña Esther** (✆ **06/2920-739;** www.otavalohotel.com) for clean, inexpensive rooms right in the center of town, on Juan Montalvo 4–44. Doubles cost $40, including breakfast and taxes.

Hotel El Indio Inn This glass-fronted high-rise hotel seems a little out of place in downtown Otavalo. The rooms are large, clean, and well kept, although lacking in any style or personality. All come with a "minibar" selection of snacks and drinks, but without any fridge. Rooms are set around a pair of interior courtyards hung heavily with potted plants, and windows front only these interior courtyards. There's a game room with a pool table and an attached Internet cafe. The hotel's main restaurant, **La Cascada de Ensueños (The Waterfall of Dreams),** serves good Ecuadorean and international cuisine in a pleasant room with a wall of glass facing the street and an interior waterfall and garden, which gives the joint its name. *Note:* This place should not be confused with Hotel el Indio, which is a slightly older sister facility closer to the bus station.

Bolívar 904 y Abdón Calderón, Otavalo. www.hotelelindioinn.com. ✆ **06/2922-922** or ✆/fax 06/ 2920-325. 33 units. $53 double. Rates include breakfast and taxes. AE, MC, V. Free parking. **Amenities:** Restaurant; bar; room service. *In room:* TV, free Wi-Fi.

Hotel Otavalo 📷 This downtown option oozes colonial-era charm. Worn wooden floors, high ceilings, and rambling common areas are the highlights here. The large central courtyard area features a high atrium roof, and there are several lounge areas. I also really like the second-floor restaurant, **Quino** (p. 144), which has seating in a series of rooms and around a central veranda. Accommodations here are simple, with minimal decorations and furnishings, although the beautiful woven bedspreads do brighten things up. No. 3 features a nice view over rooftops to the hills west of town.

Roca 504 y Juan Montalvo, Otavalo. www.hotelotavalo.com.ec. © **06/2920-416.** 32 units. $42 double. DC, MC, V. Parking nearby. **Amenities:** Restaurant; bar; room service. *In room:* TV.

Hostal Rincón del Viajero ★ 🎒 There are scores of backpacker specials in Otavalo, but this place is my pick as the best of the bunch. The rooms are all kept clean and comfortable. About half have private bathrooms, and it's worth the slight splurge. The public areas and friendly service set this place apart. There is a small central courtyard and a large third-floor rooftop terrace, with a separate covered area featuring a game room and hammock area. Down below, guests gather nightly in a cozy lounge with a large brick fireplace.

Roca 11–07, btw. Quiroga and Quito, Otavalo. www.hostalrincondelviajero.com. © **06/2921-741.** 15 units, 6 with private bathroom. $20 double with shared bathroom; $25 double with private bathroom. Rates include breakfast and taxes. DC, MC, V. Free parking. **Amenities:** Restaurant; lounge; free Wi-Fi. *In room:* No phone.

Samay Inn ★ 🎒 This simple budget hotel, centrally located on Calle Sucre, just a block from Plaza de Ponchos, is a great choice in Otavalo. The rooms all have wood floors and faux-stucco walls painted with bold primary colors and an aged-wash effect. All come with 53-centimeter (21-in.) flatscreen televisions. A relaxing interior courtyard lounge on the second floor is enclosed by a tall brick wall. Interior brick arches and other design touches give this place more charm and class than you'd expect at this price. ***Note:*** As with El Indio Inn, there are two Samay Inn sites in Otavalo—don't head to the one closer to the bus station.

Calle Sucre 1009 y Calle Colón, Otavalo. samayinn@hotmail.com. © **06/2921-826.** 23 units. $24 double. Rates include taxes. DC, MC, V. Free parking. **Amenities:** Restaurant; bar. *In room:* TV.

Where to Stay Near Otavalo

VERY EXPENSIVE

La Mirage Garden Hotel & Spa ★★★ If you're looking for luxury, you won't find a better hotel in the highlands than this member of the prestigious Relais & Châteaux. Set on the grounds of a 200-year-old hacienda, all the rooms are essentially suites. Some have brass canopy beds; other beds have antique wood frames. Crystal chandeliers brighten the rooms, while plush Oriental carpets decorate the floors. The spacious bathrooms come with extra-large showers. Queen Sofía of Spain stayed in stately no. 114, and I'm sure she must have felt right at home. Turndown service consists of lighting the fire in your private fireplace and slipping two hot-water bottles into your bed. The spa here is opulent and luxurious, with Greco-Roman baths and Egyptian energy soaks. Indulge in clay wraps and full-body massages, or treat yourself to a purification performed by a local female shaman. The outdoor gardens are also magnificent, while the restaurant offers the best fine-dining experience in the region.

At the end of Calle 10 de Agosto, Cotacachi. www.mirage.com.ec. © **800/327-3573** in the U.S. and Canada, or 06/2915-237. Fax 02/2915-065. 23 units. $366 double; $427–$671 suite. AE, DC, MC, V. Rates include breakfast and dinner, and taxes. **Amenities:** Restaurant; bar; lounge; concierge; small exercise room; Jacuzzi; solar-heated indoor pool; room service; full spa services; steam room; tennis court. *In room:* TV, hair dryer, free Wi-Fi.

EXPENSIVE

Ali Shungu Mountain Lodge ★ After decades in town, the owners of the popular and longstanding Ali Shungu Hotel have found peace and quiet on a high hillside just outside Otavalo. Here you'll find four large, fully equipped guesthouses; two have one bedroom, the others two bedrooms. Both varieties have full kitchens and large, comfortable living rooms. The one-bedroom units have a large dining room, which is used as the second bedroom in the other houses. There's a working woodstove, and the wraparound windows provide good views. Highest up the hill is the complex's main restaurant and lounge area. Locally produced organic fruits and vegetables are featured as much as possible at the excellent restaurant here. Sixteen hectares (40 acres) of private reserve surround the property. Several hours of guided horseback riding are included in the room rates, and there are trails through the neighboring cloud forest for self-guided hiking.

1.9km (1¼ miles) outside Otavalo, near the village of Yambiro. www.alishungumountaintoplodge.com. © 08/9509-945. 4 units. $110 double. Rates include breakfast and taxes. No credit cards. Free parking. **Amenities:** Restaurant; lounge. *In room.* Hair dryer, no phone, free Wi-Fi.

Casa Mojanda Casa Mojanda is located only about 10 minutes outside Otavalo, but the isolated 7.2-hectare (18-acre) property is nestled in a valley surrounded by mountains and rolling green hills. The vistas are phenomenal, unspoiled by any man-made structures. The rustic-chic cabins all have either tile or hardwood floors, antique dressers, small reed floor coverings, and tons of personal touches; several have their own fireplaces. You can enjoy the spectacular views from the comfort of your own bed. No. 6 is great for families: It has a kitchenette, a separate living room, and separate bedrooms. The gorgeous dining area, filled with antiques and local crafts, serves as the heart of the hotel. This is where you can enjoy scenic vistas as well as divine home-cooked meals, all made with food grown in the hotel's organic biodynamic gardens. The English-speaking owners are charming and can help with kayak and mountain-bike rentals, as well as horseback-riding tours.

Mojanda Lakes (mailing address: P.O. Box 160), Otavalo. www.casamojanda.com. © 06/2991-010 or 09/9731-737. 10 units. $150 double. Rates include breakfast and dinner. No credit cards. **Amenities:** Restaurant; lounge; wood-fire-heated cedar hot tub; free Wi-Fi. *In room:* No phone.

Hacienda Cusín ★★ ☺ This 17th-century hacienda is a fabulous choice in the Otavalo area, especially if you're looking for a mix of luxury and history. Cusín sits on over 4 hectares (9¾ acres) of lush gardens and cobblestone courtyards overflowing with bougainvillea, orchids, and palm trees. Rooms are located in the renovated one-story hacienda and come with antique furnishings and high ceilings. The garden cottages are of somewhat more recent construction and come with working fireplaces. The owner's suite is large enough for a family of four, and even if you don't choose this room, the entire hacienda is an extremely kid-friendly operation. All units have spacious bathrooms with lovely blue tiles. The friendly staff can help you arrange activities, including the popular overnight horseback-riding trip to Volcán Imbabura. Spanish-language classes are also available. The restaurant serves a wonderful dinner by candlelight, so there's no need to leave the property after dark.

Calle Chiriboga, San Pablo del Lago (mailing address: P.O. Box 123), Otavalo. www.haciendacusin.com. © 06/2918-013. Fax 06/2918-003. 42 units. $105–$120 double; $150 garden cottage; $350–$450 suite. All rates include breakfast. Suite rates include lunch and dinner. AE, DC, MC, V. **Amenities:** Restaurant; bar; massage; free Wi-Fi. *In room:* No phone.

Hacienda Pinsaquí ★ 📷 Originally a colonial-era textile enterprise, Hacienda Pinsaquí is one of Ecuador's great historic hotels. Simón Bolívar once stayed here. The hacienda immediately transports you back in time with its antique floors that have the scent of old wood. The homey smell of well-worn fireplaces permeates the air. The narrow, old-fashioned hallways are filled with flowers fresh from the gardens. And the rooms are sumptuous; each is unique, but all have a touch of old-fashioned country elegance. No. 8 has a magnificent canopy bed and beautiful antique furniture, as well as a separate sitting area where you can gaze out onto the property's wonderfully landscaped gardens. This room also has a sunken Jacuzzi tub, near a large window overlooking the gardens. All units have working fireplaces and colonial-era decor (though in general, the bathrooms aren't perfect). Once you leave the comfort of your room, you can walk around the property's gardens or explore the area by horseback—the hotel offers guided riding tours. Superb meals are served in an elegant dining room.

Pan-American Hwy., Km 5, Otavalo. www.haciendapinsaqui.com. ✆ **06/2946-116** or 09/9727-652. Fax 06/2946-117. 30 units. $139 double. Rates include tax and breakfast. AE, DC, MC, V. **Amenities:** 2 restaurants; bar; mountain bike rentals; room service; Internet for a fee. *In room:* No phone.

MODERATE

Hacienda Guachala 🔔   Dating to 1580, this claims to be the oldest hacienda in Ecuador. At one point, the hacienda covered over 40,000 hectares (98,800 acres). It was here that García Moreno, who lived in the hacienda for 7 years, planted the first eucalyptus trees in Ecuador, many of which still flourish on the grounds. The hacienda then passed on to the family of Neptali Bonifaz, the country's first democratically elected president, and it remains in the Bonifaz family today.

Rooms here are more rustic than those at most of the other converted haciendas, but the prices are also substantially lower. All but two rooms feature working fireplaces. Nos. 1 through 10 are my favorites. There's a small pool under a greenhouse roof, with tropical fruits and flowers planted around it. The hacienda's large church has been converted into a small museum that contains historic photos from the Bonifaz family and some pre-Inca pottery.

Km 70, Pan-American Hwy., on the road to Cangahua, Cayambe. www.guachala.com. ✆ **02/2363-042.** Fax 02/2362-426. 31 units. $59 double. AE, DC, MC, V. Free parking. **Amenities:** Restaurant; small covered pool; Internet for a fee. *In room:* No phone.

Where to Dine in & Around Otavalo

In addition to the places listed below, with advance reservations, you can treat yourself to some fine dining at the restaurant at **La Mirage ★★★** (see above). You can also get great meals at **Hacienda Cusín ★★** (see above).

If you're looking for somewhere with a view, I suggest dining at a restaurant overlooking Lago San Pablo, a beautiful little lake considered sacred by the local indigenous populations. The restaurant of **Hostería Puerto Lago** (✆ **06/2920-920;** www.puertolago.com; Lago San Pablo and Pan-American Hwy., Km 5½, Otavalo) sits right on the lake and serves delicious fresh grilled trout in addition to the usual Ecuadorean and Continental offerings. Almost every table has a lake view with magnificent Volcán Imbabura in the background. The restaurant is open Sunday through Thursday 7:30am to 9:30pm, and Friday, Saturday, and holidays 7am to 10:30pm.

Buena Vista ★★ ECUADOREAN/INTERNATIONAL   Set on the second floor with a view over Plaza de los Ponchos, this casual spot is a popular meeting ground and bistro. The menu features a mix of sandwiches, nachos, burgers (both veggie and beef), and several different pasta entrees. You can also get a grilled local trout, or chicken or steak in a mushroom sauce. This place is small and often crowded, and the one balcony table is a hot commodity. At night they play contemporary lounge tracks. This a good place to come for drinks and a mellow time among friends. In

TREE tomato

When is a tomato not a tomato? When it's a tree tomato. Although the *Cyphomandra betacea* belongs to the same family (Solanaceae) as its more universally recognized bright red cousin, the tree tomato grows as a small perennial shrub up in the hills and looks like a colorful egg when ripe. Its succulent, tomato-like flesh is tart enough to pucker your lips—don't even think about eating the skin, which is more like a shell.

Tree tomatoes were cultivated by the Incas and probably originated in one of the Andean countries between Chile and Colombia. Today they're grown commercially in New Zealand and Australia, as well as in Ecuador.

In Ecuador, the tree tomato, or *tamarillo*, flourishes at 1,500 to 3,000m (4,920–9,840 ft.), and you will see them growing in the highlands. You can find both the tart golden-orange and smoother deep-red varieties in any market around the country. Being rich in natural pectin, they make perfect setting agents for jellies and jams—orange and tree tomato is a sublime combination. You will most commonly find *tamarillo* served as a fruit drink or skinned and stewed as a dessert compote. It is also a popular local ice-cream flavor.

With supposed medicinal properties to treat everything from respiratory disease to obesity, stress, and colds—as well as improving your immune system and lowering cholesterol—the tree tomato seems to be a bit of a wonder fruit. And it's pretty good with rum, too.

addition to the food offerings, you'll find a lending library and variety of board games to help you wile away the time. These folks have a sister restaurant, **Aly Allpa,** on the street level, just a door down.

Calles Salinas 5-11, 2nd Floor, Plaza de los Ponchos. ✆ **06/2925-166** or 06/2920-289. www.buenavistaotavalo.com. Main courses $3–$6.30. DC, MC, V. Mon noon–10pm; Wed-Fri and Sun 10am–10pm; Sat 8am–10pm.

Café Pachamama ★★ ECUADOREAN/INTERNATIONAL   The cozy restaurant of this popular hotel is one of the best in the city. Heavy wooden tables are spread around the large central dining room, which features terra-cotta tile floors and a fireplace. Local and regional art and handicrafts serve as decor, and there's a small bar in one corner. I like to grab one of the tables near the long wall of picture windows, especially at lunchtime. The restaurant uses locally grown organic produce whenever possible. The delicious tomato-basil soup is a house specialty. For a main dish, I recommend the lasagna or the spinach cheese pie. For lunch, you can get excellent sandwiches on homemade bread, or one of their massive hamburgers. Breakfasts are also excellent and worth it if you want a change from traditional Ecuadorean morning fare; this is the only place around where you can get fresh waffles with homemade raspberry syrup.

Calles Quito and Miguel Egas. ✆ **06/2920-750.** Reservations recommended. Sandwiches $5.25–$6.50; main courses $7–$8.50. DC, MC, V. Daily 7:30am–8:30pm.

Pizza Siciliana Otavalo PIZZA/ITALIAN   There are several pizza joints in Otavalo, but this is my favorite. The ambience is warm and cozy, with rugged wood tables and chairs, plenty of exposed wood all around, and a large brick fireplace in one corner. Pizzas have a medium-thin and crisp crust, and come with a wide range of possible toppings. There are also over a dozen pasta dishes on the menu, including a rich meat lasagna. In addition, you can get hamburgers, sandwiches, and even barbecued ribs. There's live Andean music here most Friday and Saturday nights.

Calle Morales 5-01, near Calle Sucre. © **06/2925-999.** Main courses $5.50–$8. MC, V. Daily noon–10pm.

Quino Restaurante ECUADOREAN/SEAFOOD   While seafood features prominently on the menu here, there's plenty more for you to try. You should definitely start things off with one of their excellent *ceviches.* But for a main course, I prefer the *steak a la criolla,* which comes bathed in onions and peppers. If you do opt for fish, I'd go for the fresh mountain trout, *trucha al ajo macho,* served in a rich garlic sauce. With simple, glass-topped tables and minimal decor, there's not much ambience here. Nevertheless, it's almost always full and lively.

Calle Roca 7-40, near Calle Juan Montalvo. © **06/2924-994.** Reservations recommended Sat–Sun. Main courses $4–$8. MC, V. Daily 8am–9:30pm.

Restaurante Mi Otavalito ★ 🏠 ECUADOREAN   This lively and popular place is my favorite option for local cuisine. The menu features a wide range of fish, meat, poultry, and specialty items. I especially like the simple grilled trout. Tables are spread throughout several rooms connected by arched brick doorways. Some of the walls feature a mix of wood and woven-mat paneling. There's a small brick fireplace in the back. Most days during lunch and dinner, local bands play Andean folk music; they're working for tips, so don't be stingy.

Calle Sucre 11-19, near Calle Morales. © **06/2920-176.** Reservations recommended Sat–Sun. Main courses $5–$7.50. MC, V. Daily 9am–9pm.

Otavalo After Dark

While not a raging party town, Otavalo has several cozy bars and clubs. It's easy to find a place with a local group playing traditional Andean music. By far the most raging party spot is **Peña la Jampa** ★ (© **06/2927-791;** www.lajampa.com), on Avenida 31 de Octubre and the Panamerican Norte, which churns out Spanish rock, merengue, and salsa. This place is open Friday and Saturday from 9pm until 2am. The cover is usually $3 to $5.

For a more mellow, boho scene, try **Casa de Arte Da Pinto** ★ (© **06/2920-058**), Calle Colón 4–10, between Bolívar and Sucre. This place features creative artwork on the walls, tables, and floors, and serves up pizzas, burgers, beer, and wine. **The Red Pub** ★ (© **09/4411-373**), Calle Morales 5–07 and Modesto Jaramillo, is another good option for a some drinks and good cheer. It is open Tuesday through Sunday from 4:30pm until 2am, with "happy hour" from 8 to 9pm and live music most weekends. **Buena Vista** (see above) is another popular spot.

An Isolated & Historic Hacienda

Hacienda Zuleta ★★★ 🏠   This elegant old hacienda belonged to the former president and diplomat Galo Plaza. The massive plaza at the still-working farm is quite impressive. The majority of rooms carry the name of a prominent family member. "Galo," which is located in the oldest part of the hacienda, is a large room with a high-peaked ceiling featuring exposed beams that date back to 1691; there's a claw-foot bathtub in the bathroom. Many units face an open-air courtyard or small garden, and most have a working fireplace or woodstove, which comes in handy in this high-mountain climate. Be sure to ask to visit Galo Plaza's library, an impressive two-story room containing historic memorabilia, a massive book and art collection, and a portrait of the former president, painted by Guayasamín. The farm here produces excellent cheeses, and the local community produces renowned embroidery works. Horseback riding is taken seriously here—their horses are well trained and beautiful, and a wide range of tours are available. The hotel oversees a condor-recovery project, where injured condors are cared for and where wild condors often visit.

Hacienda Zuleta can arrange transportation for you. If you are coming on your own, there are several routes—your best bet is to check in with the hotel to find out which is in the best condition.

Angochahua, Imbabura (mailing address: Tamayo N24-607 y Colón, Quito). ✆ **06/2662-182** or 06/2662-232. www.haciendazuleta.com. 15 units. $388–$656 double. Rates include all meals, nonalcoholic drinks, guided tours and activities around the hacienda, and taxes. Children 2 and under free; children 3–5 75% discount; children 6–12 50% discount. Slight discounts for multiday stays. AE, DC, MC, V. Free parking. **Amenities:** Restaurant; lounge; free mountain bikes; room service. In room: No phone, free Wi-Fi.

IBARRA

115km (71 miles) N of Quito; 535km (332 miles) NE of Guayaquil; 20km (12 miles) N of Otavalo

Often overlooked by tourists, Ibarra is the capital of Imbabura province and the main business, transportation, and governmental hub for Ecuador's northern highlands. Founded in 1606, Ibarra was almost completely destroyed by a massive earthquake in 1868. Ibarra is nicknamed La Ciudad Blanca (The White City), owing to the surviving whitewashed colonial-era buildings that define its downtown. Situated at the foot of the Volcán Imbabura, at an altitude of 2,225m (7,300 ft.), Ibarra enjoys a year-round springlike climate, and it's located at the junction between the market town of Otavalo, the humid Chota valley, and the coastal region.

Perhaps the biggest draw in Ibarra is its satellite burg, **San Antonio de Ibarra** ★ (5km/3 miles south of downtown), a small artistic community renowned for its wood-carving and artisans. Another of Ibarra's biggest attractions, **Laguna Yahuarcocha**, also lies just outside the city.

Essentials
GETTING THERE
BY BUS Buses leave Quito's northern **Terminal Terrestre Carcelén** (✆ **02/3961-600**) for Ibarra roughly every 30 to 45 minutes between 8am and 8pm. Two main bus companies, **Transportes Andina** (✆ **02/3824-816** in Quito, or 06/2950-833 in Ibarra) and **Cooperativa Expreso Turismo** (✆ **02/2565-941** in Quito, or 06/2951-110 in Ibarra), alternate the departures. The ride takes a little under 3 hours, and the fare is $3.

The main bus terminal in Ibarra (✆ **06/2644-676**) is located southwest of downtown, on Calle Espejo and Gómez de la Torre. Taxis are always waiting at the bus station and charge $1 for a ride to the city center.

There are also frequent buses from Ibarra north along the Pan-American Highway to Tulcán.

BY CAR To reach Ibarra by car, take the Pan-American Highway (E35) north out of Quito. It's a fairly straight shot, and Ibarra is located just off the highway. You will first pass through the towns of Calderón and Cayambe, and then just skirt Otavalo. There are two $1 tolls between Quito and Ibarra. The ride takes around 2 hours.

ORIENTATION

Ibarra has a compact downtown, parts of which still feature rough cobblestone streets and whitewashed buildings from the colonial period. The Pan-American Highway skirts the town to the west before turning north for Tulcán. The city's central park, Parque Pedro Moncayo, occupies a full city block and has well-tended gardens and plenty of benches. It is anchored on the north by the city's cathedral. One block west lies a similar little park, Parque La Merced, which fronts Iglesia La Merced, while 1 block east is the San Agustín church, which features its own little plaza out front.

GETTING AROUND

Ibarra's downtown is quite easily navigated on foot. Nonetheless, taxis are always available. If you can't flag one down, call **Radiotaxi** (✆ **06/2612-333**) or **Taxi Lagos de Ibarra** (✆ **06/2606-858**).

VISITOR INFORMATION

There's an **iTur information office** (✆ **06/2608-489;** www.touribarra.gob.ec) on the corner of Sucre and Oveido, offering maps and advice on attractions, tours, and accommodations. It's open Monday through Friday 8am to 12:30pm and 2 to 5:30pm.

FAST FACTS To contact the **police,** dial ✆ **101** or **06/2950-444.** The main **post office** (✆ **06/2643-135**) is located on Salinas 6–71, between Oveido and Pedro Moncayo. **Hospital San Vicente de Paul** (✆ **06/2611-568**) is located just west of downtown, on Luis Vargas Torres and Pasquel Monge.

There are several banks and plenty of ATMs around the center of Ibarra. A branch of **Banco Pichincha** (✆ **06/2643-097**) is just off Parque Pedro Moncayo on Calle Flores 5–18, near Calle Sucre, and a branch of **Banco del Pacífico** (✆ **06/2957-714**) is on the corner of Pedro Moncayo and Olmedo.

For Internet, try **Nando's Cyber Café** (✆ **06/2950-632**), on Av. Pérez Guerrero 6–50 and Bolívar; **Internet Lago Azul** (✆ **06/2641-851**), on Pedro Moncayo 5–78 and Bolívar; or **Ejecutivo Internet** (✆ **06/2956-866**), on Bolivar and Colon.

What to See & Do in Ibarra

Aside from visiting the local churches and people-watching from a bench at one of several downtown parks and plazas, there's not much of interest for tourists in Ibarra proper. The most popular attractions, San Antonio de Ibarra and Laguna Yahuarcocha (see below), are just outside the city limits.

While **Iglesia de la Merced, Iglesia San Augustin, Iglesia Santo Domingo,** and **Cathedral** are all worth a quick visit, my favorite church in Ibarra is **Basílica de la Dolorosa** ★, located several blocks south of downtown, on Calle Sucre. This somber stone-and-brick church features two high clock towers, several large stained-glass murals, and a bright neon sign over the ornately carved wooden alter reading OH, MADRE, DOLOROSA.

The local branch of **Museo del Banco Central de Ecuador (Ecuador Central Bank Museum;** ✆ **06/2602-093**) has a respectable collection of Inca and pre-Inca relics. The museum is located at the corner of calles Sucre and Oviedo. It is open Monday through Friday from 8:30am until 5pm and Saturday 10am to 4pm. Admission is $1.

Museo de Arte Religioso (✆ **06/2955-255**), on Plaza Boyacá (Bolívar and Rafael Troya), is a small museum housing colonial-era Dominican art attached to **Iglesia Santo Domingo.** With its large carved wooden doors, this church houses

THE minga

If you want something done, you do it yourself, right? Not in the Ecuadorean highlands. The minga is a quintessentially South American phenomenon still strongly evident in many Andean communities. Derived from the Quichua word minka, meaning roughly "working together," it evokes the concept of a community mutually collaborating to achieve a task for the benefit of everyone, and a tradition predating the Incas.

The minga can apply to many different projects, such as helping with the harvest, building or repairing a neighbor's house, or, in more modern times, picking up trash along a dirty city street or equipping a children's playground.

The Incas exploited the practice to great effect within the highland farming communes (ayllus) under their domain, which partly helps explain their success in expanding and supplying their once-vast empire.

The work carried out is done free of charge and in shifts for the common good. Mingas, it's important to note, take place in addition to a worker's normal job. In the highland Andean villages, the communities decide what needs to be done—say, a new drainage ditch, road repair, or the potato harvest. Laborers bring their tools to the site of the task in question, and although the project may be back-breakingly hard, there is an almost festive atmosphere as the volunteers come and go.

The minga philosophy—that what you give, you get back—is still alive and well. Orphans, the elderly, and the infirm all make their contributions, too, however small, and receive shelter and food in return.

the famous La Virgin del Rosario painting and fronts a small park with a statue of liberator Simón Bolívar. The museum is open daily from 9am to noon and 2 to 6pm. Admission is 50¢.

If you fancy a stroll around the town's pretty plazas, head to the palmed **Parque Pedro Moncayo,** located on Bolívar between Flores and Sucre in the heart of Ibarra, surrounded by the Municipal Palace and Roman-style cathedral; alternatively, wander on down to **Parque La Merced,** with a huge Virgin statue towering over its namesake church.

For a reasonable daily fee, you can use the pool, sauna, gym, and other facilities at either Hotel Montecarlo or Hotel Ajavi (see below).

Tip: Try to catch a local match of *pelota de guante,* a popular game played with a soft ball and large circular leather paddles with large nails embedded in them. This is a team sport, played on a large field, whose rules can best be described as a rough blend of team tennis (without a net) and dodge ball. Ask around town, and you should be able to find a game to watch, especially on Saturday afternoons, after the main market activity winds down.

What to See & Do Nearby
SAN ANTONIO DE IBARRA ★

Cedar wood is abundant in Imbabura province. Take a trip to the small town of San Antonio de Ibarra, and you can see how local woodcarvers transform this raw wood into a centuries-old form of high art. The town, nestled in the Imbabura foothills, is full of galleries selling wood figurines in almost every shape and size; all are beautifully hand-painted. Many are religious themed, although there are plenty of artisans making secular decorative and functional pieces as well. The best stores are on the main street, 25 de Noviembre, and along Calle Ramón Teanga, whose colonial-era charm has been restored. This cobblestone road now features brightly painted buildings, which are a mix of residential homes, tourist shops, galleries, and artisans' workshops. All along the street are broad brick sidewalks with iron, antique-style street lamps.

Tip: I recommend starting your tour of San Antonio de Ibarra near the church known locally as La Capilla del Barrio del Sur. This diminutive blue church is near the top of the restored section of Calle Ramón Teanga. Catty-corner to the church is **Escultura Cisneros** (📞 06/2932-354), the workshop of Saul and Alfonso Cisneros, prominent local sculptors. From here, walk downhill for several blocks, stopping in at whatever shops strike your fancy, before jogging over toward the town's central plaza and the main Av. 25 de Noviembre. Heading out of town on this avenue, be sure to stop at **Asociación de Artesanos** (📞 06/2933-538). This large space exhibits works by local artisans and also has a large gallery that often hosts traveling exhibitions. For a real treat, try calling on **Alcides Montesdeoca** (📞 06/2932-106), a renowned maker of large Virgin Mary sculptures used in prominent Holy Week processions around the world. Alcides can usually be found at his home workshop, on Calle Bolívar 5–38.

GETTING THERE   San Antonio de Ibarra is located 5km (3 miles) south of Ibarra, just off the Pan-American Highway. Any bus from Ibarra to Quito or Otavalo will drop you off at the entrance to San Antonio de Ibarra, although it's 10 blocks or more uphill from here to the center of town, so be sure to hop on one of the similarly frequent direct buses to San Antonio proper. These leave roughly every 20 minutes from Ibarra's Terminal Terrestre throughout the day. The one-way fare is 20¢. A taxi ride here should cost around $3.

LAGUNA YAHUARCOCHA (YAHUARCOCHA LAKE)

This small lake is a popular local spot for picnics and small-boat outings, and has a racetrack on its shores. But for me, it holds more interest as a historical site. The lake's name means "Blood Lake," in reference to a fierce battle in 1495 in which Inca King Huayna Capac massacred thousands upon thousands of the local Cara people. The massacre was so intense that the lake allegedly turned red.

GETTING THERE   Laguna Yahuarcocha is located 3.2km (2 miles) north of Ibarra, just off the Pan-American Highway. Frequent buses leave Ibarra's main bus terminal for Yahuarcocha. The fare is 30¢. Alternatively, a taxi ride here should cost around $3 to $4.

Where to Stay in Ibarra
MODERATE
Hacienda Chorlavi ★ ☺   Dating from 1816, this hacienda was originally a Jesuit monastery. While only 12 of the rooms are housed in the original building, all have a colonial-era style and feel. The suites are very large, with king-size beds, modern bathrooms, and floors featuring a mix of wood and stonework. My favorite is no. 55, a separate little cottage fronting a small garden plot. For standard rooms, I recommend either those in the original building or those in the block (nos. 26–35), which is located near the pool. The hacienda has extensive facilities, which include tennis, squash, and volleyball courts, as well as gentle, well-trained horses. And they

specialize in rides for children. Excellent **Ecuadorean cuisine** is served in an antique dining room, as well as around the central stone courtyard of the main building. Even if you're not staying here, you might consider coming for a meal (see below). ·

Km 5, Panamericana, Ibarra (5km/3 miles south of Ibarra, on the Pan-American Hwy.). www.hacienda chorlavi.com. ✆ **06/2932-222** or 06/2932-223. Fax 06/2932-224. 54 units. $65 double; $88 suite. Rates include breakfast and taxes. AE, DC, MC, V. Free parking. **Amenities:** Restaurant; Jacuzzi; small outdoor pool; room service; sauna; steam room; outdoor squash court; outdoor tennis court; free Wi-Fi. *In room:* TV.

Hotel Ajavi   Located just a few minutes from the center of the city, this resort-style hotel offers modern, comfortable rooms with a somewhat minimalist feel. The two suites are quite large, each featuring a Jacuzzi tub in the bathroom. The province's largest hotel, Ajavi has expansive grounds and beautiful gardens. The hotel features a range of amenities and facilities, including a health club with up-to-date equipment and a full offering of massages and treatments.

Av. Mariana Acosta 1638, Ibarra. www.hotelajavi.com. ✆ **06/2955-555** or 06/2955-221. 60 units. $65 double; $100 suite. AE, DC, MC, V. Free parking. **Amenities:** Restaurant; bar; casino; gym; Jacuzzi; heated pool; room service; sauna; steam room. *In room:* TV.

INEXPENSIVE

Hotel Giralda ★ 🍴   This modern business-class hotel has the most comfortable rooms and best facilities in Ibarra proper. Indeed, it's the only hotel I know of at this price where you're greeted by a uniformed doorman. The rather tacky decor won't be featured in *Architectural Digest,* but it's not so garish as to be disturbing. Rooms are of good size, with two or three twin beds or one queen-size bed. Bathrooms feature sparkling black tile. This place is located slightly east of the city center, on Avenida Atahualpa, which is the start of the route to Hacienda Zuleta (p. 144).

Av. Atahualpa y Juan Francisco Bonilla, Ibarra. www.hotelgiralda.com. ✆/fax **06/2956-002** or ✆ 09/9589-692. 32 units. $49 double. Rates include taxes. AE, DC, MC, V. Free parking. **Amenities:** Restaurant; bar; Jacuzzi; pool; room service; sauna; steam room; tennis court. *In room:* TV, minibar, free Wi-Fi.

Hotel Montecarlo   Located a few blocks from downtown, this hotel offers perfectly acceptable rooms at affordable prices and has many of the same amenities you'll find at Hotel Giralda (see above). Most of the rooms have large picture windows, and those on the fourth floor have pretty good views. The owners and staff are extremely friendly and accommodating.

Calle Jaime Rivadeneira 5–55 y Oviedo, Ibarra. montecarlohotel@gmail.com. ✆ **06/2958-266.** 35 units. $45 double. Rates include breakfast buffet and taxes. AE, DC, MC, V. Free parking. **Amenities:** Restaurant; bar; small gym; Jacuzzi; small indoor pool; room service; sauna; steam room. *In room:* TV, free Wi-Fi.

Where to Dine in Ibarra
MODERATE

Hacienda Chorlavi ★ ECUADOREAN/INTERNATIONAL   Even if you're not staying here (see above), I recommend coming for a meal. There's an elegant dining room in the old hacienda building, but I prefer the tables set on the veranda and patio of the central courtyard with its beautiful central fountain. The menu is far more refined than anything else you'll find in or around Ibarra. The Chorlavi trout comes in a rich cream sauce, while the *carne colorado* is a spicy beef stew served with

Ibarra is famous across Ecuador for its *helado de paila,* a handmade sherbet. Although *helado* translates as "ice cream," Ibarra's *helado de paila* is made simply from fruit juice, fruit pieces, ice, and sugar churned by hand with a wooden paddle in a large copper bowl, or *paila,* over ice and salt.

My favorite flavors are *maracuyá* (passion fruit) and *tomate de árbol* or *tamarillo* (tree tomato). Other popular flavors include *mora* (blackberry) and *guanábana* (soursop).

The tradition was apparently begun in Ibarra in 1897 by Rosalía Suárez, who originally used ice gathered from the (now-extinct) glacier atop Volcán Imbabura. Her descendants still run the original **Heladería Rosalía Suárez** (*(C)* **06/2950-107**), on Calle Oviedo 7–79 and Olmedo. Today there are shops and stands selling *helado de paila* throughout the country. But if you're in Ibarra, be sure to stop here, where they've been dishing up this treat for more than a century.

llapingachos (potato and cheese patties) and *mote* (hominy). The *cuy de hacienda* (guinea pig) is a house specialty, and portions range from filling to huge. On weekends and holidays, local Andean bands accompany most lunches and dinners.

5km (3 miles) south of Ibarra, on the Pan-American Hwy. *(C)* **06/2932-222.** www.haciendachorlavi. com. Reservations recommended. Main courses $6–$14. DC, MC, V. Daily 7–10am, noon–4pm, and 7–9:30pm.

INEXPENSIVE

Café Arte ★ 🎁 ECUADOREAN/INTERNATIONAL   Opened 15 years ago, this eclectic and arty spot wears many hats. It's part gallery, part cafe, part bar, part performance space, and part restaurant. And it seems to excel on almost all fronts, so be sure to stop in here if you're in Ibarra. In addition to showing the owner's own work, this large space often has rotating exhibits of local and visiting artists. The menu ranges from sandwiches, chicken wings, and burgers to grilled mountain trout and filet mignon. There are a host of Mexican-style plates, including tacos and burritos, and specialty drinks are named after famous painters. Expect to find some sort of live entertainment on weekends, which might range from a poetry reading or cinema to a jazz combo, local punk-rock outfit, or metal band.

Calle Salinas 5-43, btw. Flores and Oveido. *(C)* **06/2950-806.** Reservations recommended Sat-Sun. Main courses $3–$7. MC, V. Mon-Thurs 5–11pm; Fri-Sat 5pm–midnight.

Ibarra After Dark

Ibarra is a relatively quiet town after sundown. My favorite nightspot is **Café Arte** ★★ (see above). Another good option is **Sambuca Amnesia** ★, on Oviedo 6–36 and Bolívar (http://sambucalibre.blogspot.com). If you're looking to boogie, head to **Zoom Disco** (*(C)* **06/2609-527**) or the nostalgically named **Studio 54** (*(C)* **06/2953-985**), located out on the highway to Laguna Yahuarcocha.

En Route North: El Angel Ecological Reserve ★

At altitudes ranging from 3,500 to 4,800m (11,480–15,744 ft.), this reserve comprises 15,700 hectares (38,779 acres). Visitors have been known to spot condors, as well as Andean foxes and deer. The park is perhaps most famous for the fields of *frailejón* found here; the *frailejón* is a striking plant with soft, furry leaves and tall central stalks that can grow to heights of some 1.8m (6 ft.). A few small lakes dot the vast and varied topography as well.

The gateway to the park is the tiny town of El Angel, where there's a **park office** (© 06/2977-597). Admission is $2 per person per day, and camping is allowed. Note that the park is often cold and wet, so come prepared.

If you need a place to stay in El Angel, try **Hostería El Angel** (© 06/2977-584; www.ecuador-sommergarten.net); they can also help you arrange a guided tour of the reserve.

To get here, turn off the Pan-American Highway near Pusir and follow signs to Mira and El Angel. If you're coming from Tulcán, make your turn at San Gabriel and follow the signs to El Angel. **Transportes Espejo** (© 02/2474-251 in Quito, 06/2959-917 in Ibarra, or 06/2977-103 in El Angel) has roughly one bus every hour leaving Quito's northern bus terminal **Terminal Terrestre Carcelén** (© 02/3961-600) for El Angel; the trip takes around 3½ to 4 hours. You can also get here with Transportes Espejo from both Ibarra and Tulcán; the ride is about 2 hours from Ibarra and 1½ hours from Tulcán.

The principal entrance to the park, El Voladero, is 16km (10 miles) outside El Angel, along the old road to Tulcán. For a few dollars, you can hire a 4WD taxi in El Angel to take you there.

TULCAN

240km (149 miles) N of Quito; 660km (409 miles) NE of Guayaquil; 145km (90 miles) N of Otavalo

The capital of Carchi province, Tulcán is a small but bustling border town. At almost 3,000m (9,840 ft.), it's usually cool—even quite cool—here. This is the principal land crossing between Ecuador and Colombia, and Tulcán has become a predominantly commercial city, with a brisk business in cross-border trading. For tourists, it's most likely just a transfer point on a journey either to or from Colombia.

Essentials
GETTING THERE
BY PLANE   Saereo (© 1800/723-736; www.saereo.com) operates one flight on Wednesday, Friday, and Sunday from Quito's international airport to the **Aeropuerto Teniente Coronel Luis A Mantilla** (© 06/2980-555; airport code: TUA). The flight takes 30 minutes and costs around $135 round-trip. Outbound and return schedules may vary, so call in advance for ticket information. Tulcán's airport is located 2km (1¼ miles) north of the city center. Taxis are always waiting to meet incoming flights and charge around $1 for the ride into town.

BY BUS   About five different bus lines have regular service making the 5-hour run to Tulcán from Quito's northern bus terminal **Terminal Terrestre Carcelén** (© 02/3961-600), with at least one bus every 15 minutes between 5:30am and 10pm, and at least one bus every half-hour around the clock. The one-way fare costs $5.

Tulcán's bus terminal is located at the southern end of the city, near the junction of Avenida General Arellano and Calle Bolívar. Taxis, which are plentiful, charge around $1 for the ride to the city center.

BY CAR   To reach Tulcán by car, take the Pan-American Highway (E35) north out of Quito. Follow the directions above to Otavalo (p. 128) and Ibarra (p. 145), and then continue on to Tulcán. The ride takes 4 to 4½ hours.

ORIENTATION

Tulcán is a long, narrow city running roughly southwest to northeast. Avenida General Arellano is the main artery through town, although 1 block east of Arellano, Calle Bolívar, as well as its parallel Calle Sucre, is where the city's business and civic life thrives. The central Plaza de la Independencia is bounded on either side by calles Sucre and Olmedo. About 5 blocks north, between Avenida General Arellano and Calle Bolívar, is the larger Parque Isidro Ayora.

The Colombian border is 6km (3¾ miles) north of downtown.

GETTING AROUND

You'll have no trouble flagging down a taxi. If you do, call **Cooperativa de Taxis Rápido Nacional** (☏ **06/2980-420**). Rides around town should not exceed $1, and a trip to the border should cost around $4.50.

Minivans leave for the airport and the border throughout the day from the northeast corner of Parque Isidro Ayora. The fare is 50¢ to the airport and $1 to the border.

VISITOR INFORMATION

There's a basic **tourist information office** (☏ **06/2980-487**) on the southeast side of Parque de la Independencia, on Calle Olmedo. You'll also find an **iTur tourist information booth** (☏ **06/2985-760**) near the entrance to the Municipal Cemetery on Cotopaxi. Both are open Monday through Friday during business hours.

Tips: Tulcán has the reputation of being a rough and dangerous border city. Colombia's ongoing insurgency and drug trafficking are no help, either. Use common sense—don't wander far from the city center or popular tourist spots, try not to travel alone, and use taxis to get around, especially at night.

FAST FACTS   To contact the **police,** dial ☏ **101.** For a medical emergency, you can call **Cruz Roja** (**Red Cross;** ☏ **06/2980-100**) on Olmedo and Junin, or head to **Hospital de Lea** (☏ **06/2980-396**), on Calle Junín and Avenida General Arellano, or **Hospital Provincial** (☏ 06/2981961), on 10 de Agosto and España. The main **post office** (☏ **06/2980-552**) is on Calle Bolívar, between Junín and Boyacá.

For your banking needs, head to **Banco Pichincha** (☏ **06/2985-020**), on 10 de Agosto and Sucre. This bank will change money into Colombian pesos, as will **Casa de Cambio** (☏ **06/2985-731**), on Calle Ayacucho and Sucre. If the bank and Casa de Cambio are closed or inconvenient, you'll find plenty of individual money-changers hanging out at Parque Isidro Ayora and on Plaza de la Independencia. You'll probably get better rates for pesos in Tulcán—either at the official bank, Casa de Cambio, or with these money-changers—than you will at the border.

As elsewhere in Ecuador, you'll have no problem finding an Internet cafe here. I recommend **Compu Café Net** (☏ **06/2984-949**), on calles Ecuador and Bolívar; **Planeta Internet** (☏ **06/2985-739**), on Bolivar between Junin and Ayacucho; or **Café Net,** on Olmedo and Ayacucho, which is closer to the center of town.

There is a **Colombian consulate** (☏ **06/2890-559**) in Tulcán at Av. Manabí 58–087, across from Parque Isisdro Ayora (although you should be able to handle all immigration formalities at the border itself).

What to See & Do

Tulcán's greatest attraction is its **Cementerio Municipal (Municipal Cemetery)** ★, with its extravagant topiary gardens. These were begun in 1936 by José María Azael Franco. In 1984, the Ecuadorean government designated the gardens a National Patrimony Site. Today Franco's sons carry on the tradition, and Franco is buried beneath some of his creations, with one of his quotes prominently displayed: "A cemetery so beautiful, it invites one to die." While the cemetery is the town's crowning achievement, Franco's work and influence can be seen all over Tulcán, where locals have taken to shearing and shaping just about every bush and tree they can lay their clippers on. The Municipal Cemetery is located about 2 blocks north of Parque Isidro Ayora.

Although not particularly tourist oriented, the Sunday market is packed with goods, clothes, and electrical appliances, and it's worth a visit if you are on the prowl for a deal. **Museo German Bastidas Vaca** (© 06/2980-172), on Cotopaxi and Panamá, houses an interesting repertoire of artifacts from the Carchi province dating from pre-Columbian to contemporary times, including pieces by the famous Ecuadorean artist, Guayasamín. Admission is $1, and it is open Monday through Friday 9am to 4pm and Saturday 9am to 1pm.

If you fancy venturing closer to the border, you can take a trip to **La Paz** hot springs or to the somewhat warmer **Aguas Hedionas,** with their extremely high sulfur content. Check the local bus companies, **Cooperativa 11 de Abril** (© 06/2985-432) and **Transportes Velotax Norte** (© 06/2980-633), for bus schedules. You can also go to Volcán Chiles, on the border with Colombia, an ideal spot for trekking, climbing, and nature walks.

If you want to arrange a tour around this area or to El Angel, or if you just need help with logistical arrangements, contact **Eccotur** (© 06/2980-368), on Calle Sucre 51–029 and 10 de Agosto.

Where to Stay & Dine in Tulcán

Tulcán has a rather wide range of hotel and restaurant options (although tourists staying here are usually only in transit). Among the best are **Hotel Azteca** (©/fax 06/2960-417), on Bolívar and Atahualpa, offering clean double rooms with cable TV and hot water at around $16; and the pricier **Hotel Sara Espindola** (© 06/2986-209), on Sucre and Ayacucho, at $88 per double. Fronting the main Parque de la Independencia, the Sara Espindola gets the nod for its location. For budget travelers, another option is **Hotel Lumar** (© 06/2980-402), on Sucre and Pichincha, which has doubles, with cable TV, for $28.

Tip: Hotel rooms fill up fast in Tulcán on weekends, when Colombian shoppers flock to town to take advantage of bargains their slightly stronger currency buys them in Ecuador. Therefore, if you're going to stay here on a weekend, be sure to make reservations.

Your best dining bets are probably the restaurants at the first two downtown hotels mentioned above. Being this close to the border, be sure to look out for and sample some Colombian cuisine. *Pollo sudado,* which translates literally as "sweaty chicken," is a tasty braised-chicken-and-potato dish, while *bandeja paisa* is a plate piled high with various fried foods, similar to the Ecuadorean dish *chugchucaras,* which is popular around Latacunga (p. 163).

Tulcán After Dark

Hotel Azteca and Sara Espindola (see above) both have bar-discos that get particularly packed on weekends. Most bars and clubs can be found in and around Calle Bolívar, including **T-Kila** (© 06/2986-346), and **Canela Son** (© 06/2981-899) and **Tropicana** (© 06/2983-335), both on Junin. If you want to try your luck at blackjack, poker, or slots, head to **Rey Casino Internacional** (© 06/2980-952), on Sucre and Ayacucho.

Crossing into Colombia

The Pan-American Highway passes through Tulcán, over the Rumichaca bridge and on into the Bolívar province of Colombia. The closest Colombian town to the border is Ipiales, about 2km (1¼ miles) north of the bridge.

The border process is relatively painless and cost-free. Ecuadorean and Colombian immigration officials have their stations on either side of the bridge. If you're heading into Colombia, you will have the option of either a 30- or a 90-day visa. (Be sure to specify the latter if you think you'll need it.) The border offices are open daily from 6am until 8pm.

There are money-changers on both sides of the border, but you're best off changing for some Colombian pesos in Tulcán.

Given the precarious security situation in Colombia, you should always check with your home consulate, fellow travelers, and knowledgeable locals before heading across.

THE CENTRAL SIERRA

Heading south out of Quito, the Pan-American High-way passes through high Andean terrain that Alexander von Humboldt called La Avenida de los Volcanes, or "Avenue of the Volcanoes." This is some of Ecuador's most beautiful mountain territory, with snowcapped peaks, high-altitude paramos, and massive tracts of cattle and sheep pasture patrolled by Andean condors overhead. Volcán Cotopaxi is the most impressive and striking of the peaks here, owing to its near-perfect volcanic cone covered in glacial ice. This imposing behemoth is still active and a must-summit for any serious mountain climber.

This region features a host of other towering snowcapped peaks, including Volcán Chimborazo, Volcán Rumiñahui, and the twin Iliniza peaks. Throughout the area, you can find isolated haciendas that have been converted into fabulous little hotels and inns. As you follow the Avenue of the Volcanoes south, you eventually hit the popular tourist towns of Riobamba and Baños. The latter is named after the hot springs, or *baños,* located at the foot of towering Volcán Tungurahua.

COTOPAXI NATIONAL PARK ★★★

60km (37 miles) S of Quito

At 5,897m (19,342 ft.), Cotopaxi is one of the world's highest continuously active volcanoes and Ecuador's second-highest peak. Your first encounter with the almost perfectly cone-shaped and snow-covered Cotopaxi might be from a plane overhead; I've been on flights that have come so terrifyingly close to the volcano that I almost felt I could reach out and touch it. From above, it's hard to determine where the clouds end and the glaciers begin. The snow glimmers in the sunlight and magically blends with the bright blue sky—and what a sight! But you don't need a plane—on a clear day in Quito, from many vantage points, you can see Cotopaxi rising high and mighty above the clouds.

The first documented summit of Cotopaxi was on November 28, 1872, by the German climber Wilhelm Reiss and his Colombian partner, Angel Escobar.

Essentials

GETTING THERE

BY PLANE The closest airport with regular traffic is Quito's **Aeropuerto Internacional Mariscal Sucre** (☎ 02/2944-900). See "Arriving," in chapter 5.

BY BUS & TAXI Frequent buses leave Quito's southbound bus terminal, **Terminal Terrestre Quitumbe** (☎ 02/3988-200), heading south along the Pan-American Highway. **Transportes Latacunga** (☎ 03/2800-765), **Cooperativa de Transportes CIRO** (☎ 03/2801-285), and **Cooperativa de Transportes Cotopaxi** (☎ 03/2800-752) bus lines take turns running the route to Latacunga and Ambato, with a bus leaving roughly every 20 to 30 minutes from 6am to 9pm, and somewhat less frequent service throughout the rest of the evening and early morning. A one-way trip to Latacunga costs $1.50.

There are two main entrances to the park and a third, lesser-used entrance. By far, most visitors use the main southern entrance, also known as El Chasqui. If you are going to the park by bus, be sure to ask the driver to drop you off at the El Chasqui entrance to Cotopaxi National Park. From here, you can hire a taxi to take you to the park entrance and on to the museum or other spots inside the park for around $8 to $15. Be sure to specify to the taxi driver exactly where you want to be dropped off, because the entrance gate (*control sur*) is several miles before any of the more popular attractions inside the park.

If you're going to the northern entrance (*control norte*), you can get off any of the above buses at the entrance to Machachi or, better yet, take the **Carlos Brito** (☎ 02/2315-192) bus from Quito's **Terminal Terrestre Quitumbe** into Machachi; here you can transfer to one of the twice-daily local buses to El Pedregal, although that will still leave you several kilometers to go to the park entrance. Your best bet is to hire a truck-taxi in Machachi to take you all the way into the park for around $20 to $30.

BY CAR No matter which entrance you decide to use to access the park, begin by heading south out of Quito on the Pan-American Highway (E35). To enter the park through the **northern entrance,** exit at Machachi and drive through the town, following the signs for El Pedregal and Cotopaxi National Park. This 21km (13-mile) stretch of dirt road is sometimes very rugged, especially during rainy periods, and a high-clearance 4WD is necessary. This is the route to take if you are staying at Hacienda El Porvenir or Hostería Tambopaxi (see reviews later in this chapter). Once inside the park, it's another 16km (10 miles) to the museum and parking area.

Although slightly farther from Quito, the **southern park entrance** is more popular and has better access roads. To reach this entrance, continue on the Pan-American Highway past Machachi for another half-hour or so, until just before the village of Lasso. You will see the signs on your left side indicating the turnoff for the southern entrance to Cotopaxi National Park. This entrance and route are best if you plan to visit, or base yourself out of, the park's museum and nearby campsites.

There is a **third entrance** to the park located about 16km (10 miles) south of Machachi, before the principal southern entrance. This entrance is often referred to as El Boliche and is the least used and least convenient for most travelers visiting the park.

A 4WD vehicle is recommended whichever route you take, although if you drive slowly and carefully, a normal sedan can usually use the southern entrance route.

BY TRAIN On Saturdays, Sundays, and public holidays, visitors can take a train that runs along the pretty Quito–Boliche–Machachi route and takes passengers to

The Central Sierra

the El Boliche recreational area right inside Cotopaxi National Park. The scenic ride, which takes just over 4 hours in total, departs the Estacion Eloy Alfaro in Chimbacalle at 8:15am and costs $15 per person. You can purchase tickets at Bolívar Oe5–43 and Garcia Moreno in Quito or at the **railway's main office,** located on Quilotoa and Sangay, Estacion Eloy Alfaro, in Chimbacalle (☎ **02/2951-400,** ext. 133; www.ferrocarrilesdelecuador.gob.ec). Check the website for current information on routes and schedules.

ORIENTATION

There are two main entrances to Cotopaxi National Park; see "Getting There," above, for more information on accessing these entrances. Most visitors use the principal southern entrance, or *control sur,* also known as El Chasqui. This is the closest entrance to the small museum and visitor center.

Inside the park are a series of trails, dirt roads, and campsites. The road from the southern entrance forms a very rough semicircle around the foot of Volcán Cotopaxi. About 10km (6¼ miles) from the entrance gate, you'll come to the museum, as well as to a small restaurant, souvenir stand, and campsite. Beyond the museum to the north lies Laguna de Limpiopungo, a small high-mountain lake with a pretty campsite beside it. Beyond Laguna de Limpiopungo, the road forks. The left fork leads toward

Tambopaxi (p. 163) and the northern entrance (*control norte*). This road actually forks again, with a secondary road leading into the much less frequently visited eastern area of the park. The main right fork heads sharply south toward the cone of the volcano and the Refugio José Rivas (4,800m/15,744 ft.), some 9km (5½ miles) away.

VISITOR INFORMATION

Whether you enter the park from the northern or southern entrance, you will be given a park map when you pay your entrance fee. Park rangers at each entrance gate can give basic information and recommendations, although their English may be limited or even nonexistent. Most travelers visit with a guide or as part of a guided tour, and unless you are a very experienced climber and hard-core camper, I recommend you do so as well.

There are no banks, shops, or other major services inside the park. The main ranger headquarters (© **09/9820-493** or 02/2812-768) is located by the small museum. The park admission is $10 per day, and camping costs another $2 per person per day. A bunk at the Refugio José Rivas costs $10 per night. This refuge is the most common jumping-off point for summit attempts.

What to See & Do in Cotopaxi National Park ★★★

Looking down from a plane at a volcano is one thing, but climbing it, camping on its flanks, riding a horse or mountain bike across the paramo, or hiking around it are much more rewarding. The high Andean paramo here features wild horses and llamas grazing. Below the volcano, the flat plains are peppered with volcanic boulders that give stark evidence of the power and fury of Cotopaxi's relatively recent eruptions. And everywhere you turn, there are fantastic views of the snow-covered crater—that is, when it's not shrouded in low cloud cover.

Climbing to the summit is serious business, and not for those in merely average physical condition or with no experience at high altitudes. Nonetheless, every year, thousands of intrepid climbers take out their ice axes, strap on their crampons, and conquer the summit. An embarrassing admission: I've never done it. But according to those in the know, the climb is not terribly technical or difficult. On the other hand, I have met several experienced climbers who have been severely affected by the altitude and were forced to turn back early. Be sure to spend several days in Quito and at higher altitudes acclimating before you attempt to summit Cotopaxi. Even if you're feeling fine at 2,800m (9,184 ft.), the air will feel a whole lot thinner at 5,000m (16,400 ft.), especially if you're exerting a lot of energy. You should also note that the climb typically starts at about 11pm to midnight, and you will be going uphill on glaciers for about 8 continuous hours before you reach the top. This way, you reach the crater in the early morning light, before the clouds settle in.

Fortunately for the less adventurous and less fit, you really don't need to climb Cotopaxi to enjoy it. A host of outfitters in Quito, and all the hotels close to the volcano, organize day trips to the national park. Many day trips bring you to the small museum and visitor center, which has a somewhat sad collection of stuffed animals, including an Andean condor, as well as a relief map of the volcano and some explanatory materials. From here, these trips commonly take any number of short to midlength hikes around the park, most commonly to the Laguna de Limpiopungo. The museum is located at 4,500m (14,760 ft.) above sea level, and most of the hikes around the park take place at this general altitude; note that, even at this altitude, the air is quite thin and it's not uncommon to feel lightheaded.

Cotopaxi National Park

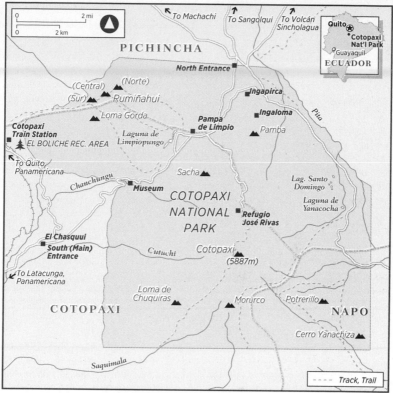

ORGANIZING A CLIMB TO THE TOP   It's very important to make sure that you're climbing Cotopaxi with an experienced guide and good equipment. The best companies provide one guide for every two climbers. The finest and most experienced outfitters include **Adventure Planet Ecuador ★** (☎ **02/2863-086;** www.adventure planet.ec) and **Safari Ecuador ★★** (☎ **02/2552-505;** www.safari.com.ec). Rates run $190 to $300 per person for a 2-day/1-night trip to the summit, depending on the size of your group.

The above companies also organize longer treks around the park, as well as climbs to the summits of other nearby peaks, including Rumiñahui, Iliniza Norte, and Iliniza Sur, all of which are good practice climbs to tackle before attempting Cotopaxi.

VISITING AS PART OF A DAY TRIP   Just about every tour desk and tour operator in Quito offers a day trip to Cotopaxi. The details may vary some, but most head first to the small museum and then spend anywhere from 1 to 3 hours hiking. In addition, most operators offer options for mountain biking or horseback riding.

The best general tour operators, in my opinion, are **Metropolitan Touring ★★** (☎ **02/2988-200;** www.metropolitan-touring.com) and **Surtrek ★★** (☎ **866/978-7398** in the U.S. and Canada, or 02/2500-530 in Ecuador; www.surtrek.com). Day

ANDEAN condor

While hiking around Cotopaxi National Park, our guide pointed out a tiny pinprick silhouette almost beyond the scope of our sight. Was he right in assuring us it was an Andean condor? I don't know, but it was the nearest I've ever come to seeing one in the wild. *Vultur gryphus,* Ecuador's national bird, is not easy to find these days, despite its 3m (9¾-ft.) wingspan, 11-kilogram (25-lb.) body, and legs and claws the size of a man's forearm and fist. It is the biggest raptor on the planet, but according to estimates, a mere 80 birds remain in isolated populations around Antisana, Cotopaxi, El Altar, and El Angel, and near the Papallacta Pass.

Dating back to the Pleistocene age, the Andean condor once thrived in an era when mastodons were their primary source of carrion. They nearly went extinct along with their large food sources but made a comeback when Spanish settlers began introducing massive sheep and cow herds on the high Andean paramo.

The condor boasts other impressive stats. Maturing at around 7 years of age, condors can live to 60. They mate for life, with both sexes incubating the egg, which is laid every 2 years (so junior gets nearly 2 years of parenting before leaving home). An overall glossy black plumage gives way to a neat white neck ruff into which apparently high-soaring birds tuck their bald heads when flying at subzero temperatures. That lack of head and neck feathers ensures that the carrion-eating condor easily keeps itself free of germs after tucking into a carcass. The condor can spot a dead animal from miles away and is known to follow smaller raptors on the hunt to get in on the meal—because no other bird will mess with a condor, it has a guaranteed place at the table. Oh, and it turns out that the condor is not in the vulture family: Biochemical studies now place it genetically with storks!

As usual, the main threat to this magnificent creature is humans. Although it is a carrion feeder, the condor has historically had a reputation for preying on young animals, placing it in direct conflict with highland farmers. Most ranchers will kill condors on sight, and it has been a traditional rite of passage for a young man to bag a bird to prove his virility. In the past, local communities would lure a condor into traps baited with rotting meat. The captive bird was then strapped to a bull depicting Spanish domination over the conquered native population. If the condor succeeded in flying free, it was a sign of good fortune for the community.

Condors need lots of air space and land to thrive, and evidence suggests that breeding programs and reintroductions into the wild can succeed. An ambitious Nature Conservancy/USAID–supported program, embracing nearly 2.2 million hectares (5.4 million acres) ranging from Antisana, Cotopaxi, Cayambe, and dropping to the Amazon rainforests to the east, might help tip the balance. With a multifaceted, functional-landscape approach, the **Condor Bioreserve** aims to protect the main watershed providing Quito's drinking water, defend indigenous reserves, and encourage farmers to create wildlife corridors. Keep your eyes open, keep your head in the air, and hope.

trips to Cotopaxi run $40 to $90, depending on the size of your group and whether lunch is included. The park entrance fee is rarely included.

If you want to tour the park on a mountain bike, contact **Aries Bike Company** (✆ **02/2380-802;** www.ariesbikecompany.com), **Safari Ecuador** ★★

(© **02/2552-505**; www.safari.com.ec), or **Surtrek** ★★ (© **866/978-7398** in the U.S. and Canada, or 02/2500-530 in Ecuador; www.surtrek.com).

For horseback-riding tours of Cotopaxi, I recommend **Ilalo Expeditions** ★ (© **09/7778-399**; www.ilaloexpeditions.com), **Hacienda La Alegría** ★★ (see below), or **Safari Ecuador** (© **02/2552-505**; www.safari.com.ec).

Mountain-bike or horseback excursions to Cotopaxi run around $50 to $90, depending on the length of the tour and several other variables, such as group size and equipment requirements.

Where to Stay & Dine in & Around Cotopaxi

The intimate and upscale **Hacienda Umbria** ★★ (© **09/9407-471** or 02/6034-151; www.haciendaumbria.com) is another excellent option. The hotel and its owner, chef, and sommelier, Alvaro Samper, offer up a wonderful culinary, cultural, and scenic feast. You might also check out the new **CotopaxiPungo** ★ (© **09/9551-215**; www.hotelsebastian.com), which is expected to open in 2011. Owned and run by the folks behind Hotel Sebastian (p. 94) in Quito, this place will have 18 rooms with excellent volcano views. Moreover, the hotel is located close to 11 beautiful and seldom-visited Andean waterfalls.

All the lodges and haciendas listed here are very isolated. If you're staying at one of them, you will most likely take all your meals there. The only real restaurant of note to visit separately while visiting the park is at **Hosteria Tambopaxi** (p. 163). There's also a simple little restaurant next to the national park's museum.

VERY EXPENSIVE

Hacienda San Agustín de Callo ★★★ 🏠   Built inside the remains of an old Augustine monastery—which was itself built on top of an ancient Inca temple and residence—this is one of the most unique hotels in Ecuador. Accommodations are large and beautifully appointed, and most rooms have hand-painted murals. My favorite rooms are those with exposed Inca stone walls, but every room has something going for it, including those in a newer building, which have Jacuzzi tubs and great views of Cotopaxi. The lounge area features an original portrait of the owner, Mignon Plaza, painted by Oswaldo Guayasamín. The main dining room is built inside a classic Inca structure, with trapezoidal window niches and a more modern large window overlooking the garden and perfectly framing the volcano.

Lasso, Cotopaxi (mailing address: Tamayo N24-607 y Av. Colon, Quito). www.incahacienda.com. ©/fax **02/2906-157** reservations office in Quito, or ©/fax **03/2719-160** at the hacienda. 11 units. $348–$398 double. Rates include 3 meals daily, and daily tours and activities. Rates higher during peak periods. AE, DC MC, V. **Amenities:** Restaurant; bar; mountain bikes. *In room:* TV, Internet.

EXPENSIVE

Hacienda Hato Verde ★   Although this converted home is over 120 years old, it has a more modern feel than most of the other haciendas, while still retaining its fair share of colonial-era charm. All the rooms have heavy iron beds, antique armoires, and wood-burning stoves; most units have dark, polished wood floors. In general, the bathrooms are on the small side, although they are very attractive, with interesting tile work and hip, modern fixtures. Paintings throughout the hacienda are by Sussy Palacio, the mother of one of the owners. The main lounge area is a beautiful room with heavy stone walls, high ceilings supported by exposed wood beams, and a massive stone fireplace. With advance notice, televisions can be put into any room. The owners are avid equestrians who specialize in horseback-riding tours and adventures. A full, hearty breakfast is included in the room rate.

Km 55, Pan-American Hwy., on the entrance road to Mulalo, Lasso, Cotopaxi. www.haciendahatoverde. com. ©/fax **03/2719-348** or 09/5978-016. 9 units. $183–$244 double. Rates include full breakfast. AE, MC, V. **Amenities:** Restaurant; bar. *In room:* No phone.

Hacienda La Alegría ★ ☺   This lovely hacienda is quite close to Quito. The entrance is striking, with a flowing fountain—made from a massive stone spewed out during one of Cotopaxi's eruptions. The owners are equestrians, and horseback riding is the specialty here. Multiday horse treks into the high paramo and exploration of Cotopaxi National Park are available. This is also a great place to learn how to ride; they take particularly good care of beginning and young riders. The best rooms are the two newer units in back of the main building, with wood floors and masonry fireplaces. Each has a queen-size and twin bed downstairs and two more twins in a large loft with a small skylight. The rooms in the older main house have more character and an antique feel, but not all have private bathrooms. Half of the still-working milking barn has been converted into a game room and lounge.

40km (25 miles) south of Quito, near the town of Aloag (mailing address: Alonso Torres N4302 y Beck Rollo, Edificio El Roble, Apt. 201, Quito). www.haciendalaalegria.com. © **02/2462-319** or 09/9802-526. 6 units, 3 with private bathroom. $130 double. Rates include full breakfast. AE, DC MC, V. **Amenities:** Restaurant; bar. *In room:* No phone.

MODERATE

Hacienda La Carriona   This is one of the closest hacienda options to Quito. The rooms in this over-200-year-old farm vary widely; most have high ceilings, painted brick walls, and exposed-beam ceilings. I like nos. 1 through 8, which are in the oldest part of the hacienda and have Persian rugs and antique beds and furniture. The best room is no. 36, a large suite with a big stone fireplace. It opens onto a small garden in back. The hotel has a small outdoor pool and pretty gardens. There's even a small bullring where nonfatal bullfights are sometimes held. The hacienda can arrange golf packages, too—one of Quito's better 18-hole courses is located just 5 minutes away, and there are two roughed-in practice holes on the hacienda's expansive grounds. La Carriona is only about 40 minutes from Quito's airport; it will be even closer to the new airport once it's open.

Km 2.5 on the road to Amaguana, Sangoloquí. www.haciendalacarriona.com. © **02/2331-974** or 02/2332-004. Fax 02/2332-005. 30 units. $110 double; $128 junior suite; $150 suite. Rates include full breakfast and taxes. AE, DC MC, V. **Amenities:** Restaurant; bar; small gym; Jacuzzi; small outdoor pool; sauna; steam bath; free Wi-Fi. *In room:* TV.

Hostería La Ciénega ★   This hacienda has been in the family of the Marques de Maenza since the 17th century. In 1802, Alexander von Humboldt took up residence in unit no. 8, the massive top-floor suite, which has soaring arched ceilings and crystal chandeliers. I actually prefer no. 7—similar in size and feel, but with a much larger balcony. The rest of the rooms vary considerably, and some are in severe need of maintenance and overhaul. Nos. 30 through 35, located in a row close to the chapel, are all good bets. For a view of Cotopaxi, ask for no. 6, an end room on the second floor with a small balcony overlooking the volcano and three oversized twin beds. In addition to the impressive main-entrance driveway, the central courtyard garden and beautiful private chapel are magnificent examples of the grand colonial-era opulence of this classic estate.

Km 20, Pan-American Hwy., Lasso, Cotopaxi (mailing address: Calle Cordero 1442 y Av. Amazonas, Quito). www.hosterialacienega.com. © **02/2549-126** reservations office in Quito, or 03/2719-093 at the hacienda. Fax 02/2228-820. 34 units. $89 double; $140–$181 suite. Rates include full breakfast and taxes. AE, DC MC, V. **Amenities:** Restaurant; bar; tennis court. *In room:* No phone.

INEXPENSIVE

Hacienda El Porvenir ★ 🎁 Located near the north entrance to Cotopaxi National Park, this is a working hacienda that specializes in dairy cattle and the wild Andean fighting bull—there are more than 300 head of the latter on the grounds. In the main building's second floor, there are a series of units with shared bathrooms and steeply pitched ceilings—however, the roof cuts into the space of the rooms. A wonderful honeymoon suite in the main building has a picture window, a woodstove, and a brass bed. In a separate building, you'll find a couple of more suites and hacienda rooms, some with great views of the Cotopaxi volcano. Besides treks and summits inside the national park, horseback riding and mountain biking are prime activities here, and the hacienda also runs a nearby zip-line canopy tour. This hacienda is also known as Tierra de Volcanes, although the owners actually run several small haciendas close to Cotopaxi under that brand name, and they organize a wide range of multiday adventure tours, including a "Traveling with Meaning" tour combining adventure with conservation and community service activities.

4km (2½ miles) from the park entrance, on the road btw. Machachi and the northern entrance to Cotopaxi National Park (mailing address: Via Lactea #350 y Chimborazo, Cumbaya). www.tierradelvolcan. com. ✆ **02/2041-520** or 09/4980-121. 19 units, 9 with private bathroom. $40 double with shared bathroom; $88–$132 double with private bathroom. Rates include full breakfast. Lower rates in the off season. Camping $4 per person, not including meals. AE, MC, V. **Amenities:** Restaurant; bar; TV lounge; mountain-bike rental. *In room:* No phone.

Hosteria Tambopaxi 🎁 Located inside Cotopaxi National Park, this makes a perfect base for folks wanting some comfort before and/or after climbing to the summit. It also makes a great base for less strenuous hiking and trekking around the park. A lunch stop for day-trippers, Tambopaxi also has four clean, comfortable dorm rooms with shared bathrooms above the restaurant. These are large, with a mix of twin and bunk beds crammed in tightly. For a bit more money, you can opt for one of the individual rooms with private bathrooms located in a separate building. The second-floor room on the south side of this building has a fabulous volcano view. Camping is allowed here. The **dining room** features a red-tile floor, rustic wooden tables and chairs, and wraparound picture windows with views of the paramo and the volcano.

Inside Cotopaxi National Park, 9km (5½ miles) from the village of El Pedregal (mailing address: Diego de Almagro N26-105 y La Pinta, office #9, Quito). www.tambopaxi.com. ✆ **02/2220-241** reservation number in Quito, or 09/9448-223 at the lodge. 10 units, 6 with private bathroom. $6 per person camping; $16 per person in dorm room; $85 double private bathroom. Rate for the private bathrooms includes breakfast. MC, V. **Amenities:** Restaurant; bar. *In room:* No phone.

LATACUNGA

89km (55 miles) S of Quito; 47km (29 miles) N of Ambato; 335km (208 miles) N of Guayaquil

Latacunga is a bustling midsize city located just across a river from the Pan-American Highway, southwest of Cotopaxi. The snowcapped volcano towers imposingly and impressively over the city, forming a beautiful backdrop from many spots. Latacunga is the capital of Cotopaxi Province and a major market and industrial center for this region. Few tourists use it as a base for exploring Cotopaxi National Park, and I highly recommend the more picturesque and inviting nearby haciendas listed above—though budget travelers and those depending on buses for transportation may find themselves, by design or by chance, needing to overnight in Latacunga. If that's the case, don't despair: This is a pleasant and friendly city. Latacunga is also the main jumping-off point for those touring the so-called Quilotoa Loop (p. 167).

Although Cotopaxi is relatively quiet at the moment, it has pretty much completely destroyed Latacunga on three occasions, in 1742, 1768, and 1877. Stubborn and loyal, the undeterred residents have continued to rebuild in this precarious spot.

Essentials

GETTING THERE

BY BUS   Very frequent buses leave Quito's southbound bus terminal, **Terminal Terrestre Quitumbe** (✆ 02/3988-200), heading south along the Pan-American Highway to Latacunga. **Cooperativa de Transportes CIRO** (✆ 03/2801-285), **Cooperativa de Transportes Cotopaxi** (✆ 03/2800-752), and **Transportes Latacunga** (✆ 03/2800-765) bus companies take turns running the route, with a bus leaving roughly every 20 to 30 minutes between 6am and 8:30pm, with somewhat less frequent service throughout the rest of the evening and early morning. The ride costs $1.50 and takes around 2 hours. Alternatively, you can catch any bus heading to Ambato or Baños—just ask to be let off in Latacunga.

Latacunga's main bus terminal is right on the Pan-American Highway, near one of the bridges a couple of blocks away from the town center. Buses heading to other towns such as Ambato will drop passengers off at the corner of 5 de Junio and Cotopaxi, a 10-minute walk from the center. Taxis are always waiting around the bus terminal and along the southern edge of the main market.

BY CAR   To reach Latacunga by car, head south out of Quito on the Pan-American Highway (E35). Latacunga is located just off the highway, across the Río Cutuchi. The ride takes a little over an hour and a half.

ORIENTATION

The heart and majority of the city lies on the eastern side of the Río Cutuchi, with the Pan-American Highway passing along the western bank of this river. There are several bridges over the river: The most popular one, farthest to the north, takes you on to Calle Félix Valencia, which runs along the northern edge of the market and Plaza El Salto. A second bridge crosses the river on Av. 5 de Junio, which runs along the southern edge of this large market area. The main north-south thoroughfare through town is Avenida Amazonas; this broad avenue is dotted with monuments, sculptures, and antique-style lampposts strung along the central divider. Most of the hotels, restaurants, shops, and bars are clustered around or near Parque Vicente Léon, the town's main plaza.

GETTING AROUND

You can easily walk anywhere in Latacunga, but taxis are also plentiful. A ride to anyplace in town should be $1 to $2. If you can't flag down a taxi, call **Taxis los Nevados de Cotopaxi** (✆ 03/2802-766) or **Cooperativa de Taxis Universidad de Cotopaxi** (✆ 03/2809-100). Taxis are always waiting around the bus terminal and along the southern edge of the main market.

VISITOR INFORMATION

There's a basic tourist information booth (Mon–Fri 8am–6pm) inside the main bus terminal. There's also an official **Captur** (✆ 03/2814-968) tourist information office on Avenida Sánchez de Orellana and Guayaquil, in Plazoleta de Santo Domingo, which is open Monday through Friday from 8am to noon. At both places, you can get maps and brochures, but your best source of information will probably be the local tour agencies (see below).

FAST FACTS The main **police station** (📞 03/2812-666, or 101 in an emergency) is on Calle San Martín. The main **post office** is at the corner of Quevedo and General Maldonado (📞 03/2811-394). **Hospital General Latacunga** (📞 03/2800-331 or 03/2800-332) is near the southern edge of the city, on Calle Hermanas Paez 1–02 and 2 de Mayo.

You'll find a branch of **Banco de Guayaquil** (📞 03/3730-100) on General Maldonado 7–20 and Orellana, and a branch of **Banco Pichincha** (📞 03/2810-304) on Quito 71–95 and Salcedo, across from Parque Vicente León.

Internet cafes are abundant in Latacunga, especially around the downtown. Check out **AJ Cyber Café** (📞 03/2806-415), on Quito 16–25 and Salcedo, or **Discovery Net** (📞 03/2806-557), on Salcedo 4–16.

What to See & Do in Latacunga

Aside from strolling around this somewhat attractive city and visiting its few parks and churches, there's not much of interest for tourists in Latacunga. The majority of travelers use Latacunga as a base to tour surrounding areas. However, the main plaza, **Parque Vicente León,** has pretty gardens, including some topiary sculptures. On the south side of Parque Vicente León is the city's main **cathedral,** a rather unspectacular large church that is most notable for the tile mosaics atop its spires and domes.

Los Molinos de Monserrat is the city's best museum. It features a modest collection of Inca and pre-Inca artifacts, as well as colonial-era art. This place is housed in the ruins of an old river-powered mill and has a beautiful setting just above the river. Reached by a footbridge is the museum's sister institution, **Casa de la Cultura** (📞 03/2813-248). The art gallery and theater make this a good place to check for any music, theater, or dance performance. You'll find Los Molinos de Monserrat and Casa de la Cultura on Antonia Vela 3–49 and Padre Salcedo. The museum is open Tuesday through Friday from 8am to noon and 2 to 6pm. Admission is $1.

Casa de los Marqueses de Miraflores (📞 03/2811-382) is a colonial-era mansion—one of the few that have survived—that has been converted into a small museum, with various rooms dedicated to exhibits ranging from archaeological finds to religious art. There's a good display and explanation of the city's Mama Negra festival (see the box "Fiesta de la Mama Negra") and celebrations. The museum, located on Sánchez de Orellana and Abel Echeverría, is open Monday through Friday from 8am to 1pm and 2 to 5pm, and Saturday from 9am to 1pm. Admission is free.

Fiesta de la Mama Negra

Latacunga is known across Ecuador for its celebration of the Virgen de la Merced (Virgin of Mercy), better known locally as Mama Negra (Black Mama). Each year on September 23 and 24, Latacunga's streets host a wild party, with dancing and parades, street food, fireworks, and carnival rides. The festivities exhibit a mix of indigenous, Spanish, and even African influences. Mama Negra is also celebrated, to slightly lesser extent, every November 11, which is Latacunga's Independence Day.

Tuesday and Saturday are market days in Latacunga, when the already substantial Plaza El Salto market swells with vendors who take over Plaza Chile and every bit of sidewalk and alley nearby. This is a working local market heavy on fruits, vegetables, housewares, and clothing, but you can find some artisans' wool clothing, as well as assorted handicrafts.

On a clear day, and if you're feeling energetic, head out to the east end of town on Calle Maldonado, to **Mirador de la Virgen del Calvario,** a high lookout point with great views of the city, countryside, and snowcapped peaks. Several blocks east of the small Parque Bolívar, you'll see a steep flight of steps and, above and beyond that, the sculpture of the Virgin of Calvary. Another good place to walk during the day is on the paved walkway that runs along the river.

Several tour agencies in town offer guided tours and expeditions to Cotopaxi National Park, the famous Saquisilí market, Lake Quilotoa, and the Quilotoa Loop (p. 167). Local operators include **Tovar Expeditions ★** (✆ 03/2811-333; www.tovarexpeditions.com), on Guayaquil 5–38 and Quito, and **Grievag Turismo** (✆ 03/2810-510; www.greivagturismo.com), on Quito and Padre Salcedo. Tovar is probably better for climbing and adventure tourism, while Grievag is better for traditional tours.

See "What to See & Do in Cotopaxi National Park," earlier in this chapter, for more details on the types of tours and adventures available to park visitors.

Where to Stay in Latacunga

Nearly all the hotels in Latacunga fill up every Wednesday night, and often on Thursday night, too, due to the Thursday market in **Saquisilí** (see "The Quilotoa Loop," below). On these nights, and during the Mama Negra festivities (see above), it's absolutely imperative that you have a reservation.

Hostal Tiana ✦ Run by a Dutch-Ecuadorean couple, this inexpensive and inviting hostel is geared toward budget travelers. Located in one of the town's oldest houses, Tiana offers rustic, clean, and spacious rooms in the center of the city. Units are either dorms with bunk beds or private rooms with individual twin beds. All the rooms share a few well-kept and immaculate bathrooms and showers. The **cafe-restaurant** offers excellent breakfasts, light bites, and evening meals. Guests absolutely rave about the coffee here.

Guayaquil 5-32 y Quito, Latacunga. www.hostaltiana.com. ✆ **03/2810-147** or 08/5737-829. 7 units. $8 per person dorm room; $20 double in private room. Rates include full breakfast and taxes. **Amenities:** Restaurant; free Wi-Fi. *In room:* No phone.

Hotel Makroz Located in the heart of downtown Latacunga, this is arguably one of Latacunga's plushest hotels. The four-story building is painted peach and yellow, and the carpeted rooms are comfortable and well equipped. Most have large picture windows that let in plenty of light. Some units come with minifridges and small stereo systems. The hotel restaurant is dependable and reasonably priced. *Note:* Street-facing rooms can be noisy.

Av. Félix Valencia 8-56 y Calle Quito, Latacunga. www.hotelmakroz.com.ec. ✆ **03/2800-907.** Fax 03/2807-274. 25 units. $50 double with private bathroom. Rates include breakfast. AE, DC, MC, V. **Amenities:** Restaurant; bar; room service. *In room:* TV; hair dryer, minibar.

Hotel Rodelu If you're spending the night in Latacunga, this is your best option. The rooms are bright and cheery, although the decor is definitely dated. Still, they have clean tile floors, cable television, and wooden headboards and furnishings. Ask to see a few units, because some are pretty compact. The hotel is located right near Parque Vicente Léon and has a popular pizzeria on the ground floor, as well as its own little garden area.

Calle Quito 16–31 y Padre Salcedo, Latacunga. www.rodelu.com.ec. © **03/2800-956.** Fax 03/2812-341. 19 units. $44 double. Rates include taxes. AE, DC, MC, V. **Amenities:** Restaurant; bar; room service. *In room:* TV.

Where to Dine in Latacunga

Latacunga's local specialty, *chugchucaras,* won't win any fans at the American Heart Association. This insane concoction is served up with piles of fried pork skins, fried plantains, fried potatoes, fried white-corn kernels that are pretty close to popcorn, some fried cheese empanadas, and seemingly anything else they can dig out of the deep fryer. *Chugchucara* restaurants abound in Latacunga. A massive *chugchucara* plate should run $4 to $6. If you want to try this local treat—and if you think your heart can take it—head to the area around calles Ordóñez and Quijano, where you'll find a string of dedicated *chugchucara* restaurants.

For good Chinese fare, head to **Chifa China** (no phone), on Antonia Vela 6–85 and 5 de Junio. For Italian fare, try **Pizzería Buon Giorno** (© 03/2804-924), on Sánchez de Orellana and General Maldonado. Another good option is the **Restaurant Rodelu** (© 03/2800-956), belonging to its namesake hotel, which serves up tasty pizzas and a la carte dishes. You can find more traditional Ecuadorian fare at **Restaurante Club Cotopaxi** on Tarqui and Quito (© 03/2800-305). For a great cup of coffee, light lunches, cakes, and cookies, head to the cafe-restaurant at **Hostal Tiana** (© 03/2810-147), on Guayaquil 5–32 and Quito.

El Copihue Rojo ★ ECUADOREAN/INTERNATIONAL This is my favorite restaurant in Latacunga. Steaks, chicken, and fish are grilled over wood coals. They also serve up a range of pastas and some local Ecuadorean fare, such as fresh Andean trout simply sautéed with garlic. The dining room is large and sometimes crowded, especially on weekends. This is a great place to come for the filling *menú ejecutivo* lunch special for around $3.

Quito 14–30, btw. Maldonado and Tarqui. © **03/2801-725.** Main courses $4–$7. MC, V. Mon–Sat 10am–9pm.

Latacunga After Dark

Latacunga is a relatively quiet city, which only really gets going on weekend nights. I recommend the popular bar **Galaxi** (© 03/2811-185), located up the hill east of town in Barrio el Calvario and open only Friday and Saturday nights. Another hot nightspot is the nearby **Skyway** (© 03/2813-016), on Av. Oriente 137 and Napo, which has either karaoke or dancing Thursday through Saturday. Otherwise, you can head to Calle Padre Salcedo, where you'll find a cluster of local bars and nightspots.

The Quilotoa Loop ★

One of the most popular trips based out of Latacunga is a circuit known as the **Quilotoa Loop.** The entire loop is about 200km (124 miles). While it is possible to do the trip in 1 day, I recommend spending a night or two at the **Black Sheep Inn** (see below). The roads, rough and rugged for much of the loop, pass through beautiful, isolated mountain villages and hamlets, many of whose inhabitants cling to their ancient indigenous heritage and ways. You can make the trip in either direction.

Whichever direction you choose, **Laguna Quilotoa ★★**, a beautiful, high-mountain lake formed in the broad crater of an extinct volcano, is roughly the halfway point and prime destination of this route. The views of the emerald-green lake are striking from the parking area, but many folks are tempted to hike down the steep slopes of the crater to the water's edge. The distance to the water seems deceptively short and the climb down is relatively quick, but the climb back up is quite steep and can take over an hour. Local vendors, touts, and guides are always on hand in the parking lot, and several will offer to sell you a mule ride back to the top. If you want to save yourself the hike, be sure to arrange this before you head off downhill. The mule ride should cost around $4 to $5. Other hiking options include the narrow and rugged trail around the crater rim, where the views are spectacular. There's a $2 entrance fee to visit the Quilotoa lagoon and crater.

Of the towns strewn along the Quilotoa Loop, perhaps the most famous is **Saquisilí,** a small indigenous village on the northeastern end of the loop, not very far from the Pan-American Highway. The weekly **Thursday market ★** is perhaps the most authentic in Ecuador, and quite distinct from what you find in Otavalo, which many feel has become far too touristy. This market is a traditional highland market with scores of vendors, and hundreds, if not thousands, of locals arriving from villages throughout the central Sierra to buy, barter, and trade for foodstuffs, household items, herbs, tools, animals, and just about anything and everything else imaginable. A similar market, albeit somewhat smaller, is held every Saturday in the town of Zumbahua and is easily combined with a visit to Laguna Quilotoa.

GETTING THERE　　The Quilotoa Loop can done by rental car, organized tour, or local buses. Most folks first head west out of Latacunga toward Tigua and then on to Zumbahua, where the loop goes north before reaching Laguna Quilotoa. Heading north from Quilotoa, the first major village is Chugchilán, followed by Sigchos, after which the route begins heading east again toward Saquisilí, close to where you meet up again with the Pan-American Highway, a little bit north of Latacunga.

If you're doing the loop by bus, arm yourself with some patience, plenty of warm clothing, snack food and energy bars, a good map of the region, and a sense of adventure. Local buses plying this circuit run erratic schedules and are often overcrowded. Still, every day countless locals make the various legs of this journey between the many small villages; and, if you wait long enough, you will be able to catch an onward ride in a bus or pickup truck.

For comprehensive and up-to-date information on bus schedules, check the websites of, or contact directly, the Black Sheep Inn or Hostal Llullu Llama (see below). Alternatively, you can head to the main bus terminal in Latacunga and inquire there. **Transportes La Iliniza** (① 03/2716-346) has two daily departures to Chugchilán, at 11 and 11:30am. The journey takes about 4 hours and is the halfway point on the loop. **Reina de Sigchos** (① 03/2714-027) and **Nacional** (① 03/2721-152) take turns with almost hourly bus departures through Saquisilí to Sigchos. **Cooperativa Vivero** (① 03/2723-251) has a couple of buses daily that head to Saquisilí, Isinlivi, Zumbahua, and Quilotoa. Most buses on the circuit spend the night and depart very early the next morning. **Cooperativa de Transportes Cotopaxi** (① 03/2800-752) buses leave roughly every hour for Quevedo and will take you as far as Zumbahua, from where you can make onward connections around the circuit. The fare for the entire circuit should cost about $6, with the current one-way fare between Latacunga and Chugchilán costing about $2.50.

Quilotoa Loop

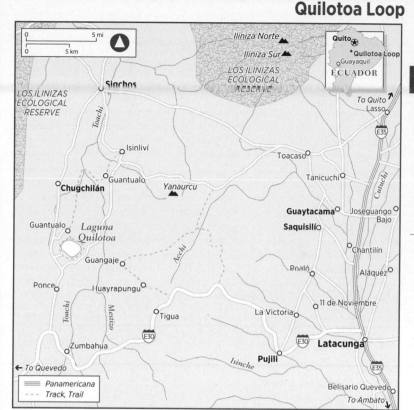

Where to Stay Along the Quilotoa Loop

There are a host of small, humble hostels and budget hotels all along the Quilotoa Loop; most are very basic and cater to locals and rugged backpackers. The two places listed below are striking exceptions, however, and I highly recommend that you choose one of these as your overnight midpoint or, better yet, as a base for exploring the area.

Black Sheep Inn ★★ 🎒 Environmental awareness and global consciousness are the hallmarks of this lodge, which was voted one of the top 10 ecoresorts by *Delta Sky Magazine* and top 50 ecolodges by *National Geographic Adventure* in 2009. There's a large dorm room, which can sleep 10, along with nine private rooms with sleeping lofts and wood-burning stoves. The immaculate shared bathrooms (five units have private bathrooms) feature composting toilets, and they recycle every type of material possible. All meals are vegetarian. Built on a hillside outside Chugchilán, the hotel has a fabulous view over the Río Toachi canyon. The lodge has its own organic permaculture gardens, as well as llamas, guinea pigs, and, of course, black sheep. There's a small swimming pond with a waterslide, a climbing wall, gym equipment, and a 9-hole Frisbee golf course. This is a great base for exploring the area, and a range of hikes and treks are available.

P.O. Box 05-01-240, Chugchilán, Cotopaxi. www.blacksheepinn.com. © **03/2708-077** or 09/9635-405. 10 units, 5 with private bathroom. $35 per person in dorm room; $120 double with shared bathroom; $160 double with private bathroom. Rates include breakfast, lunch, dinner, and taxes. No credit cards. June 15–Aug 31 and Nov 15–Mar 15. **Amenities:** Restaurant; bar; small exercise room; hot tub; sauna; small spa; swimming pond; Wi-Fi ($6/hr.). *In room:* No phone.

Hostal Llullu Llama ★   If you simply remember that the double *L* in Spanish is pronounced as a *y*, you'll have no problem saying the name of this delightful mountain retreat. The rooms in this converted farmhouse are bright and cheerful, and come with a mix of bed options, from bunks to twins to double beds for couples. Most units have thick adobe walls and varnished wooden floors with woven reed mats used as throw rugs—and, in some instances, as wallpaper. The decor is complemented with local handicrafts. The Llullu Llama features a wood-fired sauna and a range of tours and treks. Though the hotel is located slightly off the actual Quilotoa Loop, it still makes a great base for exploring the area. Your best bet for transportation, if you don't have your own rental car, is to arrange things with the lodge in advance.

Isinlivi, Cotopaxi. www.llullullama.com. © **03/2814-790** or 08/5737-829. 9 units, 4 with private bathroom. $18 per person in dorm room; $19 double with shared bathroom; $21 double with private bathroom. No credit cards. **Amenities:** Restaurant; bar; sauna. *In room:* No phone.

En Route South: A Couple of Quick Stops

You'll know you've reached **San Miguel de Salcedo** when you see the large sculpture of one of the locally produced ice-cream sticks, or *helados de sabores*. These homemade conical treats are sold all over this small roadside city, which places a lot of civic pride in them. You can pretty much stop anywhere and find a shop selling *helados de sabores*. Flavors vary and include such staples as vanilla, chocolate, strawberry, and blackberry. I like some of the local fruit varieties, such as *granadilla*, a tart member of the passion-fruit family. Salcedo is located about 15km (9¼ miles) south of Latacunga.

Located just off the Pan-American Highway, another 12km (7½ miles) south of Salcedo, the **Laguna de Yambo** is a popular spot to stop, stretch your legs, and take a gander at the lime-green waters of this lake formed in an extinct volcanic crater. Unlike Quilotoa, however, this lake appears stagnant and polluted. The lake's greatest claim to fame is the legend that it "swallowed a train"; if you look down the steep sides of the extinct crater, you can see the railroad tracks that run alongside it. Apparently, at one point, a train derailed and disappeared into the lake, and divers and salvage workers never found a trace. On a clear day, you can look beyond the lake and catch a glimpse of Volcán Tungurahua in the distance. If you're heading to Baños, this is a good reference point and marker.

AMBATO

138km (86 miles) S of Quito; 47km (29 miles) S of Latacunga; 288km (179 miles) N of Guayaquil

Despite its reputation as a cultural center that gave birth to, or was the home of, various prominent authors and intellectuals, and the fact that it is the largest city in the central Ecuadorean highlands, Ambato is rightly bypassed by most tourists. While it's an important commercial hub for the region and has the largest Monday market in the country, Ambato holds little of interest for visitors. Most folks breeze through on their way to someplace else. Moreover, with Baños (see below) and a couple of truly beautiful haciendas nearby, I see very little reason to overnight in Ambato.

Ambato is known as the City of Flowers and Fruits, and you can find an overwhelming abundance of both in the city's markets. Ambato is also sometimes called the City of the Three Juans, because three prominent Ecuadorean writers and intellectuals—Juan León Mera, Juan Montalvo, and Juan Benigno Vela—either hailed from the city or spent much time living and writing there. Montalvo was a prominent novelist whom some have called the Cervantes of South America, while Mera was both a poet and a novelist, but is most famous for writing the country's national anthem. Benigno Vela is best known as a critic and essayist.

Essentials

GETTING THERE

BY BUS   Buses frequently leave Quito's southbound bus terminal, **Terminal Terrestre Quitumbe** (© 02/3988-200), heading south along the Pan-American Highway to Ambato. **Transportes Ambato** (© 02/3824-759 in Quito, or 03/2849-504 in Ambato) and **Transportes Transandina** (© 02/3824-747 in Quito, or 03/2849-566 in Ambato) are the main bus lines, although another half-dozen or so companies are in the mix, with buses leaving roughly every 20 to 30 minutes between 3:30am and 8pm. The ride takes about 2½ hours and costs $2.50. From Ambato, there are frequent bus connections to most other major destinations around Ecuador.

The main bus terminal in Ambato, **Terminal Terrestre** (© 03/2520-859), is located in the Ingahurco sector, a little over 1.5km (1 mile) northeast of downtown, on Avenida de las Américas and Colombia. Frequent local buses connect the bus terminal and downtown Ambato—look for a bus that says CENTRO. The fare should be around 25¢. You can also take one of the many taxis you will find waiting at the bus terminal; a ride anywhere in Ambato should not exceed $2.50, and most short rides are just $1.

BY CAR   To reach Ambato by car, head south out of Quito on the Pan-American Highway (E35). The ride takes around 2 hours. There's a bypass around Ambato, but the Pan-American Highway itself, and most of the flow of traffic, actually goes right through downtown on its way south and toward Riobamba.

ORIENTATION

If you enter Ambato from the north, you'll pass by a traffic circle with the sculpture of a large, naked woman holding some flowers and welcoming you to the city. The main downtown area is bounded by the parallel avenidas Rocafuerte and 12 de Noviembre, and by the calles Sevilla and Olmedo. All the city's major parks, churches, and markets are found within this compact area.

GETTING AROUND

The city is large, spread out, and located on relatively hilly terrain, making walking long distances problematic. Luckily, taxis are abundant and inexpensive. If you can't simply flag one down, call **Cooperativa Taxi Amigos** (© 03/2417-900) or **Taxi Ejecutivo** (© 03/2418-000).

Ambato has an extensive network of local urban buses. For most tourists, the only bus route of importance is the one between downtown and the main bus terminal. Buses from the center to the bus station are marked TERMINAL and leave from the south side of Parque Cevallos. From the terminal to downtown, look for buses marked CENTRO.

VISITOR INFORMATION

The Ministry of Tourism runs a friendly **i-Tur** tourist information office (© **03/2821-800**), in the Eugenia Mena Cultural Center on Rocafuerte and Lalama, in the center of town. They can provide information on local attractions and tours.

FAST FACTS   To reach the **police,** dial © **101** or 03/2415-558. The main office is on Av. Atahualpa 568 and Avenida Quis Quis. **Hospital Provincial Docente Ambato** (© **03/2821-058**) is on Avenida Pasteur and Unidad Nacional.

You'll find the main branch of **Banco de Guayaquil** (© **03/3730-100**) on the corner of Mera and Sucre. The main branch of **Banco Pichincha** (© **03/2422-031**) is at Lalama 3–20 and Cevallos. ATMs can be found scattered around the city. The **post office** (© **03/2829-765**) is located on Castillo 410 and Bolívar.

Internet cafes abound in Ambato, especially around downtown and Parque Montalvo.

What to See & Do in Ambato

Ambato's picturesque downtown park, **Parque Juan Montalvo,** is a solid-square-block area with tall palm trees, pretty gardens, plenty of bench seating, and criss-crossing footpaths. It's very busy on weekdays during lunch and in the early evening, as well as throughout the day and into the night on weekends. On the northeast side of the park is the city's massive modern **cathedral,** with its soaring domes.

On the northwest corner of the park (Montalvo 3–50 and Bolívar) is the Greek-style **Casa de Montalvo** (© **03/2824-248**), the restored birthplace and residence of one of the town's famous Juans; it houses **Museo de Reliquias Montalvinas,** which features a collection of old Ambato relics, including traditional dress, manuscripts, photos, and literature from the Montalvo collection and era. The museum is open Monday through Friday 9am to noon and 2 to 6pm, and Saturday from 9am to 2pm. Admission is 50¢.

La Quinta de Mera (© **03/2820-419**) is the home and retreat formerly belonging to another of the three Juans, writer Juan León Mera. Today the small estate is a beautiful place to get away from the bustle of downtown Ambato and admire stunning views over the Ambato River. Located on Avenida Circunvalación in the parish of Atocha, the house boasts luscious French- and Oriental-style gardens; a natural museum displaying the late author's possessions, art, and literature; and beautiful botanical gardens housing over 250 plant and flower species. It's open Wednesday through Sunday from 9am to 4:30pm; admission is $1. La Quinta is located a little over 1.5km (1 mile) north of downtown. You can walk here or take a taxi for around $1.

The arty Atocha sector also boasts the **Centro Cultural La Liria** (© **03/2425-085;** contactos@fiestasdeambato.com), on Avenida Circunvalación, which displays collections of handicrafts, typical dress, and photography of old Ambato. This center was donated by the families of Juan León Mera, Juan Montalvo, and Luis Alfredo Martínez. It's open Monday through Friday 8:30am to 5pm; admission is free.

For a great view, head to the **Monumento a la Primera Imprenta (Monument to the First Printing Press),** located on a high point northwest of downtown. On a clear day, you'll have no problem seeing the plume of smoke from Volcán Tungurahua. A taxi here should cost $2 to $2.50 each way.

Ambato is famous for its markets. These are working traditional markets where locals and highland dwellers sell and barter for food, clothing, tools, animals, seeds, spices, and just about everything else imaginable. The city is particularly well known for its fruits and flowers. The biggest market day is Monday, with Wednesday and Friday not far behind. Really, though, Ambato's bustling **Mercado Central** and

Flowers & Fruit

Befitting a town known as the City of Flowers and Fruits, Ambato celebrates the yearly Carnaval season with a major blowout party known as **La Fiesta de las Flores y de las Frutas**. For 2 solid weeks, Ambato hosts a near-constant stream of parades, open-air concerts, beauty contests, bullfights, and street fairs with portable amusement park rides. The exact dates vary, but the celebrations coincide with traditional Latin American Carnaval periods and tend to occur around mid-February and early March, preceding Ash Wednesday and the beginning of Lent. During this fiesta, hotel rooms are sold out long in advance. For up-to-date information, see www.fiestasdeambato.com.

Mercado Modelo have ample offerings pretty much every day of the week. The Mercado Central is located on Av. 12 de Noviembre, a block northeast of Parque 12 de Noviembre. The Mercado Modelo is located on the southeastern side of Avenida Cevallos, about 2 blocks northeast of Parque Cevallos. On Monday and other market days, vendors fill the city streets all around these two markets. Only a small amount of arts and craftworks is available, but you can certainly buy hand-woven wool clothing and traditional Andean headwear.

For organized tours, contact your hotel tour desk; **Metropolitan Touring ★★** (✆ 03/2820-616; www.metropolitantouring.com), inside the Centro Comercial Caracol, on Av. Los Capulies 59–62; or **Delgado Travel** (✆ 03/2423-070; www.delgadotravelsa.com), on Juan León Mera 6–13 and Sucre. Options include city tours and trips to Cotopaxi or Baños.

Where to Stay & Dine in Ambato

In addition to the places listed below, **Quinta Loren ★** (✆ 03/2460-699; www.quintaloren.com) is a pretty, upscale option in a quiet residential neighborhood outside of downtown, while the **Gran Hotel** (✆ 03/2824-235; Rocafuerte 11–33 and Lalama) is another good choice for budget travelers right in the city center.

Ambato's dining scene has improved over the last year or so, with a greater selection of restaurants popping up around town. Although most tourists opt for dinner at their hotel restaurant, if you do decide to venture out, you'll find good pizzas and Italian ice cream at **Hotel Pizzería Fornace** (✆ 03/2823-244), on Datiles and Guaytambos, and decent Continental fare and local Ecuadorean cuisine at the popular **El Alamo Chalet** (✆ 03/2824-704), on Cevallos 17–19 and Montalvo; **Las Gallinas de Pinllo** (✆ 03/2821-830), on Pinllo, 50m (164 ft.) from Parque Central; or **El Fareon** (✆ 03/2821-252), on Bolívar 1442 and Lalama. For Argentinean-style steaks and grilled feasts, try **Parilladas El Gaucho** (✆ 03/2828-969), on Bolívar and Quito, or **Las Delicias de George** (✆ 03/2826-627), on the corner of Cevallos and Francisco Flor. An excellent spot to sample the local specialty handmade ice cream, *helado de paila*, is at **Oasis Café** (✆ 03/2825-535; www.heladeriaoasis.com), on the corner of Sucre 04–10 and Mariano Eguez.

Hotel Ambato This is a comfortable, if run-of-the-mill, well-located business-class hotel in downtown Ambato. Most of the rooms come with two twin beds, so if you're a couple, be sure to specify that you want a *matrimonial*. The rooms on the higher floors have great views of the surrounding mountains and river below. There's one presidential suite, which is large and has a separate sitting area featuring a plush

IT'S CHICHA time

If you drive through the Ecuadorean countryside at night, you may notice a red light in a window or the doorway of a home, which usually means the owners are selling homemade *chicha:* a fermented beverage popular in the Andes since the days of the Incas.

Sometimes considered a beer, though it lacks carbonation, *chicha*—the Spanish pronunciation is *chee-cha*—is made and consumed by indigenous groups across the Americas. It can be brewed from various fruits and vegetables, but in the Andes, it is usually made from yellow corn, and sometimes called *chicha de jora.*

To make *chicha,* corn kernels are soaked in water until they germinate, then are boiled and fermented for several days, usually in large clay vessels. The result is a milky yellow liquid, sweet at the beginning of fermentation and becoming sour as it progresses. The alcohol content increases the longer the liquid is fermented, but it never gets any stronger than beer.

Chicha is used in Andean indigenous rituals as a sort of holy water that is drunk, and it's copiously consumed during traditional village festivals (though it's being steadily replaced by beer). It is also given to visitors as an act of respect, and if you are offered an earthenware cup of the beverage upon arriving at an Ecuadorean village, Emily Post would probably recommend that you drink it whether you like it or not.

If you visit an indigenous village in the Oriente, you may be given *chicha* made from cassava, a tropical tuber known as *yuca* in Spanish. The cassava *chicha* is thicker and doesn't have much flavor, but that doesn't keep folks in the rainforest from consuming it regularly. Also in the Oriente, you are expected to place your cup upside down, on the ground, when you've finished your *chicha.*

If you travel to other parts of Latin America, you'll find that the word *chicha* is also used to refer to nonalcoholic fruit drinks. In Peru, a traditional beverage is *chicha morada,* made by boiling purple corn, pineapple rinds, and an applelike fruit called *membrillo;* it's especially popular with children because it leaves the tongue and lips lavender.

The uncertainty created by the existence of alcoholic and nonalcoholic beverages with the same name is sometimes clarified by using the term *chicha fuerte* (strong *chicha*) to distinguish the alcoholic beverage. And to make things just a little more confusing, there is the popular Latin American idiomatic expression, *"ni chicha, ni limonada,"* which translates as "neither *chicha* nor lemonade," and means about the same thing as "neither fish nor fowl." Now, put that in your cup and drink it!

sofa and a couple of chairs, as well as a private little bar. The hotel's **restaurant** has a wide-ranging menu and is one of the more dependable bets in Ambato. And speaking of betting, there's even a small casino on-site that's popular with locals and visiting businesspeople.

Guayaquil 01–08 y Rocafuerte, Ambato. www.hotelambato.com. © **03/2421-791.** Fax 03/2421-790. 59 units. $68 double. Rates higher during holidays. Rates include breakfast and taxes. Free parking. AE, DC, MC, V. **Amenities:** Restaurant; bar; cafe; casino; room service. *In room:* TV.

Hotel Casino Emperador ★   Easily the most luxurious option in Ambato proper, this high-rise of reflective glass is well located, wonderfully equipped, and very comfy. Rooms are large and well done, with more sense of style than you will find at many modern hotels in Ecuador. On the top of this six-story building, you'll find a small spa with a rooftop pool and Jacuzzi. The hotel's restaurant also enjoys a high perch, with walls of windows providing a fabulous view. On-site is a somewhat refined little piano bar, as well as a small but spiffy casino and upbeat disco with regular resident and guest DJs.

Av. Cevallos 10–14 y Lalama, Ambato. www.hotelcasinoemperador.com. ✆ **03/2424-460.** 63 units. $104 double; $165 executive suite. Rates include breakfast buffet and taxes. Higher rates during fiestas. Free parking. AE, DC, MC, V. **Amenities:** Restaurant; bar; disco; casino; small, well-equipped exercise room; Jacuzzi; pool; room service; sauna; steam bath. *In room:* TV, hair dryer, minibar, free Wi-Fi.

Hotel Miraflores   Located in an upscale neighborhood southwest of downtown, this charming and friendly hotel has contemporary business-class rooms. Units are carpeted and cozy, with wooden furnishings and fireplaces. The hotel grounds feature extensive and immaculately kept gardens. If you'd like to stay in Ambato but be outside the hustle and bustle of the city, this hotel is a great choice.

Av. Miraflores 227 y Las Rosas, Ambato. www.hmiraflores.com.ec. ✆ **03/2460-204** or 03/2460-509. 35 units. $57 double; $73 junior suite. Rates include breakfast and taxes. Rates higher during fiestas. Free parking. AE, DC, MC, V. **Amenities:** Restaurant; bar; room service. *In room:* TV, free Wi-Fi.

Ambato After Dark

Ambato's nightlife is pretty tame. It picks up some on Thursday and through the weekend. The most popular nightclub in town is the **Coyote Disco Club,** Av. Bolívar 20–57, near Guayaquil (✆ **03/2822-424**). This is a large club with loud music and dancing. A young crowd dominates **Cervecería Búfalo,** Olmedo 681 and Juan León Mera (✆ **03/2841-685**), or you can check out **Bar Ginos** (✆ **03/2822-445**), on Lalama 222 and Cevallos. For a slightly more sophisticated scene, check out the **Emperador Disco-Bar** (✆ **03/2424-460**), located in its namesake hotel (see above).

If you're in a gaming mood, the casino at **Hotel Casino Emperador** (see above) is a good bet.

En Route to Baños: Two Haciendas in the Hills

About halfway between Ambato and Baños, a side road heads toward the small village of Patate, beyond which are two delightful haciendas. The road on which these two haciendas are located connects to an alternative and rugged gravel road to Baños, a little over 16km (10 miles) away.

Hacienda Leito ★★ 👜   This classic hacienda features a beautiful fountain near the entrance, at the end of the centuries-old stone driveway. The main building, where you'll find the restaurant and lounge, houses antiques and colonial-era artwork. All rooms have fireplaces, wood floors, and exposed wood beams. A couple larger suits come with a balcony and view of Volcán Tungurahua. The meals are excellent, with elegant candle-lit dinners. The extensive spa features a large indoor swimming pool and expansive lounge areas. There are several massage and treatment rooms, as well as a Jacuzzi, a sauna, and a steam room. A small museum contains pre-Columbian artifacts and archaeological finds. Horseback riding is excellent here, and tours around the hacienda and Baños area are offered.

8km (5 miles) along the Via Ecologica from Patate, or 17km from Baños. www.haciendaleito.com. ✆ **03/2859-329.** ✆/fax 03/2859-331. 29 units. $134 double; $180 suite. Rates include breakfast and dinner. DC, MC, V. **Amenities:** Restaurant; bar; mountain bikes; Jacuzzi; massage; indoor pool; sauna; smoke-free rooms; spacious spa; steam room; free Wi-Fi. *In room:* No phone.

Hacienda Manteles ★   This hotel has the feel of a homey mountain lodge. There are seven rooms in the main building, while the other units are spread between two buildings slightly below. The best room—the end unit on the main floor of the main building—has a king-size bed facing a large picture window with a view of Volcán Tungurahua. I find the main house's attic rooms a bit cramped, while the four-bedroom Family House is an excellent option for a family or group of friends; its two front rooms have great views of the volcano. Around the hacienda are beautiful gardens, with fruit trees, organic vegetable gardens, and ornamental flowers and orchids. These folks own 200 hectares (494 acres) of primary cloud forest and specialize in tours of their own private reserve and neighboring (and seldom-visited) Llanganates National Park. One of the great features here is a beautiful nearby waterfall.

11km (6¾ miles) from Patate, Baños. www.haciendamanteles.com. ✆/fax **02/2233-484** reservations office in Quito, or 09/4614-275 cellphone at the hacienda. 16 units. $135 double. Rates include breakfast, dinner, and a guided hike to the nearby waterfall. AE, DC, MC, V. **Amenities:** Restaurant; bar. *In room:* No phone.

BAÑOS ★★

176km (109 miles) S of Quito; 55km (34 miles) N of Riobamba; 288km (179 miles) N of Guayaquil

Strategically located on the jungle's doorstep and at the foot of Volcán Tungurahua, the charismatic town of Baños de Agua Santa offers both adventure and relaxation. Indeed, it's extremely popular among local and international tourists alike. Tourism is well established, and a wide variety of activities are offered, from adrenaline-pumping extreme sports to a soothing soak in the hot springs. At an altitude of 1,800m (5,904 ft.), Baños has a warm and mostly sunny climate, and it's an excellent base from which to explore the jungle and neighboring protected areas, such as Parque Nacional Sangay, a UNESCO World Heritage Site since 1983.

Baños is chiefly famous for its thermal pools (hence the name Baños, or "Baths"), which are nourished by the mineral-rich naturally heated springs of Tungurahua itself. Locals rave about the health benefits of taking a soak, claiming that the springs, with their high mineral and sulfur content, can alleviate anything from muscular pain to kidney ailments.

Essentials
GETTING THERE
BY BUS   Transportes Amazonas (✆ 02/3824-847 in Quito, or 03/2740-242 in Baños) and **Expreso Baños** (✆ **02/3824-845** in Quito, or 03/2740-225 in Baños; www.coopexpresobanios.com) leave from Quito's southbound bus terminal, **Terminal Terrestre Quitumbe** (✆ **02/3988-200**), approximately every 15 to 20 minutes from 4am to midnight. Return buses follow roughly the same schedule. The trip takes from 3½ to 4 hours and costs $3.50 each way.

Baños is also connected, with less frequent service, to Tena, Coca, Puyo, and Guayaquil. The main bus terminal in Baños is located on calles Reyes and Espejo, just a short walk from the town's center.

Tip: If you arrive by bus, you will be besieged by touts offering you hotel deals and telling you that the hotel you wanted to go to is full or closed. They are almost always lying and are working on a commission basis, so their information is extremely biased.

BY CAR   To reach Baños by car, begin by heading south out of Quito on the Pan-American Highway (E35) to the city of Ambato. The highway weaves its way right

ACCOMMODATIONS ■

Finca Chamanapamba **17**
Hospedaje Santa Cruz **7**
Hostal La Posada del Arte **9**
Hostal Plantas y Blanco **10**
Luna Runtun Adventure Spa **19**
Samari Spa Resort **18**
Sangay Spa-Hotel **13**

DINING ◆

Café Hood **4**
Casa Hood **5**
Café Mariane **3**
Le Petit Restaurant **8**
Restaurant Moni **15**
Swiss Bistro **6**
Quilombo **11**

ATTRACTIONS ●

Acuario & Serpentario
San Martín **1**
Balneario Las Peñas **14**
Basílica de Nuestra Señora
de Agua Santa **16**
La Piscina de la Virgen **12v**
Zoológico San Martín **2**

through the center of Ambato. Near the southern end of Ambato, you'll see the well-marked turnoff for Pelileo and Baños. Follow the signs and Hwy. E50 to Baños. The ride takes around 3½ hours. Along the final stretch between Pelileo and Baños, you'll pass fallen ash, volcanic rocks, and the remnants of destructive lava flows from an August 2006 eruption. Be aware that mudslides (lahars) from heavy rains can occasionally cause the temporary closure of this route.

From Guayaquil, take the Pan-American Highway northeast through Riobamba and Penipe, and cross Río Chambo into Baños. The road between Penipe and Baños is also subject to mudslides from Volcán Tungurahua; it's best to get the all-clear before setting off. The Guayaquil–Baños route takes approximately 5 hours.

ORIENTATION

Baños is a compact little town nestled against the flanks of the Volcán Tungurahua. The downtown area is only about 11 by 7 blocks, and the main roads through the city run in an east-west direction. The Río Pastaza runs just outside the downtown area. The center features two small, pretty parks, **Parque Palomino Flores (Parque Central)** and **Parque Sebastián Acosta (Parque de la Basílica);** the majority of tourist infrastructure is along the main streets on either side of these two parks. The bus terminal, located near the center of town on calles Reyes and Espejo, is a short walk from most hotels and hostels. The hills of Bellavista are to the south, accessible by following a trail south off Calle Maldonado.

GETTING AROUND

It's unlikely you'll need bus transportation to get around Baños, except perhaps to go to El Salado thermal baths, which are a couple of kilometers outside the town center. The bus to El Salado departs from Calle Rocafuerte, just beside the artisans market. The fare is 15¢.

Getting around in a taxi is extremely convenient—many cooperatives offer a set rate to tourist attractions. A trip to the town *mirador* (lookout point) costs around $10; a taxi trip to and from the volcano *mirador* costs around $15; a waterfall tour costs approximately $30 and lasts 2½ to 3 hours. If you can't flag down a taxi, call **Cooperativa de Taxi 16 de Diciembre** (℃ 03/2740-416).

VISITOR INFORMATION

Tourist information is easily accessible in Baños. The friendly official **tourist office** (℃ 03/2740-483; www.baniosadn.com.ec) is on calle Halflants, near Rocafuert, by Parque Central; there you can get detailed information, maps, tourist guides, or general help with your trip. The office is open daily from 8am to noon and 2 to 5:30pm, and is usually staffed by someone who speaks English. A similar office with similar hours, run by the **local tourism chamber** (℃ 03/2741-660; www.camaradeturismo.com), is located on the side of the Basilica. Most tour operators are also a good source of information and are willing to help without any commitment on your part. In business over 20 years, **Expediciones Amazónicas ★** (℃ 03/2740-506; www.amazonicas.baniosxtreme.com), on Oriente 11–68 and Halflants, is one of the town's most experienced tour operators, specializing in a wide range of extreme sports. **Geotours** (℃ 03/2741-344; www.geotoursbanios.com), calles Ambato and Thomas Halflants, is also highly recommended for adventure and extreme sports, especially rafting; they provide bilingual, professionally trained and certified guides. Another leading operator is **Rainforestur** (℃ 03/2740-743, or 02/2239-822 in Quito; www.rainforestur.com), at Ambato 800 and Maldonado, known for its excellent jungle and mountain expeditions and trilingual guides. They also have an office in Quito on Amazonas 420 and Robles (℃ 02/2239-822) if you wish to check out or book tours in advance.

FAST FACTS   To contact the local **police,** dial ℃ 03/2740-101 (or ℃ 101 in an emergency); the police station is located on Calle Oriente 251 and Juan León Mera. For a medical emergency, head to the local **hospital** (℃ 03/2740-367), on Montalvo and Pastaza, or to **Hospital Betesda** (℃ 03/2740-643; www.hospitalbetesda.com), on De Los Rosales. A number of **pharmacies** are located along the main street, Calle Ambato.

Banco Pichincha (℃ 03/2740-961) is on the corner of calles Ambato and Thomas Halflants. **Banco del Pacífico** (℃ 03/2740-336) is on the corner of Thomas Halflants and Rocafuerte. Both have ATMs accepting international cards and can change traveler's checks.

The **post office** (℃ 03/2740-901) is located on Calle Ambato by Parque Central. **Internet cafes** are plentiful in Baños, with rates starting at 25¢ for 15 minutes; just head along Ambato or surrounding streets, and you'll find a spot. Most have cheap international-calling capabilities and are generally open from 8am until late.

What to See & Do in Baños

It's worth taking a peek inside the town's semigothic **Basílica de Nuestra Señora de Agua Santa** ★, which was finally completed in 1944, after Belgian priest Thomas Halflants had begun construction 40 years earlier. The interior displays interesting pictures telling stories of the supposed miracles performed by the Virgin of Holy Water in and around the town. There are always hawkers selling candles and religious trinkets outside, and it gets pretty crowded on Sundays and during religious festivals. Upstairs from the church is a small museum (50¢) with religious artifacts, paintings, and, for some odd reason, stuffed animals. You won't be missing much if you skip the museum.

Housing a variety of local fauna, and several endangered species, **Zoológico San Martín** ★ (② 03/2741-966) is a pretty and well-run little zoo. If you can't make it to the Galápagos, you can see one of the giant tortoises here. There are various monkey and bird species native to the nearby Amazon basin, and a pair of Andean condors, kept in a very large enclosure. Overall, they have over 350 animals. Located some 3km (1¾ miles) outside Baños, in the San Martín sector along the road to the parish of Lligua, the zoo is perfect for a half-day trip and great for kids. It's open daily 8am to 6pm. Admission is $2. If you come to the zoo, you should definitely combine it with a visit to the neighboring **Acuario & Serpentario San Martín** (**San Martin Aquarium & Serpentarium**; ② 03/2740-994), which features a host of aquariums and terrariums filled with a variety of native fish and reptile species. This place is open Monday through Sunday 7am to 6pm and charges an extra $1 per person.

> ### You Can Drink the Water
>
> Local legend has it that the waters emerging from a spring at the base of the **Cascada de la Virgin de Aguas Santas** (Virgin of Holy Waters Waterfall) possess healing properties. This is the main waterfall in town, located just to the side of its namesake hot springs. Pilgrims come here all the time to drink of the waters. If you don't have your own container, you can buy a plastic bottle at the small shop here.

All the local tour agencies and hotel desks offer sightseeing tours to the nearby waterfalls and other area attractions. Your best bet is to sign on for an organized *chiva* **tour.** These take place in open-air, brightly painted buses. They are often party scenes, especially at night. The most popular *chiva* tours are to a string of nearby waterfalls during the day or to the volcano lookout at night. **Volcano tours** usually leave around 9pm and cost around $5. These last a few hours, and if you're really lucky, you'll see the red glow of Tungurahua's erupting molten lava. **Waterfall tours** ★★ cost between $5 and $10 per person and take about half a day. Most end up at the powerful rushing waterfall **El Pailón del Diablo (The Devil's Cauldron)** ★★ or the pretty **Manto de la Novia (Bride's Veil)** ★. Along the way, you can take a ride on a *tarabita,* a cable car crossing the river, which is a fun way—if more than a little scary—to appreciate the splendid scenery. The *tarabita's* open-air mesh cars offer little in the way of enclosure and dangle by seemingly thin wires over rivers and gorges. A half-dozen or so waterfalls and an equal number of *tarabitas* are found along the route between Baños and El Pailón del Diablo. A ride on a *tarabita* usually costs $1 per person. **Tip:** If you reach El Pailón del Diablo and are limber, and not claustrophobic, be sure to make the final climb, scramble, and crawl to the uppermost lookout, which allows you to actually walk behind the waterfall. Be prepared to get wet.

As an alternative, you can do the waterfall tour via ATV or dune buggy. If this interests you, check in with the folks at **Moto Sport Adventure** (℗ **08/5213-544,** or 08/4549-974; www.motosportadventure.com), on Calle 16 de Diciembre and Martínez. Rates run around $10 to $15 per hour, and guided tours are available.

SOAKING IN THE HOT SPRINGS

No trip to Baños is complete without a visit to the town's namesake hot springs. Unfortunately, none are what I would deem very attractive or well kept. The following are my favorites. The most popular—and, therefore, busiest—thermal pools are **La Piscina de la Virgen** ★ (℗ **03/2740-462**), Martínez and Montalvo, featuring three pools of differing temperatures, from pretty cool to very hot. Many people find the medium-temperature pool just right. This place is located beneath the town's waterfall, across from the Sangay Spa-Hotel. Brave bathers can take a cold shower in the waterfall before or after a hot soak. It is open daily 4:30am to 5pm and 6 to 10pm. Admission is $2.

Just a little bit up the road from La Virgen, **Balneario Las Peñas** (℗ **03/2740-462**) is the town's largest and most modern thermal bath complex, which is also popular with local families. Also called Las Modernas, it features several pools, including one that's very large, with crisscrossing water slides that children love. It's open daily from 4:30am to 4:30pm and from 6 to 10pm. Admission is $2 during the daytime and $3 at night.

If you're looking to pamper yourself and aren't staying at a hotel with an in-house spa, head to **Stay in Touch,** on Montalvo and Ibarra (℗ **03/2740-973**), which offers full-body and deep-tissue massages and shiatsu from $20 to $30 per hour. Alternatively, opt for Carmen Sánchez's treatments at **Chakra,** Eloy Alfaro and Martínez (℗ **03/2742-027;** www.chakramassages.com), for Swedish massage, reflexology, and facials. Or, for a slight splurge, take advantage of the spas at Luna Runtun (p. 183) and Samari (p. 183).

ACTIVE ADVENTURES & OUTDOOR ACTIVITIES

Baños is a popular and, in many ways, perfect destination for those looking to participate in outdoor adventure pursuits, especially extreme sports such as white-water rafting, bridge jumping, canyoneering, mountain climbing, horseback riding, and mountain biking. Tour operators and experienced guides are plentiful, and prices are extremely reasonable. See above, under "Visitor Information," for recommended and reputable operators that can organize nearly any of the tours and activities listed below.

Whatever you sign up for, be sure to know your own physical limits before setting out. Also, always bring plenty of water and sunscreen.

Party Time in the Old Town

An excellent time to visit Baños is during its celebration of Nuestra Señora de Agua Santa (Our Lady of Holy Water), held each year throughout October, which features fireworks, parades, dancing in the streets, and all-out revelry. The city's founding is also celebrated heartily on and around December 16. Book accommodations in advance if you're planning a trip during these dates, and be forewarned that hotels often charge a premium during these fiestas.

CANYONEERING & BRIDGE JUMPING   If you'd prefer to climb the waterfall rather than navigate the river at the foot of it, try **canyoneering,** a sport proving to be increasingly popular among visitors. Canyoneering involves hiking in a mountain canyon through rivers and with periodic rappel descents, usually on the face of a waterfall. Around Baños, canyoneering is possible on the Chamana, San Jorge, Río Blanco, and Cashuano waterfalls. Half-day tours cost around $30 to $45, and a full day between $75 and $90. Try the excursions organized by **Expediciones Amazónicas, Geotours,** or **Moto Sport Adventure** (see "Visitor Information," above).

   Bridge or **swing jumping** is another of the daring outdoor pursuits offered up in the area. A rope is fastened to one end of a bridge and clipped to the jumper's harness; unlike in bungee jumping, the jumper pushes outward from the bridge, swinging pendulum-like when the rope becomes taut. Jumps, which cost $10 to $15, take place off the San Francisco bridge by the bus terminal, or off the bridge crossing the Río Blanco (along the road to Puyo), with different platform heights available, depending on how bold you are. During the week you should organize jumps through local operators. On weekends and holidays, you can head straight to the bridge.

CLIMBING, HIKING & TREKKING   The forests, mountains, volcanoes, and national parks around Baños offer opportunities for all sorts of hiking, climbing, and trekking adventures. Hiking up to Bellavista, to the white cross overlooking town, is a popular option. Take the trail that begins at the southern end of Maldonado.

   Volcano climbing is also an old favorite, although **ascending Volcán Tungurahua is not recommended at present,** owing to recent activity and the ongoing threat of eruption. Many operators have limited their climbing tours on Tungurahua because of eruptions in August 2006, February 2008, and, most recently, May 2010, and the danger of mud flows. But the now-extinct El Altar and still-active El Sangay can be ascended; check with local tour guides for up-to-date information on climbing conditions. All-inclusive trips usually range in duration from 2 days to a week and cost $80 to $100 per person per day. A minimum of two participants is usually required. Lower-altitude trekking on the flanks of these volcanoes, as well as inside Sangay and Llanganates national parks, is better suited to those seeking shorter, less strenuous trips. Day trips with relaxed hiking start at around $45.

HORSEBACK RIDING & MOUNTAIN BIKING   All the local tour agencies and hotel desks can help you arrange horseback-riding and mountain-bike tours through the lush mountainous terrain here. Rates range from $6 to $12 per hour for a guided tour.

   If you're going mountain biking, one popular option is the so-called Ruta de las Cascadas (Route of the Waterfalls), ending up at El Pailón del Diablo, which is predominantly a descent. With advance coordination, your tour company will pick up you and your bikes at the end so you can make the more arduous ascent back to Baños in a motor vehicle. Alternately, you can just flag down any of the frequent local buses and pile on with your bike and equipment.

TRIPS TO THE AMAZON   Situated on the Oriente's doorstep, Baños makes for a superb base from which to explore Puyo and the nearby Amazon basin. For 1-day to 10-day trips deep into the heart of the rainforest, expect to pay approximately $30 to $55 per day per person for budget-oriented tours, and more if you want a bit of comfort and luxury. June through September are usually the most popular months for jungle tours, so book in advance, if possible. Come prepared if embarking on longer trips; be sure to have appropriate clothing, waterproofing, insect repellent, sunscreen,

TUNGURAHUA: BACK WITH A bang

After an 80-year period of inactivity, which led many experts and inhabitants to believe that the volcano was dormant, Tungurahua unexpectedly returned to life in October 1999, spurting ash and lava for 2 weeks. Baños and surrounding villages were evacuated, and roads leading to and from the area were closed. While the eruptions were relatively minor, evacuees spent not weeks, but months waiting for a major eruption, which never materialized.

Impatient to return to their homes, locals began to pour back into the town after a showdown with the military, and by summer 2000, Baños was back to business as usual. The first half of 2006, nevertheless, marked a period of increased seismic activity, and August 2006 saw the biggest eruption since 1916, with lava flows and incandescent rocks destroying nearby villages and causing several fatalities. Following months of relative calm, February 2007 and December 2008 were again times of increased activity, with ash, gases,

lava flows, and lahars (volcanic mudslides) prompting authorities to close roads. The volcano erupted most recently in May 2010, with ash reaching as far afield as the provinces of Bolívar, Chimborazo, Los Rios, and Guayas, and causing airports and schools over the country to grind to a halt.

The volcano remains on orange-red alert, and at present, **climbers are strongly advised against ascending Tungurahua** because a large eruption is always possible. The refuge, situated at 3,800m (12,464 ft.), remains partly destroyed. Tungurahua is constantly monitored, and security measures are in place with a number of designated "safe spots" in the town's surrounding hills in the event of evacuation. Visitors to the area should be aware of the possibility of eruption, although, in this case, seismologists estimate that Baños would not be in the immediate path of danger due to its position. For further information on Volcán Tungurahua's current status, check out www.volcano.si.edu.

and malaria tablets. **Rainforestur** (p. 178) probably offers the best selection of jungle tours around.

WHITE-WATER RAFTING ★   The majority of white-water rafting trips offered out of Baños are half-day tours on Río Pastaza or Río Patate, but more experienced rafters can also book full-day or 2-day trips on Class IV and V sections of the Río Pastaza. Rates range from $30 to $50 per person for a half-day and $70 to $90 for the longer trips. Novices are welcome, and all gear is provided by the operator. Most of the shorter trips spend about 2 hours on the river, in Class II to Class III waters. Some operators also offer full-day excursions. All of the operators mentioned above offer rafting excursions, or check in with **Team Adventure** (© 03/2742-195; www. teamecuador.com) on Oriente and Thomas Halflants.

BRUSH UP ON YOUR SPANISH

With its host of language schools, Baños is a great place to brush up on your rusty Spanish or to dive in for some intensive first-time learning. Schools here offer courses for all levels, and you can opt for group or one-on-one classes. Check out **Ciudad de Baños Language School** (© 03/2740-317; www.escueladeidiomas.banios.com), on Ambato 5–22 and Eloy Alfaro, offering one-to-one classes at $6 per hour and $14 per night for a homestay, including meals. Alternatively, **Mayra's Spanish School**

(© 03/2742-850; www.mayraspanishschool.com), on Montalvo and 16 de Diciembre, offers weekly packages for $120 per week, including 4 hours of lessons per day, a homestay, and three daily meals.

Where to Stay in Baños

EXPENSIVE

Luna Runtun Adventure Spa ★★   Located some 6km (3¾ miles) above town, Luna Runtun offers spectacular views of Baños, Llanganates National Park, and the smoking Volcán Tungurahua. With spacious and cozy rooms, and a wonderful in-house spa, Luna Runtun promises a relaxing, romantic stay. However, if you want to get active, you can hike several excellent trails right from the grounds here and take part in any number of organized adventure activities. The higher-priced rooms generally offer better views, and some come with fireplaces. The imperial suites have two bedrooms with kitchenette—perfect for families. Homegrown, organic ingredients are used in a range of dishes at the restaurant, which specializes in local Andean cuisine. The hotel's pools and Jacuzzis are great places to soothe your aching muscles while taking in the fabulous views. And the spa offers a wide range of treatments.

Caserio Runtun, Km 6 (mailing address: P.O. Box 18-02-1944), Baños de Agua Santa. www.lunaruntun. com. © 03/2740-655 or 03/2740-835. Fax 03/2740-376. 30 units. $207 double; $268 deluxe double; $329 presidential suite; $537 imperial suite. Rates include breakfast, dinner, and taxes. AE, DC, MC, V. **Amenities:** 2 restaurants; bar; lounge; babysitting; 4 Jacuzzis; 4 outdoor pools; sauna; well-equipped spa; steam bath; free Wi-Fi. *In room:* Hair dryer, minibar.

Samari Spa Resort ★★★   Built around the remnants of a 300-year-old Jesuit monastery, this spa and resort offers the most elegant and luxurious accommodations in the Baños area. Rooms feature red-tile floors, brick walls, and beautiful stone work in the bathrooms. The deluxe rooms have a tiny separate sitting area (I think you'd do just as well in a standard room). However, the junior suites feature a king-size bed, fireplace, integrated sitting area, and Jacuzzi tub. Rooms on the second floor have high ceilings with exposed wood beams and planking. The gorgeous spa is modern and well equipped, and built around a large, inviting pool under a glass roof. A wide range of massages and treatments are offered. A taxi here from downtown is just $1.

Km 1 on the road to Puyo, Baños de Agua Santa. www.samarispa.com. © 03/2741-855. Fax 03/2741-859. 37 units. $153 double; $214 deluxe double; $254 junior suite. Rates include breakfast, taxes, and use of the spa facilities. AE, DC, MC, V. **Amenities:** Restaurant; bar; lounge; babysitting; 2 pools; room service; sauna; well-equipped spa; steam bath; outdoor tennis court; free Wi-Fi. *In room:* TV, hair dryer, Internet, minibar.

MODERATE

Finca Chamanapamba ★   Located beside the Chamana waterfall, this intimate, homey lodge, run by a German couple, offers excellent views of the River Ulba and Volcán Tungurahua. A quiet hideout, with two of its own man-made waterfalls, the Finca is 4km (2½ miles) outside central Baños and is a great choice if you wish to escape the hustle and bustle of the town but still be within reach of attractions and activities. The two-story cabanas are spacious and equipped with king-size beds, private bathrooms, and balconies. The owners will gladly help you arrange climbing or horseback-riding trips, or give advice on how best to explore the natural beauty of the area; you can even go trekking right from the ranch itself or bathe in the cool waters at the foot of the falls. The ranch's restaurant is quite good, and the menu features several German specialties. Given space restrictions, try to book in advance.

Km 4, Ulba, Chamana, Baños de Agua Santa. www.chamanapamba.com. © **03/2742-671** or 03/2740-641. 3 units. $80 double. Rates include buffet breakfast. No credit cards. **Amenities:** Restaurant; room service. *In room:* No phone.

Sangay Spa-Hotel ☺   Situated across the street from the Cascada de la Virgen waterfall, and right on the doorstep of the hot springs of the same name, this is one of the town's most popular moderately priced hotels. Rooms are pleasantly decorated and relatively spacious, although many show their age. You can choose colonial, cabana, or executive rooms and suites—the latter being the newest and best of the bunch. Established in 1930, and currently run by English climber Brian Warmington, Sangay offers both recreation and relaxation, with tennis and squash courts, a large swimming pool with a water slide, and spa facilities that include steam baths and a wide range of massage and spa treatments. This hotel is popular with tour groups and families, which may put off those looking for a romantic getaway, although it's well located and a good deal for the money.

Plaza Isidro Ayora 100, Baños de Agua Santa. www.sangayspahotel.com. © **03/2740-490.** Fax 03/2740-056. 65 units. $50–$85 double; $135 suite. Rates include buffet breakfast. AE, DC, MC, V. **Amenities:** Restaurant; bar; Jacuzzi; massage; pool; room service; sauna; spa; squash court; steam bath; lighted outdoor tennis court. *In room:* TV, hair dryer.

INEXPENSIVE

In addition to the places listed below, budget hounds seem to like **Hospedaje Santa Cruz** (© **03/2740-648;** santacruzhostal@yahoo.com), on calles 16 de Diciembre and Martínez.

Hostal La Posada del Arte ★ 🎁   Located close to La Virgen waterfall, on a quiet side street abutting the volcano's base, this place is a definite step up from the rest of the budget hostels in town. Rooms feature interesting pieces by Ecuadorean artists and soothing yet bold colors on the walls. The best rooms have waterfall views and private balconies. Some have fireplaces. The family suite is large and features a Jacuzzi tub. Even if you don't get a room with a view, you can enjoy the scenery from the hotel's rooftop patio. The restaurant here serves excellent local and international fare. These folks also run the nearby Casa del Abuelo Bed & Breakfast, and Casa Azul.

Calle Ibarra y Montalvo, Baños. www.posadadelarte.com. © **03/2740-083.** 15 units. $39–$53 double; $63 suite. Rates include breakfast. AE, DC, MC, V. **Amenities:** Restaurant; lounge. *In room:* No phone, free Wi-Fi.

Hostal Plantas y Blanco   One of the town's most popular budget hostels, Plantas y Blanco has a convivial backpacker atmosphere and attractive rooftop terrace decorated with plants, plants, and more plants (hence the name). Double rooms are fairly spacious and comfortable, and some offer pretty views of town; the singles, however, are on the small side. Try to book in advance, because it tends to get quite full here. The rooftop restaurant serves up tasty breakfasts and offers entertainment with a great collection of board games, music, and free Internet available on shared computers and through Wi-Fi.

Martínez y 12 de Noviembre. option3@hotmail.com. © **03/2740-044.** 22 units. $9.50 per person, including taxes. No credit cards. **Amenities:** Restaurant; steam bath; free Wi-Fi. *In room:* No phone.

Where to Dine in Baños

There is no shortage of restaurants in Baños. Most cater to budget travelers and international backpackers and serve a range of Italian, Ecuadorean, Mexican, French,

Chinese, Mediterranean, and vegetarian fare at reasonable prices. If you are feeling really adventurous, you can try the local specialty, *cuy* (roasted guinea pig), which is sold from stalls near the market.

In addition to the places listed below, you can try **Quilombo** (*©* 08/5532-144), on Montalvo and 12 de Noviembre, for Argentine-style grilled meats; or **Casa Hood** (*©* 03/2742-668), on Martinez between Eloy Alfaro and Halflants, for international cuisine and an extensive vegetarian menu.

Café Hood ★ INTERNATIONAL   This eclectic joint exudes an upbeat backpacker's vibe and serves delicious international cuisine, including pastas, curry, Mexican, Thai, Greek, Turkish, and vegetarian options. Portions are definitely generous. You can opt to chill out with a hot chocolate while playing board games or browsing the book exchange. Don't be confused or fooled: There's also a Casa Hood and Café Good in town, both serving similar fare.

Maldonado and Rocafuerte. *©* **03/2740-573.** Main courses $4–$8. MC, V. Thurs-Tues 10am–10pm.

Café Mariane ★★ 🍴 MEDITERRANEAN   This long-standing local institution offers an impressive selection of mouthwatering Mediterranean and French dishes in an attractive yet rustic setting. Their newer dining room features more space and a roaring fireplace. The steak au poivre is excellent, as is the Moroccan-style chicken. Be sure to save room for a dessert crepe. The restaurant offers free Wi-Fi for diners and is part of the new Hostal Jardín de Mariane.

Av. Montalvo, btw. Halflants and Ely Alfaro. *©* **03/2741-947** or 09/5223-555. Reservations recommended. Main courses $5–$9. MC, V. Daily noon–11pm.

Le Petit Restaurant FRENCH   This popular Baños restaurant, situated inside Le Petit Auberge hotel, serves tasty French fare—everything from crepes and hors d'oeuvres to fondue and chateaubriand. On a cold evening, their French onion soup can't be beat. The decor is warm and cozy, with dim lighting and a mix of wood paneling, woven mats, and exposed bricks on the walls. The relaxing and rustic ambience makes it the perfect place for a romantic meal, or you can relax and enjoy a drink and fondue with friends.

16 de Diciembre 240 y Montalvo, inside the hotel Le Petit Auberge. *©* **03/2740-936.** lepetitbanos@ yahoo.com. Main courses $4.50–$15. MC, V. Tues-Sun 8am–3pm and 6–10pm.

Swiss Bistro ★ SWISS   The Swiss Bistro offers a cozy and rustic dining experience with a European feel and excellent service. Delicious raclette and tasty meat, cheese, and chocolate fondues are just some of the treats on the menu of this little slice of Switzerland. A personal favorite, the *röstis,* a potato pancake, is served here with a range of toppings, including melted Gruyere cheese, ham, mushrooms, and more. You can also choose from a variety of meat, poultry, and fish plates, as well as rich desserts and a decent selection of wines.

Martinez, btw. Eloy Alfaro and 16 de Diciembre. *©* **03/2742-262.** www.swiss-bistro.com. Main courses $5.50–$15. No credit cards. Mon 6pm–midnight; Tues-Sat noon–midnight; Sun noon–4pm.

Baños After Dark

For a small town, Baños has a very vibrant nightlife. In fact, it feels a lot like Quito's Mariscal district, in miniature. Stroll down Eloy Alfaro, off Ambato, and you'll find a string of bars and dance clubs pumping out pop, rock, salsa, and reggaetón until the early hours. *Peñas*—bars hosting traditional live music—are also popular among locals and visitors alike. Dance clubs and *peñas* charge an average of $3 admission.

For dancing, **Trébol Discoteque ★★** (✆ **03/2740-428**), Montalvo and 16 de Diciembre, opposite Parque Montalvo, is the town's top spot. It stays open until near dawn and is an excellent "after-hours" spot. **Leprechaun ★** (✆ **03/2741-537**), Eloy Alfaro and Oriente, is another popular party joint (especially among foreigners), with an upbeat atmosphere, a diverse musical repertoire, and an outdoor bar on busy nights, while **Santo Pecado** (✆ **03/2742-396**), Eloy Alfaro and Ambato, blasts out Latin beats, including reggaetón, and gets pretty full. **El Reventador** (✆ **03/2740-490**), which belongs to and is attached to the Sangay Spa-Hotel (see above), is pretty popular.

A recommended *peña* is **Mocambo ★** (✆ **03/2742-733**), Eloy Alfaro between Ambato and Oriente, which extends over three floors. A great place to mingle and people-watch, it has a great cocktail menu, pool table, and balcony. **Café-Bar Barbass,** Eloy Alfaro and Ambato (✆ **03/2742-470**), and **Jack Rock ★**, Eloy Alfaro 541 and Ambato (✆ **03/2741-329**), are the town's rock bars. **La Abuela Tabaco y Ron,** Eloy Alfaro and Ambato (✆ **03/2740-923**), is a smaller, cozier, more subdued cafe/bar, perfect for chilling out with a cold beer or cocktail.

RIOBAMBA

188km (117 miles) S of Quito; 55km (34 miles) S of Baños; 233km (145 miles) N of Guayaquil

Shadowed by five spectacular snowcapped peaks in the heart of the Ecuadorean central highlands, Riobamba is an enchanting small city, with attractive 18th-century architecture, pretty peaceful parks, interesting museums, and charming churches. At an altitude of 2,750m (9,020 ft.), the town enjoys a principally springlike climate, similar to that of Quito, with plenty of cloudless days perfect for taking in the stunning views of the surrounding landscape. As capital of **Chimborazo province** and a commercial hub, Riobamba boasts a fair amount of hustle and bustle, particularly on weekends, when the town comes alive with street traders and indigenous market sellers arriving from surrounding villages to hawk their goods and produce.

Founded in 1534 and known, perhaps a tad pompously, as The Sultan of the Andes, Riobamba was the original Ecuadorean capital under Spanish rule before suffering a devastating earthquake in 1797. The earthquake almost completely destroyed the town and led to its relocation to the current site. Popular among tourists who principally come here to experience the exhilarating **Nariz del Diablo (Devil's Nose)** train ride, which famously zigzags up a solid rock face, Riobamba also serves as the perfect base from which to embark on climbing and trekking tours and trips to the beautiful lakes nearby.

Situated close to several towering peaks, including the country's tallest, **Chimborazo** (6,310m/20,697 ft.), Riobamba is a bit of a minimecca for serious mountain and rock climbers.

Essentials
GETTING THERE
BY BUS Buses depart Quito's southbound bus terminal, **Terminal Terrestre Quitumbe** (✆ **02/3988-200**), for Riobamba every 10 to 15 minutes between 3am and 9pm. **Transportes Riobamba** (✆ **02/3824-742** in Quito, or 03/2960-766 in Riobamba) is one of a half-dozen or so bus lines that alternate on this route. The return bus schedule is pretty much the same. The ride takes a little under 4 hours, and the one-way fare is $4.

Riobamba

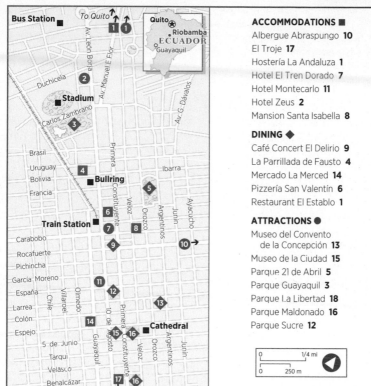

ACCOMMODATIONS ■
Albergue Abraspungo **10**
El Troje **17**
Hostería La Andaluza **1**
Hotel El Tren Dorado **7**
Hotel Montecarlo **11**
Hotel Zeus **2**
Mansion Santa Isabella **8**

DINING ◆
Café Concert El Delirio **9**
La Parrillada de Fausto **4**
Mercado La Merced **14**
Pizzería San Valentín **6**
Restaurant El Establo **1**

ATTRACTIONS ●
Museo del Convento
    de la Concepción **13**
Museo de la Ciudad **15**
Parque 21 de Abril **5**
Parque Guayaquil **3**
Parque La Libertad **18**
Parque Maldonado **16**
Parque Sucre **12**

Riobamba's **Terminal Terrestre** (© 03/2962-005) is on the northwestern out-skirts of town, on Avenida de la Prensa and Avenida León Borja. There is regular service to and from this terminal to Quito, Guayaquil, Cuenca, Guaranda, and Santo Domingo de los Colorados. Taxis always await arriving passengers, and a ride into the town center should cost you only $1.

Buses heading for Baños, Puyo, Macas, Tena, and jungle destinations need to be caught at the **Terminal Oriente** (no phone), on Espejo and Luz Elisa Borja, several blocks northeast of downtown.

BY CAR From Quito, head south on the Pan-American Highway (E35) and con-tinue along this route, passing through Latacunga and Ambato, until you reach Rio-bamba. The ride takes around 3½ hours.

If setting out from Guayaquil, take E70 east to El Triunfo, passing by Durán on the way. At El Triunfo, head northeast on E60 to Riobamba. This ride takes around 4 hours.

Keep abreast of the latest travel information if you plan on journeying between Riobamba and Baños, as the road running parallel to Río Chambo is subject to closure by authorities due to mud flows (lahars) from the currently active Volcán Tungurahua.

BY TRAIN As part of a national program to revive the country's railways, the government has been working on restoring the Riobamba train station and nearby rail lines. Currently, travelers can take the Riobamba-to-Palmira day tour, which passes by Lake Colta, La Balbanera church, Guamote, Palmira, and back to Riobamba again. Trains depart at 6:30am daily from the main Riobamba station and return at 4:30pm, costing $11 per person. For more information, call the reservations office at ✆ 03/2961-038 or check out the website at www.ferrocarrilesdelecuador.gob.ec.

Work on the Devil's Nose run is ongoing and expected to be complete in 2011. See below for more details.

Work to connect Riobamba with Quito and the rest of the Central Sierra may take a little more time. The Riobamba train station (✆ 03/2961-909) is located in the heart of downtown, on Carabobo and León Borja.

ORIENTATION

Riobamba has an orderly gridlike layout; streets, particularly around the central area, have an attractive colonial appearance, with pretty 18th- and 19th-century buildings. The main avenues through town, running in a northeast-to-southwest direction, are León Borja (which becomes 10 de Agosto, heading southeast) and Primera Constituyente.

The town center has several parks. **Parque Sucre,** occupying a square city block, is pretty much the center of town, although the Catholic cathedral, post office, and local museum are all clustered around **Parque Maldonado.** The largest park, **Parque Guayaquil,** is located toward the northern end of León Borja, next to the **Estadio Municipal** (soccer stadium), a little bit up from **Plaza de Toros** (bullring).

GETTING AROUND

Even though Riobamba is a bit spread out, it's easy to get around town. Local buses run up and down Avenida León Borja. From a small terminal a couple of blocks away from the main bus station, buses depart to surrounding areas that you may wish to visit. Fares cost 20¢ to 30¢.

But because taxis are so plentiful and economical, I still recommend them as the preferred means of travel. A ride anywhere around the city or to the bus terminals should usually be around $1 and should almost never exceed $2. Rides to outlying hotels and restaurants listed below should cost only a few dollars. If you can't flag down a cab, call **Cooperativa Los Alamos** (✆ 03/2606-699) or **Cooperativa de Taxis Terminal Terrestre** (✆ 03/2966-990).

VISITOR INFORMATION

For general tourism inquiries, maps, and helpful advice, visit the **municipal tourist office,** on León Borja and Brasil (✆ 03/2947-389; uniturismorio@yahoo.es). Local tour agencies are also excellent sources of information. For all-purpose tours and to book the Devil's Nose (see below), head to **Metropolitan Touring ★★** (✆ 888/572-0166 in the U.S. and Canada, or 02/2988-200 in Ecuador; www.metropolitan-touring. com), on León Borja and Lavalle. For hiking, trekking, mountain biking, or other adventure tours, see the companies recommended below.

FAST FACTS To contact local **police,** dial ✆ 03/2961-913, or ✆ 101 in an emergency. There are two police stations in town, the main one on Primera Constituyente, near the corner of 5 de Junio, and a more centrally located one on León Borja, near the corner of Lavalle.

For medical attention, head to **Hospital San Juan** (✆ 03/2963-098; www. hospiesaj.med.ec), on Veloz and Autachi, or to **Hospital Policlínico** (✆ 03/2945-915), toward the south end of town, on Olmedo 11–01 and Cuba. There are **pharmacies** all over town, with several on the main drag of León Borja.

You'll find the major branches of **Banco de Guayaquil** (✆ 03/2945-001), **Banco Pichincha** (✆ 03/2967-416), and **Banco del Pacífico** (✆ 03/2942-242), all within a few blocks of each other in the heart of the downtown core. All have ATMs and foreign currency exchange facilities.

The main **post office** is on 10 de Agosto 22–72 and Espejo (✆ 03/2969-942). There are plenty of **Internet cafes** around the center; one of the best is **El Puente Informático** (✆ 03/2960-292), on Guayaquil and Carabobo. I also like **EcoNet** (✆ 03/2951-658), on Rocafuerte and 10 de Agosto. Internet rates run around $1 per hour. Most hotels and hostels offer laundry services, but as an alternative, check out **Lavendería Donini** (✆ 03/2961-063), on León Borja and Brasil.

What to See & Do in Riobamba

Riobamba has a couple of minor city attractions, but most folks use the city as a base for tours, activities, and excursions outside town.

Riobamba's city parks are perfect for people-watching. Relandscaped in 1911, **Parque Maldonado** has pretty gardens, tall trees, and flowing fountains, and it fronts the city's picturesque cathedral. **Parque Sucre** has a splendid fountain of Neptune, while **Parque La Libertad** fronts the pretty 19th-century basilica. Toward the north end of the city, **Parque Guayaquil** (also called **Parque Infantil**, or **Children's Park**) is the largest in Riobamba, located near the city's main football stadium, with a small lagoon, rowboats, and a large abstract sculpture strangely resembling a cow; there's also a children's playground. For a panoramic view, head to **Parque 21 de Abril,** from where you can marvel at the scenery, particularly the plumes of smoke coming off Volcán Tungurahua.

Museo del Convento de la Concepción ★★ (✆ 03/2965-212), on Argentinos and Colón, is the town's best and most prestigious museum, with a fine collection of 18th-century religious artifacts. Housed in a former convent, the collection here is large and spread out, some of it in the rooms, known as cells, which were occupied by the prospective nuns. The museum's prize possession, a priceless gem-encrusted .9m-tall (3-ft.) monstrance, was stolen a couple of years ago, but a replica sits in its place. Still, the museum's remaining abundance of silver, gold, art, sculpture, and artifacts more than makes up for its loss. It's open Tuesday through Saturday from 9am to 12:30pm and 3 to 6pm. Admission is $2. Ask at the entrance, and you should be able to hire a bilingual guide for a few more bucks.

Alternatively, check out the city museum, **Museo de la Ciudad** (**Museum of the City;** ✆ 03/2951-906), on Primera Constituyente and Espejo; it houses exhibitions on Old Riobamba and its surroundings. The collection also features pieces by contemporary local artists, and the museum frequently projects both national and Latin American cinema. Set in a pretty restored building, the museum is open Monday through Friday 8:30am to 12:30pm and 1:30 to 4pm, and Saturday from 8am to 4pm. Admission is free.

Riobamba really comes alive on Saturday, with its famously colorful regional market, as villagers from all over the province pour into the city to sell their produce and handicrafts. The most activity occurs around calles 5 de Junio and Argentinos, where vendors principally sell produce. Tourists are better off heading to the charming market in **Parque La Concepción** (Orozco and Colón). **La Condamine** is a smaller daily market on Carabobo and Colombia. On nonmarket days, you can find **handicrafts** in a number of shops located along León Borja close to the train station. Check out **The Tagua Shop** (📞 03/2942-215; http://joyasdetagua.blogspot.com), at León Borja 35–17 and Ibarra, which sells a wide range of handicrafts carved from the extremely hard nut of the *tagua* tree; or nearby on the same street, try **Almacén Taller Rescate Artesanías de Chimborazo** (no phone), which specializes in woven bags and woolen goods.

While in Riobamba, don't miss out on a trip to the region's beautiful lakes. The **Lagunas de Ozogoche,** composed of 60 lakes, is a stunning spot, as is the **Lagunas de Atillo,** both of which are about a 3-hour drive outside the city. A closer option is the **Laguna de Colta,** just 20 minutes away. All the local tour agencies and hotel tour desks can arrange these trips.

From Riobamba, you can also visit surrounding indigenous villages. Easily accessible by bus, the small village of **Guano,** famous for its carpet- and rug-weaving industry, is located some 9km (5½ miles) north of the city. You can also head a few kilometers farther to **Santa Teresita** to visit **Parque Acuatico Los Elenes** (no phone) hot springs and spa, where you'll find amazing views of Volcán Tungurahua. The complex is open Thursday through Monday from 6am to 6pm, and admission costs $3. Buses to both these villages leave from Riobamba at the stop located on Pichincha and New York.

An excellent time to come and experience the typical Ecuadorean highlands culture of Riobamba is during its annual fiestas. The festivities take place on and around April 21, when the town comes alive with music, drinking, dancing, street parades, and fireworks to commemorate the 1822 Battle of Tapi, and Ecuador's independence from Spanish rule.

GETTING BUSY OUTDOORS

Several operators organize climbing, trekking, and mountain-biking tours to the surrounding snowcapped peaks and their outskirts.

CLIMBING & TREKKING   For climbers, Chimborazo is the prized peak: At 6,310m (20,697 ft.), it's the tallest mountain in Ecuador. This is a very high-altitude climb and somewhat technical, too. Only those in good shape and with sufficient skills and experience should attempt it. Trips can also be arranged to Sangay, the Ilinizas, Cotopaxi, and other peaks. If high-altitude climbing is beyond your reach, you can do a multiday trekking-and-camping tour at slightly lower elevations. Destinations include the flanks of Chimborazo, as well as sections of the ancient Inca trail. Organized tours usually last from 2 to 7 days and cost from around $75 to $150 per person per day. Be sure to go with a reputable, licensed guide, particularly if you are a novice. Recommended operators are **Expediciones Andes Marco Cruz** ★★ (📞 03/2364-278; www.expediciones-andinas.com), **Julio Verne Travel** ★ (📞 03/2963-436; www.julioverne-travel.com), and **Andes Trek Expeditions** (📞 03/2951-275; Quito office: 📞 02/2074-006; www.goandestrek.com).

MOUNTAIN BIKING & HORSEBACK RIDING   The terrain and scenery make this a top-notch spot to go mountain biking or horseback riding. Local operators arrange everything from half-day to multiday tours, depending on your fitness level. The most popular destinations are the Ozogoche and Atillo lakes, Chimborazo, and

El Altar. Expect to pay $10 to $75 per day, depending on the number of participants. These rates usually do not include admission to national parks or protected areas. Check out **Biking Spirit** (© 03/2963-981; www.bikingspirit.com), the biking division of Andes Spirit, on Duchicela 1446 and Esmeraldas; **Pro-Bici** (also known as **Ciclotur;** © 03/2941-880; www.probici.com), Primera Constituyente 23–51 and Larrea; or **Metropolitan Touring** (© 03/2969-600; www.metropolitan-touring. com), on León Borja and Lavalle.

THE DEVIL'S NOSE TRAIN RIDE ★★

For decades, many tourists came to Riobamba solely to embark on the exhilarating **Nariz del Diablo (Devil's Nose)** train ride, which winds through some fantastic scenery and daring zigzags up a solid 100m (328-ft.) rock face. The tight switchbacks and sheer drop-offs are enough to make the hairs stand up on the back of anyone's neck.

At press time, the Devil's Nose is currently undergoing reconstruction and is expected to begin operations again by late 2011. Check out the railway's website, **www.ferrocarrilesdelecuador.gob.ec**, for further information and updates.

The typical journey is a round-trip run from Riobamba to Sibambe, with the Devil's Nose itself on the stretch between Alausí and Sibambe. Alternatively you can get off the train at Alausi and either stay the night or head to Cuenca by bus. On the day of your trip, try to arrive early, to get a good seat. Head toward the middle to rear of the train; those sitting closest to the front get the worst of the soot and fumes from the train's exhaust. The best views are reputedly on the right side. Local touts will rent you a cushion for the trip for around $2, a recommended investment.

Where to Stay in Riobamba

In addition to the places listed below, those looking to climb Chimborazo or just wanting to spend the night at high altitude—some 4,000m (13,120 ft.)—should check out **Estrella del Chimborazo** (© 03/2364-278; www.expediciones-andinas.com), a unique option run by local legend and mountaineer Marco Cruz.

EXPENSIVE

Albergue Abraspungo ★★ This country-style inn, housed in a pretty whitewashed building, offers splendid accommodations, attentive service, and great dining. Decorated in a *mestizo* (mixed) architectural style, as the owners like to call it, the warm, spacious rooms—most have fireplaces—show a mix of decor and design influences, relying heavily on Spanish colonial and local Ecuadorean styles. The walls around the hotel are adorned with antique photographs of the breathtaking regional landscape. Located on the outskirts of Riobamba along the road to Guano, this is the perfect spot to relax away from the hustle and bustle, but close enough to explore the town and take advantage of all the local tours and activities. The friendly tour desk staff here will happily help you plan excursions.

Km 3.5, Vía Guano (mailing address: P.O. Box 06-01-979), outskirts of Riobamba. www.abraspungo. com.ec. © **03/2364-031.** Fax 03/2364-277. 42 units. $109 double. Rates include breakfast and taxes. Free parking. AE, DC, MC, V. **Amenities:** Restaurant; bar; lounge; massage; room service; tennis court. *In room:* Free Wi-Fi.

MODERATE

El Troje El Troje is a pretty whitewashed rustic hostería surrounded by luscious green palm trees in a peaceful setting away from the hustle and bustle of the town.

Rooms, some of which have their own fireplace, are done in rustic yet contemporary style. The hotel features a pool and small spa offering a range of treatments. There's also a very good restaurant serving local Andean and international fare and lovely gardens.

Km 4.5 Vía Riobamba-Chambo (mailing address: P.O. Box 060150). www.eltroje.com. © **03/2622-201.** 48 units. $55 double; $83 suite. Rates include breakfast and taxes. AE, DC, MC, V. **Amenities:** Restaurant; Jacuzzi; pool; room service; sauna; sports courts. *In room:* TV, phone.

Hostería La Andaluza ★

Located some 16km (10 miles) outside the town center in the small indigenous village of Chuquipogyo, this hotel is housed in a charming old hacienda. Standard rooms are in the old part of the hacienda, while suites and junior suites are in a newer wing. All have the same colonial-era decor. The hacienda is relatively large and popular with groups, although it still manages to maintain an intimate ambience. Take a stroll around the gardens, unwind in the Turkish baths, sweat it out in the sauna, let loose in the game room, or meander through the hostería's surroundings on horseback.

Pan-American Hwy., Km 16, Vía Ambato, Chuquipogyo, Chimborazo. handaluz@andinanet.net. © **03/2949-370.** 55 units. $73 double; $85 suite. Rates include breakfast and taxes. Free parking. AE, DC, MC, V. **Amenities:** Restaurant; bar; gym; room service; sauna; steam room. *In room:* TV, hair dryer.

Hotel Zeus

A somewhat large, contemporary place, rooms here are colorful and attractively decorated, and, from the upper floors, there are splendid views of the surrounding landscape. I recommend that you opt for one of the executive rooms or suites rather than a standard. It's worth paying a little extra so you can enjoy the stunning views of snowcapped volcanoes while you soak in the bathtub, which is set beside a picture window. Suites come with a minibar, microwave, DVD player, and Jacuzzi tub. This hotel even has a small, on-site ethno-anthropologic museum.

León Borja 41–29, Riobamba. www.hotelzeus.com.ec. © **03/2968-036** or 03/2968-037. 65 units. $54 double; $75 suite. Rates include breakfast and taxes. Free parking. AE, DC, MC, V. **Amenities:** Restaurant; bar; small gym; room service. *In room:* TV, safe.

Mansión Santa Isabella ★

Located just a couple of blocks from the train station, this new boutique hotel is the best and most atmospheric option in Riobamba proper. My favorite rooms are located around a second-floor interior balcony with a solarium roof. All are relatively simple, with wood beds, local artworks on the walls, and contemporary bathrooms. Most rooms have wide-plank wood floors, although a few are carpeted. There's an excellent restaurant on the main floor and a wine cellar and bar, **La Cueva del Cura,** in a cozy basement space with antique stone walls.

Veloz 28–48, btw. Carabobo and Magdalena Davalos, Riobamba. www.mansionsantaisabella.com. © **03/2962-947** or 08/1069-809. 12 units. $60 double; $100 suite. Rates include breakfast. AE, DC, MC, V. **Amenities:** Restaurant; bar. *In room:* TV, hair dryer, free Wi-Fi.

INEXPENSIVE

In addition to the places below, backpackers, especially those leaving early on the Devil's Nose train ride, swear by **Hotel El Tren Dorado** (© **03/2964-890;** www.hosteltrail.com/trendorado), Carabobo 25–35 and 10 de Agosto, a friendly and comfortable stopover right near the train station. Doubles with private bathroom go for $26, including breakfast and taxes.

Hotel Montecarlo ⚓

This pretty 19th-century house offers comfortable accommodations in the center of town, with elegant, cozy rooms, an attractive courtyard, and a good restaurant. Trips to climb or hike around Chimborazo can be arranged at the tour desk here. This is definitely one of the better budget options in Riobamba, and it's only a couple of blocks from the train station.

10 de Agosto 25–41, btw. García Moreno and España, Riobamba. www.hotelmontecarlo-riobamba.com. ✆ 03/2953-204 or ✆fax/03/2960-557. 22 units. $33 double. Rates include continental breakfast and taxes. Free valet parking. DC, MC, V. **Amenities:** Restaurant; bar; free Wi-Fi. *In room:* TV.

Where to Dine in Riobamba

Inexpensive restaurants serving typical Ecuadorean fare are found all over town, particularly close to the train station, where there are several *almuerzo* (lunch) eateries, as well as in the relatively tidy **Mercado La Merced (La Merced Market;** on Guayaquil btw. Colón and Espejo), open from 7am to 6pm.

In addition to the places listed below, I've heard good reports on **Café Concert El Delirio** (✆ 03/32966-441), on Primera Constituyente 28–16 at Rocafuerte, a couple of blocks from the train station. Located in an old colonial home allegedly once belonging to Simón Bolívar, this place sometimes has live music.

La Parrillada de Fausto STEAKHOUSE/GRILL   This cozy place offers steaks and a variety of chicken and fish dishes grilled over a charcoal flame. The fresh-grilled mountain trout is excellent. The ambience here is warm and inviting, and the restaurant is ideally located right in the center of Riobamba.

Uruguay 20–30 y Unidad Nacional. ✆ **03/2967-876.** Main courses $7–$10. MC, V. Mon–Sat 11am–3pm and 6–10pm.

Pizzería San Valentín ★ ITALIAN/PIZZA   This is an excellent local Italian restaurant with a lively atmosphere. The menu features a range of tasty pizzas, pastas, and lasagnas, as well as a varied selection of Mexican dishes. You can also get hamburgers and a few vegetarian items. While I often come here to eat, this place also serves as a popular pub-style meeting spot.

León Borja 22–19 y Vargas Torres. ✆ **03/2963-137.** Reservations not accepted. Main courses $4–$9. MC, V. Mon–Sat 5pm–midnight.

Restaurant El Establo ★ INTERNATIONAL   This rustic place in the Hostería La Andaluza (see above) has open log fires and serves such culinary treats as roasted lamb with applesauce and tasty Chilean empanadas. Be sure to try their home-cured Spanish-style ham. Vegetarian options are available. During the day, large picture windows offer stunning views, and most nights you'll find a live band playing Andean music.

Pan-American Hwy., Km 16, inside the Hostería La Andaluza (see above). ✆ **03/2949-370.** Reservations recommended. Main courses $6–$10. AE, MC, V. Daily 7am–11pm.

Riobamaba After Dark

Unlike Baños, Riobamba is not exactly renowned for its nightlife—your best bet is to venture to and around the eastern end of León Borja, where there are a handful of bars and *discotecas,* principally frequented by locals and often open only Thursday through Saturday. If Latin or electronic tunes are your style, check out the popular and trendy **Tentadero ★** (✆ 09/8271-757; www.eltentaderobar.com), on Avenida León Borja and Angel León. The **Vieja Guardia** (✆ 03/2940-735), on Manuel E Flor 40–43 and Carlos Zambrano, is a well-established pub, popular among the locals. The best laid-back bars for drinks are **Pizzería San Valentín ★** (see above) and **La Cueva del Cura ★★**, inside the Mansión Santa Isabella (see above).

A Detour West: Guaranda

As the capital of the province of Bolívar, **Guaranda** is a charming, relatively small provincial town set among seven lush green hills—hence its nickname, "Rome of the Andes." It has pretty views of the surrounding rolling patchwork pastures. While there isn't an extensive repertoire of things to do, Guaranda is a perfect place for taking leisurely walks and hikes, doing some horseback or bike riding, and visiting the colorful Saturday food market. It also makes for an excellent base from which to explore the giant Volcán Chimborazo or the nearby village of Salinas de Bolívar, where you can see the famous Salinerito cheese-makers at work and indulge in chocolate to your heart's content. Other popular local activities include picnics and barbecues at Las Cochas Lake and visits to El Indio de Guaranga, a large monument towering over the town, in honor of its namesake 16th-century Indian chief.

Guaranda's claim to fame is its annual **Carnaval ★★**, arguably the country's best. Local and international visitors pour into town by the hundreds to celebrate in traditional Guarandeño style with folk music, dancing, street parades, beauty contests, and plenty of alcohol, as well as massive public water, egg, and flour fights. *Fritada con mote* (fried pork with white Andean corn) is typical Carnaval fare in Guaranda, traditionally accompanied by a shot of the infamous Pájaro Azul (Blue Bird), a locally brewed alcoholic concoction that would work well as paint stripper. But it's extremely popular: The locals won't let you go home without trying it! Carnaval is 5 solid days of crazy festivities leading up to Ash Wednesday.

Your best bet for accommodations is **Hotel Cochabamba** (✆ **03/2982-124**), on García Moreno and 7 de Mayo, which charges around $25 for a double and is the most comfortable and conveniently located hotel in downtown Guaranda. Alternatively, check out the slightly more expensive and luxurious **Hotel La Colina** (✆ **03/2980-666**), at Guayaquil 117, a 10- to 15-minute walk up the hill (the splendid views are worth it). A double room here costs approximately $65 and includes breakfast and taxes, and use of the pool and Jacuzzi. Another good option is **Hotel Tambo del Libertador** (✆ **03/2980-634**), on Avenue Guayaquil opposite the Provincial Police Office, with doubles at $40, including breakfast and taxes. **Hostal de las Flores** (✆ **03/2984-396**), at Pichincha 4–02 and Rocafuerte, is set in a charming building and has rooms with a balcony and cable TV for around $16 per person. Try to book far in advance if you plan to travel to Guaranda during Carnaval; the town gets packed and hotel rates rise somewhat.

When hunger strikes, check out the numerous inexpensive restaurants around the town near Plaza Roja; most serve typical Ecuadorean cuisine, including the region's specialty, *cuy* (roasted guinea pig). **Restaurante Cochabamba** (✆ **03/2982-124**), at García Moreno and 7 de Mayo, belongs to its namesake hotel, serves some great international dishes, and is one of the town's more upmarket restaurants. **Los 7 Santos** (✆ **03/2980-612**), on Convención de 1884 and 10 de Agosto, is without doubt the trendiest eatery, with tasty, inexpensive international and Ecuadorean fare; the open fire makes for a cozy ambience and the artsy decor is a welcome change of pace for Guaranda. For Italian cuisine, try the excellent **Pizzería Buon Giorno** (✆ **03/2985-406**), Circunvalación, 2 blocks from Plaza Roja; locals rave about the scrumptious lasagna and delicious pizzas. **Restaurante La Bohemia** (✆ **03/2980-269**), on the corner of Convención de 1884 and 10 de Agosto, serves tasty chicken, meat, and seafood dishes in a rustic atmosphere.

For nightlife, Guaranda has few *discotecas,* most open only on weekends and during Carnaval. Check out **No Bar,** at Azuay and Pichincha, which pumps out typical electronic tunes and infectious reggaetón vibes.

GETTING THERE   The drive to Guaranda, by bus or car, certainly makes for some breathtaking views, particularly at dawn or dusk. Along the way, you'll ascend 4,000m (13,120-ft.) mountain passes, with huge ravines dropping off from the roadside, and pass right by Volcán Chimborazo.

Express Atenas (© **02/3824-746**) has modern buses heading to and from Guaranda approximately every hour from Quito (trip time: 5 hr.; $4.50), and less frequently from Guayaquil (trip time: 4 hr.; $4.50).

You can get here from Riobamba, on **Flota Bolívar** (© **03/2982-061** in Guaranda, 02/3824-837 in Quito, 03/2941-832 in Riobamba), which runs buses roughly every 90 minutes between Guaranda and Riobamba from 4am until 5pm. The ride takes about 2 hours and costs around $2.

The Guaranda bus terminal is a $1 taxi ride or 15-minute walk from Plaza Roja.

CUENCA & THE SOUTHERN SIERRA

8

Most visitors to Ecuador don't take the time to explore the southern Sierra, which is a shame. This region, often called El Austro, offers rich and varied rewards for all sorts of travelers. The colonial city of Cuenca is the region's de facto hub, not to mention its main attraction. One of South America's best-preserved and most charming colonial-era cities, Cuenca is compact and vibrant, and readily offers up its many charms: a wide range of wonderful boutique hotels in restored mansions, a plethora of excellent restaurants and bars, and some of Ecuador's best shopping outside of Otavalo.

A few hours from Cuenca sits **Ingapirca,** Ecuador's principal Inca ruins, as well as **Cajas National Park,** a nature lover and bird-watcher's paradise. South of Cuenca is the city and province of Loja. The Andean mountain peaks aren't quite as high or imposing here as they are in the central Sierra, but they still provide numerous opportunities for hiking, trekking, wildlife viewing, and camping. **Loja** is one of the oldest cities in Ecuador, and thanks to its remoteness, it retains much of its old-world ambience.

Just outside Loja are **Podocarpus National Park** and the isolated mountain hamlet of **Vilcabamba.** Podocarpus, one of the country's most biodiverse national parks, is a must-see for any serious bird-watcher. Vilcabamba, for its part, is world-renowned for the remarkable longevity of its inhabitants, and it has become a pilgrimage destination for those seeking a bit of spiritual healing.

CUENCA ★★

442km (274 miles) S of Quito; 250km (155 miles) SE of Guayaquil; 254km (157 miles) S of Riobamba

Cuenca is Ecuador's third-largest city, but it feels more like a charming old-world town, with cobblestone streets and a rich collection of colonial-era churches, plazas, and buildings. A good deal of the city's colonial architecture remains intact; Cuenca is a UNESCO World Heritage Site. Before the Spanish arrived here, Cuenca was the second-largest city in the Inca empire (after Cusco). The foundations of former Inca palaces

became foundations for the city's churches and government buildings. Amazingly, when the Incas conquered the area in the late 1400s, the Cañari had already been living here for centuries. The Incas—not unlike what the Spanish would eventually do—used stones from the Cañari structures to build their temples and palaces. Several excellent museums here are dedicated to the city's rich and varied past. **Museo del Banco Central** sits right next to the **Pumapungo** archaeological site, which was an Inca palace. Not only can you see the artifacts on display in the museum, but you can also tour the ruins of the palace, as well as its accompanying botanical gardens. A few blocks away, the **Todos Los Santos** archaeological site symbolizes the three layers of history; in a single area, you'll see structures built by Cañari, Inca, and Spanish settlers.

The Cañari (also spelled Kañari) people were the first-known inhabitants of Cuenca, building a city here around A.D. 500 called Guapondeleg. Their language and customs are largely a mystery, although several nearby villages still have names that end in -*deleg*, a common Cañari suffix. Around 1480, the Cañari were conquered by the Incas, who called the city Tomebamba, the current name of the main river that runs through the city center. Tomebamba was one of the preferred cities of Inca King Huayna Capac, who spent much of his time here. But the Inca reign was short-lived—they were vanquished by Pizarro and the Spanish conquistadors in 1534. The Spanish city of Santa Ana de los Cuatro Ríos de Cuenca was founded here in 1557.

Outside Cuenca, there's also plenty to see and do. **Ingapirca,** Ecuador's most impressive Inca ruins, is only 2 hours away, and **Cajas National Park,** which is full of scenic hiking trails and peaceful blue lagoons, is an hour north of the city.

Essentials
GETTING THERE
BY PLANE **Aerogal** (© 888/723-7642 in the U.S. and Canada, or **1800/2376-425** toll-free in Ecuador; www.aerogal.com.ec), **Air Cuenca** (© 02/3300-335 reservations in Quito, or 07/4084-410 in Cuenca; www.postges-ec.com), **Lan Ecuador** (© 1800/101-075 toll-free in Ecuador; www.lan.com), and **Tame** (© 1800/500-800 toll-free in Ecuador; www.tame.com.ec) all offer daily flights to Cuenca from Quito and Guayaquil.

One-way tickets cost $45 to $70 to or from Guayaquil, $55 to $90 to or from Quito. All planes arrive at **Aeropuerto Mariscal Lamar** (© 07/2867-120; www.aeropuertocuenca.ec; airport code: CUE), located on Avenida España, about 1.6km (1 mile) northeast of downtown.

Taxis are always waiting for incoming flights, and a ride from the airport to the center of town costs about $3.

BY BUS Cuenca is connected to the rest of Ecuador by regular bus service. Several bus lines leave from Quito's southbound bus terminal, **Terminal Terrestre Quitumbe** (© 02/3988-200), at least every hour, around the clock, for the 8- to 10-hour ride. **Flota Imbabura** (© 02/3988-237 in Quito, or 07/2839-135 in Cuenca) and **Cooperativa Express Sucre** (© 02/3988-248) are the main companies making this run. The fare runs around $10.

From Guayaquil, a cooperative of five different bus lines take turns departing from the main bus terminal roughly every half-hour throughout the day. The buses use two different routes, alternating each departure via either Cajas or Cañar. The former route is faster, taking about 4 hours, while the latter route takes around 5 hours. The fare costs around $8. Cuenca is also connected by frequent daily bus service to Loja, Macas, Machala, and Sigsig.

The **Cuenca bus terminal** (© 07/2842-023) is on Avenida España, about 1.6km (1 mile) northeast of the center of town, just before and across the street from the airport. Taxis are always waiting here. A ride from the terminal to the center of town costs about $3.

BY CAR If you are driving from Quito, take the Pan-American Highway (E35) south through Latacunga, Ambato, and Riobamba, all the way to Cuenca. The drive takes about 8 hours.

Coming from Guayaquil, the best route is to take E70 east out of town to the junction with E25 south. Near the town of Jesús María, take the exit for Miguir and El Parque Nacional Cajas, and follow this scenic road to Cuenca. The ride should take around 3½ hours. *Note:* In the rainy season (mid-Oct to early May), this route is sometimes hit with landslides.

Alternatively, you can take E70 east all the way to the town of Zhud, where it connects with E35 south, which will take you in to Cuenca. This route should take you about 4½ hours.

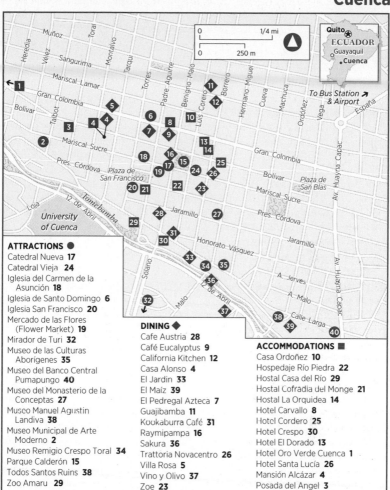

ATTRACTIONS ●

Catedral Nueva **17**
Catedral Vieja **24**
Iglesia del Carmen de la
   Asunción **18**
Iglesia de Santo Domingo **6**
Iglesia San Francisco **20**
Mercado de las Flores
   (Flower Market) **19**
Mirador de Turi **32**
Museo de las Culturas
   Aborígenes **35**
Museo del Banco Central
   Pumapungo **40**
Museo del Monasterio de la
   Conceptas **27**
Museo Manuel Agustin
   Landiva **38**
Museo Municipal de Arte
   Moderno **2**
Museo Remigio Crespo Toral **34**
Parque Calderón **15**
Todos Santos Ruins **38**
Zoo Amaru **29**

DINING ◆

Cafe Austria **28**
Café Eucalyptus **9**
California Kitchen **12**
Casa Alonso **4**
El Jardin **33**
El Maíz **39**
El Pedregal Azteca **7**
Guajibamba **11**
Kookaburra Café **31**
Raymipampa **16**
Sakura **36**
Trattoria Novacentro **26**
Villa Rosa **5**
Vino y Olivo **37**
Zoe **23**

ACCOMMODATIONS ■

Casa Ordoñez **10**
Hospedaje Río Piedra **22**
Hostal Casa del Río **29**
Hostal Cofradia del Monge **21**
Hostal La Orquidea **14**
Hotel Carvallo **8**
Hotel Cordero **25**
Hotel Crespo **30**
Hotel El Dorado **13**
Hotel Oro Verde Cuenca **1**
Hotel Santa Lucía **26**
Mansión Alcázar **4**
Posada del Angel **3**

ORIENTATION

In Spanish, *cuenca* means "river basin," and four separate rivers run through the broad, flat valley here, eventually merging southeast of the city to form the Río Cuenca. The **Río Tombebamba** runs right through Cuenca, and the central core of the city lies along and a few blocks north of this river's bank. Three blocks north of the river, **Parque Calderón** is essentially the heart of Cuenca. On the southwest corner of the park is **Catedral Nueva,** and on the southeast corner is **Catedral Vieja.** From here, you can easily walk to all the hotels, restaurants, banks, and attractions in town. Running parallel to the Río Tombebamba is **Calle Larga,** where you will find several hotels and restaurants, as well as the **Todos Santos ruins** and

Museo del Banco Central. Several sets of stairs lead down from Calle Larga to **Calle 3 de Noviembre,** where you'll find a pretty riverside pathway.

GETTING AROUND

Taxis are abundant in Cuenca. A ride anywhere in town should cost no more than $2. A ride up to **Mirador de Turi** should cost from $4 to $5. If you can't flag one down, call **Radio Taxi Ejecutivo** (② 07/2809-605) or **Taxi Paisa** (② 07/2863-774).

If you want to rent a car while in Cuenca, contact **Hertz Rent A Car** (② 07/2869-420; www.hertz.com), which has an office at the airport.

VISITOR INFORMATION

The main **tourist office** (② 07/2850-521) is located on Mariscal Sucre on the south side of Parque Calderón. These folks also maintain desks inside the main airport and bus terminals. The friendly staff can give you maps and help you get your bearings. You can also head to one of the local tour operators: **TerraDiversa** ★ (② 07/2823-782; www.terradiversa.com), on Calle Hermano Miguel 5–42, 1½ blocks north of Calle Larga; or try **Hualambari Tours** ★ (② 07/2830-371; www. hualambari.com), Av. Borrero 9–69, next to the post office. The owners of TerraDiversa are former tour guides who know all of Ecuador extremely well, while Hualambari is the local representative of Grayline Tours. Both companies can provide a wealth of information and can arrange a wide variety of tours around Cuenca, the region, and the entire country.

FAST FACTS The main **police station** is on Calle Luis Cordero, near Córdova (② 101). The main office of the National Police is on Avenida Vallejo and Calle Espejo. You'll find the **post office** on the corner of Borrero and Gran Colombia (② 07/2838-111). It's open Monday through Friday from 8am to 12:30pm and 2:30 to 6pm, and Saturday from 9am to noon.

Clínica Hospital Monte Sinai (② 07/2885-595), Miguel Cordero 6–111 and Avenida Solano, is the best hospital in Cuenca. **Fybeca** is a 24-hour pharmacy with several locations, including one at Bolívar 9–74 and Padre Aguirre.

Internet cafes are abundant in Cuenca; two of my favorites are **Hol@net** (② 07/2843-126), Borrero 5–90 and Juan Jaramillo, and **Cuenc@net Café** (② 07/2837-347), Calle Larga 602 and the corner of Hermano Miguel. Banks and ATMs are ubiquitous in Cuenca, and you'll find more than a half-dozen outlets within a block or two of Parque Calderón. For laundry service, head to **La Química Automática** (② 07/2823-945), Borrero 7–34 on the corner of Presidente Córdova, or to **Durán e Hijos** (② 07/2837-720), at Avenida Huayna Capac and Guacayñan.

What to See & Do in Cuenca

PARQUE CALDERÓN & NEARBY ATTRACTIONS

Parque Calderón is the historical heart of Cuenca and the center of the action. Here you'll find both Catedral Nueva and Catedral Vieja. **Catedral Vieja (Old Cathedral)** ★, also known as Iglesia del Sagrario, is the oldest structure in the city. Construction began in 1557 and utilized stones taken from the nearby Inca ruins of Pumapungo. Because cities can't have two cathedrals, once Catedral Nueva opened in 1967, the old one ceased functioning as a house of worship. Today it houses a modest museum of religious art. The museum (② 07/2834-636) is open Monday through Friday from 9am to 1pm and 2 to 6pm, and on weekends from 10am to 1pm. Admission is $2.

In 1885, construction began on **Catedral Nueva (New Cathedral)** ★★, also known as Catedral de la Inmaculada Concepción, but it wasn't completed for almost another 80 years. It has a mix of styles—Romanesque on the outside with Gothic windows. It is modeled on the Battistero (Baptistery) in Florence. The two massive blue domes are distinctive and visible from various vantage points around the city. The floors are made of white marble imported from Italy, while the stained-glass windows contain a mix of Catholic and indigenous symbols (the sun and the moon, for example). In 1985, when the Pope visited this cathedral and saw the Renaissance-style main altar (which is modeled on the one in St. Peter's in Rome), he looked confused and asked, "Am I in Rome?" The cathedral is open Monday through Friday from 7am to 4:30pm and Saturday from 9am to noon.

Around the corner, on Padre Aguirre and Sucre, is **Iglesia del Carmen de la Asunción.** The church is not open to the public, but from the outside, you should take note of its unique stone entrance and neon-lit altar. The church sits on the delightful and colorful **Mercado de las Flores (Flower Market)**. In the early part of the 20th century, women weren't allowed to work. To create a diversion for them, the men of the city decided to set up this little market for the use of women only. Nowadays, anyone can wander around the fresh-smelling market. Ecuador is one of the world's largest exporters of flowers, and some beautiful varieties are found here. At the market, you'll find folk remedies for all sorts of illnesses, too. Nearby, on Presidente Córdova and Padre Aguirre, is **Iglesia y Mercado de San Francisco.**

> ## Purple Petals Aplenty
>
> Beginning in late October and lasting through much of November, majestic jacarandas bloom across Cuenca. These tall trees, with broad canopies and a striking purple flower, have been planted in abundance throughout the city, especially along the Río Tomebamba and the long, broad Avenida Huayna Capac.

In addition to the places mentioned below, if you're interested in archaeological finds, stop by the small **Todos Los Santos** ★ archaeological site. Discovered in 1972, the short loop path here takes you through overlapping constructions by the Cañari, Inca, and Spanish cultures. As you walk the path, you will see the remains of massive Spanish milling stones alongside an Inca-period wall with four of the style's classic trapezoidal niches, as well as pieces of wall that date to the era of the Cañari. The site is located at the intersection of Calle Large 2–23 and Avenida Manuel Vega (a few blocks down from Museo del Banco Central). At the entrance to the site, you'll find **Museo Manuel Agustín Landiva** (✆ 07/2832-639; http://museo-landivar. arqueo-ecuatoriana.ec), which has a small collection of archaeological artifacts and also serves as a gallery space for young Cuencan artists. The museum and archaeological site are open Monday through Friday from 8am to 1pm and 3 to 5pm, Saturday from 9am to noon. Admission is $1.50. It should take you only about 30 to 40 minutes to tour both the site and the museum.

For a bird's-eye view of Cuenca, take a taxi up to **Mirador de Turi** ★. In Quichua, *turi* means "twins," and from this site, you can see twin mountains in the distance. A taxi here should cost about $4 to $5 each way. You can—and really should—combine a visit here with a visit to the ceramic gallery **Taller E. Vega** (see below).

Museo de las Culturas Aborígenes ★ This amazing private collection includes more than 8,000 Ecuadorean archaeological pieces dating as far back as 500

B.C. Some of the most interesting are the pre-Inca urns that were used to bury the dead in an upright position, and the flutes made from the bones of different animals. The collection ranges far and wide, with works by the Valdivia, Machalilla, Tolita, Yasuni, and Quitis peoples. In addition, this place has an excellent gift shop and a pleasant little courtyard cafe and bakery.

Calle Larga 5-24 y Mariano Cueva. ✆ **07/2839-181.** Admission $2.50. Mon–Fri 8:30am–noon and 2-6pm; Sat 9am–1pm.

Museo del Banco Central Pumapungo ★★ ☺ This massive museum, archaeological site, and botanical gardens is the pride and joy of Cuenca. The museum itself covers several floors in a modern building next to the Central Bank building. Exhibits range from rooms filled with colonial and religious artwork to walk-through re-creations of typical dwellings from the various regions of Ecuador, to an entire numismatic section that chronicles the country's currency from spondylus shells through the now-defunct sucre. **Tomebamba Hall** ★ is a highlight. The museum was constructed over the ruins of an Inca palace—Pumapungo—and in this room, you will learn the history of the Incas in Cuenca, as well as see archaeological artifacts found in the area. Afterward, you can exit and walk behind the museum to see the actual archaeological site, which has a few llamas wandering around it. The complex is set on a high hillside, from which the views are wonderful. In addition to the Inca archaeological excavations, Museo del Banco Central has beautiful botanical gardens and a small aviary on its extensive grounds. This museum complex is huge, and you really need at least 2 to 3 hours to see it. Groups of more than four people can ask for a free bilingual guide.

Calle Larga y Av. Huayna Capac. ✆ **07/2831-255.** Admission $3 adults, $1.50 children 6–18, free for children 5 and under. Mon–Fri 9am–6pm; Sat 9am–1pm.

Museo del Monasterio de la Conceptas ★ This small museum was a former monastery, originally founded in 1599. The nuns' rooms and common areas of the two-story adobe structure, which dates to the 17th century, are now all wonderfully curated art galleries; the theme is religious art. One of the highlights is an impressive collection of gruesome crucifixes by local artist Gaspar Sangurima. In one of these sculptures, you can see the carved heart through the gaping wounds in Christ's chest. The central courtyard is lushly planted and features a cherimoya tree that bears fruit each fall. Don't miss visiting the back patios, where you'll find the monastery's kitchen, as well as the old indoor cemetery with empty burial crypts.

Calle Hermano Miguel 6-33, btw. Presidente Córdova and Juan Jaramillo. ✆ **07/2830-625.** Admission $2.50 adults, $1.50 children 8–18, free for children 7 and under. Mon–Fri 9am–1pm and 3-5:30pm; Sat-Sun and holidays 10am–1pm.

Museo Municipal de Arte Moderno Luis Crespo Ordóñez Art and sculpture adorn the many rooms and hallways of this old adobe home. It's hard to predict what type of art you'll see when you visit this museum—there are no permanent exhibits. But the museum does display the best of Ecuadorean modern art—previous shows have included works by Guayasamín, Tábara, and Oswaldo Muñoz Mariño. The museum is also famous for hosting **Bienal Internacional de Pintura,** a biannual exposition of Ecuadorean and American art. Even if you're not an art lover, it's nice to come here and relax in the peaceful colonial courtyard.

Calle Sucre 15-27 y Coronel Tálbot. ✆ **07/2831-027.** Free admission. Mon–Fri 8:30am–1pm and 3-6:30pm; Sat 9am–1pm.

Museo Remigio Crespo Toral Perhaps the best reason to visit here is simply to tour through the neo-baroque French-style mansion that houses the museum and overlooks the Río Tomebamba. Exhibits here focus on the history of both Cuenca and Ecuador. The museum possesses a large collection of archaeological pieces, a massive coin and metalworks collection, and a good selection of colonial art. The first museum founded in Cuenca, this is a great place for history buffs.

Calle Larga 7-07 y Presidente Borrero. ☏ **07/2833-208.** Free admission. Mon-Fri 9am-1pm and 3-6pm; Sat-Sun and holidays 9am-1pm.

Zoo Amaru ☺ Located right in the center of town, this small zoo rambles through several rooms of an old home. A series of terrariums house a collection of snakes, reptiles, insects, and amphibians, while a large open pen is home to a rather good-size crocodile. Fish tanks contain several different species, but by far the biggest attraction is the piranhas. A 40-minute guided tour in English is included in the entrance fee.

Benigno Malo 4-64 y Calle Larga. ☏ **07/2826-337.** www.zooamaru.com. Admission $2.50 adults, $1.50 children 4-12. Mon-Fri 9am-1pm and 3-6pm; Sat-Sun and holidays 10am-5pm.

LEARNING SPANISH

Whether you want to just brush up on your rusty Spanish skills or dive in for intensive instruction, contact **Nexus Language & Culture** (☏ **07/4090-062**; www.nexus.edu.ec), which offers small-group and private classes. The school is located on a hill overlooking Río Tomebamba. Prices run between $9.50 and $11 per hour for classes, which are either one-on-one sessions or three students per teacher, depending upon current demand. A homestay with a local family can be arranged for just $15 per day, which is quite a bargain, considering that it includes three full meals. Nexus can also help arrange volunteer opportunities in and around Cuenca.

SPORTS & OUTDOOR ACTIVITIES

Cuenca may be Ecuador's third-largest city, but if you venture just a few kilometers outside the city center, you'll find yourself at one with nature. For the best hiking in the area, head to **Cajas National Park** (see "Side Trips from Cuenca," later in this chapter). **Hualambari Tours** ★ (☏ **07/2830-371**; www.hualambari.com) and **Terra Diversa** ★ (☏ **07/2823-782**; www.terradiversa.com) both offer horseback-riding and mountain-biking expeditions through the outlying mountains and forests, stopping at small towns along the way. Day trips run $45 to $90 per person, including lunch, equipment, and transportation. Multiday trips and expeditions can also be arranged.

HOT SPRINGS & SPAS

Located just a few miles outside of downtown Cuenca, the small town of Baños is blessed with natural hot springs and a couple of excellent places to soak your weary bones. *Baños* means "baths," and the town is appropriately named for these hot springs. Volcanically heated, these waters do not have a heavy sulfur smell, which is an added plus.

Piedra de Agua ★★★ (☏ **07/2892-496**; www.piedradeagua.com.ec) is the highlight here. A lovely complex carved into and around an outcropping of red volcanic rock, this place features several hot pools, a cold plunge, a mud bath, steam rooms, saunas, and private grottos. There's also an excellent restaurant serving health-conscious spa cuisine, and a wide range of massages and other treatments are offered. Entrance to the hot pools and cold plunge runs $10. However, for $30, you get full run of the facilities, including the mud bath, steam rooms, and saunas. Admission for children 12 and under is half-price. Treatments run an extra $40 per hour. The hot springs are open Monday and Wednesday through Saturday from 9am to 10pm, and Sunday from 9am to 7pm.

A nearby hotel option, **Hosteria Duran** ★ (© 07/2892-485; www.hosteria duran.com), also has hot pools and natural steam baths. You can use the hotel's pools and facilities for $5, or opt for a more public pool, also run by the hotel, near its entrance, for just $2.50.

A taxi to Baños should cost only around $5.

SHOPPING

Cuenca is a shopper's paradise. Ceramics and Panama hats are the best buys here, but, in general, you can find an excellent selection of folksy handicrafts, as well as some higher-end art and ceramic works. If you're here on a Sunday, you should hop on a bus to, or sign up for a tour of, the nearby villages of **Sigsig, Chordeleg,** or **Gualaceo.** They all host active Sunday markets where you can buy some very high-quality, locally produced handicrafts. All the local tour agencies offer day trips to these villages, and even on nonmarket days, you can find good arts and handicraft works here.

In Gualaceo, be sure to stop in at **Tejemujeres** ★ (© 07/2839-676; www. tejemujeres.com), a local cooperative of textile artisans that produces and sells beautiful handcrafted sweaters. The river that flows right through Gualaceo is a popular spot for a swim or picnic on sunny days. If you make it to Chordeleg, be sure to check out the fine silverwork and jewelry in the numerous shops that ring the town's central park. I like **Mar de Plata** (© 09/2223-781) for good-quality wares.

ARTS & HANDICRAFTS   Walk down any street in the center of Cuenca, and you are sure to find scads of stores specializing in handmade crafts. I especially like **La Esquina de las Artes** ★★ (© 07/2831-118), a complex featuring a restaurant, coffee shop, and cultural center, as well as a broad selection of local artwork and crafts; it's located on Av. 12 de Abril and Agustin Cueva. In the evenings, this place sometimes has live music, theater, or poetry readings.

CERAMICS   For hundreds of years, Cuenca has been a center for ceramics. Walk into any museum in the area (see above), and you'll see examples of beautiful pre-Inca jugs and vases.

For a more contemporary and personalized experience, I recommend visiting **Taller E. Vega** ★★★ (© 07/2881-407; www.eduardovega.com), located just below the Mirador de Turi. Eduardo Vega is a ceramicist and one of Ecuador's most famous artists. Monumental sculptures and murals by Vega can be found around Cuenca, as well as in Quito. A visit to his hillside workshop and gallery is worthwhile just for the views, but you'll also have a chance to glimpse a bit of his production process and to buy from his regularly changing collection of decorative and functional works, handicrafts, and wonderful jewelry. Most organized city tours stop here. If you're coming to Taller E. Vega on your own, I recommend calling in advance to be sure it's open.

JEWELRY   The spondylus shell was used as currency by early civilizations of Ecuador. At the custom jewelry shop **Spondylus** ★ (© 07/2455-890; www. spondylus.cuencanos.com), you'll find the shiny shell integrated into a wide range of pendants, earrings, and bracelets. You'll also find plenty of beautiful pieces in silver, either plain or with assorted gemstones. This shop is located on Miguel Cordero 2–22 and Cornerlio Merchán, on the south side of the Tomebamba River.

PANAMA HATS   You may be surprised to learn that Panama hats have always been made in Ecuador: For generations, the people on the coast have been using local

THE PANAMA hat

If a rose by another name would still smell as sweet, then a hat invented, designed, and manufactured in Ecuador would look as stylish and protect you from the sun just as well if, for example, it were called a Panama hat.

The Panama hat is endemic to Ecuador, with Panama mistakenly receiving credit for the hat's origin over a century ago. These lightweight woven hats made a splash at the 1855 World's Fair in Paris. When they were shipped from Ecuador, they went via Panama, their last port of call before landing in Europe. By the end of the World's Fair, Panama had gotten the credit for producing the hat, and the Emperor Napoleon III became perhaps the first in a long line of celebrities associated with the headpiece.

As far back as the 16th century, Ecuadoreans were wearing and weaving hats from *paja toquilla,* a fiber from the leaves of the *Carludovica palmata* palm. The fibers from these plants were boiled and dried and then painstakingly crafted into the final product. Cities in Manabí province—Azogues, Biblian, Sigsig, Montecristi, and Jipijapa—developed into major centers for the production of these hats. A single artisan can take anywhere from 3 to 6 months to craft

just one **superfino** (super-fine) hat. Major production was moved to Cuenca in 1836 and then spread throughout the provinces of Azuay and Cañar, now the largest centers of hat production in Ecuador. The popular style of today is still called **Montecristi,** after the town where, to this day, the finest-quality Panamas are still woven (p. 268).

After taking Paris by storm, the hats began covering the heads of American troops during the Spanish-American war (1898). Gold miners who arrived in California by way of the Isthmus of Panama also donned these light and breathable hats, whose popularity escalated further when a photograph circulated of U.S. President Theodore Roosevelt wearing one. Other prominent politicians to wear Panama hats included Winston Churchill and Nikita Khrushchev. The Panama hat also has its fair share of Hollywood cred, having graced the heads of stars as diverse as Clark Gable, Humphrey Bogart, Orson Welles, Sean Connery, Paul Newman, Bruce Willis, and Danny Glover.

Today, despite the popularity of the Panama hat, few, except those who visit Ecuador, know its true origins. But a toquilla straw hat by any name keeps the sun off your head and looks pretty sharp, to boot.

straw to create finely woven hats. The trade was moved inland, and Cuenca is now the major hub for the production of Panama hats. **Homero Ortega P. & Hijos ★★★** (© 07/2809-000; www.homeroortega.com) makes the highest-quality Panama hats in the world; patrons include the queen of England. You can visit the factory and learn how the hats are made, and afterward you can browse in the elegant boutique. The store is located a few minutes outside the center of town, at Av. Gil Ramírez Dávalos 3–86.

   Casa Paredes Roldán-Sombreros Barranco (© 07/2831-569; www.sombreros ecuatorianos.com), at Calle Larga 10–41 between General Torres and Padre Aguirre; and **K. Dorfzaun ★** (© 07/2807-537; www.kdorfzaun.com), Av. Gil Ramírez Dávalos 4–34 and Alcabalas, also sell finely crafted hats. Both of these latter stores also have informative displays and offer tours explaining and demonstrating the process of weaving a Panama hat.

Panama hats in Cuenca vary greatly in price and quality, running from around $10 to $12 for a basic version, to around $150 to $250 for a *superfino.* That *superfino,* though, may cost over $1,000 in a boutique shop in New York, Los Angeles, or London.

Where to Stay in Cuenca

VERY EXPENSIVE

Mansión Alcázar ★★★   An elegant oasis in the heart of Cuenca, this meticulously renovated house once belonged to the president of Ecuador. A beautifully tiled enclosed courtyard with a fountain leads to plush accommodations on two floors. Out back, there's a lovely garden filled with lavender and rose bushes. Each room is unique, but all have one thing in common: Every piece of furniture was made in Cuenca. Elegant antiques and fine objets d'art give the rooms that old colonial feel. Suites have wrought-iron four-poster beds; no. 207 has a mural of angels on its ceiling, but no. 202 is my favorite, with a view over the garden. Bathrooms have Cuencan marble, and each one has distinctly hand-painted walls. It's worth the splurge for one of the suites, as several of the standard rooms, especially those on the first floor, are quite small. The beautiful **Casa Alonso** (p. 210) overlooks the garden and is one of the best restaurants in town.

Calle Bolívar 12–55, btw. Tarqui and Juan Montalvo, Cuenca. www.mansionalcazar.com. ℂ **800/327-3573** toll-free in the U.S. and Canada, or 07/2823-918 in Ecuador. Fax 07/2823-554. 14 units. $202 double; $269 suite. Rates include full breakfast, afternoon tea, and taxes. AE, DC, MC, V. Free parking. **Amenities:** Restaurant; bar; lounge; room service; free Wi-Fi. *In room:* TV, hair dryer.

EXPENSIVE

Hotel Carvallo ★   The intimate Carvallo is full of understated elegance. Yet another lovingly restored old house in the heart of the downtown, the Carvallo boasts cozy rooms with blue walls and armoires made from local black-walnut wood. Some units have terrific views of the city; no. 303 has a lovely view of Cuenca's red-tiled rooftops. The bathrooms are small but well equipped and very clean. Request a bathrobe at check-in, and they'll deliver one to your room. The honeymoon suite comes with a king-size bed, plush comforter, and giant candelabra.

Gran Colombia 9–52 y Padre Aguirre, Cuenca. www.hotelcarvallo.com.ec. ℂ/fax **07/2832-063.** 30 units. $100 double; $180–$200 suite. Rates include full breakfast. MC, V. Parking nearby. **Amenities:** Lounge; room service. *In room:* TV, hair dryer, minibar, free Wi-Fi.

Hotel Crespo   This hotel has been in business since 1942. The original building, more than 140 years old, is built on the steep hillside over the Río Tomebamba. The rambling structure covers some five stories, and there's no elevator; ask for a room

---

Retirement Haven

Given its mild climate, safe streets, affordable real estate, and low cost of living, Cuenca has exploded in recent years as a destination for foreign expatriates and retirees. You can see them sitting on park benches reading books on sunny days, and working on their Spanish in restaurants and bars at night. This phenomenon hasn't gone unnoticed, and in 2010, *International Living* magazine named Cuenca its number-one retirement destination in the world.

close to the lobby if climbing several flights is a problem for you. The rooms have an old-fashioned charm, with wood paneling and furnishings, and colorful hand-painted moldings, although the decor can feel a bit dated. The ceilings are charming, designed to look like antique tin ceilings. The bathrooms feature marble tiles, lots of counter space, and a telephone. The best rooms have views of the river. No. 408, with both river and mountain views, is my favorite. Overall, this is a good choice but not nearly as elegant or as intimate as Mansión Alcázar (see above) or the Santa Lucía (see below).

Calle Larga 7–93, Cuenca. www.hotel-crespo.com. © **07/2842-571.** Fax 07/2839-473. 39 units. $114 double. Rates include taxes. AE, DC, MC, V. **Amenities:** Restaurant; bar; room service. *In room:* TV, hair dryer, minibar, free Wi-Fi (in most rooms and public spaces).

Hotel Oro Verde Cuenca   The Oro Verde is a somewhat uninspired business-class hotel—although it does have extensive grounds and facilities, including a pool and one of the better health clubs in the city. The Oro Verde is located on the outskirts of the downtown area, and you can't walk from here to the colonial center of Cuenca. Fortunately, a taxi costs only about $4 each way. Free airport pickup can be arranged if you contact the hotel a day before. Discounts abound here, so be sure to ask for "promotional" or "corporate" rates when making your reservations.

Av. Ordóñez Lazo (P.O. Box 01-01-1274), Cuenca. www.oroverdehotels.com. © **888/400-0074** in the U.S. and Canada, or 07/4090-000 in Cuenca. Fax 07/4090-001. 77 units. $100–$110 double; $120–$140 suite. Rates include buffet breakfast. AE, DC, MC, V. Free parking. **Amenities:** 2 restaurants; 2 bars; free airport transfers; babysitting; well-equipped health club; small outdoor pool; room service; sauna. *In room:* TV, hair dryer, minibar, free Wi-Fi (in most rooms).

Hotel Santa Lucía ★★★ 👬   Hotel Santa Lucía is housed in a wonderfully restored downtown mansion that dates to 1859. Meticulous attention to detail—in both decor and service—is a hallmark. The large, enclosed courtyard, which contains a 100-year-old magnolia tree and beautiful baby palms, leads to spacious, comfortable accommodations. Rooms have the amenities of a large luxury hotel, including plasma-screen televisions. No. 212 has a view of the cathedral and a small, private balcony overlooking the street. All but four of the spacious bathrooms have tubs, and many feature multihead spa showers. Antiques adorn the hallways, and fresh flowers are arranged daily. In the courtyard, **Trattoria Novacentro** (see below) serves authentic Italian cuisine, and the **Inti** restaurant focuses on Ecuadorean cooking, both old and new, while the bar **Moshi Moshi** is a classy haunt for a few drinks.

Antonio Borrero 8–44 y Sucre, Cuenca. www.santaluciahotel.com. © **07/2828-000.** Fax 07/2842-443. 20 units. $133–$145 double; $153–$177 suite. Rates include full breakfast and taxes. AE, DC, MC, V. Free valet parking. **Amenities:** 2 restaurants; bar; lounge; babysitting; concierge; room service. *In room:* TV, hair dryer, minibar, free Wi-Fi.

MODERATE

Casa Ordóñez (© **07/2823-297;** www.casa-ordonez.com), on Mariscal Lamar 859 between Benigno Malo and Luis Cordero, is another excellent option in this price range.

Hotel Cordero   This is a high-rise, business-class hotel in the heart of the old colonial center. The rooms are all of good size and well equipped, although they are rather plain. All have at least one queen-size bed, and many come with a bidet in the large bathroom. Most rooms have large windows, or even walls of glass, and those on the third and fourth floors have good views. No. 403 is a huge suite with a Jacuzzi in a large glass-enclosed room with its own wet bar. The suite has a sitting room, bedroom, and principal bathroom. The hotel has a small gym and indoor parking. If you don't have a room with a view, be sure to visit the rooftop terrace, which provides a sweeping 360-degree panorama of the city. There's a small shopping arcade just off the lobby, and the hotel is just a block from Parque Calderón.

Bolívar 6–50 y Antonio Borrero, Cuenca. www.hotelcordero.com. © **07/2825-363.** ©/fax 07/2825-834. 23 units. $65 double; $150 presidential suite. Free parking. AE, DC, MC, V. **Amenities:** Restaurant; bar; room service. *In room:* TV, free Internet, minibar.

Hotel El Dorado ★★ You won't find any colonial-era vibes here. The hip El Dorado is bold and brash, with lots of glass and polished stainless steel in the entrance and lobby. A glass-and-steel staircase leads up to the rooms, and there are several waterfalls scattered around the building. The rooms—all spacious and well lit—have a clean, minimalist decor. Some units on the higher floors have good views. I particularly like no. 512, which has a good view of the cathedral dome. The two-room presidential suite has a Jacuzzi tub, glass sinks and elegant bathroom fixtures, and a Zen-style water fountain on the writing desk. Several floors are smoke-free, and there's one room that's well set up for travelers with disabilities. The hotel's small spa covers the necessary bases but isn't quite as large or well equipped as I would have expected.

Gran Colombia 7–87 y Luis Cordero, Cuenca. www.eldoradohotel.com.ec. © **07/2831-390.** Fax 07/2831-663. 42 units. $80 double; $120 junior suite; $150 presidential suite. Rates include buffet breakfast. AE, DC, MC, V. Free parking. **Amenities:** 2 restaurants; bar; babysitting; small, well-equipped health club and spa; room service; sauna; steam room; smoke-free rooms. *In room:* TV, hair dryer, minibar, free Wi-Fi.

INEXPENSIVE

In addition to the places listed below, **Hostal Casa del Río** (© **07/2829-659;** www.casadelrio.cuencanos.com) is a pretty well-kept backpacker's option, with a mix of shared and private bathrooms, on the hillside overlooking the Tomebamba River. Some of the rooms here even have a river view.

Hospedaje Río Piedra The rooms in this modern four-story building are large, clean, and well equipped; those facing the street have huge picture windows. Many units, however, have frosted windows opening only onto the interior hallways. Some rooms come with kitchenettes, and most have fairly small bathrooms. The hotel has attractive artwork and stained-glass pieces in the public spaces, and a small cheerful restaurant.

Presidente Córdova 8–40 y Luis Codero, Cuenca. www.hotelriopiedra.net. © **07/2843-821.** ©/fax 07/2839-679. 32 units. $46 double. Rates include full breakfast and taxes. AE, DC, MC, V. Free parking. **Amenities:** Restaurant; bar; lounge; room service; free Wi-Fi. *In room:* TV, minifridge.

Hostal Cofradía del Monje 👜 Located across from Plaza San Francisco and right next to the San Francisco church, this cozy hostel inhabits yet another meticulously restored old home. The rooms are on the second floor, and the atrium-covered central courtyard houses the *hostal*'s popular **restaurant.** All rooms have polished wood floors with Persian rugs, flatscreen TVs, and small bathrooms. They also feature hand-painted wall murals, high ceilings, and ornate steel light fixtures. Nos. 1 through 5 have views of the cathedral and the lively market on Plaza San Francisco. Your best bet is to ask for room no. 2, a corner unit that has French doors opening onto two little balconies—one on each side of the corner.

Presidente Córdova 10–33 y Padre Aguirre, Cuenca. www.hostalcofradiadelmonje.com. ©/fax **07/2831-251.** 7 units. $42–$50 double. Rates include full breakfast. AE, MC, V. Parking nearby. **Amenities:** Restaurant; bar; lounge. *In room:* TV.

Hostal La Orquídea Take a moment to marvel at the ornate and beautifully restored facade before entering this excellent budget option. Once you're inside, a high atrium roof lets plenty of light into the central lobby area. The rooms are simple and plain, with wood floors and minimal decorations. Most have anywhere from two to four twin beds, so be sure to specify that you want a *matrimonial,* or queen, if you're traveling as a couple. Nos. 11 and 12 have small balconies overlooking the street. The suite here is really better described as an apartment with three bedrooms, two bathrooms, a full kitchen, and living and dining rooms. This suite also has a private rooftop terrace with a view of the San Alfonso Church steeple. There's a small restaurant tucked into the back of the ground floor serving inexpensive Ecuadorean cuisine, as well as a full breakfast for under $2.

Antonio Borrero 9-31 y Bolívar, Cuenca. *C* **07/2824-511.** *C*/fax 07/2835-844. 14 units. $20–$25 double; $80 suite. MC, V. Parking nearby. **Amenities:** Restaurant; lounge. *In room:* TV, minifridge.

Posada del Angel *C* If you're looking for a bit of colonial charm with artistic touches—at budget prices—this is the hotel for you. After an extensive renovation of the 120-year-old large colonial house, the Posada del Angel is a whimsical, airy place. Bright yellow and blue are the themes here. You enter through a large enclosed courtyard, and most of the rooms, which come in all shapes and sizes, are found around the first two floors. All are simply furnished and very clean, and all but three have beautiful hardwood floors. Some rooms have wrought-iron lamps made in Cuenca and attractive wooden armoires. Most of the tiled bathrooms are tiny but sparkling. For some privacy, ask for one of the remote rooms located on the third or fourth floors. Several lounge areas and covered courtyards are spread around the rambling structure.

Bolívar 14-11 y Estévez de Toral, Cuenca. www.hostalposadadelangel.com. *C* **07/2840-695.** *C*/fax 07/2821-360. 22 units. $47–$49 double. Rates include full breakfast. MC, V. Free parking. **Amenities:** Lounge; free Wi-Fi. *In room:* TV.

A QUIET OPTION ON THE OUTSKIRTS

Hostería Caballo Campana ★ ☺ Nestled on a hillside on the edge of the town of Baños (see above), this working horse ranch is an excellent option for those who prefer some country charm to the colonial-era city vibe in Cuenca proper. Rooms are cozy and well equipped. Most come with a working fireplace, and all have small televisions. The "Bird of Paradise" honeymoon suite is the choice room, with a four-poster bed and private Jacuzzi. The extensive grounds include a network of trails for both hiking and horseback riding, as well as a large children's play area.

Misicata, Sector Huishil Km4, Baños. www.caballocampana.com. *C* **07/2892-361.** Fax 07/2892-043. 18 units. $94 double; $121–$132 suite. Rates include breakfast buffet. MC, V. Free parking. **Amenities:** Restaurant; lounge; free Wi-Fi. *In room:* TV.

Where to Dine in Cuenca

Cuenca has excellent restaurants, inviting cafes, and wonderful bakeries. In addition to the places listed below, there's plenty of street food available all over town. You'll see *cuy* (guinea pig) and whole pigs on spits or recently roasted, as well as empanadas and *llapingachos,* all for sale by street vendors. While not an option for those with sensitive stomachs, if you've got a sturdy intestinal tract, this is a tasty and inexpensive way to go.

In addition to the places listed below, sushi lovers should head to **Sakura** (*C* **07/2827-740**), at the bottom of the stairway on Calle Larga at Hermano Miguel

The hip restaurant and bar **Zoe** (📞 07/2841-005), at Borrero 7–61 between Sucre and Córdova, is another good option. **Guajibamba** (📞 07/2831-016), on Luis Cordero 12–32, is a good place for local cuisine, including cuy, while **Vino y Olivo** ★★ (📞 09/4091-083), inside **La Esquina de las Artes** (see above), serves excellent tapas and Mediterranean fare, with a good selection of wines by the glass and bottle.

For breakfasts, lunch, and light fare, locals are flocking to the new **Kookaburra Café** (📞 07/2840-423), on Calle Larga 9–40, between Benigno Malo and Padre Aguirre, while the aptly named **California Kitchen** (📞 08/3111-740), on Gaspar Sanguriana and Borrero, serves up California-style contemporary American cooking.

EXPENSIVE

Casa Alonso ★★★ 🏠 NEW ECUADOREAN/FUSION   Housed in the elegant Mansión Alcázar hotel (see above), this place serves up the most inventive and elaborate cuisine in Cuenca. As an example, a between-course sorbet might be served on edible, sugarcoated rose petals. Chef Clayton Carnes has a fantastic culinary imagination and the skills to make it taste good on the plate, to boot. Local ingredients are used whenever possible. The homemade fettuccini is made with quinoa flour and dressed with some rabbit cacciatore, while the pork tenderloin is wrapped in prosciutto and is served with a complex but perfectly balanced mix of apple, goldenberries, goat cheese, and a sauce made from chirimoya and taxo, two local fruits. The refined restaurant has two main dining areas, and I prefer the glassed-in room just off the garden.

Calle Bolívar 12-55, btw. Tarqui and Juan Montalvo, Cuenca. 📞 **07/2823-918.** www.mansionalcazar.com. Reservations recommended. Main courses $10–$21. AE, DC, MC, V. Daily noon–3pm and 6:30–10pm.

Trattoria Novacentro ★★ 🏠 ITALIAN   Occupying the sunken central courtyard area of the classy Hotel Santa Lucía (see above), this place serves the best Italian fare in the city and holds its own as a chic and refined choice any night of the week. Service is formal and attentive. White linens cover the tables, and the seating is in uniquely designed steel chairs with plush white cushions. The high atrium courtyard is beautiful by day but is particularly romantic, with its dim lighting, at night. There's a wide range of classic Italian antipasti and pasta dishes, as well as daily specials. For a main course, I like the perfectly grilled steak and arugula. You can also get fresh grilled fish expertly prepared, or spicy shrimp fra diavolo. The wine list is extensive and fairly priced. For dessert, order a piping-hot shot of espresso and classic tiramisu.

Antonio Borrero 8-44 y Sucre, Cuenca. 📞 **07/2828-000.** Reservations recommended. Main courses $8.50–$23. AE, DC, MC, V. Mon-Sat noon–10:30pm; Sun noon–4pm.

Villa Rosa ★★ ECUADOREAN/INTERNATIONAL   This longstanding favorite has a beautiful setting: the enclosed courtyard of an old Cuencan home elegantly restored with marble floors, crisp white tablecloths, and comfortable wooden chairs. The creative cuisine here has its roots firmly in traditional Ecuadorean cooking. The owner, Berta Vintimilla, bakes the delicious empanadas herself, and they are excellent as an appetizer; the recipes for many of the Ecuadorean specials come from her family. Main courses include sea bass with crab sauce served with rice and vegetables, tenderloin of beef, jumbo langoustines with fennel, and a variety of daily specials. The service is excellent, the wine list is reasonable, and every ingredient used in the kitchen is of the highest quality. Note that the restaurant is closed on weekends, except for groups of a substantial size who have made reservations.

Gran Colombia 12-22 y Tarqui. 📞 **07/2837-944.** Reservations recommended. Main courses $8.50–$18. AE, DC, MC, V. Mon-Wed noon–3pm and 7–10:30pm.

MODERATE

El Jardín ★ INTERNATIONAL   This elegant restaurant is located inside Hotel Victoria. The dimly lit dining room features a wraparound wall of glass with views of the Río Tomebamba and the city lights below. Tables feature abundant place settings and overlapping gold-on-green tablecloths. There are stained-glass fixtures overhead, as well as on the entrance door. The menu is hand-drawn on an oversize piece of thick parchment paper. Options range from spaghetti carbonara to veal cordon bleu. There are usually one or two daily specials, as well as a daily pie or cake for dessert. Everything is wonderfully prepared and presented. The wine list is relatively short and relies heavily on Chilean vineyards.

Calle Larga 6-93, inside Hotel Victoria. ℂ **07/2831-120.** Reservations recommended. Main courses $6.50–$21. AE, DC, MC, V. Daily noon–3pm and 6:30–10:30pm.

Tiestos ★★★ 🍴 ECUADOREAN   This new restaurant has taken Cuenca by storm. Owner and chef Juan Carlos Solano serves up rich and delicious food in clay cooking pots, or *tiestos*, from a small seven-burner open kitchen. Every meal begins with the almost ceremonial laying out of eight different bowls of homemade pickled chiles and chimichurris, ranging in heat from mild to blistering, but all delectable. The signature main dishes are meant to be shared and range from tender filets of beef in a tomato cream sauce to large langostinos in a butter, parsley, and garlic sauce, to chicken curry with macadamia nuts. You can also get a few individual main dishes, as well as rich, luscious desserts. The dining room is intentionally rustic, and waiters wear *toquillo* straw hats, white shirts, and black vests. These folks, thanks to their success, have just bought their own building two blocks away, at Juan Jaramillo 4–89 and Mariano Cueva, although they don't plan on moving their restaurant operations there until late 2011.

Juan Jaramillo 7-34 y Borrero. ℂ **07/2835-310.** www.tiestosrestaurante.com. Main courses $8.50–$18. AE, DC, MC, V. Tues–Sat noon–3pm and 6:30–10pm; Sun noon–3pm.

INEXPENSIVE

Cafe Austria INTERNATIONAL   This pleasant little corner slice of Old Europe is a great place for a breakfast, coffee break, drink, or full meal. The menu features some Austrian classics such as Wiener schnitzel and Viennese goulash. You can also get pastas, sandwiches, or empanadas. For dessert, they've got apple strudel, as well as Linzer torte and other goodies. The restaurant is spread around a large room on two levels. Some arty black-and-white photos adorn the wall, as does a bust of Wolfgang Amadeus Mozart. I recommend grabbing a table by one of the wraparound windows, to take in the passing parade as you enjoy your food and drink. There's a small bar near the entrance; happy hour is every weekday from 8 to 9pm.

Benigno Malo 5-95 y Juan Jaramillo. ℂ **07/2840-899.** Main courses $4–$6.50. V. Daily 7:30am–11pm.

Café Eucalyptus ★★ TAPAS/INTERNATIONAL   This is Cuenca's hippest and most happening restaurant and bar. Folks flock here (especially on weekend nights) to gather for drinks and appetizers. There's seating on two floors—head upstairs if you want to find a somewhat quieter table, or stick to the main floor and bar area to people-watch and mingle. The food here is tapas-style and tapas-size; most people order several and share them. Selections are truly international (more than 50 dishes from 20 different countries) and include hot Cuban sandwiches, cheese quesadillas, pad thai, French bread with tapenade, and stuffed peppers with rice, raisins, and parsley. The liquor and wine list is quite impressive, and there are a number of wine

Fanesca—Holy Week Soup

If you're lucky enough to be in Cuenca for Semana Santa, or Holy Week, be sure to try the seasonal specialty, *fanesca,* a thick soup of salted cod. The soup contains 12 different beans or grains, representing the 12 apostles. It has a cream or milk base and is thickened with ground pumpkin seeds.

Fanesca is usually served with a hard-boiled egg in the bowl, and often with an empanada and some tubers such as cassava or plantain. The traditional meal in Ecuadorean homes on Good Friday, *fanesca* is served in the majority of local restaurants for most of Holy Week.

choices by the glass. Eucalyptus also has the only draft beer in the city, including Llama Negra, which is made in Quito and is a dark stout beer similar to Guinness.

Gran Colombia 9-41 y Benigno Malo. ℭ **07/2849-157** or 09/1001-740. www.cafeeucalyptus.com. Tapas $4.50–$14. AE, DC, MC, V. Sun–Tues noon–midnight; Wed–Sat noon–2am; Sun 5–11pm.

El Maíz ★ ECUADOREAN   This is the place to come for local cooking; it's set in a beautifully renovated old house with a lovely outdoor patio for alfresco dining. The indoor dining room feels like somebody's house, with wood floors, red tablecloths, and a gracious waitstaff. There are two outdoor seating areas: a lower patio with colorful tiles overlooking a courtyard full of plants, and an upper terrace with a lovely view of the green hills. Appetizers include the usual offerings of *humitas,* empanadas, and *locro de papas.* The main courses are terrific and unique. My favorites include the chicken in pumpkinseed and white-wine sauce, beef medallions in a pear sauce, and *hornado cuencano* (roasted pork served with *llapingachos*—mashed potatoes with cheese). Rotating monthly specials are tied to national holidays and celebrations. For dessert, try the *almíbar de babaco* (a compote of a local fruit, tart and sweet).

Calle Larga 1-279 y Calle de los Molinos. ℭ **07/2840-224.** Main courses $4.50–$10. MC, V. Mon–Sat noon–9pm.

El Pedregal Azteca ★★ MEXICAN   Since 1989, María and Juan Manuel Ramos have welcomed diners into their cozy restaurant. Everything is homemade, even the tortillas; the owners bring some of the ingredients back from Mexico to ensure that the food is of the highest quality. A wide range of Mexican cuisine is served up here, from fish *Veracruzana* to three types of *chilasquiles.* The *enchilada de mole* is delicious, as are the tacos filled with your choice of stuffing. For dessert, the *arroz con leche* (rice pudding) is divine and comes with fresh vanilla and plump raisins, although I sometimes prefer the sweet, fried beignetlike *buñuelos.* Live music on Friday and Saturday nights fills the place with a youngish crowd; weekday nights, on the other hand, are quiet.

Gran Colombia 10-29 y Padre Aguirre. ℭ **07/2823-652.** Main courses $4–$9.50. MC, V. Mon–Sat noon–3pm and 6:30–11pm.

Raymipampa ★ 🍴 ECUADOREAN/CUENCAN   This popular local institution is located right next to Catedral Nueva. The bustling dining room features a loft area with tables under a low ceiling made of exposed log beams over much of the main dining area. The walls feature imitation baroque bas-reliefs. I like grabbing a table near the front windows, which have a view of Parque Calderón. The menu features a range of meat, poultry, and seafood. You can also get traditional Ecuadorean fare, such as *humitas* and *tamales de maíz.* I like the complete breakfast, an excellent deal at around $2 that includes coffee, fresh juice, two eggs, two fresh-baked croissants, and local cheese. Broken plates and bent silverware have been fashioned into an interesting little sculpture hanging near the entrance.

Benigno Malo 8-59, btw. Sucre and Bolívar. Ⓒ **07/2834-159.** Reservations not accepted. Main courses $3.50–$7. MC, V. Daily 8:30am–11pm.

Cuenca After Dark

Cuenca used to be a sleepy, provincial city, but local young folk and visiting tourists have turned this into a respectable little party city. For quiet drinking and conversation, **Wunderbar Café ★★★** (Ⓒ 07/2831-274), right off the stairs below Calle Larga and Hermano Miguel, and **La Parola ★★** (Ⓒ 09/9910-234), on Calle Larga 5–89 and the Escalinata, are both popular spots. Early birds will appreciate the Wunderbar Café's happy hour, which begins at 11am and runs until 7pm, while you really can't beat the views from the open-air patio of La Parola. You also can't go wrong at the bars at either **Hotel Santa Lucía** or **Mansión Alcázar,** which are much more refined and mellow (see "Where to Stay in Cuenca," earlier in this chapter).

One of Cuenca's top hangout spots is **Eucalyptus ★★** (see "Where to Dine," above), which has a popular Ladies' Night every Wednesday and a rowdy salsa night every Saturday. Other good spots for mingling with the local crowd include **Tal Cual** (Ⓒ 07/2801-459) and **Sankt Florian** (Ⓒ 07/2833-359), both located on Calle Larga, near Hotel Crespo (p. 206); and **Tinku ★** (Ⓒ 07/2838-520), on Calle Larga 4–68 at the corner of Alfonso Jerves.

Gabbia Live Disco ★★ (Ⓒ 07/2836-641), on Presidente Cordova 5–58 and Hermano Miguel, is the top place for dancing, with live bands and DJs and several rooms and dance floors to choose from. **La Mesa Salsoteca ★** (Ⓒ 07/2833-300), on Gran Colombia 3–35 between Machuca and Ordóñez, is a more classic local dance hall, with a heavy mix of salsa, merengue, and other tropical rhythms.

Note: Many venues are open only Wednesday through Saturday. Sunday, Monday, and Tuesday are very quiet nights in Cuenca, and hardly anybody ventures out late. Covers are sometimes charged and usually range from $2 to $6, which may include a drink or two.

Side Trips from Cuenca

Hualambari Tours ★ (Ⓒ 07/2830-371; www.hualambari.com), **TerraDiversa ★** (Ⓒ 07/2823-782; www.terradiversa.com), and **Metropolitan Touring ★★** (Ⓒ 02/2988-200; www.metropolitan-touring.com) all offer a wide range of day trips out of Cuenca, including trips to the two attractions listed below.

PARQUE NACIONAL CAJAS (CAJAS NATIONAL PARK) ★★

After you've seen the museums and historic sights in Cuenca, it's great to get away from the city and immerse yourself in the area's natural wonders. Cajas is only about 32km (20 miles) west of the city (about a 1-hr. drive), but it feels worlds away. Unlike many other areas in Ecuador, the park was formed by glaciers, not volcanic activity. Covering about 29,000 hectares (71,630 acres), the park has 232 lakes. The terrain and ecosystems are varied here, allowing for an impressive variety of flora and fauna. In high-elevation cloud forests, bird species range from the masked trogon and gray-breasted mountain toucan to the majestic Andean condor. The famed Inca Trail runs through the park. One of my favorite hikes is up **Tres Cruces,** which offers spectacular views of the area and the opportunity to see the Continental Divide. I also recommend the hike around **Laguna Quinoa Pato;** the vistas of the lake are impressive, and as you walk on the trails, you'll have a good chance of spotting ducks. From the main visitor center, you can explore the flora of the humid mountain-forest climate—mosses, orchids, fungi, and epiphytes are common. The forest is full of polylepis trees, one of the few trees in the world that grows up to an altitude of about 3,000m (9,840 ft.). *Note:* It can get extremely cold here, so wear warm clothing.

GETTING THERE & VISITING THE PARK Cajas is huge, and much of its wildlife is elusive. I highly recommend exploring the park with a guide. Both Hualambari and TerraDiversa (see above) have excellent naturalist guides. If you want to go on your own, head to the main terminal in Cuenca and catch any Guayaquil-bound bus that takes the route via Molleturo and Cajas. These buses leave roughly every hour throughout the day. Ask to be dropped off at La Toreadora. Return buses run on a similar schedule and are easy to catch from the main road outside the visitor center. Admission to the park is $10 for adults, $5 for children under 12. If you have any questions, call the park office (✆ **07/2829-853**).

INGAPIRCA ★

Ingapirca is the largest pre-Columbian architectural complex in Ecuador, and it's definitely the most interesting. However, anyone familiar with the massive ruins of Machu Picchu or of the Mesoamerican Maya will find this site small by comparison. The Incas arrived here around 1470. Before then, the Cañari people had inhabited the area. It's believed that both the Cañari and Incas used Ingapirca as a religious site. It was common for the Incas to build their religious palaces over the ruins of a conquered culture. When the Incas conquered the area, they ordered all Cañari men to move to Cusco. In the meantime, Inca men took up residence with Cañari women, to subtly impose Inca beliefs on the local culture. Ingapirca, then, exhibits a mix of Cañari and Inca influences. For example, many of the structures here are round or oval-shaped, which is very atypical of the Incas. In fact, Ingapirca is home to the only known oval-shaped sacred Inca palace in the world.

Ingapirca means "the wall of the Inca," and you can see some fine examples of the famed Inca masonry here. The highlight of the site is **El Adoratorio/Castillo,** an elliptical structure believed to be a temple to the sun. If you're here on June 21, you can watch as the sun projects light on certain symbols. Nearby are the **Aposentos,** rooms made with tight stonework, and thought to have been used by the high priests. Most of the remains from the Cañari culture have been found at **Pilaloma,** at the south end of the site (near where you first enter). *Pilaloma* means "small hill," and some archaeologists surmise that this was a sacred spot, especially because it is the highest point in the area. Eleven bodies (mostly of women) have been found here—perhaps the circle of stones was some sort of tomb. On a hill behind the entrance, near the parking area, is a small museum with a relief map of the site and a collection of artifacts and relics found here.

This site is administered and run by the local community. Llamas graze among the archaeological ruins. If you're lucky enough to visit before or after the large tour buses arrive, you'll find the place has a very peaceful vibe to it.

GETTING THERE The site (✆ **07/2215-115**) is open daily from 8am to 6pm; admission is $6. It's best to visit Ingapirca with an experienced guide because most of the resident guides here do not speak English, and all the explanations inside the museum are in Spanish only. A full-day trip to Ingapirca out of Cuenca—including transportation, lunch, and guided tour of the ruins, but not the admission fee—

should cost $30 to $50. If you want to go to Ingapirca on your own, catch a bus from the main bus terminal in Cuenca. **Cooperativa Cañar** (© 07/2844-033) operates buses that stop at the site; they depart at 9am and 1pm, and the 2-hour ride costs $3 each way. The return buses leave Ingapirca at 1 and 4pm. On weekends, there's only the 9am bus, which returns at 1pm.

Staying Near the Site

Posada Ingapirca 🏨 Perched on a hill just above its namesake ruins, this converted farmhouse has cozy rooms in a remote, rural setting. Perfectly fitted Inca stones form the hearth of the beautiful fireplace here. The rooms are all carpeted; have exposed rustic, log-beam ceilings; and come with little electric heaters. The decor features colorful woven blankets and local handicrafts. Some rooms have their own fireplaces. The views are great from the large picture windows of the second-floor rooms, but those on the ground floor have a wonderful tile-and-stone shared veranda. Posada Ingapirca is located just a couple of hundred yards from the entrance to the archaeological site.

Ingapirca, Cañar Province. www.grupo-santaana.net. © **07/2827-401** or 09/3997-434. 23 units. $50–$65 double. Rates include full breakfast. AE, DC, MC, V. **Amenities:** Restaurant; bar; lounge. *In room:* No phone.

En Route South: Saraguro

Located 141km (87 miles) south of Cuenca and 64km (40 miles) north of Loja, **Saraguro,** along with a handful of neighboring towns, is home to a unique and traditional indigenous group known by the same name. The Saraguro are most recognized for their use of black ponchos and shawls, which some claim they wear in memory and mourning of Atahualpa, who was killed by the Spanish in 1533. Both Saraguro men and women wear their hair in a single long braid, and the women often wear beautiful beaded necklaces. The Saraguros also are known for using distinctive broad-brimmed hats. The everyday use of their traditional dress, however, is greatly decreasing with globalization, and the Atahualpa legend has been called into doubt. Today Saraguros can be found throughout the region, particularly in Loja and Vilcabamba (see below). The forests and hills surrounding the town of Saraguro are a rich area for bird-watching and a beautiful spot for those wanting to see a bit of rural Ecuador.

Of interest in Saraguro is the fact that the principal church and other public buildings were built using Inca stones cut, carved, and transported from Cusco during the reign of Huayna Capac. The stones were part of a temple destined for Quito. But when a lightning storm struck the convoy transporting them near Paquishapa and Saraguro, it was thought to be a bad omen and the project was abandoned.

Hotel options are severely limited in Saraguro. Your best bet is **Inti Samana Wasi** (© **09/2280-035** or 09/3862-707; www.intisamanawasi.com), on Av. 10 de Marzo, near the Pan-American Highway; it's a simple and inexpensive hostel charging $12 per person per night, including breakfast, with clean rooms and a friendly staff.

LOJA

647km (401 miles) S of Quito; 415km (257 miles) SE of Guayaquil; 205km (127 miles) S of Cuenca

Off the beaten track and not on most traditional tourist itineraries, Loja is the capital city of the southern province of the same name. This small burg is little-visited and serves predominantly as a gateway to the more popular and even more remote village of Vilcabamba (see later in this chapter). That said, Loja is a clean, quiet, and pleasant city nestled between two rivers. In addition to a colonial-era vibe, there's a whimsical side to Loja: At the entrance to the city, you'll see a castlelike bridge and clock tower, which show both medieval and Tudor architectural influences and feature various public murals.

Founded in the beautiful Cuxibamba Valley in 1548 by Alonso de Mercadillo, Loja is one of the oldest cities in Ecuador. It was also the country's first to be wired for electricity, in 1896, using electricity generated by a nearby hydroelectric dam. As you enter the city, a large sign over the main road in proclaims Loja THE MUSICAL CAPITAL OF ECUADOR, owing to the fact that the city has produced its share of popular artists. The hills and valleys surrounding Loja are home to some of Ecuador's prime coffee plantations.

Essentials

GETTING THERE

BY PLANE   Tame (© 1800/500-800 toll-free in Ecuador; www.tame.com.ec) has three daily departures from Quito to Loja's **Aeropuerto Camilo Ponce Enríquez** (© 07/2677-140; airport code: LOH)—also known as La Toma—in Catamayo, about 45 minutes outside Loja. **Saereo** (© 1800/723736 in Ecuador; www.saereo.com) flies the Guayaquil-Loja route with two daily flights Monday through Saturday and one flight on Sunday. Fares run $80 to $95 each way, and the flight takes around 50 minutes from Quito and 40 minutes from Guayaquil.

There are always taxis waiting for arriving flights. A cab ride from the airport to Loja should cost around $6. From the airport into Loja, buses also run about every hour between 6am and 9pm. The fare is around $1.

BY BUS   Transportes Loja (© 02/3824-753 in Quito or 07/2570-505 in Loja), **Transportes Santa** (© 02/3824-873 in Quito or 07/2570-084 in Loja), and **Transportes Viajeros** (© 02/3824-741 in Quito) are the main bus companies with service to Loja, via Cuenca, from Quito's southern Terminal Terrestre Quitumbe (© 02/3988-200). About a dozen different buses leave throughout the day for the 11- to 13-hour journey. The fare is around $16 or $17.

Transportes Loja and **Transportes Viajeros** have roughly hourly service between Loja and Cuenca. This ride takes about 4½ hours, and the fare is $8. **Transportes Loja** (© 04/2130-311 in Guayaquil) also has regular service to Guayaquil, a 12-hour ride.

In Loja, the main bus station, Terminal Terrestre (© 07/2570-407), is on Av. 8 de Diciembre and Juan José Flores. In addition to the major cities listed above, you can find regular bus connections between Loja and Huaquillas, Machala, and Vilcabamba.

BY CAR   To drive from Quito to Loja, follow the directions to Cuenca (p. 196). In Cuenca, stay on the Pan-American Highway (E35), which takes you right in to Loja.

If you are coming from Guayaquil, follow the directions to Machala (p. 258). From Machala, continue south on E25 until the town of La Avanzada, where you will take the well-marked exit for E92 to Loja.

ORIENTATION

The highways into Loja from Cuenca, Machala, and the airport enter the city from the north, near the divergence of the Malacatus and Zamora rivers—the heart of the city lies between these two rivers. The main north-south thoroughfares in town are avenidas Iberoamérica and Universitaria, which are parallel and straddle the Malacatus River. Parque Central is the physical and social center of Loja, with every major hotel, restaurant, shop, and attraction of note within easy walking distance. The Universidad Nacional de Loja (National University of Loja) is located south of downtown.

GETTING AROUND

Local buses and *taxi rutas* (shared taxis that cruise a specific route, picking up and dropping off passengers as necessary) circulate around the city. Fares run 10¢ to 60¢. You can also find numerous traditional taxis. A ride anywhere in town, including to or from the bus terminal, should be just $1.50. If you can't flag one down, call **Taxis Sevilla de Oro** (📞 07/2584-493) or **Taxis Libertador Bolívar** (📞 07/2571-902).

To rent a car in Loja, contact **Bombuscaro Rent A Car** (📞 07/2577-022), on 10 de Agosto between Avenida Universitaria and 18 de Noviembre, or **Scape Rent-a-Car** (📞 07/2561-554; www.scaperentacar.com) on Bernardo Valdivieso 02-41 between Juan de Salinas and Felix de Valdivieso. Rates run from $40 to $90 per day.

FAST FACTS The main **police station** (📞 **101** for emergencies, or 07/2578-344) is located outside of the center of town, on Avenida Argentina near Avenida Bolívar. The main **post office** (📞 07/2571-600) is on the corner of calles Colón and Sucre. **Hospital Loja** (📞 07/2570-540) is on Avenida Iberoamerica and Samaniego. At Juan Jose Pena E Rocafuerte and Av. 10 de Agosto, on the southwest corner of the main plaza, you'll find the **Ministry of Tourism** (📞 07/2572-964). There's also an **iTur** (📞 07/2570-407) information office on the corner of Bolívar and Eguiguren.

Several banks are located near the central park, and other branches and ATMs are spread around town. **Banco Pichincha** is on Valdivieso and 10 de Agosto, and **Banco de Guayaquil** is on Jose Antonio Eguiguren and Olmedo. Internet cafes and *cabinas telefónicas* can be found all over Loja, particularly around downtown, as well as at or near any hotel.

What to See & Do in Loja

For most visitors, the first sight to catch their eye is **Puerta de la Ciudad (Door to the City),** a castlelike clock tower that actually forms a bridge over the main road into town. The tower, which features a couple of side turrets, displays a re-creation of the coat of arms granted the city by King Phillip II of Spain in 1571. It was from here that expeditions were to be launched to conquer the Amazon and to seek the mythical city of El Dorado. Inside this structure, you'll find a few shops and galleries, as well as a simple little second-floor cafe. The top of the tower provides a nice lookout point from which to take in the lay of the land.

Public parks and plazas abound in Loja. **Parque Central ★** is a classic colonial-era construction with the city's Catholic church on the eastern side and the Palacio Municipal (Municipal Palace) on its north side. The **Catedral ★**, which has an ornately painted interior, is worth a visit. This is one of the largest churches in Ecuador, and it received a major overhaul and restoration in 2004. In mid-August, the famous statue of the Virgin of El Cisne is brought to the cathedral for the celebrations in her honor. **Museo del Banco Central** (📞 07/2573-004), on 10 de Agosto between Bolívar and Valdivieso, has a collection of archaeological relics and displays illustrating local historical events. This museum has seven rooms, with sections dedicated to the Inca and pre-Inca civilizations, colonial-era art, natural history, and significant Loja citizens. The museum is open Monday through Friday from 9am to 1pm and 2 to 5pm. Admission is free. **Casa de la Cultura ★** (✆ **07/2571-672**), on Colon 1312 and Valdivieso, is one of the town's most important cultural hubs, playing host to a number of different events, including art, music, drama, and film exhibitions. See **www.loja.cce.org.ec** for up-to-date information on what's going on.

About 5 blocks south of Parque Central is **Plaza San Sebastián ★**, also known as Plaza de la Independencia (Independence Sq.). It was here, on November 18, 1820, that the local populace gathered to declare independence from Spain. At the center of the plaza stands a towering 32m-tall (105-ft.) clock tower. Around the plaza, colonial-era buildings have been lovingly restored, and on the south side of the plaza stand the pretty blue-and-white Iglesia de San Sebastián and its attached convent. Both are beautifully maintained.

Another notable little city park, **Plaza San Francisco,** gets its name from the neighboring San Francisco church and convent. At the center of this plaza is a large sculpture of Alonso de Mercadillo, the city's founder, mounted on a marvelous steed.

Perhaps Loja's most striking church is **Iglesia de Santo Domingo ★★**, located at **Plaza Santo Domingo.** Dating to 1557, this church features interior paintings and frescos by Fray Enrique Mideros, who also painted the churches in Ibarra, Latacunga, and Baños.

Much of Loja's colonial architecture has been destroyed by earthquakes, fire, and the passage of time, so you absolutely must take a stroll up **Calle Lourdes ★**, which has a picturesque row of well-restored and -maintained colonial homes and buildings with ornate plaster facades, carved wood window frames and doors, cobblestone streets, and stone-and-tile sidewalks. Antique street lamps and fresh paint complete the picture. Scattered among the residential homes, you'll find art galleries and other shops. Calle Lourdes is south of the center of town; the best section is between avenidas Bolívar and 18 de Noviembre.

There are excellent hiking and bird-watching opportunities all around the mountains and forests outside Loja. The primary destination for these activities is Podocarpus National Park (see below). If you want to do any serious hiking, bird-watching, or any other adventure activity in the area, I recommend that you contact **Biotours** (✆ **07/2579-387;** www.ecuadorsur.wordpress.com/biotours), **Podocarpus Travel** (✆ **07/2588-010**), or **Vilcatur** (✆ **07/2571-443**). All have trained bilingual guides and a wide range of possible tour options.

Loja isn't a particularly great shopping town, but if you want to browse some excellent local arts, handicrafts, and handmade clothing, head to **Arte Sano ★**, on Calle Lourdes between Sucre and Bolívar (✆ **07/2574-242**).

Where to Stay in Loja

In addition to the hotels listed below, **Quo Vadis Hotel ★** (✆ **07/2581-805;** www.quovadishotel.com.ec) is an upscale option close to the bus terminal, with doubles at $85, while **Grand Hotel Loja** (✆ **07/2572-200;** www.grandhotelloja.com), with doubles at $55, is another downtown option offering good value, with plenty of modern amenities.

Budget travelers might want to check out **Cristal Palace Hotel** (✆ **07/2574-682**), on Av. Universitaria 09–10 and Rocafuerte.

EXPENSIVE

Grand Victoria Boutique Hotel ★★   This hotel is the classiest and most luxurious option in Loja. The large central lobby is crowned with a three-story atrium roof

THE Virgin OF EL CISNE

Located some 70km (43 miles) northwest of Loja, El Cisne is one of Ecuador's major religious pilgrimage sites. The impressive **Basílica del Cisne (El Cisne Basilica)** here is home to a famous sculpture of the Virgin Mary carved by Diego de Robles in the 16th century. Locals call the sculpture *La Churona,* which translates roughly as "The Curly Headed Girl." The first church to house this holy figure was begun in 1594; the current basilica was finished in 1934 and is impressive in size and in the amount of detailed craftsmanship. The beautiful church sits on a high hillside in a remote rural area. The main celebrations for the Virgin del Cisne occur on August 15. Two days later, carried by thousands of devotees, she begins a 3-day trek to Loja, where she will stay for the next couple of months. Based out of the main cathedral in Loja, during this period, the statue is taken to various churches in the region. In Loja, the main celebration for the Virgin del Cisne occurs on September 8, a celebration that was officially decreed by Simón Bolívar himself on a visit to Loja in 1822. On November 1, the Virgin and her followers begin their return pilgrimage to El Cisne.

and lit by a large chandelier. The spacious rooms and suites here feature thick carpets, plush beds and beddings, elegant furnishings, and a host of amenities. My favorites have balconies overlooking the town. The hotel actually has three different dining options, as well as a small spa and indoor pool. Service is professional and attentive.

Bernardo Valdivieso 06–50 y Jose Eguiguren, Loja. www.grandvictoriabh.com. ✆ **07/2583-500.** 38 units. $110 double; $120–$160 suite. Rates include breakfast. AE, DC, MC, V. Free parking. **Amenities:** 3 restaurants; bar; concierge; Jacuzzi; small indoor pool; room service; small spa; steam bath. *In room:* TV, hair dryer, minibar, free Wi-Fi.

MODERATE

Bombuscaro Hotel The exterior of this hotel is striking, with three spires of tinted glass rising six stories over Loja. Inside the entrance, the elegant lobby features an abundance of shiny marble. Rooms are large and well appointed, and have firm beds and attractive furnishings. The two presidential suites come with a private Jacuzzi in a large bathroom. Some of the units on the higher floors have really wonderful views. The hotel provides free daily newspaper delivery and has a modest little business center, as well as an in-house tour operation and car-rental agency.

Av. 10 de Agosto, btw. Av. Universitaria and 18 de Noviembre, Loja. www.bombuscaro.com.ec. ✆ **07/2577-021.** Fax 07/2570-136. 35 units. $58 double; $82 junior suite; $91 presidential suite. Rates include continental breakfast and taxes. AE, DC, MC, V. Free parking. **Amenities:** Restaurant; bar; free airport transfers; room service; free Wi-Fi. *In room:* TV.

Hotel La Castellana ★ One of the newer hotels in Loja, this high-rise business-class hotel provides comfortable, well-equipped rooms at a good price. Most have carpeted floors, two queen-size beds, and good views from large windows. The decor is understated but tasteful and contemporary. The junior suites are obviously larger and come with a king-size bed, a sitting area with a plush couch, and a stocked minibar. The hotel has a Jacuzzi, steam room, and sauna, as well as a dependable little **restaurant** serving local and international fare. The Castellana is located just west of downtown, across the Río Malacatus.

Av. Lauro Guerrero 10–57, btw. Azuay and Miguel Riofrío, Loja. www.lacastellana.com.ec. ⓒ **07/2573-790.** 32 units. $56 double; $73 junior suite. Rates include continental breakfast. AE, DC, MC, V. Free parking. **Amenities:** Restaurant; bar; Jacuzzi; room service; sauna; free Wi-Fi. *In room:* TV.

Hotel Libertador ★   This longstanding hotel has excellent facilities and amenities. The carpeted rooms are large and tastefully decorated; most have large picture windows that let in lots of light. The junior suites actually have small solarium sitting areas that are quite inviting. On the fourth floor, you'll find the hotel's pool and spa area, which has a small but pretty pool under an arched atrium ceiling. This pleasant oasis also has a small gym, Jacuzzi, sauna, and steam bath, not to mention pretty views of the city.

Colón 14–30 y Av. Bolívar, Loja. www.hotellibertador.com.ec. ⓒ **07/2560-779.** Fax 07/2572-119. 58 units. $61 double; $78 suite. Rates include buffet breakfast. AE, DC, MC, V. Free parking. **Amenities:** Restaurant; bar; exercise room; Jacuzzi; small indoor pool; room service; sauna; steam bath; free Wi-Fi. *In room:* TV, hair dryer.

Where to Dine in Loja

Loja is a midsize city with plenty of restaurants, although most cater to the local crowd, and very few stand out. The local specialty is the *tamal lojano,* a large *tamal* of fresh ground corn filled with a mix of shredded pork or chicken and other goodies, which include hard-boiled eggs, beans, carrots, and onions—all of which is wrapped in the local *achira* plant leaf.

In addition to the place listed below, Loja has its share of international restaurants. The best of these include **Pizzería Forno di Fango** (ⓒ 07/2582-905 www.forno difango.com.ec), on the corner of 24 de Mayo and Azuay, for brick-oven pizzas, pastas, and Italian cuisine; and **Mar y Cuba** (ⓒ 07/2585-154), on Rocafuerte 09–00 and 24 de Mayo, for Cuban cooking and fresh seafood. Vegetarians should head to **El Paraíso Vegetariano** (ⓒ 07/2576-977), on Calle Quito 14–50 between Sucre and Bolívar, which has a good menu of meat-free entrees and snacks.

Casa Sol ★ 📖 ECUADOREAN/LOJANO   This is the place to come for Lojano cooking. Grab a seat on the second-floor balcony and start things off with the local specialty, *tamal lojano,* or some *empanadas de yuca.* If you want to really go native, order fresh roasted *cuy,* or guinea pig—it's prepared as well here as it is anyplace in Ecuador. A daily *menú ejecutivo* for around $2.50 makes for a filling lunch.

24 de Mayo 07–04, on the corner of José Antonio Eguiguren. ⓒ **07/2588-597.** Main courses $3–$10. No credit cards. Daily 8am–10:30pm.

Loja After Dark

Loja has two universities and the self-proclaimed reputation of being the country's music capital. Indeed, there is a vibrant music scene here. On weekends, bands often play in Parque Central.

The most popular bars in town include **Casa Tinku** ★★ (ⓒ 08/5568-759), on Calle Lourdes between Avenida Bolívar and Sucre; and **Santo Remedio** ★ (ⓒ 08/4738-910), on Mercadillo between Bolívar and Valdivieso. Both attract a college crowd and frequently feature live bands and guest DJs. **La Fiesta** ★ (ⓒ 07/2578-441), on Av. 10 de Agosto 10–59, between 24 de Mayo and Juan José Pena, is Loja's all-out salsa and merengue dance club. For a quieter time, try **Siembra** (ⓒ 07/2561-347), on the corner of Macara and Mercadillo, an intimate bar that serves local fare, grilled meats, and pizzas; or **El Viejo Minero** ★ (ⓒ 07/2585-878), on Sucre 10–76 near Azuay, a down-home, no-frills watering hole popular with local college students that sometimes features live local folk music. **Discoteca VIP** (© **07/2575-087**), on Rodriguez and Carrion, is another popular spot.

Between Loja & Vilcabamba: Podocarpus National Park ★★

Naturalists and bird-watchers covet this little-visited national park. **Podocarpus National Park** begins just south of Loja and covers a vast area that descends toward the Amazon basin. The park runs from a high of 3,700m (12,136 ft.) down to some 1,000m (3,280 ft.), and contains ecosystems that range from high paramo (moor) to cloud forest and rainforest—with a total area of 146,280 hectares (361,312 acres). The sheer size and variety of ecosystems in Podocarpus make this an incredibly rich park in terms of biodiversity. Over 600 species of birds have been identified here. The park is named after several endemic species of the *Podocarpus* genus. Other park residents include the spectacled bear, jaguar, sloth, and tapir. Camping is allowed at several campsites in the park, and there are a few rustic cabins located near each of the entrance ranger stations. For more information on these, contact the **park office** (© **07/2571-534** or 07/2577-125) in Loja.

Several well-marked and -maintained trails leave from the Cajanuma park ranger station. The terrain is mostly moist cloud forest and high-altitude paramo, and rain is common throughout much of the year. A short loop trail leads through the cloud forest to a beautiful lookout point. Longer hikes, which require overnight camping, bring you to a series of stunning small mountain lakes. I recommend that you visit with a guide. In Loja, contact **Biotours** (© **07/2579-387**; www.ecuadorsur.wordpress.com/biotours), **Podocarpus Travel** (© **07/2588-010**), or **Vilcatur** (© **07/2571-443**). In Vilcabamba, contact Jorge Luis Mendieta, at **Caminatas Andes Sureños** (© **07/2673-147**; www.vilcabamba.org/caminatasandessurenos.html). A full-day tour of the park, with transportation, lunch, and naturalist guide, should run around $30 to $45 per person.

Mining firms and loggers covet this park as much as naturalists and bird-watchers do. Much of the park has been ceded to mining interests, and mining activities and illegal logging pose a major threat to the delicate ecosystems here. Both the **Nature Conservancy** (www.nature.org) and the Ecuadorean **Fundación Ecológica Arcoiris** (www.arcoiris.org.ec) are working to protect the park. Contact either of these organizations for more information or if you are interested in volunteering in the park.

GETTING THERE & VISITING THE PARK   The principal entrance to the park is the Cajanuma entrance, some 14km (8¾ miles) south of Loja, on the road to Vilcabamba. From the highway turnoff, a rugged road leads another 8km (5 miles) to the park ranger station. A taxi from Loja all the way to the ranger station should cost around $6 to $10 each way. If you want to arrange a round-trip ride, set a pickup time with a driver you trust. Alternatively, any of the many buses running the Loja-to-Vilcabamba route will drop you off and pick you up near the exit to the park entrance. See "Getting There," under "Vilcabamba," below, for more details. There's a bit of a hike into the park from where you'll be dropped off. Admission is $10 per person per day. Camping costs an additional $3 per person in a tent or $5 for a bunk in one of the cabins.

On to Peru

Loja is often used as a land-based jumping-off point for onward travel to Peru. The border crossing here is less commonly used than that at Huaquillas (p. 263). From

Loja, the Pan-American Highway heads first west, then south, to the Ecuadorean border town of Macará. The Peruvian town on the other side of the border is La Tina. Both of these towns are tiny and of little interest to travelers. In fact, the first Peruvian city that most travelers head to is Piura, several hours south of the border. A half-dozen buses or more leave daily from Loja's main bus terminal to Macará. The ride takes around 5 hours, and the fare is $5. In addition, **Transportes Loja** (© **07/2570-505**) has three daily direct buses to Piura, Peru. I highly recommend you book one of these, as the bus will wait for you to complete immigration formalities (otherwise, you'll have to take two different buses). The entire ride takes 8 to 9 hours, and the fare is around $9.

If you decide to head first to Macará, the border formalities are relatively straightforward and painless, and the entire scene is mellower than at Huaquillas. The Ecuadorean immigration office is just before the bridge over the river that separates the two countries. There's a Peruvian checkpoint on the other side of the bridge, but you will have to take care of formal Peruvian immigration procedures in Sullana, 130km (81 miles) to the south. There is plenty of taxi and onward bus service between Macará and La Tina, and from La Tina on to Sullana and Piura.

VILCABAMBA ★★

40km (25 miles) S of Loja

The remote and picturesque valley of Vilcabamba has earned the nickname "Valley of Longevity" because residents here allegedly live to ripe old ages far beyond the norm. The reasons given for this range from clean air, clean water, and clean living, to extraterrestrial influences, to the work of the gods—in Quichua, *Vilcabamba,* sometimes spelled *Huilcobamba* or *Huilco Pamba,* means "Sacred Valley." However, scientific studies have cast doubt on any quantifiable longevity effects here. I doubt a visit to Vilcabamba will add any years to your life, but if stress and the daily grind have been getting you down, it just might cure what ails you.

Located at 1,470m (4,823 ft.) above sea level, Vilcabamba enjoys a pleasant, temperate climate, with warm days and slightly cool nights. There's great hiking, birdwatching, and horseback riding all around the area.

Essentials
GETTING THERE
BY PLANE   The nearest airport to Vilcabamba is **Aeropuerto Camilo Ponce Enríquez** (© **07/2677-140**; airport code: LOH), outside Loja. See "Getting There," under "Loja," earlier in this chapter, for details. Taxis are always waiting for incoming flights. A ride from the airport to Loja costs about $6 to $8. From Loja, you can take one of the very frequent buses or minivans to Vilcabamba (see below). A direct taxi ride from the airport to Vilcabamba should cost around $30.

BY BUS   Vilcabamba Turis (© **07/2640-065**) and **Sur Oriente** (© **07/2571-755**) make the run between Loja and Vilcabamba roughly every 15 minutes between 6am and 9pm. The fare is $1, and the ride takes about an hour. Both leave from the main terminal in Loja, and in Vilcabamba, they arrive at and leave from the corner of Avenida Eterna Juventud and Jaramillo, 1 block south and 1 block west of the central plaza.

BY CAR   To drive to Vilcabamba, follow the directions to Loja (see earlier in this chapter) and then take E39 south to Vilcabamba. The drive takes around 45 minutes.

Map legend:

ACCOMMODATIONS ■
Hostería Izhcayluma **9**
Jardín Escondido **3**
Le Rendezvous **7**
Madre Tierra **1**

DINING ◆
El Punto Café **5**
Hostería Izhcayluma **9**
Jardín Escondido **3**
La Roca **2**
Madre Tierra **1**
Shanta's **8**
Timothy's Bar & Grill **4**

---- Track, Trail
⊠ Post Office

ORIENTATION

Vilcabamba is a tiny town. The main downtown area measures only 4 square blocks or so, with a main plaza at its core. The town's principal Catholic church is on the south side of this plaza.

GETTING AROUND

You can easily walk anywhere in town. Walking and horseback riding (see below) are the main means of transportation here. Numerous vans and shared taxis make the run to Loja, and a few locals with pickup trucks serve as taxis for runs around the valley. Most rides cost $1 to $3. If you can't find one on the street, call **Trans Vilca-mixto** (✆ 07/2640-044).

FAST FACTS   There's an **information office** (✆ 07/2640-090) on the north-east corner of the main plaza and a small **hospital** (✆ 07/2640-188) 1 block north of the main plaza, on Avenida Eterna Juventud. If you need to contact the local police, dial ✆ 07/2640-096.

There are no banks in Vilcabamba, but a **Banco de Guayaquil** ATM lies just off the main plaza, next to the tourist information office. This ATM isn't always depend-able, so it's best to come with enough cash to get by. There are a couple of Internet cafes in town. The best option is **Vilcanet** (℗ 07/2640-147; www.vilcanet.net), on the southwest side of town on Huilcopamba near Juan Montalvo. To pick up some good reading material, head to **Craig's Book Exchange** (www.vilcabamba.org/CraigBook.html), about 1km (½-mile) out of town on Avenida Diego de la Vaca toward Yamburara.

What to See & Do in Vilcabamba

The most popular activity here is horseback riding. Horses, with riders and without, are common in the streets. Various individuals and small tour companies offer guided horseback tours around the area, and most hotels here either have their own horses and guides or can set you up. If you want to do it on your own, check in with **Centro Equestre** (℗ 07/2673-151; centro-12@latin.mail.com) or **Caballos Gavilan** (℗ 09/0161-759; www.caballosgavilan.wordpress.com). Rides run around $15 to $20 for a half-day tour or $30 to $50 for a full-day tour, including lunch.

The same terrain that makes horseback riding so rewarding is also perfect for mountain biking. If you prefer pedal power to horsepower, ask at your hotel or contact the information office (p. 223).

There's plenty of good hiking all around the Vilcabamba valley. Perhaps the most popular hike is to the top of the Mandango rock formation. From the town and several vantage points around the valley, this rock formation looks quite a bit like a face staring up toward the sky, and locals call it "The Sleeping Giant" or "The Sleeping God." It's a sometimes steep and strenuous 2-hour hike to the top, but the views are worth it. Another popular hiking destination is Podocarpus National Park (see above). If you want to do any guided hiking, a longer trek, or some serious bird-watching, contact Jorge Luis Mendieta, at **Caminatas Andes Sureños** (℗ 07/2673-147; www.vilca bamba.org/caminatasandessurenos.html). Jorge Luis is an extremely knowledgeable and enthusiastic guide.

If you're sore from hiking, biking, or horseback riding, consider heading to **Hostería Izhcayluma** ★ (see below) or **Madre Tierra** ★ (see below) for a massage or spa treatment. Individual treatments begin at around $10 for a short session to $40

Long, Strange Tripping

It's a long way to Vilcabamba, but for many visitors here, this is where their tripping begins. The **San Pedro cactus** grows heartily here. Known as the Holy Cactus, San Pedro is a bucket term given to some 30 different species of Andean *Trichocereus* cacti. All are tall and columnar and contain the psychotropic alkaloids used to make mescaline. Its ritual and shamanic use in Ecuador and Peru dates to at least 1400 B.C. Locals and expatriates around Vilcabamba often offer to guide travelers on a San Pedro cactus trip. These trips run the gamut from very conscientious and well-guided ritual experiences to bonfire party scenes. In most cases, it is illegal, and considered a jailable offense, to take San Pedro cactus. However, apparently some shamans are licensed to provide the experience. I cannot advocate or recommend any specific guides or shamans, but only caution you that if you do decide to venture into this realm, be forewarned that this is a very strong psychedelic substance, and you should be very sure you trust and feel comfortable with whomever you choose to guide you.

for a 90-minute massage. Other options range from hot mud treatments to facials, to Reiki sessions.

For some reason, people from across Ecuador flock to Vilcabamba in late February for the annual **Carnaval** celebrations. During this period, the sleepy and peaceful little town becomes a major party destination, with bands, parades, street vendors, and pretty much nonstop partying.

Where to Stay in Vilcabamba

In addition to the places listed below, **Jardín Escondido** (☎ 07/2640-281; www.vilcabamba.org/jardinescondido.html), just off the town's central plaza, has pleasant doubles for $35 to $40.

Hostería Izhcayluma ★★   This delightful place has a range of room styles in a range of prices, from shared-bathroom dorm rooms to private cabins and suites. The latter are the top choice. Each of the five cabins is set on the edge of a hillside, with plenty of room and privacy. Each also has a large balcony, with chairs and a hammock, overlooking spectacular views. Still, even the dorm rooms here are pleasant; they have high ceilings, plenty of light, and no bunk beds. The beautiful outdoor pool was designed to resemble a natural pond, with lush plantings all around and a small waterfall. The open-air restaurant and dining room features panoramic views of the Vilcabamba valley. These folks have a small spa offering massage, mud treatments, and Reiki sessions. For less holistic pursuits, there's a bar with a pool table and dartboard. The outdoor fire pit is a popular reunion spot.

2km (1¼ miles) south of Vilcabamba, on the road to Zumba. www.izhcayluma.com. ☎ **07/3025-162** or 09/9153-419. 20 units. $10 per person in dorm room; $30 double room; $38 double cabin. Rates include breakfast buffet and taxes. No credit cards. **Amenities:** Restaurant; bar; free mountain bikes; outdoor pool; small spa; free Wi-Fi. *In room:* No phone.

Le Rendezvous ★   Located 2½ blocks from the central plaza—and close to the river—this is my favorite hotel right in Vilcabamba. The rooms are spotless, with whitewashed adobe walls and terra-cotta tile floors. All are of good size and feature firm beds. Each opens onto the hotel's lush and perpetually flowering gardens, and comes with a hammock hung on its front veranda. Two newer *cabañas* have multiple bedrooms (one with two, one with three), making them a good option for families or groups traveling together. The French owners are extremely personable and knowledgeable, and they care a good deal about the area.

Diego Vaca de Vega 06–43 y La Paz, Vilcabamba. www.rendezvousecuador.com. ☎ **09/2191-180.** 14 units. $26 double. Rates include breakfast and taxes. Rates higher during peak periods. No credit cards. **Amenities:** Restaurant; bar. *In room:* TV, no phone, free Wi-Fi.

Madre Tierra   This was Vilcabamba's original mystical mountain retreat. To say artistic touches abound would be an understatement. Carved wood, eclectic tile work and stone masonry, stained glass, and hand-painted art are everywhere. Every room is distinct: Many have exposed brick walls, some have glass skylights, and most have interesting stone, tile, and brick floors. The range in room prices reflects both the size and location of the room. The best rooms come with a private balcony, with a hammock and fabulous view. (There are excellent views from the hotel's common grounds.) You'll find an inviting outdoor pool with fabulous landscaping and stone work, and a beautiful tiled Jacuzzi. The small spa offers a range of treatment and beauty options, and organic and wholesome food is served, much of it grown on-site.

2km (1¼ miles) before the town of Vilcabamba, on the road to Loja (mailing address: P.O. Box 288, Loja, Ecuador). www.vilcabambamadretierra.com. ☎ **07/2640-269** or 09/4464-972. 27 units. $35–$55 double. Rates include breakfast. AE, DC, MC, V. **Amenities:** Restaurant; bar; Jacuzzi; midsize outdoor pool; steam bath. *In room:* Hair dryer.

Where to Dine in Vilcabamba

Two of the best restaurants in Vilcabamba are those at **Madre Tierra** and **Hostería Izhcayluma** (see above). Both serve excellent international fare, with an emphasis on fresh, healthy ingredients. The views from the restaurant at Izhcayluma are particularly beautiful. Just make sure you call ahead and make reservations. **El Punto Café** (☎ 09/7487-310), on the southwest corner of Vilcabamba's central plaza, is a great spot for some coffee or a snack. And you will also do well at both **Timothy's Bar & Grill** (☎ 09/3412-069) and **La Roca** (☎ 07/2640-364), two bar-restaurants in the heart of town.

Jardín Escondido 🎁 MEXICAN/INTERNATIONAL   The Jardín Escondido, or Hidden Garden, has wonderful covered and open-air seating in a large, central garden and courtyard at the interior of its namesake hotel. When the weather's nice, I love the heavy wrought-iron tables, with canvas shade umbrellas, out in the center of this spread. The heart of the menu is Mexican cuisine, with everything from burritos and enchiladas to spicy, dark chicken *mole*. But there are also some pizzas and pastas, as well as a few local specialties. On Saturday nights, there's usually live music.

Calle Sucre, btw. Agua de Hierro and Diego Vaca de la Vega. ☎ **07/2640-281.** Reservations recommended during high season. Main courses $3–$10. No credit cards. Daily 8am–11pm.

Shanta's 🎁 ECUADOREAN/INTERNATIONAL   This small thatch-roof place looks as if it might fall down with the first stiff wind. This is probably more bar than restaurant, but they serve good food. Grab one of the several tables, or sit at the bamboo bar. The main offerings include a range of pizzas and pastas, which are well prepared, although they wouldn't wow anyone in Naples or Rome. You can also get a thick steak or grilled chicken. The signature appetizer here is the sautéed frogs' legs, which are almost as much of a novelty as the owner's long handlebar mustache.

Diego de la Vaca, east of downtown, over the 2nd bridge. No phone. Main courses $3–$7. No credit cards. Daily noon–2am.

Vilcabamba After Dark

Vilcabamba is a remote town known for its peace and tranquillity. The nightlife here is very subdued. But the increase in tourism has given rise to a few bars in town. **Shanta's** (see above) is my favorite spot, with a laid-back drinking scene; the drink specialty is a shot of a local cane liquor that's kept in a bottle with a coral snake pickling inside!

In town, the most happening spot is **Timothy's Bar & Grill** (☎ 09/3412-069), which feels a bit like a cross between a pub and sports bar and shows live sporting matches on its television. Or you can check out whether anything's going on at **La Roca** (☎ 07/2640-364), which sometimes has live music on weekends.

GUAYAQUIL & THE SOUTHERN COAST

Quito may be the historical and political capital of Ecuador, but Guayaquil is the country's largest city and its economic motor. It's also the primary gateway to the Galápagos Islands, with virtually every flight to and from the archipelago touching down here. Guayaquil has undergone an impressive transformation and today boasts a beautiful riverfront promenade, the Malecón Simón Bolívar, and a host of excellent hotels, restaurants, shops, clubs, and casinos.

Guayaquil is also the gateway to vast stretches of Ecuador's Pacific coast and several prime beaches. This area has been dubbed **Ruta del Sol,** or "Route of the Sun," with everything from large resort destinations to tiny beach getaways, to secret surf spots. At the northern end of Ruta del Sol lies **Machalilla National Park** and **Isla de la Plata,** a lovely offshore island often described as an alternative to the Galápagos Islands. That is a stretch, but the wildlife viewing and snorkeling at Isla de la Plata are superb. Tourists and Ecuadoreans looking for some fun in the sun aren't the only ones to take advantage of this section of coast. Late June through September, the waters here are a prime mating and breeding ground for humpback whales, and an excellent place to get up close and personal with these amazing mammals.

Finally, since I'm talking about gateways, just 253km (157 miles) south of Guayaquil lies Peru—many travelers heading by land down to Machu Picchu, Cusco, and Lima will pass through here en route.

GUAYAQUIL ★

250km (155 miles) NW of Cuenca; 420km (260 miles) SW of Quito; 966km (599 miles) E of the Galápagos

Guayaquil is Ecuador's most populous and economically vibrant city. Still, most visitors to Ecuador look upon Guayaquil as only a necessary overnight stop on the way to the Galápagos Islands. But that is changing, and the city continues to reinvent itself at a dizzying pace. At the helm since 2000, Mayor Jaime Nebot has instituted a far-reaching urban-renewal project that has already had impressive results. The **Malecón Simón Bolívar**—the city's main riverfront promenade—and the restored and

LA RIVALIDAD: QUITO & guayaquil

The fierce and ongoing political rivalry between the country's two principal cities, Quito and Guayaquil, was first publicly expressed in 1830 by independence heroes Juan José Flores and Vicente Rocafuerte, during the Republic's declaration of independence. During the latter half of the 19th century, García Moreno's decision to grant the Catholic Church almost absolute authority over conservative Quito increased the polarization between the Sierra and coastal regions. This regional division was even more firmly entrenched with the rise to power of Liberal leader Eloy Alfaro, who reversed García Moreno's act and called for the separation of church and state. The back-and-forth battle for presidential power between the Liberals from Guayaquil and Conservatives from Quito dominated the political landscape during the late 19th and early 20th centuries.

The rivalry inevitably spread from politics and religion to include nearly every aspect of the social, economic, and cultural life of the country. And it is still raging strong today—both Quito and Guayaquil claim to be the country's most important city. Guayaquil bases its case on the fact that it is the country's largest and most economically important city, functioning as Ecuador's major shipping port and commercial center. Quito, on the other hand, claims its supremacy on the basis of its political power, its better educational opportunities, and its role as the country's physical and administrative center.

Stereotypes also exist: Those from Guayaquil consider themselves much more open-minded, liberal, cheerful, and boisterous than their counterparts in the capital, while Quiteños regard themselves as more hardworking, better educated, and generally calmer than Guayaquileños. Today one of the fiercest battlegrounds for this historic rivalry takes place on the fields and in the stands whenever the cities' *fútbol* teams compete.

revitalized waterfront neighborhoods of **Cerro Santa Ana (Santa Ana Hill)** and **Las Peñas** are emblematic of Nebot's impact. Whereas crime was once rampant and problematic, Guayaquil is now a relatively safe and tourist-friendly city. Perhaps the city's greatest problem is the sometimes-oppressive heat and humidity. Nevertheless, you'll find early mornings, late afternoons, and evenings all very agreeable for taking in the city's pleasures.

Although Guayaquil was founded in 1537, it lacks the colonial architecture that you find in Quito and Cuenca. A devastating fire ravaged the city in 1896, almost completely leveling it. Virtually no buildings escaped the blaze, and today the city has a more modern and contemporary feel than any other major city in Ecuador.

Essentials
GETTING THERE
BY PLANE All international and national flights arrive at the **José Joaquín de Olmedo International Airport** (© **04/2391-603;** airport code: GYE), which is located about 10 minutes north of downtown Guayaquil, just next door to the now-defunct Simón Bolívar International Airport. Many international flights to Quito first touch down in Guayaquil, and outgoing international flights often similarly stop in Guayaquil to pick up and discharge passengers.

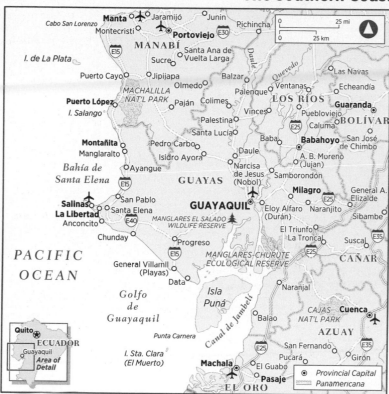

Aerogal (© 888/723-7642 in the U.S. and Canada, or 1800/2376-425 toll-free in Ecuador; www.aerogal.com.ec), Icaro (© 1800/883-567 toll-free nationwide; www.icaro.aero), Lan Ecuador (© 1800/101-075 toll-free in Ecuador; www.lan.com), and Tame (© 1800/500-800 toll-free in Ecuador; www.tame.com.ec) all offer numerous daily flights between Guayaquil and Quito. Aerogal, Lan, and Tame also offer a couple of daily flights between Guayaquil and Cuenca. One-way tickets range from $60 to $90 to or from Quito, and from $50 to $70 to or from Cuenca.

Your hotel may provide a shuttle service from the airport. If not, it's incredibly easy to catch a taxi. As you exit Customs in the international arrivals area, you'll see a desk with friendly staff who will arrange a taxi for you. You pay at the desk and receive a voucher, which you then present to a driver, who will be waiting for you once you exit the terminal. A taxi to the downtown area should cost no more than $10.

Tip: The airport provides free wireless connections throughout the terminal.

BY BUS Guayaquil is connected to the rest of the country by extensive and frequent bus service. From Quito, buses leave the main southern terminal (**Terminal Quitumbe;** © 02/3988-200) at least every half-hour for Guayaquil; the 8 hour ride

Guayaquil

ACCOMMODATIONS ■
Apart Hotel Kennedy **31**
Courtyard By Marriott **30**
Grand Hotel Guayaquil **15**
Hampton Inn **8**
Hilton Colón Guayaquil **32**
Hotel Oro Verde Guyaquil **17**
Iguanazú Hostal **24**
Mansión del Río **2**
Manso Boutique Hostal **9**

Sheraton Guayaquil **33**
Tangara Guest House **21**
UniParkHotel **13**

DINING ◆
Asia de Cuba **23**
El Vigia **3**
Hemisferios de Don Francis **37**
La Canoa **11**
La Parrilla del Ñato **25**

La Trattoria da Enrico **22**
Lo Nuestro **27**
Manso Mix **9**
Noe Sushi Bar **29**
Pique y Pase **20**
Puerto Moro **35**
Red Crab **26**
Resaca **6**
Riviera **28**
Tantra **36**

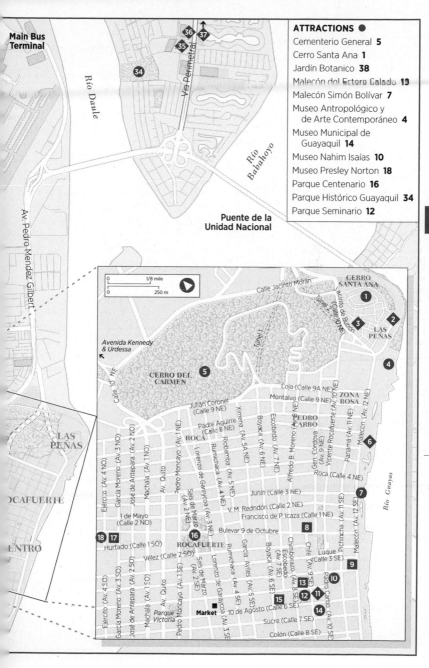

Main Bus Terminal

Río Daule

Av. Pedro Méndez Gilbert

Vía Perimetral

Río Babahoyo

Puente de la Unidad Nacional

ATTRACTIONS ●

Cementerio General **5**
Cerro Santa Ana **1**
Jardín Botanico **38**
Malecón del Estero Salado **19**
Malecón Simón Bolívar **7**
Museo Antropológico y de Arte Contemporáneo **4**
Museo Municipal de Guayaquil **14**
Museo Nahim Isaías **10**
Museo Presley Norton **18**
Parque Centenario **16**
Parque Histórico Guayaquil **34**
Parque Seminario **12**

9

GUAYAQUIL & THE SOUTHERN COAST | Guayaquil

0 — 1/8 mile
0 — 250 m

Calle Jacinto Morán

CERRO SANTA ANA

Jacinto de Burón

Túnel 2 (Calle 10 NE)

Túnel 1

LAS PEÑAS

Avenida Kennedy & Urdessa

CERRO DEL CARMEN

Calle 10 NE

Loja (Calle 9A NE)
Montalvo (Calle 9 NE)

ZONA ROSA

Julián Coronel (Calle 9 NE)
Padre Aguirre (Calle 8 NE)
ROCA
Rumichaca (Av. 4 NE)
Lorenzo de Garaycoa (Av. 2 NE)
Seis de Marzo (Av. 2 NE)
Pedro Moncayo (Av. 1 NE)
Av. Quito

Ximena (Av. 5A NE)
Robamba (Av. 5A NE)
Boyacá (Av. 6 NE)
Escobedo (Av. 7 NE)
Alfredo B. Moreno (Av. 8 NE)
Gen Córdova (Av. 9 NE)
Vicente Rocafuerte (Av. 10 NE)
Panamá (Av. 11 NE)
Malecón (Av. 12 NE)

PEDRO CARBO

Roca (Calle 4 NE)
Junín (Calle 3 NE)
V. M. Rendón (Calle 2 NE)
Francisco de P. Icaza (Calle 1 NE)
Bulevar 9 de Octubre

Río Guayas

Ejército (Av. 4 NO)
García Moreno (Av. 3 NO)
José de Antepara (Av. 2 NO)
Machala (Av. 1 NO)
1 de Mayo (Calle 2 NO)

LAS PEÑAS

ROCAFUERTE

CENTRO

Hurtado (Calle 1 SO)
Vélez (Calle 2 SO)

ROCAFUERTE

Ejército (Av. 4 SO)
García Moreno (Av. 3 SO)
José de Antepara (Av. 2 SO)
Machala (Av. 1 SO)
Av. Quito
Pedro Moncayo (Av. 1 SE)
Seis de Marzo (Av. 2 SE)
Lorenzo de Garaycoa (Av. 2 SE)
Rumichaca (Av. 4 SE)
García Avilés (Av. 5 SE)
Boyacá (Av. 6 SE)
Escobedo (Av. 7 SE)
Chimborazo (Av. 8 SE)
Chile (Av. 9 SE)
Pedro Carbo (Av. 10 SE)
Pichincha (Av. 11 SE)
Malecón (Av. 12 SE)

Luque (Calle 3 SE)
10 de Agosto (Calle 6 SE)
Sucre (Calle 7 SE)
Colón (Calle 8 SE)

Parque Victoria
Market

231

costs between $8 and $10. Buses from Cuenca leave on a very frequent schedule as well; the 5-hour bus ride costs around $8. **Flota Imbabura** (℃ **02/2565-620** in Quito, or 04/2320-925 in Guayaquil), **Transportes Ecuador** (℃ **02/2503-842** in Quito, or 04/2297-040 in Guayaquil), and **Transportes Occidentales** (℃ **02/2502-733;** www.transportesoccidentales.com) are the main companies making the Quito–Guayaquil run.

The modern Guayaquil bus station, **Terminal Terrestre Jaime Roldos Aguilera** (℃ **04/2140-166;** www.terminalguayaquil.com), is just north of the airport. This massive complex features a range of shops, restaurants, and food courts. All buses to and from Guayaquil leave from here.

Note: If possible, it's best to travel through the Guayas province—of which Guayaquil is the capital—during daylight hours. While night buses are now generally considered safe, over the years, some bus hijackings have occurred after dark.

BY CAR   To reach Guayaquil by car from Quito, start off heading south on the Pan-American Highway (E35) until the intersection at Aloag. From here, head west on E30 toward Santo Domingo de los Colorados. In Santo Domingo, take the well-marked exit for E25 south to Quevedo. This road continues on to Guayaquil via Babahoyo.

If you're going to make this drive, I strongly recommend you do so during the daytime—road and weather conditions can make this route treacherous and hair-raising after dark.

GETTING AROUND

Guayaquil is a compact city, and it's easy to walk most places around the downtown and Malecón Simón Bolívar. However, the midday heat makes a taxi very appealing, even for short rides. Moreover, a fair number of the hotels, shopping centers, and restaurants are located outside the downtown area. Luckily, taxis are an inexpensive and efficient way to get around. It's easy to flag one down on most any street. You can also call **Cooperativa del Cerro** (℃ 08/6638-406), **Cooperativa de Taxis Centro Cívico** (℃ 04/2450-145), or **Fast Line ★** (℃ 04/2823-333). Rides within the center of the city cost only $2 to $6.

Most of the major car-rental agencies have offices in Guayaquil: **Avis** (℃ **04/2169-092;** www.avis.com), on Avenida Kennedy and Avenida de las Américas; **Budget** (℃ **04/2284-559;** www.budget-ec.com), at the airport as well as on Av. de las Américas 900; and **Hertz** (℃ **04/2169-035;** www.hertz.com), at the airport.

VISITOR INFORMATION

The Guyas Province has a **tourist information office** (℃ **04/2517-622;** www.turismoguayas.com) on the 14th floor of the Edificio Bancopark, Av. Luque 111. The office is open Monday through Friday from 9am to 5pm and provides a city map, as well as other useful information on tours and attractions. There's also a helpful **information booth** (no phone) beside Museo Nahim Isaías (p. 236), in the center of town; it is run by the municipality of Guayaquil and is open Tuesday to Saturday from 9am to 5pm.

ORIENTATION

Guayaquil is located on the western bank of the Guayas River. Avenida 9 de Octubre is the main street, running west to east through the center of the city and dead-ending at the Malecón Simón Bolivar, the large pedestrian mall on the river. Avenida Malecón runs along the river, as well as the Malecón Simón Bolívar development.

A MEETING OF giants

Not long after being appointed "Protector of Peru," and with the supposed hope of annexing Guayaquil into the newly forming Peruvian nation, Argentine independence leader **José de San Martín** met with **Simón Bolívar**—El Libertador—in the city of Guayaquil on July 26, 1822. They were also to discuss the broader future of South America, now free from Spanish rule. Details of the "closed-door" meeting remain the subject of much debate among historians. But soon after the famous Guayaquil encounter, San Martín decided to abandon the independence struggle in Peru and retire to Argentina. He later went into self-imposed exile in France, leaving Bolívar to finish the Peruvian campaign.

According to some, San Martín wanted Bolívar's assistance in supplying troops for the swift conclusion of the faltering Peruvian independence struggle. Despite their common objectives, Bolívar's refusal to cooperate, even when San Martín offered to serve under him, resulted in San Martín's withdrawal from the independence struggle. Other historians suggest that Bolívar and San Martín clashed on the subject of how the new South American nations should be organized: Bolívar favored the idea of independent republics, while San Martín wanted to retain, in some measure, the European monarchy system. San Martín was thus supposedly pressured by Bolívar to resign, as he was a hindrance to Bolívar's vision of a free and independent South America. Although a failure for San Martín, the Guayaquil meeting, which lasted no more than a few hours, was followed by a banquet and a ball at which the two independence heroes made toasts to the hasty conclusion of the war and to Bolívar's health and success in future undertakings. Today a prominent **sculpture and monument** on the Malecón Simón Bolívar commemorates the historic meeting.

The central downtown area and most of the museums are located within a block or two of the Malecón. The airport and bus terminal, as well as several major malls and popular hotels, restaurants, and bars, are north of downtown in the neighborhoods of Urdesa and Nueva Kennedy.

FAST FACTS In an emergency, dial ✆ **911.** To reach the police, call ✆ **101** or 04/2402-427, and for the **Cruz Roja (Red Cross),** call ✆ **131.** The main **post office** is located on Clemente Ballén and Pedro Carbo.

Most banks in Guayaquil are clustered around the intersection of Pedro Icaza and General Córdova; you'll find branches of **Banco Pichincha** and **Banco de Guayaquil** here. You'll also find ATMs all over the city and in all the modern malls and shopping centers.

The best hospital in Guayaquil is **Hospital Clínica Kennedy** (✆ **04/2289-666;** www.hospikennedy.med.ec), which actually has three facilities in town; the main one is at Callejón 11–A and Avenida Periodista. There are hundreds of other pharmacies around Guayaquil. The chain **Fybeca** (✆ **1800/2392-322;** www.fybeca.com) has various outlets, is open 24 hours, and offers delivery.

There are scores of **Internet cafes** in Guayaquil. Rates run around 50¢ to $1.50 per hour. Many city hotels also provide reasonably priced or complimentary Internet connections.

233

What to See & Do in Guayaquil

If you're short on time, it's still possible to get a feel for Guayaquil rather quickly, as the important attractions are quite close together (see the box "If You're Short on Time," below, for more information).

The **Malecón Simón Bolívar** ★★ is the shining star of contemporary Guayaquil. It's impressive to enter the Malecón from Av. 9 de Octubre, where you are greeted by a 1937 statue of the independence heroes Simón Bolívar and San Martín shaking hands. On either side of the statue, you can climb up lookout towers, which afford great views of the city and the river. Walk south, and you'll hit the Moorish Clock Tower, Glorious Aurora's Obelisk, a McDonald's, a minimall, and tons of inexpensive food stalls. As you head in this direction, look across the street: You'll see the impressive neoclassical **Palacio Municipal.** If you walk north from the Bolívar–Martín statue, you'll come across a lively playground and an exercise course.

On the western end of Av. 9 de Octubre is a separate riverside promenade along the narrow Estero Salado (Salt Water Estuary), known appropriately as the **Malecón del Estero Salado** ★. The Malecón here is a pleasant riverside pedestrian walkway sprinkled with little parks and plazas, benches for resting, and a few restaurants, shops, and food stands.

In addition to the Malecón Simón Bolívar, Malecón Salado, and attractions listed below, you can visit a few parks and an interesting cemetery. **Parque Seminario** ★ dates from 1880 and is adjacent to the city's principal church, a neo-Gothic cathedral whose most recent and primary construction dates from 1948. Parque Seminario is also called "Iguana Park" because a healthy population of these prehistoric-looking reptiles inhabits its trees and grounds. Much larger **Parque Centenario** is in the middle of the city, bisected by Av. 9 de Octubre. This park is a very popular lunchtime spot for downtown workers and is a pleasant place to relax and people-watch.

The massive **Cementerio General (General Cemetery; ✆ 04/2293-849)** ★ is north of the downtown area. It's also called La Ciudad Blanca, or "The White City," because of its abundance of shiny white marble. The cemetery has some impressive aboveground marble tombs and mausoleums, in a variety of styles ranging from neoclassical Greco-Roman to baroque, to Moorish. The tombs are spread across a vast hillside area and connected by paths and even streets. The cemetery was opened in 1843 and has become a major emblem of the city. The entrance is at Avenida Pedro Menéndez Gilber and Julian Coronel. The Cementerio General is open daily from 8am to 6pm.

One good way to get a feel for the city is to hop on one of the red double-decker tourist buses run by **Guayaquil Visión (✆ 04/2885-800;** www.guayaquilvision. com). These folks offer several options, including a 1½-hour loop around and through the city, passing its most important landmarks, as well as a 3-hour Gran Guayaquil tour, which makes stops for visits at Las Peñas neighborhood, Parque Seminario, the handicraft market, and Parque Histórico Guayaquil. Fares run $6 for adults and $4 for children, students, and seniors, for the basic loop trip; and $30 adults, $20 children, students, and seniors, for the Gran Guayaquil tour.

If you want to see the city from the river, you can hop on any of the little tourist boats that dock at the piers along the Malecón. These basically leave as they fill up for 45-minute to an hour cruises along the river. Rates run around $5 for a standard tour, or, if you have a group, you can negotiate for a longer cruise.

Many visitors find themselves with only a few hours in Guayaquil as they connect to or from the Galápagos. If you fall into that category, don't despair: You can still get a good feel for the city in just a few hours.

Grab a cab (or walk, if you're close) from your hotel to the **Malecón Simón Bolívar.** The Malecón area is ideally enjoyed on foot, so prepare yourself for a good 3.2km (2-mile) hike and bring protection from the sun. It's best to begin at the southern end, the corner of the Malecón and Avenida Olmedo. Here you can browse the shops selling local artifacts, and the boardwalk is breezy and airy on this end. As you walk north, you'll find many food shops (and more people). Take a break halfway; most of the food stalls here sell freshly squeezed juice that makes an excellent pick-me-up; small bottles of water are also readily available, and there are impressively clean public restrooms here, too. Definitely take a break to visit **Museo Antropológico y de Arte Contemporáneo ★★** (MAAC; see below). At the end of the Malecón, just past the MAAC, you'll find **Las Peñas ★★** neighborhood—a narrow street filled with art galleries and funky shops. After you walk around Las Peñas, climb to the top of **Cerro Santa Ana ★★** (see below) to get a fantastic view of the entire city, the river, and the surrounding countryside. You'll find many places to eat and drink on the stairs leading up to the top. This is one of the city's safest areas, with tourist police patrolling the stairs day and night.

9

GUAYAQUIL & THE SOUTHERN COAST | Guayaquil

Another alternative is to set sail on the imitation pirate brig *Henry Morgan* (✆ 04/2517-228). The Morgan sails roughly every 2 hours, beginning at 2pm on weekends. The cost for a 1-hour cruise is $4 for adults and $2 for children 12 and under. Similar cruises leave most weekday afternoons around 5pm.

GUAYAQUIL'S MAIN ATTRACTIONS

Cerro Santa Ana (Santa Ana Hill) & Las Peñas ★★★ 📷 The 465 stairs leading up Cerro Santa Ana are clearly marked so you can keep track of your progress. And while the climb is vigorous in spots, it shouldn't take more than 20 to 25 minutes from bottom to top. Avoid the midday heat and sun, and you'll find the views worth the effort. Along the entire length of the steps are restaurants, cafes, bars, art galleries, and shops, mixed in with residential housing. Many of the buildings are painted in bright and contrasting primary colors, creating a beautiful effect. At the top, you'll find the chapel of Santa Ana, along with a beautiful lighthouse. Both were built in 2002, atop the foundations of a 17th-century fort. Cerro Santa Ana is where the city of Guayaquil was first established in the mid-1500s.

If you aren't up for the climb, at least take a stroll along the cobblestone street of **Las Peñas** neighborhood, at the foot of the Cerro Santa Ana. Hugging the river's edge, this similarly restored old neighborhood is heavy on art galleries, interspersed with a few restaurants and residential buildings. At the north end of Las Peñas, you will hit the **Puerto Santa Ana,** a riverside extension of the Malecón Simón Bolívar.

At the north end of Malecón Simón Bolívar. No phone. Free admission. Daily 24 hr.

Jardín Botánico (Botanical Gardens) ★ Opened in 1979, Guayaquil's botanical gardens are home to over 325 species of native and imported tropical flora.

Well-tended paths wind through sections of ornamental plants, orchids, and brome-liads, as well as medicinal plants and herbs, fruit and lumber trees, and various crops. The orchid collection is particularly beautiful. This is a great place for urban bird-watching, with over 70 avian species on record, as well as over 60 species of butter-flies. The gardens are north of the city center, out along the main Avenida Francisco de Orellana. A taxi here should cost around $6.

Cerro Colorado, Urbanización Las Orquídeas, Av. Francisco de Orellana. ✆ **04/2560-519.** Admission $4 adults; $2 children 11 and under, students, and seniors. Daily 9am–4pm.

Museo Antropológico y de Arte Contemporáneo (Museum of Anthropology and Contemporary Art) ★★
Commanding a spectacular location on the tip of the Malecón, and known simply as the MAAC, this large and impressive museum opened in 2004. It focuses on the archaeological finds from around Ecuador. However, one section is dedicated to a large collection of Ecuadorean contemporary art, as well as to a smattering of international artists. Regularly changing temporary exhibits focus on local contemporary artists. Note that museum information and exhibit plaques are in Spanish. There's also a library, a bookstore, and a pleasant cafe. It will take you about 2 hours to visit the museum.

Malecón Simón Bolívar y Calle Loja. ✆ **04/2309-383.** www.museomaac.com. Free admission. Tues–Sat 9am–5pm; Sun and holidays 11am–3pm.

Museo Municipal de Guayaquil
If you're wondering about the history of Guayaquil, head to this museum. It starts off with pre-Columbian history, displaying artifacts similar to those found in Museo Nahim Isaías (see below). Then, as you move through the museum, you'll learn about colonial history, the independence movement, the republic, and the 20th century. On display are pistols, army uniforms, coins, and an old-fashioned car. *Note:* The exhibits are in Spanish, although some pamphlets are available in English. Give yourself about 40 minutes here.

Calle Sucre, btw. calles Chile and Pedro Carbo. ✆ **04/2599-100.** www.museoguayaquil.com. Free admission. Tues–Sat 9am–5:30pm.

Museo Nahim Isaías
This small museum displays some amazing pieces of pre-Columbian arts and functional relics found along the coastal areas near Guayaquil. Some date as far back as 4200 B.C. You'll see ceramic jugs, wonderfully expressive figurines, gold jewelry, and—my favorite—carved seashells in the shape of fish. On the second floor is a collection of colonial art, including many prominent works from the Quito School, as well as gold and silver altarpieces and wooden sculptures. Allot about 30 to 40 minutes here.

Calles Clemente Ballén y Pichincha. ✆ **04/2324-182.** www.museonahimisaias.com. Admission $1.50, 50¢ for seniors and children 12 and under. Free admission Sun and holidays. Tues–Sat 10am–6pm; Sun and holidays 11am–3pm.

Museo Presley Norton ★
This is my second-favorite museum in Guayaquil (not far behind the MAAC). Unlike at the other museums listed here, *all* the exhibits here have explanations in both English and Spanish. Formerly called Museo Archeologico del Banco del Pacífico, this museum houses a small but excellent collection of archaeological relics. The most interesting artifacts come from the Chorrera Period (1000–300 B.C.). Keep an eye out for the double-chambered whistling bottle and the descriptive figurines from this period. Give yourself about 45 minutes to an hour here.

Corner of Av. 9 de Octubre and Carchi. ✆ **04/2293-423.** Free admission. Mon–Sat 11am–7pm.

Parque Histórico Guayaquil ★ ☺ This historical theme park is a great place to learn about Guayaquil and Ecuador. You can walk along a raised pathway through several distinct ecosystems with various native fauna and flora on display. You will also pass through rows of different banana plants, some endemic to Ecuador (remember that Ecuador is the world's largest banana exporter) and a tiny cacao plantation. Historic buildings and street scenes are re-created throughout the grounds. A traditional country house replicates how rural farmers lived and what farming utensils they used. In the courtyard of a beautiful old hacienda, plays, staged twice daily, depict life on a farm in the 19th century. The boardwalk here is dubbed Malecón 1900 and gives you a glimpse into how the city looked some 100 years ago. An old-fashioned bakery and cafe serves traditional dishes in a lovely outdoor setting. An old trolley completes the picture. I recommend coming here on a weekday, if possible; this park has become extremely popular with Ecuadorean families on weekends.

Vía Samborondón, btw. avs. Esmeraldas and Central. ☏ **04/2832-958.** www.parquehistorico guayaquil.com. Wed–Sat $3 adults, $1.50 children 6–12, free children 5 and under; Sun and public holidays $4.50 adults, $3 children 6–12, free children 5 and under. Wed–Fri 9am–4:30pm; Sat-Sun and holidays 10am–5:30pm.

NEARBY ATTRACTIONS & TOURS

A number of agencies in town offer a wide range of area tours. Guayaquil is surrounded by banana, coffee, and cocoa plantations; if you have an extra half- or full day, consider taking a tour to see how these farms operate. You might also want to take a guided tour to the beaches found along Ruta del Sol (see later in this chapter). Established agencies include **Hamaca Tours & Expeditions** ★ (☏ 04/2314-797; www.hamacatours.com) and **Metropolitan Touring** ★★ (☏ 888/572-0166 in the U.S. and Canada, or 02/2988-200 in Ecuador; www.metropolitan-touring. com). Both of these agencies, as well as most of the city's hotels, offer visits to the places listed below, among many other possibilities.

Bosque Protector Cerro Blanco (Cerro Blanco Protected Forest) This place has a network of trails through mangrove and primary forests, which vary vastly with the seasons—from flowing rivers and streams and an abundance of lush vegetation in the rainy season (Jan–May) to a more typical dry-forest feel during the rest of the year. I recommend you hire one of their bilingual guides—you'll see a lot more wildlife and learn a lot more. Guides cost between $7 and $15, depending upon the length of your hike, and can handle a group of up to eight people. Resident mammals include the howler monkey, wild peccary, and ocelot. Over 200 species of birds have been spotted here, including the scarlet macaw, which is being actively protected at the Bosque. There's a restaurant, and you can use their campground or rent a rustic two-bedroom bamboo bungalow. These folks also run the nearby **Puerto Hondo,** set on the banks of a broad mangrove, where you can rent canoes and kayaks (either solo or accompanied by a guide).

Km 16, on the road to the coast (Vía a La Costa). ☏ **04/2874-946.** Admission $4 adults, $3 children 11 and under. Daily 9am–4pm. Reservations recommended prior to all visits.

Puerto El Morro ★ This small fishing village hosts a small community of guides specializing in bird- and dolphin-watching tours through the local mangroves and estuary. The Ecoclub Los Delfínes (Dolphin Eco-Club) runs a small museum at the docks here, with the skeleton of a bottlenose dolphin, as well as various displays about the local coastal ecosystems. From here, tours head out for anywhere from 90 minutes to 3 hours. Along the way, there's a good chance you will see some bottlenose dolphins. Even if you don't, the bird-watching is excellent and the scenery is beautiful. Most tours stop at a small island that is both a local crab-processing spot and a nesting ground for thousands of magnificent frigate birds. Most tour operators in Guayaquil offer day tours here. **Hamaca Tours & Expeditions ★** (✆ 04/2314-797; www.hamacatours.com), in particular, specializes in this tour.

9km east of Playas. ✆ **09/2834-542.** puertoelmorro@yahoo.com. Tours $15–$45 per person, depending upon group size and tour duration. Daily 9am–4pm. Reservations recommended.

Shopping

The **Mercado Artesanal** (✆ 04/2306-266), on Baquerizo Moreno between calles Loja and Juan Montalvo, is the best place to buy local handicrafts. You'll find over 150 stalls and shops run by area businesspeople, as well as by the artisans themselves. Everything from *tagua*-nut (vegetable ivory) carvings to Otavaleño textiles, to Panama hats and ceramics is available.

There's a similar, albeit much, much smaller, artisans market at the southern end of the Malecón Simón Bolívar. I recommend you try to support the craft works of **Pro Pueblo ★** (✆ 04/2683-598; www.propueblo.com), a local, fair-trade cooperative of artisans from around the region. Their work is sold at shops at this artisans market and at their large collection point in the coastal village of San Antonio, as well as online.

Another excellent option is the new **GYE Tienda de Souvenirs ★★** (✆ 04/2311-645), which carries unique lines of one-off products, organic chocolates, and high-end craft works. You'll find this place on the main road in Las Peñas, next to Hotel Mansion del Río (see below).

Guayaquil is full of modern shopping malls that include the **San Marino Mall** (✆ 04/2083-180), **Mall del Sur** (✆ 04/2085-110), and **Mall del Sol** (✆ 04/2690-100). Each has scores of shops, a couple of department stores, a food court and independent restaurants, and a multiplex cinema. The **Malecón Simón Bolívar** shopping center is one of the town's best located and most frequented by visitors. It's located on the Malecón near Calle Junín.

Where to Stay in Guayaquil

If there's no space at the hotels below, the **Courtyard By Marriott** (✆ 888/236-2427 in the U.S. and Canada, or 04/6009-200 in Ecuador; www.marriott.com), **Hampton Inn ★** (✆ 800/426-7866 in the U.S. and Canada, or 04/2566-700 in Ecuador; www.hamptoninn.com), and **Sheraton ★★** (✆ 800/325-3535 in the U.S. and Canada, or 04/2082-088 in Ecuador; www.sheraton.com) are all good options.

Tip: For the large resorts listed below, be sure to book online or through an agency, where you can usually get rates far, far better than the rack rates listed here.

VERY EXPENSIVE

Hotel Oro Verde Guayaquil ★★★   The Oro Verde commands a central location on Av. 9 de Octubre. Rooms are spacious and have recessed lighting, laminate wood floors, and marble bathrooms. All the standard rooms are up to snuff, but try to land one of the corner units, which are a bit bigger and boast better views. Suites come with impressive bathrooms and large plasma televisions. Club Floor rooms come with a host of perks and particularly professional and personalized service. The public areas are stately, and the restaurants are excellent. For anyone wanting to be downtown, the location is superb. All guests get access to an excellent health club. A shuttle to the airport is complimentary. This place is certified as a Smart Voyager property by the Rainforest Alliance.

Av. 9 de Octubre 414 y García Moreno, Guayaquil. www.oroverdeguayaquil.com. © **04/2327-999.** Fax 04/2329-350. 230 units. $320–$360 double; $380–$430 suite; $1,100–$1,700 presidential or Oro Verde suite. AE, DC, MC, V. Free parking. **Amenities:** 4 restaurants; 2 bars; casino; babysitting; concierge; executive-level rooms; well-equipped exercise room; Jacuzzi; tiny but pretty outdoor pool; room service; sauna; smoke-free floors. *In room:* A/C, TV, hair dryer, minibar, free Wi-Fi.

EXPENSIVE

Grand Hotel Guayaquil ★   There are two reasons to stay at this hotel. First, the location: It's only a few blocks from the Malecón and close to all the major downtown attractions. Second, the gorgeous swimming pool: Take one look at the magnificent waterfall cascading into the clear blue water, and you'll feel as though you are in a tropical resort. It provides a great escape from the heat, noise, and pollution of Guayaquil. Unfortunately, the rooms, though comfortable and generously sized, aren't as fancy as the pool. The walls are a bit thin, so to avoid hearing your neighbors as they traipse through the hallway, request a room as far from the elevator as possible. This hotel is not as luxurious or well kept as the Hilton or Oro Verde, but it does offer similar amenities, and for the price, it's a great deal.

Boyacá y 10 de Agosto (P.O. Box 9282), Guayaquil. www.grandhotelguayaquil.com. © **04/2329-690.** Fax 04/2327-251. 182 units. $124–$134 double; $195 suite. AE, DC, MC, V. Free parking. **Amenities:** 3 restaurants; 2 bars; exercise room; Jacuzzi; outdoor pool; room service; sauna; smoke-free floors; 2 air-conditioned squash courts. *In room:* A/C, TV, hair dryer, minifridge, free Wi-Fi.

Hilton Colón Guayaquil ★★   This high-rise hotel has a relaxed and charming ambience. The Hilton is a Guayaquil institution—its restaurants, banquet halls, and bars are frequented by the crème de la crème of local society. The rooms are large with big windows, and some have views of air traffic at the nearby airport. Corner suites are the most desirable—each has a lovely balcony with a great view. The marble bathrooms are huge and sparkling. The outdoor pool has a swim-up bar and a snack bar for alfresco dining. The coffee shop serves excellent Ecuadorean specials at reasonable prices, and the Portofino restaurant is an excellent, elegant Italian restaurant. There's a small shopping arcade adjacent to the hotel lobby. *Tip:* The Hilton Colón is close to the airport, making it great for people trying to catch an early flight to the Galápagos.

Av. Francisco de Orellana Mz. 111, Guayaquil. www.guayaquil.hilton.com. © **800/445-8667** in the U.S., or 04/2689-000 in Ecuador. Fax 04/2689-149. 294 units. $150–$220 double; $250–$350 suite; $1,100 presidential suite. AE, DC, MC, V. Free parking. **Amenities:** 4 restaurants; 2 bars; free airport shuttle; babysitting; concierge; executive-level rooms; exercise room; Jacuzzi; beautiful large pool; room service; sauna; smoke-free floors. *In room:* A/C, TV, hair dryer, minibar, Wi-Fi for a fee.

Mansión del Río ★★ 🎁   Set right on the main cobblestone street of the riverfront Las Peñas neighborhood, this place offers plush, cozy rooms in an intimate and elegant converted 85-year-old home. The rooms all have high ceilings, Victorian decor, and a sideways view of the river—although some are a bit on the small side. The suites are larger end units directly facing the river, with small Juliet balconies. There's an interior courtyard with a relaxing fountain, and a beautiful large, third-floor balcony area with fabulous river views. Breakfasts and high tea are served in an elegant main dining room and lounge area.

Calle Numa Pompilio 120, Barrio Las Peñas, Guayaquil. www.mansiondelrio-ec.com. © **04/2566-044** or 04/2565-827. 11 units. $114–$163 double. AE, DISC, MC, V. Free parking. **Amenities:** Lounge; free airport shuttle; concierge; room service; smoke-free floors; free Wi-Fi. *In room:* A/C, TV, hair dryer, minibar.

UniPark Hotel ★ 🍴 This large luxury hotel is located right downtown and connected to the UniPark mall, across from Parque Seminario and the cathedral, and just 3 blocks from the Malecón. The rooms are everything you would want and expect in this category. The hotel lacks the pool and extensive facilities of some of the other upscale business hotels in town, but thanks to the local glut of rooms and competition, they've made up for this by dropping their rates substantially. The UniPark has several restaurants, including a sushi bar, and there are scores more in the adjacent mall.

Calle Clemente Ballén 406 y Calle Chimborazo, Guayaquil. www.uniparkhotel.com. © **04/2327-100.** Fax 04/2328-352. 139 units. $90–$140 double. Rates include breakfast buffet and free airport shuttle. AE, DC, MC, V. Free parking. **Amenities:** 3 restaurants; 2 bars; free airport shuttle; concierge; small gym; room service; sauna; smoke-free rooms. *In room:* A/C, TV, hair dryer, minibar, free Wi-Fi.

MODERATE

Apart Hotel Kennedy ★ 🍴 Catering to business travelers, the Kennedy is catty-corner to the much fancier Hilton Colón (see above). Rooms are cool, sleek, and spacious. The large suites have separate sitting rooms and kitchenettes, which come in handy if you're here for several days. The decor aims to be elegant but comes across as a bit kitschy. Still, this is a great value. *Tip:* The rates I list below are their "corporate" rates, which are less than their rack rates. All you have to do is say you work for any company—heck, make one up—and they are usually more than happy to apply the corporate rate.

Calles Nahim Isaías y Vicente Norero, Kennedy Norte, Guayaquil. www.hotelkennedy.com.ec. © **04/2681-111.** Fax 04/2681-060. 49 units. $80 double; $95 suite. Rates include buffet breakfast. AE, DC, MC, V. Free parking. **Amenities:** Restaurant; bar; room service. *In room:* A/C, TV/DVD, hair dryer, minifridge, free Wi-Fi.

INEXPENSIVE

There are plenty of run-down and seedy budget hotels in Guayaquil, but I really can't recommend any of them. Given the heat and humidity, I think it's worth the splurge for someplace with air-conditioning and a sense of style, such as the places listed below.

Iguanazú Hostal 🍴 This cozy hideaway is located in a northern suburb at the base of a forested hill that has been declared a city reserve. Accommodations range from a large dormitory-style room with four bunk beds and a fan, to air-conditioned rooms with private bathrooms. Everything is kept spic-and-span and is decorated with style. The hostel has extensive grounds, which include well-tended gardens, a pretty and refreshing pool, and a large terrace and barbecue area. The suite is a lovely room with its own Jacuzzi, television, and private entrance to the shared terrace, which has a good view of the city. Guests have full run of the converted home's full kitchen. The owners also run a good little tour agency.

Calzada La Cogra, Manzana 1, Villa 2, Km 3.5, Av. Carlos Julio Arosemena, Guayaquil. www.iguanazu hostel.com. © **04/2201-143** or 09/9867-968. 5 units. $15 per person in dorm room; $54 double room; $72 suite. Rates include full breakfast and taxes. AE, DC, MC, V. Free parking. **Amenities:** Lounge; small outdoor pool. *In room:* No phone.

Manso Boutique Hostal ★ 🏠 This bohemian-spirited place fronts the Malecón. Rooms are located on the second and third floors of a residential apartment building. The prize rooms here have a balcony overlooking the Malecón and river beyond (though the street noise can be a problem at times). They also have some shared-bathroom private rooms and, in the back, two dorm rooms for real budget travelers. The dorm rooms, which are gender specific, actually have private bathrooms. Throughout, the decor is understated and arty, and you'll often find the art and craft

works of local artists on display or for sale here. The hotel's small restaurant special
izes in creative, contemporary cooking that uses local organic ingredients whenever
possible.

Malecón 1406 y Aguirre, Guayaquil. www.manso.com.ec. © **04/2526-644.** 12 units (8 with private
bathroom). $15 per person dorm room; $55 double with shared bathroom; $92–$116 double. Rates
include full breakfast. AE, DC, MC, V. Parking nearby. **Amenities:** Restaurant; bar; small spa; free Wi-Fi.
In room: A/C, TV, no phone.

Tangara Guest House If you're looking for homey accommodations with gracious, knowledgeable hosts (who happen to run an excellent small tour operation),
this is the place for you. Housed in a converted home in a residential neighborhood,
the rooms are nothing fancy, but they are bright, cheery, and immaculate. You'll find
a common lounge area, a couple of computers for Internet access, and kitchen
facilities that guests can use. There's also a small cafe and restaurant specializing in
vegetarian fare and seafood. This little bed-and-breakfast is close to both the University of Guayaquil and Malecón Salado.

Manuela Sáenz y O'Leary Block F, House 1, Ciudadela Bolivariana, Guayaquil. www.tangara-ecuador.
com. ©/fax **04/2282-828** or 04/2284-445. 6 units. $45–$55 double. Rates include full breakfast. AE,
MC, V. Free parking. **Amenities:** Restaurant; lounge; airport or bus terminal transfers. *In room:* A/C, TV,
free Wi-Fi.

Where to Dine in Guayaquil

Much of Guayaquil's dining scene can be found along a stretch of Avenida Víctor
Emilio Estrada in the Urdesa neighborhood. Adventurous travelers could just hop a
cab to Urdesa and walk around until something strikes their fancy.

Another popular dining destination is the residential suburb of Samborondón,
which features a string of strip malls and megamalls loaded with trendy restaurants.
Of these, standouts include the steakhouse **Puerto Moro** (© 04/2834-610; www.
puertomoro.com; Centro Comercial Las Terrazas), the Pan-Asian lounge-style **Tantra** (© 04/2833-200; www.rtantra.com; Centro Comercial Riocentro), and the
intimate high-end fusion spot **Hemisferios de Don Francis** (© 04/5019-914;
Plaza Lagos).

In addition to the places listed above and below, you can get good sushi at **Noe
Sushi Bar** (© 04/2083-389), in the Centro Comercial San Marino, and fine Italian cooking in a refined environment at **Riviera** (© 04/2883-790; www.riviera
ecuador.com), at Víctor Emilio Estrada 707 and Calle Ficus. Finally, for real traditional Ecuadorean fare, head to **Pique y Pase** (© 04/2293-309; www.piqueypase.
com), on Alejo Lascano 1617 and Carchi.

EXPENSIVE

La Trattoria da Enrico ★ ITALIAN It's worth a meal here just to marvel at the
fish tanks embedded in the ceiling. And the Mediterranean-tinged trattoria-style
cuisine is also very good. Start with some grilled octopus or mixed antipasti. There's
a wide range of pasta dishes, and the gnocchi here are light and tender. Sure, you can
get a steak pizzaiola or veal marsala, but I recommend sticking with the extensive
seafood options. A group can share the mixed seafood platter, which has a little bit of
almost everything, from prawns and langoustines to fish and calamari. This place has
an excellent wine list and frequently features a roving trio of violins and guitar.

Calle Bálsamos 504, btw. Ebanos and Las Monjas. © **04/2388-924** or 04/2387-079. Reservations
recommended. Main courses $6.75–$25. MC, V. Mon–Sat 12:30–11:30pm; Sun 7–10pm.

MODERATE

Asia de Cuba ★★ LATIN-ASIAN FUSION With stylish decor and a wide-ranging menu, this is one of my favorite restaurants in Guayaquil. The chef here favors strong flavors, and you'll find influences from countries as diverse as Thailand, India, Cuba, and Peru. Start things off with your selection from their long list of creative mojitos and martinis. Appetizers range from sushi to Peruvian-style shish kabobs to *ceviches*, to large mixed plates made to share. For a main dish, I recommend the pork in adobo sauce served with rice and beans, or the sesame-crusted seared tuna. Be sure to save room for dessert. And you can't go wrong with their signature Suspiro de Angel Asiatico, a light custard of mango, raspberry, and passion fruit, topped with toasted almonds and caramel.

Calle Datiles 205 y Primera, Urdesa Central. ✆ **04/6009-999.** www.asiadecuba.net. Reservations recommended. Main courses $7.95–$20. AE, DC, MC, V. Daily noon–3:30pm and 5pm–1am.

La Parrilla del Ñato ECUADOREAN/STEAKHOUSE This local minichain serves up good grilled meats in a lively setting. Portions are legendarily large and easily shared. The dining room is also large and nearly as "loud" as the large neon signs out front. I'd stick to the simply grilled meats and seafood, though if you're feeling adventurous, you can order a dove breast. I don't know where they get their doves, but they're big. The *brocheta mixta* is a massive shish kabob with a couple of whole sausages and large cuts of meat interspersed with grilled onions and peppers. Avoid the pastas and pizzas, which are not the strong suit here. Other outlets around town can be found in Barrio Kennedy, on Avenida Francisco de Orellana and Nahim Isaías (✆ **04/2682-338**), and at Km 2.5 on the road to Samborondón (✆ **04/2834-326**).

Av. Estrada 219 y Laureles. ✆ **04/2387-098.** Main courses $7–$16. AE, DC, MC, V. Daily noon–midnight.

Lo Nuestro ★★ ECUADOREAN The best Ecuadorean restaurant in the city, located in the hip Urdesa restaurant district, is a small, elegant eatery whose walls are filled with historical photos of Guayaquil. Ask what the fresh fish is: Seafood reigns supreme here. *Ceviches* make for the best appetizers. The grilled sea bass with crab sauce is my favorite main course. There are myriad daily specials, but traditional favorites include homemade empanadas, *seco de chivo* (goat stew), and shrimp served several different ways. Everything is of the highest quality—and meticulously prepared. This is the kind of place where you enjoy a 3-hour meal and where the waiters wheel over a liquor tray to offer you an after-dinner drink. These folks also offer home delivery.

Av. Estrada 903 y Higueras. ✆ **04/2386-398.** Reservations recommended. Main courses $7.50–$26. MC, V. Mon–Fri noon–3pm and 7pm–midnight; Sat–Sun noon–midnight.

Red Crab ★★ 📷 SEAFOOD As the name implies, crabs are the star of the show here and are served up in a variety of fashions. I recommend you go with the Creole Crab, which is a large bowl of whole crabs boiled up with spices and accompanying chunks of tubers and corn. This comes with a large wooden mallet and plastic bib. Don't wear your finest duds here. For those looking for a more refined manner of digging in, you can order just the already shelled claws, in any number of sauces, or a wide range of other seafood dishes off the extensive menu. Heck, you could even get beef stroganoff or chicken cordon bleu here—but why would you? The decor is bright and gaudy, with porthole windows ringing the restaurant, neon blue lights embedded in the ceiling, and large fish tanks spread around. This place is very popular with locals and has a loud, festive vibe. These folks also have a new, much larger space out in Samborondón (✆ **04/2831-110;** Km 2.5 Vía Samborondón).

Corner of Víctor Emilio Estrada and Laureles, Urdesa ℰ **04/2380-512** Reservations recommended.
Main courses $8–$14. AE, MC, V. Daily 11am–midnight.

INEXPENSIVE

El Vigia 🎁ECUADOREAN/INTERNATIONAL   This funky hole-in-the-wall sits on a small rise about midway up Cerro Santa Ana. You'll definitely want to grab a table on the narrow balcony fronting the steps, a fantastic spot for people-watching. This place serves equally well as a coffee shop and snack joint during the day, and as a bar and restaurant at night. The food is surprisingly good, with everything from traditional Ecuadorean fare, such as *humitas* and *hayacas,* to spaghetti Bolognese and *tortilla española.* You can order a plate of mixed appetizers *(piqueo)* to share, or head right for the main courses. I recommend the grilled tilapia, which is done in a simple garlic and olive-oil sauce. All main courses come with crisp *patacones* and salad.

Callejóns Diego Noboa y del Tesoro, Cerro Santa Ana. ℰ **04/2300-218.** Main courses $4–$10. MC, V. Sun–Thurs 10am–midnight; Fri–Sat 10am–2am.

Manso Mix ★ ECUADOREAN/VEGETARIAN   Specializing in vegetarian and healthy fare, this casual spot is quite popular. The choice seat is a small balcony table for two overlooking the Malecón. You can opt for a salad or wrap, or try one of their tasty quinoa burgers. The fresh tuna burger is also excellent. Local Ecuadorian fare is featured in such dishes as the empanadas verdes, fried pastries made of green plantains. The daily lunch special is a great deal, featuring a soup, main dish, dessert, and drink for around $4.

In the Manso Boutique Hostal, Malecón 1406 y Aguirre, Guayaquil. ℰ **04/2526-644.** www.manso.com. ec. Main courses $3.35–$6.10. Prices include tax and service. AE, DC, MC, V. Daily 11am–2pm and 4–9pm.

Puerto Pirata ECUADOREAN   Located just below the chapel and lighthouse on the top of Cerro Santa Ana, this restaurant is housed inside a faux pirate ship, hence *pirata* in the name. A shallow tile pool serves as a moat around the outside, where you'll also find a small playground, some pirate mannequins, and bronze cannons. The best seats are those on the second floor, with a view out the windows of the false stern of this fantasy ship. The food is pretty standard fare, but it's very inexpensive, and what you're coming for are the view and atmosphere. You can get simply grilled meats and fish, as well as a wide range of appetizers and *ceviches.* Some nights there's live music, which might be anything from a mellow jazz trio to a full-on salsa band.

Stair 384, El Fortín Naval Museum, Cerro Santa Ana. ℰ **04/2218-278.** Main courses $4–$10. AE, DC, MC, V. Daily noon–midnight.

Resaca ECUADOREAN/INTERNATIONAL   There are scores of restaurants along the Malecón Simón Bolívar, but this is one of the only ones close enough to have a decent view. If the weather is nice, head upstairs for the second-floor, open-air patio and grab a seat close to the river. When it's too hot or windy or rainy, you can opt for a table near one of the large picture windows that ring the main dining room. The menu here leans heavily on bar-food staples, with nachos, fried calamari, *patacones,* and onion rings to choose from. You can also get main-course plates of fresh fish or grilled steaks and chicken. For lunch, try the three-course *menú ejecutivo* for $2.75. Weekend nights usually feature live bands. *Resaca* translates as "hangover," and the late-night scene here has certainly caused its fair share of them.

North end of Malecón Simón Bolívar, near Junín. ℰ **04/3000-805.** Main courses $4.50–$9. AE, DC, MC, V. Daily 11am–midnight.

Guayaquil After Dark

Guayaquil has made great strides in reducing crime and delinquency, and its nightlife has benefited greatly. Bars, cafes, and restaurants are sprouting like mushrooms around the **Zona Rosa** and **Cerro Santa Ana** (both located toward the end of the Malecón). This is the best area to experience the city's nightlife. For more mellow options, stroll up the Cerro Santa Ana, where you'll find many bars and pubs flanking the steps leading to the top of the hill. Right at the foot of the steps is the always-popular **Diva Nicotina** ★ (© 04/2309-040), while around the corner from the steps, in Las Peñas, is the boho standout **La Paleta** ★★ (© 04/2312-329).

For dancing and a more lively time, try the Zona Rosa, a several-square-block area bordered by the Malecón to the east and Avenida Rocafuerte to the west, and by Calle Juan Montalvo to the north and Calle Manuel Luzarraga to the south. You'll find a score of bars here, and it's a relatively safe area to bar-hop. I like **Mei** ★ (© 09/9393-169), on Padre Aguirre and Panama, which has a chic, contemporary club vibe.

Locals like to head to the handful of clubs and discos found in the neighborhood Kennedy Norte, at and around **Mall Kennedy.** These clubs attract a broad mix of Guayaquil's young and restless. There's plenty to choose from, but if you want an all-out party, try **Ibiza Evolution** (© 09/7422-925) or **Fizz y Sante** (© 04/2680-865), in the Kennedy Norte neighborhood on Avenida Francisco Orellana, which has both a mellow bar scene and rocking disco area.

At the northern end of the Malecón Simón Bolívar is a four-plex **IMAX theater** ★ (© 04/2563-078; www.imaxmalecon2000.com), showing late-run IMAX-specific films. For more traditional movie fare, there are **Cinemark** multiplex theaters in both **Mall del Sur** (© 04/2085-110) and **Mall del Sol** (© 04/2692-015).

If you're in the mood for some gambling, there are large modern casinos at the **Sheraton, Oro Verde,** and **Hilton** (see "Where to Stay in Guayaquil," earlier in this chapter).

Playas: The Closest Beach to Guayaquil

On weekends and holidays, Guayaquileños (Guayaquil natives) flock to the beach at **Playas General Villamil,** known as simply Playas. Located 97km (60 miles) south of Guayaquil, this laid-back fishing village has taken its popularity with a sense of indifference, and the town lacks the feel of full-on beach destinations such as Salinas or Atacames. It also lacks the stylish and varied lodging options you can find in those resort towns. The beach itself is long and wide, with a gentle curve and hard-packed, light-colored sand. Still, on weekends and holidays, this place is packed, and the restaurants and bars that line the seafront Malecón bustle and buzz. The beach is popular with surfers, who come for the long line of beach breaks.

Artisans in Playas still produce ancient-style balsa fishing rafts, as well as finely crafted balsa surfboards. The unique fishing rafts are usually made by joining together three long balsa logs and then fitting them with a triangular sail. Some of the best balsa surfboards in the world are produced here by **El Gringo Andres** (balsaflite@ hotmail.com), a transplanted Californian.

Good lodging options are limited in Playas. The best hotels in town are the beach-front **Hostería Bellavista** (© 04/2760-600; www.hosteriabellavista.net), located toward the quieter eastern end of town; and **Hotel Arena Caliente** (© 04/2761-580; www.hotelarenacaliente.com), which is 1 block inland but near the center of the action. Both of these hotels have air-conditioned rooms and swimming pools—two very important perks here. However, the plushest spot in the area, by far, is the newly renovated **Ocean Club Hotel & Resort ★** (✆ 04/2761-276; www.ocean club.com.ec), located a little outside of Playas proper.

Playas is easily reached by heading out of Guayaquil on the coastal highway and taking the well-marked turnoff for General Villamil. Buses leave Guayaquil's main terminal for Playas roughly every 15 to 20 minutes from 6am to 8pm, with less frequent departures during the hours on either end of that time frame. **Cooperativa Villamil** (✆ 04/2140-879) is the main operator running this route. The ride takes about 1½ hours, and the fare is around $2.

SALINAS & THE SANTA ELENA PENINSULA ★

163km (101 miles) W of Guayaquil; 570km (353 miles) SW of Quito

Salinas and the **Santa Elena Peninsula** anchor the southern end of **La Ruta del Sol (The Sun Route),** a string of fishing and beach towns stretching up the southern Pacific coast. Salinas is the most developed resort destination on this stretch, with high-rise luxury hotels, casinos, vacation condos, and a prominent yacht club. Sailboats, yachts, and fishing vessels fill the protected bay here. Many of these boats can be chartered out for fishing excursions, whale-watching tours, or simple cruises.

During high season (Dec–Apr), this area gets very crowded. Hotel reservations are necessary on weekends throughout this period. In contrast, the beaches and hotels here are often deserted during the off season, especially September through November.

Essentials

GETTING THERE

BY PLANE   There's a small airport in **Salinas** (airport code: SNC) at the very tip of the Santa Elena peninsula. A massive remodeling and expansion is expected to be completed in 2011. Currently, there are no regularly scheduled commuter flights to Salinas, but that should change when the work is completed.

Most folks fly into Guayaquil and continue on to Salinas by car, bus, or taxi. See "By Plane," under "Guayaquil," for details.

BY BUS   Buses regularly leave Guayaquil's main bus terminal for Salinas between 3am and 11pm every day. During busy daytime hours, a bus leaves nearly every 5 minutes. The schedule is somewhat reduced during off hours, but there are still frequent buses. Two companies run this route, **Costa Azul** (✆ 04/2781-416) and **Libertad Peninsular** (**CLP;** ✆ 04/2140-975). The 2½-hour ride costs about $3.50.

Transesmeraldas (✆ 04/2786-670 in Salinas, or 02/2505-099 in Quito) has three daily direct buses between Quito and Salinas. The ride takes 11½ hours, and the fare is $10.

The bus station in Salinas is beside the main market, 1 block in from the Malecón.

As an alternative, **Turismo Ruta del Sol** (✆ 04/2302-984) runs hourly minivan service between Guayaquil and Salinas. The fare is $10.

BY CAR   Salinas and the Santa Elena Peninsula are connected to Guayaquil by a well-traveled and -marked highway. (Though calling it a highway may seem like a misnomer.) The road is only two lanes wide in many points and passes directly through a string of small towns and villages, where you may have to slow down for a stop sign, speed bump, or passing cow. As mentioned, though, the route is well marked, heading out of Guayaquil to the west. Salinas is 163km (101 miles) from Guayaquil. The ride takes about 2 hours.

GETTING AROUND

Local buses run continuously along the main route that connects Salinas, Santa Elena, La Libertad, and Ballenita. Fares cost from 30¢ to 75¢, depending on how long your ride is.

This route is also covered by so-called *taxi rutas,* which are taxis that operate almost like the buses, following the same set route and picking up and discharging passengers. But with a maximum of five passengers, these tend to be much faster, as they make fewer stops.

Traditional taxis are also abundant—flag one down on the street or call **Taxis Ruta del Sol** (𝄞 **04/2770-358**). A taxi between Salinas and La Libertad should cost no more than $4, and a ride around either town should be under $2.

ORIENTATION

As you drive from Guayaquil toward the coast, you will arrive at the town of **Santa Elena,** considered Km 0 on the highway (E15) that runs in both directions along the coastline—and which should not be confused with the highway *to* the coast (called *carretera a la costa*) that runs from Guayaquil to Santa Elena (E70). Santa Elena sits on a small rise above the ocean. The beach and tiny town just below it are called **Ballenita.** Located at the western tip of the Santa Elena peninsula, 13km (8 miles) west of Santa Elena and Ballenita, is **Salinas.** La Libertad lies about halfway between Ballenita and Salinas. As this area develops, the distinctions may start to fade and the resorts will start to flow one into the next, but for now, there is still some separation between these beach towns, although the distances are quite short.

Heading farther east and then north up the coast, the beach stretches for kilometers and kilometers almost uninterrupted—except for the odd rocky point and headlands—with only a few small fishing villages, tiny towns, and the periodic isolated beach hotel. Beach towns along this coast include **Punta Blanca, Montañita,** and **Olón.**

The beach in Salinas itself is divided almost perfectly in half by the jetty and docks of the **Salinas Yacht Club.** One block inland from the jetty is the town's main plaza and its pretty Catholic church.

FAST FACTS   To reach the **police,** dial 𝄞 **101** in an emergency, or 04/2775-813. **Hospital Alcivar** (𝄞 **04/5002-500;** www.hospitalalcivar.com), in La Libertad, is the most modern and best-equipped facility on this coast. It has 24-hour emergency services, as well as a 24-hour pharmacy.

The **post office** (𝄞 **04/2770-097**) is on the Malecón and Calle 2, next to the Barceló Miramar Colón hotel. There are several banks and even more ATMs along the Malecón in Salinas and in La Libertad. **Banco de Guayaquil** has branches at Malecón 417 and Avenida Bolívar in Salinas (𝄞 **04/2772-552**), and at the Paseo Shopping complex in La Libertad (𝄞 **04/2785-892**). **Banco Pichincha** has branches in Salinas on the Malecón, between calles 29 and 30 (𝄞 **04/2772-468**); and in La Libertad at Av. 4 and Calle 23 (𝄞 **04/2782-294**). You'll find a number of Internet cafes all along the Malecón and on the calles and avenidas just inland.

What to See & Do on the Santa Elena Peninsula

Most of the activity here focuses on the sand and sea. In addition to swimming and sunbathing, there are plenty of waterborne activities. Most of the beach resorts have their own watersports equipment; if yours doesn't, you'll have no trouble finding someone renting out sailboards, Hobie Cats, windsurfers, jet skis, and the like. The beach of this large, curving bay is made of a rather coarse golden sand. All along the shore, you'll find beach umbrellas, portable shade cabanas, and chaise lounges for rent. A beach umbrella and two chaise lounges should cost you $10 per day. The best stretch of beach is Playa Chipipe, which starts just beyond the Salinas Yacht Club and runs roughly west from there.

Surfers will want to head out to the far western end of the peninsula, which is also called **La Chocolatera.** This is a naval base territory, and you will have to ask permission to enter (it's almost always granted). Several shops along the Malecón rent out **surf and body boards** and offer lessons. Board rentals run from $4 to $10 per hour, depending upon the quality of the equipment. Lessons cost around $6 to $10 per hour.

Even if you're not a surfer, it's worth going out to La Chocolatera to take in the view. The point here is the westernmost point of land on South America. And during the whale season, I've sometimes seen whales swimming just offshore.

If you want to go **sport fishing,** head to the **Puerto Lucía Yacht Club** (✆ 04/2783-190; www.puertolucia.com.ec), on the waterfront between Salinas and La Libertad; or contact **Pesca Tours** ★ (✆ 04/2772-391; www.pescatours.com. ec), which has an office on the Malecón and Calle 20, as well as another office in Guayaquil. Offshore fishing provides good opportunities to catch black and blue marlin, sailfish, albacore tuna, and a whole host of other big game fish. Rates run from $250 to $800 per day for up to four people, depending upon the size and quality of the boat and how far offshore you go.

The small **Museo de Ballenas** (**Whale Museum;** ✆ 04/2778-329) features an interesting collection of exhibits about the biology and natural history of whales and dolphins. The centerpiece of the museum is a 12m (39-ft.) complete skeleton of a humpback whale. They also have partial and complete skeletons and skulls of other species, as well as explanatory materials in both English and Spanish. The museum is located on Avenida General Enriques Gallo, between calles 47 and 50. The museum is open daily from 10am until 5pm, but it's wise to call in advance because they often close if there aren't many visitors. Admission is free, but a donation is requested.

Museo Salinas Siglo 21 (**Salinas 21st Century Museum;** ✆ 04/2777-815) is another option, with a collection of local maritime relics and displays, including coins recovered from the wreck of a Spanish galleon that sank in 1664. This museum also has a good collection of regional archaeological finds of the Valdivia, Machalilla, and Chorrera peoples dating back as far as 4200 B.C. Located on the Malecón, between calles Guayas and Quil, the museum is open Wednesday through Saturday from 10am to 6pm and Sunday from 9am to 5pm. Admission is $2.

June through September, the waters off Salinas are a fantastic place to **spot humpback whales** ★★★ (see "Having a Whale of a Time," later in this chapter). Most hotels offer whale-watching excursions, or you can contact **Costa Tour** (✆ 04/2770-095 or 09/7544-444) or **Pesca Tours** ★ (✆ 04/2772-391; www.pescatours.com.ec).

When the whales aren't around, the above operations can arrange simple half-day, full-day, and sunset cruises or sailboat outings.

Finally, **bird-watchers** will definitely want to head to **Ecuasal** ★ (© 04/2325-666), a private salt company. Ecuasal's vast salt flats—where salt is harvested by evaporation from shallow pools—are a primary feeding and resting ground for a number of resident and migratory species. In fact, over 130 species have been identified here. Ecuasal has built a bird-watching tower in the midst of their 1,300 hectares (3,211 acres) of salt flats. The stars of the show are the Chilean flamingos. Anyone wanting to do some bird-watching here should contact Benjamin Haase (© **04/2778-329;** bhaase@ecua.net.ec), a leading naturalist guide, who also runs the Whale Museum (see above).

Where to Stay in & Around Salinas
EXPENSIVE
Barceló Colón Miramar ★★   This is the largest and most luxurious hotel in Salinas. Rooms are big and inviting, with clean lines and stylish furnishings. Most have a small sitting area with a couple of rattan chairs and a couch. Views from the oceanfront balconies are fabulous, and you should definitely specify that you want one of these units, preferably on a higher floor. The only downside here is that they offer only an all-inclusive system. Don't let this dissuade you from spending a few extra dollars for some fresh seafood at one of the many oceanfront restaurants around Salinas. The hotel is across the street from the beach, but it's connected to the sand by a private raised walkway over the road. The beach right in front of the hotel is pretty narrow and hard packed, but the pools are easily the nicest in the area.

Malecón, btw. avs. 38 and 40, Salinas. www.barcelo.com. © **04/2771-610.** Fax 04/2773-806. 95 units. $220–$360 double. Rates are all-inclusive and include 3 buffet meals daily, unlimited soft drinks and national liquors, and nonmotorized watersports equipment. AE, DC, MC, V. Free parking. **Amenities:** 2 restaurants; 3 bars; casino; well-equipped gym; Jacuzzi; 2 outdoor pools; sauna; smoke-free rooms; watersports equipment. *In room:* A/C, TV, minibar, hair dryer.

MODERATE
In addition to the place listed below, I've gotten great feedback about **Hotel Amira** (© **04/2770-701;** www.hotel-amira.com), a small boutique option located about one block inland from the ocean.

Farallón Dillon ★ 🛍   This is my favorite hotel along this stretch of coast. The rambling whitewashed structure is built above a quiet section of beach just outside Ballenita, on a small hillside that almost qualifies as a cliff. The rooms aren't as fancy as those at some of the newer resorts in Salinas, but they have plenty of style and character. Most face the ocean and feature bright colors and carved canopy beds. I prefer those on the second floor. There's an extensive collection of nautical memorabilia and antiques throughout. The shaded, open-air balcony restaurant is delightful, with a beautiful perch and perfect views. You can sometimes even see whales blowing their spouts from this spot. The hotel has a wonderful covered area on the beach, strung with hammocks where guests can sneak a midday siesta.

Lomas de Ballenita, Ballenita. www.farallondillon.com. © **04/2953-611.** Fax 04/2953-643. 13 units. $60 double. Rates include continental breakfast. Rates lower in the off season, higher during peak periods. DC, MC, V. Free parking. **Amenities:** Restaurant; bar; small exercise room; small outdoor pool; outdoor tennis court. *In room:* A/C, no phone.

Puerto Lucía Yacht Club Hotel ★   The high rise hotel attached to this marina and yacht club offers up modern luxury rooms with plenty of perks at great prices. The rooms are big, bright, and airy, each with a large-screen television, pretty bathroom, and private balcony overlooking the ocean. In addition to the adjacent marina, the hotel has a host of facilities and services, including a couple of pools, two lit tennis courts, a small gym and spa, and a private little patch of beach between two stone jetties. There's also a children's playground, as well as a beach volleyball court. There are two restaurants in-house and even a karaoke disco bar.

Av. Puerto Lucía, La Libertad. www.puertolucia.com.ec. 𝒞 **04/2783-190.** 24 units. $85–$130 double. Rates higher during peak periods. AE, DC, MC, V. Free parking. **Amenities:** 2 restaurants; 2 bars; well-equipped gym; Jacuzzi; 2 outdoor pools; room service; 2 lit outdoor tennis courts; watersports equipment rentals. *In room:* A/C, TV, hair dryer, minibar.

INEXPENSIVE

Hotel Chipipe   This midsize hotel is 3 blocks from the beach, in the center of town. The rooms are standard, with plenty of light, cool and shiny white tile floors, simple furnishings, solid green bedspreads and curtains, and mostly unadorned walls. Most have balconies, and a few have ocean views. The pool area is a welcome oasis, with a wide tile deck area and the hotel's open-air restaurant nearby.

Calle 12, btw. avs. 4 and 5, Salinas. www.hotelchipipe.com. 𝒞 **04/2770-553.** Fax 04/2770-556. 47 units. $35–$55 double. Rates include continental breakfast. Rates lower in the off season, higher during peak periods. MC, V. Free parking. **Amenities:** Restaurant; bar; small outdoor pool. *In room:* A/C, TV.

Where to Dine in & Around Salinas

There are scores of restaurants along the Malecón, serving mostly *ceviche*, fresh seafood, and typical Ecuadorean fare. The best of these include **Mar y Tierra** (𝒞 **04/2773-687**) and **Amazon** (𝒞 **04/2773-671**). You might also want to grab a taxi and dine at one of the open-air tables at **Farallón Dillon** (see above), which has an excellent restaurant and even better setting and view.

La Bella Italia ★ ITALIAN/SEAFOOD   Besides great pizzas and pasta dishes, these folks serve up excellent seafood. The thin-crust pizza is cooked in a wood-burning oven and comes with a wide range of toppings. I especially like the grilled shrimp. There's streetside seating in front of the restaurant, as well as an indoor dining room, with air-conditioning. But I prefer the seats on the open-air second-floor patio overlooking the Malecón and beach.

Malecón y Calle 19. 𝒞 **04/2771-361.** Main courses $3.50–$10. MC, V. Daily noon–midnight.

Salinas & the Santa Elena Peninsula After Dark

Most of the after-dark activity in Salinas, and all along the coast, is located close to the beach on the Malecón. **Longboard's** ★★ (𝒞 **08/4106-629**), Malecón 319, is one of the most popular spots, with several different rooms and environments, including an open-air patio bar, dance floor, and VIP lounge. The **Oystercatcher Bar** (𝒞 **04/2778-329**), Av. 2, between calles 47 and 50, is another good bet and is popular with expatriates. For dancing and a late-night scene, the **Praia Disco** (𝒞 **09/2312-309**), about 4 blocks inland on the south side of town, has emerged as a top spot for the young and well-heeled.

MONTAÑITA

180km (112 miles) NW of Guayaquil; 59km (37 miles) N of Santa Elena; 44km (27 miles) S of Puerto López

Montañita is a tiny beach town that has garnered a fair amount of fame among surfers and backpackers. The few streets here are densely packed with funky hostels, cheap eats, lively bars, and a handful of surf shops. You'll also find a fair number of bohemian artisans from Ecuador and other Latin American locales selling their wares or offering to braid hair, pierce some body part, or lay on a henna tattoo. If you're an avid surfer, you're looking to learn how to hang ten, or you just want to party, you'll probably love it here. If not, you may find Montañita a bit seedy and limited.

Essentials

GETTING THERE

BY BUS   **Libertad Peninsular** (**CLP;** ✆ **04/2140-975**) buses leave the main bus terminal in Guayaquil three times a day for Montañita, at 5am, 1, and 5pm. The ride takes around 3 hours. The fare is $6.

Local buses run between Santa Elena and Puerto López roughly every 15 to 20 minutes throughout the day. All these buses stop in Montañita to pick up and drop off passengers. If you're coming from Puerto López, hop on at the main bus stop in town, or anywhere along the highway heading south. The fare is around $1.50. If you're in Salinas, grab a taxi to Santa Elena and ask them to drop you off at the bus stop for Puerto López.

BY CAR   To drive to Montañita, follow the directions for driving to Salinas (see "Getting There," under "Salinas," earlier in this chapter). Montañita is located at Km 59 on the E15 coastal highway.

GETTING AROUND

You can easily walk anywhere in Montañita. That said, taxis usually hang around town to take surfers up and down the coast in search of secret spots. If you can't flag one down, have your hotel or any local business call one for you.

ORIENTATION

Montañita is a tiny town, roughly 10 blocks long (running along the ocean) and 4 blocks deep (from the coastal highway to the sea). The center of town is a tight jumble of budget lodgings, restaurants, bars, surf shops, and souvenir stands. Erosion has claimed much of the beach right in front of the town, and a large stone-barrier wall has been put in to try to slow the ocean's advance.

FAST FACTS   To contact the police, dial ✆ **101** in an emergency, or 04/2901-251. There are no banks in Montañita, but you'll find a couple of ATMs in the center of town. Still, I recommend you stock up on cash before heading to Montañita. Very few hotels or restaurants here accept credit cards. There are also no medical services and very limited supplies. Local general stores carry aspirin and other basic remedies, but the closest real pharmacies and medical care are in Santa Elena, Salinas, and Puerto López. There are several Internet cafes in town.

What to See & Do in Montañita

Surfing reigns supreme here, and there are rideable beach breaks up and down the coast. The most popular is the point break formed by a rocky headland at the north end of town. Surf competitions are often held here. The best surfing is December through May, though throughout the year you can find waves that can be big and powerful, accompanied by strong rip tides. Be careful and sure of yourself before heading out. If you want to take a lesson or rent a board, stop in at one of the little surf shops in town, or ask at your hotel. I like **Hotel Tiki Limbo** (☎ **09/9540-607;** tikilimbo@hotmail.com). For a surf-camp learning package, try **Casa del Sol** (see below).

Aside from surfing and hanging out on the beach, several hotel tour desks and in-town tour operators offer trips up to Puerto López, from where you can head out to **Isla de la Plata** to see the whales in season, or visit **Machalilla National Park** and **Los Frailes** beach. See "Puerto López & Machalilla National Park," below, for descriptions of these types of tours and activities.

While Quito, Cuenca, and Otavalo have more established Spanish schools, those looking to improve their pronunciation and vocabulary, as well as their bottom turns, can check in with **Montañita Spanish School** (☎ **04/2060-116** or 09/9184-735; www.montanitaspanishschool.com), which offers private and small-group lessons, as well as combo study packages with Spanish classes mixed with surfing, paragliding, and/or scuba diving lessons. These folks can provide hostel accommodations or set you up with a local family for a homestay.

Where to Stay & Dine in Montañita

Plenty of budget hostels and funky hotels in town cater to surfers. Most charge around $7 to $15 per person for a bed in a simple room, usually with a shared bathroom. If you really want to save some dollars, walk around the tiny town and check out a few to see if any suit your fancy. Of the backpacker hostels, my favorites are **Hostal Kundalini** (☎ **09/9541-745;** www.hostalkundalini.com.ec) and **Tierra Prometida** (☎ **09/4575-216;** hoteltierraprometida@hotmail.com).

Not surprisingly, Montañita is packed with small, simple restaurants serving the backpacker and surfer crowd. Most are pretty good, and all are inexpensive. The best and most creative restaurants in town are **Tiki Limbo** ★ (☎ **09/9540-607;** tikilimbo@hotmail.com), which serves up everything from falafel to sesame-crusted seared tuna; and **Hola Ola** (☎ **09/4575-216**), which has an equally wide-ranging menu featuring burgers, pizzas, and *ceviches,* alongside Thai-flavored grilled fish and chicken curry.

MODERATE

Hotel Baja Montañita This large resort-style hotel set on the far north end of the beach is the best-equipped hotel in Montañita, although it often feels in dire need of some upkeep and updating. A couple of two- and three-story blocks are built in a horseshoe around a midsize outdoor pool. Most of the rooms have great views of the surf. All are spacious and well kept, with whitewashed, faux-stucco walls and red-tile floors. Even though the ground-floor rooms have a private terrace, I prefer the upper rooms, which have private balconies. Suites come with kitchenettes, but I don't think they are worth the extra cost. There are also *cabañas,* which have two sleeping rooms and can sleep up to six people (some in bunk beds).

On the beach, north of town. www.bajamontanita.com.ec. ☎ **305/994-2497** in the U.S., or 04/2568-840 reservations in Guayaquil, or 04/2060-119 at the hotel. 30 units. $75–$90 double; $120–$180 suite; $120 *cabaña.* Rates include breakfast buffet. Rates lower in the off season, higher during peak periods. AE, MC, V. **Amenities:** Restaurant; bar; outdoor pool; room service; free Wi-Fi. *In room:* A/C, TV.

INEXPENSIVE

Casa del Sol ★   This rambling complex on the north end of the beach was built by and for surfers. It consists of several connected buildings, with weathered thatch roofs. The owners here specialize in surf camps at this, their home base in Montañita, as well as up and down the coastline and even in the Galápagos. All of the rooms have air-conditioning, but only a few have ocean views, which are the best bets. The oceanfront **restaurant** features a high ceiling, stone walls and pillars, and large, heavy wooden tables. The food is very good, and definitely filling.

On the beach, north of town. www.casadelsolmontanita.com. ℂ **09/2488-581.** 17 units. $30–$40 double. Rates include breakfast buffet. AE, DC, MC, V. **Amenities:** Restaurant; bar; free Wi-Fi. *In room:* A/C, no phone.

Charo's Hostal ★ 🍴   At three stories, this place qualifies as a high-rise in Montañita. It's also one of the more comfortable options, and a good deal, to boot. Most rooms here come with private balconies and ocean views. The well-tended grounds include lush gardens, strategically placed hammocks, and a small pool and separate Jacuzzi. You'll also find a popular **restaurant and bar** here.

On the beach, Montañita. www.charoshostal.com. ℂ **09/9386-474** or 04/2060-044. 27 units. $34–$40 double. Rates lower in the off season, higher during peak periods. No credit cards. **Amenities:** Restaurant; bar; Jacuzzi; pool. *In room:* A/C, TV, no phone, free Wi-Fi.

Montañita After Dark

With a high concentration of young surfers, international backpackers, and Ecuadorean hippies, you'll find a lively nightlife in Montañita. The scene is pretty informal. Street performers are common. Dancing is done in shorts and flip-flops, and there are no fancy clubs here. Your best bet is to just walk around the town until you find a bar that suits you. Perhaps the largest and most consistently happening spots are **Caña Grill** (no phone), a large, open-air joint that often features live music, and the even larger **Nativa Bambu** ★ (ℂ **04/2060-095;** www.nativabambu.com), with its soaring, open-air bamboo deck and oceanfront location. **Hola Ola** (see above) also has a popular bar and dance scene. The whole town parties big-time on the weekend closest to the full moon, with Ecuadoreans coming from all over for the wild festivities.

En Route North

Heading north from Montañita, you will pass through a series of isolated beaches and small fishing towns, with such names as Olón, San José, and Ayampe. These are great places to really get away from it all, though regular local buses running the coastal route make these spots easily accessible. Most of these beaches have one or two little hotels or miniresorts, either right on the sand or up in the hills overlooking the action.

In addition to the places listed below, you might consider the following two nearby inland options. **Red Mangrove Samai Lodge** (ℂ **888/254-3190** in the U.S. and Canada, or 05/2526-564 in Ecuador; www.redmangrove.com) is a forest retreat with an in-house spa, while **El Retiro** (ℂ **04/2399-213;** www.elretiro. com.ec) focuses more on adventure activities, with a zip-line tour, trails, suspended-bridge walkways, a climbing wall, and horses, and is located, just south of Montañita. A little farther north, about 28km (17 miles) south of Puerto Lopéz, you'll find **Hostería Atamari** ★ (ℂ **02/2227-896;** http://atamari.ec.tripod.com), a somewhat upscale hotel built on a promontory overlooking the Pacific Ocean.

Cuna Luna ★ 🎁 If you're looking for an isolated and affordable beach getaway on a beautiful stretch of the Ecuadorean coast, it's hard to beat this place. As a plus, the restaurant here is superb. All the rooms are pretty basic, with wood floors and ceilings, bamboo shades, a wall-mounted fan, and a private balcony strung with two hammocks. I'd try to land one of the second-floor units of one of the four beachfront duplexes. The small grounds here feature some pretty gardens, which help produce some of the food cooked up in the kitchen.

In San José, Km 697 on the coastal Hwy. E15. www.cunaluna.com. 📞**04/2780-735.** 10 units. $40–$55 double. AE, MC, V. **Amenities:** Restaurant; bar. *In room:* No phone.

Hostería Alándaluz ☺ This place bills itself as a *pueblo ecológico* (ecological village) and makes every effort to be self-sustainable, low-impact, and environmentally friendly. The entire expansive complex here is constructed of bamboo, stone, palm thatch, wood, or some renewable resource. Most of the toilets are self-composting. Alándaluz has organic gardens and a neighboring private reserve. The wide range in room prices reflects the variance in style, decor, and location of the *hostería's* cabins. They even allow camping, in a little campground with shared bathrooms and showers. My favorite rooms are the Cabañas Torrecilla, which are classified as minisuites. These are close to the beach and feature private balconies and small fireplaces. The massive main lodge has a soaring thatch roof, polished wood floors, and homemade bamboo furniture. Geared toward Ecuadorean families, this place features a playground, game room, and pool and Ping-Pong tables.

In Puerto Rico, 12km (7½ miles) south of Puerto López on the coastal Hwy. E15. www.alandaluzhosteria. com. 📞**04/2780-690** at the hotel, or 02/2440-790 for reservations office in Quito. 25 units. $31–$84 double; $7 per person camping. AE, DC, MC, V. **Amenities:** Restaurant; bar; outdoor pool. *In room:* No phone.

PUERTO LOPEZ & MACHALILLA NATIONAL PARK ★★

224km (139 miles) NW of Guayaquil; 103km (64 miles) N of Santa Elena; 44km (27 miles) N of Montañita

Although it's little more than a small coastal fishing village, **Puerto López** is the largest town on this section of the Pacific coast, as well as the gateway to **Machalilla National Park** ★★. Scores of fishing and tour boats bob at anchor just off the shore, and many more are hauled up on the sands each day. The town itself is rather run-down and unappealing, but this is the best place to come to book whale-watching cruises and trips out to **Isla de la Plata** ★★★, as well as tours to the land-based attractions of the popular park.

Essentials
GETTING THERE
BY PLANE The nearest airport with regular service is in **Manta** (p. 264 has information on flying into Manta), some 122km (76 miles) away, although many folks also fly into **Guayaquil** (see "Getting There," under "Guayaquil," for information on flying into Guayaquil).

BY BUS **Cooperativo Carlos Aray** (📞 02/2283-080 in Quito, or 05/2300-178 in Puerto López) and **Cooperativo Reina del Camino** (📞 02/3216-624 in Quito, or 05/2300-207 in Puerto López) both have two direct buses daily between Quito and Puerto López, one leaving in each direction very early in the morning and the other leaving close to midnight. The ride takes 10 to 12 hours, and fares run between $8 and $12.

Libertad Peninsular (CLP; ☎ 04/2140-975) buses leave Guayaquil's main bus terminal three times daily for Puerto López, at 5am and 1 and 5pm. The ride, which takes around 4 hours, costs $7.50.

Turistico Manta (☎ 05/2600-311) operates bus service between Puerto López and Manta roughly every half-hour between 4:30am and 5:30pm. The fare is $4, and the ride takes 2½ hours. If you're traveling to or from Quito, you can also head first to Manta and then take an onward bus. For information on bus connections to and from Manta, see p. 266.

Local buses run between Santa Elena and Puerto López roughly every 15 to 20 minutes throughout the day. If you're coming from Puerto López, pick one up at the main bus stop in town or anywhere along the highway heading south. If you're in Salinas, grab a taxi to Santa Elena and ask them to drop you off at the bus stop for Puerto López. The fare is around $3.

BY CAR   To reach Puerto López by car from Quito, start off heading south on the Pan-American Highway (E35) until the intersection at Aloag. From here, head west on E30 toward Santo Domingo de los Colorados. In Santo Domingo, take the well-marked exit for E25 south to Quevedo. From Quevedo you will head west again on E40 to Puerto Viejo, where you will take E9 south to Jipijapa. In Jipijapa, there is an exit for the coastal highway, E15, which runs south from Puerto Cayo, through Machalilla, and on to Puerto López. The drive should take between 9 and 10 hours.

If you're driving from Guayaquil, you can either take Hwy. E9 to Jipijapa and then jog down the coast on E15, or take E70 west out of Guayaquil to Santa Elena, where you will join E15, which follows the coast north all the way to Puerto López. Either one of these routes should take between 3½ and 4 hours.

GETTING AROUND

Puerto López is compact, and you can easily walk anywhere in town. That said, there's an abundance of motorcycle-powered "ecotaxis" that will take you anywhere in town for $1 to $1.50. A round-trip ride to Los Frailes (see below) should cost around $12 to $15, but be sure to coordinate your return pickup very well. If you can't flag down a taxi, call ☎ **09/4865-361** or 09/4195-725.

ORIENTATION

Puerto López sits along the shores of a long, gently curving beach, with a seaside street, officially called Malecón Julio Izurieta, running the length of the town. The main coastal highway, E15, passes right through the center of town, where it is called Avenida Machalilla. This is where you'll find the town's Catholic church, its main market, and, just off of the market, its bus terminal. The ocean and the Malecón are 3 blocks east of here. Most of the town's hotels, restaurants, tour agencies, and Internet cafes are located on the Malecón, Avenida Machalilla, or one the few cross-streets connecting them.

FAST FACTS   The **police station (☎ 05/2300-101)** is located on Avenida Machalilla, 1 block north of the market. In an emergency, call ☎ **911.** There's a branch of **Banco Pichincha (☎ 05/2300-140)** on Avenida Machalilla and Calle Córdova. The **post office (☎ 05/2300-236)** is on the Malecón between calles Sucre and Córdova. You'll find a couple of Internet cafes along the Malecón and on the cross-streets heading toward Avenida Machalilla.

HAVING A whale OF A TIME

If you are lucky enough to find yourself traveling between late June and early October, you have an excellent chance of catching the marvel of this coast's annual humpback whale–mating celebration. Each year, Ecuador welcomes a large population of humpback whales, which migrate from the chilly polar waters of Antarctica. Arriving off the Ecuadorean coast in June, pregnant mothers promptly give birth, while single adults find a mating partner for the next 4 months.

Humpback whales grow to about 16m (52 ft.) in length and can weigh between 30 and 50 tons. The babies are born about 3 to 4.5m long (9¾–15 ft.) and can weigh over 2 tons. The Pacific humpback whales—called *ballenas jorobadas* in Ecuador—are an especially acrobatic species, and it's not uncommon to see them breach, wave their tail fins, or even pop their heads up for a look around. It is believed that their acrobatics may be a part of their mating dance.

Humpbacks have been known to travel up to 8,050km (4,991 miles) each way on their annual breeding and feeding excursions. Because calves (young whales) aren't born with blubber, a protective layer of fat, they need to be birthed and reared in the warmer tropical waters, feeding on as much as 100 pounds of their mother's milk each day in order to develop the protective fatty layer of insulation necessary for survival. A female humpback will calve approximately every 2 to 3 years.

Humpbacks can travel at a speed of 8 to 14kmph (5–8¾ mph). But during long journeys, they average only 1.6kmph (1 mph), stopping to rest and socialize along the way. They navigate back to the freezing waters to feast on crustaceans and small fish. While in the warmer, tropical waters, they don't eat at all—but live off their blubber.

During the whale-watching months, all the hotels and tour agencies in town offer outings to see these magnificent mammals up close. Most charge $20 to $40. Some of the trips combine whale-watching time with a visit to Isla de la Plata. But be careful—the boats are small and the water can be rough. If you're prone to seasickness, be sure to take some sort of anti-motion-sickness medication before you board the boat.

What to See & Do in & Around Puerto López

Puerto López makes a great base for a wide range of activities, but by far the greatest draw here is the annual humpback whale migration, mating, and breeding event, as well as Machalilla National Park (see below). There are a host of tour agencies in town, and all the hotels here either have their own tour desk or work closely with some local tour operator. I recommend **Machalilla Tours ★** (© **05/2300-234** or 09/4925-960; www.machalillatours.org), run by Fausto Choez Castro; or **Naturis** (© **05/2300-218**; www.naturis.com.ec). In addition to whale-watching tours and visits to Isla de la Plata and Machalilla National Park, both of these operations have tour offerings ranging from surf lessons and sea-kayak trips to sport fishing and horseback riding.

If you plan on enjoying the beach right here in Puerto López, I recommend you head, in either direction, away from the center of town, where all the fishing boats—and their detritus—congregate. However, by far the best beach in this area is found inside the national park at Los Frailes (see below).

Machalilla National Park ★★ includes the offshore island **Isla de la Plata (Island of Silver)** ★★★, as well as vast tracts of forest and a couple of ancient archaeological sites. Named Isla de la Plata because Sir Francis Drake is reported to have hidden a huge treasure here, the island is located 23km (14 miles) west of Puerto López. Isla de la Plata is often considered an alternative to the Galápagos Islands, especially for those short on time or money. The bird-watching and wildlife viewing on Isla de la Plata are top-notch: You will have the chance to see albatrosses; blue-footed, masked, and red-footed boobies; frigate birds; and sea lions, all in large numbers and all of which also live in the Galápagos. There are two major loop trails here that head around either end of the island. Each trail takes about 2 hours. Really hard-core tours will hike both of them. There are also some wonderful snorkeling spots here. All the tour agencies and hotels in town offer trips out to Isla de la Plata for around $30 to $40, including a guided hike, lunch, and snorkeling gear, but not including the park entrance fee.

On the mainland, Machalilla is made up of 55,000 hectares (135,850 acres) of mostly tropical dry forest. Within its boundaries lies **Los Frailes** ★★, a long, deep crescent of beautiful beach backed by high bluffs and thick forest. Los Frailes is widely reputed to be the most beautiful beach in Ecuador, and aerial photos of this spot are common on postcards and promotional materials across the country. Be sure to bring plenty of water and sunscreen. You can visit Los Frailes on your own or as part of a guided tour, which will take you to a couple of nearby archaeological sites. From the park entrance gate at Los Frailes, there is a 3.2km (2-mile) trail down to the beach.

About 10km (6¼ miles) north of Puerto López is the village of **Agua Blanca,** which has a small archaeological museum and nearby ruins. The ruins and most of the artifacts in the museum are attributed to the Manteña people, who inhabited this region from 500 B.C. until around A.D. 1500.

Admission to Machalilla National Park, which includes access to Isla de la Plata, is $20. If you're just going to the island, the entrance fee is $15. A day pass to visit only Los Frailes costs $5. If you sign on for a tour, your tour operator will handle the park passes for you. If not, head to the **national park office** (✆ 05/2300-170) in Puerto López, on Calle Eloy Alfaro, a half-block east of the main market. The office is open Monday through Saturday from 8am to 5pm.

Where to Stay in Puerto López
MODERATE

Hostería Oceanic   Located across a dirt road fronting the beach, this place has the feel of a small resort. I prefer the individual cabins, but there are also rooms in a large two-story, thatch-roof main building. The cabins feature high ceilings and a small private balcony. All feature tile floors and colorful bedspreads, although many feature worn lawn furniture. In fact, the whole operation feels a bit worn and neglected most of the time. There's also a two-level free-form pool, with a sculpted waterfall, and a small spa.

On the beach, Puerto López. www.hosteriaoceanic.com. ✆ **09/6211-065.** 15 units. $70–$90 double. Rates include breakfast. Rates lower in the off season, higher during peak periods. AE, DC, MC, V. **Amenities:** Restaurant; bar; outdoor pool; small spa; free Wi-Fi. *In room:* No phone.

Mantaraya Lodge ★   This hotel sits on a hillside overlooking dry forest and the coastline. The buildings here feature faux-adobe walls, red-tile roofs, and a quirky architectural style. There's a topiary whale and shark near the free-form pool, which

is fed by a waterfall flowing out of a large, unheated Jacuzzi. Most of the rooms have private balconies or terra-cotta tile patios. Room no. 15 is my favorite, with a great view from its second-story perch. No. 8 is another second-floor unit with a very large balcony-terrace. The rooms don't have air-conditioning, but they do have fans, and with tile floors, high ceilings, and good cross-ventilation, it's usually pretty comfortable. The Mantaraya has an excellent tour operation, both here and in Quito (Advantage Travel), and a lot of the guests come as part of an organized package that includes room, board, and tours. This place is a certified Smart Voyager property.

On the coastal hwy., Puerto López. www.mantarayalodge.com. ✆ **02/3360-887** reservations office in Quito. Fax 02/3360-774. 15 units. $80–$120 double. Rates include full breakfast and taxes. Rates lower in the off season, higher during peak periods. AE, DC, MC, V. **Amenities:** Restaurant; bar; midsize outdoor pool; free Wi-Fi. *In room:* No phone.

INEXPENSIVE

In addition to the place listed below, a good option in the heart of town is **Hotel Pacífico** (✆/fax **05/2300-133;** www.hotelpacificoecuador.com), on the Malecón and facing the ocean. Another excellent option, although not on the beach, is the new, German-run hillside **La Terraza** (✆/fax **05/2300-235;** www.laterraza.de), with cozy rooms and great ocean views.

Hostería Mandála ★★ 🎒 This unique lodging option is located just across from the beach, several blocks north of the center of town. The setting and extensive grounds and gardens here make the place feel like a remote oasis. The brick cabins—which have a small front balcony or porch and a cloth hammock—feature artistic details and design elements made of wood, bamboo, and stone. The hotel fronts a quiet section of beach, and they've built several thatch-roof shade huts on the sand for guests to commandeer while they're enjoying the sun, sand, and sea. Still, the best feature here is the Mandála's extensive and well-tended gardens, which show off a wide range of tropical flora and feature several beautiful sculptures. These folks take their conservation and environmental protection seriously.

Malecón Julio Izurieta, north end of town, Puerto López. www.hosteriamandala.info. ℰ/fax **05/2300-181** or 09/9513-940. 20 units. $30–$60 double. No credit cards. **Amenities:** Restaurant; bar; free Wi-Fi. *In room:* No phone.

Where to Dine in Puerto López

All along the Malecón are simple restaurants serving excellent fresh seafood and Ecuadorean cooking at very reasonable rates. Of these, I like **Restaurante Carmita** (ℰ **05/2300-149**) and **Restaurante Spondylus** (ℰ **05/2300-128**). For Italian fare, try **Bella Italia** (ℰ **05/2300-361**).

Café Ballena/Whale Café ★ SEAFOOD/ECUADOREAN This place is located at the southern end of the Malecón. Run by an American couple who have been here for nearly 20 years, the restaurant is famous for its filling breakfasts—in particular, its fresh banana bread and apple pancakes. Lunch and dinner are just as satisfying. I always favor fresh grilled fish, but you can also get excellent pastas and pizzas. Save room for dessert, which might feature a fresh-baked apple pie or flourless chocolate cake. In many ways, this place is a social hub for travelers, with a lively vibe and popular book exchange.

South end of Malecón Julio Izurieta. ℰ **09/6345-291** or 09/6284-047. Main courses $4–$15. MC, V. Daily 8am–10pm. Often reduced hours in the off season.

Puerto López After Dark

This is a quiet fishing town with very limited nightlife. All of the restaurants listed above have small bars or mellow drinking scenes, and most travelers stick to these. Aside from that, you can stroll the Malecón and see if any place calls out to you.

MACHALA & SOUTH TO THE PERUVIAN BORDER

518km (321 miles) S of Quito; 191km (118 miles) S of Guayaquil; 73km (45 miles) N of Huaquillas

The capital of El Oro province, Machala is an agricultural city at the heart of Ecuador's banana belt. In fact, the city bills itself as the Banana Capital of the World, and banana plantations extend for kilometers in every direction. Most of this massive banana production is shipped out of Puerto Bolívar, about 6.5km (4 miles) west of Machala's downtown. Puerto Bolívar is a major port and shipping center. In addition to bananas, this region produces and ships large quantities of cacao, pineapples, and farm-raised shrimp. In many ways, Puerto Bolívar, its seafront Malecón packed with shops, restaurants, and bars, is more attractive to tourists than Machala.

Indeed, for most tourists Machala is simply a necessary transit stop from both Guayaquil and Cuenca on the way to Peru. While here, you can tour nearby mangroves, visit the beach at Jambelí, or take a tour of a unique petrified forest down near the Peruvian border.

Essentials

GETTING THERE

BY PLANE Tame (© 1800/500-800 toll-free in Ecuador; www.tame.com.ec) has flights Monday, Wednesday, and Friday between Quito and the new **Aeropuerto Regional de Santa Rosa** (© 07/2947-011; airport code: ETR), which services Machala. **Saereo** (© 1800/723-736; www.saereo.com) makes the run daily. Saereo also flies between Guayaquil and Santa Rosa on Monday, Thursday, and Friday. The flight takes a little over an hour, and the fare is $75 to $100 each way.

BY BUS There are a handful of direct buses from Quito to Machala each day on the **Cooperativa TAC** (© 02/2951-913 in Quito, or 07/2930-119 in Machala), **Occidental** (© 07/2930-820), and **Panamericana** (© 07/2557-133) bus lines. The ride takes around 11 hours, and the fare is about $10 to $14.

Alternatively, you can travel first to Guayaquil (see "Getting There," under "Guayaquil"), and make onward bus connections to Machala and the border. Buses leave Guayaquil's main bus terminal at least every half-hour between 4:30am and 11:30pm, on three or four different bus lines, including **CIFA** (© 07/2933-735 in Machala, or 04/2140-379 in Guayaquil) and **Ecuatoriano Pullman** (© 07/2931-164 in Machala, or 04/2140-617 in Guayaquil). About half of these buses continue on to Huaquillas (see "Heading South to Peru," below). The ride takes 3 hours to Machala and 4½ hours to Huaquillas. The fares run around $4.50 to Machala and $6 to $7 to Huaquillas.

Transportes Azuay (© 07/2823-163; www.transportesazuay.com) has frequent service between Machala and Cuenca. The ride takes about 4 hours, and the fare is $5.

CIFA and **Ecuatoriano Pullman** make the run between Machala and the border at Huaquillas. The ride takes around 1½ hours, and the fare is $2.

There's no centralized bus station in Machala, but all the major bus lines arrive at and depart from stops or terminals in the downtown area. For departures out of Machala, the terminal directions are as follows. *To Guayaquil:* **Ecuatoriano Pullman** leaves from Av. 9 de Octubre and Calle Colón, and **CIFA** leaves from Avenida Bolívar and Calle Guayas. *To Quito:* **Panamericana** buses leave from Calle Colón and Avenida Bolívar, **Cooperativa TAC** buses leave from Calle Colón and Rocafuerte, and **Occidental** buses leave from Avenida Buenavista between calles Sucre and Olmedo. *To Cuenca:* **Transportes Azuay** leaves from Calle Sucre and Calle Junín.

BY CAR To reach Machala by car, follow the directions to Guayaquil (p. 227). From Guayaquil, take Hwy. E70 east out of town until the junction with E25. Just outside the city center, E25 crosses E584, which will take you to Machala. E25 continues down to the town of Arenillas, where it connects with E50, which heads to Huaquillas and the Peruvian border.

GETTING AROUND

You should have no trouble flagging down a taxi in Machala. A ride anywhere in the city should cost less than $2, and a ride out to Puerto Bolívar should cost only $3. You can also call **Cooperativa de Taxis Machala** (© 07/2920-271) or **Taxi Colon** (© 07/2933-333).

Local buses run constantly along Av. 9 de Octubre out to Puerto Bolívar. The fare is 25¢.

You can rent a car from **Budget** (© 07/2960-586; www.budgetrentacar.com.ec), which has an office on Avenida del Periodista and the Circunvalación Norte, as well as at the airport in Santa Rosa.

ORIENTATION

Machala's downtown features a central plaza with the city's Catholic church and a small park, bordered by avenidas Rocafuerte and 9 de Octubre and by calles Guayas and 9 de Mayo. Avenida 9 de Octubre is the main avenue running through the heart of town. As it heads out of Machala to the northwest, Av. 9 de Octubre becomes Avenida Bolívar Madero Vargas, which takes you to Puerto Bolívar.

FAST FACTS The main **police** station (© 101 or 07/2933-391) is on Av. 9 de Mayo and Calle Manuel Estomba, near the airport. For a medical emergency, call the **Cruz Roja** (**Red Cross;** © 07/2930-151). **Hospital Teófilo Dávila** (© 07/2935-570) is the best medical facility in the city; it's located close to downtown, on Avenida Boyacá between calles Colón and Buenavista.

The Ministry of Tourism operates a **tourist information office** (© 07/2932-106) at Av. 9 de Mayo and Pichincha. The main **post office** is on Avenida Bolívar and Calle Montalvo. The **Peruvian Consulate** (© 07/2937-040) is at Ubrbanización Unioro, Manzana 14, Villa 11.

Most major Ecuadorean banks have a branch or two in downtown Machala.

There are plenty of Internet cafes and phone cabins all over downtown Machala. Rates run around 75¢ to $1.50 per hour. Your best bet is to find whichever Internet cafe seems most comfortable and well equipped.

What to See & Do in & Around Machala

There's little of interest to tourists right in Machala. The most popular excursion from Machala is to the beach of **Jambelí,** on the tip of a mangrove archipelago that lies just off the coast. On weekends and holidays, locals flock here. The beach is a long, narrow expanse of hard-packed gray sand; it's lined with palm trees and makeshift huts built to provide shade. Though very crowded on weekends and holidays, Jambelí is usually almost empty at other times. Be sure to bring plenty of sunscreen and mosquito repellent. There are some simple restaurants and *ceviche* shacks along the beach. Many visitors prefer to take a boat tour through the mangroves, where the bird-watching is excellent. Boat taxis leave throughout the day from the pier in Puerto Bolívar for Jambelí. Boats leave roughly every half-hour, or when they fill up, between 7am and 6:30pm. The ride takes around 20 minutes, and the fare is $1.50 each way. Alternatively, you can hire an entire boat for up to 10 people for around $12 to $20 per hour.

Down south of Machala, right near the Peruvian border, sits the **Bosque Petrificado de Puyango (Petrified Forest of Puyango)** ★ (© 07/2960-055; www.bosquepuyango.ec), a unique dry-forest reserve with a vast collection of fossilized tree trunks, plants, leaves, flowers, fruits, and mollusks. Most of the fossils are approximately 100 million years old. The most common and impressive specimens here are the Araucarioxylon trunks, which are strewn across the landscape; the largest of these is some 15m (49 ft.) long, with a diameter of 2m (6½ ft.). Puyango is 111km (69 miles) south of Machala. The reserve is open daily from 8am to 4:30pm. Admission is $1.

GOING bananas

The banana has played a vital role in Ecuador's economic history. Following an epidemic blight that wiped out many of the banana plantations in Central America during the early 1940s, Ecuador was called upon to serve as an alternative supplier of the fruit to satisfy the growing demands of the U.S. market. After the end of World War II, Ecuador enjoyed a decade-long "banana boom" that brought with it an unprecedented period of peace and prosperity. From 1948 to 1952, annual exports increased from 2 million bananas to 20 million, and by 1955, they'd reached 26 million. Banana profits were used to improve the country's infrastructure, education, and health-care system, as well as to increase salaries.

Ecuador's political scene was also affected by the country's transformation into a **Banana Republic.** President Velasco served out three full consecutive terms in office, an unprecedented and unmatched feat in the country's history. Toward the close of the 1950s, however, world banana prices dropped, sparking an economic crisis marked by high unemployment and widespread social discord. The discovery of petroleum in the late 1960s helped alleviate the problem. (Bananas still rank as Ecuador's second-most-important export, after oil, and Ecuadorean bananas account for some 30% of worldwide consumption.)

The year-round tropical climate enjoyed by the country's southern coastal regions near Guayaquil is ideal for banana production. The majority of plantations are managed by private interests, the most well-known being those belonging to ex-presidential candidate and banana magnate Alvaro Noboa, owner of the world's largest export brand, Bonita. (Noboa, not coincidentally, is the wealthiest person in Ecuador.)

Ecuadorean banana workers—who represent at least 10% of the nation's workforce—are some of the lowest paid in Latin America. Human-rights abuses on plantations continue to attract international media attention; there have been reports of violent attacks against workers and union organizers.

Where to Stay in Machala
EXPENSIVE

Hotel Oro Verde Machala ★ This hotel has modern and extensive facilities and is very popular with business and conference travelers. The carpeted rooms feature contemporary furnishings and cheery fabric patterns. Those looking to stay active or fit can play tennis or squash, or work out in the small but well-equipped gym. Less strenuous pursuits include lounging by the large pool or taking a sauna or steam bath. The pool has a large children's area, and a nearby playground makes this a good choice for families traveling with the kids. The Oro Verde is located on the eastern outskirts of downtown, in an upscale residential neighborhood.

Circunvalación Norte y Calle Vehicular, Machala. www.oroverdehotels.com. © **07/2933-140.** Fax 07/2933-150. 77 units. $135–$165 double; $400 suite. Rates include breakfast buffet. AE, DC, MC, V. **Amenities:** 2 restaurants; 2 bars; small gym; Jacuzzi; outdoor pool; room service; sauna; steam room; 2 indoor squash courts; unlit outdoor tennis court. *In room:* A/C, TV, minibar, free Wi-Fi.

MODERATE

Regal Hotel This is the best hotel in downtown Machala. I enjoy its bold architecture, with three columns of curving windows rising several stories over the busy Avenida Bolívar. The rooms vary greatly in size, and some can feel a bit cramped. All are done in a neutral, modern style familiar to anyone staying in a typical business-class hotel, with built-in wood-grained Formica furniture and matching headboard. Some come with comfortable leather sitting chairs. The hotel's restaurant is an American-style cafeteria that's popular with locals, especially for lunch.

Calle Bolívar, btw. Guayas and Ayacucho, Machala. www.regalhotel.com.ec. ©/fax **07/2960-000.** 35 units. $63 double; $76–$84 suite. Rates include full breakfast. AE, DC, MC, V. **Amenities:** Restaurant; bar; small gym; room service. *In room:* A/C, TV.

INEXPENSIVE

Gran Hotel Americano ♦ This stately old dame shows her age in places but remains a good choice and an excellent value. Most rooms come with a private balcony overlooking busy downtown Machala. The rooms themselves have received regular upgrading and upkeep and are in pretty decent shape, especially at these prices. Heck, these folks even offer free valet parking. The higher up the room, the farther removed it is from street noise, which can be an issue at times. This is predominantly a business hotel, which fills up during the week but empties out on weekends. Be sure to ask about their discounts for Friday and Saturday nights.

Av. 9 de Octubre y Calle Tarqui, Machala. www.hotelesmachala.com. © **07/2966-400.** Fax 07/2966-401. 60 units. $38 double; $48 junior suite. Rates include full breakfast. AE, DC, MC, V. **Amenities:** Restaurant; bar. *In room:* A/C, TV.

Where to Dine in Machala

Downtown Machala has loads of restaurants serving inexpensive local fare and seafood. If you're looking for Chinese food, try **Chifa Central** (© 07/2932-961), on Calle Tarqui between Av. 25 de Junio and Calle Sucre. The restaurant at the **Gran Hotel Americano** (see above) and the **Oro Mar** restaurant at the Hotel Oro Verde (see above) are both very good and popular with locals and visitors alike. For pizza and pastas, you should head to **Chesco Pizzería** (© 07/2936-418), on Calle Guayas, between Av. 25 de Junio and Calle Sucre. The best thing to do, though, is to head to nearby Puerto Bolívar, which has a string of oceanfront options specializing in excellent *ceviches* and seafood.

INEXPENSIVE

Chesco Pizzería ITALIAN/PIZZA Don't come here for ambience. The fluorescent lights are dizzying, the decor relatively sterile. Still, the thin-crust pizzas here are the best in Machala. They also have a long list of pasta options and some steak and poultry main courses. Chesco offers delivery, and there's another branch nearby on Avenida Pichincha, between calles Guayas and Ayacucho.

Calle Guayas, btw. Av. 25 de Junio and Calle Sucre, Puerto Bolívar. © **07/2936-418.** Main courses $4–$12. MC, V. Daily noon–10pm.

Pepe's ★ SEAFOOD/ECUADOREAN The food here is very similar to what you'll find at any of the other *ceviche* and seafood joints along the Malecón in Puerto Bolívar, but this place, built on stilts over the water, has the best setting. Grab one of the tables along the railing and order up a dish of the delicious shrimp *ceviche*. You can also get oysters on the half-shell, another excellent appetizer. For a main dish, find out what's the freshest catch, or splurge for some langostinos served in a rich garlic sauce. After dark, this place starts to resemble a bar scene, which is not necessarily a bad thing, and they even have karaoke on the weekends.

Malecón y Rocafuerte, Puerto Bolívar. © **07/2929-505.** Main courses $3–$12. AE, MC, V. Daily 10am–midnight.

Machala After Dark

Machala is a big city with a thriving nightlife. The city even has its own *zona rosa,* a designated area chock-full of bars, clubs, and discos. It's located on the south side of town and comprises several cross-streets between avenidas Tarqui and Colón. In the *zona rosa,* some of my favorites include **Bazza Liquid Lounge** (© **07/2933-555;** www.bazza.com.ec), **Verde Limón** (© 08/4900-193), and Jabibi Litros Bar (© 09/4857-528).

For a quieter time, try the **Golden Café Concert** (© **07/2933-555**), a refined bar and club with frequent live music performances ranging from jazz to boleros, to Latin folk. It's located on the corner of Av. 9 de Octubre and Calle Junín.

Gamblers can test their luck at the casino at the **Casinomar** (© **07/2933-140**), on Circunvalación Norte and Vehicular 7, near Hotel Oro Verde Machala.

Heading South to Peru

The road south to Peru passes right by Machala and heads down through Santa Rosa and Arenillas to the border town of Huaquillas, some 80km (50 miles) south of Machala. If you're going on to Peru, you should definitely use Machala, or even Guayaquil, as your final base in Ecuador because there are very limited services and no accommodations that I can recommend in Huaquillas. The Río Zarumilla forms the physical border between the two countries, and the Peruvian border town is Aguas Verdes. Keep in mind that the Ecuadorean immigration control point is located about 3.2km (2 miles) north of the actual border crossing, while its Peruvian counterpart is about 2km (1¼ miles) south of the river. Both are on the main road and readily identified by numerous signs.

Shameless Plug

If you're going on to Peru, you'll want to pick up a copy of *Frommer's Peru,* now in its fourth edition.

If you are planning on traveling from Ecuador to Peru, I recommend you buy a through ticket on a reputable bus line, as the border crossing here is quite rough, and I've received various reports of attacks and robberies against tourists both on the ground here and on cheaper local buses. Through tickets to Peru are sold by several bus lines in Quito, Guayaquil, Cuenca, Loja, and Machala.

Note: The border is a hectic mess on both sides and is relatively dangerous for travelers. Peru and Ecuador have had border disputes in the past, which hasn't helped matters. Keep a careful eye on your belongings, and be wary of hucksters and scam artists. Try to avoid and discourage touts. Scores of individuals offer money exchange in the streets on either side of the border, but I recommend exchanging a minimal amount there, because these dealers often give unfavorable rates, use rigged calculators, and pawn off counterfeit bills. It's best to have a good grasp of the current official exchange rate ($1 was equivalent to 2.80 soles at press time) and to see if you can exchange dollars for Peruvian soles at a bank in Machala. If not, exchange what you need to get you through to Tumbes or a bit beyond, where you'll find more reputable and less risky exchange houses.

THE NORTHERN PACIFIC COAST & LOWLANDS

E cuador's northern Pacific coast and its surrounding lowlands are often neglected or avoided by foreign visitors to the country. The region, however, is not without its charms. The beaches of the northern Pacific coast are arguably the finest in the country. Long cherished by locals, they are also finding favor with international surfers, who can't get enough of the consistent beach break at Canoa or the perfect point at Mompiche.

Manta is a major port and beach town that sits just about at the center of Ecuador's long stretch of Pacific coastline. The city has high-rise hotels, a seaside Malecón, and plenty of restaurants and nightlife, including a couple of ritzy casinos. Those looking for a more pastoral port city should head to the picturesque little peninsula that is **Bahía de Caráquez.**

From Bahía, the coastline stretches north with kilometer after kilometer of pristine beaches backed at first by dry forest and cattle lands, which give way, as you enter **Esmeraldas** province, to lush rainforests and then dense mangrove forests. Esmeraldas is rightly known as "The Green Province." It is also the epicenter of the country's Afro-Ecuadorean population, a unique cultural community with distinctive music, cuisine, and customs.

Inland, on the plains just below the Andes, lies **Santo Domingo de Colorados,** one of the country's major crossroads. From this hub, spokes head out in various directions to the coast, as well as straight south to Guayaquil. In the forests around Santo Domingo lie a couple of beautiful, isolated nature lodges.

MANTA

419km (260 miles) W of Quito; 196km (122 miles) NW of Guayaquil

Manta is a city of many faces, but at its core it's an industrial port—the second-largest port in Ecuador, after Guayaquil. Inhabited for centuries, Manta was a major trading port for the pre-Columbian Manteña people who gave the town its name. The conquering Incas also used Manta as a port. Today the city has a population of some 200,000 and is home to a large university, as well as a large airbase. It also makes a respectable stab at being a beach town, with a couple of good beaches located right near the center of the city. But Manta's appeal as a beach getaway is much

Northern Pacific Coast & Lowlands

more geared toward Ecuadoreans looking for a quick, easy weekend or holiday spot than to foreign tourists in search of holiday bliss. The latter group generally uses the city's airport as a convenient gateway to beaches north and south of Manta.

Essentials

GETTING THERE

BY PLANE **Icaro** (© **1800/883-567** toll-free nationwide; www.icaro.aero), **Tame** (© **1800/500-800** toll-free in Ecuador, or 05/2626-833 in Manta; www.tame.com.ec), and **Aerogal** (© **888/723-7642** in the U.S. and Canada, or **1800/2376-425** toll-free in Ecuador; www.aerogal.com.ec) all have several daily flights into Manta's **Aeropuerto Eloy Alfaro** (© **05/2622-590;** www.aeropuertomanta.com; airport code: MEC). There are somewhat fewer flights on weekends, particularly on Saturdays—the schedule tends to fluctuate according to demand. The flight duration is 30 minutes, and fares run from $60 to $90 each way.

The Oro Verde and Howard Johnson Manta hotels both have free shuttles awaiting every flight. There are also taxis on hand when flights land. A taxi ride into town should cost around $5.

BY BUS Buses leave from Quito's southbound Terminal Terrestre Quitumbe (℗ 02/3988-200) for Manta roughly every hour between 6:30am and 10:30pm. The two main companies plying this route are **Cooperativo Carlos Alberto Aray** (℗ 02/3988-257 in Quito, or 05/2620-877 in Manta) and **Cooperativo Reina del Camino** (℗ 02/3988-256 in Quito, or 05/2620-963 in Manta). The ride takes around 7 to 8 hours, and the fare runs from $7 to $9. The return buses leave on roughly the same schedule. There is also regular bus service between Manta and Ambato, Guayaquil, Puerto López, and Esmeraldas.

The main **bus terminal** in Manta is just north of the Tarqui bridge, 1 block in from the Malecón, on Avenida 8 and Calle 7, behind the Banco Central building.

BY CAR To reach Manta by car from Quito, start off heading south on the Pan-American Highway (E35) until the intersection at Aloag. From here, head west on E30 toward Santo Domingo de los Colorados. The quickest and best route is to continue on to Chone, Portoviejo, and finally Montecristi. In Montecristi, you will connect with E9 for the last few kilometers to Manta. The drive takes around 7 hours.

If you're driving from Guayaquil, take Hwy. E21 north out of town to the intersection with E9 north, near the town of Nobol. From here, it's a straight shot on E9 into Manta. The drive takes around 3½ hours.

GETTING AROUND

You can rent a car in Manta at **Avis** (℗ 05/2622-434 or 08/7271-179; www.avis. com), at the Centro Comercial Cocomanta on the Circunvalación; or **Budget** (℗ 05/2629-919; www.budget-ec.com), on the Malecón between calles 16 and 17. Rates run around $45 to $125 per day, including unlimited mileage and insurance.

Taxis are plentiful in Manta and constantly cruise Avenida Malecón. If you can't flag one down, call **Radio Taxi Manta** (℗ 05/2625-424) or **Seguitaxi** (℗ 05/2628-215). A ride around downtown should cost just $1. A ride from downtown to the Howard Johnson should run around $3 to $5.

ORIENTATION

The city of Manta is basically divided in two by the mellow Río Manta. The eastern half is usually described as Tarqui, as it is fronted by Playa de Tarqui (Tarqui Beach). This half of the city is predominantly residential and industrial. The western half is far more developed and of far more interest to tourists, with most of the city's hotels, restaurants, shops, and businesses. Some folks call this half Murciélago, after the main beach here, Playa Murciélago.

The seafront Avenida Malecón is the defining avenue in Manta. It hugs the coastline and runs roughly east to west, from Playa de Tarqui, over a small bridge to Bahía de Manta (Manta Harbor) and Playa Murciélago. Just beyond Hotel Oro Verde, this avenue jogs inland slightly and becomes Avenida Flavio Reyes, which continues on toward Playa de Barbasquillo and the Howard Johnson hotel. Almost everything of interest to tourists is located either on the Malecón or Avenida Flavio Reyes. The airport is located about 15 minutes east of Playa de Tarqui.

VISITOR INFORMATION

You'll find a **tourist information office** (℗ 05/2610-171; i-tur@manta.gov.ec) in the town hall, or *edificio municipal*, on Calle 9 and Avenida 4 close to the bus station. They usually have an English speaker on hand and can offer good recommendations; they'll also give you a local map. There's another, smaller tourist information office (℗ 05/2624-099) at the bottom of the steps that lead down to Malecón Esenico.

Manta

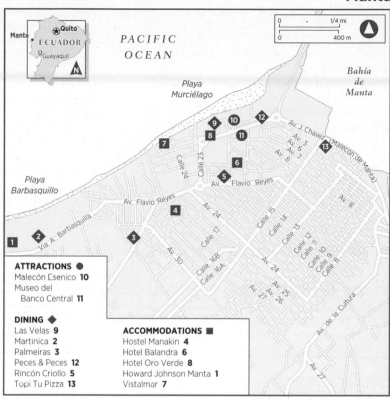

PACIFIC OCEAN

Bahía de Manta

Playa Murciélago

Playa Barbasquillo

ATTRACTIONS ●
Malecón Esenico **10**
Museo del
   Banco Central **11**

DINING ◆
Las Velas **9**
Martinica **2**
Palmeiras **3**
Peces & Peces **12**
Rincón Criollo **5**
Topi Tu Pizza **13**

ACCOMMODATIONS ■
Hostel Manakin **4**
Hotel Balandra **6**
Hotel Oro Verde **8**
Howard Johnson Manta **1**
Vistalmar **7**

This one is run by Universidad Laica Eloy Alfaro and is much less organized and useful. Your best bet for local insight and tour information is the tour desk at your hotel or the local branches of **Metropolitan Touring ★★** (☎ **888/572-0166** in the U.S. and Canada, or 02/2988-200 in Ecuador; www.metropolitan-touring.com), which has its main offices at Av. 4 1239, between calles 12 and 13. These folks are the largest tour operator in Ecuador and offer a wide range of tours and activities around Manta and all along the Pacific coast. They also have another office in the small strip mall fronting the Howard Johnson hotel.

FAST FACTS   To contact the local **police,** dial ☎ **05/2920-900** or 101. In an emergency, call **Cruz Roja** (**Red Cross;** ☎ **05/2624-212**) or head to **Hospital Rodriguez Zambrano** (☎ **05/2625-610**), on Calle 16.

There are loads of banks and ATMs all over Manta. You'll find branches of **Banco Pichincha** (☎ **05/2626-844**), on Avenida 2, between calles 11 and 12; and **Banco Bolivariano** (☎ **05/2620-504**), on Malecón Jaime Chávez Gutiérrez, next to the CAE building. The **post office** (☎ **05/2624-402**) is on the corner of Avenida 4 and Calle 8.

Most of the hotels in town, and a bunch of storefront Internet cafes, offer Internet access. Rates run around 50¢ to $1.50 per hour.

THE MANTA airbase

Since its inception, Manta's Eloy Alfaro Air Base and the presence of U.S. military forces there have been the focus of dispute and controversy. In 1999, when Ecuadorean President Jamil Mahuad announced that he would allow the United States to operate at the base, some Ecuadoreans argued that it would be an enormous affront to their country's sovereignty. Despite those protests, a 10-year lease agreement was finalized between the United States and Ecuador. During this time period, the base was used by the U.S. Air Force for operations against illegal drug trafficking in northwestern South America. Some 300 U.S. soldiers and airmen were stationed at the base at any one time. The effects this military presence was felt in the bars, restaurants, shops, and casinos of Manta. Some complained that the base led to an increase in local crime, prostitution, and drug use. However, the base was expanded and granted a civilian component in the form of Manta's **Aeropuerto Eloy Afaro.**

However, all of this is moot today. When the lease expired in 2009, the Ecuadorian government refused to renew it. Today the Manta base is one of five primary Ecuadorean Air Force air bases, and all U.S. military forces have been pulled from the country.

What to See & Do in & Around Manta

Besides the beaches and beachfront promenades, and the activities they offer, there are very few attractions in Manta. The two main beaches in Manta are **Playa de Tarqui ★** and **Playa Murciélago.** Of these, Playa Murciélago is much better suited for those looking to do some sunbathing and swimming, or to join a pickup game of beach volleyball or beach soccer. Most of Playa Murciélago is lined with a beachfront promenade called the **Malecón Escenico,** which features a concrete walkway lined with open-air restaurants and souvenir stands. There's even a climbing wall at the western end of the Malecón Escenico. You can rent a chaise lounge and shade umbrella on the sand at Playa Murciélago ($4–$6 per day).

Playa de Tarqui is, in many ways, a more atmospheric beach, where fishermen and boat builders still ply their trade. Of particular interest is the makeshift, **open-air boatyard ★★** right on the beach just east of Río Manta; here you can watch as massive wooden commercial-fishing trawlers are built by skilled artisans. Be careful of any valuables in this area, and avoid the Tarqui Malecón at night, which can be dangerous. If you walk a mile or farther east along the beach, you can also find some beautiful and deserted patches of sand for sunbathing and swimming.

West from Playa Murciélago is **Playa Barbasquillo,** which is much less developed, although it's very rocky in places, with uninspiring brown sand in others.

If it's raining or you want a small dose of culture, head to **Museo Arqueologico del Banco Central** (© 05/2626-998), on Avenida Malecón between calles 19 and 20. The small museum features a collection of pre-Columbian indigenous artifacts from the various tribes of the Manabí coast. It's open Tuesday through Saturday from 9am to 5pm, and Sunday from 11am to 3pm. Admission is $1.

Perhaps the most popular side trip out of Manta is a visit to the "Panama hat" weavers and shops in nearby **Montecristi ★**. The misnamed Panama hat is actually native to Ecuador. In a calculated move, much of the massive manufacture of these headpieces has shifted to Cuenca. Thirty years ago, there were over 2,000 hat weavers in and around Montecristi; today that number has dwindled to fewer than 50. But hats woven in Montecristi are still widely considered the best and most authentic in the country. For more information on Panama hats, see p. 205. Montecristi is located just 16km (10 miles) south of Manta. You can rent a car (see above) or sign on for a guided tour at any of the hotels in town. In Montecristi, stop at **Manufactura de Sombreros de Paja Toquilla** (✆ **09/7016-515**), on Calle 9 de Julio, the town's main street. This place has a great selection and will take you through the entire process of making one of these hats. Another good hat shop is **Modesto Hats** (✆ **09/7263-357**), on Calle 9 de Julio and Olmedo. You'll find these hats for sale in Manta, but if you want a wider selection, higher quality, and better price, it's worth a trip to Montecristi.

If you want to head farther afield, most hotel tour desks and tour operators in Manta also offer trips to **Machalilla National Park, Isla de la Plata,** and **Puerto López,** especially during whale-watching season. See chapter 9 for more information on these destinations.

Where to Stay in Manta

EXPENSIVE

Hotel Balandra ★ ☺   Although it's a couple of blocks inland from the beach, this is still one of Manta's better hotels. There's a cozy feel to the whole complex. The rooms are housed in a series of two- and three-story units. Each has a small balcony or porch. Most of the rooms feature at least one wall of exposed brick and a small sitting area with a couch. A few have kitchenettes and several bedrooms, making them good options for families. A plus for those traveling with children is the hotel's small playground area, as well as its basketball court and game room with a Ping-Pong table and other distractions. The **restaurant,** which serves good international fare, has three separate seating areas, including a beautiful outdoor terrace with views of the ocean.

Av. 7 y Calle 20, Barrio Córdova, Manta. www.hotelbalandra.com. ✆ **05/2620-545.** 31 units. $101 double; $201 *cabaña* for up to 5 people. Rates include full breakfast and taxes. DC, MC, V. **Amenities:** Restaurant; bar; small gym; small outdoor pool; room service; sauna. *In room:* A/C, TV, minibar, free Wi-Fi.

Hotel Oro Verde ★   This is the top resort hotel in Manta, and it's often booked solid. The main building forms a sort of horseshoe around the pool and faces the beach. The rooms are everything you could want in this type of hotel, with plenty of space, cool tile floors, and plenty of amenities. Every room includes a private balcony

No Hippies in These Hills

Even though the town of Jipijapa is pronounced "Hippy-Happa," don't come here expecting to find the ghosts of Abbie Hoffman or Janis Joplin. Despite its lyrical and suggestive name, this dusty roadside town south of Manta, on the highway to Guayaquil, offers little of interest to tourists. However, decades ago, Jipijapa rivaled Montecristi in the production of Panama hats. If you ask around, you might still be able to find a local artisan crafting one of these Toquilla palm hats.

with an ocean view. I actually prefer the standard rooms and junior suites over the Grand Suites, which are in a separate wing. While the latter rooms have more square footage and a kitchenette, they have diminished views—in fact, some of the Grand Suites have no ocean view at all. The Oro Verde has several **restaurant options,** including a sushi bar, as well as the city's top casino. The pool is the center of activity here, and there's a separate children's pool, with a neighboring playground.

Malecón y Calle 23, Manta. www.oroverdehotels.com. ✆ **05/2629-200.** Fax 05/2629-210. 81 units. $110 double; $140 junior suite; $170 grand suite; $250 master suite. Rates include buffet breakfast. AE, DC, MC, V. **Amenities:** 3 restaurants; 2 bars; casino; small, well-equipped gym; Jacuzzi; midsize outdoor pool; room service; sauna; free Wi-Fi. In room: A/C, minibar, TV.

Howard Johnson Manta ★★   I find the rooms and facilities here slightly more appealing than those at the Oro Verde. The hotel is right on the ocean's edge, but the beach here is rocky and not very apt for bathing, although a short walk gets you to some soft sand. The rooms are simply furnished, and some might find them a bit too austere, but I like the bright white-tile floors, white walls, and sleek beds and bureaus. Most rooms have good-sized balconies fronting the sea, and those on the higher floors have better views. Because the hotel is built into and descending down a steep hillside, the higher-floor rooms are actually closer to the lobby and restaurants. Be sure to specify you want an oceanview room. The small, modern gym has a wall of windows overlooking the sea.

Km 1.5, Vía Barbasquillo, Manta. www.ghlhoteles.com. ✆ **05/2629-999.** Fax 05/2629-989. 100 units. $110–$122 double; $124–$146 junior suite. Rates include buffet breakfast. AE, DC, MC, V. **Amenities:** 3 restaurants; 2 bars; casino; small, well-equipped gym; small outdoor pool; room service; lit outdoor tennis court; free Wi-Fi. In room: A/C, TV, free Internet; minibar.

MODERATE

Vistalmar ★★ 📖   This boutique hotel is my top choice in Manta. As you come through the entrance gate, you pass two large jade-covered horses and walk beside a pretty pond with a double Buddha fountain. The rooms and two-bedroom *cabañas* are all distinctively designed and decorated. I prefer the rooms, which share a second-floor veranda overlooking the sea. Each has one queen-size four-poster bamboo bed under mosquito netting and an exposed thatch roof, and is decorated with an eclectic mix of African and Asian art and crafts. The three *cabañas* are much more minimalist in style. Each has a sitting room and kitchenette, making them perfect for families. The small pool here is built along a steep cliff and features an infinity effect that makes it appear to blend in with the sea. A path leads down to Playa Murciélago.

Calle M-1 y Av. 24, Manta. www.hosteriavistaalmar.com. ✆ **05/2621-671.** 5 units. $70–$85 double; $75–$90 2-bedroom *cabaña;* $90–$110 deluxe suite. Rates include full breakfast. MC, V. **Amenities:** Lounge; small outdoor pool. In room: A/C, TV.

INEXPENSIVE

Hostel Manakin 🏷   There are plenty of real budget options in Manta, but most are run-down and ragged. Housed in a converted home in a residential neighborhood just a few blocks from the sea, this place is friendly, secure, and stylish. Rooms are simple yet sleek, with subdued colors on the walls offset by bright bedspreads with eye-popping geometric patterns. The common areas are very inviting and include an indoor lounge area, an outdoor garden patio, and a simple Ecuadorean restaurant.

Calle 20 y Av. 12, Manta. hostalmanakin@yahoo.com. ✆ **05/2620-413.** 9 units. $55 double. Rates include full breakfast and taxes. AE, DC, MC, V. **Amenities:** Restaurant. In room: A/C, TV, free Wi-Fi.

A Beach Retreat Just South of Manta

El Faro Escandinavio ★★ 🏠   Located in the tiny fishing village of San Lorenzo, this boutique hotel fronts a beautiful and mostly deserted stretch of beach. The eight individual bungalows are simple yet stylish, with minimalist decor, firm beds, and contemporary bathrooms. Each features a unique print by the famed artist and mime Marcel Marceau. Meals are served in the main house, where you'll also find a library, television, and large ocean-facing deck. There's a small lighthouse *(faro)* on the property, and your Norwegian/Ecuadorean hosts, Nilsen and Napo, will make sure you are well cared for during your stay.

San Lorenzo, Manabi. (San Lorenzo is located on the coastal hwy., 27km/17 miles south of Manta). www. elfaroescandinavo.com. ✆ **09/1122-336.** 8 units. $159 double. Rates include full breakfast and taxes. AE, DC, MC, V. **Amenities:** Restaurant; pool; free Wi-Fi. *In room:* A/C.

Where to Dine in Manta

In addition to the more formal restaurants listed below, you really can't go wrong at any of the open-air seafood joints that line Malecón Esenico on Playa Murciélago. All have a menu of *ceviches,* fish, shrimp, lobster, and mixed seafood plates for around $3 to $6. Of these, **Las Velas ★** (✆ **05/2629-396**), toward the western end of the strip, is my favorite, with pretty patio tables under broad canvas umbrellas. Another good option, toward the eastern end of the walkway, is **Peces & Peces** (✆ **05/2623-574**). For Ecuadorean fare and local seafood, consider **Rincón Criollo** (✆ **05/2623-183**), on Avenida Flavio Reyes and Calle 20.

Martinica ★★ INTERNATIONAL/SEAFOOD   Arty decor, attentive service, and a creative kitchen all add up to make this the top dining option in Manta. Housed in a converted home, the Martinica is far more creative and contemporary than anything else in town. Steaks and lamb are imported, and seafood options include lightly seared tuna and a carpaccio of the locally renowned Spondylus mollusk. The wine list here is fairly extensive, with good choices from Spain, Italy, Argentina, and Chile.

1 block before the Howard Johnson's (see above), Ciudela Umiña, Manta. ✆ **05/2613-735.** Reservations recommended. Main courses $7–$19. MC, V. Mon–Sat 12:30pm–midnight.

Palmeiras ★ INTERNATIONAL/STEAKHOUSE   Popular with locals and the university crowd, this place features a cool and funky open-air setting, with a stone patio floor; hanging wind chimes; and palms, ficus, and other lush tropical plants and flowers. The tables and chairs are plastic lawn furniture, although the tables do have faded tablecloths and glass-enclosed candles. The centerpiece of the menu, and of the restaurant itself, is the large, open wood-fired grill. The menu features grilled meats, poultry, fish, and seafood. You can get a whole grilled fish or a mixed seafood-and-meat platter. Portions are huge. I usually do just fine with a half-*cherna* (amberjack). The menu also features such varied options as quail breasts and pizzas.

Vía Circunvalación y Av. 29, Manta. ✆ **05/2628-637.** Main courses $5–$22. AE, DC, MC, V. Tues–Sun 4:30pm–2am.

Topi Tu Pizza ITALIAN/PIZZA   Head for the second floor of this lively open-air bar and restaurant. The tables overlook a busy roundabout on Avenida Malecón, but if you look beyond this, you'll have a view of the equally busy harbor. The pizzas here have a pretty cardboard-tasting crust, but they come with a wide range of toppings and are affordable. You can also get some simple pastas, as well as more substantial steaks and seafood dishes. I think the barbeque ribs, grilled steaks, and fresh grilled local catch are your best bets.

Av. Malecón y Calle 15. ℰ**05/2621-180** or 08/8810-791. topimanta@hotmail. Main courses $4–$22. MC, V. Daily 11:30am–1am.

Manta After Dark

Thanks to the city's steady and healthy local tourism industry, Manta actually has a relatively vibrant bar and club scene. The best and most popular bar and dance club in town is **Madera Fina** (ℰ 05/2626-573), on Avenida Flavio Reyes and Avenida 23. **West End ★** (ℰ 05/2621-587), on Avenida Flavio Reyes, and **Bar Budo ★★** (ℰ 05/2624-733), on Avenida Flavio Reyes and Calle 21, are two other popular clubs. For a more mellow night out, head to Malecón Esenico and grab a seat at one of the many outdoor restaurants and bars there.

If you want to try your luck at some gambling, head to the **Fantasy Casino** (ℰ 05/2629-444), at Hotel Oro Verde. This is a big, modern, glitzy casino with all the tables, games, and machines you could want. There's also the flashy **Casino del Mar ★** (ℰ 05/2611-440; www.casinodelmar.com), in the small strip mall attached to the Howard Johnson hotel.

Heading North: An Isolated Beach Getaway

The road north from Manta to Bahía de Caráquez passes a series of small, isolated beach towns, which get by on small-scale fishing much more than on tourism. Still, if you really want to get away from it all, and have a car or driver of your own, this might be right up your alley. The first major beach north is **San Jacinto,** which is precious little more than a few houses on either side of the highway. But **Hotel San Jacinto** (ℰ 05/2615-516; www.hotelsanjacinto.com) is an interesting option, in a worn old building with a pool, restaurant, and weekend disco, not to mention a perfect location right on the beach.

North of San Jacinto lies **San Clemente,** which is home to the hotel listed below. In addition, when the tide is low, you can actually drive directly on the sandy beach from San Clemente almost all the way to Bahía de Caráquez, cutting many kilometers and quite some time, off your trip. Most locals use this route, and even some of the bus companies take advantage of the savings in time and distance. You probably shouldn't try this on your own because the "exits" off the beach aren't marked, but ask around town, or flag down someone who is beginning this route and ask to follow him or her.

Palmazul ★★ 🛎 Set on a pretty stretch of sand on the remote beach of San Clemente, Palmazul is probably my favorite beach hotel in Ecuador. Each room faces the ocean and features a full wall of windows and sliding glass doors letting out onto a private balcony. The large pool features spacious deck areas and a range of chaise lounges and cozy beds all around. The food at the Cocomar restaurant here is excellent, and you'll find a range of treatments and massage therapies offered at their in-house spa. San Clemente is located about 40 minutes drive north of Manta and 20 minutes south of Bahía de Caráquez.

San Clemente, Manabi. www.manabihotel.com. ℰ**05/2615-018** or 09/8247-454. 22 units. $117 double. Rates include full breakfast. AE, DC, MC, V. **Amenities:** Restaurant; bar; large outdoor pool; small spa; free Wi-Fi. *In room:* A/C, no phone.

BAHIA DE CARAQUEZ ★

340km (211 miles) W of Quito; 280km (174 miles) NW of Guayaquil; 120km (74 miles) N of Manta

Known simply as Bahía, or "the Bay," this quiet little port city is one of the safest, friendliest, and homiest spots in Ecuador. It's located at the mouth of the Río Chone, whose shifting bottoms and shallow channel have limited Bahía's usefulness as a port, while saving it from the woes that often accompany heavy industry and commercial shipping. In addition, a whole host of tours and adventures can be organized out of Bahía, ranging from bird-watching to boating, to visiting an archaeological site.

In 1999, Bahía declared itself an "Eco-City," and efforts to promote recycling, conservation, and environmental awareness were instituted by a combination of local and outside actors.

Essentials

GETTING THERE

BY PLANE   There is a small airport in San Vicente, **Aeropuerto Los Perales** (✆ 05/2674-042), just across the bay from Bahía. There are occasional charter flights into San Vicente, but the nearest commercial airport is Manta (p. 265), which is connected to Bahía by regular bus traffic.

BY BUS   Cooperativa Reina del Camino (✆ 02/3824-875 in Quito, or 05/2695-818 in Manabí province) has three buses daily between Quito and Bahía, at 10am, and 1 and 11:30pm, leaving from either Terminal Terrestre Quitumbe or the private bus depot on 18 de Septiembre and Manuel Larrea. The ride takes between 8 and 9 hours, and costs $9.20.

There's much more frequent bus service between Guayaquil and Bahía, with buses leaving roughly every 2 hours around the clock. Both **Cooperativa Reina del Camino** (✆ 04/2130-757 in Guayaquil) and **Coactar** (✆ 04/2130-078 in Guayaquil, or 05/2690-014 in Bahía) do this route. The 6-hour ride costs $6 to $8. There is also regular bus service connecting Bahía and Portoviejo and Manta.

The main bus terminal is located about 6km (3¾ miles) outside central Bahía. Taxis are always waiting for arriving passengers, and there's regular city bus service to the center of town as well.

BY CAR   To reach Bahía by car from Quito, start off heading south on the Pan-American Highway (E35) until the intersection at Aloag. From here, head west on E30 toward Santo Domingo de los Colorados, and then go on to Chone. In Chone, there's a well-marked turnoff for the road to Bahía. The ride should take around 6 to 7 hours.

GETTING AROUND

BY TAXI   Taxis are abundant in Bahía, though largely unnecessary if you are sticking closely to the downtown and Malecón area. There are actually two types of taxis to choose from: traditional car cabs, and what the locals call "ecotaxis," which are bicycle-powered rickshaw-type contraptions, with the driver pedaling behind a small sitting area with two wheels on either side. There's a two-person maximum in the ecotaxis. A normal cab ride anywhere around town will run you $1 to $2. The ecotaxis charge about half as much.

ORIENTATION

Bahía is a long, narrow city that follows the inner coast of the bay out to the end of a jutting peninsula. All along the bay shore and out to the peninsula's point is a sidewalk promenade, the Malecón. The peninsula runs roughly north-south, with the point located at the northern end, where there's a small lighthouse. A few small parks, the ferry docks, and the Repsol service station, all located on the Malecón and the 2 blocks inland from here, define the heart of downtown. At its widest, Bahía spans only 5 or 6 blocks. The central north-south avenue, located inland from the Malecón, is Avenida Bolívar, along which you'll find the town's greatest concentration of shops, banks, and other businesses.

FAST FACTS   The **post office** (✆ 05/2691-177) is on the Malecón at no. 1414 in the Centro Comercial Molina Jalil. The Ministry of Tourism maintains an **information desk** (✆ 05/2691-124) at Av. Bolívar 700 and Calle Mateus. There are several banks and ATMs in the small downtown area. The biggest and best of the bunch is **Banco de Guayaquil** (✆ 05/2692-205), at the corner of Avenida Bolívar and Calle Río Frío.

There are Internet cafes all around the center of Bahía.

What to See & Do in Bahía

My favorite thing to do in Bahía is walk around the quiet town and along the seafront Malecón. Be sure to stop in at the small Catholic church, inaugurated in 1906; it's made of zinc brought in from France. Several interesting tour and activity options are also available.

Museo Arqueológico del Banco Central (Central Bank Archaeological Museum) ★ (✆ 05/2690-817) is definitely worth a visit. Spread over three floors, the museum focuses on the history and archaeology of the coastal people of pre-Columbian Ecuador, although one large room is dedicated to modern art. Still, the heart and soul of the collection are relics and artifacts of the Las Vegas, Machalilla, Valdivia, Tolita, Bahía, and Jama peoples who inhabited this coast for centuries before the arrival of the Spanish. At the entrance lobby, you'll find a massive balsa raft, with a mast and mannequins, a replica of the way it's believed ancient rafts looked. The museum is open Tuesday through Saturday from 8:30am to 4:30pm. Admission is free.

You should also take a trip to **Mirador La Cruz** ★, a lookout located on a high hill directly behind the city. You can make the brisk hike up here in about 15 minutes, or you can grab a cab. You can see the giant cross that is the lookout's namesake from just about anywhere in town. The view is wonderful and really allows you to get a feel for the lay of the land and the bay.

The beaches right in and around Bahía are passable but unspectacular. Both to the north and south, however, you will find excellent beaches. Heading south, you'll come to the beaches of **Chirije** ★ (see below), **San Clemente,** and **San Jacinto,** which are really part of one very long stretch of almost deserted beach, broken up by the occasional rocky outcropping and small house or settlement. Heading north, you'll find a similar situation with the beaches of **San Vicente, Briceño,** and **Canoa** ★ (see below). Canoa can be easily reached by boat taxi and bus from Bahía. If you want to visit any other of these beaches, you'll have to hire a car or taxi. Be sure to bring some food and plenty of water and sunscreen, as there are very few restaurants or services.

If you want to get out on the water, check in with the folks at **Club Marina 69** (✆ 05/2691-057), who rent out small boats, sailboats, and jet skis ($40–$75 per hr.). They will also take you water-skiing or parasailing ($35), or, if you've got a group, they will tow you all behind a speedboat on a large, inflatable banana ($3 per person, minimum six people). Club Marina 69 is located on the Malecón, next to the Repsol gas station.

ACCOMMODATIONS ■
Casa Grande Boutique
  Guesthouse **1**
Hostal Coco Bongo **4**
La Piedra **2**

DINING ◆
Arena Bar **3**
Puerto Amistad **8**

ATTRACTIONS ●
Church **6**
Mirador La Cruz **7**
Museo Arqueológico del Banco
  Central (Central Bank
  Archaeological Museum) **5**

Bahía de Caráquez ✪ **Quito**
ECUADOR
○Guayaquil

PACIFIC OCEAN

Río Chone

ⓘ *Tourist Information*

Market ■

0   200 yds
0   200 m

Land-based tours center on bird- and wildlife-watching. Bird-watchers will want to take a trip to **Isla del Corazón,** located in the Río Chone estuary upstream from Bahía. Isla del Corazón is a large mangrove island with a raised wooden walkway and trail through the mangroves. A range of water birds can be spotted here, including a particularly healthy colony of frigate birds. The best way to visit Isla del Corazón is on a guided tour. Alternatively, boats can be hired near the docks in Bahía to tour these islands for around $12 to $15 per hour, though your captain and guide will most likely not speak English.

South of Bahía lies the archaeological site of **Chirije** ★. Although barely excavated, early indications are that Chirije was once a major indigenous settlement, and probably an important port and trading center. You can even stay at some simple beachfront cabins here (see below). To visit Chirije, you should sign up for a tour in town or contact the hotel listed below.

Local tour agencies **Bahía Dolphin Tours** ★ (ⓒ **09/9171-935;** www.bahia dolphintours.com) and **Guacamayo Tours** (ⓒ **05/2691-107;** www.guacamayotours. com) are both reputable and well run. Both offer a range of nature, adventure, and wildlife-viewing tours, as well as city tours.

10

THE NORTHERN PACIFIC COAST & LOWLANDS

Bahía de Caráquez

275

Guacamayo Tours also offers multiday participatory stays on its Río Muchacho organic farm, located up the coast from Bahía 10km (6¼ miles) north of Canoa. Bahía Dolphin Tours is the place to go if you want to take some surf lessons.

Bahía is not a shopper's paradise. Along the Malecón, you'll find a line of souvenir stands and kiosks that sell all sorts of trinkets, T-shirts, and arts and crafts. But the general selection and quality are rather lacking.

Where to Stay in Bahía

VERY EXPENSIVE

Casa Ceibo ★★ This classy boutique hotel is just a bit outside the center of the city and seems somewhat out of place in this sleepy port town. However, if you're looking for luxury in Bahía, this is your best bet. The large rooms feature wood floors, flatscreen televisions, and ample bathrooms equipped with Jacuzzi tubs. The large outdoor pool is ringed with plush, shade-covered lounges, and there's even a clay tennis court. Spa treatments are offered, and the food is excellent.

Km 5.5, Av. Sixto Duran Ballen, Bahía de Caráquez. www.casaceibo.com. ✆ 05/2399-399. 18 units. $400–$500 double; $600–$700 suite. Rates include full breakfast. AE, DC, MC, V. **Amenities:** Restaurant; bar; gym; outdoor pool; sauna; steam bath; outdoor tennis court. *In room:* A/C, TV/DVD, hair dryer, free Wi-Fi.

MODERATE

Casa Grande Boutique Guesthouse ★ Located in a converted home, this intimate bed-and-breakfast is a welcoming and homey option out on the northern end of the peninsula, right near the lighthouse. Rooms are large, with dark-stained wood floors and private bathrooms. In a backyard garden, which has a view of the ocean, there's a pretty free-form pool encircled by a broad brick deck, and the house is chock-full of excellent Ecuadorean artwork. A large, common second-floor balcony offers a good sea view. These folks also have a unique beach hotel down in Chirije (see below).

Av. Circunvalación Virgilio Ratti 606, Bahía de Caráquez. www.casagrandebahia.com. ✆ 09/9171-935 or 05/2690-257. 7 units. $70–$90 double. Rates include full breakfast. MC, V. **Amenities:** Lounge; bar; outdoor pool. *In room:* A/C, TV, no phone, free Wi-Fi.

La Piedra ★ ☺ The largest and fanciest hotel in town, La Piedra is located at the tip of the peninsula. The hotel is built in an open horseshoe around a midsize pool and deck area and fronts a narrow patch of beach. All the rooms—sparsely furnished—are spacious, with cool tile floors. I prefer those on the second story, with their high ceilings and slightly better views. Each room opens onto a shared veranda. The second-floor nos. 217 and 218, as well as room no. 302, are my favorites because each has a private seafront balcony. This is a good choice for families with kids, as it's the only true beachfront hotel in Bahía, and they also have a game room, pool table, and beach volleyball court.

Av. Circunvalación Virgilio Ratti 802, Bahía de Caráquez. www.hotellapiedra.com. ✆ 888/790-5264 in the U.S. and Canada, or 05/2690-780 in Bahía. Fax 05/2690-154. 42 units. $79 double; $97 junior suite. Rates include breakfast and taxes. AE, MC, V. **Amenities:** 2 restaurants; bar; free Wi-Fi. *In room:* A/C, TV.

INEXPENSIVE

Hostal Coco Bongo ✍ Located a block inland from the water, this is my top budget choice in Bahía. All the rooms are on the second story and feature wood floors and a variety of bed arrangements, although most have bunk beds. There's a large television in a common lounge area, as well as a shared balcony facing a small park and the bay. With its cheery *hostal* vibe, the Coco Bongo often has evening activities, which range from DVD movie nights to Latin dance and capoeira classes.

Malecón Alberto F. Santos 410 y Arenas, Bahía de Caráquez. www.cocobongohostal.com. © **08/5440-978.** 5 units. $25 double. Rates include taxes. No credit cards. **Amenities:** Lounge. *In room:* TV, no phone.

Where to Dine in Bahía

MODERATE

Puerto Amistad ★ INTERNATIONAL This is easily the best restaurant in Bahía. Set on a large open-air dock extending into the bay, Puerto Amistad, with its bamboo-and-thatch roof, is a cool and pleasant place to be, day or night. Options range from sandwiches and quesadillas to a number of main courses. The restaurant claims to have the best hamburgers in Ecuador, and they are pretty good, as are their grilled steaks. Still, I usually opt for one of their excellent fish and seafood platters. For a main course, I recommend the shrimp curry over white rice or the *filete a la Gloria,* a piece of fresh mahimahi in a caper sauce. There's a good wine list to go along with the extensive menu. Puerto Amistad caters to cruising sailors who anchor just off the dock and use the shore facilities. So in addition to being a great place to mingle with some water-worn old salts, you'll find a book exchange, laundry service, and free Wi-Fi.

Malecón Alberto F. Santos, south of the passenger ferry dock. © **05/2693-112.** Main courses $5–$10. DC, MC, V. Mon–Thurs noon–midnight; Fri–Sat noon–2am (Sun noon–midnight during holiday season).

INEXPENSIVE

Arena Bar ITALIAN/PIZZA I like the funky, eclectic vibe of this simple pizza joint. The pizzas are pretty good, with a medium-thin crust and a wide range of topping choices. You can also get pasta dishes and homemade lasagna. Vegetarians should try the vegetarian parmesan, which is excellent. There are a few tables out on the sidewalk and more inside two abutting dining rooms. Most of the tables are made of heavy cross-sections of tree trunks. The decor relies heavily on photo collages of celebrities, ranging from Madonna, Marilyn Monroe, and Andy Warhol to Julio Cortázar, Compay Segundo, and Che Guevara. There's also some original art and a wall of masks over the small bar area.

Av. Bolívar. © **05/2692-542.** Main courses $3–$7; large pizzas $8–$14. MC, V. Mon–Sat noon–2pm; daily 5pm–midnight.

Bahía After Dark

Bahía is definitely a quiet town after dark. When locals want to really party, they usually head up the coast to Canoa (see below).

If you want a pleasant couple of drinks in a beautiful setting, head to **Puerto Amistad** (see above), which has a beautiful setting out over the water. In addition to their **Sweet Home Alabama** bar area, which gets going on weekends, they've got a large-screen television that shows major sporting events.

A Remote Beach Hotel South of Bahía

Chirije 🎁 This small collection of rooms and *cabañas* sits just off the beach a few kilometers south of Bahía and is backed by a vast expanse of untouched tropical dry forest. Everything here is built with bamboo and thatch, and solar energy is used to heat the water and power some of the lights. The best rooms are the two A-frame units, which feature a sleeping loft and have a balcony and an ocean view. There's a small museum with some very interesting artifacts, as well as a display illustrating the process of archaeological digging in this area. The hotel's restaurant and bar overlook the sea. The restaurant features a huge tree trunk as its center support and serves fresh seafood and local fare. Kilometers of deserted beach run in either direction.

On the beach in Chirije, Manabí (mailing address: c/o Casa Grande, Av. Circunvalación Virgilio Ratti, Bahía de Caráquez). www.chirije.com. © **09/9171-935.** 4 units. $85 double. Rates include full breakfast, archaeological tour and transfer from Bahía. No credit cards. The best way to get here is to coordinate transportation with the hotel. You can drive here along the beach at low tide, and there is also a more circuitous inland route. No matter what, you need to reserve ahead. **Amenities:** Restaurant; bar. *In room:* No phone.

CANOA ★

359km (223 miles) W of Quito; 299km (185 miles) NW of Guayaquil; 19km (12 miles) N of San Vicente

Canoa is a long, straight stretch of salt-and-pepper-colored sand backed by a few dirt roads, which are packed with budget hotels, dimple restaurants, funky bars, and souvenir shops. Behind the town is a steep wall of low cliffs, with a high bluff on top. Parasailers and hang-gliders often use this bluff as a takeoff point for their flights. Surfers come to Canoa for the kilometers of uncrowded beach breaks.

Essentials

GETTING THERE

BY PLANE   There is a small airport in San Vicente, just 19km (12 miles) south of Canoa. There are occasional charter flights into San Vicente, but the nearest commercial airport is in Manta. See p. 265 for details.

BY BUS   There's no direct bus service to Canoa. You must first make your way to Bahía de Caráquez. See p. 273 for details. From Bahía, local buses make the run to Canoa roughly every half-hour between 6am and 9pm. The fare is 50¢ for the 30-minute ride.

BY CAR   To reach Canoa by car from Quito, start off heading south on the Pan-American Highway (E35) until the intersection at Aloag. From here, you will head west on E30 toward Santo Domingo de los Colorados, and then on to Chone. After about 24km (15 miles), there's a well-marked turnoff for the road to San Vicente and Canoa. The ride should take around 7½ hours.

GETTING AROUND

Everything in Canoa is within walking distance. There are always taxis around town, if you need a ride down to San Vicente, or to one of the hotels on the outskirts of town. If you can't flag one down, have your hotel call you a cab. The ride between San Vicente and Canoa costs around $5 or $6.

ORIENTATION

Canoa is a tiny beach town. The main highway between Bahía de Caráquez and the northern beaches of Esmeraldas runs parallel to the coastline and passes right through Canoa. Several dirt access roads run the 4 blocks through town, from the highway toward the sea. *Tip:* Canoa has few services. There are no banks, so if you need to exchange or withdraw money, do so in San Vicente or Bahía (see above). You'll find a couple of Internet cafes in town, and some of the hotels provide Internet connections as well.

What to See & Do in Canoa

Like Montañita to the south, Canoa has a good beach for surfing, and, in fact, I prefer Canoa's over Montañita's—it's a much longer beach, with far more peaks to choose from. When the waves are small, this is an excellent beach for beginning surfers. Several little stands and shops around town rent out surf and boogie boards, and if you ask around town you should even be able to find someone to give you lessons.

The bluff above and behind Canoa has become a popular take-off spot for hang-gliders and parasailers. The 150m (492-ft.) bluff, along with frequent updrafts and an expanse of deserted beach for a landing site, makes this one of the top spots of aerial soaring in Ecuador. Occasionally, you can find a local or visiting pilot with a tandem rig to take you for a ride. For good information on aerial sports in this region, or to set up a tour in advance, contact Mauricio at **Volando Ecuador** (© 02/2248-524 in Quito or 09/8571-144; www.volandoecuador.ec). Or simply ask around town or at your hotel, or head to Hotel Sol y Luna (see below).

To arrange surf lessons, board rentals, or any number of organized tour activities, check in with **Canoa Thrills** ★ (© 09/0336-870; www.canoathrills.com), which operates out of the Surf Shak restaurant, right on the beach. These folks offer a fun sea kayaking tour through some local cave formations.

Aside from surfing and technical airborne sports, there's not much to do in Canoa except for sunbathing, swimming, beachcombing, and lying in a hammock. Locals sometimes rent out horses for horseback rides along the beach. Look for them on the beach, or ask at your hotel.

Where to Stay in Canoa
MODERATE
Hotel Canoa's Wonderland ★   This beachfront hotel is your best bet if you're looking for something a tiny bit upscale in Canoa. All of the rooms come with air-conditioning or fans and televisions, and have oceanview balconies. Try to land one of the second-floor units closest to the ocean. There's a small pool and relaxing hammock area, as well as a pool table and a common TV room where movies are often shown.

Beachfront at Calle San Andrés, Canoa. www.hotelcanoaswonderland.com.ec. © 05/2616-363. 20 units. $50–$90 double. Rates include buffet breakfast and taxes. Rates higher during peak periods. DC, MC, V. **Amenities:** Restaurant; bar; free Wi-Fi. *In room:* AC, TV/DVD.

INEXPENSIVE
In addition to the places listed below, check out **Hostería Canoa** (© 05/2616-380; www.hosteriacanoa.com), a couple of kilometers from the town, which will set you back $43 for a double room, including breakfast plus taxes.

Hotel Bambú   This is the most popular budget hotel in town, and it's almost always packed to the gills with backpackers and surfers. Overflow traffic can pitch or rent a tent here, but I recommend trying to reserve a room in advance. Accommodations are rustic and show the effects of constant wear. The best feature here is the open-air restaurant and common area fronting the hotel and facing the sea. Tree-trunk tables are set in the sand under palm and sea-grape trees. There's also an area with hammocks and a beach volleyball court, as well as billiards and Ping-Pong tables. *A bonus:* These folks offer up a free drink for every bag of beach trash you collect.

On the northern end of the beach, Canoa. www.hotelbambuecuador.com. © 05/2616-370 or 09/9263-365. 17 units. $13 double with shared bathroom; $22–$25 double with private bathroom; $30 suite. DC, MC, V. **Amenities:** Restaurant; bar. *In room:* No phone.

Hotel La Vista 🏄 I like the thatch-and-heavy-timber construction of this beach-front hotel. Every room here has a balcony with a hammock. The choice room is the fourth-floor penthouse, which, thanks to the height, has the best view. Accommodations come with a variety of bed options, from several twins or bunk beds to queen-size beds for couples. Suites come with cable television and a small kitchen area with a fridge. Be sure to ask for a fan, because there's no air-conditioning, and not every room is equipped with a fan. The hotel has a restaurant, as well as a large sandy area in front with a thatch roof.

On the beach, near the center of town, Canoa. www.lavistacanoa.com. ✆ **09/2288-995.** 10 units. $24–$30 double; $40–$50 suite. DC, MC, V. **Amenities:** Restaurant; bar. *In room:* No phone.

Where to Dine in Canoa

In addition to the places listed below, you can get excellent and wide-ranging international fare at the beachfront **Shamrock Dance Bar** (✆ **09/7812-752**), and good bar food at the **Surf Shak** (✆ **09/7942-293**), which is also on the beachfront and offers up free Wi-Fi.

Café Flor ★ 🏄 INTERNATIONAL Café Flor's owners used to run a popular restaurant in Macas, but they have been happily settled here on the coast for a few years. The menu covers a lot of ground, from vegetarian burritos to thin-crust pizzas, with main courses ranging from garlic shrimp over rice to baked pork *pernil* served with two fried eggs on top. Breakfasts are excellent. You can get a shrimp, onion, and pepper omelet or homemade pancakes. Their fresh-baked banana bread is delicious, and I like to buy a few extra slices to have as snacks on the beach. When the weather is cool and dry enough, grab one of the tables outdoors in a sandy garden. The folks here also rent out a few budget rooms above the restaurant.

2 blocks inland, center of town. ✆ **08/2676-048.** http://cafeflorcanoa.blogspot.com. Main courses $3–$6. AE, DC, MC, V. Daily 8:30am–11:30pm.

Restaurante Costa Azul 🏄 SEAFOOD/ECUADOREAN There are lots of local restaurants serving seafood and Ecuadorean fare, but this is my favorite. The menu is quite long, with everything from steaks to pastas, but you should stick to the seafood. Start things off with mixed *ceviche* or fried calamari, and then inquire what's freshest. You can get lobster here—a great deal, at $9. This open-air, beachfront joint is set on a raised wooden deck with plastic lawn chairs and long wooden tables covered with clear plastic sheets over lace tablecloths.

On the beach road, center of town. ✆ **09/9633-141.** Main courses $2.50–$9. No credit cards. Daily 8am–9pm.

Canoa After Dark

Although there are no major clubs or discos, the surfers, backpackers, and Quito vacationers like to party here in Canoa. Most of the action centers on the few open-air bars near the center of town, which include **Coco Bar** (✆ **09/9574-189**), the **Surf Shak ★** (see above), and **Coco Loco** (✆ **08/7646-459**). Ask around town to find out what's going on, or simply walk until you find something that suits you. One place that regularly gets folks dancing is the **Shamrock Dance Bar,** which takes up two floors of a three-story building right on the beachfront in the center of town.

North Along the Coast: From Canoa to Esmeraldas

As you drive north along the coast from Bahía de Caráquez and Canoa toward Atacames and Esmeraldas, the lowland dry forest and scrub give way first to cattle ranches and farms, and then later to thick tropical rainforest and moist forests. The change is quite pronounced and, in fact, happens almost immediately as you pass the sign announcing the start of Esmeraldas province.

At Km 342 is **Pedernales,** a rather undeveloped and, at times, forlorn little beach town—though one that's on the rise. Relatively new highways make this the closest Pacific beach to Quito, by car or bus. Pedernales is a long, straight beach of salt-and-pepper-colored sand, which almost disappears at high tide. Like Atacames (see later in this chapter), the beach itself is strung with a line of simple, open-air thatch-roof restaurants and bars, and backed with a few low-end hostels and hotels. The town, located on a hill behind the beach, is a jumble of shops and businesses, with a busy central park that is fronted by an interesting modern church. If you decide to stay in Pedernales, I recommend **Hotel Mr. John** (© 05/2680-235), which fronts the beach and features many rooms with private balconies; or the newer **Royal Hotel** (© 05/2681-218), on the south of the beachfront, with air-conditioned rooms, Internet access, restaurant, and a swimming pool. For food, you'll definitely want to try the seafront **La Choza** (© 05/2680-388; joslive27@hotmail.com).

MOMPICHE

At Km 261, you'll find the entrance to **Mompiche ★**, which is a mile or so toward the sea from the highway. For decades, Mompiche was almost entirely the domain of a few savvy Ecuadoreans and surfers who came for the steady and almost always uncrowded left point break here. Today it is home to the country's first and only all-inclusive megaresort, the Royal Decameron Mompiche (see below). If you want to visit Mompiche and not stay at the Decameron, try the **Hostería Gabeal** (© 09/9696-543; mompiche_gabeal@hotmail.com), with doubles at $15 per person.

Royal Decameron Mompiche ★   This is Ecuador's only large-scale all-inclusive resort. It features several hundred clean, contemporary, spacious rooms; a host of dining options (predominantly buffet); and plenty of pools and a wide range of activity options. There's a nightly revue-style show and all-you-can-drink bars at nearly every turn. That said, the beach right in front of the hotel is small and rather unappealing, although they will ferry you over to a much better nearby beach on Portete island. My biggest gripe here is the cattle-car feel of the operation. Meal reservations at the a la carte restaurants open each day at 7am and book up quickly. Heavy charges are levied for lost keys or towels. And the staff could use a little work on their hospitality. Most visitors here fly in to Esmeraldas as part of a package. *Note:* It's more than a 2-hour drive from Esmeraldas to the resort.

Mompiche. www.decameron.com. © **02/6046-969** reservations office in Quito, or 06/2997 300 in Mompiche. Fax 02/6046-989. 282 units. $168–$305 double. Rates include food, drinks, a range of activities, and taxes. AE, DC, MC, V. **Amenities:** 4 restaurants; 6 bars; disco; babysitting; large health club; 5 free-form pools; smoke-free rooms; tennis court; watersports equipment. *In room:* A/C, TV, hair dryer, Wi-Fi for a fee.

ESMERALDAS

319km (198 miles) W of Quito; 472km (293 miles) N of Guayaquil; 185km (115 miles) W of Santo Domingo

When the Spanish first landed here in 1526, they were greeted by indigenous peoples wearing all manner of emerald jewelry and adornments, so they named the place Esmeraldas, meaning "emeralds." The local tribes never provided the Spaniards with much in the way of riches, and the conquistadors soon sought their fortunes elsewhere. Today Esmeraldas is the main port and transportation hub for this region and the capital of the province. It is also a major oil-processing and shipping point, with the completion of a Trans-Andean pipeline bringing in fresh crude from El Oriente.

And while there are scores of hotels and some decent beaches here, most visitors make a beeline to Atacames and its surrounding beaches, which are much, much nicer (see later in this chapter).

Still, if you're coming out to this neck of the woods, you'll almost certainly pass through Esmeraldas. Moreover, Esmeraldas serves as a good gateway for the very remote northernmost section of Ecuador's Pacific coast, which includes San Lorenzo and La Tolita.

Essentials

GETTING THERE

BY PLANE   Tame (© 1800/500-800 toll-free in Ecuador, or 06/2729-040 in Esmeraldas; www.tame.com.ec) has two daily flights Monday to Friday and one daily flight at weekends between Quito and Esmeraldas's **Aeropuerto General Rivadeneira** (© 06/2714-581; airport code: ESM). The schedule on these flights changes periodically, and departure times vary throughout the week, so it's always best to check current schedules while booking. Flight time is 30 minutes, with fares running from $50 to $75 each way.

Taxis meet all incoming flights. A taxi from the airport to Esmeraldas should run you around $10 to $15.

BY BUS   Several bus lines have regular daily service to Esmeraldas from Quito. Buses leave at least every hour from around 7am to 11:30pm. Bus lines running this route include **Trans Esmeraldas** (© 02/3824-791 at Quitumbe, and 02/2505-099 at their Santa María terminal) and **Transportes Occidentales** (© 02/2502-733 in Quito, or 06/2723-772 in Esmeraldas). About half of all the regular buses, from both lines, leave from Quito's **Terminal Terrestre Quitumbe** (© 02/3988-200), while the other half leave from private bus terminals run by each line. Trans Esmeraldas's private terminal is on Calle Santa María 870 and Avenida 9 de Octubre, while Transportes Occidentales is on 18 de Septiembre 954 and Versalles. The ride takes around 6 hours and costs $6 to $7. The buses in Esmeraldas all stop and leave from a variety of stops located within a 1-block radius of the town's main plaza.

There is also frequent bus service between Esmeraldas and Guayaquil, as well as periodic connections throughout the day between Esmeraldas and other major cities, including Manta, Ambato, and Santo Domingo.

BY CAR   To reach Esmeraldas by car from Quito, start off heading south on the Pan-American Highway (E35) until the intersection at Aloag. From here, head west on E30 toward Santo Domingo de los Colorados, and from there follow the well-marked highway (E25) straight into Esmeraldas. The ride should take a little over 5 hours.

ESMERALDAS: ECUADOR'S AFRICAN COdSL?

Though only about 3% of Ecuador's population trace their roots to Africa, 70% of the people in Esmeraldas province are Afro-Ecuadorean. Most of its inhabitants are the descendents of maroons—escaped slaves who lived in free communities.

Legend has it that the first Africans arrived in Esmeraldas in 1553, when a slave ship ran aground off the coast and the captives escaped. What is certain is that by the late 16th century, the area had a thriving maroon population that attracted a steady trickle of runaways from the gold mines and sugar plantations of Colombia. The Africans mixed with local Indians, who shared their knowledge of the region's flora and fauna, and established communities known as *palenques* along the main rivers and the coast, some of which were fortified to fend off Spanish attacks.

Though the maroon leaders maintained sporadic relations with colonial authorities in Quito, for the better part of the 17th century, Esmeraldas virtually operated as an independent state ruled by a series of Afro-Amerindian kings. The Spaniards referred to the region as La República de los Zambos, or "Zambo Republic," the term *zambo* being used to designate the offspring of an Indian and an African in the colonial caste system.

Though a few military campaigns made unsuccessful attempts to subdue the area, Esmeraldas's maroon communities lived in relative freedom and isolation for most of the colonial era, which allowed them to preserve a culture markedly different from that of the rest of Ecuador. It was one of dozens of areas in the Americas where escaped slaves managed to establish autonomous enclaves during the colonial era, but in terms of numbers and organization, Esmeraldas was one of the most important. It rivaled Palmares, a maroon kingdom near the Brazilian city of Bahía, which it took the Portuguese a century to subdue.

Just as the African traditions preserved in Palmares gave birth to the *samba* and *batucada,* Esmeraldas, too, has its traditional music, sometimes called *currulao.* This rhythmic style combines drums and marimbas—a xylophone-like instrument of African origin—and is usually accompanied by the gyrating hips of dancers, who are capable of shaking it for hours, despite the equatorial heat.

As it did in most of the world, the 20th century brought rapid change to Esmeraldas, eroding many of the region's traditions. Nevertheless, you can still get a taste of the province's African heritage by savoring an *encocado*—a coconut seafood stew—or by tracking down a bar with a band that plays *currulao.*

If you are coming from Manta or Bahía de Caráquez, I recommend taking the coastal road, which heads first to Jama and then to Pedernales, before continuing up the coast to Muisne, Atacames, and eventually Esmeraldas.

Esmeraldas is also connected by paved road to La Tola, Borbón, and San Lorenzo to the north. This paved road actually also hooks up with another paved road that loops around northern Ecuador, connecting San Lorenzo with Ibarra.

GETTING AROUND

Taxis are plentiful and inexpensive in and around Esmeraldas. Rides around town are just $1. A ride out to Las Palmas will cost around $2.50.

Frequent bus service connects Esmeraldas with Atacames and the beaches southwest down the coast. These buses leave from around the central plaza roughly every 20 minutes between 6am and 10pm. The direct buses to Atacames are the most frequent, although a dozen or more also continue on and stop in Sua, Same, Tonchigue, and Muisne. Some even continue on to Mompiche.

ORIENTATION

The center of Esmeraldas sits on the banks of the Río Esmeraldas, a few miles from the beach. A Catholic church faces the city's main central park, and 1 block east of this is the city's Malecón, which runs along the river. Most of the banks, shops, and services are located within a 2-block radius of this central park. The **Las Palmas** beach area, 3.2km (2 miles) north of the town center, is reached by heading out Avenida Bolívar.

FAST FACTS   There's a **tourist information office** (℗ 06/2714-528; www. turismoesmeraldas.com) on Av. Bolívar 221, between Calle Mejía and Calle Salinas. It is open Monday through Friday from 9am to 5pm. **Banco Pichincha** (℗ **06/2728-741**) has a branch in downtown Esmeraldas, as well as one out in Las Palmas. Both have 24-hour cash machines.

Hospital Delfina Torres (℗ 06/2713-216) is on Avenida Libertad and Manabi. The **post office** (℗ **06/2726-834**) is on Av. Colón 1811, between avs. 10 de Agosto and 9 de Octubre. The main **police station** is on the corner of Avenida Bolívar and Calle Cañizares, or call ℗ **101** in an emergency. You'll find Internet cafes all over downtown and in Las Palmas.

What to See & Do in Esmeraldas

The main attraction in town is **Museo de Arqueología Regional (Museum of Regional Archaeology;** ℗ 06/2727-078; free admission; Mon–Fri 9am–4:30pm). Housed in the Centro Cultural Esmeraldas (Esmeraldas Cultural Center), which also has a small library, bookshop, and gift store, this modern museum's collection features over 500 pieces of ceramic, bone, gold, and iron. There's a good selection of pieces from the La Tolita indigenous group.

The main beach area of Esmeraldas proper is **Las Palmas,** located 3.2km (2 miles) north of town. The beach is a long, broad stretch of brown sand, which usually has gentle waves and is good for swimming. The seaside Malecón here is packed with simple open-air restaurants and bars. During Esmeraldas's annual Carnaval, which celebrates the town's Afro-Ecuadorean heritage, Las Palmas is ground zero for some impressive revelry. Each year the celebrations coincide with the locally produced **Festival Internacional de Música y Danza Afro (International Festival of African Music and Dance),** and feature dancing in the streets, organized parades, and marimba band competitions. As with other Carnaval and Mardi Gras celebrations around the world, Esmeraldas's Carnaval occurs each year in the period prior to Lent.

If you want to do any organized tours, check in with your hotel desk or contact **Delgado Travel** (℗ 06/2723-723; www.delgadotravelsa.com), Calle Sucre 627 and Calle Cañizares, a large national tour agency. Possible tours include sport fishing, whale- and dolphin-watching, and visits to La Tolita (see below) and the mangrove forests of the Cayapas Mataje Ecological Reserve.

Where to Stay in Esmeraldas

Aparthotel Esmeraldas This high-rise (five stories) downtown hotel gives you plenty of space, comfort, and amenities for the price. The rooms are almost stylish, with shiny tile floors and modern furnishings. Overall, it's probably the plushest option in town, but that is definitely not saying much. Located several blocks north of the central park, the Aparthotel Esmeraldas is popular with businesspeople.

Av. Libertad 407 y Ramón Tello, Esmeraldas. www.aparthotelesmeraldas.net. ℂ **06/2728-700.** ℂ/fax 06/2728-704. 44 units. $55 double; $87 suite. Rates include breakfast and taxes. DC, MC, V. **Amenities:** Restaurant; bar; room service; free Wi-Fi. *In room:* A/C, TV, minibar.

El Cisne ✦ This is a clean, dependable, and safe bet right in the heart of Esmeraldas. The rooms are decidedly simple and could use a bit more decoration and style, but they'll definitely do for a night or two. The restaurant serves good Ecuadorean cuisine and local specialties. El Cisne is located just a block and a half from the main plaza, close to a host of restaurants, shops, and bus stops.

Av. 10 de Agosto 416, btw. Olmedo and Colón, Esmeraldas. www.hotel-elcisne.com. ℂ **06/2721-588.** ℂ/fax 06/2723-411. 35 units. $24 double. No credit cards. **Amenities:** Restaurant; bar. *In room:* No phone.

Hotel Cayapas Because I'd almost always rather stay at the beach than in town, this is my top choice in Esmeraldas. It's in Las Palmas, right on the beachfront, and the rooms here are cheerful and well appointed. They even have a pretty little garden in back. The hotel's restaurant is very good, with excellent seafood and local specialties.

Av. Kennedy 100 y Valdéz, Las Palmas, Esmeraldas. www.hotelcayapas.com. ℂ **06/2721-318.** Fax 06/2721-319. 30 units. $35 double. Rates include breakfast and taxes. DC, MC, V. **Amenities:** Restaurant; bar. *In room:* A/C, TV.

Where to Dine in Esmeraldas

The food in Esmeraldas province is distinct. Making ample use of the fresh seafood and other local ingredients, including coconuts, it is more like Caribbean cuisine than typical Ecuadorean fare. Local dishes include *encocado* (seafood in a slightly spiced coconut-milk broth), *empanadas de verde* (fried stuffed patties made with a plantain crust), and *tapao* (a fish and plantain stew).

Las Redes SEAFOOD/ECUADOREAN   Facing the main plaza and church, this popular downtown joint can get packed, especially midweek when local workers and businesspeople come for the daily *plato ejecutivo,* a three course lunch for around $2. The seafood and local fare are top-notch here. Try the *encocado de camarones* (shrimp in a coconut-milk broth).

Av. Bolívar, fronting the main plaza. ℂ **06/2723-151.** Main courses $2–$10. MC, V. Daily 7am–10pm.

Nuevo Amanecer SEAFOOD/ECUADOREAN   This casual place fronts the beach in Las Palmas and has an extensive menu of seafood dishes, including a wide range of *ceviches.* However, you can also get a thick steak or a chicken breast grilled over an open flame. But I recommend that you stick with the seafood. The *tapao* (fish and plantain stew) here is excellent.

Malecón, Las Palmas. ℂ **06/2725-339.** Main courses $3–$11. DC, MC, V. Daily 8am–9pm.

Esmeraldas After Dark

If you stay in the city itself, I recommend sticking very close to the bars, clubs, and restaurants around the central plaza. Esmeraldas has a reputation of being somewhat unsafe after dark. Single women should take particular caution. **Bar Asia,** on Avenida Bolívar near the main plaza, is a good option. If you're feeling lucky, you can always head to the casino at the **Aparthotel Esmeraldas** (see above).

The best nightlife to be had in the vicinity is on the beach in **Las Palmas.** Your best bet is to simply walk the Malecón here and stop into a few of the many open-air beachfront bars. However, be careful, because this area can also get dodgy at night. Stick to well-worn and well-lit areas, and don't go wandering on the beach at night.

North from Esmeraldas: San Lorenzo & La Tolita

Heading north from Esmeraldas, the vegetation and terrain turn quickly from forest and pastureland to an immense area of mangroves, rivers, and canals. The main town up here is **San Lorenzo,** an Afro-Ecuadorean city that feels a world apart from the rest of the country. San Lorenzo was once connected by railroad to Ibarra, but the train no longer runs all the way to San Lorenzo, and a road has been built to take its place.

There aren't many recommended places to stay in San Lorenzo. The surest bet in town is the **Gran Hotel San Carlos,** calles Imbabura and Juan José Flores (© 06/2780-284), which offers acceptable rooms—some that even have air-conditioning and televisions at around $20 for a double room.

One of the most unique places to visit in Ecuador is situated on a small island in the midst of mangrove forests outside San Lorenzo. **La Tolita** ★ is an archaeological site, believed to be the remnants of one of the oldest pre-Columbian cultures in Ecuador. The people here smelted and worked with platinum, silver, and gold. It's not clear if La Tolita was a residential site or a purely ceremonial one. *Tola* is the word for a small, elevated mound or grave. When the area was first discovered, there were over 50 *tolas* on the island, many of which have since been plundered and destroyed. One of the most fascinating parts of a visit to La Tolita is Santiguero Beach, where, instead of sand or stones, the shore is littered with millions of shards of pre-Columbian pottery.

Most of the mangrove forests around San Lorenzo are protected as part of the **Cayapas-Mataje Ecological Reserve.** There are no real services or trails in this reserve; in fact, it is principally accessible by boat. A boat ride through the rivers, canals, and lagoons here provides an excellent opportunity to spot hundreds of waterfowl, as well as caiman and other wildlife. The mangrove trees in this reserve are the tallest in the world, with some reaching nearly 60m (197 ft.).

You can hire a boat in San Lorenzo to take you to La Tolita or through the Cayapas-Mataje Reserve. You can ask around at the docks and usually find a boat and guide for around $12 to $15 per hour. But I think it's best to make day-trip arrangements through a hotel or tour agency in Esmeraldas or Atacames.

Warning: Although San Lorenzo is practically on the Colombian border, it is not recommended that you cross into Colombia here. Ongoing guerrilla activity and drug-trafficking activities make the area on the Colombian side rather dangerous for tourists.

By far, the best place to stay in this region is **Kumanii Lodge** ★ (© 800/747-0567 in the U.S. and Canada; www.kumanii-lodge.com), located in the Chocó Rainforest. The lodge is run by members of the local Chachi indigenous and Afro-Ecuadorean tribes. Accommodations are a bit rustic, but the wildlife viewing, cultural interaction, and sense of isolation definitely make it worthwhile. You can either fly directly into a small airstrip near the lodge or take a 2 ½-hour boat ride upriver from the coastal mangrove town of Borbón.

ATACAMES & THE BEACHES WEST OF ESMERALDAS ★★

349km (216 miles) W of Quito; 442km (274 miles) N of Guayaquil; 30km (19 miles) SW of Esmeraldas

This is my favorite beach destination in Ecuador. Leaving Esmeraldas and heading west—or, more precisely southwest—along the coastline, you'll come to a string of beaches, most of which have broad swaths of white or cream-colored sand fronting a blue-green sea. These beaches run the gamut from bustling tourist resort towns with a jumble of hotels and condos, to isolated getaways with just a few cabins, to secluded secret spots where surfers pitch tents and ride wave after wave.

Just outside Esmeraldas is **Tonsupa ★**, a beautiful wide beach that is the fastest-growing destination in the area, which makes sense, as it is so close to the city and airport. A little farther southwest is **Atacames ★**, the most developed beach resort town on this coast. The seafront Malecón in Atacames is jampacked with hotels, bars, restaurants, and shops.

One of the most undeveloped beaches along this coast, **Sua ★**, is located between two high bluffs, with a handful of fishing boats anchored offshore. Much larger is **Same ★★**, with its broader beach backed with scores of vacation condos. Many of these condos are whitewashed and set on the surrounding hillside in such a way that Same has a Mediterranean feel. Sua is around 6.5km (4 miles) southwest of Atacames, Same around 13km (8 miles) southwest of Atacames.

Beyond Same lie ever more remote and out-of-the way beaches and small fishing villages, including Tonchigue and Galera. At Galera, the coastline turns and heads south to the isolated little island of **Muisne.**

Essentials

GETTING THERE

BY PLANE The nearest airport to these beaches is in Esmeraldas (p. 282). There are always taxis waiting for incoming flights. A taxi from the airport in Esmeraldas costs about $20 to $30.

BY BUS **Trans Esmeraldas** (✆ **02/3824-791** at Quitumbe, 02/2505-099 at their Santa María terminal, or 06/2721-381 in Esmeraldas; www.transesmeraldas. com) buses leave from Quito for Atacames roughly every hour between 7am and 11pm, with sporadic but less frequent service during off hours. About half of Trans Esmeraldas buses leave from Terminal Terrestre Quitumbe (✆ **02/3988-200**), the main bus station in the south, with the rest leaving from Esmeraldas's own terminal, on Calle Santa María 870 and Avenida 9 de Octubre. While not a hard-and-fast rule, the departure site alternates pretty much one-for-one throughout the day. **Panamericana** (✆ **02/2569-428**) also runs the route leaving from their terminal on Avenida Colon and Reina Victoria, conveniently located in La Mariscal. The 6½ to 7-hour trip costs $8 to $10. The bus stops in Atacames are all near the main park and Catholic church, east of the main bridge.

Local buses run between Atacames and Esmeraldas roughly every 20 minutes between 6am and 10pm. Those between Esmeraldas and destinations farther down the coast also leave consistently throughout the day. These buses stop in Atacames, Sua, Same, Tonchigue, and Muisne. Some continue on to Mompiche.

BY CAR   To reach Atacames and the surrounding beaches, follow the directions to Esmeraldas (p. 282). On the outskirts of the city of Esmeraldas, you will see a well-marked exit for the coastal road that passes by Atacames, Same, Sua, and Muisne.

GETTING AROUND

You'll have no trouble flagging down a taxi or one of the open-air motorcycle-powered cabs in Atacames. You can also call **Taxis Alfa Omega** (© 06/2760-710). Taxis to the neighboring beaches cost $6 to $12 each way. If you do get a ride to one of the neighboring beaches, it's a wise idea to arrange a specific pickup for your return trip.

ORIENTATION

The town of Atacames is divided into sections by the curving Río Atacames, which enters the town as a narrow river but broadens considerably as it flows parallel to the ocean, toward the north end of town, before finally joining the sea. The main coastal highway runs through the center of Atacames and then southwest down the coast, with well-marked turnoffs for all of the other beach towns mentioned here.

FAST FACTS   To contact the local **police,** dial © 06/2735-065, or 101 in an emergency. The **post office** (© 06/2731-441) is on Espejo.

There's a branch of **Banco Pichincha** (© 06/2731-029) on Calle Calderon, on the corner of Espejo. While there's no bank in Same, there is a cash machine in the small convenience store just outside the Club Casablanca hotel. There are a handful of Internet cafes all over Atacames. Just head to the Malecón and pick one that has working air-conditioning and modern-looking equipment. Same and Sua each have one or two little Internet cafes on their main roads as well.

What to See & Do in & Around Atacames

Sunbathing, swimming, and relaxing are the main activities here. While there are sometimes good waves to be caught at the beach breaks all up and down this section of coast, serious surfers will want to head to the point break at **Mompiche** (see "North Along the Coast: From Canoa to Esmeraldas," earlier in this chapter). You can rent jet skis and Hobie Cats from a variety of stands set up on the beach. Rates run from $10 to $20 per hour.

If you want to do any organized tours, check in with your hotel desk or contact **Delgado Travel** (© 06/2723-723; www.delgadotravelsa.com), a large national tour agency with an office in Esmeraldas. Tours include sport fishing, whale- and dolphin-watching, and visits to La Tolita and the mangrove forests of the Cayapas-Mataje Ecological Reserve (see "North from Esmeraldas: San Lorenzo & La Tolita," above).

Where to Stay in & Around Atacames

The beach hotels here tend to fill up on Friday afternoon and empty out on Sunday. If you're arriving on the weekend or during a holiday week, I recommend you have a reservation. Midweek, almost every place is nearly empty.

MODERATE

Hotel Club del Sol ★   This is my top choice for a beachfront, modern, resort-style hotel in Atacames. Located in the center of town, just in front of the stadium, this place is popular with well-to-do Ecuadoreans. Rooms are spacious and well kept, with bold-colored walls and flashy floral bedspreads. The large pool and poolside bar and restaurant are the center of the action here, and where most guests spend most of their time. However, the beach is just across the street.

On the Malecón, Atacames (mailing address: Av. Universitaria #550 Oe5-284 y 18 de Septiembre, Quito). www.hotelclubdelsol.com. ✆ **02/2529-412** reservations in Quito, or 06/2760-660 in Atacames. 55 units. $78 double. AE, DC, MC, V. **Amenities:** Restaurant; bar; large outdoor pool. *In room:* A/C, TV, minifridge.

Hotel Juan Sebastián   One of the most popular beach hotels in Atacames, this massive place caters to Ecuadorean families, as well as to Quiteño revelers. Accommodations come in a variety of sizes, with several multiroom options, many featuring bunk beds for large families or student groups. In my opinion, the best rooms are the individual cabins; they give a bit more privacy and isolation, which is welcome when this place is really cranking. The hotel's pool area is a free-flowing affair, built to resemble a series of connected lagoons. The bar, located right near the pool, has a giant TV screen for karaoke and is often pretty happening at night.

On the Malecón, Atacames (mailing address: Wilson E8-22 y Av. 6 de Diciembre, Quito). www. hoteljuansebastian.com. ✆/fax **06/2731-049** in Atacames, or 02/2561-990 in Quito. 65 units. $60–$90 double; $90–$120 suite. Rates include breakfast buffet. Lower rates in the off season. AE, DC, MC, V. **Amenities:** Restaurant; bar; large free-form outdoor pool; free Wi-Fi. *In room:* A/C, TV.

INEXPENSIVE

In addition to the places listed below, if you want to stay in picturesque, isolated Sua, your best bet is the simple **Hostal Chagra Ramos** (✆ **06/2731-006**), which is a very basic hotel beautifully located on a piece of land that stretches from the beach up a small hillside.

Hotel Cielo Azul ★ ☺   This a great option on the beach. The hotel is built in an L-shape around a small pool and Jacuzzi, and faces the sea. The spotless accommodations are plenty roomy and have cool tile floors and private balconies or patios. I prefer the second-floor rooms, with ocean views. Most of the offerings here are two-bedroom suites, set up for families, with a master bedroom for the parents and a mix of twins and bunk beds in the second bedroom. The pool area is very popular with guests and features a small stone waterfall, as well as a poolside restaurant serving excellent seafood and local cuisine.

Av. 21 de Noviembre, near the stadium, Atacames. www.hotelcieloazul.com. ✆/fax **06/2731-813** or 09/4662-783. 13 units. $45–$59 double; $112 suite. Rates include full breakfast and taxes. Lower rates in the off season. Children 11 and under 50% discount. AE, DC, MC, V. **Amenities:** Restaurant; bar; small outdoor pool. *In room:* AC, TV, minifridge, no phone, free Wi-Fi.

Hotel Der Alte Fritz 🍴   This German-Ecuadorean-owned and -run hotel is located in a bright white five story building on the Malecón. Rooms are large and immaculate, with plenty of light. Most have a private balcony and cable television. You might want one of the rooms in the taller section of the building, toward the rear. Those fronting the Malecón can get noisy at night. The hotel has a good tour operation with a wide range of available tour options, as well as a popular restaurant on the ground floor facing the beach.

On the Malecón, Atacames. www.deraltefritz-ecuador.com. ✆/fax **06/2731-610.** 30 units. $30–$40 double. Rates include full breakfast and taxes. No credit cards. **Amenities:** Restaurant; bar. *In room:* No phone.

Where to Dine in & Around Atacames

All the beach towns here have their share of simple seaside restaurants serving fresh fish, *ceviche,* and local cuisine. Pick any one that seems sanitary and inviting, and you can't go wrong. One of my favorite seafood spots on the Malecón is **Marcos** (© **06/2760-126**). In addition to the place listed below, you can get good pizzas and pastas, and an excellent ocean view, at **Pizza Terraza** (© **06/2733-320**), in Same. In addition, you'll find great grub at **Der Alte Fritz** (see above).

Sea Flower Restaurant ★★★ 🍴 INTERNATIONAL   If these folks hadn't built up such a stellar reputation, it'd be a real surprise to find this type of dining in a simple restaurant in Same. They focus on fresh seafood—as most beach restaurants do—but this place stands out. Salads are served in a giant abalone shell, which itself is set in a massive slab of wood. A range of seafood is served in a variety of styles—in a spicy coconut milk broth, over spaghetti, simply grilled, or sautéed with garlic. The *pescado a la portuguesa,* a fresh filet of mahimahi baked in a terra-cotta bowl with a subtle passion-fruit and tomato sauce, is served piping-hot in the same clay bowl in which it was cooked. All meals come with a salad and fresh-baked bread. But save room for dessert. The service is casual yet professional, and the ambience is rustic beach elegance, with thick cotton tablecloths, heavy Mexican glassware, and an eclectic mix of jazz, blues, and world music.

1 block inland from the beach, Same. © **06/2733-369** or 09/8147-536. Reservations recommended. Main courses $6–$25. DC. Daily 11am–3pm and 6–10pm. Hours reduced in the low season.

Atacames After Dark

Atacames has a well-deserved reputation as a party town. The beachfront Malecón is lined with an almost uninterrupted string of open-air thatch-roof bars that have loud reggae and Latin music and cheap drink specials. This is the perfect strip for a leisurely pub crawl, stopping in at whichever spot seems the most happening or appealing. Many of these shacks have celebrity-sounding knock-off names such as **Friend's Bar, Cheer's, Hard Rock Café,** and **Planet Atacames.** In addition, I like **Jamaica Bar, Tsunami Bar,** and **Madera Fina.** Two of the more established dance clubs include the **Scala Disco** (© **06/2720-404**) and **Ludos** (© **06/2731-225**), both on the Malecón.

There's much, much less nightlife to be had at the beaches west of Atacames; in fact, they are rather dead after dark—though that can be a good thing to some travelers.

Muisne: Almost Your Own Island

One of the most remote beach destinations in Ecuador, **Muisne** is a small island fishing community located some 42km (26 miles) southwest of Atacames. There's no road directly here, although the buses leaving Esmeraldas and Atacames will say MUISNE. The buses leave you at a small pier in the village of El Relleno, from which you take one of the nearly constant little boats across the Río Muisne to the island. The fare is 20¢. The boat-taxis run throughout the daylight hours and often into the early evening. Pedal-powered ecotaxis await the boat-taxis and will take you to the tiny village, and anywhere else on the island, for $1. There are only a couple of places to stay on the island. The beachfront **Hostal Playa Paraíso** (© **06/2480-192**) is your best bet, with rustic rooms and individual cabins going for around $20 for a double. The beach in Muisne is long, broad, and almost always nearly deserted. Ask at the hotel or around town, and you should be able to organize a boat tour through nearby mangroves. Aside from that and sunbathing, there's not much else to do here except enjoy the beach, sea, and tranquillity.

SANTO DOMINGO DE LOS COLORADOS

134km (83 miles) W of Quito; 287km (178 miles) N of Guayaquil; 185km (115 miles) E of Esmeraldas

Set in the lowlands just below the western slope of the Andes, Santo Domingo de los Colorados is a major transportation hub connecting coastal and southern Ecuador with Quito and the rest of the country. It is also in the center of some of the country's most productive agricultural lands, where bananas, palm nuts, pineapples, cacao, and more are grown.

The city gets its name from the local indigenous group, the Tsachilas, who paint their hair a bright red using an achiote paste. Seeing this, the early Spaniards dubbed them *los colorados* (the colored ones). When the area was colonized and converted by Dominican priests, the town was christened Santo Domingo de los Colorados.

Essentials

GETTING THERE

BY BUS   Buses leave Quito for Santo Domingo roughly every 15 minutes between 5:30am and 7pm, and somewhat less frequently during the remaining hours. Several bus lines work this route: **Trans Esmeraldas** (© 02/3824-791 in Quito, or 02/2750-355 in Santo Domingo; www.transesmeraldas.com) and **Cooperativa Zaracay** (© 02/2750-244 in Quito, or 02/2763-716 in Santo Domingo) are the main providers. All buses leave from the **Terminal Terrestre Quitumbe** (© 02/3988-200). The 3-hour ride costs $3.

Santo Domingo is also connected by frequent bus service to cities such as Guayaquil, Ambato, Ibarra, Esmeraldas, Manta, Pedernales, and Portoviejo. Less frequent direct service runs between Santo Domingo and Bahía de Caráquez, Cuenca, Lago Agrio, Coca, Mindo, and Riobamba.

Santo Domingo's main bus terminal is located about 3.2km (2 miles) north of the center of town, just off Avenida Abraham Calazacón, near this avenue's intersection with Avenida Esmeraldas and Avenida de las Tsachilas. Taxis are always available at the bus station. A ride to downtown will cost $1.

BY CAR   If you're driving from Quito, start off heading south on the Pan-American Highway (E35), until the intersection at Aloag. From here, head west on E30 straight to Santo Domingo de los Colorados. The road from Aloag descends precipitously and provides a mix of hair-raising, white-knuckle switchbacks and spectacular views. On a clear day, you can even see the Pacific Ocean in places. The ride should take about 2½ hours.

From Guayaquil, you can head to Quevedo on either Hwy. E23 or E25. From Quevedo, E25 continues on direct to Santo Domingo. From Guayaquil, the trip takes around 3½ hours.

GETTING AROUND

Taxis are plentiful in and around Santo Domingo. A ride to or from the bus station, or anywhere around downtown, should cost $1 to $2. Flag one down on the street, have your hotel call one for you, or try **Taxis Progreso** (© 02/2750-531).

For a cheap city tour, you can hop on any bus marked CENTRO or TERMINAL, which will run a short circuit around town, and between the central plaza and the main bus terminal. The fare is 25¢.

ORIENTATION

The main road from Quito enters Santo Domingo and becomes Avenida Quito, which passes through the heart of the downtown area. The central plaza is bordered by Avenida Quito on the south and has the city's Catholic church on its north side. The park here is large, with paths and benches set amid gardens and grass lawns. There's a large market area several blocks west of the main plaza.

FAST FACTS   The **post office** (© 02/2759-071) is on Avenida de los Tsachilas, near Calle Río Baba. There's a branch of **Banco de Guayaquil** (© 02/2761-212) at the corner of avenidas Quito and Abraham Calazacón, and a branch of **Banco Pichincha** (© 02/2758-165) at Avenida La Paz and Calle Santa Rosa. Both have 24-hour ATMs.

To contact the **police,** dial © 02/2750-225. The regional **hospital** (© 02/2750-336) is located at Km 1 on the road to Quito. Several Internet cafes are located around the downtown area, as well as near the bus station, and most hotels in town also offer access.

What to See & Do in Santo Domingo

There is very little of interest to tourists right in Santo Domingo, although you can use this busy city as a base for a reasonable range of activities, including rainforest hikes, bird-watching excursions, visits to a Tsachila community, and white-water rafting trips. For any organized tours or activities around Santo Domingo, contact **Delgado Travel** (© 02/2760-036; www.delgadotravelsa.com), at Calle Cocaniguas 148 and Avenida Quito, or **Turismo Zaracay** (© 02/2750-546; www.turismo zaracay.com), Avenida 29 de Mayo and Cocaniguas.

The best attraction close to Santo Domingo is the **Jardín Botánico La Carolina ★** (© 02/3702-868; www.pucesd.edu.ec), located just a few kilometers outside the city center at the Km 2 marker on the road to Chone. These botanical gardens have a broad series of well-marked, self-guided trails, and they will even provide a bilingual guide if you reserve in advance. Exhibits include ornamental and medicinal plants, orchids, and native and introduced hardwoods. The bird-watching here is often excellent. The Jardín is open daily from 9am to 4pm, and admission is $1.50; children get in at half-price.

Even if you're not staying there, bird-watchers and nature enthusiasts can tour the trails and forests at **Tinalandia ★** (see below). All the tour agencies in town offer day trips here for around $30 per person. Alternatively, you can head directly to Tinalandia, which offers lunch and free run of its trails and facilities for $20 per person.

Where to Stay & Dine in Santo Domingo

In addition to the hotels listed below, you can try **Milenio Hotel** (© 02/3710-516; www.mileniohotelecuador.com), on Avenida Quevedo and Juan Pio Montufar, with doubles at $35 to $40.

There's no great dining scene in Santo Domingo. In many cases, your best bet will be your hotel restaurant. **La Tonga,** belonging to Grand Hotel Santo Domingo (see below), is arguably the best. If you find yourself in the city and hungry, head to **D'Marco** (© 02/2751-099), on Calle Río Mulaute, near Calle Río Baba; or to **Restaurante Timoneiro** (© 02/2751-642), on Avenida Quito near Tsachila.

RED-HAIRED boys

Although they number only some 3,000, the Tsachila are one of the most distinctive indigenous groups in Ecuador, well known for their healers and shamans. Today the Tsachila live in eight community groups in the area surrounding Santo Domingo. Most dedicate themselves to farming and cattle ranching. As part of their traditional dress, the men use a thick paste made from the achiote seed to mat down and color their hair, and wear a knee-length wraparound skirt with black-and-white horizontal stripes, tied at the waist with a red belt. For ceremonies and healings, men and women paint their bodies with horizontal black lines said to be indicative of the snake or serpent spirit. In Santo Domingo, it's rare, but not unheard of, to see Tsachila in their traditional garb.

MODERATE

Grand Hotel Santo Domingo ★

This is easily the best hotel in steamy Santo Domingo. It's hard to miss this four-story white-concrete behemoth with tinted windows, which seems a bit out of place in this hot, rugged agricultural city. Inside, though, you'll find a cool oasis. Rooms have an almost stately feel, with subdued tones and dark-wood furniture and trim. Most have Jacuzzis and either a private balcony or patio overlooking the central pool area. The **restaurant** here is the best and fanciest in town.

Río Toachi y Galápagos, Santo Domingo de los Colorados. www.grandhotelsantodomingo.com. ✆ **02/2767-947.** Fax 02/2750-131. 41 units. $83 double. AE, DC, MC, V. **Amenities:** Restaurant; bar; small gym; Jacuzzi; small outdoor pool; room service; sauna; free Wi-Fi. *In room:* A/C, TV, free Internet, minibar.

Hotel Zaracay

Located just on the outskirts of Santo Domingo, this is a sprawling complex with extensive grounds and pleasant gardens. Rooms here are spacious and well equipped, although the decor is rather lifeless and dated. In addition to the tennis court and pool, there are volleyball and basketball courts. This is a popular place for Ecuadorean business conferences and weekend retreats, and there's even a small casino. The hotel is named after Joaquin Zaracay, a famous contemporary Tsachila chief.

Km 1.5 on the road to Quito, Santo Domingo de los Colorados. www.hotelzaracay.com. ✆ **02/2750-316.** Fax 02/2754-535. 61 units. $85 double. AE, DC, MC, V. **Amenities:** Restaurant; bar; casino; small exercise room; small outdoor pool; outdoor tennis court. *In room:* A/C, TV, minifridge, free Wi-Fi.

INEXPENSIVE

Hotel Del Pacífico

The best option right in downtown Santo Domingo, this hotel offers modern, comfortable accommodations just 2 blocks in either direction from the main plaza and main market. All the rooms are spacious and well appointed, but the suites are especially large, with separate sitting areas and such upgrades as a king-size bed, air-conditioning, a 29-inch television, a minibar, and a hair dryer, which aren't included in the standard accommodations. Every room does come with one, two, or three queen-size beds; a small wooden desk and chair; and a fan. Located in the heart of the city, street noise can sometimes be a problem here.

Av. 29 de Mayo 510, btw. Ibarra and Latacunga, Santo Domingo de los Colorados. hoteldelpacifico@hotmail.com. ✆ **02/2752-806.** 40 units. $35 double; $78 suite. AE, DC, MC, V. **Amenities:** Restaurant; bar. *In room:* TV.

Santo Domingo After Dark

There's plenty of nightlife in Santo Domingo, although much of it is rough and ragged. Prostitutes hang around the main plaza after dark, and tourists should be very careful about walking around then. I recommend that you take a taxi to and from any bar or nightclub. **Habana Blues ★** (© **09/6069-810**) is the best and liveliest club in town, with a large dance floor and private VIP section. It is located on Calle Pallatanga and Avenida Quito.

Nature Lodges near Santo Domingo

Kashama ★★ 🏨 This delightful jungle lodge and spa is set in lush forests on the shore of the Río Blanco. Located just 20 or so minutes away from Santo Domingo, it feels much, much more isolated. The rooms are all distinctively designed and decorated, with an emphasis on local materials. All units are spacious and bright, with white walls offset by colorful wood and paint accents. There's a large outdoor pool here with a tall sculpted waterfall filling one end. The Cascada Spa offers a wide range of traditional spa and massage treatments, many of them integrating local herbs, muds, or ritual into the deal. Nearby nature trails include a hike to a beautiful waterfall with a perfect wading pool below it. Rafting, horseback riding, kayaking, tubing, rappelling, and trips to the local indigenous communities are also offered.

Km 26 on the road to Esmeraldas, Valle Hermoso, Santo Domingo de los Colorados. www.kashama. com. © **02/2773-193.** ©/fax 02/2773-465. 21 units. $95 double; $135 junior suite; $169 suite. Rates include breakfast, activities, and taxes. AE, DC, MC, V. **Amenities:** Restaurant; bar; Jacuzzi; outdoor pool; sauna. *In room:* TV.

Tinalandia Unlike Kashama, which lies in the lowlands west of Santo Domingo, Tinalandia is in the foothill slopes of the Andes east of the city in moist cloud forest. The bird-watching here is spectacular, with over 350 species recorded. The main lodge sits high on a steep bank over a small river. I find the rooms a tad dark and dated. A wide range of tours and activities are offered, but bird- and wildlife-watching are the strong suits. There's a pretty midsize pool, with a great views of the surrounding forests.

Km 16 on the road to Santo Domingo (mailing address: Urbanización El Bosque 2da. Etapa Av. del Parque, Calle 3era., Lote 98 no. 43–78, Quito). www.tinalandia.com. ©/fax **02/2449-028** or 09/9467-741. 16 units. $107 per person double. Rates include taxes, breakfast, lunch, and dinner. No credit cards. **Amenities:** Restaurant; bar; midsize outdoor pool; 9-hole golf course. *In room:* No phone.

EL ORIENTE

E l Oriente, which means "The East," is a vast area that stretches from the eastern slopes of the Andes to the border with Peru. El Oriente contains over 25% of the nation's territory. This region is commonly called the Amazon (Las Amazonas) because the rivers here—created by melting snow from the Andes—flow into the Amazon. The rainforests of El Oriente have been home to Native Americans for thousands of years. Because of the natural barrier formed by the Andes, the people here have lived in almost complete isolation. Some tribes have had contact with the "outside world" only since the 1970s, when oil was discovered. Since then, development has increased dramatically with the construction of new roads, such as the controversial Macas-to-Guamote road, which runs through national parkland. Various tribes inhabit Ecuador's Amazon basin, including the Shuar, Cofán, Huaorani, and Quichua. Their languages and lifestyle are markedly different from those of Ecuadoreans on the opposite side of the Andes. In order to adapt to somewhat harsh conditions, inhabitants of El Oriente have developed a special relationship with the natural resources of the area. When you take a trip to this region, you will usually have the opportunity to meet some of the indigenous people, who will share their land with you and teach you some of their age-old secrets, such as how to farm, fish, hunt, or use medicinal herbs and plants.

In addition to learning about the local cultures, you will most certainly enjoy the incredible biodiversity that exists here. Fifty-seven percent of all mammals in Ecuador live in the Amazon basin, and there are more than 15,000 species of plants in Ecuador's rainforest. You'll have the chance to see more than 500 species of tropical birds, as well as freshwater dolphins, monkeys, sloths, anacondas, boas, turtles, and, if you're extremely lucky, the rare and elusive jaguars.

A robust ecotourism business has developed here over the past couple of decades. Excellent jungle lodges have been built to blend in with the natural environment. Naturalist guides from these lodges take visitors on all sorts of excursions: walks through the forest to learn about the medicinal properties of the local plants; fishing trips to catch piranhas; early-morning bird-watching expeditions to see parrots, macaws, and other tropical species; visits to traditional indigenous villages; nighttime canoe rides in search of caimans; and outings where you can paddle downriver in a dugout canoe. Just be sure to bring plenty of mosquito repellent!

El Oriente comprises six provinces, but it is generally divided up into two areas: the **northern Oriente** and the **southern Oriente.** For the purposes of this guide, the lodges on and around the Río Napo, Río Coca, and Río Aguarico—which are reached by the gateway cities of Lago Agrio,

Coca, and Tena—constitute the northern Oriente. This area has been most affected by the oil industry; charges of environmental destruction and uncompensated profit from indigenous lands and resources have been common, and conflicts and protests have periodically occurred (see "Down & Dirty in the Jungle," on p. 298). This is also the area that has been most developed for tourism. The southern Oriente, which includes everything south and east of the gateway city of Puyo, is much less developed. However, this area is more directly accessible by land from Ambato, Riobamba, and Baños, making it a good place to visit if you plan to be in one of those cities.

How to Visit El Oriente: Jungle Lodges & Independent Travel

By far, the easiest way to visit El Oriente is with an organized trip to one of the well-established jungle lodges. These trips usually last 4 or 5 days. Depending on where you're staying, the journey generally involves a commercial flight to Coca or Lago Agrio. Some lodges, such as Kapawi (p. 320), can be reached only by a charter flight. All the jungle lodges listed below either include transportation from Quito in their packages or can arrange transportation for you. *Note:* Because many of these lodges are extremely isolated and difficult to reach, I strongly encourage you to book your trip in advance, either before you come to Ecuador or while you're in Quito, Baños, Cuenca, or Guayaquil.

If you're looking to reduce costs—or if you want to conveniently combine some time in Baños or Riobamba with a visit to an Amazon-basin nature lodge—consider staying at one of the lodges in or around Tena or Puyo. Most of the lodges listed in these sections are easily accessed by bus, taxi, or rental car.

Climate

Guarded by the high Andes mountains to the west, the lowland rainforests of El Oriente have a climate that's hot and wet most of the time. Well, it's *always* hot and often wet. Annual rainfall throughout much of this region ranges from 300 to 450cm (118–177 in.), with some areas getting even more. The wettest months are March through June, the driest August through November. During the rainy season, you'll find swollen rivers, muddy trails, and frequent downpours. In the drier months, things dry up some—but never completely. Some of the smaller rivers, canals, and lagoons either dry up or become impassable. Rain is possible throughout the year, and it's a good idea to pack rain gear and fast-drying clothes. All the lodges listed in this chapter provide thick rubber boots for hiking.

LAGO AGRIO & CUYABENO WILDLIFE RESERVE

Lago Agrio: 259km (161 miles) NE of Quito; 674km (418 miles) NE of Guayaquil; 700km (434 miles) NE of Cuenca

Sitting on the shores of the Aguarico River, **Lago Agrio** (Sour Lake) is the main port city and access point for Ecuador's northern Amazon basin. It is the capital of Sucumbíos province and has a population of nearly 70,000. Officially known as Nuevo Loja (New Loja) because the early settlers were predominantly from Loja, the town is almost universally known now as Lago Agrio, or simply Lago. The name Lago Agrio was given to the town by Texaco oil company workers, as the home base for this firm is in Sour Lake, Texas.

National Capital
Provincial Capital
Panamericana

Today Lago Agrio is a rough, dirty, and generally unappealing industrial town, and most of the forests and rivers immediately surrounding the town have been clear-cut or polluted by the oil industry. The town serves almost entirely as a necessary transportation hub for those seeking to visit the **Cuyabeno Wildlife Reserve ★★** and the remote jungle regions farther down the Aguarico and Zabalo rivers.

Essentials

GETTING THERE

BY PLANE Tame (© **1800/500-800** toll-free in Ecuador, or 06/2830-113 in Lago Agrio; www.tame.com.ec) has one daily flight Monday through Thursday and Saturday, and two flights on Fridays from Quito to the recently remodeled **Lago Agrio Airport** (© **06/2830-442;** airport code: LGQ). **Aero-VIP** (© **1800/2376-425** toll-free nationwide, or 06/2830-333 in Lago Agrio; www.aerogal.com.ec) has two flights daily Monday through Friday and one flight on Sunday. The flight takes 30 minutes one-way from Quito, and the fare is around $70 one-way or $135 round-trip on either airline.

DOWN & DIRTY IN THE jungle

For most travelers, Lago Agrio is simply the gateway to Cuyabeno Wildlife Refuge and some of Ecuador's remote jungle lodges. But this Ecuadorean oil town is also the battleground for an ongoing multibillion-dollar lawsuit filed by a coalition of environmental groups against U.S. oil giant Chevron.

The suit's 88 Ecuadorean plaintiffs claim to represent 30,000 people affected by water contaminated by oil operations in the area. It accuses Texaco, which merged with Chevron in 2001, of improperly dumping 18.5 billion gallons of wastewater into pits, swamps, and streams in the Lago Agrio area between 1971 and 1992.

Chevron claims that Texaco's Ecuadorean subsidiary, working together with the state-owned oil company PetroEcuador, operated within the local laws when it dumped oil-contaminated water. (The alternative would have been to use the more expensive process of reinjecting wastewater, as is mandated in the U.S.) The company, which extracted 1.5 billion barrels of oil from the area over the course of 3 decades, points out that it paid $40 million to "remediate" oil sites when its concession expired and was subsequently given a release by the Ecuadorean government.

Environmentalists say the U.S. company cleaned up very little of the mess it made and claim the company dumped more oil in the Ecuadorean rainforest than was spilled during the Exxon *Valdez* disaster. They say Chevron-Texaco—the second-largest U.S. oil company—should spend billions to clean up the oil it left

behind and provide medical care for communities affected by it.

The lawsuit was originally filed in New York in 1993, but after a decade of languishing in the U.S. legal system, an appellate court ruled that the case should be heard in Ecuador. A group of environmental lawyers consequently filed suit in Lago Agrio, *Aguinda v. Chevron-Texaco,* in which they hope to apply a relatively new Ecuadorean law that mandates that companies cover the cost of cleaning up their pollution.

Environmentalists believe a victory against Chevron would set an important precedent for the developing world, where big corporations often get away with mistreatment of the natural environment. Tragically, despite all the noise made about Texaco, oil companies working in the Amazon basin continue to dump wastewater into streams and rivers, even though they could easily inject it back into the earth at a cost of just a few dollars per barrel.

At this writing, the case continues to make its way through the Ecuadorean court system. Several judges have been recused or removed from the case, and Texaco has been accused of using both strong-arm tactics to intimidate Ecuadorean lawyers and stalling tactics to bog down the local legal system. Still, many expect Chevron to lose the case and face anywhere from $23 billion to $115 billion in damages.

See the websites **www.chevron toxico.org**, **www.texacotoxico.org**, and **www.amazonwatch.org** for updates and information on the case.

The airport is located about 3.2km (2 miles) southeast of town. Taxis are always waiting to meet incoming flights, and a cab ride between the airport and downtown should cost around $2.

BY BUS Buses leave from Quito's southbound Terminal Terrestre Quitumbe (© 02/3988-200) for Lago Agrio roughly every hour or so from 6am to 10:30pm. Two main bus lines, **Transportes Baños** (© 02/3824-843) and **Putumayo**

(© 02/3824-807 in Quito, or 06/2833-819 in Lago Agrio), make the run. The ride takes about 7 to 8 hours, and the fare is around $7. In Lago Agrio, the Putamayo station is located on the south end of town, on avenidas Río Amazonas and 12 de Febrero, while the Transportes Baños terminal is north of downtown on Avenida Progreso. Return buses follow roughly the same schedule.

BY CAR To get here by car, take the highway (E20) east out of Quito to the remote town of Baeza. Here the road forks, with the well-marked northern fork (E45) heading to Lago Agrio. It's 88km (55 miles) from Quito to Baeza, and another 170km (105 miles) from Baeza to Lago Agrio. To get to the highway toward Baeza from downtown Quito, head north on Avenida Eloy Alfaro to Avenida de los Granados and then turn right. This road becomes Hwy. E20. Follow any signs to Papallacta, Tumbaco Baeza, or El Oriente. The ride should take about 7 hours.

GETTING AROUND

Taxis are readily available all around town. If you can't flag one down on the street, call **Taxis El Cofan** (© 06/2831-519), or have your hotel call for you. Fares should be just $1 to $2 anywhere in town.

ORIENTATION

Lago Agrio is a compact little city. There is a small park or plaza at the corner of avenidas 12 de Febrero and 18 de Noviembre, an intersection that more or less defines the center of the city. However, most of the hotels, restaurants, and tour agencies are located a few blocks south of here, along avenidas Quito and Colombia.

FAST FACTS To contact the local **police**, dial © 06/2830-101, or 911 in an emergency. There are branch outlets of **Banco de Guayaquil** (© 06/2832-314; avs. Quito and 12 de Febrero) and **Banco Pichincha** (© 06/2831-602; I Hotel Cofán). Both have 24-hour cash machines. If you need any medical care, head to **Clínica González** (© 06/2830-728; avs. Quito and 12 de Febrero). The local **post office** (© 06/2830-115) is situated on avs. Rocafuerte and 12 de Febrero. A branch of the local **pharmacy** is located on Av. Quito 417 between Fco. de Orellana and Av. 12 de Febrero. For **Internet access,** check out the facilities inside the Centro Cultural on Orellana between Venezuela and Cofanes.

What to See & Do in & Around Lago Agrio

There's very little to do or see in Lago Agrio itself. For a vast majority of tourists, the town is essentially a transfer point on an itinerary into the deeper reaches of Ecuador's Amazon basin. Just 3.5km (2¼ miles) outside town is the namesake lake, where local authorities have put together a small tourism project dubbed **Parque Ecológico Recreativo Lago Agrio (Lake Agrio Ecological Recreation Park),** or PERLA, a 110-hectare (272-acre) park, which features a few nature trails, a swimming pool, lakeside picnic tables, and other recreational facilities, including canoe and rowboat rentals and a cafe/restaurant.

If you're not already traveling here as part of a package tour to one of the lodges listed below, the best way to explore this area is to sign up for a trip with one of the local tour agencies in Lago Agrio.

Magic RiverTours ★★ (© 06/2831-003; www.magicrivertours.com), at Lotización 18 de Diciembre, Calle Primera and Pacayacu, offers a 5-day tour of the Cuyabeno Wildlife Reserve for $320 per person. Travel is by nonmotorized canoes, and accommodations are in a mix of rustic lodges and tents. They also customize longer or shorter tours to your liking.

For something even more unique, you might check out tours offered by the **Cofán Nation** ★★ (✆ 02/2470-946; www.cofan.org), who offer multiday guided tours that allow visitors a firsthand experience of the lifestyle, culture, and ecology of this forest-dwelling tribe. Depending on group size and tour duration, trips cost between $85 and $120 per person per day, including all accommodations, meals, and activities. *Tip:* The Cofán Nation website includes an extensive online dictionary of the Cofán language.

> ### En Route: A Stop at Papallacta Hot Springs
>
> If you're traveling to Lago Agrio or Coca by land, consider coordinating your trip so that you stop here for the night, or at least to take a soak in the Papallacta Hot Springs. These **soothing sulfur springs** ★★ are perhaps the best hot springs in Ecuador. For more information on the springs and their namesake resort, see p. 126.

The **Cuyabeno Wildlife Reserve** ★★ is one of the largest and richest in Ecuador, with over 655,781 hectares (1.6 million acres) of protected land. The terrain is very wet, with numerous lagoons, rivers, and lakes. These waters are home to freshwater river dolphins, as well as to piranha, manatee, anaconda, and five species of caiman. The rainforest canopy and dry land are home to a wide range of tropical flora and fauna. The Siona, Shuar, Cofán, and Secoya indigenous people live here. Almost all tours offered out of Lago Agrio, as well as those from the remote lodges listed below, take part either entirely or partially within the Cuyabeno Wildlife Reserve. There's a $20 entrance fee to the reserve, which is usually collected by your hotel, tour agency, or canoe captain.

Where to Stay & Dine in & Around Lago Agrio

In addition to the places listed below, **Hotel Araza** (✆ 06/2830-223), at avs. Quito 610 and Narvaez, is another good lodging option, with clean, air-conditioned rooms. There are no notable dining options around Lago Agrio. Most travelers choose to eat in their hotel restaurant, call it a night, and wake early for a tour into the Cuyabeno Wildlife Reserve. Of the hotel restaurants in town, the Italian fare at **D'Mario** (see below) is a local favorite. When it's not too hot and muggy, their street-side tables are a great spot to sit and people-watch while enjoying a drink or meal.

Hotel D'Mario ★ 🍴 This is the most popular option in Lago Agrio. Accommodations are immaculate, though the least expensive rooms are rather small and don't have hot water. It's worth a bit of a splurge for more space, hot water, and more modern decor. The hotel has a small pool in a central courtyard area, plus a small but surprisingly well-equipped gym. The **restaurant** here is one of the better and more popular spots in town.

Av. Quito 263 y Pasaje Gonzanama, Lago Agrio. www.hoteldmario.com. ✆/fax **06/2830-172** or 06/2830-456. 17 units. $22–$45 double. Rates include continental breakfast. DC, MC, V. **Amenities:** Restaurant; bar; small exercise room; Jacuzzi; small outdoor pool; sauna. *In room:* A/C, TV, minibar, free Wi-Fi.

Hotel El Cofán This well-located and neat little hotel is a good value. If you end up having to overnight in Lago Agrio and can't find space in D'Mario, you'll appreciate the tidy air-conditioned rooms, which come with cable television, to boot. You might also enjoy the ample common areas, the small gym, or the billiards table in the bar. The **restaurant** here serves good Ecuadorean and international fare.

Avs. 12 de Febrero 1915 y Quito, Lago Agrio. ✆ **06/2830-527.** Fax 06/2830-456. 30 units. $36–$60 double. DC, MC, V. **Amenities:** Restaurant; bar; room service. *In room:* A/C, TV, minibar.

Stay Away from the Border

The **Colombian border** is only 15km (9¼ miles) north of Lago Agrio. Instead of being an attraction, though, the border is mostly a source of trouble. The Colombian side of the border is a particularly lawless area, marked by guerrilla and drug-trafficking activity. Some of this spills over from time to time into Ecuador, and this region is a periodic scene of tension between the two countries. What this means for tourists is that the border area, and any crossing, should definitely be avoided. Moreover, Lago Agrio itself is best used only for transfers in and out of the hotels and jungle lodges listed below.

NEARBY JUNGLE LODGES

In addition to the places listed below, other remote jungle lodges to consider include **Siona Lodge ★** (✆ **09/8430-679;** www.sionalodge.com) and **Tapir Lodge** (✆ **02/2926-670;** www.tapirlodge.com).

Cuyabeno Lodge ★   While still decidedly rustic on many levels, this rainforest lodge provides some of the best accommodations inside or near the Cuyabeno Wildlife Reserve. Set on a small rainforest island in the middle of the reserve's Laguna Grande (Big Lagoon), the duplex bungalows feature loads of dark-stained wood and high thatch ceilings. All the bungalows have private bathrooms, mosquito netting over the beds, and large screened windows. Bunk bed–equipped dorm rooms with shared bathrooms are also available for budget travelers. Tasty, simple meals are served family style in the main lodge building. A host of tour and activity options are offered, including trips to their rainforest observation tower.

Laguna Grande, Reserva Faunística Cuyabeno (mailing address: Neotropic Turis, Pinto E4-360 y Av. Amazonas, Quito). www.neotropicturis.com. ✆ **02/2521-212** office in Quito, or 09/9803-395. Fax 02/2554-902. 14 units. 5-day/4-night tour $270 per person shared bathroom; $430 double occupancy private bathroom. Rates include round-trip transportation from Lago Agrio, all meals, nonalcoholic beverages, daily tours, and taxes. Rates do not include the $20 park entrance fee. MC, V. **Amenities:** Restaurant; bar. *In room:* No phone.

Jamu Lodge   This jungle lodge sits on the Cuyabeno River a few minutes downstream from the Laguna Grande. Accommodations are a series of raised duplex wooden bungalows with thatched roofs. The whole complex is connected by a series of raised wooden walkways. The cabins have private bathrooms, shared verandas, and no electricity. Light is provided by candles and oil lanterns. All the standard wildlife-viewing hikes and canoeing are offered. On a trip to the local Siona community, you can learn how to make cassava bread from the *yuca* root.

Laguna Grande, Reserva Faunística Cuyabeno (mailing address: Jose Calama E-615 y Reina Victoria, Quito). www.cabanasjamu.com. ✆ **02/2220-614** office in Quito, or 09/5281-035. 18 units. 5-day/4-night tour $250–$285 per person. Rates include round-trip transportation from Lago Agrio, all meals, nonalcoholic beverages, daily tours, and taxes. Rates do not include the $20 park entrance or $2 community visit fees. MC, V. **Amenities:** Restaurant; bar. *In room:* No phone.

Lago Agrio After Dark

There's really not a lot of action that's of interest to tourists here. Be forewarned, much of the bar scene in Lago Agrio is dominated by oil workers, and it can be a bit rough and seedy at times. If you're looking for a drink or some late-night carousing, your best bet is to head to one of the bars along Avenida Quito.

11

EL ORIENTE | Lago Agrio & Cuyabeno Wildlife Reserve

COFÁN chief **RANDY BORMAN**

Born to American parents in the oil town of Shell, Ecuador, in 1955, Randall Bruce Borman eventually rose to occupy the role of chief of the Cofán Nation. Randy's parents were missionaries who lived with the Cofán. They learned and spoke the language and adopted most trappings of the local lifestyle. Randy was raised almost entirely as a Cofán, although he did receive a modern Western education, including studies at Michigan State University and the Universidad Católica in Quito.

Seeing the destruction of the traditional Cofán lifestyle and ecosystem, Randy led a group of Cofán downriver and founded the village of Zabalo, on the banks of the Zabalo River. Since the establishment of this village, Randy and the Cofán Nation have fought hard not only to protect their heritage, customs, and language, but also to preserve the natural habitat that gives them sustenance.

Founded in 1977, the Cofán Community Ecotourism project is often considered the first true community-based tourism project in the world. Today the Cofán Nation, with only some 1,000 people, continues its struggle to survive.

En Route: Salto de San Rafael & Volcán Reventador

Along the main route to Lago Agrio lies the spectacular Salto de San Rafael (San Rafael Falls). At 145m (476 ft.), San Rafael Falls is the tallest waterfall in Ecuador. But these falls are not only tall; they're also raging and powerful. The trail head to the falls is marked CAMPAMENTO SAN RAFAEL Y LAS CASCADAS. It's a hike of a little over 1.6km (1 mile) to the lookout across from the base of the falls. The trail can be slippery and muddy at times. Sometimes a local guard will charge $1 admission, though at other times you'll just waltz on through. The rich rainforest and cloud forest here are excellent for bird-watching.

Across the road from the entrance to San Rafael Falls, and just a little to the east, is a trail leading up Volcán Reventador. At 3,485m (11,431 ft.), Reventador is one of the most active volcanoes in Ecuador. If you want to hike the trail and even attempt a summit, you should definitely go with a guide who knows the area and who is up-to-date on current volcanic activity. Any of the tour agencies out of Quito, Lago Agrio, or Coca should be able to set you up with a qualified guide. San Rafael Falls and Volcán Reventador are located just off Hwy. E45 on the way to Lago Agrio, about an hour and a half outside Baeza.

EL COCA & THE LOWER RÍO NAPO ★★

Coca: 300km (186 miles) E of Quito; 60km (37 miles) S of Lago Agrio

Although officially christened **Puerto Francisco de Orellana,** this riverside port city is known universally as **El Coca** (or simply "Coca"). The capital of Orellana province, Coca, like Lago Agrio, is a relatively young boomtown carved from the jungle to service the oil industry. Not surprisingly, it's seedy and rough around the edges. And, like its northern neighbor, Coca is a gateway to several isolated jungle lodges.

ACCOMMODATIONS
& DINING ■
Cuyabeno Lodge 8
Jamu Lodge 9
La Selva Jungle Lodge 2
Napo Wildlife Center 3
Sacha Lodge 1
Sani Lodge 4
Siona Lodge 11
Tapir Lodge 10
Yarina Lodge 5

ATTRACTIONS ●
Cuyabeno Wildlife Reserve 7
Yasuní National Park 6

Coca sits on the banks of the Río Napo, which, along with its tributaries, canals, and lagoons, is home to some of the best nature lodges in Ecuador's Amazon basin. Most of the lodges listed below are located a 2- to 3-hour boat ride downstream from Coca. The wildlife viewing here is top-notch.

Essentials

GETTING THERE

BY PLANE Coca is just a 30-minute flight from Quito, and numerous flights connect the two cities. **Aero-VIP** (© **1800/2376-425** toll-free nationwide; www. aerogal.com.ec), **Icaro** (© **1800/883-567** toll-free nationwide; www.icaro.aero), and **Tame** (© **1800/500-800** toll-free in Ecuador, or 06/2881-078 in Coca; www. tame.com.ec) all have several daily flights from Quito to Coca Monday through Friday, with fewer flights on Saturday and Sunday. These schedules are fluid and frequently altered according to demand. Fares run from $45 to $80 each way.

Aeropuerto El Coca (© **06/2880-185;** airport code: OCC) is located on the northern outskirts of town. Taxis meet all incoming planes; a ride from the airport into town should cost $2.

BY BUS Various bus companies service the Coca route. The best is **Transportes Baños** (© 02/3824-843 in Quito, or 06/2880-946 in Coca), which has several daily buses from the southbound Terminal Terreste Quitumbe (© 02/3988-200) in Quito to Coca. These buses go via Loreto, and the ride takes about 9 hours. Buses to Coca via Lago Agrio leave every half-hour between 6am and 11:30pm. Both **Transportes Baños** and **Putumayo** (© 02/3824-807) make this run, which is longer and takes about 11 hours. The fare via either route is around $15. Return buses follow roughly the same schedule.

BY CAR To get here by car, take the highway (E20) east out of Quito to the remote town of Baeza. Here the road forks, with the well-marked northern fork (E45) heading to Lago Agrio, the southern fork to Tena. You can get to Coca via either route, but it's faster to head south toward Tena and then take the turnoff for Coca. To get to the highway to Baeza from downtown Quito, head north on Avenida Eloy Alfaro to Avenida de los Granados and turn right. This road becomes Hwy. E20. Follow any signs to Papallacta, Baeza, or El Oriente. The ride should take about 8 hours.

GETTING AROUND

Taxis are relatively plentiful around Coca; no ride, including out to the airport, should cost more than $2. If you can't find a cab on the street, have your hotel call one for you, or try **Taxis Amazónicos** (© 06/2881-333) or **Taxis Río Napo** (© 06/2880-169).

Most travelers come here as part of an organized tour or sign on for an organized tour with one of the local agencies. In this case, transportation down the Río Napo is included. However, it is possible to either jump on one of the regular water taxis that ply this river or rent one for yourself. Motorized launches can be hired at the main dock at the end of Calle Napo. A boat holding 8 to 10 passengers should cost between $60 and $80 for a ride to most destinations along the Napo.

ORIENTATION

Unlike Lago Agrio, Coca has a riverside promenade, or Malecón, which is quite attractive, albeit very, very short. You'll find a mix of brick and wooden walkways strewn with park benches and minor attempts at landscaping running along the riverbank. The downtown area of Coca is about 6 square blocks, with the Río Napo defining its southern boundary and the bus terminal defining its northern limits.

FAST FACTS For police, dial © 06/2880-101, or 911 in an emergency. **Hospital Francisco de Orellana** (© 06/2880-139) is on Avenida Labaka about a half-mile outside of downtown. **Banco Pichincha** (© 06/2811-103), near the corner of avenidas Quito and Bolívar, has a 24-hour cash machine. There's also an ATM at the airport. The **post office** (© 06/2881-411) is on Calle Napo, near the corner of Cuenca. There are various Internet cafes in downtown Coca; I like **Samy Café Net** (© 06/2880-362), on Calle García Moreno, between Napo and Quito.

What to See & Do in & Around the Lower Río Napo

There is very, very little for a tourist to do or see in Coca. If you've got some time to kill before heading down the Napo River on a tour or to a lodge, you should head to the riverfront **Malecón** for a pleasant stroll and then stop at one of the simple bars or restaurants for refreshments or a bowl of *ceviche*.

ORELLANA'S journey OF DISCOVERY

In a time when even the most remote regions of the Amazon basin seem to be easily accessible, it is hard to comprehend the challenges faced by the Spanish conquistadors. Few of that era's stories are as incredible as **Francisco de Orellana**'s—a man for whom an Ecuadorean province and its capital city are named, and who "discovered" and navigated the length of the Amazon.

That amazing journey began in Quito, but Orellana's tale started several decades earlier, in the south of Spain. Like most conquistadors, he came from the Spanish province of Extremadura, where conditions were grim enough to make joining expeditions to the Americas—from which few people returned—seem like a good idea. Orellana traveled to the West Indies at age 17 and cut his teeth in Central America. In 1535, he joined an expedition led by his cousin Francisco Pizarro that conquered the Inca empire and captured unfathomable amounts of gold.

Orellana was rewarded for his military service with the governorship of Guayaquil, but the desire for glory, or perhaps simple greed, drove him to join an expedition to find El Dorado, a mythical empire awash with gold. That expedition, led by Francisco's brother Gonzalo Pizarro, departed Quito for the jungles east of the Andes in 1541, with 220 Spaniards, horses, indigenous porters, llamas, and livestock. By the time the group reached the confluence of the Coca and Napo rivers, half the men had deserted or died, and the food stores had run out. They built two boats, and

Pizarro sent Orellana downriver with 50 men to raid indigenous villages for food. But once he had the goods, Orellana was unable to return against the strong current, so he decided to go with the flow. What followed was an 8-month journey down increasingly wide and voluminous rivers, ending at the Atlantic Ocean. They floated past countless indigenous settlements, including one where the riverbank was lined with human heads skewered on posts. But the mythical golden city was not to be found. Some Indians were friendly, but for much of the trip, the conquistadors' boats were attacked by poison arrows. According to Orellana, one such attack was led by fierce women, like the Amazons of Greek mythology, for whom the big river was subsequently named.

On August 26, 1542, Orellana and the remnants of his crew reached the Atlantic, where they sewed their blankets into sails and made their way to a Spanish outpost in the Caribbean. Orellana then returned to Spain, where he regaled the king and aristocracy with tales of his discovery and obtained a grant to establish two colonies on the river. In 1544, he set sail with four ships and 400 men, but Orellana's luck had run out: One ship sank en route, and disease, hunger, and enemy arrows claimed most of his crew once they reached the Amazon delta. Unable to establish a viable colony, Orellana fell ill and died in November 1546. The expedition's 44 survivors sailed to the Caribbean, where a Spanish ship rescued them.

Yasuní National Park ★★   While the Galápagos National Park covers more area, Yasuní National Park is Ecuador's largest land-based park, with some 962,000 hectares (2.4 million acres). Yasuní encompasses several parks and reserves, including the Huaorani Reserve, and has been declared a UNESCO Biosphere reserve. The park—much of which has seen little or no human presence—comprises vast tracks of lowland tropical rainforest, swampland, rivers, and lagoons. Several indigenous groups have their lands and homes protected within the park and still live very simple lives as subsistence farmers, hunters, and gatherers.

Yasuni's wildlife is astonishing and hasn't yet been fully studied or counted. Among the more striking denizens are the jaguar, tapir, harpy eagle, and anaconda. Tours through Yasuni must be made with a guide, either through one of the remote lodges in this region or as part of a tour out of Coca. There's a $25 entrance fee to visit, which is usually collected by your lodge or tour operator and is good for the length of your stay in the region. Yasuni National Park is located to the east and south of Coca, with the Río Napo forming its northern boundary.

Yasuni has recently received worldwide media attention after the Ecuadorian government announced the **Yasuni–ITT Initiative** to leave the 900 million barrels of as-yet untapped oil underground in the Ishpingo-Tiputini-Tambococha (ITT) fields situated in the heart of the biosphere reserve, in return for compensation from the international community for lost profits. Alternately, exploiting the ITT would create carbon emissions of around 436 million tons. The initiative has already gained the support of several countries in a worldwide bid to reduce carbon emissions and help slow climate change. For more information on the Yasuni–ITT Initiative, see www. sosyasuni.org or www.liveyasuni.org.

Where to Stay & Dine in & Around Coca

The restaurants at the two hotels listed below are by far the best and most dependable in town. If you fancy trying the local fare, check out **La Casa del Maito** (✆ 06/2882-285), on Napo and Espejo, or **Pizza Choza** (✆ 06/2881-025), on Rocafuerte and Napo, for good pizzas and pasta. You can get good burgers, burritos, and bar food at **Papa Dan's** (see below).

INEXPENSIVE

In addition to the hotel listed below, budget travelers can head to **Hotel San Fermin** (✆ 06/2880-802; www.wildlifeamazon.com), on Quito and Juan Monalvo, offering simple yet comfortable accommodations with air-conditioning and hot water. Doubles go for $22 to $28.

Hotel Auca ★   This six-story brick-and-glass building towers over Coca. As you approach the fancifully carved front doors, you can almost feel the cool air-conditioning that awaits inside. This place has the most modern and comfortable accommodations in town, but it lacks the riverfront setting of La Misión (see below). Still, if comfort is your priority, I'd choose this place. There's a range of room styles here, and I'd recommend the slight splurge for the minisuites, which come with minibars and free Wi-Fi. Behind the imposing facade is a large garden area, with hammocks for lounging, although the loud pet macaws might make it hard to take a siesta. The **restaurant** serves safe and dependable Ecuadorean and international fare. A favorite of oil workers, Hotel Auca is set in the middle of town, about 4 blocks from the waterfront Malecón.

Av. Napo, btw. Rocafuerte and García Moreno, Coca. ✆ **06/2880-127** or ✆/fax 06/2880-600. 80 units. $44–$48 double; $54 minisuite. Rates include breakfast. AE, DC, MC, V. **Amenities:** Restaurant; bar; small gym. *In room:* TV.

Hotel La Misión ☺   This longstanding riverfront hotel is the major social and transportation hub in Coca. Units vary widely in comfort and style; the best are the second-floor units facing the river. Still, many of the rooms here feel quite worn and dated. The hotel's best feature is its riverfront pool and boardwalk area, with three midsize pools—one with a spiral water slide—and separate children's pool. There are also several shady thatch-roofed areas and an unheated Jacuzzi. The worst feature here? The sad little collection of domesticated toucans, monkeys, and other local fauna.

On the waterfront Malecón and av. 12 de Febrero, Coca (mailing address: Edificio Alamo, 18 de Septiembre E4-76 y Amazonas, Quito). www.hotelamision.com. ☎ **06/2880-544.** Fax 06/2880-263. 85 units. $39 double; $62 suite. DC, MC, V. **Amenities:** Restaurant; bar; small gym; Jacuzzi; 3 outdoor pools. *In room:* A/C, TV, no phone.

Coca After Dark

For a quiet drink, my favorite bar in town is **Papa Dan's** (☎ **06/2880-907**), a simple, open-air joint on the Malecón facing the river; they have good bar food and rocking music. **Bar Emerald Forest Blues** (☎ **06/2882-280**), on the corner of calles Quito and Espejo, is also good. The liveliest spot in town for late-night fun is the downstairs bar and disco at Hotel La Misión (see above), called **El Bunker de Galeth** (☎ **06/2880-260**). If you're lucky, you'll be in town on an evening when this same hotel's floating bar, **Big Bang,** heads out onto the Napo River for a night of partying. The floating barge features an airplane fuselage for the bar's structure. Check with the hotel (☎ **06/2880-260**) to get the barge-bar's current schedule and to reserve a spot. For dancing, you might also try **La Jungla Disco Club** (☎ **09/7832-433**), on the Malecón.

Jungle Lodges on the Lower Río Napo

In addition to the options listed below, the folks at Hotel La Misión have a floating-barge hotel, similar to the *Manatee* listed below. The **Flotel La Misión** (☎ **06/2880-544** for reservations; www.hotelamision.com), offering a 3-day/4-night cruise, is much more rustic, and I prefer the *Manatee* for this type of trip.

Note: Salt licks, or parrot licks, are impressive sights. On sunny days, you can find hundreds, if not thousands, of parrots of various species gathering on these patches of exposed red clay to extract salt and other nutrients. The sight and sound of a parrot lick is not to be missed. Two of these licks are found on the grounds of Napo Wildlife Center, and visits here are included in their package prices. Just about all the lodges and riverboats in the region offer day trips to the parrot licks, although there's always a surcharge. However, be forewarned: There's often a long period of waiting for the birds to appear, and they sometimes don't show up at all.

EXPENSIVE

La Selva Jungle Lodge This place has been going strong for more than 2 decades. Each wood-and-thatch cabin has a large, screened picture window for cross-ventilation, as well as a private bathroom. At night, a pair of kerosene lanterns provides light. La Selva is about 2 hours downriver from Coca; from the disembarkation point on the Napo River, it's a half-hour hike across a rickety raised pathway to the shores of Garzacocha (Heron) Lagoon, where you'll be met by a dugout canoe to transport you across to the lodge. One of the nicest features here: The lagoon is safe for swimming.

Río Napo (office address: Calle Mariana de Jesús E7-211 y La Pradera, Quito). www.laselvajunglelodge. com. ☎ **888/636-3341** in the U.S., or 02/2545-425 reservations in Quito. 17 units. 4-day/3-night tour $717 per person; 5-day/4-night tour $852 per person. Rates include round-trip transportation from and to Coca, all meals and nonalcoholic beverages, daily tours, and taxes. AE, MC, V. **Amenities:** Restaurant; bar; small spa. *In room:* No phone.

Napo Wildlife Center ★★★ 🗽 This lodge is perhaps the area's best run, as well as the most environmentally and socially conscious. A joint venture with the local Añangu Quichua community, the Napo Wildlife Center is involved in conservation efforts. The lodge consists of 12 lakefront bungalows, which are quite large and come with one king-size bed in the main living area and a twin-size bed in a small nook. There's also a hammock on each bungalow's private balcony overlooking the lake. A favorite of bird-watchers, the Napo Wildlife Center has excellent guides, and the grounds here are home to two parrot licks. The 36m (118-ft.) observation tower is one of the tallest in the area, and there's another observation tower just off the bar area. No motorized vehicles are allowed near the lodge, which is inside the Yasuni National Park. From Coca, it's a 2-hour motorboat ride on the Río Napo, then either a 2-hour paddle or a 2km (1¼-mile) hike to the lodge.

On Añangu Lake, off the Lower Río Napo, Coca (Quito office: Rio Yaupi N31–90 y Av. Mariana de Jesús). www.napowildlifecenter.com. ✆ **866/750-0830** in the U.S., or 02/6005-893 reservation office in Quito. 12 units. 4-day/3-night tour $760 per person; 5-day/4-night tour $950 per person. Rates include round-trip transportation from and to Coca, entrance fee to Yasuni National Park, all meals and nonalcoholic beverages, daily tours, and taxes. AE, DC, MC, V. **Amenities:** Restaurant; bar. *In room:* No phone.

Sacha Lodge ★ This is another upscale lodge on the lower Napo River. The large rooms feature high thatched ceilings, varnished wooden floors, relatively modern bathrooms, ceiling fans, and two double beds. Located on Pilchicocha Lake, the cabins are connected to the main lodge via a network of raised and covered walkways. One of the nicest features here is a 275m-long (902-ft.) canopy walkway, located some 30m (98 ft.) above the forest floor. You'll also find an observation tower built around a giant kapok tree, and a butterfly enclosure and breeding project. Meals are served family style in a gorgeous open-air dining room and bar area, and the food is plentiful, varied, and quite tasty.

On a small lagoon off the Lower Río Napo, Coca (mailing address: Julio Zaldumbide 397 y Valladolid, Quito). www.sachalodge.com. ✆ **800/706-2215** in the U.S. and Canada, or 02/2566-090 reservations in Quito. Fax 02/2236-521. 26 units. 4-day/3-night tour $729 per person; 5-day/4-night tour $920 per person. Rates are for double occupancy and include round-trip transportation from and to Coca, all meals and nonalcoholic beverages, daily tours, and taxes. 30% discount for children 11 and under. AE, DC, MC, V. **Amenities:** Restaurant; bar. *In room:* No phone.

MODERATE

Sani Lodge The local Sani Island indigenous community owns and runs this lodge. While you are here, you will hear a lot about "the community," and you will almost certainly visit the home of one or more members. The lodge is set on a narrow black-water lagoon that is home to a healthy population of black caimans, as well as to the odd piranha, electric eel, anaconda, and freshwater sting ray—swimming is discouraged. The lodge also has kilometers of excellent trails and a 30m-tall (98-ft.) bird observation tower. The individual wooden bungalows are simple, with firm beds under mosquito netting and tiny porches. A two-story building houses four large rooms, which each features a king-size bed and small balcony. Though overall the Sani is a good lodging option, the operation and coordination can be rough around the edges. Camping is also allowed at a nearby campsite with covered platforms and permanent tents, and common showers and bathrooms.

On a small lagoon off the Lower Río Napo, Coca (mailing address: San Ignacio 134 y Av. 6 de Diciembre, San Ignacio bldg., 3rd Floor, Office #8, Quito). www.sanilodge.com. ✆ **02/2543-492** reservations in Quito, or 09/4341-728. 14 units. 4-day/3-night tour $627 per person; 5-day/4-night tour $814 per person. Rates include round-trip transportation from and to Coca, all meals and nonalcoholic beverages, daily tours, and taxes. AE, MC, V. **Amenities:** Restaurant; bar. *In room:* No phone.

INEXPENSIVE

Yarina Lodge   This rustic lodge caters to budget-minded travelers. The bamboo-and-thatch cabins are arranged around a large, open, grassy clearing. Each cabin has a tiny front porch, anywhere from two to four twin beds—each with mosquito netting—and a private bathroom. All sorts of tour options are available, including visits to local communities and overnight camping excursions in the jungle. This is one of the closest lodges to Coca, although these folks also operate Yuturi Lodge, which is very isolated, some 5 hours by boat from Coca, on the banks of the Río Yuturi.

Rio Napo, Coca (mailing address: Av. Amazonas N24-240 y Colón, Quito). www.yarinalodge.com. $\mathcal{C}$/fax **02/2504-037** or 02/2503-225 reservations in Quito. 27 units. 4-day/3-night tour $360 per person; 5-day/4-night tour $450 per person. Rates are for double occupancy and include round-trip transportation from and to Coca, all meals, daily tours, and taxes. DC, MC, V. **Amenities:** Restaurant; bar. *In room:* No phone.

A Unique Riverboat Lodge on the Río Napo

Manatee Amazon Explorer ★ 📔   For a different experience of Ecuador's Amazon basin, you might consider booking a berth on this converted river barge. The boat is based out of Coca and cruises up and down the Napo and Aguarico rivers. Side trips to hike in the rainforest, to visit parrot licks, to paddle on isolated lagoons, and to visit local communities are all offered. The cabins are compact yet cheerful, and there are plenty of common areas and deck space, which you can enjoy during the cruise. By boat, you actually see more of the Amazon basin than by staying at a land-based lodge. The longer itineraries here include visits to both Yasuni National Park and Cuyabeno Wildlife Reserve, as well as to Limoncocha Biological Reserve and the flooded area of Lagartococha.

Río Napo, Coca (mailing address: Advantage Travel, Av. Gaspar de Villarroel y 6 de Diciembre, Ed. Ritz Plaza, Quito). www.manateeamazonexplorer.com. $\mathcal{C}$ **02/3360-887** or 02/3360-888 reservations in Quito. 14 units. 4-day/3-night tour $650 per person; 5-day/4-night tour $870 per person. Rates are for double occupancy and include round-trip transportation from and to Coca, all meals and nonalcoholic beverages, daily tours, and taxes. Rates do not include $25 entrance fee to Yasuni National Park or $20 entrance fee to the parrot lick. AE, DC, MC, V. **Amenities:** Restaurant; bar. *In room:* A/C, no phone.

TENA & THE UPPER RÍO NAPO ★

Tena: 186km (115 miles) SW of Quito; 79km (49 miles) N of Puyo

The capital of Napo province, Tena is an attractive and quiet city in the Ecuadorean lowlands. In addition to holding the provincial seat, Tena claims to be the cinnamon capital of Ecuador, and there are cinnamon farms in and around Tena. The town sits at the convergence of the Tena and Puno rivers. Because of its location close to the Andean foothills, Tena has emerged as one of the top spots in Ecuador to go whitewater rafting or kayaking.

Unlike the jungle lodges listed above, the rainforest lodges, tours, and adventures available from Tena are often accessible by car or 4WD vehicle and do not necessarily involve long boat journeys. Also, because Tena is located in the Andean foothills, slightly above sea level, it's a bit cooler here than in the true lowland regions of El Oriente.

Essentials

GETTING THERE

BY PLANE   At the time of writing, Tena's new airport is currently undergoing construction and set to be ready by the time you read this. There is currently no scheduled air traffic to the terminal.

BY BUS   Several bus lines leave from Quito's southbound Terminal Terrestre Quitumbe (© 02/3988-200) for Tena. The main bus lines serving this route include **Transportes Baños** (© 02/3824-843 in Quito, or 06/2886-285 in Tena), **Expreso Baños** (© 02/3824-845 in Quito, or 06/2886-256 in Tena; www.coopexpreso banios.com), **Transportes Amazonas** (© 02/3824-847 in Quito, or 06/2887-213 in Tena), and **Flota Pelileo** (© 02/3824-827 in Quito, or 06/2886-502 in Tena). There's at least one bus per hour between 6am and 7pm, and they run less frequently throughout the rest of the evening hours. The trip takes about 5 hours; return buses follow roughly the same schedule. Fares run around $6. There is also frequent bus service between Tena and Ambato, Coca, and Puyo, as well as less frequent direct service between Tena and Baños, Misahualli, Lago Agrio, and Guayaquil.

BY CAR   To get here by car, take the highway (E20) east out of Quito to the remote town of Baeza. Here the road forks, with the well-marked southern fork (E45) heading to Tena. It's 88km (55 miles) from Quito to Baeza and another 98km (61 miles) from Baeza to Tena. Tena can also be reached from Baños, via Puyo. To take this route, follow the directions to Puyo below and then head north 79km (49 miles) on E45 to Tena.

GETTING AROUND

Taxis are plentiful around Tena. No ride around town should cost more than $1 or $2. Most of the taxis are white pickup trucks, which are well suited for rides on the rough dirt roads that abound off the main thoroughfares all around the area. If you can't easily flag one down or have your hotel call one for you, try **Taxi Central** (© 06/2886-426) or **Taxi Tena** (© 06/2886-658).

ORIENTATION

Tena is spread out on both sides of the Río Tena, with one pedestrian and one vehicular bridge connecting the two halves of the city. The Río Tena makes a severe "S" right in the heart of downtown, so you're never very far from the river. Tena's main plaza is just over the western end of the pedestrian bridge. The bus station is a little over 1km (½ mile) south of the pedestrian bridge on Av. 15 de Noviembre, between Avenida Montero and Calle del Chofer.

FAST FACTS   The **police station** (© 101 in an emergency, or 06/2886-101) is on the main plaza. The **post office** (© 06/2886-418) is at Calle Olmeda and García Moreno, northwest of the vehicular bridge. For emergencies, there's **Hospital José María Velasco Ibarra** (© 06/2886-305), south of town on Av. 15 de Noviembre.

   Banco Pichincha (© 03/2887-600) has a branch at the corner of Avenida Amazonas and Calle Juan León Mera, with a 24-hour cash machine. There are several Internet cafes located in the downtown area, especially around the central plaza.

What to See & Do in & Around Tena

Tena is a quiet city, but an often pretty and safe town in which to stroll. The cathedral fronting the main plaza is an attractive blue-and-white building with two steeples. There are several stone-and-sand beaches on the Tena and Puno rivers, where locals wash their clothes or swim. The main attraction in town is **Parque Amazónico** (© 06/2887-597; parquelaisla@yahoo.es), a small zoo and botanical garden located on an island at the confluence of the Tena and Puno rivers. Typically, the park is reached via a small bridge located on the riverfront a couple of blocks south of the main pedestrian footbridge. However, flooding in 2010 destroyed the park's

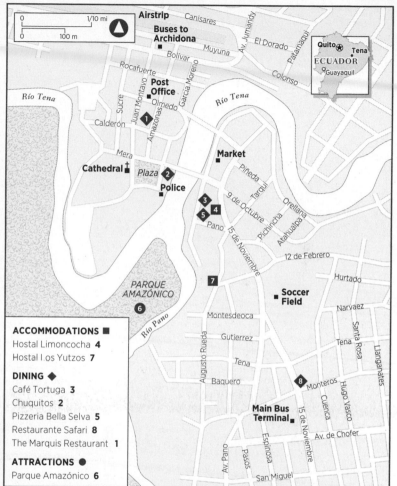

ACCOMMODATIONS ■
Hostal Limoncocha **4**
Hostal Los Yutzos **7**

DINING ◆
Café Tortuga **3**
Chuquitos **2**
Pizzeria Bella Selva **5**
Restaurante Safari **8**
The Marquis Restaurant **1**

ATTRACTIONS ●
Parque Amazónico **6**

footbridge. Currently, the park is open only by appointment and reached via a short boat ride. Admission is $2.

Many folks enjoy visiting the nearby town of **Archidona.** Just 10km (6¼ miles) north of Tena on the road to Baeza, this small, somewhat downtrodden town maintains a sense of timeless tranquillity, with some remnant architecture evocative of its colonial past. The two-tone painted black-and-white-striped church is said to be an imitation of the main Catholic church in Siena, Italy. This is quite a stretch; still, it's worth a quick visit if you find yourself in Archidona.

Just a few kilometers north of Archidona are the **Cuevas de Jumandy** (**Jumandy Caves;** ⓒ **06/2889-185**). This extensive cave system is a popular tourist destination. There's a basic little recreation complex near the entrance, with a couple of pools, slides, and playground areas. The main cave entrance is lit with floodlights, but the caves are best seen as part of a guided tour, which allows you to explore much farther and includes a strong flashlight or headlamp, as well as rubber boots—a help on the moist and muddy hike. Bring a bathing suit: One of the more adventurous parts of the guided tours is the chance to swim in the cool interior pools and rivers. In fact, if you intend to explore the caves deeply at all, you'll have to wade or swim. Most guided tours combine the Jumandy Caves with a stop in Archidona. The caves are open daily from 8am to 6pm. Admission is $5 and includes a 45-minute guided tour.

While a host of guided tours of the local rainforests are possible, I recommend signing up for a visit to the **Jatun Sacha Biological Station** (© 02/2432-240; www.jatunsacha.org), a 3,500-hectare (8,645-acre) private reserve and field station. Developed to promote environmental education and conservation, Jatun Sacha has well-maintained trails and a rotating stable of biologists, guides, and volunteers. Over 565 species of birds and nearly 800 species of butterflies have been spotted here. Jatun Sacha is about 25km (16 miles) south of Tena and can be reached by road or by river.

If you want to do any adventure or organized tours, check in with **Agencia Limoncocha** ★ (© 06/2887-583; http://limoncocha.tripod.com), on Avenida Sagrado Corazón de Jesús; **Hakmatecuad Travel Agency** (© 06/2886-853; hakmatecuad@gmail.com), at 12 de Febrero and Marañón 167; or **Amarongachi Tours** (© 06/2888-204; www.amarongachi.com), at Av. 15 de Noviembre 438. All offer full- and multiday tour options.

GET WET

Tena provides access to some of the best **white-water rafting and kayaking** ★★★ in the country. You have the choice of everything from Class III to Class V rapids. The most popular rivers are the Upper Napo, or Río Jatunyacu, a long and almost constantly moving Class III affair, and the Río Misahuallí, a rough and rugged Class IV+ that is wet and wild. The Misahuallí, in particular, is gorgeous, passing through virgin forest and a deep gorge, and includes a portage around the rushing Casanova Falls. The scenery along both rivers is beautiful. The Jatunyacu is no slouch, either; its name in Quichua means "Big Water." For beginners, children, or timid adventurers, there's the Río Anzu, a much gentler yet still moving Class II and Class III ride.

The best local rafting operators are **Agencia Limoncocha** ★ (© 06/2887-583; http://limoncocha.tripod.com), **Ríos Ecuador** ★★ (© 06/2886-727 in Tena, or 02/2904-054 in Quito; www.riosecuador.com), and **River People Rafting** (© 06/2887-887; www.riverpeoplerafting.com). Rafting trips run $50 to $80 per person, depending on which river you run and the size of your group. Any of the above companies can arrange for experienced kayakers to kayak these rivers.

Where to Stay in Tena

Hostal Limoncocha   There's nothing fancy about this budget hostel in downtown Tena. But the rooms are clean and spiffy, with hand-painted murals, and they're definitely inexpensive. Given the very modest price increase, I definitely recommend one of the rooms with a private bathroom and air-conditioning. These rooms also have small televisions with a handful of cable channels. The best reason for staying here is the fact that these folks run one of the better local tour and rafting agencies. There's no restaurant, but breakfast is served for $2.50 per day, and guests can use the communal kitchen. Limoncocha also has a rustic jungle lodge set beside a beautiful river, some 28km (17 miles) outside Tena, in the Quichua area of Serena.

Av. del Chofer y Sagrado Corazón de Jesús, Tena. http://limoncocha.tripod.com. © **06/2887-583.** 13 units, 6 with private bathroom. $6–$7 per person with shared bathroom; $16–$20 double with private bathroom. No credit cards. **Amenities:** Bar; free Wi-Fi. *In room:* TV, no phone.

Hostal Los Yutzos ★ This riverfront hostel should be your first choice in Tena. Wonderfully located and well managed, the place stands head and shoulders above the competition in town. The rooms are simple, but most are quite spacious, with firm beds, large windows, and a homey vibe. The more expensive units have air-conditioning and more room, and the best have river-view balconies. Even if you don't land a room with a private balcony, the rambling building features several common lounge areas overlooking the river, and lush gardens. Los Yutzos also has a slightly less expensive and more basic annex, where the rooms have no air-conditioning or televisions, but you still get Wi-Fi access.

Augusto Rueda 190 y Av. 15 de Noviembre, Tena. www.uchutican.com. © **06/2886-717** or 06/2887-897. Fax 06/2886-769. 31 units. $49 double. Rates include breakfast and taxes. MC, V. **Amenities:** Bar; smoke-free rooms; free Wi-Fi in lobby. *In room:* TV, minibar.

Where to Dine in Tena

In addition to the places listed below, check out **Pizzeria Bella Selva** (© **06/2887-964**), on the Malecón de Tena, for decent pizzas and pasta, or **Restaurante Safari** (© **06/2888-257**), on Av. 15 de Noviembre and Monteros, for some traditional Ecuadorean cuisine.

MODERATE

The Marquis Restaurant ★★ INTERNATIONAL/STEAKHOUSE This is the fanciest place in town, although that's not exactly a monumental achievement, because no one else is trying to fill this niche. In fact, the atmosphere in this open-air, family-run restaurant is quite relaxed and informal. That said, they do an excellent job, especially on grilled steaks and chicken. You can also usually get homemade pasta, or perhaps a Spanish-style tortilla. They have the only decent selection of wine in town. Portions are quite large, and you can opt for a fixed-price menu, including appetizer, main course, and dessert, for around $12.

Av. Amazonas 251 y Calle Olmedo. © **06/2886-513.** Reservations recommended. Main courses $5–$25. DC, MC, V. Mon–Sat noon–4pm and 5:30–11pm.

INEXPENSIVE

Café Tortuga 🛗 INTERNATIONAL Located beneath the Hostal Brisa del Río, this homey cafe specializes in iced coffees, fresh-baked desserts, and homemade crepes. For more filling fare, you can get a hearty fresh salad, a sandwich served on a baguette, or an American-style hamburger or a vegetarian crepe. For a snack, I also like the *empanada de verde,* with a meat filling and "dough" made from ripe plantains. The large, open front door and windows face the Malecón and river below.

On Calle Orellana (Malecón), just south of the footbridge. © **06/2887-304.** cafetortuga@yahoo.com. Main courses $2.50–$4. No credit cards. Tues–Sat 7:30am–11pm; Sun–Mon 7:30am–12:30pm.

Chuquitos ★ ECUADOREAN This place fronts the main plaza on one side and the Río Tena on the other. You'll want to grab a river-view table in the open-air dining room or on the open deck below it. The food here is simple but well prepared and ample. The menu is quite extensive, and on top of the standard meat, poultry, and seafood dishes, they have such odd options as frogs' legs and *cuy* (guinea pig). The freshwater fried fish—see if they have piranha—is excellent. This is one of the most popular places in town, and justifiably so.

On Calle García Moreno, fronting the main plaza. ✆ **06/2887-630.** Main courses $3–$8. DC, MC, V. Mon–Sat 7:30am–9:30pm.

Cositas Ricas ECUADOREAN/INTERNATIONAL   This is another popular spot, especially with tourists, because it's attached to the **Hostal Traveller's Lodging,** a budget hostel. The broad menu here caters to its international youth crowd, with a good selection of vegetarian options in addition to the typical Ecuadorean and diner-style fare. Breakfasts here are filling and a good deal, at around $2. Be sure to try the fresh juices or fruit smoothies. You can also get pizzas and pastas at their neighboring addition, the **Pizzería Dolce Vita.**

Av. 15 de Noviembre, btw. 9 de Octubre and Calle Tarqui. ✆ **06/2886-372.** Main courses $3–$7. DC, MC, V. Daily 7am–10pm.

Jungle Lodges Outside Tena

A couple of the lodges listed below are located on the Upper Río Napo. All these lodges use both Tena and the tiny river outpost town of Misahuallí as transportation points, although by far most tourists arrange for their transportation via Tena.

In addition to the places listed below, you can't go wrong at **Yachana Lodge** (✆ 02/2523-777; www.yachana.com). I also recommend, **Cabañas Shangrila** (✆ 06/2888-204; www.amarongachi.com), a rustic lodge set on a high hillside over the Anzu River, with spectacular river and forest views.

VERY EXPENSIVE

Hamadryade Lodge ★★ 🏠   This new little lodge is the fanciest and most stylish option in the area. The four spacious individual cabins are awash in varnished hardwoods, and large, open living areas overlook the forest and river below. The lush and beautifully landscaped grounds make for wonderful bird-watching. Owners Sebastian and Melanie Cazaudehore are personable and knowledgeable hosts. The French-inspired food here is outstanding, using local, organic ingredients whenever possible, and is usually prepared personally by Sebastian himself.

11km (6¾ miles) south of Tena, on the road to Pto. Misahuallí. www.hamadryade-lodge.com. ✆ **800/327-3573** in the U.S. and Canada, or 08/5909-992 in Ecuador. 4 units. $260–$360 double. Rates include breakfast and dinner. AE, DC, MC, V. **Amenities:** Restaurant; bar; small pool. *In room:* No phone.

EXPENSIVE

La Casa del Suizo ★   A large pioneering lodge on the banks of the Napo River, La Casa del Suizo offers up cozy rooms and loads of activities. Popular with groups, this lodge feels a bit more like a resort than the other jungle lodges listed in this chapter. The best rooms sit on a high hillside with great views of the river below and rainforest beyond. All come with a ceiling fan and private balcony equipped with an inviting hammock. The lodge borders the small village of Ahuano and offers walks through the town, visits to local artisans, and tours of a wonderful nearby butterfly garden, as well as rainforest and river excursions farther afield. Meals are served buffet style.

On the Río Napo, 15km (9¼ miles) south of Tena (mailing address: Julio Zaldumbide y Wilson, Segundo Valladolid, Quito). www.casadelsuizo.com. ✆ **800/706-2215** in the U.S. and Canada, or 02/2509-504 in Ecuador. 75 units. $94 per person per day. Rates are based on double occupancy and include all meals, daily tours, and taxes. Rates do not include transportation to the lodge, which can be arranged as an add-on. AE, DC, MC, V. **Amenities:** Restaurant; bar; large outdoor pool. *In room:* No phone.

MODERATE

Cabañas Aliñahui   This pretty jungle lodge offers clean and comfortable rooms in a great setting fronting the Río Napo. The rooms are housed in duplex cabins. Each cabin is built up on raised stilts, with a hammock and lounge area on a concrete platform below the rooms. Each duplex has one common bathroom. The spacious rooms have wooden floors and walls, thatched roofs, and large, screened picture windows. Most rooms have either two or three twin beds. Meals are served buffet-style in a large, open-air dining room with a view of the river. Tours include rainforest hikes, trips to the nearby Jatun Sacha Biological Station (see above), and canoe trips. One of my favorite activities here is floating an inner tube on the Napo River.

On the Río Napo, 25km (16 miles) south of Tena, Napo (mailing address: Inglaterra 1373 y Av. Amazonas, Edificio Centro Ejecutivo, 7th Floor, Office 702, Quito). www.ecuadoramazonlodge.com. ⓒ/fax **02/2274-510.** 16 units. 3-day/2-night tour $165 per person; 4-day/3-night tour $185–$195 per person; 5-day/4-night tour $235 per person. Rates are based on double occupancy and include all meals and nonalcoholic beverages, daily tours, and taxes. No credit cards. **Amenities:** Restaurant; bar. *In room:* No phone.

Cotococha Amazon Lodge ★   The wood-and-thatch bungalows here are rustic yet inviting. Request a room that fronts the river. My favorites are nos. 13 and 14, housed in a two-story cabin facing the river and farthest from the main lodge. None has electricity, although they all have hot-water showers and small private balconies. A host of tour and activity options are available. One of the most popular activities here is taking an inner tube out on the Napo.

On the Río Napo, 10km (6¼ miles) south of Tena, on the Puerto Napo-to-Ahuano rd., Napo (mailing address: Av. Amazonas N24–03 y Wilson, Segundo Piso 3, Quito). www.cotococha.com. ⓒ/fax **02/2234-336.** 21 units. 3-day/2-night tour $190 per person; 4-day/3-night tour $320 per person. Rates are based on double occupancy and include all meals, daily tours, and taxes. Rates do not include beverages or transportation to the lodge, which can be arranged as an add-on. DC, MC, V. **Amenities:** Restaurant; bar. *In room:* No phone.

Hacienda Hakuna Matata ★★   This family-run place sits on the banks of the gentle Inchillaqui River. There are three types of rooms—it's worth the slight price increase to get a Lodge or Supreme cabin, which are larger and have wraparound, covered verandas. Units have wood furnishings, large picture windows, and private bathrooms. Horseback riding, hiking, and river rafting are a few of the many popular activities. A new pool, in the shape of a palm tree, is a welcome and welcoming addition. A lunch-and-dinner package is an extra $28 per person per day.

10km (6¼ miles) northwest of Tena, Napo (mailing address: Apartado Postal 165, Correo Central, Tena). www.hakunamat.com. ⓒ/fax **06/2889-617.** 14 units. $70–$90 double. Rates include full breakfast and taxes. DC, MC, V. **Amenities:** Restaurant; bar; pool. *In room:* No phone.

INEXPENSIVE

Huasquila Amazon Lodge   This lodge offers excellent opportunities to enjoy Ecuador's Amazon basin at a great price, with the added perk of easy road access. The wood-and-thatch cabins are a good size, and their decor features work by local artisans. Each unit comes with two twin beds and a private bathroom. Available tours and activities include rainforest hikes, horseback riding, visits to indigenous communities, and a tour to see nearby stone hieroglyphics. For an additional fee, white-water rafting can be arranged. The lodge is 4 to 5 hours from Quito.

3km (1¾ miles) west of Cotundo, about halfway btw. Baeza and Tena (mailing address: Av. Amazonas N22–131 y Veintimilla, Edificio Espinoza, 801, Quito). www.huasquila.com. ⓒ **02/2908-491.** Fax 02/2237-224. 12 units. $99 per person. Rates are based on double occupancy and include all meals and nonalcoholic beverages, daily tours, and taxes. DC, MC, V. **Amenities:** Restaurant; bar; babysitting. *In room:* No phone.

PUYO & THE SOUTHERN AMAZON BASIN ★

Puyo: 237km (147 miles) SE of Quito; 79km (49 miles) S of Tena; 61km (38 miles) SE of Baños

Puyo is the capital of Pastaza province and the principal gateway to the southern Amazon basin. It sits on the banks of the small Río Puyo, at the major road junction connecting Tena and the northern Oriente with Macas and other points in the southern Oriente. Despite not having any major oil industry, such as Coca's or Lago Agrio's, Puyo is the largest city in El Oriente, with nearly 25,000 inhabitants.

Located at the edge of the Andean foothills at an altitude of some 950m (3,116 ft.), Puyo has a slightly cooler and more pleasant climate than you'll find at the lower elevations of the Amazon basin. But it is very humid and moist here.

Essentials

GETTING THERE

BY PLANE Although the small airports here and in the nearby oil town of Shell receive some charter traffic, no regular commuter service is offered to Puyo.

BY BUS Various bus lines leave from Quito's southbound bus terminal Terminal Terrestre Quitumbe (☎ 02/3988-200) for Puyo. The main bus lines servicing this route include **Cooperativo San Francisco** (☎ 02/3824-752 or 02/3824-775 in Quito, or 03/2885-327 in Puyo), **Expreso Baños** (☎ 02/3824-845 in Quito, or 03/288-756 in Puyo), and **Transportes Amazonas** (☎ 02/3824-847 in Quito, or 03/2886-696 in Puyo). Buses leave approximately every hour from 4am to 7:30pm, with less frequent service throughout the rest of the evening hours. The trip takes about 5 hours, with fares costing $5. Return buses follow roughly the same schedule. There is also frequent bus service between Puyo and Ambato, Macas, Riobamba, and Tena, as well as less frequent direct service between Puyo and Baños, Coca, Lago Agrio, and Guayaquil.

BY CAR The most direct route to Puyo from Quito is via Baños, and, in fact, most visitors driving to Puyo come through Baños. Leaving Quito, take the Pan-American Highway (E35) south to Ambato. Just south of Ambato, take the well-marked turnoff for Pelileo, Patate, and Baños. This road continues on through Baños to Puyo. The drive should take around 4½ hours. Alternatively, you can reach Puyo from Tena. To take this route, follow the directions for reaching Tena (p. 309) and continue south on E45 to Puyo, which is a little over an hour's drive.

GETTING AROUND

Taxis are plentiful and inexpensive in Puyo. Any ride around town should be $1 to $2. If you can't readily flag down a taxi, call **Taxi Puyo** (☎ 03/2885-231) or **Taxi 12 de Mayo** (☎ 03/2889-516).

ORIENTATION

The main road from Baños enters Puyo from the south and becomes Avenida Alberto Zambrano. You'll find the main bus terminal along this avenue, a few blocks before hitting the heart of downtown. The central part of the downtown area is north off Zambrano, and its hub is the central park and main Catholic church found at the intersection of Avenida Bolívar and 9 de Octubre.

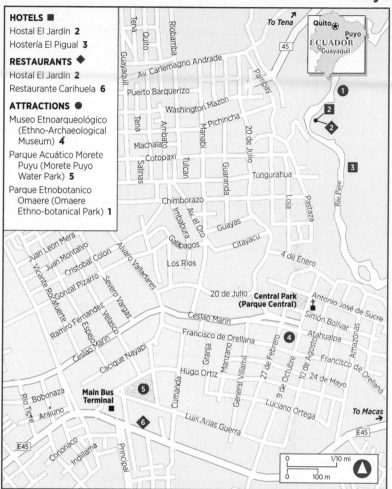

HOTELS ■
Hostal El Jardín **2**
Hostería El Pigual **3**

RESTAURANTS ◆
Hostal El Jardín **2**
Restaurante Carihuela **6**

ATTRACTIONS ●
Museo Etnoarqueológico (Ethno-Archaeological Museum) **4**
Parque Acuático Morete Puyu (Morete Puyo Water Park) **5**
Parque Etnobotanico Omaere (Omaere Ethno-botanical Park) **1**

FAST FACTS The **Ministry of Tourism** (☏ 03/2885-819) has an information booth at its offices on Avenida Francisco de Orellana, between Calle Vilamil and 27 de Febrero. They can give you information on local tours and accommodations.

To reach the local **police**, dial ☏ 03/2885-101, or 911 in an emergency. In the case of a medical emergency, head to the reasonably well-equipped **Hospital Provincial Puyo** (☏ 03/2885-335), on Calle Ramiro Fernández, between calles Espejo and Juan de Velasco. **Banco Pichincha** (☏ 03/2886-792) and **Banco del Austro** (☏ 03/2883-923) both have branches with ATMs in downtown Puyo.

What to See & Do in & Around Puyo

The main attraction in town is **Parque Acuático Morete Puyu** (⊘ 03/2885-123). This water playground is located just behind the main bus terminal and features a series of pools and water slides. There's even a wave pool here. Open Wednesday through Sunday from 8am to 5pm, the park has a $4 entrance fee. This place is very popular with local families and kids, especially on weekends and holidays.

Just off the main plaza in town is the small **Museo Etnoarqueológico (Ethno-Archaeological Museum),** Atahualpa, between avs. 9 de Octubre and 10 de Agosto (⊘ 03/2885-605). The museum has a collection of artifacts, tools, and ceramics from the various indigenous communities of the region, as well as informative displays in Spanish. The museum is open Monday through Saturday from 10am to noon and 1 to 4:30pm. Admission is $1.

Just a short walk from the town's riverside malecón is **Parque Etnobotanico Omaere** ★ (Omaere Ethno-botanical Park; ⊘ 08/5250-864; www.fundacion omaere.org), where you can learn about the different plants from the region and their importance to the local indigenous cultures. Guided walks last an hour or two and the park is open daily from 9am to 5pm. Admission is $3 per person.

Jardín Botánico Las Orquídeas ★ (⊘ 03/2884-855; www.jardinbotanicolas orquideas.com) is another pretty little privately run botanical garden with well-groomed paths, ponds, and an extensive collection of tropical orchids. These botanical gardens are located about 3.2km (2 miles) south of Puyo, on the road to Macas. They are open daily from 8:30am to 4pm, but it's best to call ahead and confirm. Admission is $5 and includes a guided walk through the gardens.

If you're coming here independently and want to organize a trip into the rainforest, or if you want to sign up for adventure sports, you should check in with **Madre Tierra** ★ (⊘ 03/2889-572; www.madreselvaecuador.com). They offer a range of single-day adventures and tours, as well as multiday combination tours. Options include river rafting, mountain biking, canyoneering, rainforest excursions, and tours of local indigenous communities. They can also arrange for Spanish classes and a homestay with a local family, or set you up with a volunteer gig. They also offer shamanic journeys with guided experiences with the local hallucinogenic vine Ayahuasca.

Where to Stay & Dine in Puyo

Puyo is a bustling town in the heart of the lowland jungle. It's not nearly as much of a tourism gateway as its northern neighbors, but it is starting to catch up. There are a number of unmemorable but acceptable budget lodgings in town, many of which are rock-bottom accommodations for backpackers; I recommend spending a few extra dollars for the comfort offered by the inexpensive places listed below.

Aside from the restaurant at **Hostal El Jardín** (see below), you might try **Restaurante Carihuela** (⊘ 03/2883-919), on Avenida Alberto Zambrano near the bus station, which specializes in grilled meats.

Hostal El Jardín ★   The outgrowth of a popular river-view restaurant, this *hostal* offers tidy, spacious rooms on large, well-tended grounds just off the Río Puyo. The rooms are pretty bare, with little more than their varnished wood walls and ceilings, a couple of beds with fluffy comforters, and large picture windows. I'd opt for one of the second-floor units, but those on both the first and second floors have access to shared verandas with sitting areas and some hammocks. There's a small spa here

Macas is the southernmost major town in the Oriente. It's a small jungle town on the banks of the Río Upano with very little in the way of tourism infrastructure. Indeed, it's really only for those looking to get as far away from it all as possible.

There are a handful of budget lodgings around the small downtown area. Of these, I recommend **Hotel Heliconia** (📞 **07/2701-956**), in the heart of downtown on Avenida Soasti and 10 de Agosto. You can't miss this six-story building, the tallest in Macas.

If you want to arrange any tours or adventure activities out of Macas, check in with **Planeta Tours** (📞 **07/2701-328**; planeta_ms@hotmail.com), on Calle Domingo Comin and Avenida Soasti. Tours that include a visit to the indigenous Shuar community, jungle, lakes, and waterfalls will set you back around $75 per person per day, including basic accommodations.

You can get to the town by bus from Quito, Cuenca, or Puyo, but the ride involves taking one bus as far as a narrow footbridge over the Río Puyo and then transferring to a waiting bus on the other side. Another option is to fly to Macas on **Tame** (📞 **1800/500-800** toll-free in Ecuador, or 07/2701-978 in Macas; www.tame.com.ec), which has one flight Monday through Wednesday, and Sunday, from Quito to **Aeropuerto Coronel Edmundo Carvajal** (📞 **07/2700-258**; airport code: XMS). The flight takes 40 minutes and costs $80 each way.

featuring a cozy massage room and two wood-heated hot tub Jacuzzis, and the hotel's **restaurant** is probably the best in town.

Paseo Turístico del Río Puyo, Barrio Obrero. www.eljardin.pastaza.net. 📞/fax **03/2887-770.** 10 units. $56 double. Rates include full breakfast and taxes. MC, V. **Amenities:** Restaurant; bar; 2 Jacuzzis; small spa. *In room:* No phone, free Wi-Fi.

Hostería El Pigual ☺ This complex is a sort of country club and weekend retreat for Ecuadoreans, and also caters to tour groups. All rooms are plenty large, with tile floors, white walls, dark stained-wood furniture and exposed beam ceilings, and minimal decor. You'll pay a little more for a deluxe room, but this will get you a mini-bar and a private balcony or porch. I recommend units on the second floor, with views of the river. There are two-floor units with a queen-size bed below and several twins upstairs, making this a good option for those traveling with children. On the grounds are a children's playground and a game room. There is also a large indoor sauna, steam, and Jacuzzi facility, with high ceilings and brick walls.

At the end of Calle Tungurahua, Barrio Obrero. www.elpigualecuador.com. 📞/fax **03/2887-972.** 21 units. $62–$69 double; $93–$110 deluxe. Rates include breakfast and dinner. Rates slightly lower mid-week. AE, MC, V. **Amenities:** Restaurant; bar; Jacuzzi; midsize outdoor pool; sauna; steam bath. *In room:* TV, minibar.

A Jungle Lodge Outside Puyo

Las Cascadas   Run by the very able folks at Surtrek, this remote, rustic lodge sits amid lush gardens. You have your choice of rooms in one of three duplex cabins or in the main lodge. Rooms in the main lodge are smaller but have access to a wonderful third-floor balcony lounge. The duplex rooms are much larger, and each comes with a spacious private garden-level balcony of its own, with a hammock or two. The signature experience here is a rainforest hike to one of a couple of nearby jungle waterfalls, or *cascadas*.

40km (25 miles) outside of Puyo (mailing address: Surtrek, Reina Victoria N24-151 y Calama, 4to piso, Quito). www.surtrek.com. © **866/978-7398** in the U.S. and Canada, or 02/2500-530 in Ecuador. 11 units. 3-day/2-night tour $540 per person; 4-day/3-night tour $700 per person. Rates include round-trip transportation from Quito, 3 meals daily, all guided tours, taxes, and a stop at the Papallacta hot springs on the way home. AE, MC, V. **Amenities:** Restaurant. *In room:* No phone.

A Very Isolated Nature Lodge

Kapawi Ecolodge & Reserve ★★★   Kapawi is an excellent example of sustainable tourism in action. This lodge has been developed with the cooperation and participation of the local Achuar community, who are the sole owners and operators. All the structures here were built using traditional methods and environmentally friendly technology. The cabins, set on stilts over a black-water lagoon, are rustic in a handsome way; they're extremely comfortable, with polished wood floors, thatched roofs, and bamboo walls. After a hard day of hiking or canoeing, you can relax in a hammock on your own balcony as you gaze at the river. The food here is so good that it's hard to believe you're in the middle of the jungle. *Note:* To get you here, the lodge will arrange a private charter flight—it's the only route in.

On the Río Pastaza, Pastaza province (mailing address: Mariscal Foch E7-38 y Reina Victoria, Edificio Reina Victoria, Quito). www.kapawi.com. © **02/6009-333** reservations office in Quito. Fax 02/6009-334. 18 units. 4 days/3 nights $799–$879 per person; 5 days/4 nights $999–$1,079 per person; 8 days/7 nights $1,699–$1,779 per person. Round-trip airfare from Quito is an additional $344 per person. Rates are for double occupancy and include accommodations, all meals, all nonalcoholic beverages, guide services, and daily excursions. Rates do not include a $10 one-time fee, plus $2.50 per person per day, given to the Achuar community; or taxes. Half-price for children 11 and under, accompanied by two adults. AE, DC, MC, V. **Amenities:** Restaurant; bar; library. *In room:* No phone.

THE GALÁPAGOS ISLANDS

The Galápagos Islands offer some of the best wildlife viewing in the world, not only because the animals themselves are beautiful and interesting (and, in many cases, endemic), but also because many of them are seemingly fearless of humans. Through a quirk of evolution, large predators failed to evolve here, meaning, for example, that the famous blue-footed booby will perform its awkwardly elegant two-step mating dance right under your nose, oblivious to your presence. Mockingbirds will hop onto your shoes. Sea lions will do figure-eights to show off their swimming prowess as you snorkel among them. The local penguins are, admittedly, a bit aloof, but even they aren't above using a snorkeler as a human shield as they attempt to sneak up on schools of fish. In the Galápagos, you don't have to get downwind and peer through the bushes to glimpse the wildlife; you do, however, have to be careful not to step on marine iguanas sunning on the rocks or trip over a sea lion sleeping on the beach as you position yourself to take a photo.

The Galápagos Islands were formed over 5 million years ago by volcanic eruptions. These (and the ongoing formation and development of the islands) occurred primarily over a relatively localized hot spot. However, due to continental drift, the islands are slowly but steadily migrating eastward. Today the most active islands are Fernandina and Isabela, the westernmost islands, although several others have ongoing volcanic activity. The islands' geographic isolation, over 960km (597 miles) off the continental coast, has led to the evolution of numerous endemic species here. This, combined with the animals' fearlessness of humans, played a key role in Charles Darwin's development of the theory of natural selection.

The first European to discover the Galápagos Islands was the Spanish priest Father Tomás de Berlanga, who landed here in 1535. In the centuries that followed, the islands were frequented by various settlers, pirates, fishermen, and whalers. Today only five of the islands are populated— Santa Cruz, San Cristóbal, Floreana, Isabela, and Baltra.

Nearly every visitor to the Galápagos arrives by plane, and only three airlines make the flight from the mainland. Seats are often booked solid far in advance, and fares are certainly not cheap. The best way to see the islands is with a package tour out of Quito or Guayaquil. Most packages include airfare and a berth on a local cruise ship, or a planned land-based itinerary. The ships that tour the islands vary widely in size and quality. My advice: Spend as much money as you can afford. But no matter what you can pay, you won't be disappointed. The wildlife here, which so beguiled Charles Darwin and Herman Melville in the 19th century, is no less astonishing now than it was when they visited.

ESSENTIALS

Getting There

With very, very rare exceptions, travelers come by commercial jet to the Galápagos Islands. **Aerogal** (⌀ 888/723-7642 in the U.S. and Canada, or 1800/2376-425 toll-free in Ecuador; www.aerogal.com.ec), **Lan Ecuador** (⌀ 1800/101-075 toll-free in Ecuador; www.lan.com), and **Tame** (⌀ 1800/500-800 toll-free in Ecuador; www.tame.com.ec) all offer daily flights to **Baltra Airport** (airport code: GPS), right off Santa Cruz Island, while **Aerogal** and **Tame** also service **Puerto Baquerizo Moreno** (airport code: SCY), on San Cristóbal Island. Note, however, that there are sometimes last-minute changes to flight schedules owing to inclement weather. Always check and double-check with your airline and the cruise company to confirm the airport that will be used for your particular itinerary.

Round-trip fares cost around $400, including local taxes and airport fees. During the low season (mid-Sept through mid-Dec, and mid-Jan through mid-June), flights are sometimes a little bit less expensive.

Upon arrival you must pay a $100 fee to the **National Park** (www.galapagospark. org), which is good for the duration of your stay. This fee must be paid in cash, so plan ahead and have it ready. Children under 12 pay $50. There is also a $10 "transit tax" that you must pay at a special booth in the airport before checking in for your flight to the Galápagos.

If you booked a boat tour before you arrived, the airfare and ticket booking should already be included. You can usually expect someone to pick you up at the airport and escort you through the logistics of arriving in the Galápagos and finding the way to your ship. If you're traveling on your own and you have a choice of flights (and airports), I don't recommend flying into San Cristóbal; there is very little tourist infrastructure here. There are a handful of hotels on the island, and you can book last-minute tours and day trips from its port city of Puerto Baquerizo Moreno. But if you plan to base your touring out of a hotel on land, or if you're looking for a last-minute berth on a boat, the place to be is Puerto Ayora, on Santa Cruz, which is accessed from the Baltra Airport.

All flights from the mainland originate in Quito and stop in Guayaquil. If you plan on flying to the Galápagos the day after you arrive in Ecuador, I recommend spending the night in Guayaquil. Most flights to the Galápagos leave Quito early in the morning and then stop for more than an hour to pick up passengers in Guayaquil. You can have a more relaxed morning, and gain precious sleep time, if you board the plane there.

In addition to the two airports mentioned above, a small airstrip on Isabela Island is used for provisioning and inter-island commuter traffic.

Getting Around

The Galápagos archipelago consists of 13 big islands, 6 small islands, and more than 40 islets. **Santa Cruz** is the most populated island; its main town, Puerto Ayora, is the major city in the Galápagos. From here, you can arrange last-minute tours around

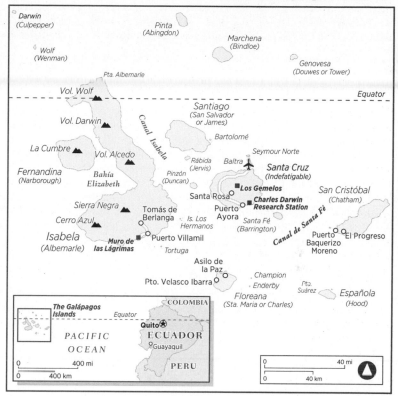

the islands, day trips, and scuba-diving excursions. Santa Cruz is also home to the Darwin Research Station, where you can see giant land tortoises. **San Cristóbal** is the second-most-populated island. Several tour boats begin their journeys from its port, Puerto Baquerizo Moreno. While serving as the official capital of Galápagos province, the town of Puerto Baquerizo Moreno is small. Moreover, there's not much to see on this island. **Isabela** is the largest island but only the third-most populated. In general, most visitors stop here only on a guided tour. For more information about individual islands in the Galápagos, see the appropriate sections below.

To enjoy the best of what the Galápagos have to offer, I recommend exploring the islands by boat. More than 100 tourist ships ply the seas. All boats need a permit and must register with the national park, so it's very difficult to use your private craft. If you're prone to seasickness, you might prefer just taking short day trips from Puerto Ayora to Santa Fe, Plaza Island, North Seymour, and Bartolomé.

Flights between the islands aren't frequent, but the local Galápagos airline **EME-TEBE** (© **800/481-3163** in the U.S., or 02/2956-934; www.emetebe.com) offers service on tiny propeller planes among Santa Cruz, San Cristóbal, and Isabela islands. Fares are $199 for a single flight segment, or $299 for two flight segments.

Visitor Information

The main **tourist information office** (℡ **05/2526-614;** turismo@santacruz.gov.
ec) in the Galápagos is in Puerto Ayora, on Avenida Charles Darwin, close to the
corner of Charles Binford. It is open Monday through Friday from 8am to noon and
2 to 5:30pm.

Note: The Galápagos Islands are 6 hours behind GMT, 1 hour behind mainland
Ecuador.

Exploring the Galápagos
WHEN TO GO

There's never a bad time to visit the Galápagos. The peak season lasts from mid-June
to early September and from mid-December to mid-January. It's almost impossible to
find a last-minute deal at these times. The national park limits the number of visitors
to each island and coordinates each ship's itinerary, so the Galápagos will never feel
like Disney World. But if you visit in the summer, you are less likely to feel a sense
of solitude and isolation. Below is a brief summary of the seasons to help you decide
what time of year is best for you.

DECEMBER THROUGH MAY   During these months, the water and the air are
warmer, but this is the rainy season. It drizzles almost daily for a short period of time,
with the heaviest rains falling February through March. Ironically, this is also the
sunniest time of year. The end of December through the beginning of January is still
the high season, so expect more crowds than during the rest of the year.

Because the water is warmer at this time, swimming and snorkeling are more entic-
ing. On the flip side, there aren't as many fish to see as there are later in the year.
This is the breeding season for land birds, so it's a good time to watch some unusual
mating rituals. If you're into turtles, this is when you want to be here; you can watch
sea turtles nesting on the beach, and March through May, you can often see land
tortoises searching for mates around the lowland areas of the islands. Sea lions also
mate in the rainy season—it's entertaining to watch as the males fight for the females.
Around March and April, you'll see the adorable newborn pups crawling around the
islands.

In February, March, and April, flowers start to blossom and the islands are awash
in bright colors. Another benefit of traveling to the Galápagos at this time of year: The
ocean is much calmer, so you'll have less chance of getting seasick.

JUNE THROUGH NOVEMBER   June through November, the Humboldt Current makes it way up to the Galápagos from the southern end of South America. The
current brings cold water and cold weather, but it also brings water rich in nutrients
and plankton, which attracts fish and birds. During this season there always seem to

---

 You Can Look, but You'd Better Not Touch

It seems like common sense, but in no
case should you touch or in any way
disturb the wild flora and fauna of the
Galápagos. This includes plants, birds,
reptiles, and mammals—every living

thing, both on land and under the
water. Be very aware of not encroach-
ing upon any wild creature or habitat.
Do not litter, and definitely do not
attempt to feed any of the animals.

While most of the ships and boats and all of the dive shops in the Galápagos have snorkeling and diving gear for rent, you might consider bringing your own. If nothing else, bring your own mask. A good, properly fitting mask is the most important factor in predicting the success of a dive or snorkeling outing. Faces come in all sizes and shapes, and I really recommend finding a mask that gives you a perfect fit. Fins are a lesser concern—most operators should have fins to fit your feet. But I definitely prefer to have my own snorkel. If you plan on going out snorkeling or diving more than a few times, the investment will more than pay for itself.

Even during the dry season, the waters of the Galápagos are much cooler than you'd expect this close to the Equator. Most scuba companies dive with full 6mm wet suits year-round. Even if you are snorkeling, a 2 or 3mm full or "shortie" wet suit will make the experience much more enjoyable, especially from June to November, when the Humboldt Current makes the water significantly colder. I highly recommend that you find out in advance if your ship or tour operator can provide or rent you a wet suit. If not, consider buying and bringing one.

be clouds or heavy fog in the air, but it rarely rains. It can also be quite windy, and the seas tend to be rougher.

Experienced divers claim that this is the best time of year to visit the Galápagos. Unfortunately, to see the wide variety of underwater marine life, you have to brave the cold water. Because there are more fish in the sea at this time of year, there are also more seabirds searching for these fish. Albatrosses arrive on Española in June and stay until December. Penguins also like the cold water and the abundance of fish, so you're more likely to see them here during this season. On Genovesa, the elusive owls mate in June and July, and you have the best chance of spotting one during this time. Blue-footed boobies also mate now, so it won't be difficult to witness their beautiful mating ritual known as the "sky point."

The Islands in Brief

Every island in the Galápagos has its own allure. The more time you have, the richer your experience will be, but even if you have only a few days, with proper planning, you'll come home with a lifetime of memories. When you're choosing a tour operator, you should always examine the itinerary. Note that 7-day trips often make frequent stops at Santa Cruz or San Cristóbal to collect and drop off passengers. The best trips head out to far-flung places, such as Genovesa, Española, Floreana, and Fernandina, and spend only 1 day docked in Puerto Ayora, on Santa Cruz. To help you decide which trip might be best for you, here's a list of what each island has to offer.

Santa Cruz ★★ You will most likely begin and end your trip to the Galápagos on Santa Cruz. If you plan to arrange your trip on your own, you should use Santa Cruz as your base. The main city here, Puerto Ayora, is a bustling and attractive little harbor and burg, with a variety of small hotels, restaurants, gift shops, and tour operators. If you're looking for a luxury hotel getaway, this island offers the only such options on the Galápagos, with both the Royal Palm Hotel (p. 343) and Finch Bay Hotel (p. 342). This island is also home to the Charles Darwin Research Station ★★, where you can observe tortoises firsthand. Tours of the island include stops at Los Gemelos (The Twins) ★, two sinkholes that stand side by side. As you walk around Los Gemelos, you will have a good chance of spotting the beautiful vermilion flycatcher. Some companies will take you to a farm in the highlands, where you can see tortoises in the wild. It's exciting to see these enormous creatures crawling about, but I must warn you, it's either hot and sunny up here or cool and drizzly (depending on the seasons). After you see the tortoises, the tour continues on a long, boring hike to a small, unattractive lake. If you can, try to turn back after you see the tortoises. Finally, most trips make a stop at the lava tubes, where you can wander though underground tunnels created by the movement of hot lava. On the north side of the island is Cerro Dragon, which is a great place to see the unique Galápagos land iguana.

Bartolomé Bartolomé (or Bartholomew) is famous for its dramatic vistas and barren volcanic landscape. The most common anchorage here is near the oddly shaped **Pinnacle Rock** ★★. From here, you can climb 372 steps of a wooden walkway to reach the top of an extinct volcano. The vigorous but technically easy climb is a lesson in volcano geography, with cooled-off lava flows and parasitic spatter cones visible along the route to the main cone. On the way up, you will see lava cactuses and lava lizards. The view from the lookout up top is beautiful, with Pinnacle Rock below you. Be sure to ask your guide to pick out a few of the lava rocks to show how light they are. This island has one of the larger colonies of Galápagos penguins ★★★, and many snorkelers have spotted penguins off this island.

San Cristóbal ★ Most boats stop on San Cristóbal only to pick up and drop off passengers. Still, the island's main town, Puerto Baquerizo Moreno, is a pretty little port, with an attractive waterfront walkway, or Malecón. The main attraction on the island is the **Centro de Interpretación (Interpretive Center)** ★★, a small, interesting museum with exhibits on the natural,

human, and geological history of the island. If you spend any time on San Cristóbal, you will probably stop at **El Lobería** ★★, a pretty beach with sea lions, red crabs, and colorful lava gulls. It's also worth visiting **La Galapaguera de Cerro Colorado,** a natural giant-tortoise reserve. If you sail into or out of Puerto Baquerizo Moreno, you will probably pass through **Kicker Rock**—a unique rock formation set about 1.5km (1 mile) offshore. Take note of San Cristóbal's fishing and commuter craft at anchor; many are ringed with strands of barbed wire to keep off sea lions. Boats without the barbed wire almost always have one or two of these large sea mammals lounging around on the aft deck or sunning on the prow.

Santiago ★ Also called **James Island,** Santiago was a major base where early buccaneers and pirates stocked up on fresh water and food. Santiago is also a case study in the potential destruction caused by introduced species. Supposedly, a couple of pairs of feral goats, left here as a future source of food by buccaneers in the 18th century, reproduced to the point where they numbered over 100,000. Recent efforts have greatly reduced the size of the herds of wild goats, but they are still wreaking havoc on certain native species, including giant tortoises. Most of the sea lions in the Galápagos are California sea lions. But on Santiago Island, you will have the chance to see the only endemic species of sea lion in the Galápagos, which is incorrectly called the Galápagos fur seal. After you see the fur seal, you will have an opportunity to take advantage of the excellent snorkeling here ★★. If you're lucky, you'll see sea turtles. The island is also full of coastal birds such as great blue herons, lava herons, oystercatchers, and yellow-crowned night herons.

Española ★★★ This relatively small island features a beautiful cliffside hike, with majestic views. May through December, albatrosses settle down here to mate and take care of their young. In May and June, if you arrive early in the morning, you can witness the beak-cracking mating ritual of the albatross. Later in the season (Sept–Dec), you can see the little chicks. There must be some sort of aphrodisiac on this island, because this is also a great place to see blue-footed boobies doing their mating dance, where the male extends his wings and lifts his beak at his prospective mate. If the female likes what she sees, she mimics her suitor.

Fernandina ★★★ This is the westernmost island in the archipelago and one of the best for wildlife encounters. The largest colony of marine iguanas lives here. These cold-blooded animals hug and cuddle with each other to warm up after swimming. Flightless cormorants also inhabit the island; even though these birds can't fly (they are the only flightless cormorants in the world), they still dry their wings in the sun, just like their flying ancestors used to do millions of years ago. At something around 1 million years of age, Fernandina is the youngest of the Galápagos Islands and one of the most volcanically active. Major eruptions here were recorded as recently as 1995. Hikes over the cooled lava here are fun and rewarding. Be sure to visit the brackish mangrove lagoon, where it's common to see a mixed menagerie that includes sea turtles, sea lions, marine iguanas, and large sting rays.

Isabela ★★ Just to the east of Fernandina, this is the largest island in the Galápagos, formed by the volcanic activity and eventual joining of six different volcanoes—five of which are still active. Darwin's Lake provides an excellent backdrop for dramatic photos of the sea. The island is home to several different species of the giant Galápagos land tortoise, which can commonly be seen in several protected areas. Isabela is particularly prized by bird-watchers; owing to its size, the island has a high species count. One of the common species here is the flamingo, found in its namesake **Pozo de los Flamingos (Flamingo Pond),** close to the main town of Puerto Villamil. Among the main attractions on Isabela is **El Muro de Lágrimas (The Wall of Tears)** ★, a stone wall that was used as a torture mechanism for prisoners kept in a penal colony here

during the mid–20th century. Isabela also has several great hiking and mountain-biking options. Perhaps the most popular is to **Cerro Negro** (a massive, still-active crater often nestled in clouds) ★★ and on to **Cerro Chico** ★★, which offers spectacular panoramic views. In town, you can also see graffiti that dates back to 1836. Tour companies in town, and ships stopping here, usually offer *panga* (dinghy) rides around Tagus Cove, where you will have the opportunity to see the Galápagos penguins.

Rábida ★ Rábida, also known as **Jervis Island,** has a beautiful red-sand beach that is almost always heavily populated with sea lions. If you get too close to a female or child, the local bull male will probably make his presence known. Just behind the beach is a small saltwater lagoon that is a good place to see flamingos. A small loop trail leads to the top of a hill, with some good views of the island's coastline. In my opinion, the waters off Rábida offer the best snorkeling in the islands. I have found myself swimming simultaneously with sea lions and penguins here. Unfortunately, I arrived too late in the day, and the marine iguanas weren't interested in joining us; otherwise, I would have scored a wonderful trifecta.

Genovesa (Tower) ★ Home to **Darwin Bay** and the popular hiking trail known as **"Prince Philip's Steps,"** Genovesa is located on the far northeastern end of the archipelago. It's a long, often rough sail here, and only the longer tours include a visit to Genovesa. Almost every Galápagos tourist brochure has a picture of a frigate bird puffing up its red neck in an attempt to attract females; on Genovesa, you'll have ample opportunities to see these birds in action. This island is also home to the largest colony of red-footed boobies on the archipelago. On another side of the island, you can see masked boobies and storm petrels. If you're lucky, you might spot the elusive short-eared owl—as these guys don't have predators, they are the only owls in the world that are diurnal. Genovesa is also home to both sea lions and the endemic Galápagos fur seal.

Floreana ★★ This small island, the first to be inhabited, is rich in lore and intrigue (see "An Island Whodunit?" on p. 354). Today some 100 people live on this island, which is seldom visited by tourists. If you do come here, hopefully your itinerary includes a stop at **Post Office Bay** ★, where a barrel full of letters and postcards sits on the beach. It's a tradition begun by early whalers: If you see a letter or card addressed to someone in your town or country, you are supposed to carry it and post it from home. In exchange, feel free to leave a letter or postcard of your own for someone else to return the favor. A hike on Floreana often passes by the island's main lagoon, a seasonal nesting site for pink flamingos.

CRUISES

Choosing a Boat Tour

Scores of companies offer trips through the Galápagos, and trying to sift through all the tourist brochures and offers is daunting. First and foremost, let me warn you that you tend to get what you pay for here. There are four classes of boats: economic, tourist class, first class, and luxury. The **economic boats** have shared dormitories and bathrooms, inexperienced (and non-English-speaking) guides, and mediocre food. On a **tourist-class boat,** you may have your own private quarters, but expect them to be cramped. You probably won't have air-conditioning or hot water, and your guide might not have a good command of the English language. **First-class ships** have excellent guides, small but private cabins with hot water and air-conditioning, and passable food. The main difference between first-class and **luxury** service is the food; some luxury boats also have swimming pools or Jacuzzis, but the cabins are not necessarily much bigger.

Another word of caution: Don't expect your cruise in the Galápagos to be a typical pleasure cruise; the boats are used mainly for lodging and transportation purposes. During the day, small dinghies, known as *pangas,* will transport you to the actual islands. Schedules are packed with activities and often include early wake-up calls and full, grueling days. Once you're on land, the excursions often involve long

---

Ship or Shore?

For many, the most important decision to make when planning a trip to the Galápagos is whether to take a cruise or visit the islands from a hotel base on land. The standard advice is that those prone to seasickness are better off staying on land. This may be true, but if you plan to take day trips from Santa Cruz Island to any of the other popular island sites, you will most likely be doing so on a very small boat. Conversely, if you book a cruise on one of the larger ships, you will be on a boat that is much more stable in rough seas, and most of the travel is done at night,

while you are hopefully asleep or, at the very least, supine.

If you're looking to avoid a regimented experience with a bit of the cattle-car feel, avoid the larger ships, and be sure to ask in advance the number of passengers per naturalist guide. I recommend you **find a tour with no more than 10 tourists per naturalist guide.**

Yogi Berra said, "When you come to a fork in the road, take it." I personally think the best way to go is to do both. My ideal Galápagos tour is a 4- or 5-night cruise, followed by 3 nights at a hotel on one or more of the islands.

Scuba-Diving Trips

The waters surrounding the Galápagos offer **some of the best diving in the world ★★★**. If you want to dive here, you have two options: Book a tour on a dedicated dive boat—and dive every day—or take a nondiving cruise and then spend a couple of extra days in Puerto Ayora and arrange diving excursions from there. Two of the best diving outfitters in Puerto Ayora are SCUBA Iguana (© 05/2526-497; www.scuba iguana.com), located at the end of Avenida Charles Darwin, right by the entrance to the Darwin Research Station; and **Sub-Aqua ★** (© 05/2526-633; www.galapagos-sub-aqua.com), on avs. Charles Darwin and 12 de Febrero. You can also dive out of Puerto Barquerizo Moreno on San Cristóbal, or Puerto Villamil on Isabela.

hikes, some with steep climbs. The Galápagos are not a place for relaxing—expect to participate in strenuous activities.

Moreover, **size matters.** The larger ships, in general, are the most luxurious, with the greatest number of amenities. These are also much more stable and enjoyable when the seas get choppy. Still, even the best of these have a slight cattle-car feel to their operation. When you're exploring the islands with 100 other people, the islands lose some of their mystique. Plus, you always feel a bit rushed, because there is always a group behind you, waiting for you to continue on your way. If you're looking for a more intimate experience, you'll want to book one of the smaller yachts. These have a bit more flexibility and often afford the ability to linger a bit more on the island tours.

Trips to the Galápagos venture out to the high seas, and the waters can be rough. Be sure to bring anti-seasickness medication with you. Ginger (candied or powdered) also helps settle small stomach upsets and is an alternative to medication. If you know that you are prone to seasickness, you'll definitely want to book on one of the larger ships, which are much more stable and comfortable. Also note that although the lower cabins tend to be a bit darker, with portholes as opposed to larger windows, these cabins are also the most stable. (In other words, you're more likely to become seasick when you're sleeping higher up.)

Recommended Tour Operators & Ships

Every travel agency and tour operator in Quito and Guayaquil offers package tours to the Galápagos, as do many international operators. In most cases, they just book space, either by reserving in advance or on a first-come, first-served basis, on the set number of boats touring the archipelago. Profit margins are very low, and prices tend to be standardized—meaning it's very rare for any agency or operator to severely undercut another for the same berth on any one boat or ship. Below I list recommended Ecuadorean and international tour operators specializing in Galápagos trips, as well as descriptions and contact information, when possible, for my favorite boats and ships.

ECUADOREAN & INTERNATIONAL TOUR OPERATORS

Butterfield & Robinson ★★ (© 866/551-9090 in the U.S. and Canada; www. butterfield.com) specializes in the very high-end market. One of its most interesting options is a trip designed for families with children over 8 years old. The trip provides a wealth of activities and adventures for parents and children to enjoy both together

NOT YOUR TYPICAL passenger: CHARLES DARWIN & THE GALÁPAGOS ISLANDS

Charles Darwin was only 22 years old when he set sail on an around-the-world cruise aboard the HMS *Beagle* in 1831. After several years surveying the coast of South America, the *Beagle* reached the Galápagos Islands in September 1835 and spent 5 weeks charting the archipelago. While there, Darwin made careful note of the biology and geology of the islands, and collected numerous specimens. Darwin visited only four of the islands—San Cristóbal, Santiago, Isabela, and Floreana. But his observation of species differentiation, particularly among the tortoises and finches, intrigued and inspired the young scientist. While Darwin is often credited with the discovery of the theory of evolution, what he really developed was the theory of natural selection, which explains how and why evolution occurs. Central to Darwin's theory was his recognition of the geological age and isolation of the volcanic islands; he was convinced that wildlife on the Galápagos came from mainland South America, changing and adapting over time to fill in specific niches defined by the particular ecosystem of the islands. Even though Darwin had formulated most of his most important ideas in just the few years following his visit to the Galápagos, he didn't publish his seminal work, *On the Origin of Species,* until 1859. Prior to that, in 1839, he published *The Voyage of the* Beagle, which chronicled his trip.

and apart. These folks charter out the luxury cruise ship *Isabela II* and pay particular attention to the small details. Of course, this level of service and luxury doesn't come cheap: A 9-day/8-night trip ranges from $7,000 to $12,500 per person.

Ecoventura ★ (© **800/633-7972** in the U.S. and Canada, or 04/2839-390 in Ecuador; www.ecoventura.com) operates four first-class ships: the 16-passenger dive boat M/Y *Galapagos Sky* (see below), and the three identical 20-passenger boats M/Y *Eric, Flamingo I,* and *Letty.* Each of the latter three has two guides for every 20 people, a large sun deck, a bar, two sea kayaks, and snorkeling equipment. In addition to providing personalized service and excellent local guides, Ecoventura is environmentally friendly. Don't expect super-luxurious cabins or over-the-top food, but you can count on this operation having the most experienced guides in the islands.

Galacruises Expeditions (© **02/2509-007** in Ecuador; www.galacruises.com) runs five ships of their own and can book passage on a wide range of other boats and ships. Their boats range from tourist-class monohulls to modern luxury catamaran yachts. They do full-service tours around Ecuador and the region.

KLEIN Tours ★ (© **888/810-6909** in the U.S., or 02/2430-345 in Ecuador; www.kleintours.com) is one of the oldest companies operating boats in the Galápagos, and their experience shows. The company maintains three first-class ships: the 20-passenger M/Y *Coral,* the 26-passenger M/Y *Coral II,* and the 110-passenger M/V *Galápagos Legend.* The guides are excellent and knowledgeable. The M/Y *Coral* is the more deluxe option of the two smaller vessels, with a top-deck Jacuzzi and fine rooms. The *Legend* has large cabins, a swimming pool, massage service, and a jogging track.

Linblad Expeditions ★★ (© **800/397-3348** in the U.S. and Canada; www.expeditions.com) is another luxury-oriented tour agency with decades of experience in the Galápagos, and a particular commitment to protecting the environment and raising environmental awareness. The company operates three luxurious cruise ships here, the *National Geographic Explorer,* the *National Geographic Islander,* and the *National Geographic Polaris.* Their 10-day program costs $4,980 to $8,040 per person. Various extensions are available, as is a Machu Picchu combination tour.

Metropolitan Touring ★★★ (© 888/572-0166 in the U.S. and Canada, or 02/2988-200 in Ecuador; www.metropolitan-touring.com) runs three luxury ships (M/V *La Pinta,* M/V *Santa Cruz,* and M/V *Isabela II*) and one luxury hotel (Finch Bay Hotel; p. 342) and is one of the largest and most professional tour agencies in Ecuador. Consider booking with them especially if you want to mix and match time on shore with time on a ship, or if you want to design a package that includes a Galápagos excursion as well as trips to other destinations in Ecuador. Their 48-passenger *La Pinta* combines the comforts and smooth ride of a large ship with an intimate, small-group experience.

Overseas Adventure Travel ★ (© 800/493-6824 in the U.S. and Canada; www.oattravel.com) offers good-value itineraries, often combining a Galápagos cruise with time in Ecuador's Amazon or a side trip to Machu Picchu. Tours are limited to 16 people and are guided by experienced naturalists. Their 15-day Galápagos-and-Amazon package starts at $4,695 per person, including round-trip airfare from Miami.

Quasar Náutica (© 866/481-7790 in the U.S. and Canada, 0800/883-0827 in the U.K., or 02/2446-996 in Ecuador; www.quasarnautica.com) operates two large yet intimate yachts in the Galápagos. Their largest ship, the M/V *Evolution,* features 16 double staterooms. This vessel harkens back to the early 20th century and features a wonderful aft-deck dining room. The smaller M/V *Grace* is a classic and historic yacht that was actually the wedding present given by Aristotle Onasis to Prince Rainer and Grace Kelly—hence the name.

Surtrek ★★ (© 866/978-7398 in the U.S. and Canada, or 02/2500-530 in Ecuador; www.surtrek.com) is one of the better Quito-based general tour/adventure tour operators. And their Galápagos connections and experience are top-notch. They can book a wide range of cruises and mixed itineraries, and are often good at finding last-minute bargain berths on ships.

Tauck ★★ (© 800/788-7885 in the U.S. and Canada; www.tauck.com) is a well-established soft-adventure tour company catering to higher-end travelers. They do an excellent job across the board and have various itineraries, ranging from a combination Galápagos-and-Peru trip to a family excursion through the Galápagos. Tauck always charters an entire ship, usually one of the better luxury cruise ships plying these waters.

INDIVIDUAL SHIPS & BOATS
Luxury & First Class
M/V Celebrity Xpedition ★★★ LUXURY   It's hard to beat Celebrity for luxury and pampering. This 92-passenger vessel has several stateroom categories, and if you can afford it, the suites all feature private balconies. The 296-foot ship is wonderfully appointed and features several bar, lounge, and dining areas, as well as a small spa, sauna, and requisite top-deck Jacuzzi. Tours and service are top notch, as are the food and overall pampering, and most drinks, tips, and extra charges are already included in the rates. Their 10-day packages include 3 nights at the JW Marriott in Quito, two pre-cruise, and one post-cruise.

1050 Caribbean Way, Miami, FL 33132. © **800/647-2251** toll-free in the U.S. and Canada, or 316/554-5961. Fax 305/373-4384. www.celebritycruises.com. 7-night cruises from $4,000 per person. Rates include accommodations, all meals and drinks, guide services, and transfers btw. the dock and airport, as well as crew and staff gratuities and the $100 national park fee.

M/V Galápagos Explorer II ★★ LUXURY   The *Galápagos Explorer II* is one of the most luxurious ships in the Galápagos. The 100-passenger cruise ship offers all the amenities you could want: swimming pool, two Jacuzzis, a couple of bars, first-class food, research center, nightly naturalist lectures, library, game room, and a doctor on board. Most important, all the accommodations are exterior-facing suites, each with a small sitting area, a minibar, and a TV/DVD.

Urbanización Santa Leonor, Manzana 5, Solar 10, Guayaquil. ☎ **800/613-6026** in the U.S. and Canada, or 04/2285-711 in Ecuador. Fax 04/2287-651. www.galapagosexplorer.com. 3 nights $1,490–$2,155 per person; 4 nights $1,985–$2,880 per person; 7 nights $3,260–$4,730 per person. Rates include accommodations, all meals, guide services, and transfers btw. the dock and airport. Rates do not include airfare, hotel-to-airport transfers in Quito or Guayaquil, gratuities, or the $100 national park fee.

M/V La Pinta ★★★ LUXURY   This is my favorite of the large luxury cruise ships working the Galápagos. This newer ship was launched in 2008. Every cabin has an ocean view, through a large floor-to-ceiling picture window. Connecting rooms are perfect for families. And Wi-Fi is offered throughout the ship. The common areas are inviting, and the 48-passenger maximum is small enough that it's easy to interact with other guests and not feel overwhelmed by the masses. The guides are all well trained and very pleasant, and the ship's standard 7-night/8-day itinerary is excellent.

Av. de la Palmeras N35–74 y Av. de las Orquídeas, Quito. ☎ **888/572-0166** in the U.S. and Canada, or 02/2988-200 reservations in Quito. Fax 02/3341-250. www.metropolitan-touring.com. Rates run around $4,656 per person double occupancy for a 7-night cruise. 3- and 4-night itineraries are also available. Rates include accommodations, all meals, guide services, and transfers btw. the dock and airport. Rates do not include airfare, hotel-to-airport transfers in Quito or Guayaquil, gratuities, or the $100 national park fee.

M/V Santa Cruz ★★ LUXURY   This is another fabulously run large ship. Almost every cabin has an ocean view—many with large picture windows, and a couple with balconies. The common areas are inviting, and the 90-passenger maximum is just small enough that it's easy to interact with other guests and not feel overwhelmed by the masses. Well-done buffet meals are served for breakfast and lunch, while dinners are more formal, with a limited selection of nightly a la carte items. The main deck area features a large open-air bar and a popular, well-heated Jacuzzi. There's Wi-Fi aboard, and they even offer limited free Internet access from a common computer in the small library, which has a good selection of natural history and fiction. Run by Metropolitan Touring, the guide staff and over service are excellent.

Av. de la Palmeras N35–74 y Av. de las Orquídeas, Quito. ☎ **888/572-0166** in the U.S. and Canada, or 02/2988-200 reservations in Quito. Fax 02/3341-250. www.metropolitan-touring.com. Rates begin around $3,711 per person double occupancy for a 6-night cruise. 3- and 4-night itineraries are also available. Rates include accommodations, all meals, guide services, and transfers btw. the dock and airport. Rates do not include airfare, hotel-to-airport transfers in Quito or Guayaquil, gratuities, or the $100 national park fee.

S/S Mary Anne ★★ 🛏 FIRST CLASS   This is the most unique vessel touring the Galápagos. Launched in 1997, the *Mary Anne* is a true three-masted, square-rigged barkentine. Over 197 feet long, including its bowsprit, it carries over 93 sq. m (1,001 sq. ft.) of sail and a maximum of 16 passengers. That's a lot of ship for very few passengers. When all its sails are set, it's an impressive sight. Heck, even at anchor, it's pretty special. If you choose this vessel, you'll truly feel transported back in time. The air-conditioned cabins aren't quite as large and luxurious as the offerings of some of the other luxury cruise ships listed here, but what you sacrifice in creature comforts you more than make up for in character and ambience. The ship carries kayaks for guest use and one naturalist guide, which is a bit thin if they are booked to capacity. These folks also run several other sail and motor vessels.

Mariana de Jesús E7-113 (326) y Pradera, Quito. ℂ **02/3237-330** in Quito. Fax 02/3238-309. www.angermeyercruises.com. 7 nights from $3,700 per person. Rates include accommodations, all meals, nonalcoholic beverages, guide services, snorkeling equipment, and transfers btw. the dock and airport. Rates do not include airfare, hotel-to-airport transfers in Quito or Guayaquil, gratuities, or the $100 national park fee.

Tourist & Economy Class

M/S Angelique SUPERIOR TOURIST This is a beautiful 75-foot wooden schooner. Its foremast even carries a couple of square sails, making it seem like a classic sailing ship. The berths near midship are larger than those closer to the bow, but the midship cabins are also closer to the engine, so it's a trade-off. I'd opt to be a bit farther away from the engine.

Ramírez Dávalos 117 y Av. Amazonas, Quito. ℂ **02/2505-599.** Fax 05/2226-715. www.kempery.com. Rates for a 3-night cruise begin at $930 per person double occupancy; for a 7-night cruise, rates begin at $1,680 per person double occupancy. Rates include accommodations, all meals, nonalcoholic beverages, guide services, and transfers btw. the dock and airport. Rates do not include airfare, hotel-to-airport transfers in Quito or Guayaquil, gratuities, or the $100 national park fee.

M/S Sulidae ★ 🗲 TOURIST This is one of my top choices among the tourist- and economy-class options, but then again, I'm partial to sailboats—or, at least, to motor-sailers. This 62-foot motor-sailer features teak decks, red sails, and the feel of a working sailboat. Down below, there's plenty of varnished wood, and the boat is well maintained. The bunks are compact, but all have private bathrooms and even air-conditioning. Traditional sailboat enthusiasts will find its massive aft quarters a bit unsightly, but they greatly increase the room and comfort inside.

Mariscal Foch 746 y Av. Amazonas, Quito. ℂ **02/2906-665.** www.galapagossulidae.com. 7 nights $1,350 per person. Rates include accommodations, all meals, nonalcoholic beverages, guide services, snorkeling equipment, and transfers btw. the dock and airport. Rates do not include airfare, hotel-to-airport transfers in Quito or Guayaquil, gratuities, or the $100 national park fee.

M/Y Sea Man II SUPERIOR TOURIST Of the many small tourist-class motor yachts plying the Galápagos Islands, this spacious catamaran is one of the best, but also one of the most expensive. This boat carries a maximum of 16 passengers in eight double staterooms. The wood-floored cabins are a bit small, but they all have air-conditioning, which is not always the case with tourist-class yachts. And the intimate boat and excellent crew help compensate for the lack of space. Plus, when you're awake, you don't spend that much time in the cabins anyway. There's a large sun deck on the uppermost level. This is a fully equipped dive boat, and scuba diving will run you an additional $80 per dive, with all equipment included.

Galacruises Expeditions, 9 de Octubre N22-118 y Veintimilla, Edificio El Trébol, Quito. ℂ/fax **02/2509-007** in Quito. www.galacruises.com. 4 nights $1,900–$2,400 per person; 7 nights $3,400–$3,800 per person. Rates include accommodations, all meals, nonalcoholic beverages, snorkel gear, guide services, and all transfers btw. Quito or Guayaquil and the Galápagos. Rates do not include gratuities or the $100 national park fee.

Dedicated Dive Boats

In addition to generally having better equipment and dive masters, the dedicated dive boats tend to design their itineraries in order to visit the archipelago's top dive sites, particularly those around Wolf and Darwin islands. Most feature an average of four dives per day, although some days you may go down five times. Night diving is not allowed in the Galápagos.

ORGANIZING A LAST-MINUTE trip TO THE GALÁPAGOS

There's no way around it—trips to the Galápagos are expensive. But if you book a cruise at the last minute, you can sometimes save substantially off the regular rates. Most boats would rather sell a few spaces at steep discounts than send the ship out with empty staterooms. Unfortunately, it's not easy to find a last-minute price, and you run the risk of not finding space. During the high season (June–Sept and late Dec–early Jan), it's especially difficult, although there are sometimes spots to fill from last-minute cancellations. Even during the low season, you shouldn't expect to come to Ecuador and immediately find a boat leaving the next day. In some cases, you may have to wait a week to 10 days before you find an opening.

Your best bet for finding a discount is to hit several of the budget-oriented travel agencies in the Mariscal district of Quito, or along Avenida Charles Darwin in Puerto Ayora. I've found the following agencies to be some of the best at arranging a last-minute Galápagos cruise.

In Quito

o **Ecoventura** ★ operates four ships and yachts in the Galápagos. Through their website (www.ecoventura.com), they sometimes offer last-minute deals at reduced rates. If there are no special discounts on the website, stop in or call their local offices in Ecuador. They have an office at Almagro N31–80, Edificio Venecia (✆ 02/2907-396); in Guayaquil, their office is in the Edificio Samborondón Business Center, Torre A Piso 3 (✆ 04/2839-390). At both offices, you can try to book a last-minute berth at last-minute prices.

o **Quasar Náutica** (✆ 800/481-7790 in the U.S. and Canada, 0800/883-0827 in the U.K., or 02/2446-996 in Ecuador; www.quasarnautica.com), at Jose Jussieu N41-28 and Alonso de Torres, is one of the larger cruise operators in the Galápagos, with a fleet of boats and a permanent office in Puerto Ayora.

o **Surtrek** ★★ (✆ 866/978-7398 in the U.S. and Canada, or 02/2500-530 in Ecuador; www.surtrek.com), on Av. Amazonas 897 and Wilson, is an excellent and very accommodating Quito-based operator, with great Galápagos connections and good last-minute deals.

o **Zenith Ecuador Travel** ★ (✆ 02/2529-993; www.zenithecuador.com), at Juan León Mera N24-264 and Luis Cordero, has access to information on about 100 boats that ply the waters around the Galápagos Islands. Give the staff your dates and your requirements, and they'll talk to their contacts and try to find you a special last-minute deal. Ask to speak to the owner, Marcos Endara, and tell him you are a Frommer's reader.

In Puerto Ayora

o **Moonrise Travel Agency** (✆ 05/2526-589; www.galapagosmoonrise.com), on Avenida Charles Darwin near the corner of Charles Binford, is an excellent family-run local operation that specializes in booking last-minute trips on a number of different vessels (all classes and sizes).

Caution: Diving in these waters is not for beginning divers. There are often strong currents, cold waters, and limited visibility. Much of the diving is in relatively deep water. The payoff comes in the size, number, and diversity of large marine life. Due to the nature of the diving here, I recommend taking a boat with Nitrox facilities. If you are not already Nitrox certified, you can take a course onboard and dive with Nitrox tanks the entire time.

M/V Galápagos Aggressor I & II ★★ 🎁 LUXURY   Part of the worldwide *Aggressor* fleet, these identical live-aboard vessels provide state-of-the-art dive technology and guiding services along with top-notch accommodations, cuisine, and creature comforts. Living, dive, and common areas are all well designed and roomy. These 98-foot ships carry a maximum of 14 divers, so the experience is always intimate and personal. While scuba diving is the focus, several land tours are included in the weeklong itinerary. This boat has Nitrox facilities, as well as full film-developing equipment. Underwater still and video cameras can be rented.

P.O. Box 1470, Morgan City, LA 70381. ℂ **800/348-2628** in the U.S. and Canada, or 04/2681-950 in Ecuador. www.aggressor.com. 7-day itinerary $4,495–$5,395 per person double occupancy. Rates include accommodations, all meals and beverages, unlimited diving, and transfers btw. the boat and airport. Rates do not include airfare, hotel-to-airport transfers in Quito or Guayaquil, gratuities, the $100 national park fee, or $75 port fee.

M/V Galápagos Sky ★ LUXURY   This modern 98-foot vessel carries a maximum of 16 divers in eight staterooms. The air-conditioned staterooms are certainly comfortable, but I find the accommodations and amenities a notch better across the board on the two *Aggressors*. Still, this is a very well-run and reputable operation, and serious divers will not be disappointed here. Food and diving services are excellent, and they have top-notch facilities, including Nitrox tanks and training.

Km 1.5 Vía Samborondón, Samborondón Business Center, Torre A, Piso 3, Guayaquil. ℂ **800/633-7972** in the U.S. and Canada, or 04/2839-390 in Ecuador. www.ecoventura.com. 7-day itinerary $4,595–$4,795 per person double occupancy. Rates include accommodations, all meals and beverages, unlimited diving, and transfers btw. the boat and airport. Rates do not include airfare, hotel-to-airport transfers in Quito or Guayaquil, gratuities, or the $100 national park fee.

PUERTO AYORA & SANTA CRUZ ISLAND ★★

Santa Cruz is the principal base for tourism operations around the Galápagos, and Puerto Ayora is the island's main city. In fact, Puerto Ayora is the largest settlement in the archipelago. If you're arriving on your own, this the best place to base yourself and organize your trip. Puerto Ayora is a bustling little port, with some 15,000 inhabitants. The Galápagos National Park headquarters is here, as is the Charles Darwin Research Station.

Just off the north coast of Santa Cruz lies the small but very crucial island of Baltra. It's home to both the busiest airport on the Galápagos and the most important deepwater port, where cruise and cargo ships come to refuel, unload cargo, and pick up and discharge passengers. The only major paved road on the island, outside of the city streets, is the road that connects Puerto Ayora with the dock at the narrow Canal de Itabaca (Itabaca Canal), which separates Santa Cruz and Baltra islands.

Essentials

GETTING THERE

All flights from Quito and Guayaquil to Santa Cruz land at **Aeropuerto Seymour** (✆ **05/2521-165;** airport code: GPS), on the small island of Baltra, just off Santa Cruz's northern coast. In addition to desks at the airport, **Tame** (✆ **1800/500-800** toll-free nationwide, or 05/2526-527 in Puerto Ayora; www.tame.com.ec) has its main local offices on Avenida Charles Darwin and 12 de Febrero; **Aerogal** (✆ **1800/2376-425** toll-free nationwide, or 05/2526-797 in Puerto Ayora; www.aerogal.com.ec) has its offices on Avenida Baltra, between 10 de Marzo and Indefatigable; and **Lan Ecuador** (✆ **1800/101-075** toll-free in Ecuador; www.lan.com) has its offices on Avenida Charles Darwin, between calles Islas Plazas and 12 de Febrero.

Once you land at the airport, a free shuttle bus will take you to a ferry crossing of the Itabaca Canal to Santa Cruz. If you are going to the town of Puerto Ayora, take the bus marked CANAL. The ferry costs 80¢, and a regular bus will be waiting for you on the other side. From here to Puerto Ayora, the ride takes about 40 minutes and costs $3.50. You can also go to Puerto Ayora by taxi—you'll find a host of them waiting at the crossing. The fare should run you from $15 to $20.

If you are going to directly board a boat or ship and are not being met by a representative of that ship, you may need to take the free bus from the airport terminal marked MUELLE. This bus takes you to the dock in Baltra, where many of the ships wait to pick up passengers. Be sure to check this out in advance with your ship.

Tip: If you are flying out of Baltra, allow at least an hour to get from downtown Puerto Ayora to the airport.

VISITOR INFORMATION

The Ministry of Tourism runs a **tourist information office** (✆ **05/2526-614;** turismo@santacruz.gov.ec) on Avenida Charles Darwin, close to the corner of Charles Binford. It is open Monday through Friday from 8am to noon and 2 to 5:30pm. There are several small local tour operators along Avenida Charles Darwin. All of these offer a range of tour options and can help you try to find a last-minute berth on a boat or cruise ship.

ORIENTATION

Puerto Ayora is a port town set around a broad and deep harbor known as Bahía Academia (Academy Bay). The principal road in town, Avenida Charles Darwin, pretty much hugs the coastline and runs from the main dock in town to the Charles Darwin Research Station. All along its length, Avenida Charles Darwin is peppered with restaurants, shops, tour agencies, bars, and hotels. Almost everything of interest to tourists in Puerto Ayora is within walking distance, although a few tourist attractions and destinations on the island do lie outside of town.

GETTING AROUND

Everything in Puerto Ayora is within easy walking distance, including the Charles Darwin Research Station. If you're really lazy, you can take a taxi around town for about $1. If you want to tour other sites around the island on your own, you can hire a taxi for about $10 per hour. If you can't flag one down on the street, have your hotel arrange one for you. Alternatively, you can rent a bike, which will cost you only around $10 per day.

If you're staying on one of the boats at anchor, or if you just want to visit someplace more easily reached by watercraft, head to the main dock at the southern end of

ACCOMMODATIONS ■
Angermeyer Waterfront Inn **4**
Hostal Estrella del Mar **9**
Hostal Mainao **14**
Hotel Salinas **6**
Hotel Silberstein **16**
Hotel Sol y Mar **11**
La Perigrina **15**
Palo Santo Spa **2**
Red Mangrove
  Adventure Lodge **17**

DINING ◆
Angemeyer Point Restaurant **3**
Café Hernan **5**
Il Giardino **13**
Isla Grill **12**
La Garrapata Restaurante **10**
Red Sushi **17**
Ristorante La Dolce Italia **7**
The Rock **8**

ATTRACTIONS ●
The Charles Darwin
  Research Station **18**

ⓘ Tourist Information

Avenida Charles Darwin and grab one of the many water taxis. Rides cost 60¢ during the day and just $1 at night to any boat at anchor or any nearby pier.

FAST FACTS To contact the local **police,** dial ✆ **05/2526-101,** or 911 in an emergency. Their headquarters are located on Avenida Charles Darwin and 12 de Febrero. For the local **fire department,** dial ✆ **05/2526-111.**

You can get a cash advance, exchange traveler's checks, or use the ATM at **Banco del Pacífico** (✆ **05/2526-282**), on Avenida Charles Darwin near the corner of Charles Binford.

The hospitals in the Galápagos can provide for emergency care, but any serious condition or long-term treatment should be dealt with on the mainland or back at home. The main hospital in town (✆ **05/2526-103**) is located right near the main docks, near the intersection of avenidas Charles Darwin and Baltra. If you need a pharmacy, try **Farmacia Edith** (✆ **05/2526-487**) or **Farmacia Vanessa** (✆ **05/2526-392**), on Avenida Baltra and Tomás Berlanga, across from the hospital.

Internet access is a bit slower and more expensive here than on the mainland, but it has been catching up. Reliable Internet cafes include **Galápagos Online** (✆ **05/2527-169**), on Avenida Charles Darwin between Baltra and Islas Plaza, and

Choza.Net (✆ **05/2527-010**), on Avenida Baltra. Rates run $1 to $3 per hour. The **post office** (✆ **05/2526-575**) is located at the far end of Avenida Charles Darwin, right across from the main dock.

What to See & Do on & Around Santa Cruz Island

There's plenty to see and do here. By far the most popular and convenient way to visit the various attractions and partake in the different active adventures listed below is by signing up for a tour. A host of tour agencies are located along Avenida Charles Darwin, and most local hotels can arrange any tour on Santa Cruz, on surrounding islands, and on the water, including every tour and activity listed below.

Kids enjoy the small playground, basketball court, and skateboard half-pipe in the small public park fronting the harbor, just off the main docks on Avenida Charles Darwin.

Of the local tour agencies, I like **Moonrise Travel Agency ★** (✆ **05/2526-589;** www.galapagosmoonrise.com), on Avenida Charles Darwin near the corner of Charles Binford. An excellent local tour outfit and source of information, Moonrise has staff who are friendly and can help arrange a last-minute cruise of the Galápagos, independent tours around the islands, and any of the local tours listed below.

Take note: When there are no cruise passengers in town, many of the shops close down or operate on very reduced hours.

MAIN ATTRACTIONS

CHARLES DARWIN RESEARCH STATION ★★   This is the primary tourist attraction on Santa Cruz and a major player in the protection and propagation of the very endangered Galápagos tortoise. The main attraction here is an interpretive walk through the grounds of the active breeding center. The guided tour takes you through the life cycle and natural history of these massive land reptiles. You'll see juveniles as well as representatives of the 11 Galápagos tortoise subspecies. This is a great place to actually note the difference in shell shapes of the various subspecies. As you walk the trails, you'll find various corrals holding the tortoises; with a guide's supervision, you can enter some of these for a close encounter with the denizens.

The Charles Darwin Research Station (✆ **05/2526-146;** www.darwinfoundation. org) is located at the end of Avenida Charles Darwin, about a 10- to 15-minute walk from the main dock in Puerto Ayora. It is open daily from 7am until 6pm. There is no entrance fee, and bilingual guides are provided. To offset the free admission, however, I recommend that you make a small donation to the Charles Darwin Foundation.

CERRO CHATO TORTOISE RESERVE   After you've learned about the giant tortoise and seen a few captive specimens at the Charles Darwin Research Station, you might want to head out to see these fascinating reptiles in their natural environment. This reserve, located southwest of the small inland town of Santa Rosa, is best visited as part of a guided tour. Most of these tours also stop at the bulk of the other attractions listed in this section. Some include horseback riding or mountain biking.

CERRO CROCKER, MEDIA LUNA & PUNTADO   These three volcanic peaks are the highest spots on the island and are more or less clustered together near the center of the island. Although it's only 864m (2,834 ft.) high, it's still a vigorous hike to the top of Media Luna (Half Moon), the tallest of the three. The rewards include excellent bird-watching on the way, as well as a wonderful panoramic view from the top.

UNWANTED guests

Numerous threats, including illegal fishing, burgeoning populations, and large-scale tourism, threaten the fragile ecology of the Galápagos Islands. But perhaps the greatest threat to the native species and delicate ecosystems here come from introduced species. Since the early 19th century, even as Darwin made his groundbreaking visit, the Galápagos Islands have seen populations of feral goats, pigs, cattle, and donkeys established to supplement food sources for passing ships or for the incipient resident communities. These species were accompanied by a whole host of accidental tourists—rats and insects stowed away on ships, escaped pet cats and dogs, and discarded fruit and vegetable seeds. Today it is estimated that some 300 invertebrates, 24 vertebrates, and 480 or so plants have been introduced, either on purpose or inadvertently, throughout the archipelago.

Prior to 1964, no objective scientific studies had been made to reveal the full impact of the invasive plants and fauna that compete against, dominate, or just plain decimate the delicate native and endemic species here. Increasingly expansive introductions, lack of control, and less-than-transparent government interests reached such a point that UNESCO, in 1995, threatened to list the Galápagos as an "endangered World Heritage Site." This surely would have meant stringent outside regulations and reduced tourism income for the Ecuadorean government. The Special Law for the Conservation of the Galápagos Islands was passed in 1998 by the Ecuadorean Congress.

With two primary objectives—the eradication of existing feral species and the prevention of further introductions—UNESCO has received multimillion-dollar funding for community education programs, quarantines, and rapid-response actions when new and unwelcome "settlers" are identified. The early results of eradication efforts have shown some promising results. Still, the complexity of the situation continues to include a mix of increased human populations; fishing issues; and the near impossibility of eliminating even a single species, such as goats or feral cats.

This is not a situation that can be fixed quickly—it's likely, in fact, that *Frommer's Ecuador 2050* will include a sidebar similar to this one in its Galápagos chapter.

CERRO DRAGÓN ★ Cerro Dragón (Dragon Hill), on the north side of Santa Cruz, was established as a breeding and protection area for the endangered and unique Galápagos land iguana. There's a great loop trail here that offers excellent opportunities to see the land iguanas, as well as many bird species, including the Darwin finch. If you're lucky, you may see flamingos in the large, brackish mangrove lagoon. Cerro Dragón is accessible only by sea, and you'll definitely need to sign up for a boat tour to visit here.

LOS GEMELOS (THE TWINS) The Twins are two impressively large craters that straddle the main road almost halfway between Puerto Ayora and the Itabaca Canal. This popular destination sits at a high point on the island in an area of dense cloud forest. There are easily accessible lookouts for both craters just off the highway, and a couple of nearby trails through the forests offer excellent bird-watching. If you're lucky, you'll catch a glimpse of the brightly colored vermilion flycatcher.

I'm So Lonely

Discovered in 1971 by a National Parks expedition out hunting feral goats, Lonesome George is believed to be the sole survivor of the Isla Pinta tortoise subspecies. Previously, the last recorded sighting of an Isla Pinta tortoise had been in 1906. Lonesome George was brought to the Charles Darwin Research Station for a variety of reasons. Scientists, for example, are frantically trying to find a mate for him so that the species doesn't become extinct. They've even offered a $10,000 reward to anyone who finds another Isla Pinta tortoise. They have also tried to breed Lonesome George—estimated to be between 70 and 80 years old—with closely related female species, but so far these attempts have been unsuccessful. Hopes were high in 2008, when eggs were discovered in the nest of one of the closely related females who shares her pen with George. However, none of 13 incubated eggs successfully hatched. Still, neither George nor the local scientists are giving up easily, and the lone surviving Isla Pinta tortoise continues to share his pen with not one, but two, closely related females, Georgette and Georgina.

PLAYA DE LOS ALEMANES & LAS GRIETAS ★ Playa de los Alemanes (German Beach), a beautiful white-sand beach, is good for sunbathing and swimming. The beach sits right in front of Finch Bay Hotel (p. 342). It is best enjoyed between mid- and high tide, as it recedes very far during low tide, leaving a semi-muddy bottom and lots of rocks exposed at pure low tide. To get here, take a water taxi at the main dock in Puerto Ayora and ask the driver to drop you at Angemeyer Point. It's only a few minutes' hike from there to the beach.

A 20-minute hike from Playa de los Alemanes will bring you to Las Grietas (The Grottos), where a couple of steep, narrow canyons contain calm pools filled with a mix of fresh- and saltwater. Las Grietas is an excellent place for a refreshing dip and pretty good for snorkeling. More adventurous types can jump off the surrounding rocks into the deep pools. Although relatively short, the hike here is mostly over rough and uneven lava rocks. Be sure to wear sturdy shoes.

TORTUGA BAY ★★ Located just west of Puerto Ayora, Bahía Tortuga (Tortuga Bay) is one of the best and most beautiful beaches in the Galápagos. The first beach you come to is a long stretch of white sand. Be careful here: The waves and undertow are often very strong, and several drownings have occurred. If you really want to swim, head over to the far western end of the beach, where there is a calmer, protected area. Tortuga Bay is just 2.5km (1½ miles) outside of Puerto Ayora and is reached via a well-marked and paved path. Ask anyone in town to point you to the trail head, from which a gentle and very scenic hike should take about an hour each way.

ADVENTURE ACTIVITIES

MOUNTAIN BIKING & HORSEBACK RIDING The largely uninhabited wild terrain of Santa Cruz Island is well suited for both mountain-bike and horseback exploration, and a variety of rides are possible. Several shops along Avenida Charles Darwin rent mountain bikes, although I think you're best off signing up for a tour. For those in less than competitive shape, I recommend one of the tours that take the gear and participants first by van to the highlands so that most of the biking is downhill. Rates run from $10 to $20 per day. Quality varies widely, so check out a few possibilities first. **Red Mangrove Aventura Lodge** (see below) offers both full-day mountain-biking and full-day horseback-riding tours around Santa Cruz Island.

ON & UNDER THE WATER

BOAT TOURS TO OTHER ISLANDS   Water taxis can be hired at the main dock, at the southern end of Avenida Charles Darwin. Rates run from around 80¢ for a short ride across Academy Bay, to around $10 or $15 per hour for longer excursions. If you want to visit a specific island to do some wildlife viewing or snorkeling, you're best off signing on for an organized tour with a reputable operator.

GLASS-BOTTOM BOAT   To see the underwater world of the Galápagos, check out **Aqua View Glass Bottom Boat** (© 05/2527-303; www.galapagosaquatours. com), which has daily excursions at 9am and 2pm. The trips last 4 hours and include a stop or two to snorkel, as well as a snack. The ride passes around Punta Estrada and takes in Las Grietas (The Grottos). The cost is $30 per person.

PADDLING AROUND   The bays and mangroves around Santa Cruz are great spots for kayaking. Most of the tour agencies in town offer guided sea-kayak excursions. If you just want to rent one on your own, head to the **Lonesome George Tour Agency** (© 05/2526-241), which is on Avenida Baltra, just off Avenida Darwin; they have a small fleet of kayaks available for around $10 per hour, and they also offer full-day guided kayak tours.

SNORKELING & SCUBA DIVING ★★★   The snorkeling and scuba diving around the Galápagos Islands is some of the best in the world. In addition to the vibrant fish life, you can often count on a close underwater encounter with a sea lion or sea turtle. Really lucky divers and snorkelers will catch glimpses of an underwater marine iguana or Galápagos penguin. For scuba divers, the ante gets upped, and prized sightings include schools of scalloped hammerhead sharks, manta rays, and the occasional whale shark. Almost all the tour agencies and hotel tour desks in town can arrange for a snorkel or dive trip.

There's good snorkeling all around Santa Cruz. One of the most popular spots is called La Lobería (The Sea Lion Colony), a small island located about a 15-minute boat ride from Puerto Ayora. You are almost guaranteed a close in-water encounter with a playful sea lion here. Equipment rental runs around $8 to $12 per day for fins, mask, and snorkel. A guided tour or boat excursion to snorkel will run you $20 to $45, depending upon the length of the outing and the distance traveled to the snorkel spot.

For scuba diving, I recommend you use either **SCUBA Iguana ★** (© 05/2526-497; www.scubaiguana.com), located on Avenida Charles Darwin, right below the Darwin Research Station; or **Sub-Aqua** (© 05/2526-633; www.galapagos-sub-aqua.com), on Avenida Charles Darwin and Avenida 12 de Febrero. Both operations are very professional and have excellent gear and dive masters. A two-tank dive outing, including all gear, should run you $90 to $150, including lunch. My favorite dive sites easily accessible from Puerto Ayora include Gordon Rocks, Mosquera Islet, and North Seymour Island.

SURFING ★★   The Galápagos Islands are not only one of the world's most exotic surf destinations; but they are also blessed with numerous point, reef, and beach breaks. With the isolation of the archipelago, and the fact that most people come here to interact with wildlife or to scuba-dive, these breaks are almost always uncrowded. While San Cristóbal is the islands' most popular surf destination, there are several good surf spots around Santa Cruz—and depending upon the swell direction, one or more is almost always working. Just beyond the Charles Darwin Research Station lie the spots of La Ratonera and Bazán. You'll almost always find locals surfing here because they're so close to town. Farther afield, but still within walking distance, you can surf the break at Tortuga Bay. A short boat ride will bring you to prized surf spots such as Ola Escondida (Hidden Wave) and Punta Barba Negra (Black Beard Point). You can easily hire a **water taxi** (see above) to take you to any of the more remote surf spots. Itinerant surfers should check in at the **Lonesome George Tour Agency** (© 05/2526-241), where you can rent boards.

A LITTLE PAMPERING

If you want a massage, facial, or pedicure, head to the Asian-themed **Chi Spa** (© 09/5139-784), located toward the end of Avenida Charles Darwin.

Shopping

Most folks don't come to the Galápagos to shop, and most of what you will find here is pretty standard tourist fare. The entire length of Avenida Charles Darwin is strewn with simple souvenir shops and T-shirt outlets. But there are a few exceptions. The best local art and high-end crafts can be found at **Galería Aymara** ★★★ (© 05/2526-835; www.galeria-aymara.com), on Avenida Charles Darwin and Los Piqueros. These folks have an amazing and very varied stable of artists and craftspeople stocking this large and well-run gallery. Another good option, although I find it pricey, is **Angelique Art Gallery** (© 05/2526-656), on Avenida Charles Darwin near the corner of Indefatigable. For high-end, one-off jewelry, head to **Joyería Lugi** ★★ (© 05/2526-868; www.lugigalapagos.com), run by a transplanted Swiss artisan, Beat Luginbuhl. You can also check out **Galápagos Jewelry** ★ (© 05/2526-044; www.galapagosjewelry.com), on Avenida Charles Darwin, between Isla Floreana and Indefatigable. They have an excellent selection of original pieces, many in the shapes and images of local flora and fauna. They also have smaller storefronts inside the Puerto Ayora hotels Hotel Silberstein and Royal Palm Hotel, and in two high-end hotels in Quito, the JW Marriott and Swissôtel Quito, as well as in Guayaquil and Cuenca. Finally, if you want to take home a classic image of the Galápagos flora and fauna, head to **Creative Force** ★ (© 05/2527-004), which features the fabulous images of photographer Daniel Fitter, available framed or unframed, in a variety of sizes.

Where to Stay on Santa Cruz Island

VERY EXPENSIVE

In addition to the places listed below, you might look into the luxurious new **Palo Santo Spa** ★★ (© 05/3015-033; www.galapagospalosantospa.com), set to open in late 2011, or the already operational **Angermeyer Waterfront Inn** (© 05/2526-561 or 09/4724-955; www.angermeyer-waterfront-inn.com). Or, for something completely different, you can check out the **Galápagos Safari Tent Camp** ★ (© 800/327-3573 in the U.S. and Canada, or 09/1794-259 in Ecuador; www.galapagossafaricamp.com), an upscale wilderness tent-camp lodge located in the island's central highlands.

Finch Bay Eco Hotel ★★★ 📷   The only beachfront hotel in Santa Cruz is a quick boat ride and short walk from downtown Puerto Ayora. It's secluded and serene amid the mangroves, with a magnificent pool and beautiful beach. Rooms feature earth tones and simple decor. Although it's definitely a splurge, I highly recommend their oceanfront premium rooms. The ecofriendly hotel uses solar power and actively pursues policies of sustainable tourism and environmental conservation. There are mountain bikes, kayaks, and snorkeling equipment available for guests. While nowhere near as luxurious as the Royal Palm (see below), I vastly prefer this hotel's beachfront location and easy access to town. When making your reservation, be sure to inquire about the all-inclusive packages, which include transfers from the airport, all meals, and daily tours on the hotel's fast private yacht, the *Sea Finch*.

Punta Estrada, Isla Santa Cruz (mailing address: Av. De Las Palmeras N45–74 y De Las Orquídeas, Quito). www.finchbayhotel.com. © **877/534-8584** in the U.S. and Canada, or 02/2988-200 reservations office in Quito, or 05/2526-297 at the hotel. Fax 02/3341-250. 27 units. $300 double; $400 ocean view. Rates include breakfast buffet and taxes. AE, DC, MC, V. **Amenities:** Restaurant; bar; lounge; bike rentals; large outdoor pool; smoke-free rooms; watersports equipment; free Wi-Fi. *In room:* A/C, hair dryer.

Red Mangrove Adventura Lodge ★★ 🎒

The Red Mangrove is close to both the Charles Darwin Research Station and downtown Puerto Ayora, yet it seems a world away. The hotel sits nestled in a grove of red mangroves on a calm and rocky bay. Rooms vary considerably in size, price, and placement. The best units are quite large, with great views of the bay. The top choice here is the Suite Mayor, with wooden floors, walls, and ceilings; wraparound floor-to-ceiling picture windows; and a telescope on its balcony for taking in the harbor sights. I also like the Suite Azul, which has a private cupola-covered gazebo on its large, second-floor balcony. There are delightful common sitting areas, a small free-form pool, and a separate hot tub. The **restaurant** has both indoor and outdoor seating and is the best sushi restaurant in the Galápagos (see review below). These folks have instituted an extensive program sustainable and responsible tourism measures.

Av. Charles Darwin, Puerto Ayora, Isla Santa Cruz. www.redmangrove.com. © **888/254-3190** in the U.S. and Canada, or 05/2526-564. 14 units. $215–$300 double; $450 suite. Rates include full breakfast. AE, DC, MC, V. **Amenities:** Restaurant; bar; free bicycles; Jacuzzi; kayak rentals; small pool. *In room:* A/C, TV, CD player, hair dryer, no phone, free Wi-Fi.

Royal Palm Hotel ★★

This plush resort sits on 200 lush, often misty hillside hectares (494 acres) a 20-minute drive from Puerto Ayora. There are 10 beautiful villas on the hillside, 4 veranda studios, and 3 spectacular suites. The villas each have a separate living/dining area, a bedroom with a king-size bed, and a huge bathroom with a large shower and separate Jacuzzi tub. The three suites are all unique—the two-bedroom, two-bathroom Imperial comes with a private-garden Jacuzzi, while the Royal has a four-poster bed and an indoor sauna. The Veranda studios are the simplest (and least expensive) units but have charming patios with hammocks and spacious bathrooms with Jacuzzi tubs. Service is exquisite and friendly, highlighted by the special greeting at the airport and the private speedboat transfers from Baltra to Santa Cruz. This hotel is a member of the Small Distinctive hotel group and certified as a Smart Voyager property.

Vía Baltra, Km 18, Isla Santa Cruz. www.royalpalmgalapagos.com. © **05/2527-409.** Fax 05/2527-408. 17 units. $375 studio; $500–$600 suite; $625 villa for 2; $875 Imperial Suite. Rates include American breakfast. AE, DC, MC, V. **Amenities:** Restaurant; bar; concierge; exercise room; outdoor pool; room service; sauna; 2 outdoor tennis courts. *In room:* A/C, TV/DVD, hair dryer, free high-speed Internet access, minibar.

EXPENSIVE

Hostal Mainao This distinct downtown option features bold Mediterranean-influenced architecture, with whitewashed stucco offset by red accents. The building itself features arched doorways and curved walls. Several of the rooms have private balconies. Decor is minimal, with white walls and thin white muslin curtains. My favorite rooms are Plazas and Genovesa—each comes with a large wraparound balcony. The Floreana is a huge suite, with a kitchenette, living room, and large balcony area as well.

Calle Matazarnos e Indefatigable, Puerto Ayora, Isla Santa Cruz. www.hotelmainao.com. ℂ/fax **05/ 2527-029** in Puerto Ayora, or 04/2296-799 in Guayaquil. 19 units. $119 double; $197 suite. Rates include breakfast and taxes. DC, MC, V. **Amenities:** Bar. *In room:* No phone.

Hotel Red Booby   Although it's located a few blocks inland from Avenida Charles Darwin and the main strip, this hotel is still a popular choice. Rooms feature sparkling white-tile floors, simple wooden furnishings, and firm beds. You'll definitely want to ask for one of the "Isabela" rooms, located on the third floor around the pool. The best and most unique thing here is this open-air rooftop swimming pool, with a large terrace area all around and good views. The more formal restaurant here serves respectable Ecuadorean and international fare, but I really like eating at the poolside grill, where you can get fresh fish, shrimp, or steaks prepared to order on their charcoal-fired grill.

Islas Plazas, btw. Tomás de Berlanga and Charles Binford, Puerto Ayora, Isla Santa Cruz. www.hotelred booby.com.ec. ℂ **05/2526-485** in Puerto Ayora, or 02/2221-505 reservations office in Quito. Fax 05/2526-486. 27 units. $110–$150 double. Rates include full breakfast. DC, MC, V. **Amenities:** Restaurant; bar; rooftop grill; small outdoor pool. *In room:* A/C, TV, no phone, free Wi-Fi.

Hotel Silberstein ★   This longstanding hotel is a good choice downtown. The building is an attractive two-story structure surrounding a small but delightful free-form swimming pool. Well-tended and relatively lush gardens give the grounds the feel of a small tropical oasis. The rooms are large, with white-tile floors and built-in beds and nightstands, although some of the bathrooms are on the small side. All share a common veranda or balcony. The hotel has a good **restaurant** serving Ecuadorean and international cuisine. In the hotel's Silberstein tour agency, which is well-run and respectable, multiday tour and dive packages are available.

Av. Charles Darwin y Piqueros, Puerto Ayora, Isla Santa Cruz. www.hotelsilberstein.com. ℂ **02/2269- 626** reservations in Quito, or 05/2526-277 at the hotel. Fax 05/2250-553. 24 units. $165 double. Rates include breakfast buffet. AE, DC, MC, V. **Amenities:** Restaurant; bar; small outdoor pool; free Wi-Fi. *In room:* A/C.

Hotel Sol y Mar ★   All the rooms in this horseshoe-shaped hotel face the bay, and all but one comes with a small bayside balcony. The rooms are contemporary and well equipped, and each features an original painting of some local wildlife, but they still feel somewhat spartan. The best decoration here is a wonderful wall relief and painting of a whale in the main second-floor hallway. Perhaps the hotel's best feature is its large bayside patio, pool, and waterfront dining area. Pelicans, herons, and the occasional sea lion can often be found here.

Av. Charles Darwin, btw. Tomás de Berlanga and Charles Binford, Puerto Ayora, Isla Santa Cruz. www. hotelsolymar.com.ec. ℂ **05/2526-281.** Fax 05/2527-015. 17 units. $195 double. DC, MC, V. **Amenities:** Restaurant; bar; Jacuzzi; pool. *In room:* A/C, hair dryer, free Wi-Fi.

MODERATE
Hotel Estrella del Mar   Located right off the water, and fronting Academy Bay, this is a good midrange option. However, even at this price, this is definitely what I would consider a budget hotel, with a budget hotel vibe. Still, everything on-site is

well maintained and neat. You'll definitely want to reserve one of the four bayside units. If you don't snag one of these, you can still enjoy the shared balcony overlooking the bay. There's no restaurant, but breakfast is served daily.

Av. Charles Darwin y 12 de Febrero, Puerto Ayora, Isla Santa Cruz. www.hotelestrellademar.com.ec. ✆ 05/2526-427 or 05/2524-288. Fax 05/2526-080. 12 units. $76 double. Rates include taxes and full breakfast. DC, MC, V. **Amenities:** Lounge. *In room:* A/C, TV, no phone.

INEXPENSIVE

In addition to the place listed below, you might check out **La Peregrina** (✆ 05/2526-323; www.laperegrinagalapagos.com.ec), a small B&B about midway along Avenida Charles Darwin.

Hotel Salinas　This place offers some of the most popular backpacker accommodations in Puerto Ayora. The three-story hotel is built in a U shape around a small garden courtyard. The least expensive rooms are very basic, with virtually no decor beyond some simple wooden beds and nightstands, and have cold-water showers. The more expensive rooms are larger and come with air-conditioning and private balconies.

Calle Isla Plaza, btw. Av. Charles Darwin and Tomás de Berlanga, Puerto Ayora, Isla Santa Cruz. www. hotel-galapagos.com. ✆ 05/2526-107. ✆/fax 05/2526-072. 20 units. $35–$60 double. DC, MC, V. **Amenities:** Restaurant. *In room:* TV, no phone.

Where to Dine on Santa Cruz Island

The restaurants at the **Royal Palm Hotel** and **Finch Bay Hotel** (see above) are both excellent. If you're not staying at either of these, you might consider a splurge and dine at one or both while in Puerto Ayora. In both cases, reservations are essential, and the food will be quite a bit more expensive than anything else you'll find around town.

For pizzas, fresh seafood, hearty breakfasts, and a range of international dishes, you can head to **Café Hernan** (✆ 05/2526-573; avs. Baltra and Charles Darwin), which has a pretty open-air dining room and laid-back vibe, while **Ristorante La Dolce Italia** (✆ 09/4554-668; Av. Charles Darwin and 12 de Febrero) offers more traditional Italian fare in a more formal setting. **The Rock** ★ (✆ 05/2527-505; Av. Charles Darwin) is a popular local joint, with large picture windows fronting the busy main street through town.

EXPENSIVE

Angermeyer Point Restaurant ★★ 📷 ECUADOREAN/SEAFOOD　This gets my vote for the best-located and most atmospheric dining spot in Puerto Ayora. This old stone house with a broad wraparound wooden deck is set on a rocky promontory facing the bay. It was the former home of local legend and painter Karl Angermeyer, who arrived here in 1937. You'll definitely want to grab one of the waterfront tables on the outdoor deck. This place is also known as La Casa de las Iguanas (The House of Iguanas), and there are always large groups of these remarkable reptiles here. The food is quite good and varied. Menu items range from lobster risotto to Thai shrimp, to beef in Jack Daniels sauce. Friday is sushi night, and there's a nightly happy hour and tapas menu.

Angermeyer Point, Puerto Ayora. ✆ 05/2527-007. Reservations recommended. Main courses $13–$22. DC, MC, V. Tues–Sun 5–10pm. To reach Angermeyer Point, you have to take a water taxi, which you board at the main dock in Puerto Ayora for around $1 each way. Or call the restaurant to make a reservation, and they should be able to arrange transport for you.

MODERATE

Il Giardino ★ ITALIAN   This new restaurant is spread out, with several open-air dining areas and a small, sometimes-busy bar. My favorite spot is the second-floor dining room, with a view of Academy Bay and the busy Avenida Charles Darwin. Start things off with the Mediterranean octopus or some spicy curried shrimp. For mains, I recommend the homemade shrimp-filled ravioli or a steak in red-wine sauce with an onion confit. Save room for dessert, which often stars their fabulous Italian gelato.

Av. Charles Darwin and Binford, Puerto Ayora. (✆ **05/2526-627.** Reservations recommended in high season. Main courses $7.50–$15; lobster $20. AE, DC, MC, V. Tues–Sun 7am–10pm.

Isla Grill ★ INTERNATIONAL/PIZZA   I enjoy the relaxed, almost loungelike vibe at this Argentine-owned spot. There's dim lighting, and the floor features broken-tile mosaic patterns. You'll find a large Argentine grill serving up perfectly done seafood and steaks, as well as a wood-fired pizza oven turning out respectable pies. Shish kabobs are served over burning coals at the table, and the mixed grill is a massive plate filled with seafood, fish, and meat—perfect for sharing.

Av. Charles Darwin and Binford, Puerto Ayora. (✆ **05/2524-461.** Reservations recommended in high season. Main courses $5.50–$24; lobster $19. AE, DC, MC, V. Daily 7am–9:30pm.

La Garrapata Restaurante ECUADOREAN   This place is a local institution. It's where the expats eat—and all the foreign guides who work on the ships. There's a great selection of fresh juices and sandwiches. The open-air dining room features low wooden chairs and round tables with linen tablecloths. But there's nothing formal about either the vibe or the service here. Main courses include a wide range of seafood and meat options, as well as some pastas. There's usually a *menú del día* (menu of the day) with soup, main course, and dessert for around $5. They even have a pretty good wine list. On weekends, sometimes there's live music.

Av. Charles Darwin and Charles Binford, Puerto Ayora. (✆ **05/2526-264.** Main courses $4.50–$18. AE, DC, MC, V. Mon–Sat 9am–4pm and 6:30–10pm.

Red Sushi ★ JAPANESE/SUSHI   The menu here is a slightly abbreviated version of what you might expect to find at any typical sushi bar and Japanese restaurant. There are a few sushi, sashimi, and maki options, as well as noodle dishes, tempura, and more substantial plates such as chicken yakitori. The fish is extremely fresh, and overall they do a very good job. Presentations are artistic, with the dishes served on colorful plates or spread on large platters made from the cross-section of a log. The hip dining room and bar features floor-to-ceiling windows with a view of the bay. Because this is the Red Mangrove's main restaurant, you can also order a range of more traditional Ecuadorean and international seafood, meat, poultry, and pasta dishes.

At the Red Mangrove Aventura Lodge, Av. Charles Darwin, Puerto Ayora. (✆ **05/2526-524.** Reservations recommended. Main courses $5.50–$18. AE, DC, MC, V. Daily noon–2:30pm and 6:30–9:30pm.

Puerto Ayora After Dark

For such a seemingly sleepy little city, Puerto Ayora has a surprisingly lively, albeit limited, nightlife and bar scene. **Bongo Bar** ★★ (✆ **05/2526-264**) is the most happening place in town at night; it's located on a rooftop above and behind La Panga (see below). Bongo Bar opens at 4pm but usually doesn't get busy until after 8pm. Across the street, the **Limón y Café** (✆ **05/2526-510**) is another lively downtown bar that sometimes gets the crowds up and dancing, while **The Rock** (see above) is your boat bet for a mellower bar scene. If you're looking for the best dance club in town, head to **La Panga** (℃ 05/2527-199). Finally, for a real local scene, head to **La Taberna del Duende** (℃ 05/2527-320), which is located inland from the main tourist strip on Calle Juan León Mera and San Cristóbal.

PUERTO BAQUERIZO MORENO & SAN CRISTOBAL ISLAND

The second-most-important island for tourism in the Galápagos, San Cristóbal is a large island at the eastern end of the archipelago. The main settlement here, Puerto Baquerizo Moreno, is the provincial capital of the Galápagos. Still, it is a small city, and much less developed and less active than Puerto Ayora, on Santa Cruz Island.

Aside from the capital city, there's only one other settlement of note on San Cristóbal, El Progreso. Located several kilometers inland from the port, El Progreso was actually the first spot settled on the island. In 1879, Ecuadorean businessman Manuel Cobo set up a notorious prison camp here, using the free prison laborers to farm sugarcane, harvest sea-turtle meat, and slaughter and skin the island's feral cattle. Conditions on Cobo's prison farm were said to be cruel, and Cobo himself was a bit of a dictator; he even issued his own currency. An inmate uprising in January 1904 ended Cobo's life, although one of the town's main streets is still named after him.

Essentials

GETTING THERE

All flights from Quito and Guayaquil to San Cristóbal land at **Aeropuerto San Cristóbal** (℃ 05/2520-156; airport code: SCY), which is just a few blocks west of downtown Puerto Baquerizo Moreno.

Both of the major airlines, **Tame** (℃ 1800/500-800 toll-free nationwide, or 05/2521-351 in Puerto Barquerizo Moreno; www.tame.com.ec) and **Aerogal** (℃ 1800/2376-425 toll-free nationwide, or 05/2521-118 in Puerto Barquerizo Moreno; www.aerogal.com.ec), have desks at the airport.

Taxis are always waiting to meet incoming flights. A taxi to any hotel in town should cost only $1.

VISITOR INFORMATION

The chamber of tourism runs a **tourist information office** (℃ 05/2520-358) on Avenida Charles Darwin and Teodoro Wolf. It is open Monday through Saturday from 8am to 5pm. They can provide orientation and some brochures, but you're probably better off going to one of the small tour operators that are concentrated around the tiny downtown area. All offer a range of tour options and can help you try to find a last-minute berth on a boat or cruise ship, or to book a hotel room.

FAST FACTS   To contact the local **police,** dial ℃ 05/2520-101, or 911 in an emergency. Their headquarters are located on Avenida Charles Darwin and Calle Española. The **post office** (℃ 05/2520-373) is located on Avenida Charles Darwin and Calle Española.

The hospitals in the Galápagos can provide for emergency care, but any serious condition or long-term treatment should be dealt with on the mainland or back at home. There is a small **hospital** in Puerto Baquerizo Moreno (℃ 05/2520-118), on Avenida Quito and Charles Darwin. In an emergency, you can call the **Red Cross** at ℃ 05/2520-125. If you need a pharmacy, try **Farmacia Jane** (℃ 05/2520-242), on Avenida Charles Darwin and Teodoro Wolf, or **Farmacia Nicole** (℡ **05/2520-676**), on Avenida Charles Darwin and 12 de Febrero.

You can get a cash advance, exchange traveler's checks, or use the ATM at **Banco del Pacífico** (℡ **05/2520-365**), on Avenida Charles Darwin, near the main dock. There are several Internet cafes along the Malecón and scattered around the downtown area. Rates run from $1 to $3 per hour.

ORIENTATION

Almost all the hotels, restaurants, shops, and tour operators of any importance on San Cristóbal are located in a compact area around Puerto Baquerizo Moreno's Malecón (the town's seafront promenade), which is about 10 blocks long. The main part of the downtown extends inland from the Malecón for just some 3 blocks, where it is bordered by Avenida Alsacio Northia, the town's primary east-west thoroughfare. At the far eastern end of the Malecón lies Playa de Oro (Gold Beach). A little beyond this is the island's small museum and interpretive center. The airport lies on the western outskirts of town.

GETTING AROUND

Almost everything in Puerto Baquerizo Moreno is within easy walking distance, including even the airport, although if you have any baggage, you're best off taking a taxi. Taxis are readily available, and a ride anywhere in town should cost $1. If you want to tour other sights around the island on your own, hire a taxi for around $10 per hour. If you can't flag one down on the street, have your hotel arrange one for you or call **Coop La Galapaguera** (℡ **05/2520-900**).

If you're looking for a commuter flight to one of the other islands, contact **Emetebe** (℡ **800/481-3163** in the U.S., or **05/2521-427**; www.emetebe.com), which has a desk at the airport. Fares are $199 for a single flight segment or $299 for two flight segments.

What to See & Do on & Around San Cristóbal

As on Santa Cruz, there are plenty of land- and water-based tour options on San Cristóbal. If you're visiting the island on your own and you're not part of a guided tour, you'll probably want to check in with one of the many tour agencies—there are a handful in Puerto Baquerizo Moreno, all located right around the downtown area. Of these, I recommend **Turisgal,** Avenida Charles Darwin and Teodoro Wolf (℡ **05/2520-969**), and **Galakiwi,** Avenida Charles Darwin and Española (℡ **08/8102-663**; www.galakiwi.com). Another option is to contact the very helpful folks at **Come To Galapagos** (℡ **05/2520-348**; www.cometogalapagos.com), who live on the island and design and book custom tours to San Cristóbal and neighboring islands.

 Sinking Feeling

The popular bay and anchorage just off Puerto Baquerizo Moreno is called Bahía Naufragio, or Shipwreck Bay. Over the centuries, the bay has claimed several vessels, and today scuba divers—and marine life—get to enjoy the benefits.

One of the most popular activities for travelers here is walking along the **Malecón,** a beautiful waterfront promenade, which features several fountains, sitting areas, children's playgrounds, and even an enclosed saltwater swimming area, replete with two water slides (although it's more common to find sea lions rather than people enjoying this pool).

Puerto Baquerizo Moreno

ACCOMMODATIONS ■
Casa Opuntia **3**
Hotel Casablanca **5**
Hotel Miconia **4**
Hotel Orca **2**

DINING ◆
Deep Blue **6**
La Playa **10**
Miconia **4**

ATTRACTIONS & NIGHTLIFE ●
Centro de Interpretación
   (Interpretation Center) **1**
Malecón **7**
Parque Ecológico Artesanal **8**
El Barquero **9**

The Galápagos Islands

Darwin   Pinta
 Wolf   Genovesa
      Marchena   Equator
GALÁPAGOS   Santiago
NAT'L PARK
Fernandina   Santa   **Puerto**
                    Cruz   **Baquerizo**
Isabela   **Moreno**
                           San
      Santa María   Cristóbal
                Española

PACIFIC
OCEAN

Passenger Pier 2

Cargo Pier

Naval Zone

Av. Armada Nacional

Av. Charles Darwin

Ignacio Hernández

Cobos

Española

Av. Isabela

J. José Flores

5   3
   4
7 6
   8
9
Basketball Court ■

Basketball Court ■

Av. Alsacio Northia

Av. 12 de Febrero

Av. Quito

10

0   1/10 mi
0   100 m

Airport

For a great panoramic view of the island, hire a taxi to take you to the **Mirador de la Soledad,** located a little bit above Progreso. Just below the lookout, you can visit **La Iglesia de Soledad,** a small church built into the rock here.

MAIN ATTRACTIONS

CENTRO DE INTERPRETACIÓN (INTERPRETIVE CENTER) ★
This humble little museum features exhibits and displays on the human, natural, and geological history of San Cristóbal and the Galápagos Islands. It's worth a visit. There are several rooms, all well laid out, with a mix of dioramas, artifacts, illustrations, and written explanations (in English and Spanish). I particularly like the relief model of the entire Galápagos archipelago, which shows both the underwater and above-sea-level topography. The **Interpretive Center** (© 05/2520-358), on Avenida Alsacio Northia, Sector Playa Mann, is open daily from 7am to noon and 1 to 5pm. Admission is free, and it's about a 15-minute walk from downtown. Alternatively, if you take a taxi here, it should cost you just $1 each way.

EL PROGRESSO
The only major road on the island connects the downtown port with El Progreso, the site of Manuel Cobo's infamous prison and work camp. If you visit, you can tour the ruins of the old farmhouse and see Cobo's grave. **La Casa del**

Ceibo (© 05/2520-248) is a good place for a lunch break, and adventurous souls can inquire about the tree-house room for rent in the giant ceiba tree. Several buses a day leave downtown Puerto Baquerizo Moreno for El Progreso. The fare is just 25¢, and the ride takes about 10 minutes.

LA GALAPAGUERA DE CERRO COLORADO   On the far southeastern end of the island is this protected area of dry forest, which is also a wild-tortoise habitat. A hike along the trails here is an excellent way to do some bird-watching and wildlife viewing; you'll also have the opportunity to see one of the endemic San Cristóbal giant tortoises in their natural habitat. At the entrance is a small information center and a corral with one captive tortoise, Genesis. There are several well-maintained trails, with some bilingual self-guided information plaques. If you don't come here as part of a guided tour, a round-trip taxi should cost you $25 to $30. *Tip:* This should not be confused with La Galapaguera, another protected habitat of giant tortoises, which is located on the far northeastern end of the island.

LAGUNA EL JUNCO   Formed in the crater of a dormant volcano, this is one of the few freshwater lakes in the Galápagos. It's only 240m (787 ft.) in diameter and barely 6m (20 ft.) deep. If you're lucky, you may observe the rare phenomenon of a giant frigate bird washing the salt off its wings in the freshwater lagoon.

LA LOBERÍA   La Lobería, or Sea Lion Colony, is a pretty crescent-shaped beach with a large colony of sea lions. You will probably also see some blue-footed boobies and an endemic mockingbird here, as well as marine iguanas. This is a popular surf spot and, therefore, a bit rough for casual bathing, so if you go swimming, try to choose a calm section of the beach—one that is also far from any territorial bull sea lion. La Lobería is about a 40-minute walk northwest of downtown. You can hire a taxi here for around $3 or $4.

AN ADVENTURE ACTIVITY

MOUNTAIN BIKING   The sparse car traffic, relatively subtle rise in altitude, and abundance of off-road trails and paths make San Cristóbal an excellent place to explore on a mountain bike. Most rides begin on the 6.5km (4-mile) paved road to El Progreso. But that's where the pavement ends, and a variety of destinations are possible from there. One of the more popular rides is to El Junco (see above). This 19km (12-mile) ride is mostly uphill on the way there, but welcomingly downhill on the way home. All the tour agencies and hotel desks in town can arrange a guided mountain-bike tour, or they can find you a bike to rent.

ON & UNDER THE WATER

KAYAKING   There's some great kayaking all around San Cristóbal. You can choose to either paddle around Bahía Naufragio or to venture farther afield. If you want to rent a kayak, check at **Hotel Orca** (see below) or with any of the tour agencies in town. Rental rates run $5 to $10 per hour, or $15 to $30 per day. All the tour agencies in town offer guided half- and full-day kayak trips as well.

SNORKELING & SCUBA DIVING ★★★   As you'll find throughout the archipelago, the snorkeling and scuba diving out of San Cristóbal are excellent. Snorkelers often have close encounters with sea lions and sea turtles, while scuba divers frequently come across schools of hammerhead sharks, eagle rays, Galápagos sharks, and the rare whale shark. Some of the popular dive spots include **Roca Ballena (Whale Rock), Isla Lobos (Sea Lion Island), Punta Pitt (Pitt Point),** and the **Caragua Wreck.**

Chalo Tours (℃ 05/2520-953; chalotours@hotmail.com), at Española and Ignacio Hernández, and **Wreck Bay Diving Center** (℃ 05/2521-663; www.wreckbay.com), at Avenida Charles Darwin and Teodoro Wolf, are the two most established dive operators on the island. Rates for a two-tank dive outing, including all gear and lunch, are $100 to $150. A snorkel outing, including equipment, should cost $25 to $50 per person. In both cases, the higher-priced trips involve greater travel time and distance to the dive or snorkel spot.

SURFING ★★ San Cristóbal has the most consistent and best-developed surf spots in the Galápagos, if not the entire country. Some of the better-known breaks include **La Lobería, Punta Carola,** and **Tango Reef.** If you're a surfer, you should definitely contact the local surf association, **Dive & Surf Club** (℃ 09/4096-450). They can help get you orientated and even provide you with permits and transportation to breaks that are located inside protected areas or offshore from San Cristóbal. *Caution:* The surf here is not for beginners, and there are no surf schools, board-rental outfits, or mellow beach breaks. If you come to the Galápagos to surf, you should probably know what you're doing and bring your own gear. If you want to sign up for a surf tour with an operator that has lots of local experience, check out **Casa del Sol** (www.casasol.com).

SWIMMING While you can swim in the protected harbor from Playa de Oro, I recommend taking a taxi out of town to one of the several rather spectacular beaches found on the west side of the island. Of these, Cerro Brujo and Puerto Grande are the best, although Playa Ochoa and Playa Mangelcito are also beautiful. None of these beaches are ever crowded.

Shopping

The shopping options on San Cristóbal are quite disappointing and nowhere near as interesting as those on Santa Cruz. All you'll find here are run-of-the mill souvenirs and T-shirts offered up at a host of small shops along the Malecón and scattered around downtown. If you venture inland from the Malecón, you can try your luck at **Parque Ecológico Artesanal** (℃ 05/2520-240), a complex of shops arrayed around a small garden area on Avenida Alsacio Northia, at the corner of Manuel Cobo. However, I find that the offerings here are no better than those near the waterfront.

Where to Stay in Puerto Baquerizo Moreno
EXPENSIVE
Hotel Miconia This hotel is located right on the Malecón, facing the harbor, just steps away from the town's main dock. Rooms are simple, and a few are a bit too spartan for my tastes. The better units have colorful walls and some wall decorations. The best room here (I think it's the best room in town) is the Presidential Suite, which is a third-floor end unit with a king-size bed, flatscreen plasma TV, and large private balcony overlooking the harbor. Facilities include a popular restaurant (see below), a small gym with a shiny varnished wooden floor, and a small interior courtyard with a tiny pool and separate Jacuzzi.

Av. Charles Darwin, across from the main dock, Puerto Baquerizo Moreno, Isla San Cristóbal. www.miconia.com. ℃ **05/2520-608** or 09/4276-507. 21 units. $132 double; $169–$205 suite. Rates include breakfast. DC, MC, V. **Amenities:** Restaurant; bar; Jacuzzi; small pool. *In room:* A/C, TV, no phone.

MODERATE

In addition to the places listed below, **Casa Opuntia** (© 05/2520-632; www.opuntiagalapagoshotels.com) is a hotel overlooking the harbor, with clean, bright rooms and a pretty, free-form pool.

Hotel Casablanca ★ ✦ Rambling up four stories, this cozy and creative hotel is my top choice in town. Rooms feature hand-painted wooden beds and unique art and design touches throughout. Most have views of the harbor. The suite is a fourth-floor room housed in a sky-blue painted dome, with a large private wraparound terrace, a television, and a minifridge. The "Genovese" room features a king-size bed, shared bayfront veranda, and a beautiful mermaid mural.

Av. Charles Darwin, across from the main dock, Puerto Baquerizo Moreno, Isla San Cristóbal. jacquibaz@ yahoo.com. ©/fax **05/2520-392**. 7 units. $60–$90 double. DC, MC, V. **Amenities:** Restaurant. *In room:* A/C, no phone.

Hotel Orca This two-story yellow beachfront spot is located on Playa de Oro, at the eastern end of the bay, a short walk from the heart of downtown. The rooms are large and well kept, if relatively plain and uninspiring. The best units are those on the second floor, with a large shared balcony and ocean views. You'll have to pay a little more for one of these, but it's well worth it. Reservations are often absolutely necessary here because tour groups frequently book up the entire place. The hotel has an excellent tour operation that specializes in diving packages and island-hopping vacations.

Av. Charles Darwin, on Playa de Oro, Puerto Baquerizo Moreno, Isla San Cristóbal. ©/fax **05/2520-233** or 09/7228-132. Fax 05/2520-682. 20 units. $90–$120 double. DC, MC, V. **Amenities:** Restaurant; bar. *In room:* A/C, TV, minifridge, no phone.

Where to Dine in Puerto Baquerizo Moreno

There are a host of simple local restaurants serving Ecuadorean cuisine and fresh seafood all around the downtown. Of these, **Deep Blue** (© 05/2520-990), at Avenida Charles Darwin and Española, is a good bet. In addition to the place located below, **La Playa** (© 05/2521-511), at the south end of the waterfront, is an excellent local joint with good fresh seafood and a great view of the harbor.

Miconia ★ 🍴 ITALIAN/SEAFOOD This is my favorite restaurant in Puerto Baquerizo Moreno. Just the view from one of the second-floor bayside tables would probably be enough to earn it this honor, but the food and service are also good. Most folks opt for the pizzas or pastas, but there's also a wide range of fresh seafood. This close to the water, I definitely recommend fresh fish or shrimp; they are best just sautéed in oil and garlic.

Av. Charles Darwin, across from the main dock, Puerto Baquerizo Moreno. © **05/2520-608**. Main courses $7.50–$16. AE, DC, MC, V. Daily 7am–9:30pm.

Puerto Barquerizo Moreno After Dark

Puerto Baquerizo Moreno is a pretty, quiet town when night falls. By far the best and most popular bar here is **Iguana Rock ★** (© 05/2520-418), located on Calle Juan José Flores and Avenida Quito, about 4 blocks inland from the Malecón. This place occasionally has live music, and even when there's no band playing, the bar is lively and inviting—plus, there's a pool table. If Iguana Rock isn't happening, check out what's happening at **El Barquero ★** (© 05/2520-516), on calles Ignacio Hernández and Manuel Cobo.

STAYING ON OTHER ISLANDS

While the vast majority of tourists stay either on boats or ships, or at one of the hotels on either Santa Cruz or San Cristóbal, it is possible to stay on the much less developed islands of Isabela or Floreana. Staying at either of these will definitely give you the sense of being off the beaten path, while still allowing you access to all the same types of tour and activity options available to those who choose a more traditional route.

You can get to Isabela from either Santa Cruz or San Cristóbal on a commuter flight with **EMETEBE** (© 800/481-3163 in the U.S., or 02/2956-934; www.emetebe.com), or via a boat ride from Puerto Ayora or Puerto Barquerizo Moreno. Isla Floreana can be reached only by boat, and it's a slightly shorter ride to Floreana from Santa Cruz than from San Cristóbal. Boats leave regularly for both of these islands from Puerto Ayora and Puerto Barquerizo Moreno. The fare is between $25 and $35 one-way. Any hotel or tour agency on the archipelago can help you arrange a ride. Or, you can call **Ferry Transmartisa** (© 05/2526-360; www.transmartisa.com.ec), which has regular daily service between Santa Cruz and Isabela. However, if you plan to stay on either one of these islands, you should probably reserve your room and arrange transportation in advance.

Alternatively, you can book a complete island-hopping tour in advance. Most tour agencies in Ecuador can arrange such a trip, or you can try **Red Mangrove Galápagos Lodges** (© 888/254-3190 in the U.S. and Canada, or 05/2526-524 in Ecuador; www.redmangrove.com), which specializes in island-hopping tours and has comfortable hotels on three of the islands.

On Isabela Island

Isabela is a picturesque little island with a burgeoning tourism scene. Despite its remote and undiscovered feel, the island has many attractions and activities to keep visitors busy. Snorkeling and scuba diving are excellent here, and there are a host of great hikes, mountain-biking trails, deserted beaches, and wildlife-viewing opportunities.

Some of the most popular tours and activities are hikes to the massive crater of the still-active **Cerro Negro** ★★ (also called Sierra Negra) and beyond to the impressive lookout at **Cerro Chico** ★, or to **El Muro de Lágrimas (The Wall of Tears),** a stone wall that was used as a torture mechanism for prisoners kept in a penal colony here during the mid–20th century. On a visit to the Wall of Tears, you actually have the opportunity to see Galápagos tortoises in the wild. Other options include a boat ride to **Los Tintoreros** ★, a small island where you can see sea lions, marine iguanas, and nurse sharks in a small, man-made-but-natural-looking canal flanked by a walkway. **Los Tuneles** ★ is another popular snorkel spot, with lava tunnels and arches, and abundant marine life in shallow waters. There is also a tortoise-hatching facility, or **Galapaguero,** with a small museum and pens with a couple of dozen tortoises representing several different species. For any of these or other tour options, ask at your hotel or contact **Papi's Tours** (© 05/2529-392) or **Tropical Adventures** (© 05/2529-085; www.tropicaladventures.com.ec). For scuba-diving and snorkel tours, check in with **The Isabela Dive Center** (© 05/2529-418; www.isabeladivecenter.com.ec).

Note: There is no bank or ATM on Isabela, so be sure to bring enough cash for your stay.

AN island WHODUNIT?

Steel dentures, silk underwear, love triangles, food poisoning, and unaccounted-for corpses: The sordid details surrounding the early settlers on Floreana Island have all the trappings of a Carl Hiaasen murder mystery.

When German philosopher and dentist Dr. Friedrich Ritter set off with lover Dora Strauch in 1929, he foresaw the lack of dental facilities on his island utopia, so he removed both his and Dora's teeth, replacing them with just a single set of steel dentures. Sharing is caring?

Their written dispatches tempted other dreamers to venture onto Floreana's arid shores. Most gave up quickly when faced with the daunting challenges of physical and spiritual survival there, but not Heinz and Margaret Wittmer. They established a home with Heinz's son Harry and soon enough gave birth to Rolf, the first Galápagos-born citizen.

This challenging idyll was shattered with the arrival of the self-described Baroness Eloise Wagner von Bosquet and her entourage of three "companions," Rudolph Lorenz, Robert Philippson, and Felipe Valdivieso. Valdivieso quit Floreana almost immediately. The newly self-enthroned "Empress of Floreana" exercised almost complete control over the tiny community's supplies and communications. Clad only in her favorite silk underwear, she controlled access to the supply ships and bathed naked in the island's only reliable water source. She also played her various lovers against one other and frequently denied visitors access to the island. Some say she brought Dr. Ritter into her complicated web of lovers.

Things came to a head in 1934. Primary lover Lorenz had been degraded to servant in favor of Philippson. After a violent dispute, Lorenz took refuge with the Wittmers. In March 1934, the Wittmers found Lorenz alone and hysterical; he told them that the Baroness and Philippson had left Floreana on an American yacht to seek new shores. Lorenz soon arranged to be taken to the mainland.

The Baroness and Philippson were never seen or heard from again. Lorenz and a Norwegian fisherman named Nuggerud disappeared. Dr. Ritter, a vegetarian, was poisoned from eating contaminated chicken. Two severely decomposed corpses were eventually discovered 260km (161 miles) north on barren Marchena Island. Evidence suggests that they were Lorenz and Nuggerud, who apparently had starved to death.

Dora Strauch finally returned to Germany to publish her version in *Satan Came to Eden,* while Margaret Wittmer wrote *Floreana: A Woman's Pilgrimage to the Galápagos.* Both volumes contain firsthand accounts of the events mentioned above, but the early Floreana history remains, in many ways, a mystery.

WHERE TO STAY & DINE

In addition to the places listed below, **Hotel Albemarle** ★ (© **05/2529-489;** www.hotelalbemarle.com) is an upscale beachfront hotel in the center of town. For backpackers, the best of the budget bunch is **Caleta Iguana** (© **05/2529-330**). Finally, if you're looking for something a little different, the folks at **Red Mangrove** (see below) also run a "deluxe" campground, **Campo Duro,** set on the slopes of Cerro Negro, amid a tortoise-rehabilitation zone.

The two hotels listed below, and the Albemarle mentioned above, have the best restaurants in town; however, they are also the priciest. Aside from these, you might also try **El Encanto de la Pepa** ★ (☎ 05/2529-284) or **El Toque del Sabor** (☎ 05/2529-442), two simple open-air restaurants that face the town's small central park.

For sunset and drinks, you can't beat the **Sea Lion Café** (☎ 08/2603-022), which is located out at the end of the dock jutting off the center of town. For later-night drinking, head to **Bar de Beto** (☎ 05/2529-015).

Iguana Crossing ★★★   This new beachfront boutique hotel is easily the most luxurious option on Isabela. The large rooms feature contemporary design touches, plush linens and amenities, and plenty of modern conveniences. All have large and abundant windows letting in lots of light and letting out onto wonderful vistas. The hotel's infinity-effect pool is delightful, as are the rooftop bar and Jacuzzi. The food at the in-house restaurant is excellent as well. Located on the outskirts of town, this place sits on a beautiful and isolated stretch of beach, bordering protected national park land.

Puerto Villamil, Isla Isabela. www.opuntiagalapagoshotels.com. ☎ **800/217-9414** in the U.S. and Canada, or 02/6046-800 in Ecuador. Fax 02/2544-073. 13 units. $288–$360 double; $366–$488 suite. Rates include full breakfast and taxes. AE, DC, MC, V. **Amenities:** Restaurant; 2 bars; concierge; Jacuzzi; outdoor pool; room service; free Wi-Fi. *In room:* A/C, TV, hair dryer, MP3 docking station.

La Casa de Marita ★ 👜   Containing a delightful collection of rooms and suites, this little hotel fronts a beautiful crescent-shaped beach a few blocks from the heart of downtown Puerto Villamil. Rooms vary in size and design, but all show the owner's attention to detail and style. A top room in the house is the large Mango Suite, with a private ocean-view and Jacuzzi-equipped terrace. My preference, though, is the Mediterranean Suite, with its contemporary design and large bayside balcony. Quite a few of the rooms have two twin beds, so be sure to specify if you want a queen or king. The third-floor restaurant and dining room features modern glass-topped tables and a great view of the ocean from many tables.

Puerto Villamil, Isla Isabela. www.casamaritagalapagos.com. ☎ **05/2529-301**. Fax 05/2529-201. 19 units. $72–$92 double; $130–$180 suite. Rates include breakfast buffet and 1st night's minibar consumption. AE, MC, V. **Amenities:** Restaurant; bar; room service; free Wi-Fi. *In room:* A/C, TV, minibar.

Red Mangrove Isabela Lodge ★★   The four duplex Santa Fe–style buildings here are set in somewhat tight rows, so the oceanfront unit is by far the best of the bunch. The rooms in this building let out directly onto the large, common wood deck, which fronts a pretty little beach. This unit also features a beautiful rooftop patio, which the others lack. Aside from that, the rooms are all pretty much identical, with two queen-size beds, exposed beam ceilings, and contemporary decor. This hotel is part of the Red Mangrove group, and they have an excellent in-house tour operation, which gives you the ability to build your own island-hopping tour.

Puerto Villamil, Isla Isabela. www.redmangrove.com. ☎ **888/254-3190** in the U.S. and Canada, 05/2526-564 on Puerto Ayora, or 05/2529-030 at the lodge. 8 units. $222 double. Rates include full breakfast. AE, DC, MC, V. **Amenities:** Restaurant; free Wi-Fi. *In room:* A/C, hair dryer, MP3 docking station.

On Floreana Island

Floreana is the most isolated and undeveloped of the inhabited islands on the Galápagos, with just some 150 permanent residents and very little tourism infrastructure. This is a great place to come to get away from it all, or to dig into the island's sordid history (see "An Island Whodunit?," above).

THE GALÁPAGOS tortoise

The giant Galápagos tortoise (*Geochelone elephantopus*) is the most distinctive animal on the entire archipelago. In fact, the name Galápagos comes from the Spanish word *galápago*, which is what the early Spanish explorers and conquistadors called these tortoises, because their shells resembled riding saddles. Fifteen subspecies of giant tortoise have been recorded. Of these, four are confirmed extinct, and another, the Isla Pinta subspecies, is on the verge of extinction (see "I'm So Lonely," earlier in this chapter).

Given the geological isolation and workings of evolution, almost every major island on the archipelago has one or more distinct subspecies. The various subspecies can be divided into two general classes, based on the shapes of their shells. Generally speaking, shells are dome-shaped or saddle-backed. The domed tortoises tend to live in higher, moister environments, and their plentiful food is found close to the ground. Their shells have very little curvature above their necks. Conversely, the saddle-backed tortoises live in more desertlike, arid environments, and they often have to reach high for their favorite foods. Hence, their shells are characterized by the large open arch above their neck areas, allowing them to make these reaches. Domed-shell tortoises tend to be larger than their saddle-backed brethren, too—though most are large by nearly any standard.

For millions of years, the Galápagos tortoise had virtually no natural predators. Eggs and hatchlings were vulnerable to certain hawks and owls, but beyond that, they lived a totally unthreatened life until people arrived. Early explorers, settlers, and pirates found the tortoise to be an invaluable and easy source of food, and thousands upon thousands of tortoises were slaughtered. These same early settlers introduced non-native species, such as goats, pigs, dogs, and rats, that devastated the island's tortoise habitat and, in some cases, the reptiles themselves. Today several subspecies remain threatened or in danger of extinction, while many others have stable and growing populations, thanks to the efforts of conservationists, scientists, and the Charles Darwin Foundation.

WHERE TO STAY & DINE

Red Mangrove Floreana Lodge   This is the most comfortable lodging option on Floreana. That said, the individual wood cabins here are still rather basic. Each comes with one full-size matrimonial bed and a bunk bed. The best feature is the isolated beachfront location and broad, shared front deck, built over volcanic rock just steps from the water's edge. There's an in-house **restaurant** serving up hearty and tasty fare, including plenty of fresh seafood. The main town and several sea lion nesting beaches are short walks away.

Playa Negra, Puerto Velasco Ibarra, Isla Floreana. www.redmangrove.com. © **888/254-3190** in the U.S. and Canada, or 05/2526-564 in Puerto Ayora, or 05/2524-905 at the lodge. 10 units. $167 double. AE, DC, MC, V. **Amenities:** Restaurant. *In room:* A/C, CD player, hair dryer, no phone.

PLANNING YOUR TRIP TO ECUADOR

W ith so many distinct attractions, regions, and destinations, there are a variety of ways to visit Ecuador. A large majority of tourists do so as part of an organized package tour to the Galápagos, often with an "add-on" excursion to some other popular destination in the country. Whether or not you are traveling on your own or with a package, there are many factors to take into consideration, from the basics of where and when to go, to more subtle decisions about how to get around and how to stay in touch with loved ones while on the road—or the high seas. This chapter will answer these questions and many more.

GETTING THERE
By Plane

There are two international airports in Ecuador. All flights into Quito land at **Aeropuerto Internacional Mariscal Sucre** (© 02/2944-900; www.quiport.com; airport code: UIO). Most international flights also touch down in Guayaquil's **José Joaquín de Olmedo International Airport** (© 04/2391-603; airport code: GYE). If you plan to go to the Galápagos immediately after you arrive in Ecuador, it's best to fly into Guayaquil. All international passengers leaving by air from Ecuador must pay a departure tax, which is $26 from Guayaquil and $42 from Quito.

THE MAJOR AIRLINES
FROM NORTH AMERICA **American Airlines, Continental Airlines, Delta, LAN, Taca,** and **Copa Airlines** all have regular flights from a variety of North American hub cities. There are no direct flights from Canada to Ecuador, so Canadians have to take a connecting flight via the United States.

FROM THE U.K. There are no direct flights from the United Kingdom to Ecuador. British travelers can fly to the United States (Atlanta, Miami, Houston, or New York) and then hook up with a direct flight (see "From North America," above). **Iberia** and **LAN Airlines** offer daily, nonstop service between Madrid and Ecuador; convenient daily connections are available from London and a plethora of other European cities, including

Dublin, Paris, and Berlin. **KLM** offers service from many cities in England to both Guayaquil and Quito via Amsterdam and Bonaire. Otherwise, you will have to fly via a major U.S. hub city and connect with one of the airlines mentioned above.

FROM AUSTRALIA & NEW ZEALAND   To get to Ecuador from Australia or New Zealand, you'll first have to fly to Los Angeles or some other U.S. hub city, where you can connect with one of the airlines mentioned above.

GETTING INTO TOWN FROM THE AIRPORT
It's easy and inexpensive to get from both of the international airports to their respective downtown areas. Depending upon whether you are arriving in Quito or Guayaquil, see the corresponding chapters' "Getting There" sections for more details.

All the major rental-car agencies operating in the country have desks at these airports. See "Getting Around," below, for more information.

By Bus
It is possible to travel by bus to Ecuador from Peru. (I don't recommend traveling from Colombia due to kidnapping incidents near the border.) From Peru, the most popular border crossing is from Tumbes to Huaquillas in Ecuador. See chapters 8 and 9 for more information.

By Car
It's possible, but very difficult and impractical, to travel to Ecuador by car. For all intents and purposes, this is not an option for travelers. For more information about driving in Ecuador, see "Getting Around," below.

GETTING AROUND

Because Ecuador is one of the smallest countries in South America, traveling from one end to the other is not too difficult. The bus routes are comprehensive. The roads, however, can be a bit rough, and the buses are often hot and crowded. If you're short on time, I recommend flying, which is cheap and efficient. If you're traveling only a short distance, though—say, from Quito to Otavalo (around 2 hr.) or Riobamba (under 4 hr.)—then a bus, shuttle, rental car, or car and driver may be your best bet.

By Plane
Most of Ecuador's major cities and tourist destinations are serviced by regular and reliable commuter air traffic. In some places, remote destinations can best be reached by charter flights, organized by the lodges themselves.

> ### New Quito Airport
>
> Construction is almost complete at the sprawling new Quito airport, located 24km (15 miles) east of the current facility. The new airport will be 15 times larger and is expected to open in mid-2011. Taxi fares to many hotels will likely double, and the trip to town will take about 40 to 50 minutes.

Aerogal (© **888/723-7642** in the U.S. and Canada, or **1800/2376-425** toll-free in Ecuador; www.aerogal.com.ec), **Icaro** (© **1800/883-567** toll-free in Ecuador; www.icaro.aero), **Lan Ecuador** (© **1800/101-075** toll-free in Ecuador; www.lan.com), and **Tame** (© **1800/500-800** toll-free in Ecuador; www.tame.com.ec) are the main commuter airlines.

CAR-RENTAL tips

Although it's preferable to use the coverage provided by your home auto-insurance policy or credit card, check carefully to see if the coverage really applies in Ecuador. Many policies exclude 4WD vehicles and off-road driving—much of Ecuador can, in fact, be considered off-road. It's possible at some car-rental agencies to waive the insurance charges, but you will have to pay all damages before leaving the country if you're in an accident. If you do take the insurance, you can expect a deductible of $750 to $2,100. At some agencies, you can buy additional insurance to lower the deductible. To rent a car in Ecuador, you must be at least 21 years old and have a valid driver's license and a major credit card in your name.

With the exception of the Galápagos, which is quite expensive, most flights cost between $60 and $120 for a one-way fare. See the destination chapters for detailed information on flight schedules, times, and fares.

By Car

In general, I don't recommend renting a car in Ecuador. For the most part, the roads are in bad condition, and because signs are nonexistent, it's very easy to get lost. For short-distance journeys, it's much more economical to take a bus or even a taxi.

Nevertheless, if you're an adventurous type and you want to see the country from the privacy of your own car, you can certainly get a rental.

Budget (© 02/3300-979; www.budget-ec.com) and **Hertz** (© 02/2254-257; www.hertz.com) are the main rental-car agencies, with offices at both major international airports.

Because the roads are so poorly maintained, I recommend that you rent a 4WD, which are offered by all the agencies listed above. Rates run between $45 and $150 per day, with unlimited mileage and insurance, depending upon the type of vehicle you rent.

One very interesting option is to use **Rent 4WD.com ★** (© 02/2544-719; www.rent-4wd.com), which gets you a large, modern four-wheel-drive vehicle; unlimited gas and mileage; and driver, for just $198 per day. They even cover the driver's lodging expenses.

GASOLINE (PETROL)   Gasoline, or *gasolina* in Spanish, is sold as *extra* and *super,* both of which are unleaded. *Super* is just higher octane. Diesel is available at almost every gas station as well. Most rental cars run on premium, but always ask your rental agent what type of gas your car takes. Gas stations are widely available along the highways and in all major cities, towns, and tourist destinations. But make sure to have a full tank when you're heading to a remote destination. At press time, a gallon of *super* costs around $2.10. Note that gas in Ecuador is sold by the gallon.

ROAD CONDITIONS   Most of the major highways in Ecuador are in pretty decent shape. But once you venture off the major thoroughfares, the situation deteriorates dramatically.

Even the major highways and tourist destinations are only sporadically marked with up-to-date signs and markers. And once you get off the beaten path, you may not encounter any signs or indications as you pass intersection after intersection.

Value Added Tax Refunds

In an effort to boost foreign tourism, the government decided in 2011 to return to tourists the 12% value added tax (i.v.a.) on all purchases for goods and services over $50. The procedures aren't simple, but the savings can be substantial. These purchases must be made with either a MasterCard or Visa at a business specifically affiliated with this program. To date, participating businesses include a range of hotels and gift shops; most participants prominently display a "Tax Free" sign or decal. At the moment of purchase you must ask for a specific tax return form, or "annex," to turn in upon your departure from the country. Then, when departing from either the Quito or Guayaquil international airports you will have to go to the SRI-CAE (www. sri.gob.ec) counter in the check-in area. Be sure to bring all of your original receipts, as well as a copy of your passport's most important pages—those including all of your pertinent data, as well as the page with the most recent Ecuadorean entrance stamp. At the desk you'll have to fill out forms and turn them in with your receipts and passport copies. From that moment on, you should expect a refund to your credit card within 120 days. At the SRI-CAE desk, you will also need to have any goods in question available for inspection.

Always keep an eye out for the sudden appearance of a pedestrian, bicycle rider, dog, or cow, even on major highways. It's best to avoid driving at night, as very few roads or highways are illuminated.

MAPS   Car-rental agencies and the Ministry of Tourism information centers at the airport and in downtown Quito have adequate road maps. For more information on maps, see "Maps," in "Fast Facts," p. 367.

RENTER'S INSURANCE   Even if you hold **your own car-insurance policy** at home, coverage doesn't always extend abroad. Be sure to find out whether you'll be covered in Ecuador, whether your policy extends to all persons who will be driving the rental car, how much liability is covered in case an outside party is injured in an accident, and whether the *type* of vehicle you are renting is included under your contract.

DRIVING RULES   A current foreign driver's license is valid for the length of your 90-day tourist visa. Seatbelts are required for the driver and front-seat passengers.

Official driving rules are often ignored. Drivers seldom use turn signals or obey posted speed limits. Transit police are a rarity, but they will bust you for speeding. So keep to the speed limit (usually 60–90kmph/37–56 mph) if you don't want to get pulled over. Never pay money directly to a police officer who stops you for any traffic violation. Speeding and traffic tickets are usually charged to your credit card by your rental-car company.

BREAKDOWNS   Be sure your car is in excellent working order. Emergency services, both vehicular and medical, are extremely limited once you get far from Quito, Guayaquil, or any of the major tourist destinations. If you are a AAA member, contact the local affiliate **Aneta** (℃ **1800/556-677;** www.aneta.org.ec), which can provide free towing, as well as other emergency services.

If you're involved in a breakdown or accident, you should contact the police. Throughout Ecuador, you can reach the police by dialing ℭ **101** in an emergency. The tourist police may be of help and are more likely to have someone on hand who speaks English. In Quito, the number for the tourist police is ℭ **02/2543-983.**

If your car breaks down and you're unable to get well off the road, check to see whether there are reflecting triangles in the trunk. If there are, place them as a warning for approaching traffic, arranged in a wedge that starts at the shoulder about 30m (98 ft.) back and angle gradually toward your car. If your car has no triangles, try to create a similar warning marker using a pile of leaves or branches. Finally, although not rampant, there have been reports of folks being robbed by seemingly friendly good Samaritans who stop to feign assistance.

By Bus

In Ecuador, all roads lead to Quito. From Quito, you can find a bus to every corner of the country, but don't expect to get anywhere quickly. Locals seldom board buses at the actual bus terminals. Instead, buses leave the station empty and then drive very slowly through the outskirts of town, picking up passengers along the way. This adds considerable time onto most bus rides. Still, for relatively short distances, buses are your best and cheapest option. The journeys between Quito and Riobamba, Baños, Otavalo, and Cotopaxi are best served by buses, which leave frequently for these destinations. The road between Cuenca and Guayaquil is also a popular bus route. For specific information on bus schedules, fares, and companies, see the destination chapters throughout this book.

TIPS ON ACCOMMODATIONS

You'll find a whole range of accommodations in Ecuador. Still, there are very few truly high-end luxury hotels and resorts. Most are in Quito or Guayaquil and are geared toward business travelers.

The country's strong suit is elegant, **midrange boutique hotels,** many housed in old colonial-era homes or haciendas. The antique furnishings and cozy rooms will make you feel as though you are an Ecuadorean aristocrat living in the 18th century. In fact, throughout the Andean highlands, you will find a string of these lovely converted haciendas. Some are in buildings over 200 years old.

On the other end of the spectrum are **jungle lodges,** usually built in the style typical to the Amazon basin (thatched roofs, bamboo walls, and so on). Accommodations are usually basic; the more expensive ones, such as Kapawi Ecolodge & Reserve (p. 320) and Napo Wildlife Center (p. 308), have private bathrooms, but hot showers are a rarity.

In general, inexpensive accommodations are easy to find. In Quito, you can rent a clean room, with private bathroom and television, for little more than $25; in smaller towns, you can find a bed for as little as $15 a night.

In the Galápagos, most visitors spend their nights sleeping on ships. The general rule is that if you don't pay a lot, you won't get a lot. The least expensive boats have dorm-style common sleeping rooms and one shower for everyone onboard.

Heads-Up
When hotels quote prices, they rarely include the hefty tax. Unless otherwise noted, expect to pay an additional 22% in taxes on the prices quoted by hotels and listed throughout the book.

One good website and Ecuadorean travel operator, **Exclusive Hotels & Haciendas of Ecuador** (www.exclusivehotelshaciendasecuador.com), functions as a one-stop booking agent for various high-end boutique hotels and haciendas around the country.

Tip: If you're traveling on a budget and staying in some of the less expensive hotels, one item you're likely to want to bring with you is a towel. Your hotel might not provide one, and even if it does, it might be awfully thin.

> ### Speak Up
>
> If you are booking directly with your hotel (by phone, fax, or e-mail), remember that most hotels are accustomed to paying as much as 20% in commission to agents and wholesalers. It never hurts to ask if they will pass some of that on to you. Don't be afraid to bargain.

Throughout this book, I separate hotel listings into several broad categories: **Very Expensive,** $200 and up; **Expensive,** $100 to $200; **Moderate,** $50 to $100; and **Inexpensive,** under $50 double.

Frommer's uses a zero- to three-star-rating system. A truly special bed-and-breakfast, run with style and aplomb, may get two or three stars, even though the rooms do not have televisions or air-conditioning. Likewise, a large resort with a host of modern amenities may receive one or no stars. Every hotel listed is in some way recommended. This book is selective, and I've done my best to list the best options in each price range and each region.

For tips on surfing for hotel deals online, visit Frommers.com.

TIPS ON DINING

In major cities such as Quito, Cuenca, and Guayaquil, you'll find tons of Ecuadorean restaurants, as well as an excellent selection of international cuisines. In Quito, there is everything from cutting-edge fusion cuisine to Thai food and sushi. Throughout the country, you'll also be able to find authentic pizza joints, as well as Chinese restaurants, known as *chifas*.

While you're in Ecuador, you should definitely try *comida típica* (typical food). *Ceviche de camarones* (shrimp marinated in a tangy lemon juice and served with onions and cilantro) is one of the most popular dishes in Ecuador—you'll find it on almost every menu. *Ceviche* is often served with a side of salty popcorn, fried corn, and fried plantains. The salt complements the tart lemon flavor. Other local specialties include *seco de chivo* (goat stew in a wine sauce), *empanadas de verde* (turnovers made with fried green bananas and filled with cheese), *tortillas de maíz* (small round corn pastries, served with avocado), and *humitas* (a sweet corn mush mixed with eggs, served in a corn husk). In the Sierra, where it can get very cold, locals often have a soup called *locro de papas* (a creamy potato soup with cheese). In Cuenca, *mote pillo con carne* (huge potato-like pieces of corn, mixed with onions and eggs, served with a fried piece of meat and *tortillas de papa*—the Ecuadorean version of potato pancakes) is one of the more popular local dishes.

Fixed-price lunches *(almuerzos del día)* are also common in smaller restaurants. For about $2.50 to $3, you will get soup, a main course, dessert, and fresh juice.

I separate restaurant listings throughout this book into three price categories based on the average cost per person of a meal, including tax and service charge. The categories are **Expensive,** more than $25; **Moderate,** $12 to $25; and **Inexpensive,** less than $12. Prices on menus don't include tax or tip. Expect to pay an extra 22% in tax and service charges above the prices listed throughout this book and on menus. Although a 10% tip is typically included in the bill, if the service is particularly good and attentive, you should probably leave a little extra.

For a more detailed discussion of Ecuadorean cuisine and dining, see "*Llapinga-chos, Cuy* & Pilsener: Ecuadorean Food & Drink," in chapter 2.

[FastFACTS] ECUADOR

American Express
American Express has two travel offices in Ecuador—one in Quito, the other in Guayaquil—both run by **Global Tours** (www.global tour.com.ec). In **Quito,** the office is located on Av. República El Salvador 309 and Calle Suiza (⌀ **02/ 2265-222**). In **Guayaquil,** the office is located in the Edificio Las Cámaras, on Avenida Francisco de Orellana and Alcivar (⌀ **04/ 2680-450**).

Area Codes Ecuador's country code is **593.** Cities and provinces have single-digit area codes: Pichincha province and Quito 2, Guayas province and Guayaquil 4, Azay province and Cuenca 7, and so on.

Business Hours In general, business hours are weekdays from 9am to 1pm and 2:30 or 3 to 6:30pm. In Quito and Guayaquil, most banks stay open all day from about 9am to 5pm, but some still close in the middle of the day, so it's best to take care of your banking needs early in the morning. Most banks, museums, and stores are open on Saturday from 10am to noon. Everything closes down on Sunday.

Car Rental See "Getting There by Car," earlier in this chapter.

Cellphones See "Mobile Phones," later in this section.

Crime See "Safety," later in this section.

Customs Visitors to Ecuador are legally permitted to bring in up to $1,250 worth of items for personal use, including cameras, portable typewriters, video cameras and accessories, tape recorders, personal computers, and CD players. You can also bring in up to 2 liters of alcoholic beverages and 200 cigarettes (1 carton).

It is illegal to bring out any pre-Columbian artifact from Ecuador, whether you bought it, you discovered it, or it was given to you.

Disabled Travelers Ecuador is severely behind the times in making structural changes to address the needs of its own citizens with disabilities—not to mention visitors with disabilities. In most cities, sidewalks are narrow, crowded, and uneven. Few hotels offer wheelchair-accessible accommodations, and there are no public buses equipped to handle those in wheelchairs. The Quito trolley system can handle wheelchair passengers, although its near-constant overcrowding makes this better in theory than in practice. A few of the higher-end large hotels in Quito and Guayaquil have specific wheelchair-accessible rooms and bathrooms.

However, **Ecuador For All ★★** (⌀ **02/2237-224;** www.ecuadorforall.com) is a full-service travel agency geared toward arranging trips for travelers with disabilities and their friends and families. Tour options range from day trips from Quito, to longer excursions to all of the country's major destinations, including the Galápagos Islands and Amazon basin. Different tours and support services are tailored to travelers with physical, hearing, and visual disabilities.

Doctors If you get sick, consider asking your hotel staff or concierge to recommend a local doctor—even his or her own. Your home country's embassy or consulate can also provide a list of area doctors who speak English. Also see "Hospitals," later in this section.

Drinking Laws

The legal drinking age is 18, although it's almost never enforced. At discos, however, you often need to show a picture ID for admittance. Everything from beer to hard spirits is sold in specific liquor stores, as well as at most supermarkets and even convenience stores.

Driving Rules

See "Getting Around," earlier in this chapter.

Drugstores

A drugstore or pharmacy is called a *farmacia* in Spanish. Drugstores are quite common throughout the country. Those at hospitals and major clinics are often open 24 hours a day. **Fybeca** (☏ 1800/2392-322; www. fybeca.com) has the largest chain of pharmacies in Ecuador and makes deliveries.

Electricity

The majority of outlets in Ecuador are standard U.S.-style two- and three-prong electric outlets with 110 to 120V AC (60 Hz) current.

Embassies & Consulates

The embassy of the **United States** in Quito is at Av. Avigiras E12-170 y Av. Eloy Alfaro (☏ 02/3985-000; http://ecuador.usembassy. gov); there is a U.S. Consulate in Guayaquil at Avenida 9 de Octubre y García Moreno (☏ 04/2323-570; http://guayaquil.us consulate.gov)

The embassy of **Canada** in Quito is at Av. Amazonas 4153 y UNP, Edificio Eurocenter, 3rd Floor (☏ 02/2455-499; www. canadainternational.gc.ca); the Canadian Consulate in Guayaquil is at Avenida Juan Tanca Marengo y Orrantea (☏ 04/2158-333).

The embassy of the **United Kingdom** in Quito is at Avenida Naciones Unidas y República de El Salvador, Edificio Citiplaza, 14th Floor (☏ 02/2970-800; http:// ukinecuador.fco.gov.uk); the U.K. Consulate in Guayaquil is at General Córdova 623 y Padre Solano (☏ 04/2560-400).

There is no Australian Embassy in Ecuador, but there is an **Australian Honorary Consul** (☏ 04/6017-529; ausconsulate@unidas. com.ec) in Guayaquil, on Rocafuerte 520 in the Fundación Leonidas Ortega Building.

Emergencies

In an emergency, call ☏ 911. Alternately, you can dial ☏ 101 for the police only.

Family Travel

All children, no matter how young, will need a valid passport to enter Ecuador. By law, minors under 18 need no special permission to enter or leave Ecuador. However, I recommend that adults traveling with children who are not their own carry documented permission from the parent or guardian of record, and contact a local Ecuadorean embassy or consulate before traveling.

Hotels in Ecuador often give discounts for children under 12, and children under 3 or 4 are usually allowed to stay for free. This varies according to the hotel; but in general, don't assume that your kids can stay in your room for free.

Hotels offering regular, dependable babysitting service are few and far between. If you will need babysitting, make sure that your hotel offers it, and be sure to ask whether the babysitters are bilingual. In most cases, they are not. This is usually not a problem with infants and toddlers, but it can cause problems with older children.

To locate accommodations, restaurants, and attractions that are particularly kid-friendly, look for the "Kids" icon throughout this guide.

Gasoline

Please see "Getting There By Car," earlier in this chapter.

Health

In general, the health care system in Ecuador is pretty good and can handle most emergencies and common illnesses. Although pharmacies are well stocked and widespread, you should still carry with you sufficient supplies of any prescription medicines you may need. Most over-the-counter remedies commonly available at home should be relatively available in all but the most remote destinations around Ecuador, although you may have some trouble figuring out what the local equivalent is.

Pack prescription medications in your carry-on luggage, and carry prescription medications in their original containers, with pharmacy labels—otherwise, they won't make it through airport security. Also bring along copies of your prescriptions, in case you lose your pills or run out. Carry the generic name of prescription medicines, in case a local pharmacist is unfamiliar with the brand name.

If you suffer from a chronic illness, consult your doctor before your departure. For such conditions as epilepsy, diabetes, or heart problems, wear a **MediCAlert identification tag** (© 888/633-4298; www.medicalert.org), which will immediately alert doctors to your condition and give them access to your records through MedicAlert's 24-hour hot line.

Malaria Because mosquitoes can't live at high altitudes, malaria is not a risk in Quito, Cuenca, Baños, or Otavalo. Although located at sea level, there's no malaria risk in the Galápagos, either. But because there is a small risk of malaria for travelers who plan on spending time in the jungle areas of El Oriente or the Pacific lowlands, the Centers for Disease Control recommends that you protect yourself by taking the drugs mefloquine, doxycycline, or Malarone. However, I'm not a huge fan of malaria vaccinations. Insect repellent and protective clothing are probably your best protection against malaria and other mosquito-borne illnesses.

Dietary Red Flags Travelers to Ecuador should be very careful about contracting food-borne illnesses.

Always drink bottled water. Avoid beverages with ice unless you are sure that the water for the ice has been previously boiled. Be very careful about eating food purchased from street vendors. Some travelers swear by taking supplements such as super bromelain, which helps aid in the digestion of parasites; consult your doctor to find out whether this is a good option for you. In the event you experience any intestinal woe, staying well hydrated is the most important step. Be sure to drink plenty of bottled water, as well as some electrolyte-enhanced sports drinks, if possible.

Bugs, Bites & Other Wildlife Concerns Although Ecuador has Africanized bees (the notorious "killer bees" of fact and fable), scorpions, spiders, and several species of venomous snakes, your chances of being bitten are extremely minimal, especially if you refrain from sticking your hands into hives or under rocks in the forest. If you know that you're allergic to bee stings, consult your doctor before traveling.

Snake sightings, much less snakebites, are very rare. Moreover, the majority of snakes in Ecuador are nonpoisonous. If you do encounter a snake, stay calm, don't make any sudden movements, and don't try to handle it. As recommended above, avoid sticking your hand under rocks, branches, and fallen trees.

Scorpions, black widow spiders, tarantulas, bullet ants, and other biting insects can all be found in Ecuador. In general, they are not nearly the danger or nuisance most visitors fear. Watch where you stick your hands, and shake out your clothes and shoes before putting them on to avoid any unpleasant and painful surprises.

High-Altitude Hazards Of concern in areas of high altitude is **altitude sickness.** Common symptoms include headaches, nausea, sleeplessness, and a tendency to tire easily. The most common remedies include taking it easy, abstaining from alcohol, and drinking lots of bottled water. To help alleviate these symptoms, you can also take the drug acetazolamide (Diamox); consult your doctor for more information.

Tropical Sun Limit your exposure to the sun, especially during the first few days of your trip and, thereafter, from 11am to 2pm. Use a **sunscreen** with a high protection factor, and apply it liberally. Remember that children need more protection than adults. Don't be deceived by cool weather or cloud cover. I've been foolish enough to think I didn't need sunscreen on a severely overcast day, and paid the price with a painful sunburn.

Riptides Many of Ecuador's beaches have large surf and riptides, strong currents that can drag swimmers out to sea. A riptide occurs when water that has been dumped on the shore by strong waves forms a channel back out to open water. These channels have strong currents. If you get caught in a riptide, you can't escape the current by swimming toward shore; it's like trying to swim upstream in a river. To break free of the current, swim parallel to shore and use the energy of the waves to help you get back to the beach.

Holidays Official holidays in Ecuador include New Year's Day (Jan 1), Easter, Labor Day (May 1), Simón Bolívar Day (July 24), National Independence Day (Aug 10), Guayaquil Independence Day (Oct 9), All Souls' Day (Nov 2), Cuenca Independence Day (Nov 3), and Christmas Day (Dec 25). The country also closes down on some unofficial holidays, including Carnaval (Mon and Tues prior to Ash Wednesday), Battle of Pichincha (May 24), Christmas Eve (Dec 24), and New Year's Eve (Dec 31). Foundation of Quito (Dec 6) is observed as a holiday only in Quito.

Hospitals The best and most modern hospitals can be found in Quito and Guayaquil. **Hospital Vozandes** (☎ 02/2262-142; www.hospitalvozandes.org; Villalengua 267 and 10 de Agosto) and **Hospital Metropolitano** (☎ 02/3998-000; www.hospital metropolitano.org; Mariana de Jesús and Occidental) are the two most modern and best-equipped

hospitals in Quito. Both have 24-hour emergency service and English-speaking doctors. For hospitals in other cities, see the "Fast Facts" for each individual city.

Insurance Before leaving home, find out what medical services your health insurance covers. You may have to pay all medical costs up front and be reimbursed later. As a safety net, you may want to buy travel medical insurance, particularly if you're traveling to a remote or high-risk area where emergency evacuation might be necessary. If you require additional medical insurance, try **MEDEX Assistance** (☎ 410/453-6300; www.medexassist.com) or **Travel Assistance International** (☎ 800/821-2828 or 410/987-6233; www.travelassistance.com).

Canadians should check with their provincial health plan offices or contact **Health Canada** (www.hc-sc.gc.ca) to find out the extent of their coverage and what documentation and receipts they must take home in case they are treated overseas.

Travelers from the **U.K.** should carry their European Health Insurance Card (EHIC), which replaced the E111 form as proof of entitlement to free/reduced-cost medical treatment abroad (www.ehic.org.uk). Note, however, that the EHIC covers only "necessary medical treatment," and for repatriation costs, lost money, baggage, or

cancellation, travel insurance from a reputable company should always be sought (www.travelinsuranceweb.com).

For information on traveler's insurance, trip cancellation insurance, and medical insurance while traveling, please visit **www.frommers.com/planning**.

Internet & Wi-Fi Internet access is available almost everywhere in Ecuador, including in the Galápagos islands. However, don't expect to be able to log on at any of the more remote jungle lodges. Connections in major cities cost 50¢ to $1 per hour. In smaller, more remote towns and the Galápagos, the connection can cost up to $3 per hour.

Language Spanish is the language most commonly used in business transactions. Indigenous languages such as Quichua are also widely spoken throughout the country. Shuar is common in the Amazon basin. It's best to come to Ecuador with a basic knowledge of Spanish. Outside the major tourist sights, it can be difficult to find people who speak English.

Legal Aid If you need legal help, your best bet is to first contact your local embassy or consulate. See "Embassies & Consulates" above for contact details. Alternately, you can ask at your hotel or at a local tour agency that works frequently with foreign visitors.

LGBT Travelers Ecuador is a predominantly Catholic, socially conservative country, and in general terms, the nation is considerably homophobic. Public displays of same-sex affection are rare. For these reasons, the local gay and lesbian communities are pretty discreet. While Quito and Guayaquil have something of a gay and lesbian scene, with several bars and clubs catering to this clientele, the situation gets radically worse outside these large, modern metropolitan centers. **Ecuador Gay** (✆ **02/2529-993;** www. ecuadorgay.com) is a Quito-based travel agency geared specifically toward a gay and lesbian clientele, while **Galápagos Traveller** (✆ **877/829-9006** in the U.S. and Canada; www. galapagostraveller.com), is a recommended LGBT-friendly Ecuadorean travel agency.

Mail Post offices are called *correos* in Spanish. Most towns have a central post office, usually located right on the central park or plaza. In addition, most hotels will post letters and postcards for you. Most post offices in Ecuador are open Monday through Friday from 8am to 12:30pm and 2:30 to 6pm, and Saturday from 8am to 2pm. It costs around $1 to mail a letter to the United States or Canada, and $1.40 to Australia and Europe. From time to time, you can buy stamps at kiosks and newsstands. But your best bet is to mail your letter and buy your stamps from the post office itself, especially because there are no public mailboxes.

However, it is best to send anything of value via an established international courier service. Most hotels, especially in major cities and tourist destinations, can arrange for express mail pickup. Alternately, you can contact **DHL** (✆ **02/3975-000;** www.dhl.com), **FedEx** (✆ **02/6017-818;** www.fedex.com), **EMS** (✆ **1700/267-736;** www. correosdelecuador.com.ec), or **UPS** (✆ **02/3960-000;** www.ups.com).

Maps Corporación Metropolitana de Turismo (**Metropolitan Tourism Corporation;** www.quito.com. ec) hands out excellent city maps of Quito and the entire country at all their desks, which include those at both the major international airports in Quito and Guayaquil. The most detailed map available is produced by **International Travel Maps** (www.itmb. com), available online from the website listed or from www.amazon.com.

Medical Requirements No specific shots or vaccines are necessary for travelers to Ecuador, although vaccinations against hepatitis A are always a good idea. In addition, some countries, including Costa Rica, require proof of a yellow fever vaccine for tourists who have visited Ecuador.

For more on medical concerns and recommendations, see "Health," above.

Mobile Phones Ecuador uses **GSM** (Global System for Mobile Communications) networks. If your cellphone is on a GSM system and you have a world-capable multiband phone, such as many Sony Ericsson, LG, Motorola, or Samsung models, you can make and receive calls across civilized areas around much of the globe. Just call your wireless operator and ask for "international roaming" to be activated on your account. Per-minute charges can be high, though—$1.50 to $4 in Ecuador, depending upon your plan.

There are several competing cellphone companies in Ecuador. All have numerous outlets and dealers around the country, including at both international airports, and all these outlets and dealers sell prepaid GSM chips that can be used in any unlocked tri-band GSM cellphone, as well as new phones with or without calling plans. These chips cost around $7 to $10 and usually include a dollar or two of calling time. If you're not carrying your own GSM phone, you are probably best off just buying one. Scores of storefronts around town, including those at the airport, sell already activated phones, with a few dollars of calling time loaded onto the chip. The cheapest of these phones—a fully functional phone—costs around $30. After your initial time is used up, you simply buy prepaid minutes at any cellphone store or pharmacy around the country.

The main cellphone companies in Ecuador are **Porta, Movistar,** and **Alegro.** Porta and Movistar have the best coverage.

Money & Costs Frommer's lists exact prices in the local currency. The currency conversions provided were correct at press time. However, rates fluctuate, so before departing, consult a currency exchange website such as **www.oanda.com/currency/converter** to check up-to-the-minute rates.

Since 2000, the official unit of currency in Ecuador has been the **U.S. dollar.** You can use American or Ecuadorean coins, both of which come in denominations of 1¢, 5¢, 10¢, 25¢, and 50¢. Otherwise, all the currency is in the paper form of American dollars, in denominations of 1, 5, 10, 20, 50, and 100. It's very hard to make change in Ecuador, especially for any bill over $5, and especially in taxis. If you are retrieving money from an ATM, be sure to request a denomination ending in 1 or 5 (most ATMs will dispense money in multiples of $1) so that you won't have to worry about breaking a large bill. If you are stuck with big bills, try to use them in restaurants to make change.

Some of Ecuador's major banks include **Banco de Guayaquil, Banco Pichincha,** and **Banco del Pacífico.** The country has a modern and widespread network of ATMs; you'll even find them in the Galápagos. You should find ATMs in all but the most remote tourist destinations and isolated nature lodges. While some of Ecuador's ATMs will work fine with five- and six-digit PINs, many will accept only four-digit PINs. If your ATM card doesn't work and you need cash in a hurry, contact **Western Union** (☎ **1800/989-898** in Ecuador; www.westernunion.com), which has numerous offices around Quito and other major towns and cities. It offers a secure and rapid (although pricey) money-wire and telegram service.

All major credit cards are accepted in Ecuador, although MasterCard and Visa will give you the greatest coverage, while American Express and Diners Club are slightly less widely used and accepted. Because credit card purchases are dependent upon phone verifications, some hotels and restaurants in more remote destinations, such as the Amazon basin and Galápagos Islands, do not accept them. Moreover, some add on a 5% to 10%

surcharge for credit card payments. Always check in advance if you're heading to a more remote corner of Ecuador.

Beware of hidden credit-card fees while traveling. Check with your credit or debit card issuer to see what fees, if any, will be charged for overseas transactions. Recent reform legislation in the U.S., for example, has curbed some exploitative lending practices. But many banks have responded by increasing fees in other areas, including fees for customers who use credit and debit cards while out of the country—even if those charges were made in U.S. dollars. Fees can amount to 3% or more of the purchase price. Check with your bank before departing to avoid any surprise charges on your statement.

To report a lost or stolen **American Express** card, call ☎ **1700/242-424** in Ecuador, or 336/393-1111 collect in the U.S.; for **Diners Club,** call ☎ **02/2981-300** in Ecuador, or 303/799-1504 collect in the U.S.; for **MasterCard,** call ☎ **636/722-7111** collect in the U.S.; and for **Visa,** call ☎ **410/581-9994** collect in the U.S.

For help with currency conversions, tip calculations, and more, download Frommer's convenient Travel Tools app for your

THE VALUE OF THE U.S. DOLLAR VS. OTHER POPULAR CURRENCIES

US$	Aus$	Can$	Euro (€)	NZ$	UK£
1	A$1.01	C$1.01	€.75	NZ$1.34	64p

WHAT THINGS COST IN ECUADOR	US$
Taxi from the airport to New Town	5.00–8.00
Taxi from New Town to Old Town	3.00–5.00
Double room, expensive	100.00–200.00
Double room, moderate	50.00–100.00
Double room, inexpensive	30.00–50.00
Dinner for one without wine, expensive	15.00–25.00
Dinner for one without wine, moderate	8.00–15.00
Dinner for one, inexpensive	5.00–8.00
Bottle of Pilsener beer	1.50
Bottle of Coca-Cola	1.25
Cup of coffee	1.00–1.50
Gallon of premium gas	2.10
Admission to most museums	1.00–3.00
Admission to Galápagos National Park	100.00
Airport exit tax Quito	41.80
Airport exit tax Guayaquil	26.00

mobile device. Go to **www. frommers.com/go/mobile** and click on the Travel Tools icon.

Newspapers & Magazines There are several Spanish-language daily papers in Ecuador. The most popular and prominent are *La Hora, El Universo,* and *El Comercio.*

At the airports in Quito and Guayaquil, and at the high-end business hotels, you can usually find the latest edition of the *Miami Herald* or *New York Times.* English-language copies of *Time, Newsweek,* and other popular magazines are also available at some newsstands in the most touristy areas of Quito.

Packing Everyone should be sure to pack the essentials: sunscreen, insect repellent, camera, bathing suit, a wide-brimmed hat, and all prescription medications. You'll want good hiking shoes and/or beach footwear, depending upon your itinerary. I also like to have a waterproof headlamp or flashlight and refillable water bottle. Lightweight long-sleeved shirts and long pants are good protection from both the sun and insects. Surfers use "rash guards," quick-drying lycra or polyester shirts, which provide great protection from the sun while swimming. I also recommend a travel umbrella or some rain gear (many high-end hotels provide umbrellas). If you plan to do any wildlife viewing, bringing your own binoculars is a good idea, as is a field guide (see p. 28 for recommendations).

If you're spending any time in Quito or the high Sierra, be sure to bring some warm clothing, as it gets cold at those altitudes. For more helpful information on packing for your trip, download our convenient Travel Tools app for your mobile device. Go to **www.frommers.com/go/ mobile** and click on the Travel Tools icon.

Passports A valid passport is required to enter and depart Ecuador. The websites listed provide downloadable passport applications, as well as the current fees for processing applications.

Australia Australian Passport Information Service (✆ **131-232,** or visit www.passports.gov.au).

Canada Passport Office, Department of Foreign Affairs and International Trade, Ottawa, ON K1A 0G3 (© **800/567-6868;** www.ppt.gc.ca).

Ireland Passport Office, Setanta Centre, Molesworth Street, Dublin 2 (© **01/671-1633;** www.foreignaffairs.gov.ie).

New Zealand Passports Office, Department of Internal Affairs, 47 Boulcott St., Wellington, 6011 (© **0800/225-050** in New Zealand or 04/474-8100; www.passports.govt.nz).

United Kingdom Visit your nearest passport office, major post office, or travel agency, or contact the **Identity and Passport Service (IPS),** 89 Eccleston Square, London, SW1V 1PN (© **0300/222-0000;** www.ips.gov.uk).

United States To find your regional passport office, check the U.S. State Department website (http://travel.state.gov/passport) or call the **National Passport Information Center** (© **877/487-2778**) for automated information.

Petrol Please see "Getting Around by Car," earlier in this chapter.

Police Throughout Ecuador, you can usually reach the police by dialing © **101** in an emergency. The tourist police can also help sort out problems. In Quito, the toll-free number for the tourist police is © **0800-1300.**

Safety Robberies and pickpocketing are the greatest problem facing most tourists to Ecuador. Crowded markets, public buses, and busy urban areas are the prime haunts of criminals and pickpockets. Never carry a lot of cash or wear very valuable jewelry. Men should avoid having a wallet in their back pants pocket. A woman should keep a tight grip on her purse. (Keep it tucked under your arm.) Thieves also target gold chains, cameras and video cameras, prominent jewelry, and nice sunglasses. Be sure not to leave valuables exposed or unattended in your hotel room.

Rental cars generally stand out, and they are easily spotted by thieves. Don't ever leave anything of value in a car parked on the street. Also be wary of solicitous strangers who stop to help you change a tire or bring you to a service station. Although most are truly good Samaritans, there have been reports of thieves preying on roadside breakdowns. Public intercity buses are also frequent targets of stealthy thieves. Never check your bags into the hold of a bus if you can avoid it. If this can't be avoided, when the bus makes a stop, keep your eye on what leaves the hold. If you put your bags in an overhead rack, be sure you can see the bags at all times. Try not to fall asleep during the trip. For more information on car and road safety, see "Getting Around," earlier in this chapter.

The Ecuadorean indigenous people are very uneasy about having their picture taken. Many, in the more touristy areas, have parlayed this into a means of earning a few dollars, by charging to have their picture taken. In the more remote and rural areas, a rude or disrespectful foreign shutterbug can earn the strong and sometimes vocal disdain of the local population. Always ask permission before taking photographs of people.

Political gatherings to protest current economic and social conditions are not uncommon. The most common form of this is the blockading of roads and highways. There's really little you can do to avoid this, though a fair amount of patience and some compassion will ease the bother and lower your stress levels. Many of these protests and blockades are announced in advance in the newspapers. If you have an important flight or connection and you have a long ride to the airport, ask your hotel to check on any alerts, and be sure to leave plenty of time for your drive to the airport.

Senior Travel Those 65 and older are eligible for various discounts in Ecuador, including reduced admissions to museums, some national parks, movies, and public transport. Be sure to ask before paying, if this applies to you.

Many reliable agencies and organizations target the 50-plus

market. **Elderhostel**
(📞 **800/454-5768;** www.
elderhostel.org) arranges
tour and study programs
for those ages 55 and over
(and a spouse or compan-
ion of any age) in the U.S.
and in more than 80 coun-
tries around the world,
including Ecuador. **Elder-
Treks** (📞 **800/741-7956;**
www.eldertreks.com) offers
small-group tours to off-
the-beaten-path or adven-
ture-travel locations,
restricted to travelers 50
and older. ElderTreks usually has at least one trip per
year touching down in
mainland Ecuador or cruising the Galápagos.

Single Travelers The
solo traveler is often forced
to pay a premium price for
the privilege of sleeping
alone. On package vaca-
tions, single travelers are
often hit with a "single supplement" to the base price.
To avoid it, you can agree
to room with other single
travelers on the trip, or you
can find a compatible
roommate before you go
from one of the many
roommate locator agencies.

GAP Adventures
(📞 **888/800-4100** in North
America, or 44/844-272-
000 in the U.K.; www.
gapadventures.com) is an
adventure-tour company
with a good range of regular and varied tours in
Ecuador. As a policy, they
do not charge a single supplement and will try to pair
a single traveler with a
compatible roommate.

Smoking By law, smok-
ing is prohibited in all
indoor public spaces,
including restaurants,
shops, cinemas, and offices.
(Bars and discos are
exempt.) That said, enforce-
ment is virtually nonexistent. While not as rampant
as in most of Europe, a
large number of Ecuador-
eans smoke, and smoke-
filled public spaces are
common. Bars, discos, and
clubs are often especially
smoke-filled in Ecuador.

Student Travel Check
out the **International Student Travel Confederation
(ISTC)** website (www.istc.
org) for comprehensive
travel services information
and details on how to get
an **International Student
Identity Card (ISIC),** which
qualifies students for substantial savings on rail
passes, plane tickets,
entrance fees, and more. It
also provides students with
basic health and life insurance and a 24-hour
helpline. The card is valid
for a maximum of 18
months. You can apply for
the card online or in person
at **STA Travel** (📞 **800/781-
4040** in North America;
132-782 in Australia;
087/1230-0040 in the U.K.;
www.statravel.com), the
biggest student travel
agency in the world; check
out the website to locate
STA Travel offices world-
wide. **Travel CUTS**
(📞 **866/246-9762;** www.
travelcuts.com) offers similar services for both Canadians and U.S. residents.
Irish students may prefer to
turn to **USIT** (📞 **01/602-
1906;** www.usit.ie), an
Ireland-based specialist in
student, youth, and inde-
pendent travel.

Taxes All goods and services are charged a 12%
value-added tax. Hotels and
restaurants also add on a
10% service charge, for a
total of 22% more on your
bill. There is an airport
departure tax of $26 from
Guayaquil and $42 from
Quito.

Telephones **To call
Ecuador:** If you're calling
Ecuador from abroad:

1. Dial the international
access code: 011 from the
U.S.; 00 from the U.K.,
Ireland, or New Zealand;
or 0011 from Australia.

2. Dial the country code 593.

3. Dial the one-digit area
code; for Quito, the area
code is 2.

4. Dial the seven-digit number. The whole number
you'd dial for a number
in Quito, Ecuador, would
be 011-593-2-0000-000.

**To make calls within Ecua-
dor:** Cities and provinces
have single-digit area codes
(Pichincha province and
Quito 2, Guayas province
and Guayaquil 4, Azay
province and Cuenca 7, and
so on). If you are calling
within the same area code
inside Ecuador, you simply
dial the 7-digit number.
However, if you are calling
from one area code to
another, you must dial 0
and then the area code. To
call a cellphone, you must
first dial 09 or 08 (depending upon the cellphone provider) and then the
seven-digit number.

To make international calls: To make international calls from Ecuador, first dial 00 and then the country code (U.S. or Canada 1, U.K. 44, Ireland 353, Australia 61, and New Zealand 64). Next, you dial the area code and number. For example, if you wanted to call the British Embassy in Washington, D.C., you would dial 00-1-202-588-7800.

To reach an international operator, dial ✆ 116. Major long-distance company access codes are as follows:

- **AT&T:** ✆ 1-999-119
- **Bell Canada:** ✆ 1-999-175
- **British Telecom:** ✆ 1-999-178
- **MCI:** ✆ 1-999-170
- **Sprint:** ✆ 1-999-171

For directory assistance: Dial ✆ 104.

For operator assistance: If you need operator assistance in making a call, dial ✆ 105.

Toll-free numbers: While all toll-free numbers in Ecuador begin with **1800,** there's no hard-and-fast rule about how many digits you'll find following them. Many toll-free numbers are just six digits long (after the 1800), while others are seven digits long. Calling a toll-free number in the United States from Ecuador is not toll-free. In fact, it costs the same as an overseas call.

Time   Mainland Ecuador is on Eastern Standard Time, 5 hours behind Greenwich Mean Time (GMT). The Galápagos Islands are on Central Standard Time, 6 hours behind GMT. Daylight saving time is not observed.

For help with time translations and more, download our convenient Travel Tools app for your mobile device. Go to **www.frommers.com/go/mobile** and click on the Travel Tools icon.

Tipping   Restaurants in Ecuador add a 10% service charge to all checks. It's common to add 5% to 10% on top of this, especially if you feel the service merits it. Taxi drivers don't expect tips. Hotel porters are typically tipped 50¢ to $1 per bag.

For help with tip calculations, currency conversions, and more, download our convenient Travel Tools app for your mobile device. Go to **www.frommers.com/go/mobile** and click on the Travel Tools icon.

Toilets   The condition of public facilities is surprisingly good in Ecuador. In museums, the toilets are relatively clean, but they never have toilet paper. If you have an emergency, you can also use the restrooms in hotel lobbies without much problem. Note that most buses don't have toilet facilities, and when they stop at rest stops, the facilities are often horrendous—usually smelly squat toilets. It's always useful to have a roll of toilet paper handy.

VAT   See "Taxes," earlier in this section.

Visas   Ecuadorean visas are not required for citizens of the United States, the United Kingdom, Canada, Australia, New Zealand, South Africa, France, Germany, or Switzerland. Upon entry, you will automatically be granted permission to stay for up to 90 days. Technically, to enter the country, you need a passport that is valid for more than 6 months beyond the date of entry, a return ticket, and proof of how you plan to support yourself while you're in Ecuador, but I've never seen a Customs official ask for the last two requirements. If you plan on spending more than 90 days here, you *will* need to apply for a visa at your local embassy. Requirements include a passport valid for more than 6 months, a police certificate with criminal record from the state or province in which you currently live, a medical certificate, a return ticket, and two photographs. Ecuadorean embassy locations:

In Australia: 6 Pindari Crescent, O'Malley, ACT 2606 (✆ 628/64021; fax 628/61231)

In Canada: 50 O'Connor St., Ste. 316, Ottawa, ON K1P 6L2 (✆ **613/563-8206;** fax 613/235-5776)

In the U.K.: 3 Hans Crescent, Knightsbridge, London, SW1X 0LS (✆ **020/7584-1367;** fax 020/7823-9701)

In the U.S.: 2535 15th St. NW, Washington, DC 20009 (✆ **202/234-7200;** fax 202/667-3482)

Visitor Information

From home, you can get some basic information by contacting the **Ecuadorean Tourism Ministry** (℡ **02/2507-555;** www.ecuador.travel), which also maintains helpful information desks at the international airports in Quito and Guayaquil, and in many of the major cities and tourism destinations. Most of these desks can provide you with a decent map, as well as tips on local accommodations and attractions.

In addition to the official Tourism Ministry's site, you'll be able to find a wealth of Web-based information on Ecuador. In fact you'll be better off surfing, as the ministry site is rather limited and clunky. See "The Best Websites about Ecuador" on p. 16 for some helpful suggestions about where to begin your online search.

The nonprofit **South American Explorers** (℡ **02/2225-228;** www.saexplorers.org/clubhouses/quito) is a great source for visitor information and a great means for meeting fellow travelers. Its Quito office is staffed by native English-speakers who seem to know everything about Ecuador. Membership costs $60 a year per person ($90 per couple). Members have access to trip reports (reviews of hotels, restaurants, and outfitters throughout Ecuador written by fellow travelers) and a trip counselor, as well as a host of discount offers. If you aren't a member, the staff can give you basic information that will get you on your way.

Water Always drink bottled water in Ecuador. Most hotels provide bottled water in the bathroom. You can buy bottles of water on practically any street corner. Small bottles cost about 30¢. The better restaurants use ice made from boiled water, but to be on the safe side, always ask.

Wi-Fi See "Internet & Wi-Fi," earlier in this section.

Women Travelers As is common throughout Latin America, Ecuador can be considered a typically "macho" nation. Misogyny and violence against women, while not rampant, are part of the social fabric. In general, the most prominent expression of this machismo is a steady stream of come-ons and catcalls. Ignoring them is often the best tactic. Still, women should be careful walking alone at night in big cities and throughout the country.

AIRLINE WEBSITES

Aerogal
www.aerogal.com.ec

Aeroméxico
www.aeromexico.com

Air France
www.airfrance.com

Air New Zealand
www.airnewzealand.com

Alitalia
www.alitalia.com

American Airlines
www.aa.com

Avianca
www.avianca.com

British Airways
www.british-airways.com

Continental Airlines
www.continental.com

Copa Airlines
www.copaair.com

Cubana
www.cubana.cu

Delta Air Lines
www.delta.com

Frontier Airlines
www.frontierairlines.com

Iberia Airlines
www.iberia.com

JetBlue Airways
www.jetblue.com

Lan Airlines
www.lan.com

Lufthansa
www.lufthansa.com

Quantas Airways
www.quantas.com

Southwest Airlines
www.southwest.com

Spirit Airlines
www.spiritair.com

Swiss Air
www.swiss.com

TACA
www.taca.com

Tame
www.tame.com.ec

United Airlines
www.united.com

US Airways
www.usairways.com

Virgin America
www.virginamerica.com

Virgin Atlantic Airways
www.virgin-atlantic.com

USEFUL TERMS & PHRASES

Spanish—more commonly known among the locals as castellano—is Ecuador's official language. Across Ecuador, you'll find that accents vary somewhat as you travel from the Andes to the Amazon to the coastal regions. For the traveler, the clearest and most comprehensible is certainly the Spanish spoken in the capital.

Quito is one of South America's most popular destinations for Spanish-language learners, with a vast number of language schools scattered around the city. (For a list of these schools, see chapter 2.) Coastal Spanish is generally a lot quicker, with the s and r frequently dropped, making it a little more difficult to understand.

Spoken Ecuadorean *castellano* varies from that of Spain, mainly with the pronunciation of the letters c and z, which are not lisped; *gracias* is therefore pronounced *grah*-syahss in Central and South America, not *gra-thiass*. The diminutives *-ito* and *-cito* are used extensively in Ecuador (for example, *chico = chiquito*), as is the ending *-azo*, which exaggerates the meaning of almost any adjective (for instance, *bueno* = good, and *buenazo* = really good). Just as in other Latin American countries, the plural form of *tú* is *ustedes* rather than *vosotros*, and the pronoun *vos* is frequently used among friends and acquaintances in place of *tú*. The Spanish letter *ñ* is pronounced *ny*, as in "canyon."

Indigenous groups who inhabit the Andes and Amazon jungle account for around 25% of the population; many speak Quichua as their first language, though the majority are also relatively fluent in Spanish.

Below is a list of common Spanish terms and phrases. A fair number of words originating from indigenous languages have also found their way into Ecuador's Spanish vocabulary; several of these are included here.

BASIC WORDS & PHRASES

English	Spanish	Pronunciation
Hello	**Buenos días**	*Bweh*-nohss *dee*-ahss
How are you?	**¿Cómo está usted?**	*Koh*-moh eh-*stah* oo-*stehd*
Very well	**Muy bien**	Mwee byehn
Thank you	**Gracias**	*Grah*-syahss
Goodbye	**Adiós**	Ad-*dyohss*
Please	**Por favor**	Pohr fah *bohr*

English	Spanish	Pronunciation
Yes	**Sí**	See
No	**No**	Noh
Excuse me (to get by someone)	**Perdóneme**	Pehr-*doh*-neh-meh
Excuse me (to begin a question)	**Disculpe**	Dees-*kool*-peh
Give me	**Deme**	*Deh*-meh
Where is . . . ?	**¿Dónde está . . . ?**	*Dohn*-deh eh-*stah*
the station	**la estación**	la eh-stah-*syohn*
the bus stop	**la parada**	la pah-*rah*-dah
a hotel	**un hotel**	oon oh-*tehl*
a restaurant	**un restaurante**	oon res-tow-*rahn*-teh
the toilet	**el servicio**	el ser-*bee*-syoh
To the right	**A la derecha**	Ah lah deh-*reh*-chah
To the left	**A la izquierda**	Ah lah ee-*skyehr*-dah
Straight ahead	**Adelante**	Ah-deh-*lahn*-teh
I would like . . .	**Quiero . . .**	*Kyeh*-roh
to eat	**comer**	ko-*mehr*
a room	**una habitación**	oo-nah ah-bee-tah-*syohn*
How much is it?	**¿Cuánto?**	*Kwahn*-toh
The check	**La cuenta**	La *kwen*-tah
When?	**¿Cuándo?**	*Kwan*-doh
What?	**¿Qué?**	Keh
What time is it?	**¿Qué hora es?**	Keh *oh*-rah ehss
Yesterday	**Ayer**	Ah-*yehr*
Today	**Hoy**	Oy
Tomorrow	**Mañana**	Mah-*nyah*-nah
Breakfast	**Desayuno**	Deh-sah-*yoo*-noh
Lunch	**Almuerzo**	Ahl-*mwehr*-soh
Dinner	**Cena**	*seh*-nah
Do you speak English?	**¿Habla usted inglés?**	*Ah*-blah oo-*stehd* een-*glehss*
Is there anyone here who speaks English?	**¿Hay alguien aquí que hable inglés?**	Eye *ahl*-gyehn ah-*kee* keh *ah*-bleh een-*glehss*
I speak a little Spanish.	**Hablo un poco de español.**	*Ah*-bloh oon *poh*-koh deh eh-spah-*nyohl*
I don't understand Spanish very well.	**No (lo) entiendo muy bien el español.**	Noh (loh) ehn-*tyehn*-do mwee byehn el eh-spah-*nyohl*

Numbers

English	Spanish	Pronunciation
1	**uno**	*oo*-noh
2	**dos**	dohss
3	**tres**	trehss
4	**cuatro**	*kwah*-troh
5	**cinco**	*seen*-koh
6	**seis**	sayss
7	**siete**	*syeh*-teh
8	**ocho**	*oh*-choh
9	**nueve**	*nweh*-beh
10	**diez**	dyehss
11	**once**	*ohn*-seh
12	**doce**	*doh*-seh
13	**trece**	*treh*-seh
14	**catorce**	kah-*tohr*-seh
15	**quince**	*keen*-seh
16	**dieciséis**	dyeh-see-*sayss*
17	**diecisiete**	dyeh-see-*syeh*-teh
18	**dieciocho**	dyeh-*syoh*-choh
19	**diecinueve**	dyeh-see-*nweh*-beh
20	**veinte**	*bayn*-teh
30	**treinta**	*trayn*-tah
40	**cuarenta**	kwah-*rehn*-tah
50	**cincuenta**	seen-*kwehn*-tah
60	**sesenta**	seh-*sehn*-tah
70	**setenta**	seh-*tehn*-tah
80	**ochenta**	oh-*chehn*-tah
90	**noventa**	noh-*behn*-tah
100	**cien**	syehn
1,000	**mil**	meel

Days of the Week

English	Spanish	Pronunciation
Monday	**lunes**	*loo*-nehss
Tuesday	**martes**	*mahr*-tehss
Wednesday	**miércoles**	*myehr*-koh-lehs
Thursday	**jueves**	*wheh*-behss
Friday	**viernes**	*byehr*-nehss
Saturday	**sábado**	*sah*-bah-doh
Sunday	**domingo**	doh-*meen*-goh

MENU TERMS

FISH

Atún Tuna
Calamares Squid
Camarones Shrimp
Cangrejo Crab
Ceviche Cold marinated seafood soup
Conchas Shellfish
Corvina Sea bass
Dorado Mahimahi
Encebollado Hot fish soup with onions and yuca

Erizo Sea urchin
Langosta Lobster
Langostinos Prawns
Lenguado Sole
Mejillones Mussels
Ostras Oysters
Pargo Snapper
Pulpo Octopus
Trucha Trout
Tiburón Shark

MEATS

Bistec Beefsteak
Borrego Lamb
Carne de res Beef
Cerdo/Chancho Pork
Chicharrones Fried pork rinds
Chuleta Cutlet
Conejo Rabbit
Costillas Ribs
Cuy Roasted guinea pig
Fritada Fried pork chunks

Guatita Goulash made with sheep intestines
Hornado Roasted pork
Jamón Ham
Lengua Tongue
Lomo Beef
Pato Duck
Pavo Turkey
Pollo Chicken
Salchichas Sausages

VEGETABLES

Aceitunas Olives
Alcachofa Artichoke
Arverjas Peas
Berenjena Eggplant
Brócoli Broccoli
Cebolla Onion
Champiñon Mushroom
Choclo Corn on the cob
Col Cabbage
Coliflor Cauliflower
Ensalada Salad
Espárragos Asparagus
Espinacas Spinach

Frijoles Beans
Habas Broad beans
Lechuga Lettuce
Palmito Palm heart
Papa Potato
Pepino Cucumber
Pimiento Pepper
Remolacha Beet
Tomate Tomato
Vainita String beans
Yuca Yuca
Zanahoria Carrot
Zuquini Zucchini/courgette

FRUITS

Aguacate Avocado
Banana/guineo Banana
Cereza Cherry
Chirimoya Tropical fruit with tasty white pulp, similar to soursop
Ciruela Plum

Durazno Peach
Frambuesa Raspberry
Fresa or **Frutilla** Strawberry
Guayaba Guava
Granadilla Sweet passion fruit
Limón Lemon or lime

Menu Terms

USEFUL TERMS & PHRASES

Mango   Mango
Manzana   Apple
Maracuyá   Passion fruit
Melón   Melon
Mora   Blackberry
Naranja   Orange
Naranjilla   Lulo
Nicaragua   Star fruit

Pera   Pear
Piña   Pineapple
Plátano   Plantain
Sandía   Watermelon
Tomate de árbol   Tree tomato
Toronja   Grapefruit
Uvas   Grapes

BASICS

Aceite   Oil
Ají   Chili, or hot chili sauce
Ajo   Garlic
Arroz   Rice
Azúcar   Sugar
Crema agria   Sour cream
Crema de leche   Cream
Hielo   Ice
Leche   Milk
Locro   Potato and cheese soup
Mantequilla   Butter
Mermelada   Jam/marmalade

Mayonesa   Mayonnaise
Miel   Honey
Mostaza   Mustard
Mote   Andean white corn
Pan   Bread
Pimienta   Pepper
Queso   Cheese
Quinua   Quinoa
Sal   Salt
Salsa de tomate   Tomato sauce
Tortillas   Flat corn pancakes

DRINKS

Agua aromática   Herbal tea
Agua con gas   Sparkling water
Agua purificada   Purified water
Agua sin gas   Still water
Aromática   Fresh herb tea
Batido or licuado   Milkshake
Bebida   Drink
Café   Coffee
Cerveza   Beer

Chocolate caliente   Hot chocolate
Colas   Soft drinks
Jugo   Juice
Leche   Milk
Ron   Rum
Té   Tea
Trago   Alcoholic drink
Vino   Wine

OTHER RESTAURANT TERMS

Al grill   Grilled
Al horno   Oven-baked
Al vapor   Steamed
Asado   Roasted
Caliente   Hot
Cambio   Change
Cocido   Boiled
Comida   Food
Congelado   Frozen
El baño   Toilet

Frío   Cold
Frito   Fried
Grande   Big
La cuenta   The bill
Medio   Medium
Muy cocido   Well done
Pequeño   Small
Poco cocido   Rare
Sorbete   Straw
Tres cuartos   Medium-well

HOTEL TERMS

Aire acondicionado Air-conditioning
Almohada Pillow
Baño Bathroom
Baño privado Private bathroom
Calefacción Heating
Cama Bed
Cobija Blanket
Colchón Mattress
Cuarto/Habitación Room
Escritorio Desk

Habitación simple/sencilla Single room
Habitación doble Double room
Habitación triple Triple room
Mosquitero Mosquito net
Sábanas Sheets
Seguro de puerta Door lock
Telecable Cable TV
Ventilador Fan

TRAVEL TERMS

Aduana Customs
Aeropuerto Airport
Avenida Avenue
Avión Airplane
Aviso Warning
Bus Bus
Calle Street
Cheques viajeros Traveler's checks
Correo(s) Mail, or post office
Cuadra City block
Dinero/Plata Money
Embajada Embassy
Embarque Boarding
Entrada Entrance
Equipaje Luggage
Este East
Frontera Border

Hospedaje Inn
Lancha or bote Boat
Norte North
Occidente West
Oeste West
Oriente East
Pasaje Ticket
Pasaporte Passport
Puerta de salida Boarding gate
Salida Exit
Servicios Higiénicos (SSHH) Public restrooms
Sur South
Tarjeta de embarque Boarding card
Terminal terrestre Bus station
Vuelo Flight

EMERGENCY TERMS

Ambulancia Ambulance
¡Auxilio! Help!
Bomberos Fire brigade
Clínica Clinic
Emergencia Emergency
Enfermera Nurse
Enfermo/a Sick
Farmacia Pharmacy

Fuego/incendio Fire
Hospital Hospital
Ladrón Thief
Peligroso Dangerous
Policía Police
Médico Doctor
¡Váyase! Go away!

Hotel Terms

USEFUL TERMS & PHRASES

TYPICAL ECUADOREAN WORDS & PHRASES

Acá   Here
¡Achachay!   It's freezing!
Ahí muere.   That's the end of that.
¡Arrarray!   It's scorching!
¡Ayayay!   Ouch!
Batido   Fruit milkshake
¡Chévere!   Cool!
Chifa   Chinese restaurant
Chiva   An open-topped truck
Chuchaqui   Hangover
¡Dale!   Go! Go for it!
De ley   Of course, exactly.
El/la man   Colloquial term for *man* or *woman*
Estoy cabreado/a.   I'm pissed off.
Estoy chiro/a.   I'm broke.
Fresco   Okay, fine
Gringo/a   North American/European/white person
Guagüito   Child
Loco/loca   Crazy, also used to refer to someone like "mate" or "buddy"
Longo/a   Derogatory term to refer to those from the Sierra
¿Mande?   Yes? (used when someone calls out your name)

Merienda   An evening meal
Mono/a   Derogatory term (literally meaning "monkey") used to refer to those from the coast
Nevado   Snowcapped peak
No te perderás.   Stay in touch.
¡Ojo!   Watch it! Don't take your eyes off it! Attention!
Pana   Friend, buddy
Páramo   High-altitude Andean moors or grasslands
Pelado/a   Boyfriend or girlfriend
Plata   Money, cash
¡Ponte pilas!   Wake up (to something)! Wake up and smell the coffee!
Por fa/por fis   Please (from *por favor*)
¿Qué más?   What's up?
¡Qué pena!   What a shame!
Salsateca   Discotheque exclusively playing salsa
Siga no más.   Carry on.
Simón   Yes
Tragar   To eat until you are stuffed
¡Vacán!   Cool!
Vos   You (colloquial; used instead of pronoun *tú*)

ECUADOREAN WILDLIFE

For such a small country, Ecuador is incredibly rich in biodiversity, owing to the fact that the country has such a wide range of ecosystems—from the high Andean paramo to the lowland rainforests of the Amazon basin, to the arid tropical dry forests of the southern Pacific coast. And, of course, there are the Galápagos Islands. Whether you come to Ecuador to check 100 or so species off your lifetime list or just to check out of the rat race for a week or so, you'll be surrounded by a rich and varied collection of flora and fauna. The information below is meant to be a selective introduction.

Most casual visitors, and even many dedicated naturalists, will never see a wildcat or kinkajou in the wild. But anyone working with a good guide should be able to see a broad selection of Ecuador's impressive flora and fauna.

See "The Lay of the Land" in chapter 2 for more information, as well as "Tips on Health, Safety & Etiquette in the Wilderness" and "Searching for Wildlife" in chapter 4 for additional suggestions on enjoying Ecuador's flora and fauna.

MAMMALS

Ecuador has over 350 documented species of mammals. Of these, there are over 130 bat species and almost 20 primates. Ecuador also boasts 30 endemic mammal species—astounding, given the relatively small size of the country. Note that the ocean dolphin, sea lion, and whale species have been included in "Sea Life," later in this appendix.

Jaguar *Panthera onca*   The largest cat in the New World, the jaguar measures from 1 to 1.8m (3¼–6 ft.) plus tail, and is distinguished by its tan/yellowish fur with black spots. Habitat destruction and hunting have placed the jaguar on the endangered-species list in Ecuador and throughout the Americas. **Prime Viewing:** Although they exist throughout much of Ecuador's lowlands, on

both sides of the Andean cordillera, jaguars are extremely hard to see in the wild. Nocturnal and extremely well camouflaged, jaguars are most commonly found in the Amazon basin, as well as the rainforests of the north Pacific lowlands.

Ocelot   *Leopardus pardalis*   The tail of the *tigrillo* (little tiger, as it's called in Ecuador) is longer than its rear leg, which makes for easy identification. Although occasionally active during the daytime, ocelots are predominantly nocturnal. During the daytime, they often sleep in trees. **Prime Viewing:** Lowland and midelevation forests throughout Ecuador, although most common in the Amazon basin.

Capybara   *Hydrochaeris hydrochaeris*   The capybara is the largest living rodent in the world. It can reach over 1.2m (4 ft.) in length and weigh as much as 60 kilograms (132 lb.). Capybaras are almost always found in or around water, often in large groups. **Prime Viewing:** Throughout the Amazon basin.

Paca   *Agouti paca*   Known as ***guanta*** in Ecuador, this rodent inhabits the forest floor, feeding on fallen fruit, leaves, and tubers dug from the ground. The paca is the second-largest rodent in the New World (after the capybara). **Prime Viewing:** Most often found near water throughout many forest habitats of Ecuador, from river valleys to swamps, to dense tropical forest. But because pacas are nocturnal, you're much more likely to see their smaller cousin, the diurnal black agouti or *Dasyprocta fuliginosa.*

Giant Otter   *Pteronura brasiliensis*   This endangered species is the largest otter species in the world, and can reach up to 1.8m (6 ft.) in length and weigh 34 kilograms (75 lb.). The fur is thick and soft and highly prized, contributing to the precarious status of this magnificent creature. Carnivorous, the giant otter feeds mainly on fish but will occasionally hunt caiman and snakes, including small anaconda. In Ecuador, the giant otter is sometimes called ***lobo del río*** (river wolf). **Prime Viewing:** In lakes, lagoons, rivers, and streams throughout the Amazon basin.

Brazilian Tapir   *Tapirus terrestris*   Known locally as ***danta*** or ***macho de monte,*** the tapir is the largest land mammal native to South America. Tapirs are active both day and night, foraging along riverbanks, streams, and forest clearings. **Prime Viewing:** Throughout the Amazon basin. A related sister species, the mountain tapir *(Tapirus pinchaque),* is slightly smaller and found in midelevation cloud forests and

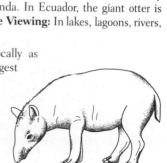

rainforests. Baird's tapir (*Tapirus bairdii*) is actually the largest of the tapir species and can occasionally be found in the moist lowland forests of the Pacific coast.

South American Coatimundi *Nasua nasua* Primarily diurnal, this raccoonlike mammal is one of few with the ability to adapt to habitat disturbances and is often inquisitive around humans. Although mostly terrestrial, coatimundi sleep, mate, and give birth in trees. Unrelated females and their respective young often travel together in large packs, while males tend to be solitary. **Prime Viewing:** Lowland to midelevation forests throughout the Amazon basin. At higher elevations, you'll find mountain coatimundi (*Nasuella olivacea*).

Collared Peccary *Tayassu tajacu* Also called *saino* or *chancho de monte,* the collared peccary is a black or brown piglike animal, with a distinct white band or collar around its neck. It travels in small groups and has a strong musk odor. **Prime Viewing:** Lowland moist and dry forests on both sides of the Andes, and throughout the Amazon basin.

Giant Anteater *Myrmecophaga tridactyla* This species can reach 1.6m (5¼ ft.) in length. The giant anteater has a long, thin nose and long front claws, and is active both day and night. This anteater is terrestrial, and its tail is not prehensile. **Prime Viewing:** Throughout the Amazon basin and the moist lowland forests of the Pacific coast.

Nine-Banded Armadillo *Dasypus novemcinctus* This is the most common armadillo species. *Armadillo* is Spanish for "little armored one," and that's an accurate description of this hard-carapace mammal. The nine-banded armadillo can reach 65 centimeters (26 in.) in length and weigh up to 4.5 kilograms (10 lb.). The female gives birth to identical quadruplets from one single egg. **Prime Viewing:** Lowlands and midelevations and along the Andean slopes, in both forests and clearings.

Kinkajou *Potos flavus* The nocturnal, tree-dwelling kinkajou has a long prehensile tail and looks a bit like a cross between a monkey and a weasel. Kinkajous average around 63 centimeters (25 in.) in length and can weigh between 6.6 and 18 kilograms (15–40 lb.). **Prime Viewing:** Strictly nocturnal and extremely hard to see in the wild, the kinkajou is found in lowland forests on both sides of the Andes.

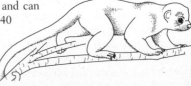

White-Bellied Spider Monkey *Ateles belze-buth* This is a large monkey (64cm/25 in.) with dark brown fur on its back and lighter—at times, nearly pure white—fur on its belly and limbs and over its eyes. One of the more acrobatic monkey species, the spider monkey is active both day and night, and travels in small to midsize bands or family groups. This species is particularly prized by Amazonian indigenous peoples for its meat. **Prime Viewing:** Found in the high canopy throughout the Amazon basin.

Mantled Howler Monkey *Alouatta palliata* The highly social mantled howler monkey grows to 56 centimeters (22 in.) in size and often travels in groups of 10 to 30. The loud roar of the male of this species can be heard as far as 1.6km (1 mile) away. **Prime Viewing:** Wet and dry forests along the entire length of Ecuador's Pacific coastal lowlands. Almost entirely arboreal, howler monkeys tend to favor the higher reaches of the canopy.

Squirrel Monkey *Saimiri sciureus* Active in the daytime, these frisky monkeys travel in small to midsize groups. Squirrel monkeys do have a prehensile tail as infants, but the tail loses this ability as they enter adulthood. The squirrel monkey is known locally as *barizo*. **Prime Viewing:** Lowland rainforests of the Amazon basin.

Three-Toed Sloth *Bradypus variegatus* The largest and most commonly sighted of Ecuador's sloth species, the three toed sloth has long, coarse brown-to-gray fur and a distinctive eye band. They have three long, sharp claws on each foreleg. Except for brief periods during which they defecate, these slow-moving creatures are entirely arboreal. **Prime Viewing:** Lowland moist forests and rainforests on both sides of the Andean cordillera. While sloths can be found in a wide variety of trees, they are most commonly spotted in the relatively sparsely leaved cecropia.

False Vampire Bat *Vampyrum spectrum* The false vampire bat has an average body size of around 15 centimeters (6 in.) and an impressive wingspan that can reach a whopping 86 centimeters (34 in.), making it the largest bat in the Western Hemisphere. Although it doesn't survive on blood, like a true vampire bat, this species is, in fact, carnivorous, feeding on other bats and small birds and rodents. **Prime Viewing:** Found in lowland to midelevation forests on both sides of the Andes and along Andean slopes.

Spectacled Bear *Tremarctos ornatus* This is the only bear species native to South America, and it is substantially smaller than its northern brethren, averaging 1.5 to 2.1m (5–6¾ ft.) in length. The spectacled bear is predominantly black with white patches on its chest and around its eyes, although the amount of white fur varies substantially from one bear to the next. Omnivorous, the spectacled bear eats everything from plants and fruits to carrion. **Prime Viewing:** Mid- to high-elevation Andean forests.

Andean Fox *Dusicyon culpaeus* Known locally as **lobo del páramo** (paramo wolf), this large fox is a member of the gray fox family. **Prime Viewing:** Found predominantly in the high Andean paramo, up to 4,500m (14,764 ft.). A nocturnal hunter, the Andean fox is best spotted at twilight.

Llama *Lama glama* Llamas are the largest of Ecuador's four camelid species—the others being the alpaca, vicuña, and guanaco. Llamas have soft-padded, even-numbered toes and a three-chambered stomach. They are an essential part of the economy and daily life of highland Andean communities, providing meat, milk, and wool, as well as serving as pack animals. **Prime Viewing:** Found predominantly in the high Andean paramo, llamas are almost entirely domesticated or ranch-herded in Ecuador. Reintroduced wild herds can be seen in Cotopaxi and Chimborazo national parks.

Amazonian Manatee *Trichechus inunguis* The Amazonian manatee is an entirely freshwater species. These "sea cows" are much smaller than their West Indian and West African brethren. The Amazonian manatee can reach lengths of 2.1 to 2.7m (6¾–8¾ ft.) and weigh up to 350 kilograms (772 lb.). The Amazonian manatee is mostly gray, with a prominent white or pink streak on its belly. **Prime Viewing:** Active both day and night, the manatee can be found throughout the Amazon basin. It prefers calmer lakes, lagoons, channels, and mangroves, although during the dry season, it will head to larger rivers and tributaries.

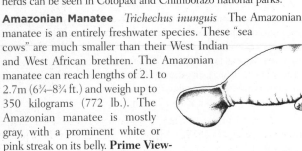

Amazon River Dolphin *Inia geoffrensis* Also known as the pink dolphin, or boto, this is the largest freshwater dolphin in the world. It reaches lengths of up to 2.6m (8½ ft.) and weighs as much as 180 kilograms (397 lb.). The Amazon river dolphin can range in color from pink to dull gray and lacks the pronounced dorsal fin of its saltwater brethren. **Prime Viewing:** Throughout the Amazon basin.

BIRDS

Ecuador is a bird-watcher's paradise, with over 1,600 identified species of resident and migrant birds. The variety of habitats and compact nature of the country make this a major bird-watching destination. The Galápagos Islands have some 60 recorded bird species, of which 28 are endemic.

White-Throated Toucan *Ramphastos tucanus* Also known as the red-billed toucan, this is one of the more common and larger toucan species in Ecuador. It averages around 6 centimeters (2⅓ in.) in length and weighs around 600 grams (1⅓ lb.). The bill of the white-throated toucan can be as much as 18 centimeters (7 in.) long. The bill is hollow, yet still heavy enough to affect the bird when it flies, giving it a swooping flight pattern. Toucans do not build nests; instead, they live in hollowed-out sections of tree trunks. Ecuador has related toucan, toucanet, and aracari species. **Prime Viewing:** Throughout the Amazon basin's lowland forests, nesting in the holes of tree trunks.

Scarlet Macaw *Ara macao* Known as *guacamaya* in Ecuador, the scarlet macaw is a long-tailed member of the parrot family. It can reach 89 centimeters (35 in.) in length. The bird is endangered, particularly because it is so coveted in the pet trade. Its loud squawk and rainbow-colored feathers are quite distinctive; it usually flies in pairs or small flocks, squawking in flight. **Prime Viewing:** The wet lowland forests of the Amazon basin.

Magnificent Frigate Bird *Fregata magnificens* The large magnificent frigate bird is a naturally agile flier and it swoops (unlike other birds, it doesn't dive or swim) to pluck food from the water's surface — or, more commonly, it steals catch from the mouths of other birds. Frigate birds have a long bill, with a sharp hook at the end. The male possesses a bright red throat pouch, which it inflates as part of its mating ritual. Immature frigate birds have white heads and bellies. **Prime Viewing:** All coastal regions of Ecuador and on the Galápagos Islands.

Blue-Footed Booby *Sula nebouxii* The largest and most emblematic of Ecuador's booby species, the blue-footed booby has bright blue webbed feet. Impervious to human presence, the bird will move only if stepped upon. The name comes from the Spanish word *bobo,* which translates roughly as "stupid" or "silly." Boobies are monogamous and have a distinct mating dance. **Prime Viewing:** On the Galápagos Islands and parts of the Pacific coast, particularly on Isla de la Plata. However, you are most likely to see them on T-shirts saying "I Like Boobies."

Osprey *Pandion haliatus* These large (.6m/2 ft., with a 1.8m/6-ft. wingspan), brownish birds with white heads are also known as "fishing eagles." In flight, the wings of an osprey "bend" backward. **Prime Viewing:** Throughout Ecuador, although predominantly near freshwater lakes, rivers, and coastal estuaries. Also found on the Galápagos Islands.

Laughing Falcon *Herpetotheres cachinnans* The laughing falcon gets its name from its loud, piercing call. This largish (56cm/22 in.) bird of prey has a wingspan that reaches an impressive 94 centimeters (37 in.). It specializes in eating both venomous and nonvenomous snakes, but will also hunt lizards and small rodents. **Prime Viewing:** Throughout the country, up to around 2,400m (7,874 ft.).

Hoatzin *Opisthocomidae hoazin* The hoatzin is believed to be an ancient species, closely related to very early bird species. Infant hoatzin actually have vestigial claws on their wings and can swim, although they lose both the claws and the ability to swim after a few weeks. The hoatzin is locally known as "smelly bird" or "stink turkey" because it has a strong, unpleasant odor. Despite its size, and thanks to its smell, the hoatzin has never been prized as a food source, widely hunted, or captured for the exotic pet trade. **Prime Viewing:** Throughout the Amazon basin. Often found on low branches near rivers, streams, and lagoons. They have a loud, raucous cry.

Andean Cock-of-the-Rock *Rupicola peruvianus* This midsize bird can reach up to 28 centimeters (11 in.). The male cock-of-the-rock features striking scarlet and orange plumage and has a large crest over its beak. The female has a duller coloring and smaller crest. This bird nests on rock walls, from which it gets its name. **Prime Viewing:** Midlevel cloud forests on both slopes of the Andes, although those on either side of the Continental Divide are considered to be of separate subspecies.

Andean Condor *Vultur gryphus* A member of the vulture family, the Andean condor is the largest flying bird on the planet, with a wingspan of around 3m (9¾ ft.). In prehistoric days, the condor feasted on the carcasses of wooly mammoths. The bird nearly went extinct owing to lack of food but was saved when Spanish settlers introduced wide-scale ranching throughout the Andean region. Today, however, the condor is again endangered—fewer than 100 are believed to exist in Ecuador. **Prime Viewing:** High-elevation Andean paramo nationwide, above 3,000m (9,843 ft.).

Yellow-Rumped Cacique *Cacicus cela* This is a mid size black bird with brilliant yellow plumage on its back and shoulders. Caciques weave large hanging nests and have several loud and distinct calls. (Some of these calls could be used as sound effects for modern video games.) This bird tends to nest in large colonies. **Prime Viewing:** Lowland moist and dry forests on both coasts, especially common throughout the Amazon basin.

Galápagos Penguin *Spheniscus mendiculus* A rare and endangered flightless bird, the Galápagos penguin is endemic to the Galápagos Islands and is the only tropical penguin species in the world. **Prime Viewing:** Galápagos Islands, predominantly on Isabela and Fernandina, although smaller populations are found on Bartolomé, Santiago, and Floreana. A truly lucky visitor will see one while snorkeling.

Flightless Cormorant *Nannopterum harrisi* Endemic to the Galápagos Islands, this is the only cormorant species in the world that lacks the ability to fly. This bird compensates with webbed feet and superb swimming abilities. Also called the Galápagos cormorant, this is one of the largest cormorant species, reaching lengths of up to 100 centimeters (39 in.). **Prime Viewing:** Galápagos Islands, on Fernandina and Isabela.

AMPHIBIANS

Frogs, toads, and salamanders are actually some of the most beguiling, beautiful, and easy-to-spot residents of tropical forests. With over 450 recorded species, Ecuador is home to nearly 10% of the entire planet's amphibian species. Only Brazil and Colombia have more amphibian species, although species density is far greater in Ecuador.

Amazon Poison-Dart Frog *Ranitomeya ventrimaculata* This small diurnal frog can range from dark blue to black, with red- or yellow-striped markings. The markings become less defined and more greenish toward the rear legs of the Amazon poison-dart frog. **Prime Viewing:** On the ground, around tree roots, amid leaf litter, and under fallen logs in rainforests of the Amazon basin.

Ecuadorean Poison-Dart Frog *Epipedobates bilinguis* With prominent yellow markings on each limb and a granular texture to its back, this is a small to mid-size member of the poison-dart family. Although not closely related, the Ecuadorian poison-dart frog is often confused with the ruby poison-dart frog (*Epipedobates parvulus*), which is similar in appearance. **Prime Viewing:** On the ground, around tree roots, amid leaf litter, and under fallen logs in rainforests around the Río Napo and its surroundings, in the Amazon basin.

Fleischmann's Glass Frog *Hyalinobatrachium fleischmanni* This is a small lime-green frog with numerous pale yellow spots on its back. The belly of the Fleischmann's Glass Frog is transparent, allowing you to see the workings of internal organs, especially in captivity against a glass terrarium. **Prime Viewing:** This nocturnal frog can be found in forests along the western coast and Andean slope, up to 1,500m (4,921 ft.).

Marine Toad *Bufo marinus* The largest toad in the Americas, the 20-centimeter (8-in.) wart-covered marine toad is also known as *sapo grande* (giant toad). The females are mottled, the males uniformly brown. These voracious toads have been known to eat small mammals, along with other toads, lizards, and just about any insect within range. They also have a very strong, toxic chemical-defense mechanism. **Prime Viewing:** This terrestrial frog can be found in lowland moist and dry forests on both coasts.

Smoky Jungle Frog *Leptodactylus pentadactylus* Also known as the South American Bullfrog, this bulbous brown frog can reach over 18 centimeters (7 in.) in length. The smoky jungle frog has prominent skin folds on its back and long, thin fingers that lack webbing. **Prime Viewing:** This nocturnal, terrestrial frog is abundant in lowland rainforests on the Pacific coast and throughout the Amazon basin.

REPTILES

Ecuador has over 400 species of reptiles, ranging from the frightening and justly feared fer-de-lance pit viper to a wide variety of nonvenomous snakes, turtles, and lizards. Note that the sea turtle species have been included in the "Sea Life" section, later in this appendix.

Boa Constrictor *Boa constrictor* Adult boa constrictors average about 1.8 to 3m (6–9¾ ft.) in length and weigh over 27 kilograms (60 lb.). Their coloration camouflages them, but look for patterns of cream, brown, gray, and black ovals and diamonds. Ecuador has numerous other boa species, including the Amazon tree boa and the beautiful rainbow boa. **Prime Viewing:** In lowland forests and mangroves on both sides of the Andean cordillera, up to about 1,000m (3,281 ft.). They also often live in rafters and eaves of homes in rural areas.

Fer-de-Lance *Bothrops asper* Known as *equis* (or "X") in Ecuador, the aggressive fer-de-lance can grow to 2.4m (8 ft.) in length. Beige, brown, or black triangles flank either side of the head, while the area under the head is a vivid yellow. Arboreal at the beginning of their life, these snakes become increasingly terrestrial as they grow older and larger. **Prime Viewing:** Countrywide up to 1,200m (3,937 ft.).

Anaconda *Eunectes murinus* This massive constrictor can weigh over 225 kilograms (496 lb.) and be more than 30 centimeters (12 in.) in diameter. Anacondas range in size from around 4 to nearly 10m (13–33 ft.), with females much larger than males. Their skins are a beautiful olive green, with large oval black spots. **Prime Viewing:** In streams, lakes, rivers, and lagoons, throughout the Amazon basin. Forget the sensationalist namesake movie; the anaconda is one of the most amazing creatures of the tropical forest, and consider yourself lucky if you spot one.

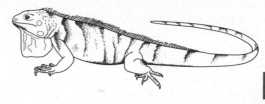

Green Iguana *Iguana iguana* Green iguanas can vary in shades ranging from bright green to a dull grayish-green, with quite a bit of orange mixed in. The iguana will often perch on a branch overhanging a river and plunge into the water when threatened. **Prime Viewing:** All regions of the country, along rivers and streams up to 1,000m (3,281 ft.).

Basilisk *Basiliscus vittatus* The basilisk can run across the surface of the water for short distances by using its hind legs and holding its body almost upright; thus, the reptile is also known as "the Jesus Christ lizard." **Prime Viewing:** In trees and rocks located near water in moist forests and rainforests along the western coast.

Marine Iguana *Amblyrhynchus cristatus* This unique reptile is the only marine iguana species on the planet. It can dive to depths of up to 15m (49 ft.) and stay submerged for up to 30 minutes, feeding on seaweed and marine algae. Darwin was unimpressed, if not downright revolted, by these creatures, calling them "imps of darkness." **Prime Viewing:** Widespread throughout the Galápagos Islands. Often found in large colonies basking on rocks to absorb the sun's heat.

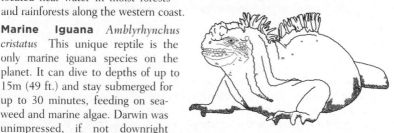

Spectacled Caiman *Caiman crocodilus* This is the most common *Crocodylia* species in Ecuador. It can grow to a length of 2.4m (8 ft.), although the average spectacled caiman measures around 1.5 to 1.8m (5–6 ft.). **Prime Viewing:** In streams, lakes, rivers, and lagoons throughout the Amazon basin.

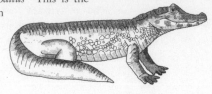

Galápagos Lava Lizard *Tropidurus albemarlensis* Lava lizards vary greatly in size and color, and various subspecies exist. In general, males are larger and more brightly colored than females. Most are between 10 and 15 centimeters (4–6 in.) in length, although specimens as large as 30 centimeters (12 in.) have been recorded. They are predominantly insectivores but have been known to exhibit cannibalistic traits. **Prime Viewing:** Galápagos Islands, except for the northern outer islands of Wolf, Darwin, and Tower. Commonly found on arid volcanic stone and sandy areas.

Galápagos Tortoise *Geochelone elephantopus nigrita/Geochelone hoodensis* The giant Galápagos tortoises—the largest in the world—are iconic on their namesake archipelago. There are various subspecies, in two major groups: those with domed shells (*Geochelone nigrita*) and those with saddleback shells (*Geochelone hoodensis*). Adults of the larger species can weigh over 295 kilograms (650 lb.). Giant tortoises are estimated to have a life expectancy of 150 to 200 years. For more information, see "The Galápagos Tortoise" (p. 356). **Prime Viewing:** Galápagos Islands.

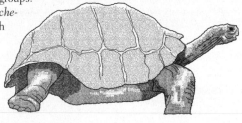

INVERTEBRATES

Creepy crawlies, biting bugs, spiders, and the like give most folks chills. But this group—made up, among others, of moths, butterflies, ants, beetles, and even crabs, includes some of the most fascinating and easily viewed fauna in Ecuador.

Blue Morpho *Morpho peleides* The large blue morpho butterfly, with a wingspan of up to 15 centimeters (6 in.), has brilliant, iridescent blue wings when opened. Fast and erratic fliers, these butterflies are often glimpsed flitting at the edges of your peripheral vision in dense forest. There are actually scores of morpho subspecies, with various color patterns and shadings. **Prime Viewing:** Low to midelevation forests countrywide, particularly in moist environments.

Leafcutter Ants *Atta cephalotes* You can't miss the miniature rainforest highways formed by the industrious little red leafcutter ants carrying their freshly cut payload to their massive underground nests. The ants do not actually eat the leaves, but instead feed off a fungus that grows on the decomposing leaves. **Prime Viewing:** In most low to midelevation forests countrywide.

Golden Silk Spider *Nephila clavipes* Often called a "banana spider," the common neotropical golden silk spider weaves meticulous webs that can be as much as .5m (1¾ ft.) across. The adult female of this species can reach 7.6 centimeters (3 in.) in length, including the legs, although the males are tiny. The silk of this spider is extremely strong and is being studied for industrial purposes. **Prime Viewing:** Lowland rainforests on the Pacific coast and throughout the Amazon basin.

Sally Lightfoot Crab *Grapsus grapsus* Also known as the red rock crab, the Sally Lightfoot crab is the most common crab found along the Pacific coast of Ecuador. It is a midsize crab whose colorful carapace can range from dark brown to deep red to bright yellow, with a wide variation in striations and spotting. **Prime Viewing:** On rocky outcroppings near the water's edge all along the Pacific coast and on the Galápagos Islands.

SEA LIFE

Ecuador has 2,237km (1,390 miles) of coastline, not including the Galápagos Islands, and some 6,720 sq. km (2,595 sq. miles) of territorial waters. These waters are home to a vast and abundant array of sea life.

Manta Ray *Manta birostris* Manta rays are the largest rays, with a wingspan that can reach 6m (20 ft.) and a body weight known to exceed 1,361 kilograms (3,000 lb.). Despite their daunting appearance, manta rays are quite gentle. If you are snorkeling or diving, watch for one of these extraordinary and graceful creatures. **Prime Viewing:** All along the Pacific coast and in the Galápagos Islands.

Whale Shark *Rhincodon typus* Although whale sharks grow to lengths of 14m (46 ft.) or more, their gentle nature makes swimming with them a special treat for divers and snorkelers. **Prime Viewing:** All along the Pacific coast and in the Galápagos Islands.

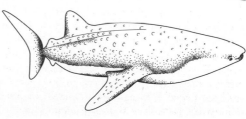

Scalloped Hammerhead Shark *Sphyrna lewini* One of the larger hammerhead species, the scalloped hammerhead shark can reach lengths of 4m (13 ft.), although most range from 2.4 to 3m (8 to 9¾ ft.). They get their name from distinct scallops located across the front of their signature hammer-shaped head. **Prime Viewing:** All along the Pacific coast and in the Galápagos Islands. Large schools of these sharks are commonly sighted while diving in the Galápagos, especially off the outer northern islands.

Humbacked Whale *Megaptera novaeangliae* The migratory humpbacked whale frequents the waters off Ecuador's Pacific coast throughout the southern, or austral, summer season. Called *ballena jorobada* in Ecuador, humpbacked whales mate and calve in the warm waters here. These mammals have black backs and whitish throat and chest areas. They can reach lengths of nearly 18m (59 ft.) and weigh as much as 48,000 kilograms (105,821 lb.). **Prime Viewing:** All along the Pacific coast, particularly the central Pacific coast from Salinas up to Puerto López and Machalilla National Park, from June to September.

Pacific Green Turtle *Chelonia mydas agassizii* Also known as the black sea turtle, the Pacific green turtle is the only sea turtle to mate and nest on the Galápagos Islands. **Prime Viewing:** All along the Pacific coast, particularly in the Galápagos Islands.

Hawksbill Turtle *Eretmochelys imbricata* The hawksbill turtle is a shy tropical species that feeds primarily on sponges. Registered on the endangered species list, the turtle has a highly prized shell. Commercial exploitation and illegal hunting exacerbate the species' continued decline. **Prime Viewing:** All along the Pacific coast and in the Galápagos Islands.

Galápagos Sea Lion *Zalophus californianus wollebacki* Called *lobo marino* (sea wolf) in Spanish, this endemic species is plentiful throughout the Galápagos Islands and is seemingly fearless of humans. Large bull males are territorial, protecting a well-defined stretch of beach, which is usually populated by a large harem of females and their young. Males are much larger and have a pronounced bump on their forehead. It is not uncommon for snorkelers and scuba divers to have close encounters with Galápagos sea lions. **Prime Viewing:** Widespread throughout the Galápagos Islands. Occasionally found along the north Pacific coast of the mainland.

Index

See also Accommodations index, below.

General Index

Accommodations